AMNESTY INTERNATIONAL
REPORT 2004

This report covers the period January to December 2003

First published in 2004 by
Amnesty International
National Office
Publications
322 Eighth Avenue
New York, NY 10001
USA

www.amnestyusa.org

©Copyright
Amnesty International Publications
ISBN 1-887204-40-7
AI Index: POL 10/004/2004
Original language: English

Printed by:
The Alden Press
Osney Mead, Oxford
United Kingdom

Cover design by Synergy

Maps by András Bereznay,
www.historyonmaps.com

CONTENTS

Preface/1
A message from the Secretary General/3
Building an international human rights agenda/5

PART 1
Africa regional overview/28-30
 A-Z country entries/31-92
Americas regional overview/94-96
 A-Z country entries/97-140
Asia/Pacific regional overview/142-144
 A-Z country entries/145-196
Europe/Central Asia regional overview/198-200
 A-Z country entries/201-268
Middle East/North Africa regional overview/270-272
 A-Z country entries/273-308

PART 2
What is AI?/311
AI's appeals/316
AI in action/319
International and regional organizations/327
Selected international human rights treaties/331
Selected regional human rights treaties/336

INDEX OF COUNTRY ENTRIES
Afghanistan/145
Albania/201
Algeria/273
Angola/31
Argentina/97
Armenia/202
Australia/147
Austria/203
Azerbaijan/204
Bahamas/98
Bahrain/275
Bangladesh/148
Belarus/206
Belgium/208
Belize/99
Bhutan/150
Bolivia/100
Bosnia-Herzegovina/210
Brazil/101
Brunei Darussalam/151
Bulgaria/213
Burkina Faso/33
Burundi/34
Cambodia/151
Cameroon/36
Canada/104
Central African Republic/38
Chad/39
Chile/105
China/153
Colombia/107
Comoros/41
Congo (Democratic Republic of the)/41
Congo (Republic of the)/44
Côte d'Ivoire/45
Croatia/214
Cuba/110
Czech Republic/216
Dominican Republic/112
East Timor (see Timor-Leste)
Ecuador/114
Egypt/276
El Salvador/115
Equatorial Guinea/47
Eritrea/48
Estonia/217
Ethiopia/50
Fiji/157
Finland/218

CONTENTS

France/219
Gambia/52
Georgia/221
Germany/222
Ghana/53
Greece/224
Guatemala/116
Guinea/54
Guinea-Bissau/54
Guyana/119
Haiti/120
Honduras/123
Hungary/226
India/158
Indonesia/161
Iran/278
Iraq/281
Ireland/228
Israel and the Occupied Territories/284
Italy/229
Jamaica/124
Japan/164
Jordan/287
Kazakstan/232
Kenya/56
Korea (Democratic People's Republic of)/166
Korea (Republic of)/168
Kuwait/289
Kyrgyzstan/232
Laos/169
Latvia/233
Lebanon/290
Liberia/58
Libya/293
Lithuania/234
Macedonia/234
Madagascar/61
Malawi/62
Malaysia/171
Maldives/174
Malta/236
Mauritania/63
Mexico/126
Moldova/237
Mongolia/175
Morocco/Western Sahara/294
Mozambique/65
Myanmar/176
Namibia/66
Nepal/178
Nicaragua/128
Niger/67
Nigeria/68
Pakistan/180

Palestinian Authority/297
Papua New Guinea/182
Paraguay/129
Peru/130
Philippines/183
Poland/238
Portugal/239
Puerto Rico/132
Qatar/298
Romania/241
Russian Federation/243
Rwanda/70
Saudi Arabia/299
Senegal/72
Serbia and Montenegro/247
Sierra Leone/74
Singapore/186
Slovakia/249
Slovenia/251
Solomon Islands/187
Somalia/76
South Africa/78
Spain/252
Sri Lanka/188
Sudan/80
Suriname/133
Swaziland/83
Sweden/254
Switzerland/256
Syria/301
Taiwan/190
Tajikistan/258
Tanzania/84
Thailand/191
Timor-Leste/193
Togo/85
Tonga/194
Trinidad and Tobago/134
Tunisia/304
Turkey/259
Turkmenistan/261
Uganda/87
Ukraine/263
United Arab Emirates/305
United Kingdom/264
United States of America/135
Uruguay/138
Uzbekistan/267
Venezuela/139
Viet Nam/194
Yemen/306
Yugoslavia (see Serbia and Montenegro)
Zambia/89
Zimbabwe/90

PREFACE

Amnesty International (AI) is a worldwide movement of people who campaign for internationally recognized human rights.

AI's vision is of a world in which every person enjoys all of the human rights enshrined in the Universal Declaration of Human Rights and other international human rights standards.

In pursuit of this vision, AI's mission is to undertake research and action focused on preventing and ending grave abuses of the rights to physical and mental integrity, freedom of conscience and expression, and freedom from discrimination, within the context of its work to promote all human rights.

AI is independent of any government, political ideology, economic interest or religion. AI does not support or oppose the views of the victims whose rights it seeks to protect. It is concerned solely with the impartial protection of human rights.

AI has a varied network of members and supporters around the world. At the latest count, there were more than 1.8 million members, supporters and subscribers in over 150 countries and territories in every region of the world. Although they come from many different backgrounds and have widely different political and religious beliefs, they are united by a determination to work for a world where everyone enjoys human rights.

AI is a democratic, self-governing movement. Major policy decisions are taken by an International Council made up of representatives from all national sections.

AI's national sections and local volunteer groups are primarily responsible for funding the movement. No funds are sought or accepted from governments for AI's work investigating and campaigning against human rights violations.

Amnesty International Report 2004

This report documents human rights issues of concern to AI during the year 2003. It also reflects the activities AI has undertaken during the year to promote human rights and to campaign against specific human rights abuses.

The core of this report is made up of entries on individual countries and territories, grouped alphabetically by region. Each of these entries gives a summary of the human rights situation in the country or territory and describes AI's specific human rights concerns there. The absence of an entry on a particular country or territory does not imply that no human rights abuses of concern to AI took place there during the year. Nor is the length of individual entries any basis for a comparison of the extent and depth of AI's concerns.

Maps of the world and of each region are included in this report to indicate the location of countries and territories. Each individual country entry begins with some basic information about the country during 2003. Neither the maps nor the country information may be interpreted as AI's view on questions such as the status of disputed territory.

The final part of the report contains information about AI and its work during the year, including some specific areas on which it has taken action (see **AI's Appeals** and **AI in Action**). The final chapter focuses on AI's work with intergovernmental organizations and includes information about which states are signatories or state parties to key international and regional human rights treaties.

AI reports

Reports published during the year are listed at the end of country entries. These are available on the AI website.

The AI Index given in this report can be used to locate a document as follows:
AI Index: ABC 56/013/2003
http://web.amnesty.org/ai.nsf/index/ABC560132003

Abbreviations for treaties

The following abbreviations have been used:

- UN Convention against Torture refers to the Convention against Torture and Other Cruel, Inhuman or Degrading Treatment or Punishment.
- UN Women's Convention refers to the Convention on the Elimination of All Forms of Discrimination against Women.
- Optional Protocol to the UN Women's Convention refers to the Optional Protocol to the UN Convention on the Elimination of All Forms of Discrimination against women.
- UN Children's Convention refers to the Convention on the Rights of the Child.
- UN Convention against Racism refers to the International Convention on the Elimination of All Forms of Racial Discrimination.
- UN Refugee Convention refers to the Convention relating to the Status of Refugees.
- European Convention on Human Rights refers to the (European) Convention for the Protection of Human Rights and Fundamental Freedoms.
- European Committee for the Prevention of Torture refers to the European Committee for the Prevention of Torture and Inhuman or Degrading Treatment or Punishment.
- UN Human Rights Norms for Business refers to the Norms on the Responsibilities of Transnational Corporations and Other Business Enterprises with Regard to Human Rights.

Amnesty International prepares for the launch of its worldwide campaign to *Stop Violence against Women* by joint campaigning with the mothers of women killed in Ciudad Juárez and Chihuahua, Mexico, AI biennial International Council Meeting, Mexico, August 2003. Irene Khan, Amnesty International's Secretary General, is seen in the centre, front row.

2

WHY HUMAN RIGHTS MATTER

A message from Irene Khan, Amnesty International's Secretary General

On 19 August 2003 the UN High Commissioner for Human Rights, Sergio Vieira de Mello, was killed in a bomb attack on the UN building in Baghdad, almost 10 years after the Office of the High Commissioner was established to uphold and promote human rights.

As one of the most prominent international human rights defenders lay dying in the rubble, the world had good cause to ponder how the legitimacy and credibility of the UN could have been eroded to such a fatal degree. Bypassed in the Iraq war and marginalized in its aftermath, discredited by its perceived vulnerability to pressure from powerful states, the UN seemed virtually paralysed in its efforts to hold states to account for their adherence to international law and their performance on human rights.

It was easy at that moment to wonder whether the events of 2003 had also dealt a mortal blow to the vision of global justice and universal human rights that first inspired the creation of global institutions such as the UN. If human rights are used as a cloak by governments to put on or cast away according to political expediency, can the international community of states be trusted to bring about that vision? And what can the international community of citizens do to rescue human rights from the rubble?

The answer came the same week that the UN office was bombed, when a group of women in Mexico won the first step towards achieving justice for their murdered daughters. Marginalized and poor, they had fought for 10 years to get that far but, finally, they compelled Mexican President Vicente Fox and the federal authorities to intervene. I was with the mothers of Ciudad Juárez when the news of this breakthrough came through. I will never forget the joy on the faces of the women and their gratitude to the thousands of people around the world whose efforts had helped bring about change. A worldwide web of international solidarity had globalized their struggle. Looking at them, I saw how much can be achieved for human rights through the dynamic virtual space of global civil society.

The challenges facing the global movement for human rights today are stark. As activists, we must confront the threat posed by callous, cruel and criminal acts of armed groups and individuals. We must resist the backlash against human rights created by the single-minded pursuit of a global security doctrine that has deeply divided the world. We must campaign to redress the failure of governments and the international community to deliver on social and economic justice.

The Baghdad tragedy was a clear reminder (though by no means the only one) of the global threat posed by those who are ready to use any means to further their political objectives. We condemn their acts unequivocally. They are guilty of abuse of human rights and violation of international humanitarian law, sometimes amounting to crimes against humanity and war crimes. They must be brought to trial but — and here we part company with some governments — in accordance with standards of international law. Human rights are for the best of us and the worst of us, for the guilty as well as the innocent. Denial of fair trial is an abuse of rights and risks converting perpetrators into martyrs. This is why we call for Saddam Hussein to be tried in accordance with international standards. This is why we oppose military commissions for the detainees at the US naval base in Guantánamo Bay, Cuba, that fail to meet international standards.

There is no path to sustainable security except through respect for human rights. The global security agenda promulgated by the US Administration is bankrupt of vision and bereft of principle. Sacrificing human rights in the name of security at home, turning a blind eye to abuses abroad, and using pre-emptive military force where and when it chooses have neither increased security nor ensured liberty.

Look at the growing insurgency in Iraq, the increasing anarchy in Afghanistan, the unending spiral of violence in the Middle East, the spate of suicide bombings in crowded cities around the world. Think of the continued repression of the Uighurs in China and the Islamists in Egypt. Imagine the scale and scope of the impunity that has marked gross violations of human rights and humanitarian law in the "forgotten" conflicts in Chechnya, Colombia, the Democratic Republic of the Congo and Nepal — forgotten, that is, by all except those who daily suffer their worst effects.

Double speak brings disrepute to human rights but, sadly, it is a common phenomenon. The USA and its allies purported to fight the war in Iraq to protect human rights — but openly eroded human rights to win the "war on terror". The war in Iraq was launched ostensibly to reduce the threat of weapons of mass destruction, yet the world is awash with small arms and conventional weapons that kill more than half a million people a year. To make matters worse, in the name of combating the so-called "war on terror", many countries have relaxed controls on exports to governments that are known to have appalling human rights records, among them Colombia, Indonesia, Israel and Pakistan. The uncontrolled trade in arms puts us all at greater risk in peace and war.

Iraq and the "war on terror" have obscured the greatest human rights challenge of our times. According to some sources, developing countries spend about US$22 billion a year on weapons and, for $10 billion dollars a year, they would achieve universal primary education. These statistics hide a huge scandal: the failed promise to attack extreme poverty and address gross economic and social injustice.

According to some analysts, there is a real risk that the targets of UN Millennium Development Goals —

such as the reduction of child and maternal mortality, getting all children to primary school, halving the number of people with no access to clean water – will not be achieved because international attention and resources have been diverted to the "war on terror".

The poor and the marginalized are most commonly denied justice and would benefit most from the fair application of the rule of law and human rights. Yet despite the increasing discourse on the indivisibility of human rights, in reality economic, social and cultural rights are neglected, reducing human rights to a theoretical construct for the vast majority of the world's population. It is no mere coincidence that, in the Iraq war, the protection of oil wells appears to have been given greater priority than the protection of hospitals.

Nor is it surprising that big business can do what it wants and get away with it, or choose not to do what it ought to do by claiming that it has no clear legal responsibility or accountability for human rights. The UN Human Rights Norms for Business, approved in 2003, are an important step towards corporate accountability but, sadly, have come under concerted attack by companies and governments.

Against this backdrop of abuse and impunity, hypocrisy and double standards, what can we do to make human rights matter?

We can show that human rights offer a powerful and compelling vision of a better and fairer world, and form the basis of a concrete plan of how to get there. They bring hope to women like Amina Lawal in Nigeria whose death sentence was set aside as a result of the massive support her case generated. They provide a tool to human rights defenders like Valdenia Paulino to fight her battles against police brutality in the *favelas* of São Paulo in Brazil. They give voice to the powerless: the prisoner of conscience, the prisoner of violence, the prisoner of poverty.

In times of uncertainty the world needs not only to fight *against* global threats, but to fight *for* global justice. Human rights are a banner to mobilize people globally in the cause of justice and truth. Thanks to the work of thousands of activists in Latin America, the tide is turning against impunity in that region. Despite the crusade by the USA to undermine international justice and ensure global immunity from prosecution for its citizens, the International Criminal Court appointed its prosecutor and began its work in earnest. Slowly, the courts in the USA and the United Kingdom have begun to scrutinize government attempts to restrict human rights in their "war on terror".

Human rights promise the certainty of equality and equity to millions of women around the world. Recent legislative changes in the status of women in Morocco will open a new chapter in gender equity in the region. Recognizing the power of human rights to universalize the struggle of women, members of Amnesty International are joining hands with women's rights activists and many others to campaign globally to stop violence against women. We call on leaders, organizations and individuals to make a public pledge to change themselves and to abolish laws, systems and attitudes that allow violence against women to flourish.

Human rights are about changing the world for the better. Using the powerful message of human rights, Amnesty International has launched a joint campaign with Oxfam and the International Action Network on Small Arms (IANSA) to achieve global control of small arms. To those who say this will not work, we point to the coalitions that led to the banning of landmines and the creation of the International Criminal Court. Combining public pressure and government support, we are determined to bring about change.

We celebrate these and other gains in this report, but we have not allowed them to obscure the very real challenges that persist. We live in a dangerous and divided world where the relevance of human rights is daily put to the test, the legitimacy of activists is questioned, and the "accountability gap" of governments, international institutions, armed groups and corporate actors is growing. It is precisely in such a world that we need a bigger humanity that will say, "This has to stop. Things must change".

There is no stronger international community than global civil society. Through its members and allies in the human rights movement, Amnesty International is committed to reviving and revitalizing the vision of human rights as a powerful tool for concrete change. Through the voices and visions of millions of men and women, we will carry the message of human rights forward.

BUILDING AN INTERNATIONAL HUMAN RIGHTS AGENDA

During 2002 and 2003 Amnesty International (AI) conducted an intensive and far-reaching analysis of human rights in the world. This analysis was the basis for the development of the organization's strategic plan for the period 2004-2006. The plan was adopted in August 2003 at the 26th International Council Meeting in Morelos, Mexico.

Under the rallying cry of "Justice for all", AI reaffirmed its commitment to defending fundamental human rights around the world and took steps to find new ways of engaging with a rapidly changing human rights environment. A key strategic direction was to clearly position AI within the broader human rights movement, building strategic alliances with others, and supporting, defending and working with other human rights defenders.

AI believes that by presenting the main features and rationale of its human rights agenda for the next few years, set out below, it will contribute to the building of a truly international human rights agenda for action which meets the challenges of our time.

Resisting abuses in the context of the 'war on terror'

The current framework of international law and multilateral action is undergoing the most sustained attack since its establishment half a century ago. International human rights and humanitarian law is being directly challenged as ineffective in responding to the security issues of the present and future. In the name of the "war on terror" governments are eroding human rights principles, standards and values. The international community appears unable or unwilling to halt this trend. Armed groups, meanwhile, continue to flout their responsibilities under international humanitarian law.

All governments have an obligation to protect the security of those under their jurisdiction. Since 11 September 2001, many have adopted draconian new "anti-terrorism" measures, arguing that the existing legal framework is inadequate for combating such threats. Yet, the term "terrorism" is most commonly used to describe a range of actions by armed political groups or individuals which are already prohibited by national and international law. For example, actions of armed political groups such as the killings of civilians by members of *al-Qa'ida*, the Communist Party of Nepal (Maoist) or ETA in Spain; the hostage-taking by members of the *Fuerzas Armadas Revolucionarias de Colombia* (FARC), Revolutionary Armed Forces of Colombia, or the *Abu Sayyaf* group in the Philippines; and the bomb attacks on civilians by members of Palestinian groups – all are crimes under international law. They are also crimes under domestic law. When committed in the context of an armed conflict they are war crimes. Some amount to crimes against humanity. Despite this, many governments have made the introduction of new legislation, often employing vague definitions of "terrorism", a political priority.

Since 11 September 2001, governments around the world have been openly pursuing repressive agendas. Many play on people's fears and sometimes prejudices. Some governments have introduced measures that break with their best judicial traditions. Others have repackaged existing repressive practices using the language of "counter-terrorism". And governments once willing to intercede with other governments on human rights issues have been more reluctant to do so.

©AI

"Humanity is in need of AI more than at any point in the past because human rights violations are not just limited to authoritarian regimes." Riad al-Turk, a prisoner of conscience held in solitary confinement in Syria for more than 18 years, during a visit with his wife, Asmah al-Feisal, to AI's offices in the UK. He spoke with gratitude of the solidarity shown by AI members towards him and other prisoners in Syria's jails. "AI's support was like a candle that lit the darkness of the cell and left the spark alive and vivid in our souls."

A Uighur woman walks past a construction site in the city of Kasghar in the Xinjiang Uighur Autonomous Region in China. The Chinese authorities continue to use the "war against terror" to justify harsh repression in Xinjiang, resulting in serious human rights violations against the predominantly Muslim ethnic Uighur community. Repression has been manifested through assaults on Uighur culture, such as the closure of several mosques. As part of China's economic development, Uighur communities have also been subjected to substantial reconstruction of their neighbourhoods and towns. This is viewed by many as another attempt to dilute their way of life and cultural heritage.

© Reuters

Unlawful killings have been perpetrated in the name of "counter-terrorism". The conflict in Colombia has worsened, with government forces, their paramilitary allies and armed opposition groups responsible for widespread killings of civilians. Unlawful killings in the context of "counter-terrorism" also continued in the Chechen Republic and the Philippines.

Governments who publicly expressed their concerns about the threat of weapons of mass destruction at the same time helped to fuel existing conflicts with large transfers of conventional weapons, including small arms. In general, the world's richest states have relaxed restrictions and increased military aid in the name of the "war on terror", even when they know the recipients are responsible for grave human rights abuses.

A very large number of countries toughened up their laws in the wake of 11 September 2001, some rushing through legal amendments in a matter of weeks. Others continued to debate "anti-terrorism" laws in 2003. Common to most such laws are vaguely worded definitions of new offences; sweeping powers to hold people without charge or trial, often on the basis of secret evidence; provisions to allow for prolonged incommunicado detention, which is known to facilitate torture; and measures which effectively deny or restrict access to asylum and speed up deportations.

Laws raising human rights concerns have been introduced since 2001 in countries as far apart as Germany and Mauritius and from Cuba to Morocco. The Prevention of Terrorism Ordinance (2002) in India provides for immunity from prosecution for officials acting in "good faith" against "terrorists". Similar provisions exist in the Russian Federation. At the end of 2003, South Korea was preparing a Terrorism Prevention Bill which could further empower the National Intelligence Service, already responsible for serious human rights violations. AI expressed concerns regarding draft "anti-terrorism" legislation in Tunisia

which, if adopted, would further undermine fundamental human rights including the right to freedom of expression.

The US naval base at Guantánamo Bay, Cuba, remained under the spotlight in 2003. Over 600 detainees continued to be held in indefinite detention at the base. They were held outside the protection of US courts, effectively in a legal vacuum without precedent. The US authorities made clear that these detainees were held primarily to be interrogated or simply to be "kept off the streets". A handful of them faced the prospect of unfair trial before deeply flawed military commissions. Other detainees were held by, or apparently on behalf of, the US authorities in secret locations around the world. The US government used

© Reuters

A demonstrator holds a placard reading "Let's stop war in Chechnya". Hundreds of demonstrators marched through Moscow, Russian Federation, in February calling for an end to the armed conflict in Chechnya.

its executive authority to remove even US citizens from the ordinary criminal justice system and place them in indefinite and incommunicado military custody as "enemy combatants", action which was being challenged in the US courts.

Security forces in Yemen embarked on mass arbitrary arrests and detentions in the immediate aftermath of 11 September 2001. In 2002 the Yemeni authorities informed AI that the government had "no option" but to break its own laws and its human rights obligations in order to "fight terrorism" and contain the risk of a US military attack against Yemen. Scores of people remained in detention in 2003. Domestic law as well as international standards also continued to be violated in Pakistan, where nationals and non-nationals were arbitrarily detained and forcibly handed over to the authorities of other countries.

Thousands of Uighurs in the Xinjiang Uighur Autonomous Region of China continued to be arbitrarily detained and accused of "separatism" or "terrorism", as part of a general crack-down which also seriously restricted their religious rights. Some were believed to have been tried unfairly and executed. Members of Islamist organizations were arbitrarily arrested in Uzbekistan, where torture remained systematic.

In the United Kingdom (UK), despite more than 500 reportedly "terrorist related" arrests since 11 September 2001, there had been only a few convictions connected with membership of or involvement with *al-Qa'ida*. In addition, 14 people remained interned under the Anti-Terrorism, Crime and Security Act (ATCSA). This law allows for the indefinite detention without charge or trial, principally on the basis of secret evidence, of foreign nationals who cannot be deported. Among other reasons, the UK has justified these measures on the grounds that its rules of evidence are too stringent to allow successful prosecutions.

A number of countries have introduced new capital offences relating to "terrorism" since 2001. They included Guyana, India, Jordan, Morocco, the USA and Zimbabwe. Executions apparently related to "terrorism" offences were reported in China. Three men convicted of the Bali bombing in Indonesia were also under sentence of death at the end of 2003.

Asylum-seekers and other non-nationals continued to be targeted by measures ostensibly designed to counter "terrorism". For example, Afghan asylum-seekers fleeing persecution who had been blocked from entering Australia by the authorities in the weeks before the September 2001 attacks remained in detention, in part as a "counter-terrorism" measure in the wake of the attacks. Such measures were undeniably a response to popular calls for greater security. However, they not only resulted in the violation of rights, such as the right to protection against forcible return to a country where the person faces serious human rights violations, but they also ignored the evidence that foreign nationals intending to enter a country to commit "terrorist" or other crimes seldom rely on the asylum channels.

Since 11 September 2001, public attitudes and government policies relating to the "war on terror" have had a detrimental impact also on the rights of women. In her January 2003 report to the UN Commission on Human Rights, the Special Rapporteur on violence against women, its causes and consequences, pointed out that the fight to eradicate certain violent cultural practices is often made difficult by what can be termed as "the arrogant gaze" of the outsider. Many feel that this "gaze" has increased since 11 September 2001.

AI believes that only a concerted effort by the world human rights community can resist and reverse the trend of increasing human rights abuses in the context of the "war on terror" and abuses by armed groups. AI's plan of action includes a determined effort to expose and oppose "counter-terrorism" measures that are contrary to international human rights and humanitarian law. AI will continue to campaign against arbitrary detention, unfair trials and discrimination. It will continue to oppose human rights abuses by armed opposition groups and work to increase their accountability. AI will also engage in critical reviews of intelligence and judicial cooperation agreements and the development of treaties on "terrorism".

Defending human rights in armed conflict

In much of the world, armed conflicts, and especially internal conflicts, are the breeding ground for mass violations of human rights. Wherever armed conflicts erupt they are invariably characterized by grave abuses on a mass scale including unlawful killings, rape and other sexual violence, torture, and the denial of the most fundamental economic and social rights.

Many internal conflicts have persisted for decades — despite significant international efforts to find solutions — and in parts of the world conflict appears

(right) During 2003 AI, Oxfam and the International Action Network on Small Arms (IANSA) launched the *Control Arms* campaign for effective arms control to make people genuinely safer from the threat of armed violence.

©Giovanni Diffidenti/Oxfam

©Reuters

A father cries over the bodies of his children in al-Hilla, Iraq, April 2003. Survivors of the attack on al-Hilla described how the explosives fell "like grapes" from the sky. The use of cluster bombs in al-Hilla by US/UK forces may have amounted to indiscriminate attacks and therefore a grave violation of international humanitarian law.

endemic. Identity issues can trigger conflict, but poverty and, paradoxically, mineral wealth, are more often harbingers of internal conflict. Conflicts over resources, fuelled by discrimination, continue, especially in poorer countries, and the number of situations in which weak states are confronted by economically powerful armed groups may increase.

Mass abuses against civilians continue, and despite significant international and national legal developments, impunity still reigns in most situations. International organizations like the UN have advanced considerably their capacity to monitor and report on human rights in conflict situations, but protection seems to depend all too often on the presence of foreign troops.

The re-emergence of international conflict, and the role of the USA in particular, pose new challenges to the UN's legitimacy. The doctrine of "pre-emptive self-defence" could lead to an escalation of international conflicts as governments, following the precedent of the US-led war on Iraq, feel less constrained about pre-empting perceived threats from other states.

2003 saw AI deeply engaged in attempting to defend human rights in conflict and to protect civilians on many fronts. Long-running conflicts that have

produced some of the past decade's most serious human rights crises in Burundi, the Democratic Republic of the Congo, Liberia and Sudan showed signs of possible breakthroughs. Elsewhere, for example in Israel and the Occupied Territories, Nepal, and Colombia, old conflicts seemed to intensify. And new armed conflicts, such as that in Iraq, brought to the fore new challenges to the human rights framework and international law.

The war in Iraq forced human rights groups to think anew about whether and to what extent they should comment on when the use of force in international relations is justified. Given the dire humanitarian and human rights situation in Iraq, whose population was already debilitated by years of internal repression and UN-imposed sanctions, many felt that the disastrous consequences of a military invasion would be so severe that they had a duty to speak out against it. Others felt that human rights advocates need to balance the foreseeable dangers with the potential benefits of toppling a regime with such an atrocious human rights record. AI urged the parties to the conflict to consider the use of force only as a last resort. As war became imminent, AI emphasized the need for all parties to adhere strictly to rules of

©AI

AI members in Senegal *(far left)* and Italy campaign for human rights in the build-up to the US-led invasion of Iraq in March.

8

international humanitarian law, explaining its concerns in the light of abuses in past conflicts. When the US/UK attack on Iraq began, AI monitored compliance by both sides with the laws of war, expressing particular concern about the use of cluster munitions by US and UK forces which resulted in the killing of scores of Iraqi civilians. After the fall of Baghdad, AI moved quickly to establish a field presence and documented violations by the occupying powers, including reports of torture and ill-treatment of detainees, and unlawful killings. AI submitted detailed concerns to the occupying powers regarding their compliance with obligations under the Fourth Geneva Convention and human rights standards, and concerning legislation and the administration of justice in Iraq.

While the world's media focused on Iraq, little attention was paid to the DRC where the conflict involved armies and armed groups from the DRC itself and several neighbouring states. Despite formal progress towards a political solution and the withdrawal of foreign armies, grave abuses continued, especially in eastern DRC. AI's work focused on the links between exploitation of the region's mineral wealth and grave abuses by all sides to the conflict. In Ituri district, where the remorseless manipulation of ethnic tensions by political leaders resulted in mass killings of civilians on the basis of their ethnic identity, AI campaigned successfully for the introduction of a UN-mandated rapid deployment force to protect civilians and then for a strengthened protection mandate for the UN Mission in the DRC (MONUC). In October, an AI delegation visited the DRC, Rwanda and Uganda. AI Secretary General Irene Khan met the Heads of State in Uganda and Rwanda and members of the DRC transitional government in Kinshasa. Contrasting the optimism in Kinshasa with the horrendous cycle of abuses in the DRC, and condemning the complicity of neighbouring states and various factions in the DRC, she pressed for an immediate end to abuses and urged that all those suspected of having perpetrated war crimes, crimes against humanity or genocide be investigated and brought to justice.

In Israel and the Occupied Territories the internationally-sponsored "road map" peace plan lacked provisions to ensure the parties' compliance with international law and failed to bring about any improvement in the situation. Meanwhile the death toll in the increasingly bitter conflict continued to mount. At least 600 Palestinians, more than 100 of them children, were killed by the Israeli army. Palestinian armed groups killed some 130 Israeli civilians, including 21 children, and some 70 Israeli soldiers. The Palestinian population of the Occupied Territories were subjected to increasing measures of collective punishment, including the destruction of hundreds of homes, large areas of farmland and commercial properties, and unprecedented restrictions on movement. Israel's construction of a fence/wall in the West Bank confined hundreds of thousands of Palestinians to enclaves cut off from their land and jobs, education, health and other essential services in nearby towns and villages. Such measures caused increased unemployment and poverty and the emergence of malnutrition. Israeli soldiers frequently delayed or refused passage to Palestinians at checkpoints, including to patients and medical personnel, and several women were forced to give birth at checkpoints; some cases resulted in death. During the year, scores of Israelis were imprisoned for refusing to perform military service because of their opposition to human rights violations by the Israeli army in the Occupied Territories.

Abuses by all sides in the long-running conflict in Colombia, which has claimed more than 60,000 lives and displaced over 2.5 million people since 1985, continued throughout 2003. Army-backed paramilitaries carried out extrajudicial executions and "disappearances", and committed torture with complete impunity. Rebel groups committed widespread abuses, including bomb attacks in which civilians were killed. The FARC also executed captured civilians and soldiers. AI pressed the US and other governments to cease military and security transfers to the Colombian security forces, which are responsible for serious human rights violations either directly or in collaboration with paramilitary forces.

In Nepal, a cease-fire between government forces and Communist Party of Nepal (CPN – Maoist) insurgents broke down in August and widespread abuses continued. State security forces were responsible for extrajudicial executions, "disappearances", torture and arbitrary detention. CPN (Maoist) forces unlawfully killed civilians, summarily executed captured soldiers, and carried out abductions. AI focused on ending impunity for abuses including "disappearances" and abductions

AI representatives from 51 countries at the UK Prime Minister's residence express concern over reported abuses of humanitarian law in the war on Iraq, March 2003.

and urged the government to invite the UN Working Group on Enforced or Involuntary Disappearances to Nepal.

The persistence, scale and severity of abuses in conflicts around the world call into question the effectiveness of the work of AI and other human rights groups in addressing these situations. It seems that the human rights movement has little impact in some of the worst ongoing conflicts. In many cases it is difficult for AI to influence the warring parties themselves, especially in weak states. However, conflicts are sustained or supported by foreign governments, private companies, international organizations, and diaspora communities. AI believes that refocusing its efforts to bring pressure to bear on such influential outside actors will result in more effective interventions to bring about real improvements in human rights for those caught up in armed conflict.

AI will intensify its efforts to hold economic actors and second states accountable for abuses committed in armed conflicts. AI will continue to scrutinize the role of transnational corporations in Sudan and the DRC; of extractive industries and other international economic interests in Colombia; and the role of military aid in perpetuating violations in many other conflicts. Building on its work on the Kimberley process – an international diamond certification scheme to eradicate the trade in diamonds mined in conflict areas – AI will help to develop clear rules on accountability of businesses and other external actors in conflict zones.

The proliferation of small arms has contributed to deepening and prolonging conflicts, claiming a massive toll on human rights throughout the world. In 2003, AI, together with Oxfam and the International Action Network on Small Arms (IANSA), launched the *Control Arms* campaign which aims to get governments to agree an international arms trade treaty by 2006. The treaty would prohibit transfer of arms to destinations where they are likely to be used to commit serious violations of human rights or international humanitarian law. AI will expand its campaigning for the enforcement of arms embargoes and for the development and strengthening of regional arms control agreements to uphold human rights and humanitarian law. AI has also joined the Cluster Munitions Coalition to push for a moratorium on the use of these weapons.

AI will continue active campaigning to end the recruitment of child soldiers and to ensure their demobilization and reintegration into society. AI will lobby at the UN for strengthened protection of civilians, including strict adherence to human rights and humanitarian law in peace-keeping efforts. And AI will seek to ensure the centrality of respect for human rights, including the rights of women, in peace processes, final agreements and post-conflict situations.

Finally, AI will engage with the process of grappling with conflict prevention and peace-building. If mass human rights violations and humanitarian crises are an inevitable by-product of armed conflict, such preventive work must be seen as a necessary activity for a human rights organization like AI.

Protecting the rights of human rights defenders

As this report shows, governments, armed opposition groups and individuals continue to erode respect for international human rights and humanitarian standards. In this environment, human rights defenders have played a unique role in documenting abuses and providing the first direct assistance to many of those whose rights have been violated. Human rights defenders include people from all walks of life and all sectors of society who work for human rights in many different ways, including activists campaigning on a range of social issues.

2003 witnessed the harassment, arrest, torture, "disappearance" and killing of human rights defenders around the world. Those targeted included campaigners seeking to compel governments to deal with gross inequalities in the distribution of wealth, access to basic health facilities, education, water and food. Many fought to protect the environment and defend social, economic and cultural rights. Others were attempting to expose crimes against humanity, extrajudicial killings, "disappearances" or torture. Many were targeted because of their insistence on the need for democratic or judicial reform or their criticism of harsh security measures.

©Paul Smith/Panos Pictures

A demonstrator from the *Ruta Pacífica*, a Colombian feminist peace movement, during a minute's silence for the dead in Colombia's war.

Over 200 children stage a bicycle parade as part of anti-gas pipeline protests in Songkhla province, Thailand, June 2003. Residents living in the area of the Thai-Malaysia gas pipeline project protested against the goverment's plan, which they said would damage their livelihoods.

©AP

Governments used many pretexts to stifle legitimate criticisms of their policies, including national security and the "war on terror". Around the world individual activists were targeted because those who benefit from the injustices of the status quo perceive them as a threat and sought to evade judicial responsibility, quash public scrutiny or silence criticisms.

The challenges faced by human rights defenders reflect national and international trends in the social, political and technological spheres. Internal or international armed conflict, flawed transitions to democracy, the so-called "war on terror", legal frameworks inconsistent with international standards,

cultural factors – all these have provided an environment encouraging human rights abuses. Human rights defenders express people's desire for justice and often expose the failure of state institutions to provide remedies for abuses.

AI's campaigning to stop violence against women highlights the efforts of those working to defend women's human rights. In doing so they challenge political, economic and social discrimination in areas such as access to basic healthcare and education. They too face the very violations they combat, as well as gender-specific human rights abuses ranging from verbal abuse to rape and other forms of sexual violence.

In November, AI published a report on the situation of activists in the Americas where over several decades more human rights defenders have been killed than in any other part of the world. The study found that in 2003 human rights defenders enjoyed no more, and in some cases less, protection than they had in previous years. Killings were a particularly serious problem in Colombia and Guatemala. In March, there was a massive crackdown on dissent in Cuba; 75 people, including several human rights activists, were arrested and sentenced to long prison terms after hasty and unfair trials. AI considered them to be prisoners of conscience.

Human rights defenders often work at great risk to their own safety. In armed conflict zones where international scrutiny is not possible either for security reasons or because the authorities do not allow international organizations to work there, human rights defenders sometimes pay for their dedication with their lives.

Palestinian human rights activists were limited in their ability to carry out their work by increasingly stringent restrictions imposed by the Israeli army on the movements of Palestinians in the Occupied Territories. At the same time international and Israeli human rights and peace activists were increasingly targeted. At least four were killed or seriously injured by the Israeli army in the space of a few weeks in March and April 2003.

> "Every time I drive on these roads and see a tank in the distance I wonder if I'll make it home to see the children again. I have a permit, for a month, but if the soldiers shoot at me and I am killed the permit won't do any good to me or my family. They can always say I was a terrorist, or that I did something suspicious that made them think I was a danger. And even if they admit making a mistake and they apologize, what good would that be if I am dead? So I try to avoid travelling as much as possible."
> A Palestinian human rights lawyer working under restrictions on freedom of movement imposed by the Israeli authorities in the Occupied Territories

In May, in the Chechen Republic, armed men killed a woman human rights activist and three members of her family. She had lodged a complaint at the European Court of Human Rights regarding the failure of the Russian authorities to follow up allegations of torture and ill-treatment during her detention in a "filtration" camp.

Courageous lawyers continued to defend human rights and press freedom in Zimbabwe, placing themselves at personal risk. In October 2003 Beatrice Mtetwa, who was named Human Rights Lawyer of the Year in December 2003, called for police assistance when her vehicle was attacked by car thieves; instead the police took her into custody for allegedly driving while intoxicated. While in police custody she was reportedly beaten by police officers and subsequently needed treatment for severe bruising and cuts to her face, throat, arms, ribcage and legs.

An important theme of AI's work in Africa has been supporting and working with human rights defenders, and campaigning for the adoption of measures for the legal protection of human rights defenders at a regional level.

For several years, AI, together with other international and national human rights nongovernmental organizations, has called on the African Commission on Human and Peoples' Rights to adopt a resolution that will recognize the fundamental rights of human rights defenders and strengthen the protection of those rights in Africa. Although the Commission has recently established a focal point on human rights defenders to streamline and better respond to information on the situation of human rights defenders in Africa, the effectiveness of such a mechanism remains a concern.

In February, AI organized a human rights defenders workshop in Somaliland with 23 Somali nongovernmental organizations working in different areas of human rights in different parts of the country, including the conflict-torn southern areas of Somalia, which remained in state of collapse. One purpose of the workshop was to enable the participants to be more effective by increasing familiarity with and use of international human rights mechanisms; to increase knowledge of effective ways of defending freedom of association and expression, justice and the rule of law, women's human rights and minority rights; and to enhance the development of humanitarian activism. This type of workshop is one of the many initiatives that AI will take to involve human rights defenders from all sectors of society, especially marginalized groups, in events aimed at strengthening human rights defence mechanisms, building coalitions and enhancing skills.

As information technology becomes more widely available, human rights defenders are increasingly using the Internet to communicate with each other, to denounce human rights violations or simply as a way of exercising their right to freedom of expression. They have not escaped repression in countries including China and Viet Nam. In Viet Nam one of these so-called "Cyberspace dissidents" was sentenced in June to 13 years' imprisonment. This was later reduced on appeal to five years, following a wave of international solidarity.

Large economic projects such as the building of dams and oil and gas pipelines have been opposed by local activists because of the threat of ecological damage and loss of farmland. In the case of the Thai-Malaysian natural gas pipeline project, activists in Thailand opposed to the pipeline were detained and some were threatened. Opponents of the Pak Mun Dam in northeastern Thailand also received threats during 2003. Some have received death threats and there have been reports of assassination attempts against others.

In many countries human rights defenders continue to struggle to gain acknowledgement of the legitimacy of their work, despite resolutions and declarations by the UN and other intergovernmental organizations such as the Organization of American States. In Tunisia, for example, the government has taken every possible step to silence and deny public space to registered human rights groups and it continues to deny official recognition to many others.

Recognizing the critical role of a wide range of human rights defenders operating in different sectors of society, AI will involve and engage human rights defenders from all social spheres, especially marginalized groups, in all aspects of its work. AI will give special attention to the increasing visibility and role of women human rights defenders. Since human rights defenders often face difficulties in advocating or making appeals for their own protection, AI will use its international status as a global human rights movement to raise the profile of human rights defenders and strengthen local spaces where human rights defenders can operate at local, regional and national levels. AI will also help and support human rights defenders to advocate and create their own protection mechanisms, to reduce dependency on international and foreign agencies.

Reforming and strengthening the justice sector

The rule of law is the cornerstone of the protection of human rights and systems of governance based on the values of the Universal Declaration of Human Rights. Yet domestic institutions that should uphold the rule of law are often seriously flawed. For example, in many countries criminal justice systems are undermined by institutionalized discrimination, lack of resources and corruption. In others, the administration of justice has been manipulated to perpetuate the domination of political elites or ethnic or religious groups. The result is continuing widespread violations of civil, political, economic, social and cultural rights.

The justice sector should provide the mechanisms to ensure redress for human rights abuses committed either by agents of the state or by private individuals. However, the history of human rights violations is also the history of failures and shortcomings in the administration of justice.

Reform of the justice system involves exposing the gaps and loopholes in domestic legislations that allow human rights to be abused with impunity, and campaigning for the removal of legislation or procedures that are instrumental in the perpetration of abuses. It involves setting up truly independent and impartial judicial institutions and promoting a vision of policing which sees the protection of human rights as integral to public security.

Perhaps the biggest challenge in the administration of justice at the domestic level is ending impunity. Impunity is more than just a failure to do justice in individual cases. It is a cancer which debilitates the very framework of the rule of law. AI's ongoing battle against impunity in countries around the world will need to address the role played by poverty, stigma and marginalization in denying access to justice to particular sectors of society.

Fresh opportunities to combat impunity and restore faith in the rule of law arose in 2003 in countries undergoing processes of democratic transition. Across the Americas, for example, a wave of anti-impunity initiatives throughout the year marked a significant step towards greater accountability of democratic institutions.

Post-conflict situations offer the opportunity to introduce new constitutions, repeal legislation that is inconsistent with international standards, and introduce into domestic law rights enshrined in human rights treaties. AI believes that constitutional processes provide opportunities to advance the rights of women, children, indigenous people and other groups at risk of abuse. In Afghanistan, AI focused its attention on

Women using an official "writer" to help with their petition to a court in Kabul, Afghanistan. Women victims of crime are routinely denied access to justice in Afghanistan. AI stressed the need for measures to protect the rights of women to be built into legal and constitutional reform.

© AI

©Reuters

©US Department of Defense

AI members stage a protest outside the residence of UK Prime Minister Tony Blair during a visit by US President George W. Bush in November. Demonstrators sought to highlight violations of the fundamental human rights of hundreds of detainees held by the US authorities in Guantánamo Bay, Cuba. (*Inset*) A US soldier watches over prisoners in Guantánamo Bay.

legislation and practices affecting prisoners, the administration of justice, the reconstruction of the police force and the rights and status of women. In its 2003 report *Afghanistan: "No one listens to us and no one treat us as human beings" – Justice denied to women*, AI stressed the need for measures to protect the rights of women to be built into legal and constitutional reform and integrated into policing and criminal justice processes. An AI delegation was present in Afghanistan in December at the time of the meeting of the Constitutional *Loya Jirga* (CLJ) in order to press CLJ delegates for a constitution fully consistent with international human rights standards. AI wrote an open letter to President Karzai raising a number of issues concerning the draft constitution, including, for example, the rights of women.

International mechanisms to provide redress for failures of domestic justice systems have evolved rapidly in the past decade. However, they remain embryonic and contested. The international and regional systems to monitor state compliance with human rights standards have also grown significantly, but face a crisis of capacity and credibility. Strengthened international justice and monitoring mechanisms would provide a safety net in the fight against impunity and an international platform for accountability. They would also have the effect of improving domestic systems in the medium to long term.

AI has campaigned tirelessly for the adoption of the Rome Statute that created the International Criminal Court (ICC). During 2003, AI urged states to adopt effective implementing legislation for the Rome Statute, including provisions giving domestic courts universal jurisdiction over the crimes of genocide, crimes against humanity, war crimes, torture, extrajudicial executions and "disappearances". AI also campaigned vigorously against US government efforts to sign bilateral agreements with other countries providing impunity for US nationals accused before the ICC. The year saw further ground-breaking initiatives to

hold perpetrators accountable through transnational judicial cooperation. For example, the Mexican Supreme Court set an important precedent for extraterritorial jurisdiction by confirming the extradition to Spain of an Argentine naval captain to face charges of genocide and terrorism.

International human rights and humanitarian standards provide a comprehensive framework for advancing demands for global justice. While the main emphasis in the coming years will be on implementation of existing standards, AI will continue to support efforts to develop new norms, particularly in areas where accountability is most lacking. So, for example, AI is contributing to efforts to create a complaints procedure for the International Covenant on Economic, Social and Cultural Rights (ICESCR). It is also promoting awareness and enforcement of the UN Norms on the Responsibilities of Transnational Corporations and Other Business

Enterprises with Regard to Human Rights, adopted by the UN Sub-Commission on the Promotion and Protection of Human Rights in August 2003, as part of attempts to ensure that companies, as powerful and influential non-governmental actors, are brought within the framework of international human rights treaties.

2003 saw unequivocal signs that a global justice movement has emerged to respond transnationally to worldwide injustice. The millions of global citizens who gathered at the World Social Forum in Porto Alegre, Brazil, who simultaneously took to the streets in solidarity with the Iraqi people or who spoke out through the Internet against the unfairness of global trade rules are all part of a diverse but universal clamour for justice, whether in the legal, economic or social sphere. The era of globalization may present us with many threats, but it also offers unprecedented opportunities to globalize the struggle for justice in all its forms. If we explore their universal reach, expansive scope and transformative potential, human rights can be a powerful driving force behind the global agenda for change.

Promoting abolition of the death penalty

When AI convened an International Conference on the Death Penalty in Stockholm, Sweden, some 26 years ago, just 16 countries had abolished capital punishment for all crimes. Today the figure stands at over 75. The momentum towards worldwide abolition continues, yet the death penalty persists and in some places its use is expanding, especially in relation to criminality and "terrorism". While some governments promote worldwide abolition, others firmly resist.

This dichotomy was shown by two related events in 2003. On 24 April the UN Commission on Human Rights passed a resolution calling on all states that still maintain the death penalty to establish a moratorium on executions, and affirming that the abolition of the death penalty "contributes to the enhancement of human dignity and to the progressive development of human rights". The resolution was co-sponsored by 75 states, seven more than had co-sponsored a similar resolution in 2002.

On the same day, a joint statement by a group of other states, dissociating themselves from the resolution, was circulated at the Commission on Human Rights. This stated that "there is no international consensus that capital punishment should be abolished" and asserted that the characterization of the death penalty as a human rights issue "must be weighed against the rights of the victims and the right of the community to live in peace and security". It was signed by 63 states, one more than had signed a similar statement the year before.

Leroy Orange, a wrongfully convicted death row inmate pardoned by Governor George Ryan, acknowledges applause during a speech by the Governor at Northwestern University Law School, Chicago, Illinois, USA, in January 2003.

©AP

2003 saw a number of key developments in the campaign to abolish the death penalty. In July the President of Armenia, Robert Kocharyan, commuted all outstanding death sentences and in September Armenia abolished capital punishment in peacetime by ratifying Protocol No. 6 to the European Convention on Human Rights. Earlier in the year the Armenian parliament had adopted a new criminal code that eliminated the death penalty in peacetime but contained a loophole that would allow its use in a case then before the courts.

Groups of prisoners had their death sentences commuted. In the USA in January, George Ryan, the outgoing Governor of the state of Illinois, commuted the death sentences of 167 prisoners and pardoned four others who he believed had been tortured into confessing to crimes they did not commit. In February it was announced that 28 prisoners, who had each spent between 15 and 20 years under sentence of death, had been released in Kenya, while the death sentences of 195 others were commuted to life imprisonment.

By the end of the year, 77 countries had abolished the death penalty for all crimes. A further 15 countries had abolished it for all but exceptional crimes, such as wartime crimes. At least 25 countries were abolitionist in practice: they had not carried out any executions for the previous 10 years or more and were believed to have a policy or an established practice of not carrying out executions. Seventy-eight other countries and territories retained the death penalty, although not all of them passed death sentences or carried out executions during 2003.

Protocol No. 13 to the European Convention on Human Rights entered into force on 1 July, having been ratified by the necessary minimum of 15 states. Protocol No. 13 is the first international treaty to provide for the abolition of the death penalty in all circumstances with no exceptions permitted. By the end of 2003 it had been ratified by 20 of the 45 member states of the Council of Europe. Ratifications of the three other international treaties against the death penalty – Protocol No. 6 to the European Convention on Human Rights, the Second Optional Protocol to the International Covenant on Civil and Political Rights, and the Protocol to the American Convention on Human Rights to Abolish the Death Penalty – stood at 43, 51 and eight states respectively at the end of 2003.

The World Day against the Death Penalty was commemorated on 10 October with local events in over 60 countries and an Internet appeal calling on the highest authorities of all countries that retain the death penalty "to ensure that executions cease immediately, and to abolish the death penalty for all crimes". The World Day was organized by the World Coalition against the Death Penalty, a coalition established in 2002 that unites national and international human rights organizations, including AI, bar associations, trade unions, and local and regional governments.

In a subsequent event, public buildings in over 100 cities around the world were illuminated on 30 November as part of the "Cities for Life – Cities against the Death Penalty" initiative. This effort was organized by the Italian organization *Sant'Egidio* with the collaboration of other organizations including AI sections.

The Fourth World Summit of Nobel Peace Laureates, meeting in Rome, adopted a final statement on 30 November stating, "After a special session, the Nobel Peace Prize Winners have agreed that the death penalty is a particularly cruel and unusual punishment that should be abolished. It is especially unconscionable when imposed on children."

> In 2003 at least 1,146 people were executed in 28 countries. At least 2,756 people were sentenced to death in 63 countries. These figures include only cases known to AI; the true figures were certainly higher.
> As in previous years, the vast majority of executions worldwide were carried out in a tiny handful of countries. In 2003, 84 per cent of all known executions took place in China, Iran, the USA and Viet Nam.

AI opposes the death penalty as a violation of fundamental human rights – the right to life and the right not to be subjected to cruel, inhuman or degrading punishment. The organization also cites other features of the death penalty – its brutalizing effect, the inherent risk of executing the innocent, the lack of a proven unique deterrent effect on crime – in support of abolition.

Alongside these considerations, one of the most powerful arguments against the death penalty is its unfairness. This unfairness encompasses recurrent aspects of the death penalty in principle and in practice, such as: its arbitrary infliction; its use following unfair trials and in cases where torture has been used; and its discriminatory use against members of racial and ethnic groups, the poor, the socially marginalized and others.

AI will work to highlight these injustices in its efforts against the death penalty in the coming years.

The use of the death penalty against child offenders – people convicted of crimes committed when they were under 18 years old – is prohibited under international law. However, a handful of countries continue to sentence to death and execute child offenders. AI will make a special effort in the coming years to end the use of the death penalty against child offenders worldwide.

The death penalty has virtually disappeared from certain regions – Latin America, Europe and the Pacific. In parts of other regions it has fallen into disuse and abolition in the near future appears to be a real possibility. In October AI launched a campaign to abolish the death penalty throughout West Africa where only four out of 16 countries have carried out executions in the past decade. AI is calling on West African countries that have not already done so to establish a moratorium on executions and abolish the death penalty in law.

Working through its membership and in collaboration with other organizations, AI continues to strive to rid the world of the death penalty.

Palestinian children on their way to school having to sneak through the wall put up by the Israeli army in the Occupied Territories. The wall/fence has cut off hundreds of thousands of Palestinians from work, education and health care facilities and from their relatives and friends.

©Eyal Dor-Ofer

Promoting economic, social and cultural rights

In June 1993, at the Vienna World Conference on Human Rights, the international community affirmed its commitment to uphold the full range of human rights as "indivisible, interdependent and inter-related". Yet, 10 years on, the systematic denial of economic, social and cultural rights, growing global inequalities and the failure of governments to significantly reduce the number of people living in extreme poverty, are among the defining human rights problems of our time.

In expanding its work to encompass economic, social and cultural rights, AI faces numerous challenges. Not least among these is the fact that many people – and many governments – continue to doubt that these rights are worthy of the same attention as civil and political rights. Various arguments are raised to justify such doubts; some of the most common are:

· financial resources are required to protect economic and social rights and therefore AI should not criticize governments which fail to fulfil these rights when such resources are lacking;

· resources and other factors make it difficult for courts to apply and enforce economic and social rights, and, if they are not enforceable through the justice system, these rights necessarily carry less force;

· enforcing these rights requires governments to take positive action, not simply to refrain from certain acts, and pushing for their implementation necessarily involves interfering in decisions on how governments should allocate budget resources;

· the best way to fulfil economic, social and cultural rights is to defend the rights to freedom of expression and association, and political participation, because in an open and democratic system citizens will be empowered to ensure their basic needs are met.

Confronting these and other arguments is an essential part of AI's work on economic and social rights. There are differences between individual human rights guarantees, not least in the degree to which they are protected in international law, but most of the common objections to economic and social rights are misguided. All human rights require governments to take positive action, including through the expenditure of resources. For example, meeting fair trial guarantees necessarily entails costs. The fact is that national courts in many countries regularly do adjudicate on rights to education, shelter, social security or access to health care. The idea that one set of rights deserves priority ignores the fact that all rights are interdependent and that political freedoms do not guarantee social justice.

During 2003, AI's experience of working on economic and social rights has demonstrated in practice the interdependence of human rights. The economic and social rights issues the organization has addressed have often arisen as a direct result of ongoing work on civil or political rights.

Some 15,000 people listen to the Chair of AI's International Executive Committee at the World Social Forum, Porto Alegre, Brazil.

©AI

Lack of respect for human rights in the Israeli-Palestinian conflict is well reported, most commonly killings of civilians, arbitrary detentions, and reports of ill-treatment. For most Palestinians, however, human rights abuses also include the ubiquitous and arbitrary restrictions placed on their movement, with whole towns, villages and neighbourhoods cut off from each other by Israeli army blockades and often placed under curfew. Even when travel is possible, military checkpoints and closures make it difficult, lengthy and potentially dangerous. Many of these restrictions amount to collective punishments or are otherwise unjustified. Freedom of movement – and its denial – is without doubt a central part of conventional civil and political rights work. Restrictions on movement, however, also have a profound impact on Palestinians' economic and social rights, not least their ability to make a living. The restrictions severely limit travel to and from work and the transport of products and services. The result has been the virtual collapse of the Palestinian economy. In 2003 AI reported in detail on these restrictions and their impact on Palestinians' right to work (see *Israel and the Occupied Territories: Surviving under siege – the impact of movement restrictions on the right to work*).

A further example of the interdependence of human rights can be seen in AI's work to expose the abuses suffered by slum-dwellers in Luanda, Angola. In previous years, AI had reported on the beatings and detentions suffered by those who mobilized to defend their homes against arbitrary and forcible evictions carried out by the government. In 2003, AI's work focused on challenging the evictions *per se*, noting that they were proceeding without due process of law and with inadequate attention to the rights of the people living there.

Similarly, AI has for many years exposed discrimination against minorities in the administration of justice, especially as regards the application of the death penalty and ill-treatment in police custody. In 2003 in Kosovo (Serbia and Montenegro), Bulgaria and Thailand, AI took action against discrimination suffered by minorities and marginalized groups regarding access to basic economic and social rights, including education, housing, work and health care.

The notion that human rights are interdependent may sound rather abstract. In practice all it means is that it is difficult to achieve sustainable progress towards implementation of any one human right in isolation. The right to effective political participation depends on a free media, but also on an educated and literate population. Rights of access to health care, to social security, or to enjoy an adequate standard of living will be better realized if a fair and effective system for the administration of justice is in place. AI will strive to demonstrate these links and in so doing to assert a holistic view of rights protection. It will be particularly important to do so in relation to extreme poverty, and the human rights issues underlying poverty.

The persistence of poverty, and in particular the situation of the more than one billion people living in extreme poverty, is well documented and also widely recognized as a matter requiring global action. All UN member states, UN agencies and the international financial institutions have committed themselves, through the Millennium Declaration, to address extreme poverty.

The Universal Declaration of Human Rights and subsequent international human rights standards hold out the promise of a life with dignity, where every person enjoys an adequate standard of living and access to those essentials that give practical meaning to such a promise – including food, water, shelter, education, work and health care. Poverty is a denial of these rights and therefore a denial of human dignity.

Those living in extreme poverty, furthermore, suffer human rights abuses as a consequence of the marginalization and exclusion that characterizes the treatment of the poor in every country. They are vulnerable to the arbitrary exercise of state power, leading to abuses of the whole range of human rights. To defend their rights, people must have access to, and equal treatment by, the police, the courts, and government offices responsible for delivering services. The poor are too often denied such access, and indeed in many cases face discriminatory treatment by such institutions.

AI developed as a movement committed to denouncing injustice. It believes that the human rights framework can and must grapple with social injustice with the same rigour that characterized its work to combat political and civil injustice. It will do this by working to ensure that marginalized and excluded communities enjoy greater access to the institutions needed to give effect to their rights and denouncing the discrimination they suffer at the hands of these institutions. AI will also insist that at a global level all governments recognize and fulfil their obligation to eradicate extreme poverty and respect basic economic and social rights.

Ending violence against women

2003 saw AI increase its work in opposing violations of women's rights and exploring the effects of gender-based violence in the home and the community committed by private individuals and groups as well as by agents of the state. AI continued to work to highlight its concerns on gender-based violence in states as diverse as Afghanistan, the DRC and Iraq.

One of the key concerns emerging from the reports published and research undertaken in 2003 was that incidents of sexual violence and even patterns of widespread and systematic violations do not necessarily come to light in the immediate aftermath of the event. Disclosure of abuse sometimes takes many years to surface.

A number of factors – such as discrimination, stigma or even the threat of being killed by their own communities – may prevent women from making public their grievances. Indifferent or ineffective justice systems, repressive governments and the lack of a public demand for accountability may also cause many years to lapse before women demand redress. The lapse of time may raise serious concerns about the possibility of fair trial for individuals accused of such abuses. However, where the state is directly implicated there can be no such concern. The Japanese state was directly involved in the sexual slavery of many thousands of so-called "comfort women" during the Second World War, and in June AI publicly expressed its support for the right of redress of surviving "comfort women" from the Japanese state. However, in April the Supreme Court of Japan dismissed an appeal filed by a group of South Korean "comfort women" demanding compensation from the Japanese government.

In July AI published a report on allegations that British soldiers had raped hundreds of Kenyan women in the 1960s and 1970s in areas of central Kenya which were used as training grounds by the British Army. AI called for a public judicial inquiry into what appeared to be a pattern of state indifference to persistent contemporary complaints.

Even where there has been timely and persistent demand for redress the state has failed to act effectively. The scale of violence and the systematic failure of the state to ensure safety for and the protection of the rights of women and girls in Ciudad Juárez and Chihuahua, northern Mexico, over the past 10 years were the subject of a major AI report published in August. The report also highlighted the role of globalization. Manufacturing industries set up in the free trade zone, where Ciudad Juárez is situated, acted as a magnet for women seeking work and led to an influx of migrants from poorer regions of Mexico. However, the environment created is one characterized by a lack of regulation and the absence of the rule of law in which hundreds of women have been killed. The women's movement and human rights organizations, and particularly the relatives of missing and murdered women, have continued a heroic struggle to demand proper investigations and to hold the state accountable for its failure to prevent or punish these crimes effectively. The intense national and international pressure on the case – including AI's campaigning on the basis of the report and a visit to the country by AI's Secretary General, Irene Khan, to meet with senior officials and President Vicente Fox – led to a number of important government initiatives to tackle the situation. However, there is a long way to go before the women of Ciudad Juárez and Chihuahua are assured of justice and safety.

In December, AI published a report on the psychological, social and economic effects on women whose husbands had "disappeared" after being arrested by the security forces in the Casamance region of Senegal. The study showed clearly the after-effects of unacknowledged deaths in the absence of judicial redress, emotional closure and economic security in the form of pension or financial compensation. The report also highlighted the cases of women rape survivors who were denied appropriate physical and psychological care as well as judicial redress.

In early 2003, AI published an account of sexual violence against women in custody in Turkey. The organization also focused its efforts on detailing the consequences for communities when violence is perpetrated by state officials. It urged the Turkish government, police and judiciary to deal effectively with violence against women in custody.

AI is also seeking to bring to public attention the effect on women of the widespread arrest and

South Korean former "comfort women" used as sex slaves by the Japanese Imperial Army during the Second World War demand compensation and redress.

detention without charge or trial of hundreds of men in many countries across the world as part of the "war on terror".

The state of insecurity following military interventions in Afghanistan and Iraq has had particularly severe implications for the safety of women and girls. Although the situations in the two countries are quite different, the collapse of state institutions has meant that the threat to women of violence in the community, whether committed by armed groups or their own families, has intensified. In Afghanistan, some women in such circumstances were also at risk of being killed if released. AI called for protection and shelter capacity to be developed as an alternative to detention for women and girls accused of *zina* crimes and at risk of violence from their families.

AI urged that the new authorities in Afghanistan and Iraq ensure that laws to protect the rights of all citizens, and in particular women and girls, were enacted and enforced.

In Africa, AI reported widespread abuses against women, including killings, torture, rape and other forms of sexual violence. The conflict in the DRC, which has seen more than three million people killed, witnessed among the highest number of mass rapes committed anywhere in the world. AI called for cases to be investigated by the DRC authorities and the International Criminal Court Prosecutor.

An AI report on child soldiers in the DRC highlighted the appalling toll the conflict has had on women and girls. Many girl soldiers testified that they were abducted and forced to join an armed group to fight on the front lines and most girls reported being raped and sexually exploited by their commanders and other soldiers in their units.

In the Occupied Territories and the DRC there is some evidence that not only do women in conflict situations face rising levels of state violence or violence at the hands of combatants, but they also face increased violence in the family.

Another developing aspect of AI's work is helping to expose the health consequences of violence against women, particularly in the context of the HIV/AIDS pandemic in Southern and East Africa, and to lobby for increased access to appropriate care and treatment as well as access to justice. International and local campaigns by other organizations have focused with increasing success on the non-discriminatory delivery of vital medicine and medical services. AI will continue to monitor the curtailment of civil and political rights and attacks on human rights defenders, including health care providers, trying to spread information about safe-sex practices or ensure access to necessary healthcare.

AI believes that the criminalization of consensual sexual relations between adults is completely unjustified and adopts as prisoners of conscience those imprisoned on such grounds. AI's work has highlighted the application of the death penalty in Nigeria where women who become pregnant outside marriage may face the death penalty under certain laws enacted in parts of the country. At the 2003 UN Commission on

Agnes Siyiankoi, the first Maasai woman to take her husband to court for beating her. In October 1998 a Kenyan magistrate found her husband guilty as charged and sentenced him to six months' imprisonment and a fine. For having the courage to speak out, Agnes Siyiankoi was severely criticized and labelled a traitor to Maasai culture.

©AP

Human Rights, AI lobbied governments to support a resolution sponsored by the government of Brazil stating that sexual orientation should not be a ground for discrimination. The resolution was deferred and AI is committed to supporting this or a similar initiative in 2004.

AI continues to campaign to hold states responsible for abuses committed by private individuals where the state has not taken appropriate action to bring the perpetrators to justice or to protect the victims. In 2003, AI Spain issued a report — *There is No Excuse* — which analysed the gaps and failures in the state's legislation and provision for women who face violence from their intimate partners.

In the UK, AI activists examined the state's denial of resources to refugee women facing domestic violence and to women whose citizenship status is insecure and dependent on an existing marriage.

AI continues to monitor legislation on domestic violence and sexual offences in many countries. It has already commented on the standards required to uphold the human rights of women in new legislation or draft constitutions drawn up in post-conflict Afghanistan and Iraq, and in Turkey, Swaziland and South Africa. AI will promote the International Criminal Court's definition of rape and its incorporation into domestic legislation. AI will also continue to campaign for states to ratify relevant international treaties, such as the Optional Protocol to the UN Women's Convention.

In 2004, AI will launch a global campaign to *Stop Violence against Women*. The campaign will concentrate on violence in the family and in conflict and post-conflict situations. It will enable AI members to work on an interrelated network of themes, to strengthen the gender dimensions of work which is already under way and to examine and challenge the multiple forms of discrimination faced by women who experience gender-based violence.

The campaign *Control Arms*, launched by AI, Oxfam and IANSA in October in 63 countries worldwide also provides an opportunity to link increasing militarization and the spread of small arms and other conventional weapons to communities with human rights abuses and in particular with violence against women.

Upholding the rights of refugees and migrants

Migration has always been an essential part of the human condition. It has been characterized by a mixture of motives – some related to social and economic rights and dynamics, and others associated with forced flight from armed conflict and human rights abuses. Among the global population of 6.3 billion people, there are an estimated 175 million migrants including over 14 million refugees and just over 1 million asylum-seekers. There are also some 25 million internally displaced people around the world.

In some respects, movement has become more available for many. For those that the global economy favours, extensive possibilities have opened up. Legal migration options for others have, however, become ever more restrictive, and the alternatives – such as people smuggling and trafficking – remain extremely treacherous. Although only about three per cent of the world's population lives outside their country of origin,

the global migration dynamic has rapidly become one of the most highly visible features of today's world.

The debate relating to the rights of refugees, migrants and displaced people has become increasingly controversial and polarized over recent years and has captured a disproportionate and unjustified amount of negative media coverage. The political will to protect refugees has seen a sharp decline over the last decade and 2003 was no exception.

Popular concerns over perceived threats to identity or ways of life in the face of rising immigration have been readily stoked by many politicians. Xenophobic and racist sentiments have featured in both developed and developing countries' responses to migration and refugee movements.

Whatever politicians decide, the reality is that migrants will continue to cross borders – with or without authorization. Some will seek to access asylum procedures. Restrictive migration control measures and security measures targeting foreign nationals risk forcing ever more people "underground" and depriving them of legal protection. Those "uprooted" from their homes are likely to experience increased vulnerability to a wide variety of human rights abuses. Those who are forced, in the absence of legal channels, to turn to smugglers and traffickers will be among those who are particularly vulnerable.

In meeting the challenges that lie ahead, and in an effort to lay the groundwork for effective advocacy for change over the coming decade, AI's work in 2003 sought to identify and highlight some key areas of law and policy that continue to impact negatively on the rights of people on the move, whether refugees, asylum-seekers or migrants.

For example, following recent changes in government in Afghanistan and Iraq, some states

A woman in Côte d'Ivoire whose house was destroyed in the conflict which erupted in September 2002.

© Sevi Gbekide / Panapress

AI members from 22 countries in Asia take part in a march to Australian Prime Minister John Howard's residence in Sydney, July 2003. Demonstrators demanded the release of child refugees and asylum-seekers held in Pacific island camps.

©Reuters

sought to pave the way for premature returns of Afghan and Iraqi refugees and asylum-seekers, despite the fact that security and human rights conditions were far from conducive to return. AI expressed concern about the timing of returns and whether they were, or would be, voluntary and sustainable. AI emphasized in particular that where conditions in a country change as a result of the violent overthrow of a regime, safety, security and human rights conditions should be even more cautiously assessed precisely because it is so difficult to make accurate assessments of the durability of change.

In Côte d'Ivoire, xenophobic sentiments were a key cause of the year-long conflict targeting not only Liberian and other refugees, but also migrant workers from neighbouring countries such as Burkina Faso. Many Burkinabè had been resident in Côte d'Ivoire for generations. Since the crisis began in September 2002, many have been forced to leave their homes and some fled Côte d'Ivoire for their country of origin where they had no meaningful social or economic links. Sent to a country which many had never even visited, they found themselves in the extraordinary position of being in a refugee-like situation, yet in their country of origin. AI documented the risks to foreign nationals in the context of a conflict fuelled by xenophobia, and raised concerns about legal, policy and practical protection gaps for refugees and migrant workers forcibly displaced by the conflict.

In early 2003 the UK, the European Union (EU) and the UN High Commissioner for Refugees (UNHCR) put forward different but related proposals to establish extra-territorial mechanisms for processing the claims

of asylum-seekers arriving in countries inside the EU. These would be closed centres to which certain asylum-seekers would be transferred and their claims considered. The UK proposal — the most controversial of the three — was to locate the centres outside the EU and was clearly designed to circumvent international legal obligations to protect refugees. Deeply concerned that a slightly modified form of Australia's controversial "Pacific Solution" would be repeated on the margins of the EU, and that compromise proposals would not sufficiently mitigate the manifest threat to the institution of asylum, in June AI published a report highlighting its fears ahead of the EU Heads of State Summit in Thessaloniki, Greece, and a key UNHCR-hosted meeting (the High Commissioner's Forum). There were clear indications that AI's intervention influenced decisions by a number of states about whether and how to proceed with such "new approaches".

As industrialized countries continue to look for new and creative ways to avoid their obligations to refugees, they are giving increasing prominence to the notion that protection can be denied in those countries because, it is claimed, they could have found "effective protection" elsewhere. On this basis, some states are seeking to shape the concept of "effective protection" to enable them to return asylum-seekers to countries where they first fled or to countries through which they travelled. AI believes that there is a continuing need for clarity on both the doctrine and the reality of "effective protection" of refugees and to ensure that the doctrine is not shaped "down" to fit the reality. AI will continue

"I am very grateful for all the help that Amnesty International gave me during my long detention. I felt very close to members from all the sections of AI in the world through the cards sending encouragement ...

It's perhaps impossible to imagine, even for one second, how those cards brought me strength, moral comfort, protection and happiness. The letters landed on the desks of all the relevant officials calling for either my release or my transfer to a medical centre which I had been refused... These letters were my great protection...

I will always be grateful to the friends and members of AI's sections and the team at the International Secretariat of AI. I reserve particular thanks for the French section who, on two occasions, sent me financial help without which I would not have been able to survive in prison because we had to pay for our own medical care..."

Letter from N'sii Luanda Shandwe, Democratic Republic of the Congo

to advocate an approach which is consistent with human rights principles.

It is increasingly evident that there is a pressing need to expand the focus of AI's work to encompass the promotion and protection of the rights of migrants in order to challenge the way in which many states label people in an effort to define away recognition – both political and legal – of their basic human rights.

Refugees, asylum-seekers and migrants continue to face human rights abuses at the point of departure, transit, arrival, stay or return. The most common abuses are discrimination, in particular on the basis of racism and xenophobia, arbitrary detention, and various forms of exploitation.

Since the end of the Cold War, the role of economic, social and cultural factors as contributory causes of conflict and flight has become more and more evident. These rights are also increasingly becoming issues in countries of asylum and transit. For example, countries such as Australia, Denmark and the UK have undermined the right to an adequate standard of living for asylum-seekers and migrants by adopting deliberately harsh policies in the name of deterrence.

The rapid decline in the political will to protect refugees, exacerbated in a number of key states by a decline in the will to protect human rights in general and those of foreign nationals in particular, represents an enormous challenge for the human rights movement.

The task facing AI and others is to persuade politicians, policy makers and the general public of the urgent need to defend the institution of asylum; to combat discrimination against refugees and migrants and to promote their rights, including economic, social and cultural rights; and to ensure that the international community identifies and implements effective mechanisms for securing protection of the rights of refugees and migrants, and for providing remedies where such rights are abused.

AI REPORT 2004

AFRICA

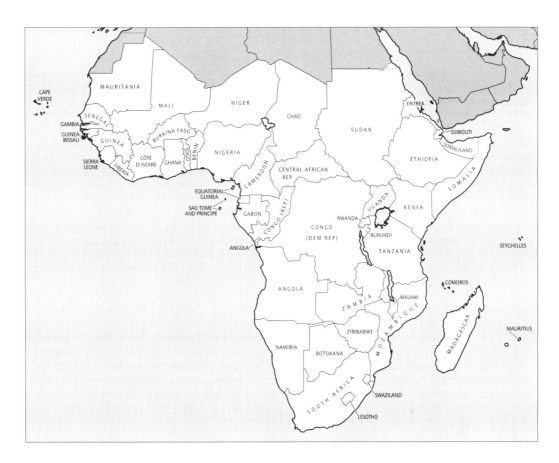

Angola
Burkina Faso
Burundi
Cameroon
Central African Republic
Chad
Comoros
Congo, Democratic Republic of the
Congo, Republic of the
Côte d'Ivoire
Equatorial Guinea
Eritrea
Ethiopia
Gambia
Ghana
Guinea
Guinea-Bissau
Kenya
Liberia

Madagascar
Malawi
Mauritania
Mozambique
Namibia
Niger
Nigeria
Rwanda
Senegal
Sierra Leone
Somalia
South Africa
Sudan
Swaziland
Tanzania
Togo
Uganda
Zambia
Zimbabwe

AFRICA REGIONAL OVERVIEW 2003

The human rights situation across the Africa region in 2003 was characterized by widespread armed conflict, repression of political opponents, persecution of human rights defenders, violence against women, and limited access to justice for the most marginalized in society. Illicit trade in resources and arms, near total impunity for past and continuing human rights abuses, and the failure of many governments to live up to professed standards of governance contributed to the denial of civil, political, economic, social and cultural rights particularly of the most vulnerable – women and children, refugees and the internally displaced, people living with HIV/AIDS, the poor and those who lack formal education. However, regional initiatives to establish greater respect for human rights progressed, including through intervention and mediation in conflict situations or in the protection of human rights defenders.

Armed conflict

Government forces and armed opposition groups frequently abused human rights in conflicts such as those in Burundi, Central African Republic (CAR), Côte d'Ivoire, Democratic Republic of the Congo (DRC), Liberia, Sudan and Uganda. Among the abuses were the use and recruitment of child soldiers as combatants and sex slaves.

In eastern DRC and particularly the Ituri district, clashes between armed ethnic groups supported by outside powers including Rwanda and Uganda cost the lives of tens of thousands of people. Men, women and children were slaughtered, raped and mutilated indiscriminately, treated as mere pawns in the power play of those benefiting from the frequently illicit exploitation of resources that has fuelled years of conflict. Tens of thousands of people were internally displaced. The intervention of a European Union-sponsored Interim Emergency Multinational Force (IEMF) in June improved the security in and immediately around Bunia in the Ituri district, where a previously deployed UN force had failed. However, after the IEMF withdrew in September, serious abuses continued outside the areas that were once again controlled by a reinforced UN Mission in the Democratic Republic of the Congo (MONUC).

A transitional government constituted in Kinshasa in July, which comprised government representatives and heads of key armed and unarmed opposition groups, faced the major tasks of rebuilding national institutions, such as a functioning independent judiciary and a credible law enforcement system, and

working with the international justice system to end impunity. In October the UN Panel of Experts on the Illegal Exploitation of Natural Resources and Other Forms of Wealth in the DRC submitted the last of four reports to the UN Security Council. The Panel had come under considerable pressure from a number of companies and governments not to repeat its previous recommendation that certain companies be investigated by their home governments for their activities in the DRC. Despite this, the Panel's fourth report again revealed the responsibility of businesses for the human rights and humanitarian crisis in eastern DRC.

In June, the then Liberian President Charles Taylor was indicted for war crimes and crimes against humanity by the Special Court for Sierra Leone – the first time such a measure had been taken against a serving head of state in Africa. He was forced to step down in August after increasing pressure from the international community and following an escalation in the conflict in Liberia. The conflict, particularly in early 2003, resulted in thousands of deaths and involved high levels of sexual violence against women and girls, and mass displacement of people within Liberia and to Côte d'Ivoire, Guinea and Sierra Leone. Charles Taylor was given refuge by the government of Nigeria which offered him implicit guarantees that he would not be prosecuted in Nigeria or surrendered to the Special Court. AI protested strongly that the Nigerian government had violated its obligations under international law, but calls to either surrender Charles Taylor to the Special Court or open an investigation with a view to determining whether to pursue criminal or extradition proceedings in Nigerian courts were ignored.

The departure of Charles Taylor from office and Liberia contributed to a stabilization of the conflict in neighbouring Côte d'Ivoire. However, the implementation of the power-sharing agreement for Côte d'Ivoire, agreed in January in Linas-Marcoussis, France, and endorsed by the UN Secretary-General, continued to face problems. No progress was made in the investigation of numerous reported human rights abuses by all parties to the conflict.

Some progress in conflict resolution was achieved elsewhere. In Burundi, a new government including several parties to the conflict was formed in November, and in Sudan new security agreements were signed in September by the government and the armed opposition group, the Sudan People's Liberation Army (SPLA). However, scores of civilians were killed in Burundi by government forces and armed groups, and in Sudan the conflict in the western province of Darfur claimed hundreds of lives and led to the displacement of hundreds of thousands of people.

In the CAR, a coup in March involving armed groups from neighbouring DRC led to the intervention of Chadian soldiers and French logistical support troops. Numerous extrajudicial executions and widespread sexual violence were reportedly carried out by several parties involved in the coup. In Uganda, a government military initiative against the armed group, the Lord's Resistance Army (LRA), led to an intensification of the conflict in the north. The LRA continued to abduct children to abuse them as combatants and sex slaves.

Economic insecurity and denial of rights

Widespread poverty, high illiteracy rates and large disparities in wealth remained major obstacles for many people in the Africa region to justice, education and adequate health care and living standards. Political rivalry including violent struggle for power and resources, as well as discrimination, led to the economic and political exclusion of large sections of the continent's population, including its youth. In spite of frequent declarations of goodwill and important regional initiatives for greater national and international investment, such as under the NEPAD (New Partnership for Africa's Development), most governments failed to live up to their promises, resulting in the spiralling deterioration of opportunities for the most marginalized and vulnerable to have access to the most basic level of livelihood.

The Africa region continued to have the highest regional rate in the world of people living with HIV/AIDS. In some countries close to 40 per cent of the population were infected, threatening a catastrophic level of human suffering and death and putting at risk the ability of society to develop in a sustainable way. While some progress was made in 2003, the majority of states and the international community continued to fail people living with HIV/AIDS in Africa by not making anti-retroviral drugs and treatment, which can also help prevent mother-to-child transmission of the virus, available to the most vulnerable.

Violence against women

Violence against women continued to be widely seen as socially acceptable, and women were frequently and blatantly denied their civil, political, economic, social and cultural rights. This seriously affected the ability of women to enjoy their sexual and reproductive rights or to gain justice for abuses of their rights. The weaker position of women in the negotiation of safe sex practices and their greater vulnerability to sexual violence led to higher infection rates of HIV/AIDS among women than among men of the same age group.

Women faced widespread discrimination in law and administrative practice. For example, there continued to be different standards of evidence for sexual "offences" such as *zina* (involving consensual sexual relations above the age of consent), and culpable homicide was used as a charge in cases of abortion and miscarriage in some states in Nigeria. As a result, women, especially those from deprived economic backgrounds and with little formal education, were more likely than men to be convicted and sentenced to death or other cruel, inhuman and degrading punishments for some crimes.

Women and girls remained the most vulnerable group in society in armed conflict and as refugees or when internally displaced. They were raped and suffered other forms of sexual violence by perpetrators from different parties to the conflicts in Burundi, CAR, Côte d'Ivoire, the DRC, Liberia, Sudan, Uganda and elsewhere.

The human rights of women were further denied by the failure of the state to protect them effectively from criminally motivated sexual violence or to support them as survivors of violence. In countries such as South Africa and Swaziland, this was largely the result of inadequate frameworks and practices of law enforcement and judicial process. In Senegal, women also faced serious obstacles in access to adequate health care and to redress for abuses committed against them and close relatives in the conflict in the southern region of Casamance over the past decades.

In several countries, legislation on domestic violence was being prepared, but progress was slow. Female genital mutilation continued to be widely practised in different forms in many countries, but only in a few have effective measures been taken at state level to eradicate the practice, despite growing campaigning by civil society to end its use.

Political repression

Political opponents were free in only a few countries in the Africa region to exercise their rights to freedom of conscience, expression and association. Governments of countries such as Cameroon, Chad, Eritrea, Ethiopia, Rwanda, Togo and Zimbabwe used malicious prosecution, arbitrary arrest and excessive force against demonstrators as tools of political repression. In some cases newspapers and radio stations were arbitrarily closed down. Journalists and human rights defenders continued to be harassed by the security forces or accused, charged and detained on grounds of libel to silence dissent and prevent criticism of government acts and policies. In some countries, detainees were denied their right to a fair trial on "security" grounds and in some instances, such as in Kenya, legislation was being prepared that would allow derogation from key human rights obligations on grounds of combating "terrorism".

In many countries, including Burundi, Eritrea, Ethiopia, Sudan, Togo and Zimbabwe, torture and ill-treatment of suspects continued to be widespread. Across the region too, the judiciary was undermined and politically influenced by governments to silence opposition. In December, the Commonwealth decided to renew its suspension of Zimbabwe because of the government's poor human rights record; Zimbabwe then withdrew from the Commonwealth.

Death penalty

The worldwide trend towards abolition of the death penalty was reflected in the Africa region, with several countries being abolitionist in law or practice. Opportunities for further progress emerged in 2003 through the work of sub-regional intergovernmental organizations such as the Economic Community of West African States (ECOWAS). However, many people remained in detention under threat of execution across the region. In Nigeria, *Sharia* (Islamic law) courts continued to hand down death sentences based on penal legislation passed since 1999, and in Zambia more than 40 people were sentenced to death for participation in an alleged coup attempt. No executions were reportedly carried out in either country. In Chad, however, nine men were executed – the first time death sentences had been carried out in the country since 1991.

Human rights defenders

Human rights defenders in the Africa region continued to play a vital role in monitoring human rights and bringing abuses to international attention. After several years of lobbying by African and international non-governmental organizations, and support from the Special Representative of the UN Secretary-General on Human Rights Defenders, the African Commission on Human and Peoples' Rights finally decided to designate a commissioner as a "focal point" to monitor abuses of the human rights of defenders in Africa, recognizing the important role they play and their specific need for protection. However, the Commission failed to adopt a declaration or binding protection mechanism to this end.

ANGOLA

REPUBLIC OF ANGOLA
Head of state: José Eduardo dos Santos
Head of government: Fernando da Piedade Dias dos Santos
Death penalty: abolitionist for all crimes
UN Women's Convention: ratified
Optional Protocol to UN Women's Convention: not signed

Efforts to consolidate peace continued. Displaced people and demobilized soldiers were resettled but many lacked basic social services and adequate food. Over 1.7 million people remained vulnerable to food insecurity. Conflict continued in the Cabinda enclave where government soldiers reportedly carried out acts of torture and extrajudicial executions. Despite a program of police reform, there were reports of beatings and extrajudicial executions by police. Political and human rights activists were briefly detained. Forced evictions occurred and thousands of victims of forced evictions in previous years remained without adequate shelter.

Background

The legacy of the war between the government and the *União Nacional para a Independência Total de Angola* (UNITA), National Union for the Total Independence of Angola, which ended in April 2002, included over a million displaced people, devastated social and economic infrastructure, and profound social inequalities generated by oil wealth and underdevelopment. Lack of government financial transparency was a significant factor in delaying a proposed post-war donors' conference.

Rehabilitation programs included assistance to an estimated 8,000 former child soldiers and one million children separated from their families during the war. Over 3,000 children lived in the streets of the capital, Luanda. Projects in two provinces drew 500,000 children into education but about a million others aged under 11 remained outside the education system.

The UN Mission in Angola (UNMA) withdrew in February. Subsequently, a small human rights office headed by the UN Resident Coordinator was established to carry out human rights promotion but not protection.

UNITA members elected Isaías Samakuva in July to replace the former leader, Jonas Savimbi, who was killed in a government attack in February 2002. The *Movimento Popular de Libertação de Angola* (MPLA), People's Movement for the Liberation of Angola, held its fifth conference in December. Political parties began preparing for elections but no election date was set.

Various professional and workers' groups protested or took strike action against poor pay and conditions. Students demonstrated in April against high public transport costs. In June state university staff went on strike over pay and conditions, resuming work 45 days later after the government agreed a salary increase.

The internally displaced and refugees

About 1.8 million people internally displaced by the war and over 90,000 refugees returned to their areas of choice, either spontaneously or through assistance programs. Despite a considerable increase in food production, up to two million people continued to need assistance. Dilapidated infrastructure and landmines hampered deliveries of food aid. In some areas, basic social services were lacking and aid agencies noted high levels of malnutrition and disease.

The reception areas that had held over 400,000 former UNITA soldiers and their families were closed in June. Many people left of their own accord. Others were transported to their homes. However, tens of thousands spent weeks in transit centres without adequate services, and there were long delays in the distribution of demobilization benefits. Government soldiers demobilized in previous years complained that they had not received retirement benefits.

Cabinda

Factions of the *Frente de Libertação do Enclave de Cabinda* (FLEC), Front for the Liberation of Cabinda Enclave, suffered heavy losses in a major government offensive in late 2002 and early 2003. The fighting caused severe displacement. Low-level conflict continued in northern Cabinda throughout the year. Government forces said they had released thousands of civilian FLEC captives. In March, state-controlled radio called on soldiers and members of the paramilitary Rapid Intervention Police to "mercilessly annihilate" FLEC fighters, claiming that they had murdered, maimed and tortured civilians, and "press-ganged" and "used them as slaves".

AI received some reports of FLEC abuses, but many more of human rights violations by government forces. Government soldiers reportedly destroyed at least 15 villages in the Buco Zau, Necuto and Belize areas, displacing and killing villagers. Soldiers posted in villages formerly under FLEC control allegedly accompanied villagers to their fields, impeding their work and increasing food shortage.

⊟ A government soldier shot dead two teenage girls in a village in Belize municipality during the temporary absence of their father in February. The soldier had been staying in their home and the girls had cooked his meals. Villagers said that he fired three shots at the younger girl, then shot her sister as she was running away.

⊟ Soldiers arrested Eduardo Brás while he was fishing near Caio Caliado village in October. The following day they entered Caio Caliado and arrested and beat his brother and four other men. Days later, seven soldiers arrested José Capita, also from Caio Caliado, at his home in Cabinda city. At the end of 2003 their families had no news of the seven men.

In a report in November, local non-governmental organizations (NGOs) detailed over 100 cases of arbitrary arrest, torture, rape, extrajudicial execution and "disappearance" in 2003. The provincial civilian authorities investigated some of the allegations, but there was no adequate response from military or civilian authorities in central government to the reports of violations of human rights and international humanitarian law by military personnel.

Criminal justice system

A commission was set up to study the criminal justice system and propose reforms, and a project to revise the penal code was initiated. Several municipal and provincial courts were rehabilitated and judges appointed. Juvenile courts were established in Luanda and other provinces. However, in many areas, access to justice was severely limited, including by the lack of human and material resources.

The police initiated a five-year Modernization and Development Plan that included restructuring, retraining, and the improvement of infrastructure, equipment and working conditions. The authorities stressed that a key objective was to improve respect for human rights.

Complaints offices where police abuses could be reported were opened in Luanda in February and subsequently in other provinces. The offices reportedly produced three-monthly summary reports, but these were not widely publicized.

Despite increased resources, police were unable to respond adequately to high levels of violent crime. Police authorities, which estimated that one third of Angolans possessed firearms, announced that they were developing a plan to collect illegally held weapons. NGOs reported cooperation from the police in their work with local communities to prepare for the surrender of weapons.

Freedom of expression and association

Human rights defenders, journalists and political activists exercised their right to monitor and criticize the government. However, some were threatened with violence. Some were arrested in connection with their work but were usually released without charge or acquitted after trial.

UNITA claimed that MPLA members attacked its offices in Huambo province in August and complained of acts of aggression and intimidation in other areas.

⌷ Riot police arrested six members of the *Partido de Apoio Democrático e Progresso de Angola* (PADEPA), Democratic Support and Progress Party, during a peaceful demonstration in Luanda in June. Three days later the six were tried on charges of holding an illegal demonstration and acquitted. The judges ruled that their detention was unlawful as they had not been brought promptly before a magistrate, and that the provincial authorities' decision to ban the demonstration was illegal.

Torture and extrajudicial executions

Reports of torture and extrajudicial executions came mainly from Luanda, where most news outlets and human rights organizations were based. The limited

information available suggested that few suspected perpetrators were brought to trial.

Early in 2003 there were many allegations that fiscal agents of the Luanda provincial government, sometimes assisted by police, beat and harassed street vendors and money changers, seizing their goods.

⌷ In March police officers beat and briefly detained a television cameraman who tried to film them ill-treating spectators at a football stadium in Luanda. A few days later fiscal agents beat two journalists who saw them steal street vendors' goods.

There were reports of extrajudicial executions by the security forces.

⌷ Manuel Mateus, a 32-year-old telecommunications worker, was extrajudicially executed in March. Two paramilitary police officers demanded bribes after his car broke down at night. His girlfriend said she saw an officer beat him with a spanner and shoot him in the foot before she fled. Relatives subsequently found his unidentified body in the morgue. The police told his relatives that an officer had shot him in self-defence, but an autopsy reportedly showed that the bullet that killed him had been fired when he was lying down. A police officer was subsequently arrested but at the end of 2003 was still awaiting trial.

⌷ Members of the Presidential Guard Unit killed Arsénio Sebastião on a Luanda beach in November because he had been singing a rap song severely critical of the government. Witnesses tried vainly to intervene as the soldiers beat, bound, stabbed and then drowned him in the sea. The perpetrators were arrested.

Forced evictions

Commercial pressure on land and the absence of security of tenure resulted in forced evictions in Luanda and other abuses in rural areas. Draft land and urban development laws failed to provide occupation rights for informal urban dwellers. This group had no effective means of obtaining or occupying land legally.

Mass forced evictions – carried out without due process, including consultation and redress – occurred in several areas of Luanda. Police forcibly evicted several families from Soba Kapassa in February, firing into the air and beating some residents. These families, and hundreds of others forcibly evicted from Soba Kapassa in previous years, received no compensation. In Benfica, 57 families were forcibly evicted in March, another 15 in April. They were rehoused on the outskirts of Luanda but many suffered loss of possessions, employment or access to schooling.

⌷ Emilia André Zunza, a 38-year-old woman with four children aged between one and 12 years, was left without shelter in Benfica after police removed the zinc sheets that formed her shelter and offered to sell them back to her. After two weeks she found accommodation with relatives.

In late 2003, over 1,400 families forcibly evicted from Boavista in central Luanda in 2001 were still living in tents. In July half of the more than 4,000 families in tents in Zango, Viana municipality, were allocated new houses. Others were subsequently rehoused.

In June, angered by the authorities' failure to provide alternative housing, former Boavista residents reportedly burned down 121 tents and occupied about 300 unfinished houses in Viana. Police and provincial government officials evicted them, beating some.

José Rasgadinho, coordinator of the Boavista residents' commission and previously detained without charge on several occasions, was arrested in September in Viana on suspicion of planning the tent-burning in June. Although the prosecutor found no grounds to charge him and ordered his release, he remained in custody for over three days because the police said they had misplaced the release warrant. Police also reportedly refused to allow him medication for hypertension.

The managers of large estates abused the rights of people whose families had built villages or homesteads on the land before the estates were privatized. On one estate in Huila province, two people arrested on suspicion of stealing cattle were reportedly tortured with cattle prods. Two of the suspected torturers were subsequently arrested but remained untried at the end of 2003. The manager of another estate in Huila province fenced off a homestead, depriving the family of direct access to water and grazing land.

AI country reports/ visits
Report
· Angola: Mass forced evictions in Luanda – a call for a human rights-based housing policy (AI Index: AFR 12/007/03)
Visit
AI delegates visited Luanda and Cabinda in April and May to undertake research.

BURKINA FASO

BURKINA FASO
Head of state: Blaise Compaoré
Head of government: Ernest Yonli
Death penalty: abolitionist in practice
UN Women's Convention: ratified
Optional Protocol to UN Women's Convention: signed

There appeared to be no progress in investigations into the alleged extrajudicial execution of more than 100 people whose bodies were uncovered in 2001 and 2002, or into the killings of a prominent journalist and three others in 1998.

Background
The crisis in neighbouring Côte d'Ivoire in September 2002 led to thousands of Burkina Faso nationals returning home, which contributed to an increasing social crisis. The two countries reopened their common border in September. However, in October the Burkina Faso authorities accused Côte d'Ivoire of being involved in an alleged coup attempt in Burkina Faso. Several people, most of them military officers, were arrested following the alleged coup attempt.

Impunity
No progress was reported in the judicial investigation commission promised in early 2002 after the human rights organization Burkinabè Movement for Human and Peoples' Rights reported that 106 bodies had been found between October 2001 and January 2002. The organization said that the bodies were handcuffed and bullet-ridden, and alleged that the victims had been extrajudicially executed by security forces during a security operation launched in October 2001. There was also no progress in the investigation into the killings of Norbert Zongo, a prominent journalist, Ablassé Nikiema, Ernest Zongo and Blaise Ilboudo in 1998.

Death penalty
On 1 April the Criminal Chamber of the Ouagadougou Court of Appeal sentenced Pierre Soulgané and Mahamady Congo to death *in absentia* for the murder and mutilation of a Belgian woman, Monique Meyer, in May 2002.

BURUNDI

REPUBLIC OF BURUNDI
Head of state and government: Domitien Ndayizeye
(replaced Pierre Buyoya in April)
Death penalty: retentionist
UN Women's Convention: ratified
Optional Protocol to UN Women's Convention: signed

Conflict raged throughout the country for most of the year. Over 100 civilians were extrajudicially executed by the armed forces. Scores of others were unlawfully killed by armed political groups. All parties to the conflict looted and destroyed property and the livelihoods of the civilian population in reprisal for perceived support of the enemy. Rape by most of the forces involved was widespread. Armed robbery by criminal gangs, sometimes with the complicity of government forces and often accompanied by rape, increased dramatically. Humanitarian organizations were increasingly targeted. In response to the rise in insecurity, the government stepped up its policy of arming the population. Politically motivated or arbitrary arrests occurred, often followed by ill-treatment or torture. A number of "disappearances" were reported. At least 5,000 people remained in detention without trial. Two soldiers were given only brief prison terms for their involvement in the killing of over 170 civilians in 2002. Freedom of expression came under attack. At least 14 death sentences were passed. About 500,000 people remained internally displaced, often without humanitarian assistance. Up to 90,000 refugees returned from Tanzania despite insecurity in Burundi. At least two people were forcibly returned to Rwanda where they "disappeared".

Background
In April President Buyoya transferred power to Domitien Ndayizeye, of the *Front pour la démocratie au Burundi* (FRODEBU), Front for Democracy in Burundi political party, thus beginning the second half of the political transition set out in the August 2000 Agreement for Peace and Reconciliation in Burundi. In October a power-sharing agreement was signed between the main armed political group, the CNDD-FDD (Nkurunziza) (*Conseil National pour la Défense de la Démocratie-Forces pour la Défense de la Démocratie*, National Council for the Defence of Democracy-Forces for the Defence of Democracy) and the Transitional Government of Burundi. A new inclusive government came to power in late November 2003.

One armed political group vowed to continue fighting – PALIPEHUTU-FNL (Rwasa) (*Parti pour la libération du peuple Hutu-Forces nationales de libération*, Party for the Liberation of the Hutu People-National Liberation Forces) – known as the FNL. An African Union force to monitor the cease-fire agreement deployed gradually throughout the year.

All parties to the conflict committed grave violations of international humanitarian law, crimes against humanity and war crimes. These included deliberate killings of unarmed civilians and other non-combatants, rape, and the recruitment of child soldiers under the age of 15.

Both government and opposition forces appeared to have obtained substantial new military equipment. Before the October agreement was signed, conflict between the CNDD-FDD (Nkurunziza) and government forces had escalated. Preparations to demobilize two marginal armed political groups paradoxically led to further recruitment, including of child soldiers under the age of 15, as the leaders struggled to prove they had fighting forces. In late 2003 fighting between the CNDD-FDD (Nkurunziza) and the FNL broke out around the capital, Bujumbura. A number of summary executions and unlawful killings took place.

In July the FNL attacked Bujumbura, occupying several districts for a week and displacing some 30,000 people. Up to 200 people died, including an unknown number of civilians. As the FNL withdrew, the government armed forces looted property, including emergency aid for the displaced. Both sides initially allowed civilians to leave but also carried out unlawful killings, the armed forces reportedly shooting dead 11 civilians in one house. The FNL shelled several districts, apparently aiming for but missing military targets, and killing at least two civilians. On the last day of the attack, a large number of child soldiers were killed, at least two as they tried to surrender. They were reported to be new FNL recruits, although the FNL denied having child soldiers in their ranks. In late 2003, the FNL extended its operations to southern Burundi for the first time.

Proliferation of small arms
The proliferation of small arms led to a dramatic increase in armed criminality. Small arms, including weapons rented by government soldiers to armed criminal gangs, were used in robberies and rapes against the civilian population. Armed criminal gangs multiplied, some formed by combatants or serving members of the government armed forces or *Gardiens de la paix* (an unpaid and untrained government militia responsible for numerous human rights abuses); former combatants or army deserters; or armed civilians with the complicity of the security forces. International humanitarian organizations were repeatedly attacked. In some provinces, the authorities responded by distributing more arms to civilians.

The rise in insecurity destroyed the health, livelihoods and foodstocks of the population. Many people slept outdoors to escape killing or rape. The government's policy of requiring an impoverished and largely displaced population to contribute to the costs of their healthcare further reduced access to medical treatment, despite international humanitarian interventions.

Violations by government forces
At least 100 unarmed civilians were deliberately and unlawfully killed by government forces in 2003, often in

reprisal for the military activities of armed political groups. Other reprisals included the systematic destruction of property and crops. In Rural Bujumbura province, the sick, the elderly and the young were sometimes bayoneted and killed after military operations. Government forces shelled indiscriminately. Following the July attack, there was heavy fighting in Rural Bujumbura, and at least 24 civilians were reportedly killed in bombing and shelling by the armed forces.

On 20 January at least 30 unarmed civilians were extrajudicially executed by government forces in Muvumu sector, Gisuru commune, in reprisal for the CNDD-FDD (Nkurunziza) killing of 10 soldiers in an ambush two days earlier.

At least nine unarmed civilians were killed in Ruziba district, Bujumbura, in October when soldiers called residents to a meeting then opened fire on them and looted their homes.

Abuses by armed political groups

Armed political groups unlawfully killed scores of unarmed civilians, suspected collaborators and several low-level government officials. Both the CNDD-FDD (Nkurunziza) and the FNL "taxed" the impoverished population, robbed scores of people and held some hostage for ransom. Both groups shelled military targets in civilian areas without taking steps to protect the civilian population, causing some civilian casualties.

Four FRODEBU members of parliament and seven other civilians were abducted by the CNDD-FDD (Nkurunziza) in June in Ruyigi province, apparently in response to reports of FRODEBU campaigning. They were released unharmed between seven and 30 days later.

In July, the CNDD-FDD (Nkurunziza) reportedly abducted three employees of international humanitarian organizations in Makamba province.

The FNL in Rural Bujumbura deliberately and unlawfully killed several local government officials, as well as people suspected of belonging to rival opposition factions. Scores of civilians suspected of passing information to the local administration or armed forces were killed or ill-treated. The FNL continued to subject civilians to "trials" for offences including collaboration, theft, adultery and drunkenness, and summarily executed an unknown number. At least eight people were summarily executed in the immediate aftermath of the July attack, suspected of collaborating with the armed forces. They included three children aged between 11 and 14.

Violence against women

The scale of rape by government and opposition forces, in particular the CNDD-FDD (Nkurunziza), strongly suggested that it was being used as a deliberate strategy and weapon of war. Civilians reported scores of cases of rape and sexual violence by armed criminal gangs; the victims included young girls.

In Ruyigi province alone, between May and August, the hospital treated 60 cases of rape. The victims were aged between nine and 77.

'Disappearances'

Several "disappearances" were reported.

In November, three men reportedly suspected of links with an anti-Rwandese armed political movement in the Democratic Republic of the Congo "disappeared" after being held in gendarmerie custody in Rumonge, southern Burundi. Two of them, both Rwandese nationals, at least one of whom was a registered refugee in Uganda, were reportedly handed over to Rwandese security forces in Bujumbura. Their subsequent fate could not be confirmed. Members of the security forces variously claimed that the third man, a Congolese national, had been handed over to the Congolese Embassy in Bujumbura or had been released.

Torture

Detainees continued to be ill-treated and tortured. Detainees were frequently tied in excruciating positions with their arms and legs behind their backs, or beaten or stabbed.

Désiré, aged 18, was detained without charge for nine days in July in central Bujumbura. He was reportedly held at a military post, where his legs and arms were tied together behind his back and he was beaten. Soldiers reportedly threatened to blow him up with a grenade or bayonet him if he did not confess to participating in the FNL July attack.

Administration of justice

In September legislation was passed to devolve jurisdiction in capital cases and cases punishable by life imprisonment to the High Courts, effectively introducing the right of appeal. The Appeal Courts had tried such cases since the reopening of the courts in 1996.

More than 5,000 prisoners out of a prison population of approximately 8,000 were awaiting trial, many on suspicion of involvement in the 1993 massacres that followed the assassination of Burundi's only democratically elected president.

The trial began in February, before the Bujumbura Court of Appeal, of five people charged with involvement in the 2001 murder of Dr Kassi Manlan, the head of the World Health Organization in Burundi, but it was repeatedly postponed. In October, four senior police or intelligence officials and a civilian were arrested in connection with the case.

Few improvements were seen in the administration of juvenile justice and children continued to be ill-treated, isolated and abused within the justice system. Under Burundian law, no child under the age of 13 may be detained. Alexandre Nzeyimana, reportedly aged 12 at the time of his arrest in April 2002, was finally released in February.

The population resorted increasingly to mob justice and lynching, and relied on armed political groups to administer "justice".

Verdict in the Itaba trial

The authorities failed to bring to justice armed forces officers responsible for the killing of between 173 and 267 unarmed civilians, many of them women and children, in Itaba commune in September 2002. In February, two officers were convicted by a military court of failing to follow orders, sentenced to four months' imprisonment – already served while awaiting trial – and immediately released. The civilian state public prosecutor ordered the case reopened, but no further investigations were known to have taken place.

International justice
The bill authorizing ratification of the Rome Statute of the International Criminal Court was adopted in June by the National Assembly. However, it was withdrawn from the Senate after the government announced its intention to make a declaration under Article 124 of the Rome Statute providing that for a period of seven years Burundi would not recognize the Court's jurisdiction over war crimes committed in Burundi or by its nationals. The Constitutional Court upheld a challenge by the National Assembly to the government's intervention and the bill was submitted to the President for signature. The bill had not been adopted by the end of the year.

Freedom of expression
Freedom of expression again came under repeated attack, although in December a less restrictive media bill was passed. In March, following the breakdown of negotiations with the CNDD-FDD (Nkurunziza), President Buyoya ordered radio stations not to mention or broadcast statements by the CNDD-FDD (Nkurunziza) or the FNL. In September, two independent radio stations were suspended for several days after they broadcast an interview with the FNL spokesperson.

The internally displaced and refugees
An estimated 500,000 people remained internally displaced. Tens of thousands were made vulnerable to disease by having to sleep outside on a regular basis to escape attack. Insecurity or obstruction by military commanders for long periods prevented access to some displaced populations, particularly in Ruyigi province, by humanitarian organizations.

Up to 90,000 refugees returned from Tanzania despite insecurity in Burundi, most because of poor conditions in the camps but also for fear of losing their land. Scores of others were forcibly returned after being arrested outside the camps.

Death penalty
At least 14 death sentences were passed and over 450 people were under sentence of death. No executions took place.

AI country reports/visits
Statements
- Burundi: Deployment of ceasefire monitors – a critical time (AI Index: AFR 16/002/2003)
- Burundi: Journalists subjected to constant attacks (AI Index: AFR 16/004/2003)
- Burundi: No justice for victims of the Itaba massacre (AI Index: AFR 16/005/2003)
- Burundi: War on civilians demands urgent action (AI Index: AFR 16/009/2003)
- Burundi: Regional summit should give priority to protection of human rights (AI Index: AFR 16/011/2003)
- Burundi: Durable peace dependent on respect for basic human rights (AI Index: AFR 16/015/2003)

Visits
AI delegates visited Burundi in July and September to undertake research. Delegates also met government authorities and visited a number of prisons.

CAMEROON

REPUBLIC OF CAMEROON
Head of state: Paul Biya
Head of government: Peter Mafany Musonge
Death penalty: retentionist
UN Women's Convention: ratified
Optional Protocol to UN Women's Convention: not signed

Security forces used lethal force against demonstrators, killing several. Political activists were prevented from holding meetings and some were briefly detained. Journalists and trade unionists were arrested for exercising their right to freedom of expression. Independent radio and television stations were closed down. Members of the Southern Cameroons National Council (SCNC) serving lengthy prison terms were not granted the right to appeal; one of them died in custody. Torture was systematic. The state failed to protect women against violence. Eight people were sentenced to death but no executions were reported.

Background
Political activity by opposition parties and repression by government and security officials increased in the run-up to presidential elections in 2004. As in 2002, the authorities banned opposition meetings and detained government critics, including political activists and journalists.

In June Nigeria agreed to implement a 2002 ruling of the International Court of Justice and return the Bakassi Peninsula and 33 border villages to Cameroon in May 2004. Nigeria undertook to withdraw its civil servants and security forces from the region before the transfer of sovereignty.

Impunity
No progress was reported on investigations into reports of extrajudicial executions in previous years or

the "disappearance" in February 2001 of nine adolescents in the Bépanda Omnisports neighbourhood in Douala.

In April Patrick Mbuwe, a former secretary of the SCNC – a group supporting independence for Anglophone provinces – was shot by men in civilian clothes and later died in hospital. Local sources suspected that the assailants were members of the security forces.

In July police shot dead five people and wounded more than 30 others during demonstrations in Douala. The demonstrators were protesting against police corruption and extortion, and the beating to death by police of a motorcycle taxi driver who reportedly failed to stop at a roadblock. No action was known to have been taken against the police responsible for using lethal force and causing deaths during the protest.

Threats against human rights defenders

In November the authorities harassed and threatened human rights defenders suspected of helping the Paris-based International Federation of Human Rights to compile a report on torture in Cameroon which was published in October. Franka Nzounkekang, director of the Human Rights Defence Group, was followed by security agents and received an anonymous telephone call threatening her assassination. The home of Alh Wakil of the Movement for the Defence of Human Rights and Freedoms was searched by security agents without a warrant. His colleague, Bouba Dirva, was told by two armed gendarmes that he was to be arrested and was then forced to pay them a large sum of money. The offices of the Douala-based Christian Action for the Abolition of Torture and the Death Penalty were under surveillance and its director, Madeleine Afité, received anonymous telephone calls.

Muzzling of independent media and government opponents

The authorities closed down or refused to grant licences to several independent radio and television stations. In February *RTA* and *Canal 2* television stations were closed down by the authorities who accused them of operating illegally. In May *Freedom FM* radio station was shut down on the eve of its inauguration. In November *Veritas* radio station, owned by the Roman Catholic Church, was ordered by the Minister of Communications to stop transmissions. Its founder, Cardinal Christian Tumi, is a known critic of the government's human rights record. In early December, *Veritas* was licensed and allowed to resumed broadcasting.

On 14 April the security forces prevented the publication of *Mutations* newspaper and seized a computer disk containing the newspaper's edition. The edition reportedly contained an article about the succession of President Paul Biya. The newspaper's editor and several journalists were arrested and briefly detained. Two days later copies of the newspaper were seized from kiosks by members of the security forces in civilian clothes.

The authorities repeatedly prevented opposition political parties and political activists from holding public or private meetings. Those targeted included the Front of Alternative Forces, some of whose leaders were briefly detained in October; the Alliance of Progressive Forces; and the Social Democratic Front.

Detention of trade unionists

In January and February Benoît Essiga, President of the Workers' Trade Union Confederation of Cameroon, and at least 13 other trade unionists were arrested and detained for several days each time. The authorities accused them of responsibility for train derailments in Central Province. They were rearrested in mid-April and released in May. They appeared to be prisoners of conscience targeted for their non-violent trade union activities.

Political prisoners

Members of the SCNC sentenced to lengthy prison terms in 1999 continued to await a decision by the Minister of Defence on their right to appeal against their convictions and sentences. One of the 18 prisoners, Daniel Ntanen, died in custody after a short illness in April. Another, Ebenezer Akwanga, who was serving a 20-year term, escaped while receiving treatment in Yaoundé General Hospital. Other detainees were in poor health and only receiving treatment offered by humanitarian organizations.

Torture and ill-treatment

In November the UN Committee against Torture expressed grave concern about systematic torture by police and gendarmes after the arrest of suspects, with perpetrators almost always enjoying impunity. It highlighted reports of severe overcrowding in prisons with life-threatening conditions amounting to cruel, inhuman and degrading treatment. As many as 72 prisoners were reported to have died in Douala central prison alone. Detainees were obliged to pay for their medical care and women and men were often not separated in custody. Only rare visits were allowed by officials of the judiciary and the National Human Rights Committee.

Violence against women

The UN Committee against Torture expressed concern that Cameroon had not passed any legislation prohibiting female genital mutilation. Provisions in the Penal Code that exempt a rapist from judicial proceedings if he marries his victim remained in force.

Death penalty

Seven people were sentenced to death in February after they were convicted of murdering a police officer in Bamenda in January 2002. In June a nurse was sentenced to death after she was found guilty of infecting her former lover's two children with HIV and hepatitis viruses by injecting them with her blood.

CENTRAL AFRICAN REPUBLIC

CENTRAL AFRICAN REPUBLIC
Head of state: François Bozizé (replaced Ange-Félix Patassé in March)
Head of government: Célestin Gaombalet (replaced Abel Goumba in December, who replaced Martin Ziguélé in March)
Death penalty: abolitionist in practice
UN Women's Convention: ratified
Optional Protocol to UN Women's Convention: not signed

Hundreds of women were raped and many of them killed by combatants involved in armed conflict. Some of the survivors contracted HIV and other diseases as a result of rape. Female genital mutilation was widely practised. Dozens of unarmed civilians were unlawfully killed. Numerous civilians, government opponents and detainees were tortured and ill-treated. Beneficiaries of an amnesty decreed by the new President included 25 people sentenced to death in their absence in 2002.

Background

Fighting between government forces and an armed political group led by former army Chief of Staff François Bozizé, which had escalated in late 2002, culminated in March in the overthrow of the government. Rebel forces captured the capital, Bangui, on 15 March. President Patassé, who had been attending a heads of state summit in Niger, stayed in exile. François Bozizé declared himself President, and in April formed a government and established a new legislative body, the National Transitional Council.

The new government created a Ministry of Justice, Human Rights and Good Governance, and a National Human Rights Commission. However, members of the security forces impeded the work of the Commission, including by denying its High Commissioner access to detainees.

In September representatives of political and civil society organizations joined a one-month "National Dialogue" to chart the country's political future. Former President André Kolingba and officials of the ruling party ousted in March were among former leaders who apologized for their part in political violence and mismanaging public affairs. The Dialogue's recommendations included establishing a conflict prevention, management and resolution structure; appointing an independent human rights commissioner; and creating a solidarity fund to compensate victims of conflicts. The Dialogue also called for the President and Prime Minister to share power under a new Constitution, and for general elections to be held by the end of 2004.

Foreign involvement in the armed conflict

Early in 2003 government forces were supported by Libyan government troops and by hundreds of combatants of the *Mouvement pour la libération du Congo* (MLC), Movement for the Liberation of the Congo, an armed political group from the Democratic Republic of the Congo. Libyan forces left the country in January. MLC fighters withdrew as the forces led by François Bozizé, reportedly with the support of Chadian government forces, took control of Bangui.

Several hundred Chadian troops were subsequently deployed as part of a peace-keeping force backed by the Central African Monetary and Economic Community (CEMAC). The CEMAC force, supported by several hundred French soldiers, was still in the country at the end of 2003.

Widespread looting of public and private property by MLC and Chadian forces was reported.

Violence against women

In late 2002 and early 2003 combatants systematically raped hundreds of women. Many women, including the elderly and children, were said to have been raped by MLC fighters, who included child soldiers, others by forces loyal to François Bozizé. Some victims were reportedly killed while resisting rape, or died from their injuries. Some who survived were infected with HIV or other diseases, and were abandoned by their partners as a result. Others became pregnant. In most cases, no action was taken against MLC rapists by the government of President Patassé, or against rapists in the forces led by François Bozizé before or after he came to power in March.

▭ After a woman testified on a privately owned radio station that she had been detained and raped by five members of a Presidential Guard unit in Bangui on 28 October, President Bozizé dismissed the alleged perpetrators and two accomplices from the army. The suspects were detained in a military barracks but had not appeared in court by the end of the year. The commander of the Presidential Guard was also removed from his post and transferred to a provincial governorship.

Female genital mutilation continued despite a 1966 law banning the practice and the existence of a government department with responsibility to campaign against it.

Extrajudicial executions

Both government and armed opposition forces unlawfully killed dozens of unarmed civilians they accused of supporting their opponents.

Numerous extrajudicial executions by forces loyal to former President Patassé came to light. They included the killings north of Bangui of at least 25 Muslims of Chadian origin for allegedly colluding with the armed opposition.

In Damara and Sibut, in the north, an improvised court martial set up by the armed opposition ordered the execution of at least 10 people. It did not respect fair trial procedures. In March a Chadian military commander reportedly ordered the summary execution of an unspecified number of civilians accused of looting. No investigation was known to have taken place and no action was taken against the officer responsible.

In August an army lieutenant reportedly shot dead two students who were among demonstrators demanding better conditions at Barthélémy Boganda College in Bangui. The officer was demoted as punishment, but was not charged or brought to trial for the killings.

Throughout the year armed men, usually in military uniform and believed to be members of the security forces, reportedly killed unarmed civilians. The victims included Barry Okonkwo Norason, shot dead in September. Soldiers at a roadblock north of Bangui robbed him and his brother as they returned from a business trip, then shot them both. His brother was injured.

Torture and other ill-treatment
Torture and other cruel, inhuman or degrading treatment were widely used by government and armed opposition forces. Chadian troops reportedly introduced a form of torture known as *arbatachar*, often inflicted on government opponents in Chad, in which the victim's limbs are tied tightly in 14 places, causing extreme pain and often resulting in death.

Soldiers tortured government officials accused of embezzling public funds and other offences soon after their arrest, threatening to kill some of them, including former government minister Gabriel Jean-Edouard Koyambounou. Nearly all the detainees were held unlawfully, often without charge, and were denied the right to challenge the basis of their arrest and detention.

Amnesty for coup plotters
In April President Bozizé decreed an amnesty for those convicted in their absence of offences related to the May 2001 coup attempt against former President Patassé. Among the beneficiaries were former President Kolingba and 24 others sentenced to death, and about 600 others sentenced to prison terms. Their trials in August 2002 had been unfair.

AI country reports/ visits
Visit
AI delegates visited the Central African Republic in September to conduct research, including into violence against women.

CHAD

REPUBLIC OF CHAD
Head of state: Idriss Déby
Head of government: Moussa Faki Mahamat
Death penalty: retentionist
UN Women's Convention: ratified
Optional Protocol to UN Women's Convention: not signed

Nine executions took place, at least four after an unfair trial. Freedom of expression came under attack. Judicial investigations continued into human rights violations under former President Hissein Habré. The impact of an oil pipeline on local people's rights and the environment remained of concern. Tens of thousands of refugees fled to Chad from conflict and state endorsed attacks in Sudan and the Central African Republic (CAR).

Background
General insecurity and violent crime increased. Sporadic armed conflict with the Movement for Democracy and Justice in Chad (MDJT) continued in the north. A peace agreement between the MDJT and the government was signed in December. A action of the MDJT rejected the agreement.

Conflict and human rights abuses in neighbouring Sudan and the CAR forced tens of thousands of refugees to seek refuge in Chad. Chadian combatants believed to include government soldiers helped CAR rebel leader, François Bozizé, to overthrow CAR President Ange-Félix Patassé in March. Several hundred Chadian soldiers, deployed in the CAR as part of a regional peace-keeping force, were involved in human rights violations, including summary executions of alleged looters, and looting.

The government facilitated negotiations between the Sudanese authorities and the Sudan Liberation Army/Movement, which resulted in a cease-fire in September.

In October President Déby's party, the Patriotic Salvation Movement, proposed amending the Constitution to allow President Déby to run for a third term in office. The proposal was met with hostility by the opposition.

Arbitrary detention
📁 Luc Maokarem Beoudou was arrested in January, detained without charge or trial for three weeks and reportedly ill-treated. He appeared to have been arrested because of an article published in 2000 by his brother, Marc Mbaiguedem Beoudou, then president of a human rights organization, who subsequently fled the country. The article accused a soldier of robbing and killing a trader.

Freedom of expression
Freedom of expression again came under serious attack.

🗀 Prisoners of conscience Bénoudjita Nadjikimo, Publication Director, and Bétoubam Mbainaye, Deputy Chief Editor, of the privately owned *Notre Temps* newspaper, were convicted of libel after an unfair trial in February. They were fined and sentenced to six months' imprisonment, and *Notre Temps* was closed for three months. They were released in April.

In October the Minister of Territorial Administration closed the privately owned radio station *FM Liberté* after it criticized President Déby, although the constitutional authority to take such action rests with the Higher Communication Council. *FM Liberté*, a vocal critic of human rights abuses, voiced concerns about increased insecurity and the Chad-Cameroon pipeline. The ban was lifted in December.

Executions

Nine men were executed in Chad in November in the first known executions since 1991. At least one person, a woman, remained under sentence of death.

🗀 Four of the executed men had been sentenced to death on 25 October for the murder of a Sudanese member of parliament and Director of the Chad Petroleum Company. Serious flaws in their trial included the use as evidence of incriminating statements allegedly made after torture.

Prisoners under sentence of death had only limited rights of recourse. They could submit a cassation plea for a retrial to the Supreme Court on grounds of gross error of fact and law, and could petition the President for clemency.

Investigations into human rights violations

Belgian and Chadian courts continued judicial investigations into human rights violations including "crimes of torture, murder and enforced disappearance" allegedly committed by former President Habré and others. A case against President Habré proceeded in Belgium despite restrictions to a law on universal jurisdiction, and related investigations in Chad reportedly concluded without charges being brought.

In September a court in the capital, N'Djaména, ruled that two police officers had no case to answer in a civil claim for damages for "unlawful violence, intentional lethal bodily harm, and aggravated grievous bodily harm". Following the killing of Brahim Selguet at a gathering of opposition supporters awaiting presidential election results in May 2001, and the wounding of several women in a peaceful protest about the elections in June 2001, lawyer Jacqueline Moudeïna, herself seriously wounded, and other victims had lodged the claim with the support of human rights groups.

Female genital mutilation

Although a law was passed in 2002 prohibiting female genital mutilation, no cases are known to have been brought to the courts. Female genital mutilation is believed to be widely practised in Chad despite efforts by the authorities and some non-governmental organizations to eradicate the practice.

Chad-Cameroon pipeline

Oil production began in October in southern Chad. The World Bank has held up the Chad-Cameroon pipeline as a model for environmental protection and for the use of revenue for development. The government admitted in 2000 using some associated funding to purchase military equipment. In 2003 exploration for new oil fields began outside the area covered by strict expenditure controls. There were continuing concerns that oil exploitation would have a negative impact on cultural, economic and social rights, that revenues would be misused and that environmental pollution would destroy rural livelihoods. Peaceful protests were organized by civil society groups when production started.

Refugees

At least 12,000 refugees and 14,000 Chadian nationals fled from the CAR into Chad, and tens of thousands of Sudanese refugees arrived from Sudan. The humanitarian situation for most Sudanese refugees was dire, with limited distribution of food and non-food items to only a minority. Attacks by Sudanese militias on refugee camps reportedly killed at least four people.

AI country reports/visits
Statement
- Chad: Amnesty International condemns executions (AI Index: AFR 20/002/2003)

Visit

In November, AI delegates visited Chad to meet Sudanese refugees and conduct research. The delegation also met Chadian government and judicial authorities, and discussed concerns including freedom of expression and the death penalty.

COMOROS

UNION OF THE COMOROS
Head of state: Assoumani Azali
Death penalty: retentionist
UN Women's Convention: ratified
Optional Protocol to UN Women's Convention: not signed

Arbitrary detention was used to intimidate and suppress political opposition. Union government forces used excessive force to break up demonstrations; one protester reportedly died as a result. Judicial independence continued to be eroded.

Background
The political stalemate which followed the devolution of power in June 2002 persisted. By the end of 2003, the issue of the separation of powers between the president of the Union and the presidents of the constituent islands had not been resolved. Legislative elections scheduled for March and April, the last step in a three-year peace process, were deferred as a result. Strikes by magistrates on Nzwani (Anjouan) led to their dismissal by the Nzwani government which took control of the judiciary in February.

Demonstrations
On 24 March government forces opened fire on primary and secondary school students demonstrating in Moroni. Three students were wounded and another was reportedly killed. A number of demonstrators were detained and allegedly beaten. The students had organized the demonstration in support of a strike by teachers over unpaid salaries which had lasted 45 days.

Conditions of detention
Prison conditions remained harsh. Cells were severely overcrowded and many had no beds or mattresses. Sanitary facilities were minimal and food had to be provided by prisoners' families.

Crack-down on opposition
Union government supporters forcibly disrupted political meetings organized by opposition parties or island governments. Political opponents of both the island and Union governments were allegedly tortured in military camps and held in unofficial detention facilities. Two ministers on the island of Ngazidja (Grand Comore) and an adviser to the island's president were arrested in February on grounds of state security. One of the ministers was detained for nearly four months before being released without charge.

Freedom of expression
A number of publications ceased operation owing to financial and political pressures. Several journalists, including Ibrahim Youssouf, were beaten by soldiers and had their equipment seized or broken when they were reporting on a demonstration that ultimately did not take place. A number of journalists were detained, including Morad Aït-Habbouche who was held from 22 to 27 September. Izdine Abdou Salam, a journalist held since November 2001, was released in February without charge.

CONGO
(DEMOCRATIC REPUBLIC OF THE)

DEMOCRATIC REPUBLIC OF THE CONGO
Head of state and government: Joseph Kabila
Death penalty: retentionist
UN Women's Convention: ratified
Optional Protocol to UN Women's Convention: not signed

Following extended peace negotiations, a transitional government of national unity was sworn in, comprising representatives of the former government, major armed groups and civil society. In practice, however, the Democratic Republic of the Congo (DRC) remained under the fragmented control of different armed forces. Conflict and grave human rights abuses continued in eastern DRC. Abuses in the east included mass unlawful killings of civilians, rape and the extensive use of child soldiers. Torture, arbitrary arrests and illegal detentions persisted throughout the country. Death sentences continued to be passed and executions resumed. By the end of 2003 around 3.4 million people remained internally displaced, in many cases in areas inaccessible to humanitarian assistance.

Background
A plan for a power-sharing coalition government, to end the conflict since 1998 that has claimed an estimated three million lives, was agreed in December 2002 in Pretoria, South Africa, in peace talks between the Kinshasa government and rebel and unarmed opposition groups. In July 2003 a transitional government led by President Kabila was established. Four Vice-Presidents were drawn from the former government, the unarmed political opposition and the two major armed political groups, the *Mouvement pour la libération du Congo* (MLC), Movement for the Liberation of the Congo, and the *Rassemblement congolais pour la démocratie-Goma* (RCD-Goma), Congolese Rally for Democracy-Goma. Ministerial posts were appointed from these groups, other armed groups and civil society. In October, the UN Special Rapporteur on the DRC noted that individuals involved in mass human rights violations had been appointed to the government.

The transitional government was mandated under the peace accord to hold free and fair national elections within 24 months and to form a unified national army. It must disarm, demobilize and reintegrate into civilian life scores of thousands of combatants who will not be integrated in the new army. A joint military command was established, but the armed groups continued to control large areas of the country.

The transitional Constitution established a number of civil institutions to support progress towards democracy, including a National Human Rights Observatory and a Truth and Reconciliation Commission. Both institutions lacked sufficient independence, proper resources and a clear mandate. One individual suspected of involvement in human rights abuses was appointed to the executive committee of the Truth and Reconciliation Commission.

In eastern DRC, mass killings took place in May in Ituri district of Oriental province, where antagonism between the Hema and Lendu ethnic groups since 1999 had been manipulated by armed political groups and Ugandan government forces for political and economic gain. In May, as the situation deteriorated, the UN authorized the deployment of an Interim Emergency Multinational Force (IEMF) to Bunia, capital of Ituri. The Force largely restored security inside the town, but did not deploy to surrounding areas where killings continued. It withdrew in September and was replaced by a reinforced brigade of peace-keepers from the UN Mission in the Democratic Republic of the Congo (MONUC). By the year's end the brigade had begun to deploy outside Bunia.

On 28 July the UN Security Council authorized MONUC forces to use "all necessary means" to protect civilians under imminent threat of physical violence in Ituri district and the Kivu provinces, and imposed an arms embargo on the same areas.

Human rights abuses in other crisis zones, notably in North- and South-Kivu provinces, continued at a high level, despite the installation of the new government. Widespread sexual violence, unlawful killings of civilians and recruitment of children into armed forces persisted. A redeployment of MONUC forces to the Kivu provinces was planned but not substantially implemented by the end of 2003. MONUC troops in the DRC numbered around 10,500 by the end of 2003, 4,800 of them deployed in Ituri.

Impunity for the perpetrators of human rights abuses remained widespread. The European Union and UN took steps towards rebuilding and reforming the judicial system, which included a review by international and national experts. In July the Prosecutor of the International Criminal Court indicated that his office would undertake a preliminary examination of alleged atrocities in Ituri.

Exploitation of natural and economic resources continued to drive the conflict. In October the UN Panel of Experts on the Illegal Exploitation of Natural Resources and Other Forms of Wealth in the DRC submitted its final report to the UN Security Council. Previous reports had named a number of international companies as engaged in resource exploitation that contributed to funding the DRC conflict. The final report referred 40 companies for further investigation by their own governments. Part of the report was not made public and allegedly accused Rwanda and Uganda of continued exploitation in the DRC and of breaking the arms embargo. The Panel was disbanded at the end of October. The majority of its recommendations remained unimplemented. Reports continued of Rwandese and Ugandan involvement in eastern DRC after their forces had officially withdrawn, allegations denied by both governments.

Unlawful killings
Ituri
Ituri district saw a dramatic escalation of violence. In March Ugandan government forces seized control of Bunia and other areas after dislodging the Hema-dominated armed group, the *Union des patriotes congolais* (UPC), Union of Congolese Patriots, their former allies. The fighting in Bunia claimed many civilian lives.

On 6 May Ugandan government forces withdrew from Ituri. Immediately afterwards, inter-ethnic killings of civilians by Lendu and Hema militia or the UPC resulted in more than 400 reported deaths in Bunia and further killings outside the town, including of two MONUC observers in Mongbwalu. MONUC forces present did not protect civilians adequately. The arrival of the IEMF in June and a reinforced MONUC brigade in September calmed the situation in Bunia, although insecurity persisted for the remainder of the year.

Massacres of civilians, however, continued in other areas of Ituri. Most of the several hundred killed were women and children, attacked with machetes, homemade weapons and small arms. Hundreds of thousands fled the violence, and at the year's end were internally displaced, often inaccessible to humanitarian aid because of continuing violence, or living as refugees in precarious circumstances.

🗇 Massacre sites included Nizi, where 22 civilians were killed on 7 July; Tchomia, where over 300 people were reported killed on 31 May and at least 80 on 15 July; Fataki, where at least 60 were killed in July and early August; and Katshele, where on 6 October 65 civilians were killed, 42 of them reported to be children.

Mambasa
In February the MLC, faced with international condemnation, tried 27 soldiers by military court for their part in large-scale killings, torture, including rapes, and other abuses by MLC and RCD-National forces in and around Mambasa, in Oriental province, in late 2002. However, by the end of the year, many of the soldiers had reportedly been released. The victims were mainly from the Nande ethnic group, who were targeted for their presumed support of a rival armed group, the *Rassemblement congolais pour la démocratie-Mouvement de libération* (RCD-ML), RCD-Liberation Movement, and the Twa community.

South-Kivu
In South-Kivu province, scores of unarmed civilians were killed in fighting between various armed groups or

in unlawful killings by all the forces involved. The fighting created massive waves of displacement. Combatants extensively looted and destroyed homes, schools, medical and nutritional centres, and religious institutions.

In the Ruzizi plain, they committed systematic abuses against civilians they accused of supporting the "enemy". In October an agreement to cease hostilities between the Congolese *mayi-mayi* militia and the RCD-Goma was signed after mediation by MONUC.

The Hauts-Plateaux region, home to a large Banyamulenge (Congolese Tutsi) population, was the scene of a continuing rebellion by a former RCD-Goma commander. RCD-Goma forces struggled to control the rebellion and reportedly used excessive, indiscriminate violence against civilians, particularly Banyamulenge. Large numbers of civilians were killed in the fighting, and up to 30,000 were displaced.

⬜ In April scores of unarmed civilians were reported to have been killed in Uvira, Walungu and Bukavu in fighting between the RCD-Goma and *mayi-mayi*.

Child soldiers

All armed forces in the DRC used children as soldiers. In the east, armed political groups actively recruited children, who reportedly constituted more than 40 per cent of their armed forces in some instances. Child soldiers, boys and girls, sometimes as young as seven, were typically subjected to ill-treatment during their training; in some camps, children died from the harsh conditions. They were often sent into combat or used as sex slaves. Some were forced to kill their own families; others were made to engage in cannibalistic or sexual acts with enemy corpses. Girl soldiers were raped and some died as a result. Child soldiers detained for breaches of discipline were tortured and ill-treated.

None of the commitments to demobilize children given by the various armed forces proved genuine, and little effort was made to support reintegration of former child soldiers into civilian life. In the east, the small numbers of children who were officially demobilized were at constant risk of re-recruitment. During visits to the DRC, AI delegates heard testimony from former child soldiers of the torture, ill-treatment and other abuse of child soldiers by combatants.

⬜ A child soldier, recruited at the age of 13 by the RCD-Goma, lost the use of his legs as a result of beatings to his spine in Mushaki training camp, North-Kivu province.

⬜ A child soldier, aged 12, who was first forcibly recruited aged seven, witnessed fighters cutting off his commander's head in fighting in Ituri. The boy was wounded in the arm and was not given proper treatment for his injury or trauma.

⬜ A former child soldier from South-Kivu, recruited when she was 12 by the RCD-Goma, was repeatedly beaten, whipped and raped by other soldiers. She had a baby as a result of these rapes.

Violence against women

Sexual violence against women of all ages, including very young girls, was used as a weapon of war by most of the forces involved in the conflict. In many cases rape was followed by the deliberate wounding or killing of the victim. Thousands of women and girls were abducted and forced to remain with armed groups as sexual slaves. The prevalence of HIV/AIDS among combatants added to the trauma and social stigma faced by these women, who feared being ostracized by their families or communities. Medical and psychological treatment appropriate to the needs of the victims was rare. Leaders of armed groups have taken few meaningful steps to protect women and girls against rape by their fighters, and few of those responsible have been brought to justice.

⬜ In South-Kivu, the UN estimated that some 5,000 women had been raped between October 2002 and February 2003, an average of 40 a day.

⬜ On 16 May a soldier forced his way into the house of Kavira Muraulu, from Mangangu near Beni, North-Kivu, and raped her. After reporting the rape to the district governor, she was attacked again at her home by the alleged rapist and other soldiers, who beat her and stabbed her with a bayonet.

Torture and illegal detention

People suspected of links with opposing armed political groups were targeted for torture and illegal detention. Human rights defenders and journalists engaged in legitimate investigation and criticism were also beaten, threatened and unlawfully detained because of their reporting on the human rights situation.

Torture techniques typically included systematic beatings or whippings of detainees, stabbing with bayonets or electric shocks. Torture was facilitated by the widespread use of private and unofficial detention centres – including underground pits (*cachots souterrains*), freight containers and the homes of security officials – particularly in areas of eastern DRC under the control of armed political groups.

Arbitrary detentions remained frequent across the DRC and virtually none of those detained were known to have had their arrest ordered or reviewed by an independent judicial official. Many spent long periods in detention without charge or trial.

⬜ Two men, Paul Mbonabihama and Ndibwami Nyanga, died as a result of torture in RCD-Goma detention in Bunagana, North-Kivu province, in January. At least three other men were also tortured. They had a hot iron pressed on their backs and heavy weights attached to their testicles, and were suspended upside-down for long periods. A woman detainee reportedly had gunpowder set alight close to her breasts and her thumbnails ripped out. No action was taken against the perpetrators.

⬜ Donatien Kisangani Mukatamwina, a member of the non-governmental human rights organization *Solidarité-Echange pour le Développement Intégral*, Solidarity-Exchange for Integrated Development, based in Uvira, South-Kivu, was arrested by the RCD-Goma in June. RCD-Goma officials detained him without charge for 13 days on the pretext that he was linked to the *mayi-mayi*, and allegedly beat and threatened to kill him.

🗀 Human rights defender N'sii Luanda Shandwe was released on 26 January, having spent nine months as a prisoner of conscience at the *Centre pénitentiaire et de réeducation de Kinshasa*, Kinshasa Penitentiary and Re-education Centre. He was detained because of his human rights activism, but was not formally charged with a criminal offence.

Death penalty

On 7 January, 15 people were executed in secret in Kinshasa, the first executions known to have taken place since December 2000 and the first following the government's suspension in September 2002 of a moratorium on the death penalty. The 15 detainees were reportedly executed at a military camp close to Kinshasa's international airport, and the bodies were buried in a common grave nearby.

The Military Court, which had conducted unfair trials and sentenced to death large numbers of people, including civilians, was abolished by presidential decree in April. Other courts continued to sentence prisoners to death.

AI country reports/ visits

Reports

- Democratic Republic of the Congo: On the precipice – The deepening human rights and humanitarian crisis in Ituri (AI Index: AFR 62/006/2003)
- Democratic Republic of the Congo: "Our brothers who help kill us" – Economic exploitation and human rights abuses in the east (AI Index: AFR 62/010/2003)
- Democratic Republic of the Congo: Ituri – How many more have to die? (AI Index: AFR 62/030/2003)
- Democratic Republic of the Congo: Ituri – A need for protection, a thirst for justice (AI Index: AFR 62/032/2003)
- Democratic Republic of the Congo: Children at war (AI Index: AFR 62/034/2003)
- Democratic Republic of the Congo: Addressing the present and building a future (AI Index: AFR 62/050/2003)

Visits

In January, February and March AI delegates visited Kinshasa, Goma in North-Kivu, and Bukavu and Uvira in South-Kivu. In July AI delegates visited Bunia and Beni in Ituri province and western Uganda. In October AI's Secretary General travelled to the DRC, Rwanda and Uganda to meet senior government and UN officials, survivors of human rights abuses, human rights activists and international humanitarian agencies.

CONGO
(REPUBLIC OF THE)

REPUBLIC OF THE CONGO
Head of state and government: Denis Sassou-Nguesso
Death penalty: abolitionist in practice
UN Women's Convention: ratified
Optional Protocol to UN Women's Convention: not signed

The government tried to prevent investigations and prosecution in French courts of senior officials accused of involvement in "disappearances" in 1999. Killings of alleged sorcerers were allowed to continue with impunity. Combatants responsible for past human rights abuses were granted an amnesty. People displaced from their homes by internal conflict faced a humanitarian crisis.

Background

In February a former Rwandese armed forces officer was arrested in the capital, Brazzaville, for his alleged role in the 1994 genocide in Rwanda and handed over to the International Criminal Tribunal for Rwanda (ICTR).

In March the government signed a peace agreement with an armed opposition group, the *Conseil national de résistance* (CNR), National Resistance Council, bringing an end to a one-year armed conflict in the Pool region. Implementation of the agreement included disarming some 2,300 CNR combatants known as *Ninjas* and releasing 40 captured combatants. In August the National Assembly approved a law granting amnesty to CNR combatants and to government forces, allied militias and mercenaries accused of any crimes committed since January 2000.

In August a President was appointed to head a National Human Rights Commission created under the 2002 Constitution. The Commission is mandated to work for the protection and promotion of human rights. Several non-governmental human rights groups questioned the independence and impartiality of the Commission.

On 12 August new members of the High Court of Justice were sworn in. The Court, composed of 17 Supreme Court judges and 19 members of the legislature, is empowered to try government officials, including the President, ministers and members of parliament. The appointment of new members, who constituted a majority of the Court's membership and included politicians, raised fears about their independence and impartiality and the motives behind their appointment.

On 1 September the government ratified the UN Convention against Torture. On 22 November the National Assembly passed a government bill to ratify the Rome Statute of the International Criminal Court.

During the last three months of 2003 the International Committee of the Red Cross provided training in international humanitarian law for as many as 1,500 armed forces officers.

Impunity: the May 1999 'disappearances'

In April the government asked the International Court of Justice (ICJ) in The Hague to rule that French courts had no jurisdiction over investigations or prosecutions of Congolese government and security officials, including President Sassou-Nguesso. In a case lodged in a French court in late 2001, the officials were accused of responsibility for the May 1999 "disappearance" of at least 353 refugees returning from the neighbouring Democratic Republic of the Congo (DRC). In June the ICJ dismissed the government's case. However, no official was brought to justice.

Investigations in the Republic of the Congo into the 1999 "disappearances" had not concluded by the end of 2003. It was reported that the investigating judge had interviewed government ministers, security officials and relatives of the "disappeared", and had charged four people – whose identities were not revealed – with unspecified offences. No one was arrested. In early November the investigating judge said the investigations had been blocked, but gave no further details. He died following an illness in mid-November and is not known to have been replaced.

In November the government was reported to have demanded that the UN High Commissioner for Refugees (UNHCR) provide documents relating to the return of refugees in 1999. In a letter to the UNHCR, the Minister of Foreign Affairs reportedly said that those alleged to have "disappeared" had actually remained in the DRC. By contrast, the Minister of Communication was reported as saying that there may have been a settling of personal accounts and unfortunate mistakes, but that the authorities "had no plan" to abduct or kill refugees.

Unlawful killings

The government failed to take action against unlawful killings. At least 13 people, five of them unarmed civilians, were killed on 15 October during a shoot-out at Mindouli in the Pool region. According to the authorities, the shoot-out began after railway officials tried to prevent former *Ninja* combatants from loading fuel containers on to a train. No action was known to have been taken against the perpetrators.

Human rights groups expressed concern in October that people were killing alleged sorcerers accused of responsibility for apparently natural deaths. In the Cuvette region alone, as many as 87 alleged sorcerers were reportedly killed between 1999 and 2003. The authorities failed to take action to prevent the killings or bring the perpetrators to justice.

Internally displaced people

More than 230,000 people had been displaced from their homes by armed conflict at the start of 2003. Many of them had no access to adequate food or medicine. The UN Office for the Coordination of Humanitarian Affairs (OCHA) reported in September that there was an acute humanitarian crisis in the Pool region.

AI country reports/ visits

Report

· Republic of the Congo: A past that haunts the future (AI Index: AFR 22/001/2003)

CÔTE D'IVOIRE

REPUBLIC OF CÔTE D'IVOIRE
Head of state: Laurent Gbagbo
Head of government: Seydou Diarra (replaced Pascal Affi N'Guessan in January)
Death penalty: abolitionist for all crimes
UN Women's Convention: ratified
Optional Protocol to UN Women's Convention: not signed

A National Reconciliation Government was established in April under the Linas-Marcoussis Agreement signed by all sides to the year-long internal conflict, but the political situation remained volatile throughout the year. In practice the country remained divided in two by a security zone controlled by French soldiers and troops of the Economic Community of West African States (ECOWAS). Human rights abuses continued to be perpetrated by all parties to the conflict, resulting in tens of thousands of civilians fleeing Côte d'Ivoire or being internally displaced within the country. Several people in the capital, Abidjan, were abducted by armed individuals, some of them members of the security forces operating during the hours of curfew. In the west, along the border with Liberia, armed opposition groups raided towns and villages, killing civilians, raping women and forcibly recruiting people. All parties to the conflict forcibly recruited civilians, in particular Liberian refugees and including children under the age of 18. Government security forces and pro-government militias targeted Ivorian and foreign journalists against a background of xenophobia and "hate speech".

Background

After the uprising in September 2002 by armed groups resulted in the division of the country, the international community made several attempts at mediation to reach a peaceful solution to the crisis. In January, all parties to the conflict signed the Linas-Marcoussis Agreement in France. The Agreement, endorsed by the UN, the European Union and the African Union, provided for the constitution of a government of national reconciliation and the regrouping, disarming and demobilizing of the forces on the ground. The first steps towards its implementation were the nomination of a Prime Minister agreed by all parties, Seydou Diarra, and the formation in April of a National Reconciliation Government, which included representatives of the armed opposition groups, renamed *Forces nouvelles*, New Forces.

Although the situation along the Liberian border remained tense, with continuing clashes between elements of the armed opposition groups and French and ECOWAS troops, the war was officially declared over in July. In September, however, government ministers representing the *Forces nouvelles* withdrew from the government after disagreement with President Gbagbo over the appointment of the Security and Defence Ministers. Tensions increased and in November, members of the armed forces and pro-government militias who claimed loyalty to President Gbagbo asked for the departure of French troops, a demand the President refused. In December the ministers representing the *Forces nouvelles* announced their return to government. President Gbagbo announced an imminent disarmament operation and his willingness to go to Bouaké in central Côte d'Ivoire, the second largest city and the *Forces nouvelles* stronghold, to announce the official end of the war. In December the government approved laws on the eligibility of presidential candidates and on rural land ownership, and President Gbagbo declared that these laws would be put to a referendum.

Extrajudicial executions and 'disappearances'
Members of the security forces, including plainclothes officers, were responsible for several extrajudicial executions and "disappearances", notably in Abidjan. Pro-government militias, their actions supported or condoned by the security forces, carried out other abuses such as intimidating and beating opponents, foreign nationals and journalists. Many of these acts occurred during curfews, when only members of the security forces were allowed to move around the city. Many of the victims were foreigners or Ivorians bearing Muslim names and suspected of supporting the armed uprising. No investigations were carried out into these abuses and the perpetrators enjoyed complete impunity.

On 19 February, Lamine Sangaré, an imam, was arrested by two gendarmes, paramilitary police officers, in Abobo, a neighbourhood of Abidjan. He refused to go with the gendarmes, who shot him dead.

At the beginning of March, armed men in uniform, claiming to be part of the security forces, in the early hours arrested Cissé Korotomou and Diakité Mamadou, who were sleeping in their house in a neighbourhood of Abidjan. They accused them of harbouring "rebels", beat Diakité Mamadou with the butt of a gun and took both men to an unknown destination. Their families had no further news of them.

Abuses by armed opposition groups
Armed opposition groups committed human rights abuses, notably in the west where they terrorized the population, raping women and forcibly recruiting civilians, including children under the age of 18.

On 24 January, in Soukourougban in central Côte d'Ivoire, armed members of the *Mouvement patriotique de Côte d'Ivoire* (MPCI), Patriotic Movement of Ivory Coast, burst into a funeral ceremony and forced the 26 people there to lie on the ground. They shot Daubge Adama as he arrived for the funeral, forced three people to bury his body, then killed them too.

Between 9 and 11 February, members of the two armed opposition groups that were formed in the west in November 2002 – the *Mouvement populaire ivoirien du grand ouest* (MPIGO), Western Côte d'Ivoire Popular Movement, and the *Mouvement pour la justice et la paix* (MJP), Justice and Peace Movement – attacked Gohouo-Zagnan, a village near Bangolo. They shot dead about 20 civilians and abducted several women, including Glao Célestine and Tahou Bah Dumas. By the end of the year their whereabouts and fate remained unknown.

Refugees and the internally displaced
From the beginning of the crisis in September 2002, hundreds of thousands of civilians – foreign and Ivorian nationals – were forced to seek safety in neighbouring countries or within Côte d'Ivoire. Liberian refugees who had lived in Côte d'Ivoire since armed conflict broke out in Liberia in 1989 were targeted by both government and opposition forces in Côte d'Ivoire. In April, thousands who had fled back to Liberia were forced to return to Côte d'Ivoire after violent clashes in eastern Liberia between Liberian government and opposition forces. Many refugees were victims of torture, extrajudicial executions and forcible recruitment by Ivorian government and opposition forces.

During a visit to Côte d'Ivoire in March, AI delegates heard testimony of forced recruitment, including of children aged under 18, organized by members of the security forces in the refugee camp at Nicla, near the village of Guiglo in the west, and in Abidjan.

Journalists targeted
Several Ivorian and foreign journalists were harassed and attacked by the security forces and pro-government militias, who accused them of being partial. In most cases, those responsible were not held to account for acts of intimidation and assault.

In January, *Reuters* correspondent Anne Boher was arrested in the town of San Pedro and detained overnight by the security forces. She was released without charge the next day.

In March a French television crew was verbally abused and physically assaulted by uniformed and plainclothes security officers while covering a press conference held by President Gbagbo in the Presidency compound.

On 21 October, Jean Hélène, a *Radio France Internationale* correspondent, was shot dead by a police officer while awaiting the release of opposition party activists outside a police station in central Abidjan. The officer was arrested and an inquiry opened. At the end of the year the trial was postponed.

Impunity

Despite commitments by all parties to the conflict to accept an international inquiry into human rights abuses since the September 2002 uprising, impunity remained the rule and fuelled further human rights abuses. The Linas-Marcoussis Agreement stated that those responsible for human rights violations "must be brought to justice before an international criminal jurisdiction". In February the UN High Commissioner for Human Rights reminded parties to the conflict that grave human rights violations were punishable as international crimes. In August parliament passed an amnesty law that covered acts of rebellion against the government but that did not apply to serious violations of human rights and humanitarian law. Despite this provision, no inquiry was opened into any of the serious and numerous allegations of abuses committed by all the parties to the conflict.

UN Security Council

The UN Security Council was involved throughout the year in the resolution of the crisis. In February it endorsed both the Linas-Marcoussis Agreement and the peace-keeping operation launched by ECOWAS and France, and authorized recourse to force by the peace-keeping troops for a duration of six months. In May it established a political mission to facilitate implementation of the Linas-Marcoussis Agreement, the UN Mission in Côte d'Ivoire (MINUCI). Following a request by ECOWAS, in November the UN Security Council discussed deploying a UN peace-keeping mission and decided to extend the MINUCI mandate for three months.

AI country reports/ visits

Reports

- Côte d'Ivoire: A succession of unpunished crimes — from the massacre of gendarmes at Bouaké to the mass graves of Daloa, Monoko-Zohi and Man (AI Index: AFR 31/007/2003)
- Côte d'Ivoire: No escape — Liberian refugees in Côte d'Ivoire (AI Index: AFR 31/012/2003)

Visit

In March AI delegates visited Côte d'Ivoire, met President Gbagbo and government officials, and carried out research.

EQUATORIAL GUINEA

REPUBLIC OF EQUATORIAL GUINEA
Head of state: Teodoro Obiang Nguema Mbasogo
Head of government: Candido Muatetema Rivas
Death penalty: retentionist
UN Women's Convention: ratified
Optional Protocol to UN Women's Convention: not signed

Despite a partial amnesty in August, more than 30 prisoners convicted in 2002 on the basis of confessions extracted under torture remained in harsh conditions that amounted to torture. At least two of them needed hospital care because of ill-treatment and medical neglect. Several members of the opposition were detained for exercising their right to freedom of expression or for membership of political opposition groups.

Background

In January President Teodoro Obiang Nguema Mbasogo, in power since 1979, was sworn in for another term of seven years following an election in which he won 97 per cent of the votes. The European Parliament criticized the flaws in the electoral process, which it described as "neither free nor fair".

Shortly after the election, the President said that he favoured a broad-based national unity government. However, he refused to meet a pre-condition of the main opposition party, the *Convergencia para la Democracia Social* (CPDS), Convergence for Social Democracy, that their Secretary General, Plácido Micó, be released from prison.

Update: 2002 FDR trial

Plácido Micó was not released until August when he and 17 other prisoners sentenced at the same trial in 2002 were granted a conditional pardon. A total of 67 people had been convicted of involvement in an alleged coup plot by the *Fuerza Demócrata Republicana* (FDR), Republican Democratic Force, an unauthorized opposition party, and sentenced to long prison terms. Many appeared to be prisoners of conscience, arrested solely because of their links with the FDR. Their trial was unfair and their convictions based on statements made under torture.

Arrests of prisoners of conscience

Several people suspected of being political opponents were arrested and detained without charge or trial.

In January, Simón María Nsue Mokuy, local representative of *Fuerzas Republicanas de Reflexión y Acción en Guinea Ecuatorial* (FRRAGE), Republican Forces for Reflection and Action on Equatorial Guinea, a grouping of political exiles in France and Spain, was arrested. He was detained incommunicado without charge or trial for six weeks solely for exercising his right to freedom of expression. He had distributed information about a meeting to be held in Paris by the FRRAGE group.

◻ In October, Bienvenido Samba Momesori, a Protestant pastor, was arrested by plainclothes police officers in the capital, Malabo, while celebrating mass at his church. His whereabouts were unknown for two weeks, until his daughter was allowed to visit him in the main Malabo prison, known as "Black Beach". One week later he was transferred. After many efforts, his relatives learned that he was held at Evinayong prison, in the continental part of the country, 300km from Malabo.

◻ In November, Rodrigo Angue Nguema, a journalist working for the French news agency, *Agence France Presse*, was detained without charge or trial for eight days and questioned about the sources of an article he had written.

Harsh prison conditions

Conditions remained harsh for prisoners sentenced in connection with the alleged FDR plot, who were held in the "Black Beach" prison. At the beginning of 2003, they remained crammed together in small, dangerously overcrowded cells. In March, two of the prisoners were transferred to hospital. One of them, Lorenzo Asu Nguema, had a broken rib as a result of being beaten. In April the conditions improved a little and the prisoners were allowed to receive family visits and reading material. However, the authorities continued to pressure them to sign "confessions" admitting guilt, asking the President for forgiveness and promising to join his ruling party.

◻ In June FDR leader Felipe Ondó Obiang was transferred to Evinayong prison, apparently because he refused to ask for a presidential pardon. He was held in conditions that amounted to torture, and his physical and mental health deteriorated. He was kept chained to the wall in his cell by his left leg, which became swollen and painful, and was held for several months in solitary confinement.

UN Commission on Human Rights

In April the UN Commission on Human Rights considered the report of a visit to Equatorial Guinea in December 2002 by the Special Rapporteur on the promotion and protection of the right to freedom of opinion and expression. His report stressed the "legal and administrative obstacles to the registration of non-governmental organizations, in particular in the field of human rights" in Equatorial Guinea. The government did not respond to his recommendations to allow the establishment of independent human rights organizations. In 2002 the Commission had ended the mandate of the Special Rapporteur on Equatorial Guinea, who monitored human rights in the country for over 20 years.

ERITREA

ERITREA
Head of state and government: Issayas Afewerki
Death penalty: retentionist
UN Women's Convention: ratified
Optional Protocol to UN Women's Convention: not signed

Hundreds of people were arrested for the peaceful expression of their opinions or beliefs. Scores of other prisoners of conscience remained held since a major crack-down on dissent in 2001, including former government leaders and journalists. Prisoners of conscience included hundreds of members of minority religions, some detained for nine years. They were held indefinitely without charge or trial, and incommunicado in secret detention places. Torture of political prisoners was reported, including of army deserters who had no right of conscientious objection to military service. Women conscripts were reportedly sexually abused. Information came to light of ill-treatment and possible extrajudicial executions of Ethiopian prisoners of war during the 1998-2000 border conflict.

Background

The ruling People's Front for Democracy and Justice (PFDJ) remained the sole permitted political party. The government made no announcement of any steps towards multi-party elections as required by the 1997 Constitution. No opposition activity or criticism of the government was tolerated, and no independent non-governmental organization was allowed. Constitutional protection against arbitrary detention and guarantees of "freedom of conscience, expression of opinion, movement, assembly and organization" were ignored. The private media remained banned. Law reform was delayed further and the Special Court, an anti-corruption tribunal of military judges that allows no legal defence representation or appeal, continued to convict defendants in secret.

A drought put a third of the country's population at risk.

Aftermath of the 1998-2000 war with Ethiopia

Fears of a new war with Ethiopia — likely to result again in huge military casualties and massive human rights abuses against civilians — intensified in late 2003. Although both sides declared they would not start war, the peace accord was thrown into question when Ethiopia rejected the April 2002 ruling of the Eritrea-Ethiopia Boundary Commission at The Hague, the Netherlands, and the UN Security Council's call for it to implement the ruling. The Commission had concluded that the small border town of Badme, which had been the flashpoint of the 1998-2000 war, was Eritrean territory. This indefinitely delayed the planned demarcation of the border. The UN Security Council extended further the UN Military Mission in Ethiopia and Eritrea

(UNMEE), which administered a buffer zone along the border.

In May the Eritrea-Ethiopia Claims Commission ruled on claims by both sides about treatment of prisoners of war (POWs) in the war. It said both sides were liable for claims through violations of the Geneva Conventions. It reported that Ethiopian POWs had been tortured – made to walk long distances barefoot, forced to do hard labour, and denied medical treatment. Some POWs were alleged to have been extrajudicially executed. Eritrea admitted that Ethiopian air force colonel Bezabih Petros died in custody but refused to say when or how. The Commission later began investigations into treatment of civilians and property claims.

Tension was exacerbated by engagement by both sides in other conflicts. Eritrea continued to host Ethiopian armed opposition groups fighting in Ethiopia (in particular the Oromo Liberation Front and Ogaden National Liberation Front), as well as the Sudanese armed opposition. Sudan and Ethiopia supported the Eritrean National Alliance (ENA), which included the Eritrean Liberation Front (ELF) and Islamist groups. Some armed activity by ENA groups was reported, such as the killing of two local humanitarian workers in August and the planting of landmines.

Prisoners of conscience
There were scores of detentions of suspected government opponents who supported calls by dissidents for democratic reforms and of others who were suspected of supporting armed opposition groups. They were arrested and secretly detained without official acknowledgement, explanation, charge or trial.

Eleven former government and ruling party leaders remained in detention as prisoners of conscience since their arrest in September 2001. No information was disclosed or known about their whereabouts or condition. They included former Vice-President Mahmoud Ahmed Sheriffo, former Foreign Minister Haile Woldetensae and former Eritrean People's Liberation Front (EPLF) intelligence chief Petros Solomon. Dozens of others also remained in incommunicado detention.

Journalists
Fifteen journalists of the private and state media remained in detention at the end of the year. Most were independent media journalists who had been detained in the September 2001 crack-down, when the entire private media, which had reported on the calls for reform, was banned.

▭ Aklilu Solomon, a reporter for the US-based *Voice of America* radio station, was detained and conscripted into the army in July after reporting adverse public reaction to the government's announcement of names of soldiers killed in the Ethiopian conflict. He had already performed the national service requirements and had medical exemption from being recalled as a reservist.

Long-term political prisoners
Hundreds or possibly thousands of government critics and opponents arrested during the first decade following

independence in 1991, about whom information was difficult to obtain, were believed to be still detained in secret military and security detention centres around the country, although some had "disappeared" and were feared to have been extrajudicially executed.

▭ General Bitweded Abaha, a co-founder of the EPLF detained from 1992 to 1997 and rearrested after a few weeks of freedom, was held in a secret security prison in Asmara, reportedly mentally ill and denied psychiatric treatment.

Military conscripts
Conscription for national service continued, with very little demobilization since it began in 1994. National service regulations oblige all men and women aged between 18 and 40 to do six months' military training and 18 months' development service, often construction work, with further reservist obligations. Military service was extended indefinitely during and after the war with Ethiopia and many reservists were recalled. The right to conscientious objection is not recognized by the authorities.

Conscripts accused of military offences were punished with torture (see below) and indefinite arbitrary detention.

▭ Paulos Iyassu, Isaac Moges and Negede Teklemariam, all members of the Jehovah's Witnesses religious group, which opposes war and the bearing of arms, remained in detention since 1994 in Sawa military barracks without charge or trial.

Religious persecution
Between February and May, police cracked down on minority Christian churches, breaking into religious services and church premises, arresting and beating church members, and torturing them in military detention centres. Those who were liable for military service were conscripted and others were provisionally released after weeks in detention, with threats of severe reprisals if they continued their religious activities. Religions other than the Eritrean Orthodox Church, the Catholic and Lutheran churches and Islam were banned in May 2002 and ordered to register with the new Department of Religious Affairs, but had been informally allowed to continue.

In August, over 200 teenage school students on a compulsory pre-conscription course at Sawa military camp were arrested for possessing bibles. Twenty-seven girls and 30 boys were held in metal shipping containers in harsh conditions. They were pressed to abandon their faith. At least 330 church members, including over 80 conscripts, were reportedly still detained in secret at the end of 2003.

Muslims suspected of links with Sudan-based armed Islamist groups were also targeted for repression. Dozens of Qur'anic teachers and government schoolteachers arrested in Keren and other towns in 1994 remained in secret detention and appeared to be prisoners of conscience.

Torture and ill-treatment
Torture continued to be used against some political prisoners and as a standard military punishment. Army

deserters and conscription evaders were tortured in military custody. They were beaten, tied hand and foot in painful positions and left in the sun for lengthy periods ("the helicopter" torture method), and suspended by ropes from the ceiling. Religious prisoners were held in Sawa and other military camps, beaten and forced to crawl on sharp stones. They were kept in overcrowded shipping containers in unventilated, hot and unhygienic conditions, and denied adequate food and medical treatment.

Violence against women

Female genital mutilation was widely practised, despite government and UN education programs. Domestic violence against women was reportedly common. Some women conscripts were reportedly subjected to rape or other sexual abuse by army officers.

Refugees

Most of the 100,000 or more Eritrean refugees in Sudan resident there for up to 30 years appealed against losing their refugee status as a result of the UN High Commissioner for Refugees' cessation of refugee status in 2002 for pre-1991 and 1998-2000 war refugees. Several hundred Eritreans fled to Sudan and other countries in 2003, mainly army deserters and others fleeing conscription.

Some 232 Eritreans who were deported by Malta in September/October 2002 were detained on arrival in Eritrea. Women, children and the elderly were reportedly released but the remainder were tortured and detained without charge or trial, at first in Adi Abeto military camp near Asmara, later on the main Dahlak Island in the Red Sea, and then at other secret military detention centres.

AI country reports/ visits
Statements
- Eritrea: Human rights appeal for 10th independence anniversary (AI Index: AFR 64/002/2003)
- Eritrea: Continued detention of prisoners of conscience and new arrests of members of religious groups (AI Index: AFR 64/004/2003)

ETHIOPIA

FEDERAL DEMOCRATIC REPUBLIC OF ETHIOPIA
Head of state: Girma Wolde-Giorgis
Head of government: Meles Zenawi
Death penalty: retentionist
UN Women's Convention: ratified with reservations
Optional Protocol to UN Women's Convention: not signed

Torture, arbitrary detention and excessive use of force by police were among many human rights violations reported. Journalists in the private media were at risk of arrest and prosecution. Several thousand people remained in long-term detention without charge or trial on suspicion of supporting armed opposition groups. Prison conditions were harsh and many prisoners were held incommunicado or were feared to have "disappeared" in secret prisons. The long series of trials continued of members of the former Dergue government on charges including genocide. Some trials were concluded and the first death sentences against defendants were imposed. There were death sentences in ordinary criminal trials too. No executions were reported during the year.

Background

Thirteen million of Ethiopia's 70 million population were dependent on food aid as a result of drought.

The National Human Rights Commission and Ombudsman's office established in law in 2000 were not yet set up.

Around 75,000 Ethiopian "illegal immigrants" in Djibouti were swiftly and harshly deported back to Ethiopia by the Djibouti government in September. Some 3,000 others, including asylum-seekers, who feared persecution because of their political opinions or for allegedly supporting the armed opposition Oromo Liberation Front (OLF), were sent to a makeshift rural refugee camp in Djibouti and allowed access to the UN High Commissioner for Refugees (UNHCR) for consideration of their asylum claims.

Ethiopia continued to face armed opposition from the OLF in the Oromia region and in the Somali region from the Ogaden National Liberation Front (ONLF), allied to the OLF and *Al-Itihad Al-Islamiya* (Islamic Unity). The OLF denied government accusations of bombing the Djibouti rail link in September.

There were inter-communal conflicts in several areas, related in some cases to federal administrative boundary changes, which resulted in a number of deaths.

Preparations started for the 2005 parliamentary elections. A new coalition of 15 groups inside and outside Ethiopia, the United Ethiopian Democratic Forces, was formed in the USA in August. The coalition was among a group of opposition parties that called for measures to guarantee free and fair elections.

Aftermath of the 1998-2000 war with Eritrea

In late 2003 a new war with Eritrea threatened, raising fears of a return to the large-scale military casualties and human rights abuses of the 1998-2000 war. Although both sides declared peaceful intentions, Ethiopia rejected the April 2002 ruling of the Eritrea-Ethiopia Boundary Commission set up under the peace accord, despite pressure from the UN Security Council. The Commission had concluded that the contested town of Badme was Eritrean territory. This indefinitely delayed demarcation of the border. The Security Council again extended the UN Military Mission in Ethiopia and Eritrea (UNMEE), which administered a buffer zone.

In May the Eritrea-Ethiopia Claims Commission found that both sides were liable for claims under the Geneva Conventions that prisoners of war were ill-treated. Ethiopia was found to have ill-treated Eritrean prisoners. The Commission later began investigations into treatment of civilians and property claims.

In the uneasy post-war peace, Ethiopia supported the armed opposition Eritrean National Alliance (ENA), while Eritrea continued to host Ethiopian armed opposition groups. In another regional conflict, Ethiopia backed factions in the Somalia Reconciliation and Restoration Council which opposed the Transitional National Government in Somalia supported by Eritrea.

Freedom of the media

The vigorous and highly critical private press continued to be a target for government repression. Dozens of journalists remained free on bond after being arrested in recent years but none was brought to trial in 2003.

A draft new press law threatened even greater restrictions on the media than its 1993 predecessor, which was used to imprison hundreds of journalists. The draft law was publicly debated and workshops were held involving government and private media, international consultants employed by the government and international media groups.

In November the Ministry of Justice closed down the Ethiopian Free Press Journalists Association (EFJA), saying it had failed to apply for renewal of its licence and had not submitted audited records. The EFJA said action was taken against it for leading opposition to the proposed press law.

☐ In October Araya Tesfamariam of *The Reporter* newspaper was severely beaten and left for dead by men in police uniform, reportedly after he received warnings from security officers and was accused of writing articles criticizing the government.

Justice and rule of law

Reports continued to be received of arrests of government opponents; arbitrary and indefinite detention without charge or trial; police shootings of criminal suspects with impunity; torture and ill-treatment of prisoners; detentions of government opponents suspected of links with armed opposition; and "disappearances" among detainees allegedly at risk of torture in secret detention centres.

The government began a series of legislative and other reforms to improve the administration of justice, with international assistance. The problems included long court delays; insufficient trained and competent judges; weak independence of the judiciary; lack of an effective, independent bar association; and poor access to justice, particularly for women.

☐ In early January, dozens of detained members of a church group, which was opposed to the official Ethiopian Orthodox Church leadership of the Lideta Church in the capital, Addis Ababa, were released on bond. They had been among several hundreds arrested in late December 2002 and tortured at Kolfe police training camp. Most had been freed with a warning. In February up to 100 other church dissidents were taken to Kolfe police camp, beaten and made to crawl across stones, sleep in the open and do harsh physical exercises. They were taken to court after two days and released on bond. None was brought to trial.

☐ No outcome was announced of government investigations into police killings of over 200 demonstrators in 2002 in protests across the country. Government opponents in Teppi and Awassa were still reportedly detained without charge or trial, while police, soldiers and local administrative officials allegedly responsible for unlawful killings seemed to enjoy impunity.

☐ On 12 December hundreds of members of the Anywaa (or Anuak) ethnic group were killed by mobs in and around Gambela town in the southwest. Civil servants, students, children and farmers were indiscriminately targeted on account of their ethnicity in reprisal for the murder of eight men – three government refugee officials, a police officer and four civilians – who were travelling nearby in a UN vehicle. The men were allegedly killed by an Anywaa gang with a grievance against the authorities. The bodies were reportedly displayed in Gambela, leading to rioting by members of the Amhara, Tigrayan, Oromo and other groups, who killed hundreds of Anywaa people and burned down homes. Over 15,000 survivors fled across the Sudan border. Police and soldiers were reportedly slow to stop the killings, and some allegedly took part in the massacre. By the end of the year, the government had not set up an independent inquiry. It stated that about 60 people had been killed, while other sources estimated the number to be at least 300.

In the zones of armed conflict, as well as in urban areas, human rights abuses against civilians suspected of links with rebels were widely alleged, although difficult to verify. In the conflict in the Oromia region, members of the Oromo ethnic group ("nationality") risked secret detention and torture. Unlawful arrests and ill-treatment were reported of opposition supporters in the Amhara and Southern regions, particularly of members of the All-Ethiopia Unity Party (formerly the All-Amhara People's Organization) and the Southern Ethiopian Peoples' Democratic Coalition.

Political prisoners were believed to number several thousands, some held for several years without charge or trial, although there were some releases through judicial review reported during the year. Held in many regions and prisons, many prisoners had access to the International Committee of the Red Cross.

◻ There was still no information about Amanti Abdissa, a former relief agency worker who was arrested in Addis Ababa in August 2000 and reportedly accused of links with the OLF, then later "disappeared" in custody.

◻ A group trial continued of 19 Oromos arrested in 1997 for alleged conspiracy with the OLF. Dinkenesh Deressa Kitila, a Total Oil company manager arrested in June 2002, was added to the defendants.

Human rights defenders

The trial of human rights defenders Professor Mesfin Woldemariam, Chair of the Ethiopian Human Rights Council, and Berhanu Nega, Chair of the Ethiopian Economic Association, was again adjourned. Falsely accused of instigating violence at demonstrations at Addis Ababa University in April 2001, they had been provisionally released on bond.

Dergue trials

The trial continued of 33 senior officials of the former government of Mengistu Hailemariam for "genocide", murder, torture and other crimes. The Zimbabwean government continued to refuse to extradite former President Mengistu to face trial. Trials also continued of up to 1,000 less senior officials accused of killing members of former Emperor Haileselassie's government and thousands of "anti-revolutionaries" during the government's "Red Terror" atrocities of 1977-1978. According to official figures in mid-2003, since the trials began in 1994, 1,017 defendants had been tried, 552 had been convicted, and 3,426 were still awaiting trial. During 2003, six were sentenced to death and others to prison terms.

Violence against women

Female genital mutilation continued to be widely practised on women and girls in many regions, despite public education programs by the government and non-governmental organizations. Women's organizations worked to improve women's access to justice and campaigned against domestic violence, rape and the forced marriage of girls where the law allowed rapists to escape punishment by marrying their victim.

Death penalty

Six defendants were sentenced to death in different Dergue trials during 2003. They were convicted of killings under former President Mengistu, including of the "disappeared" Patriarch of the Ethiopian Orthodox Church, Abune Tewoflos, in 1978. No appeals had been heard by the end of 2003. The only previous death sentences in these trials had been imposed in absentia. Almost all defendants faced a possible death penalty.

Several death sentences were also passed by ordinary criminal courts. No executions were reported.

The Ethiopian Human Rights Council launched a campaign against the death penalty.

GAMBIA

REPUBLIC OF THE GAMBIA
Head of state and government: Yahya Jammeh
Death penalty: abolitionist in practice
UN Women's Convention: ratified
Optional Protocol to UN Women's Convention: not signed

Freedom of expression came under repeated attack. Two men suspected of links with *al-Qa'ida* were unlawfully transferred to Bagram Air Base, Afghanistan, after being detained incommunicado for two months in Gambia. Trials of alleged coup plotters and political opponents continued. Female genital mutilation remained widespread. Ill-treatment by the security forces was reported.

Background

In September Gambia signed the Protocol to the African Charter on Human and Peoples' Rights on the Rights of Women in Africa.

Attacks on freedom of expression

In June the new National Media Commission was inaugurated. The Gambia Press Union lodged a legal action with the Supreme Court challenging the constitutionality of the Commission. The Commission has considerable quasi-judicial powers, including the power to force journalists to reveal sources and to impose mandatory licensing conditions, and lacks independence. However, the Supreme Court was not functioning so the legal action was not heard.

The Independent newspaper came under particular attack and several of its staff received death threats, were ill-treated or were detained. Its editor-in-chief, Abdoulaye Sey, was detained for three days in September by the National Intelligence Agency (NIA) following publication of an article critical of President Jammeh. NIA agents denied holding him, prompting fears for his safety. NIA agents also reportedly threatened that he would be killed if he continued to publish articles critical of the President. Abdoulaye Sey was released without charge.

In October, three unidentified men set fire to *The Independent*'s premises. The newspaper's security guard was beaten unconscious. A police inquiry was announced but did not appear to take place. An independent radio station, *Citizen FM*, the target of a previous arson attack, remained closed: it had been shut down in 2001 after the government accused it of not paying taxes.

Incommunicado detention and unlawful transfer of *al-Qa'ida* suspects

Bisher Al-Rawi, an Iraqi national, and Jamil Al-Banna, a Jordanian national with refugee status in the United Kingdom (UK), were secretly transferred to Bagram Air Base probably in early January even though a habeas corpus application on their behalf was pending in the courts in Banjul. The men had been detained incommunicado since November 2002, when they were arrested in Banjul on their arrival from the UK where they both lived.

A Moroccan national was briefly detained in January on suspicion of links with *al-Qa'ida* before being expelled from the country.

Fate of suspected coup plotters
In July, two men suspected of involvement in a July 1996 attack on military barracks in Farafenni were arrested shortly after returning to the country from Liberia. The circumstances of their return were unclear. They had not been formally charged by the end of the year. Three other men sentenced to death in June 1997 for involvement in the attack were still awaiting the outcome of the state's appeal against the quashing of their sentence in late 1997. All the men remained in detention.

Two armed forces officers accused of involvement in an alleged coup plot in June 2000 were acquitted in July after charges were dropped. Charges were dropped against a third defendant, Momodou Marena, in October. The men had been detained since June 2000. Hearings in the trial of three others, including Dumo Sarho, continued until the end of the year.

Trial of political opponents
In December the judge in the trial of opposition leader Ousainou Darboe and four of his supporters, charged with the murder of a government supporter in 2000, ruled that the trial should proceed even though one of the defendants would be tried *in absentia*. Defence lawyers appealed against the decision arguing it was unconstitutional. The Appeal Court had not ruled by the end of the year. The charge was believed to be politically motivated.

Lamine Waa Juwara, leader of the National Democratic Action Movement, was charged with sedition in September after calling for protests against the government which he accused of corruption and economic incompetence.

Female genital mutilation
Female genital mutilation remained widespread, especially in rural areas. There was no specific legislation in Gambia prohibiting the practice.

Ill-treatment by the security forces
There were several reports of beatings of people by the security forces outside places of detention. A journalist from *The Independent* was allegedly beaten in Banjul in August. Three people testified before Kanifing Magistrates' Court in October that they had been ill-treated in custody. One woman reportedly miscarried as a result. In May, two police officers were arrested in Brikama following accusations that they had beaten a suspect.

AI country reports/ visits
Statement
- Gambia: Open letter to members of Parliament of the Gambia (AI Index: AFR 27/005/2003)

GHANA

REPUBLIC OF GHANA
Head of state and government: John Agyekum Kufuor
Death penalty: retentionist
UN Women's Convention: ratified
Optional Protocol to UN Women's Convention: signed

A death sentence was imposed; no executions were carried out. A National Reconciliation Commission started its hearings into human rights abuses during Ghana's periods of unconstitutional government since 1957. A woman was imprisoned for practising female genital mutilation. A draft Domestic Violence Bill was still not tabled in Parliament.

Death penalty
The death penalty remained on the statute books. In April an Accra High Court sentenced Dereck George Mensah to death for murdering his employer. No executions were carried out.

The National Reconciliation Commission
Hearings began in January of the National Reconciliation Commission. Established by the government in 2002, its task was to compile a record of human rights abuses committed during Ghana's periods of unconstitutional rule since independence from colonial rule in 1957, and to make recommendations for reparations and reforms. The government appointed the Commission's members, who included judges, representatives of religious communities, academics, traditional rulers and the military. The law establishing the Commission did not require it to include representatives of non-governmental organizations among its members or to make its findings and recommendations public. It also allowed evidence to be heard behind closed doors on grounds of national security, and granted limited immunity from prosecution to witnesses who incriminated themselves with regard to that particular evidence.

Most of the people making statements in hearings before the Commission were victims of human rights violations under the military governments headed by Flight Lieutenant, later President, J.J. Rawlings. Much of the testimony involved allegations of summary executions, "disappearances", torture and other cruel, inhuman or degrading treatment. Some victims had been politically targeted. In other cases, soldiers had flogged and killed men and women they accused of hoarding and other economic crimes, looted their property and stolen from their homes and businesses.

Women's rights
Despite being made a criminal offence in 1994 by an amendment of the Criminal Code, female genital mutilation is still practised. In September a woman from Wa, Upper West Region, who had performed female genital mutilation on three girls, was convicted and sentenced to five years' imprisonment.

By the end of the year, a draft Domestic Violence Bill had not yet been tabled in Parliament. The bill aimed to strengthen official responses to complaints of violence against women and to broaden remedies available to the courts. It received wide support from women's organizations and other civil society groups.

GUINEA

REPUBLIC OF GUINEA
Head of state: Lansana Conté
Head of government: Lamine Sidimé
Death penalty: retentionist
UN Women's Convention: ratified
Optional Protocol to UN Women's Convention: not signed

Several political and trade union activists were arbitrarily arrested and detained briefly.

Background
President Lansana Conté, who seized power in 1984, was re-elected for a third term in presidential elections held in December. A new Constitution to allow President Conté to stand for another term had been approved in 2001. Mamadou Bhoye Barry, the only other presidential candidate and member of the Union for National Progress, polled less than five per cent of the vote and contested the results. Other opposition parties boycotted the elections saying they would not be free or fair. The Guinean Human Rights Organization accused the election organizers of serious and massive violations of the law.

Arbitrary arrests
Several political and trade union activists were arbitrarily arrested.
◻ In April, Diarra Doré and two other leaders of the Union of Republican Forces were arrested after their party organized a march in the capital, Conakry. They were released without charge four days later.
◻ Six members of the Independent Teachers' and Researchers' Union of Guinea were arrested in November after the union called on teachers to strike for improved pay and pensions. They were released without charge a day later.
◻ Also in November, Jean Marie Doré, a member of the National Assembly and Secretary General of the Union for Progress in Guinea, was arrested and held for 24 hours in Conakry. He had thrown doubt on a health certificate allowing President Conté to stand in the December elections.
During the year, dozens of military officers and soldiers were arrested. Some were released but others remained in detention. The reasons for the arrests were unclear.

GUINEA-BISSAU

REPUBLIC OF GUINEA-BISSAU
Head of state: (interim) Henrique Pereira Rosa (replaced Kumba Ialá in September)
Head of government: (interim) António Artur Sanhá (replaced Mário Pires in September)
Death penalty: abolitionist for all crimes
UN Women's Convention: ratified
Optional Protocol to UN Women's Convention: signed

Politically motivated arrests of human rights defenders and political opponents continued. Political activists received threats and some were prevented from leaving the country. Soldiers arrested in December 2002 and accused of attempting to overthrow the government were held without charge, often incommunicado, in harsh conditions. Some were reportedly tortured; one died as a result. The authorities failed to investigate these and other human rights violations. There were further attempts to curb freedom of expression and undermine the judiciary. Dire economic and social conditions coupled with repeated postponement of parliamentary elections increased political instability. There was a military coup in September.

Background
Non-payment of salaries led to numerous strikes in the public sector, including by teachers and hospital workers. Discontent within the military who had not been paid was aggravated by the dismissal and subsequent arrest of the Minister of Defence in April. In May the military hierarchy warned President Kumba Ialá of the dangers of military discontent and some soldiers received their salaries.

Tension heightened as parliamentary elections were repeatedly postponed. The international community withheld funding for the elections pending elections to the Supreme Court and the promulgation of the Constitution, which had been approved by the National Assembly in 2001. Elections were finally scheduled for 12 October. However, they were postponed again in September. There were numerous allegations that the ruling *Partido da Renovação Social* (PRS), Social Renewal Party, tried to rig the electoral roll.

A bloodless military coup in September deposed President Ialá. It was welcomed by most citizens of Guinea-Bissau but condemned by the international community. An interim civilian government was formed charged with organizing legislative and presidential elections within six and 18 months respectively. However, there was discontent about the choice of prime minister, and demonstrations to protest were banned by the military authorities. A National Transitional Council of military and civilians, chaired by the Chief of Staff of the Armed Forces, was set up to supervise the head of state and the government.

The judiciary was not independent and attempts by judges to be independent were punished. For instance, judges who displeased the government were often dismissed or transferred to remote areas of the country. The political authorities often ignored judicial decisions and refused to release detainees or ordered the release of others.

In December the mandate of the UN Peace-building Support Office in Guinea-Bissau (UNOGBIS) was extended until 31 December 2004.

Arrest of human rights defenders
The authorities arrested and threatened human rights activists, including trade unionists, for criticizing government policies.

⌓ João Vaz Mané, Vice-President of the Guinea-Bissau Human Rights League, was arrested in January and held incommunicado in the main police station, *Segunda Esquadra*, in the capital Bissau for 21 days before he was released without charge. He had criticized President Ialá in a radio broadcast for making funds available to Muslims to travel to Mecca while workers had not been paid. Following his release João Vaz Mané sued the authorities for unlawful arrest and detention. The case had not been heard by the end of the year.

Freedom of expression and the media
There were further attempts to curb freedom of expression. Media workers were harassed and briefly detained for reporting on the activities of opposition political activists. In February the authorities withdrew the licence of the independent radio station *Rádio Bombolom* on grounds that the licence had been granted by a previous government. The station reopened in May after it successfully challenged the decision in court. Ensa Seidi lost his job with the national state radio station after he reported on the visit to Guinea-Bissau in March of the President of the *Partido Unido Social Demócrata* (PUSD), United Social Democratic Party, who lives abroad. In September, four employees of *Radio Sintchan Occô* in the eastern town of Gabú were detained for 24 hours after broadcasting comments by an opposition politician critical of President Ialá.

Politically motivated arrests and harassment
There were politically motivated arrests and harassment of leading members of political parties and others. Members of the *Movimento Bafatá-Resistência da Guiné-Bissau* (MB-RGB – Bafata Movement-Guinea-Bissau Resistence), the PUSD and the former ruling *Partido Africano da Independência da Guiné e Cabo Verde* (PAIGC – African Party for the Independence of Guinea-Bissau and Cape Verde), were particularly targeted.

⌓ Zinha Vaz, an MB-RGB member of parliament, was briefly detained in February after she replied to comments that President Ialá made about her father. She was released without charge two days later. A ban against travelling imposed on Zinha Vaz was lifted in July.

⌓ Five PAIGC members and former government officials – Carlos Correia, Mário Mendes, Filinto Barros, José Pereira and Francisca Pereira – were detained for four days in February in connection with a decision in 1986 by the Council of State, of which they were members, to execute six members of the Balanta ethnic group convicted of an attempt to overthrow the former government of Guinea-Bissau headed by President João Bernardo Vieira. The four men and one woman were released uncharged but remained under restrictive conditions for several months.

⌓ Marcelino Lopes Cabral was arrested in April, a week after he was dismissed as Defence Minister, for allegedly making defamatory remarks. Two days later, José de Pina, a former presidential adviser, was dismissed from his post and arrested for allegedly passing information to Marcelino Lopes Cabral that the authorities considered defamatory. Both were held at the *Segunda Esquadra* until their release on bail in late June. They were not charged.

Threats against government opponents
Political opponents of the government were threatened with physical harm, including death. Members of the PUSD were particularly targeted.

⌓ PUSD member Carlos Silva Schwarz escaped unhurt after a group of men wearing uniforms of the Rapid Intervention Police opened fire on his house on the night of 28 March. He had received an anonymous letter the previous day threatening to kill him and several other politicians.

Detention of alleged coup plotters
Eleven military officers continued to be held without charge at the end of the year. They were part of a group of more than 30 soldiers arrested in December 2002 on allegations of plotting a coup. Most had been arrested previously, including Major Almane Alam Camará who had been imprisoned in 2000 and 2001 following unproved allegations of coup attempts. The 11 were held incommunicado in harsh conditions until May. Several were reportedly tortured and some needed hospital treatment. One died (see below). Three civilians, including Ernesto Carvalho, Vice-President of the National Unity party, were also arrested in December 2002, apparently in connection with the same coup allegations. They were held incommunicado in harsh conditions in the main police station in Bissau until their release without charge in May.

⌓ Second-Lieutenant Mussá Cassamá, who was arrested in December 2002, died in custody in Cumeré barracks in February, apparently as a result of torture. He had allegedly been tied and beaten. His body showed signs consistent with torture. The authorities failed to carry out an investigation into his death.

Human rights violations by police
The police violated human rights.

⌓ In June a police officer in Pixce in the south shot dead Rui António Mendes. The officer accused him of buying cashew nuts illegally and took him to the local police station. During interrogation the police officer reportedly shot him. Unconfirmed reports suggested the officer was arrested. He had not been tried by the end of the year.

◻ In May a woman was raped while in custody in the *Segunda Esquadra*. Police officers had gone to her house in the night to arrest her husband. As he was not there they arrested the woman instead and took her to the police station where she was raped by three officers. She eventually escaped and went to the UN office for help. The police officers were arrested. However, they were released the next day by the national chief of police who then ordered the arrest of the magistrate who had ordered the arrest of the officers.

◻ In April the Rapid Intervention Police reportedly used excessive force to disperse a student demonstration in Bissau. They beat students and opened fire on them. Several demonstrators were reportedly injured and at least 10 were briefly detained.

KENYA

REPUBLIC OF KENYA
Head of state and government: Mwai Kibaki
Death penalty: abolitionist in practice
UN Women's Convention: ratified
Optional Protocol to UN Women's Convention: not signed

The new government worked to improve the human rights environment in Kenya. Steps to reform the judiciary were initiated. A constitutional conference was in the process of drafting a Constitution containing a strengthened Bill of Rights. The President ordered the release of 28 death row prisoners and commuted to life imprisonment the death sentences of 195 others. Violence against women, particularly within the family, was rife. Law enforcement officials continued to use excessive force in dispersing demonstrations, and during the arrest of criminal and "terrorist" suspects. Torture in police custody persisted.

Background
Following presidential and parliamentary elections in December 2002, President Kibaki formed a government from the political parties that made up the National Rainbow Coalition, which had won a majority of parliamentary seats. Disagreements within the Coalition on implementing a pre-election power-sharing agreement were reflected in discussions about constitutional reforms at the National Constitutional Conference.

The Kenya National Commission on Human Rights was established in law in March, with a mandate to protect and promote human rights and to ensure Kenya's compliance with international human rights standards. In July, 10 commissioners were nominated.

In April the Minister for Justice and Constitutional Affairs, heading a newly created ministry with a clear human rights mandate, appointed a task force to examine whether to set up a mechanism for transitional justice. In August the task force, after public consultations, recommended the establishment by presidential decree of a Truth, Justice and Reconciliation Commission.

The security situation continued to deteriorate. In urban areas armed criminals caused deaths and destruction of property. Security forces clashed with members of the proscribed Mungiki group, which claims to represent traditional African values. More than 20 people were seriously injured in October when police, using tear gas, broke up a Mungiki demonstration in the capital, Nairobi.

Investigation of the judiciary
Following the resignation of the Chief Justice in February, his successor initiated reform of the judiciary by appointing a committee to investigate corruption, headed by Appeal Court judge Justice Aaron Ringera.

The committee's report, published in September, contains evidence of corruption, unethical conduct and other offences at the highest levels. It alleged that five of the nine Appeal Court judges, 18 of the 36 High Court judges, 82 of the 254 magistrates and 43 paralegal officers were corrupt.

Review of the Constitution

In May the nominated constitutional conference convened by the Constitution of Kenya Review Commission started its work. Difficulties in agreeing a draft for a revised Constitution emerged, and expectations that it would be adopted in 2003 were frustrated when the review process stalled. On 17 November, the date the conference was to reconvene, riot police barred the Commission Chairperson and 25 delegates from the venue. The Commission, in the absence of the Chairperson, had decided, with the Parliamentary Select Committee on Constitutional Affairs and the House Business Committee, to adjourn the conference until January 2004. No ruling had been given on a legal challenge to this decision by the end of 2003.

Violence against women

Violence against women by state officials and private individuals, particularly violence within the family and sexual violence, continued to be widespread. Many cases did not come before the courts because of unsympathetic and insensitive responses to women's complaints by the police and courts. The 2001 Domestic Violence and Family Protection Bill, which would improve victims' access to justice, was still not enacted.

Measures continued to be taken by governmental and non-governmental agencies to end female genital mutilation, but the practice remained widespread.
☐ A court in Kilgoris in November sentenced three suspects to two years' probation for subjecting a 15-year-old girl to the practice. They were convicted of an offence under the Children's Act.

The UN Committee on Elimination of Discrimination against Women, responsible for monitoring states' compliance with the UN Women's Convention, considered Kenya's third and fourth reports on compliance in January. The Committee expressed concern about the lack of information provided in the reports about violence against women.

Hundreds of Kenyan women made allegations of rape spanning a period of almost 30 years against United Kingdom (UK) soldiers during training in Kenya. Following publicity about the complaints, the allegations were debated in parliament in October. The UK Royal Military Police initiated criminal investigations. (See United Kingdom entry.)

'War against terror'

In March the authorities said that Suleiman Abdallah, in custody in Kenya after being arrested in Somalia, was suspected of membership of *al-Qa'ida* and involvement in the bombings of US embassies in Kenya and Tanzania in 1998 and of an Israeli-owned hotel in Mombasa, Kenya, in November 2002. He was reportedly handed over to the US authorities. International legal standards for the extradition of suspects were not met.

In May the government published a Suppression of Terrorism Bill which, if enacted, would allow the police to arrest suspects and search property without the authority of the courts. It provided for the incommunicado detention of suspected "terrorists" for up to 36 hours, and the extradition of suspects without internationally agreed safeguards. The bill conferred on members of the security forces immunity from prosecution for the use of "reasonable force" in the performance of their duties in fighting "terrorism".

Following reported security threats and the suspension of some international flights to and from Kenya in May and June, the police carried out extensive arrests in Mombasa and Nairobi in an "anti-terrorism" drive. On several occasions, dozens of people were detained, interrogated and released without charge.
☐ On 28 June a contingent of security officials raided the grounds of the Garissa Muslim Children's Home in a commando-style operation, and arrested 24-year-old Naveed Anwar Mohamed, who had been living at the home since his return from Pakistan in 2002. He was taken to Nairobi where he was held incommunicado, interrogated intensively for three days and released without charge after nine days.

In November the trial started of six men charged with the murder of 15 people – 12 Kenyan and three Israeli nationals – in the Mombasa hotel bombing. The trial was continuing at the end of 2003.

Torture and death in custody

The Criminal Law Amendment Act, enacted in July, amended the Penal Code, the Criminal Procedure Code and the Evidence Act to prohibit the use of confession statements or admissions of guilt as evidence in criminal proceedings if they were made under duress. The Act also abolished corporal punishment.

Widespread torture and ill-treatment of suspects and detainees continued to be reported, mainly in prisons and police stations.
☐ On 6 January, Samuel Sirare Wanyonyi was arrested and two days later died in custody at Malakisi police station in western Kenya, reportedly as a result of torture. No action had been taken to bring those responsible to justice by the end of 2003.
☐ In October, three detainees suspected of the September murder of Dr Crispin Mbai, Convenor of the Devolution Committee of the Constitutional Conference, alleged that they had been tortured by police officers to extract confessions. The Attorney General's Office announced that 22 officers were to be charged, but had not brought charges by the end of 2003.

Death penalty

There were at least 3,200 prisoners on death row. No executions took place. Kenya has not carried out any executions since the mid-1980s. On 25 February President Kibaki ordered the release of 28 death row prisoners and commuted 195 death sentences to life imprisonment.

On 10 February the Minister of Justice and Constitutional Affairs said in a statement that the death penalty would be abolished so that the fundamental right to life was respected. Other members of the government made statements in support of abolition during the year.

AI country reports/visits
Reports
· Kenya: A human rights memorandum to the new government (AI Index: AFR 32/002/2003)
· Kenya: Open letter – the International Criminal Court campaign (AI Index: AFR 32/009/2003)
Visits
AI delegates visited Kenya in July, October and November to conduct research.

LIBERIA

REPUBLIC OF LIBERIA
Head of state and government: Gyude Bryant (replaced Moses Blah in October who replaced Charles G. Taylor in August)
Death penalty: retentionist
UN Women's Convention: ratified
Optional Protocol to UN Women's Convention: not signed

As armed conflict worsened, government forces and armed opposition groups were responsible for widespread abuses against civilians including killings, torture, rape and other forms of sexual violence, and forcible recruitment of children. Hundreds of thousands of civilians were forced to flee their homes. Despite cease-fire and peace agreements, hostilities and human rights abuses continued. The UN Security Council authorized deployment of an international peace-keeping operation. Those responsible for human rights abuses enjoyed almost total impunity.

Background
From January internal armed conflict worsened and spread to previously unaffected areas. The armed opposition Liberians United for Reconciliation and Democracy (LURD) advanced towards the capital, Monrovia, and a second armed group, the Movement for Democracy in Liberia (MODEL), emerged in March in the east of the country, taking control of the strategic port of Buchanan in July.

The killing of three humanitarian workers by government forces in late March and the abduction of others aggravated an already alarming humanitarian situation. Threats to their security and looting of supplies and vehicles forced humanitarian agencies to reduce or suspend their activities. By April delivery of emergency assistance was impossible to about 70 per cent of the country.

Negotiations to resolve the conflict began in Accra, Ghana, on 4 June under the auspices of the Economic Community of West African States (ECOWAS). President Charles Taylor announced his readiness to relinquish power in the interests of peace. On that day the Special Court for Sierra Leone issued an indictment against President Taylor for crimes against humanity, war crimes and other serious violations of international humanitarian law committed during Sierra Leone's conflict. These charges related to, among other crimes, killings, mutilations, rape and use of child soldiers perpetrated by Sierra Leone armed opposition forces whom he had actively supported in order to destabilize Sierra Leone and gain access to diamond resources. The Ghanaian government ignored an international arrest warrant and calls by AI for President Taylor's arrest, and he was allowed to return to Liberia the same day.

A cease-fire signed on 17 June, which anticipated a transitional government without President Taylor, collapsed within days. LURD forces again advanced towards Monrovia. Fighting and indiscriminate shelling during June and July exacted a heavy toll on civilians in Monrovia; the UN estimated that more than 1,000 people were killed and some 450,000 made homeless. Acute shortages of food, clean water, sanitation facilities and medical care resulted in an unprecedented humanitarian crisis, and collapse of law and order left Monrovia's inhabitants, including Sierra Leonean refugees and hundreds of thousands of internally displaced people, increasingly vulnerable to human rights abuses.

As civilian casualties mounted, the UN Secretary-General, the UN High Commissioner for Refugees, international humanitarian agencies and the Liberian population called for urgent international military intervention. Indecision by the international community continued until early August when the UN Security Council authorized deployment of an ECOWAS force.

President Taylor left Liberia on 11 August, travelling to Nigeria with implicit guarantees from the Nigerian government that he would be neither prosecuted in Nigeria nor surrendered to the Special Court for Sierra Leone. While the Nigerian government argued that it was acting in the interests of peace in Liberia, AI condemned violation of its obligations under international law. In early December, Interpol allowed worldwide circulation of the arrest warrant against Charles Taylor with a view to extradition.

President Taylor was replaced by Vice-President Moses Blah. On 18 August a peace agreement was signed in Accra between the government, LURD, MODEL and political parties. The agreement provided for a power-sharing National Transitional Government of Liberia (NTGL), to take power by 14 October, elections in 2005 and inauguration of a new government in early 2006. Gyude Bryant was elected Chairman of the NTGL.

While security in Monrovia improved following deployment of ECOWAS forces, hostilities continued in Bong, Nimba and Grand Bassa Counties. ECOWAS forces were subsequently absorbed into the UN Mission in Liberia (UNMIL). Only some 6,500 of the projected 15,000 UN peace-keeping troops had been deployed by the end of the year, restricting UNMIL's capacity to deploy extensively outside Monrovia. Disarmament and demobilization of an estimated 40,000 combatants began falteringly in December and was quickly postponed.

Civilians targeted in armed conflict

Civilians lived in constant fear of undisciplined armed groups who killed, raped, forcibly recruited children and looted. After the peace agreement, violence increased in some areas as command structures broke down and combatants made last-ditch attempts to seize territory and property before deployment of UNMIL forces. The gravity of abuses against civilians prompted an emergency report by the Acting UN High Commissioner for Human Rights on 8 August which described the grievous abuses against civilians and called for international support in bringing the perpetrators to justice.

Rape and other forms of sexual violence against women and girls, including those who had been internally displaced and Sierra Leonean refugees, by government, LURD and MODEL forces were widespread. Young women and girls were abducted and forced into sexual slavery.

As violence reached a peak in Monrovia during June and July, the number of reported rapes increased significantly. Civilians fleeing continuing fighting in Bong and Nimba Counties after the peace agreement also reported rape by pro-Taylor militia, LURD and MODEL forces.

Forced recruitment of children under 18 years old – both boys and girls and some as young as 10 – by all parties to the conflict was rampant. Children in camps for internally displaced people were particularly vulnerable. Some of those resisting recruitment were beaten or shot by pro-Taylor militia. With a minimum of training, children were sent directly to the front line. Girls were forcibly recruited to provide sexual services, to carry ammunition or to cook for fighting forces.

The UN Children's Fund (UNICEF) estimated that as many as one in 10 Liberian children may have been recruited to fight in Liberia or neighbouring countries. It was estimated that more than 15,000 children, both boys and girls, among the ranks of former government and armed opposition forces needed to be disarmed, demobilized and reintegrated into their families and communities.

More than a thousand civilians were killed and many others injured in Monrovia during June and July, either in cross-fire or by indiscriminate shelling of areas with no obvious military targets, including those harbouring thousands of displaced people. While most shelling was attributed to the LURD, government forces were also responsible.

Violations by government forces and militia

Government forces, including special security units such as the Anti-Terrorist Unit, and pro-Taylor militia were responsible for summary executions, rape and forced recruitment, including of children. Scores of civilians suspected of opposing President Taylor were reported to have been summarily executed, in particular by militia. It was frequently difficult, however, to obtain detailed and corroborated information because witnesses and victims feared reprisals. For example, credible but unsubstantiated reports were received of killings by government forces of more than 350 civilians, including women and children, in villages in River Gee County in April. Harassment and looting were systematic, forcing thousands to flee their homes.

While indiscriminate shelling or stray bullets caused many civilian casualties in Monrovia from early June, others resulted from random attacks by undisciplined government forces.

Some members of militia accused of rape or caught looting were summarily executed by their commanders in June and July in Monrovia after the authorities announced that those responsible would be dealt with severely.

Abuses by armed opposition forces

Both LURD and MODEL forces were responsible for deliberate and arbitrary killings, torture and ill-treatment, rape and forcible recruitment.

Civilians in areas around Gbarnga, Bong County, reported that LURD forces had summarily killed several men in August, apparently because they were perceived to be supporters of President Taylor. LURD forces attacked internal displacement camps around Monrovia; in March a large camp known as Rick's Institute was caught in fighting, forcing an estimated 25,000 people to flee. A large number of people were reported to have been abducted by the LURD and used to carry looted property, arms and ammunition. In late June the LURD leadership made a commitment to end the use of child soldiers, threatening to punish commanders who persisted in using children. This did not appear, however, to result in any significant change.

After the peace agreement, civilians fled as villages in Bong County were attacked and looted by LURD forces. As they fled, their few remaining possessions were looted by pro-Taylor militia.

In April there were reliable reports that MODEL forces deliberately and arbitrarily killed civilians perceived to be government supporters. In November civilians fleeing attacks by MODEL forces as they advanced through Nimba County reported deliberate and arbitrary killings, rape, looting and destruction of villages.

Both groups also used civilians as forced labour, for example to carry looted property and harvest crops.

Arbitrary detention and extrajudicial execution of perceived opponents

Attempts by President Taylor's government to suppress critics were sustained and brutal. The independent media, human rights activists, members of ethnic groups such as the Krahn and Mandingo associated with the armed opposition, and others perceived as opponents were arbitrarily detained and ill-treated.

Although President Taylor announced in early June that all political prisoners and "prisoners of war" were to be freed, none was released until 11 July. Some 40 detainees were released, including Sheikh Sackor, Executive Director of Humanist Watch, who had been held without charge or trial since July 2002. After repeated adjournments of his trial, charges of treason against Aloysius Toe, a leading human rights activist arrested and imprisoned in November 2002, were finally dropped in July.

In June President Taylor claimed that a plot to overthrow him while he was in Ghana had been foiled. Two officials arrested in connection with the alleged plot, John Yormie, Deputy Minister for National Security, and Isaac Vaye, Deputy Minister of Public Works, subsequently "disappeared". On 16 July President Taylor publicly confirmed that they were both dead. Despite apparently incontrovertible evidence that government forces were responsible, there was no official investigation into the circumstances of their deaths and no one was held accountable.

The circumstances of the death in Liberia in early May of Sam Bockarie, a leading member of the Sierra Leone armed opposition Revolutionary United Front and closely associated with President Taylor, remained unclear. He had been indicted by the Special Court for Sierra Leone in March. The government claimed that he had died in a confrontation with government forces but suspicions surrounding his death were compounded by the reported murder several days later of his mother, wife and two children in Monrovia. It appeared that Sam Bockarie had been killed to prevent him giving evidence to the Special Court which would implicate President Taylor.

Refugees and internally displaced people
Protracted conflict had forced an estimated one million Liberians, a third of the population, to flee their homes, becoming either refugees in neighbouring countries or internally displaced. During 2003, there were some 500,000 internally displaced people and 300,000 refugees.

Liberian refugees in Côte d'Ivoire, indiscriminately associated with Ivorian armed opposition groups, risked summary execution by Ivorian government forces. Despite the risks, especially for Krahns and Mandingos, by February an estimated 43,000 Liberians had no option but to return to Liberia. As fighting escalated in eastern Liberia, both Liberian and Ivorian refugees were forced back and forth across the border.

Between January and March, as the LURD advanced into Grand Cape Mount County, more than 9,000 Liberians, including deserting combatants, fled into Sierra Leone.

Internally displaced people were particularly vulnerable and suffered serious abuses both in Monrovia and other parts of the country. In addition to systematic looting, extortion and intimidation, they were abducted for fighting, sexual slavery and forced labour.

As LURD forces advanced towards Monrovia in June, up to 300,000 internally displaced people and Sierra Leonean refugees were concentrated in the capital. Already living in appalling conditions, they were then caught in fighting and shelling.

Ending impunity
No action was taken to end impunity, despite repeated reminders, including by the UN Secretary-General, the Security Council, the Special Representative of the Secretary-General for Liberia and the Acting High Commissioner for Human Rights, that those responsible for human rights abuses should be brought to justice.

While providing for a truth and reconciliation commission, the peace agreement also stated that the NTGL would consider a recommendation for general amnesty to all those engaged or involved in military activities during the conflict. NTGL Chairman Gyude Bryant publicly expressed a preference for such an amnesty.

AI called on the international community, in consultation with the Liberian people, to develop a long-term strategy to end impunity, including an early international, independent investigation to establish accountability and identify an appropriate court for trying those alleged to have been responsible for crimes under international law.

International peace-keeping operation
In early August, the UN Security Council authorized deployment of an ECOWAS multinational force to support implementation of the cease-fire, to be replaced by a UN peace-keeping operation. In September the Security Council established UNMIL, with effect from 1 October, with a mandate to support implementation of the peace process, to protect UN staff and civilians and to support humanitarian and human rights assistance and security reform.

AI had called for an unambiguous mandate to protect civilians and a strong human rights component within UNMIL, stressing the need for regular and public reporting on human rights. In November it called for swift deployment of additional UNMIL troops to areas of the country where civilians continued to suffer human rights abuses.

Military assistance to government and armed opposition forces
The Panel of Experts established by the UN Security Council to monitor compliance with UN sanctions, including a ban on arms transfers and rough diamond exports in force since 2001, provided evidence that arms continued to reach Liberia. In May the Security Council renewed prohibition of all sales or supply of arms and related *matériel* to any recipient in Liberia, including the LURD and MODEL. Sanctions on timber exports came into effect in July. The Security Council demanded that states in the region cease military support for armed groups in neighbouring countries.

The governments of Guinea and Côte d'Ivoire were identified as providing assistance to, respectively, the LURD and the MODEL.

AI called for arms sanctions to remain in place and also called for UNMIL to report to the UN Security Council sanctions committee on Liberia any information relating to the transfer of military assistance to Liberia or misuse of weapons for human rights abuses.

AI country reports/ visits

Reports

- Liberia: Recommendations to the International Contact Group on Liberia, New York, 28 February 2003 (AI Index: AFR 34/004/2003)
- Côte d'Ivoire: No escape – Liberian refugees in Côte d'Ivoire (AI Index: AFR 31/012/2003)
- Liberia: Recommendations to the Security Council and Special Representative of the Secretary-General (AI Index: AFR 34/018/2003)
- Liberia: "The goal is peace, to sleep without hearing gunshots, to send our children to school; that is what we want" (AI Index: AFR 34/024/2003)

Visit

AI delegates visited Liberia in November to carry out research, and to meet the Chairman and other members of the NTGL. They also met a number of UNMIL personnel.

MADAGASCAR

REPUBLIC OF MADAGASCAR
Head of state: Marc Ravalomanana
Head of government: Jacques Sylla
Death penalty: abolitionist in practice
UN Women's Convention: ratified
Optional Protocol to UN Women's Convention: signed

Security overall stabilized after the 2002 political crisis. Despite government commitments to human rights, judicial proceedings against people associated with the previous government, including those suspected of human rights abuses during the 2002 crisis, were often unfair. Lengthy pre-trial detention coupled with poor prison conditions further undermined the rights of detainees. The government on occasion restricted freedom of expression and assembly.

Background

President Ravalomanana's party, *Tiako I Madagasikara* (TIM – I love Madagascar), dominated the political scene having won a large majority in parliamentary elections in December 2002. Some political parties that supported TIM in 2002 as part of the coalition KMMR (Marc Ravalomanana Support Committee) returned to opposition.

In March the government issued a document accusing AI of political bias and rejecting the organization's findings that both sides in the 2002 political conflict had committed human rights abuses. The government did not give substantive responses to the cases raised by AI.

In December, after debates between the Senate and parliament, the President issued an amnesty decree in relation to "crimes committed during the 2002 political crisis". The decree applies to anyone sentenced to less than three years' imprisonment and excludes those convicted of murder, torture and corruption.

In March Madagascar presented its report to the UN Committee on the Rights of the Child, which had been due since 1998. The Committee raised issues concerning gaps in the monitoring of children's rights, the fight against child labour and the reform of the juvenile justice system. In particular, the Committee recommended that the length of pre-trial detention be shortened and prison conditions improved.

The government promised to fight HIV/AIDS by allocating resources to awareness campaigns and infrastructure. Some members of parliament expressed support for the abolition of the death penalty.

Economic and social rights continued to be of serious concern, despite a government program to reduce poverty. Local and international aid organizations distributed emergency food supplies in the southeast to combat chronic hunger.

Accountability for human rights abuses

No investigations were conducted into the alleged torture of suspected supporters of former President Didier Ratsiraka during the 2002 political crisis by soldiers or supporters of the Ravalomanana government. Among such cases were those of Venance Raharimanana and Said Ibrahim, who said they were tortured after arrest in Mahajanga in June 2002.

▭ Lieutenant-Colonel Assolant Coutiti, an army officer under the Ratsiraka government, was found guilty of "inflicting injuries wilfully" on two civilians, François Xavier Rakotoarisoa and Ali Sarety, and sentenced to 15 years' imprisonment. The two men had been tortured in Antsiranana and Ambanja respectively, northern Madagascar, during the 2002 crisis.

Unfair trials and judicial proceedings

In November the Minister of Justice stated that 59 people had been tried in the capital Antananarivo for offences committed during the 2002 crisis; at least 83 people were awaiting trial; and 113 others had been freed owing to lack of evidence. No details of any convictions or information about those held in the provinces were provided. There were concerns that the trials failed to meet international standards.

▭ Judicial proceedings against former Prime Minister Tantely Andrianarivo, detained since May 2002 and accused of several offences including embezzlement and "endangering the state", were marred by irregularities. In January he was transferred from the Antanimora prison in Antananarivo to a provincial prison without his family and lawyers being warned; he was transferred back to the capital a few months later. His defence lawyers raised procedural irregularities and argued that he should be tried before the yet to be constituted High Court of Justice. The High Constitutional Court ruled that he should be tried before an ordinary criminal court on grounds of "public order". He was subsequently refused release on bail. After August his health reportedly deteriorated and in December he was transferred to hospital. His trial began on 22 December even though appeals on procedural grounds had not been fully exhausted and his lawyers had only had access to his case file half a day before the trial. He was sentenced to 12 years' forced labour. The President, during his end-of-year speech, announced that he had allowed Tantely Andrianarivo to seek medical treatment abroad.

Former State Secretary of Public Security Azaly Ben Marofo and his son Antonio were arrested on their return to Madagascar in May. They were detained without charge for six days before the investigation produced witnesses on whom to base charges. They were tried in August and found guilty of "undermining state security". Their lawyers denounced the lack of evidence presented against them at the trial. They were each sentenced to five years' imprisonment.

Poor prison conditions
Prison conditions remained poor and life-threatening. No investigation was conducted into the death in custody of Bernardo Tsano in Tsiafahy prison in July 2002, apparently caused by the poor conditions and lack of medical facilities.

On 24 October Lieutenant-Colonel Norbert Botomora died in the infirmary of Antanimora prison, reportedly of a heart attack. Other prisoners said that he had asked for help during the night but the guard refused to open the infirmary. The authorities said that security rules prohibit guards from opening the infirmary at night. Lieutenant-Colonel Norbert Botomora had been transferred from Tsiafahy prison, which has no medical facilities, a few days earlier. He had been in pre-trial detention for more than a year on charges of "threatening state security".

Restrictions on freedom of assembly and expression
In February political activist Liva Ramahazomanana was arrested as she was holding a public meeting critical of the government without authorization. She was subsequently accused of an "attempted coup d'état" with other army officers after it emerged that grenades had been left outside the Defence Ministry. She was sentenced in June to two years' imprisonment for "threatening state security".

In March demonstrators and security forces clashed in the town of Toliara during a political rally. At least four people were injured by tear gas and gun butts used by security forces. Two members of the security

forces were injured. Journalists from *TV Plus* were also beaten by security forces and had their videotape confiscated. One of them was briefly detained.

Racial violence against Merina community
Unidentified armed people committed acts of violence against people of Merina ethnic origin in provincial towns. The authorities accused an opposition party, the Committee for National Reconciliation, of being behind what appeared to be politically motivated violence.

In October, after an opposition meeting on the death in custody of Lieutenant-Colonel Botomora (see above), several merchants of Merina origin were harassed or beaten by unidentified people.

AI country reports/ visits
Statement
- Madagascar: Former Prime Minister's trial must respect international standards of fairness (AI Index: AFR 35/002/2003)

MALAWI

REPUBLIC OF MALAWI
Head of state and government: Bakili Muluzi
Death penalty: retentionist
UN Women's Convention: ratified
Optional Protocol to UN Women's Convention: signed

Politically motivated violence escalated in the run-up to the 2004 elections and there were reports of excessive use of force by police. Torture in police custody continued to be reported. Journalists perceived to be critical of the government were assaulted, threatened and arrested.

Background
On 31 March President Bakili Muluzi announced that he would not run for a third term. By the end of the year the bill seeking to amend the Constitution to enable him to run for a third term had not been withdrawn.

In September the World Food Programme stated that Malawi had mostly recovered from the serious food shortages that had put approximately 3.3 million Malawians at risk of hunger and starvation in 2002.

Policing
Police used excessive force in an attempt to quell demonstrations against a third term for the President and to break up opposition rallies. On 27 January, police fired rubber bullets and tear gas at anti-third term protesters during demonstrations organized by civic organizations. Torture of suspects and deaths in police custody continued to be reported.

⬦ Peter Mussa Gama died in custody on 12 September. He was detained by police in Blantyre for questioning about a suspected case of armed robbery. An autopsy revealed that he had died of asphyxia and that he may have been assaulted.

Freedom of expression
There was an overall decline in freedom of expression. State-sponsored attacks on independent media workers and media outlets perceived to be critical of the government intensified. In October, the Director of Public Prosecutions wrote a letter to the Regional Police Commissioner for the south and other senior police officers calling on the police to end arbitrary arrests of journalists and warning that such acts were unconstitutional.

⬦ On 8 July Daniel Nyirenda, a photojournalist with *The Nation* newspaper, was severely beaten by suspected members of the ruling United Democratic Front (UDF) youth wing in Blantyre in front of senior members of the UDF and police officers. In September a reporter with the *Daily Times* newspaper, Frank Namangale, was arrested on charges of "publishing false information likely to cause fear and alarm to the public". The Director of Public Prosecutions later ordered that the charges be dropped.

Arrests of *al-Qa'ida* suspects
On 22 June, five men suspected of being members of *al-Qa'ida* were arrested by agents of the Malawi National Intelligence Bureau and agents from the USA reported to be members of the Central Intelligence Agency (CIA). The men were held at a secret location without access to lawyers and then flown out of Malawi to an undisclosed location in US custody for interrogation. At the end of July it was reported that the five had been taken to Zimbabwe, held there for a month and then sent to Sudan where they were released after no evidence was found linking them to *al-Qa'ida*. In Kasungu district, police fired tear gas, rubber bullets and live ammunition at people demonstrating against the deportation of the five men.

MAURITANIA

ISLAMIC REPUBLIC OF MAURITANIA
Head of state: Maaouiya Ould Sid 'Ahmed Taya
Head of government: Sghaïr Ould M'Bareck (replaced Cheikh El Avia Ould Mohamed Khouna in July)
Death penalty: abolitionist in practice
UN Women's Convention: ratified with reservations
Optional Protocol to UN Women's Convention: not signed

Government forces foiled a military coup attempt. Detained suspects were reportedly tortured in custody. None had been tried by the end of 2003. Relatives of suspected plotters were detained without charge or trial. Dozens of opposition supporters and religious leaders were detained for several weeks before being released, some after an unfair trial. Privately owned newspapers were banned arbitrarily. The suspension of a member of the Bar Association raised concerns about the independence of the judicial system.

Background
In June members of the armed forces attempted to overthrow President Taya, who came to power after a coup in 1984. Dissident soldiers took control of part of the capital, Nouakchott, and attacked the presidential palace before government forces regained control. Officials later announced that 15 people, including civilians, had been killed and 68 wounded.

President Taya was re-elected on 7 November. The election was not monitored by independent observers and an opposition coalition alleged massive fraud throughout the country.

New legislation
In July Parliament adopted a law against trafficking. It provided for up to 10 years' forced labour for anyone who forcibly, or by fraud or improper inducement, trafficks someone for the purposes of exploitation.

In July a new law effectively restricted freedom of expression by making all mosques public institutions and bringing them under the control of the Minister in charge of Islamic orientation. The law provided for sanctions against anyone who would use the mosque for political or sectarian purposes or for any act incompatible with "quietude and respect". This move was part of a government campaign against Islamist opposition groups.

Release of prisoners of conscience
On 24 August, Mohammed Lemine Chbih Ould Cheikh Melaïnine, President of the *Front populaire mauritanien* (FPM), Popular Mauritanian Front, and two other prisoners, Mokhtar Ould Haibetna and Bouba Ould Hassenan, were released under a presidential pardon. They had been sentenced to five years' imprisonment after being convicted of "conspiracy to

commit acts of sabotage and terrorism" in an unfair trial in June 2001.

Detentions and unfair trials

In April, May and June dozens of opposition party supporters and imams were arrested in Nouakchott and the northern town of Nouadhibou. All were detained incommunicado for several weeks. Some were members of the *Parti de la renaissance nationale* (PRN), National Renaissance Party, which the authorities then moved to ban by sealing its headquarters in Nouakchott on 3 May. On 29 May, nine PRN members were convicted on charges of "forming an unauthorized association and reorganizing a party after it has been disbanded" although the PRN had not been banned at the time of their arrest. Some were denied lawyers of their own choice. They were given prison terms of up to six months, suspended.

In June more than 30 other detainees, mostly religious leaders, were charged with "plotting against the constitutional regime and incitement to undermine the State's internal and external public order". They were provisionally released in August. Their trial had not begun by the end of 2003. The remaining detainees were released without charge.

In November, presidential candidate Mohamed Khouna Ould Haidalla, two of his sons and at least 13 others were arrested before and after the presidential election. After several weeks of incommunicado detention, on 28 December, nine detainees were convicted of crimes related to state security: Mohamed Khouna Ould Haidalla and four others were sentenced to suspended five-year prison terms, fines and deprivation of civil and political rights; four others received suspended two-year terms and fines. The remaining detainees were acquitted of similar charges. No judgment had been given in the trial of Mohamed Khouna Ould Haidalla's younger son by the end of the year. Independent observers noted irregularities in the trial proceedings.

Coup attempt

Scores of armed forces officers were arrested following the coup attempt in June. After three months of incommunicado detention, in September at least 128 officers and soldiers were brought before a judge and charged with treason, a capital offence. They were reportedly held at a naval camp in Nouakchott, which was decreed an official prison from September by the Minister of Justice. The trial had not started by the end of 2003.

Dozens of people suspected of links with the coup plotters, including relatives, were also detained. Some were held in secret locations for several weeks. All were subsequently released without charge or trial.

In July armed forces officer Lieutenant Didi Ould M'Hamed was extradited from Senegal as a suspected coup plotter and returned to Mauritania, despite Senegal's international human rights obligations not to extradite anyone to a state where they risked serious human rights violations (see Senegal entry).

Torture and ill-treatment

Some detainees arrested after the failed coup attempt were reportedly tortured or ill-treated. The military detainees were said to have been handcuffed 24 hours a day and beaten with gun butts. Some were allegedly made to lie on the ground, their hands tied, while soldiers trampled on their backs.

Freedom of expression

Several newspapers were either suspended or banned. In June the weekly newspaper *Erraya* was banned, apparently for publishing an article deemed critical of the government.

Independence of the judicial system

In July, Mahfoudh Ould Bettah was suspended from membership of the bar for three years for allegedly usurping the title of President of the Bar Association and for insubordination. The decision was circulated to the entire judiciary before he was formally notified. There was concern that the government had engineered his removal from power after he was elected President in June 2002. The presence of the police at the vote, the challenge to the announced results, and a new vote two days later that resulted in the election of a candidate from the ruling party all contributed to suspicions of interference by the authorities.

AI country reports/visits
Reports
- Mauritania: Wave of arrests of political opponents and imams (AI Index: AFR 38/004/2003)
- Mauritania: Where is Lieutenant Didi Ould M'Hamed? (AI Index: AFR 38/008/2003)
- Mauritania: Authorities announce imminent trials but ignore defence rights (AI Index: AFR 38/012/2003)

MOZAMBIQUE

REPUBLIC OF MOZAMBIQUE
Head of state: Joaquim Alberto Chissano
Head of government: Pascoal Mocumbi
Death penalty: abolitionist for all crimes
UN Women's Convention: ratified
Optional Protocol to UN Women's Convention: not signed

Many people faced food shortages as a result of floods and drought. Important trials represented some progress in tackling corruption. Despite police reforms, there were a number of allegations of torture and of excessive use of force and firearms. There were reports of trafficking in people and body parts.

Background
Hundreds of thousands of people suffered food shortages as a result of floods in the north and centre and drought in the centre and south of the country. In June the government set up a research body to monitor its poverty reduction programs which included strategies for gender equality and combating HIV/AIDS.

In March the government declared that it had fulfilled its obligations under the Ottawa Convention by destroying its last stocks of anti-personnel landmines. Some minefields remained to be cleared at the end of the year.

Former soldiers of the *Resistência Nacional Moçambicana* (RENAMO), Mozambique National Resistance, who continued to guard RENAMO's former military stronghold in Maríngue, Sofala province, reportedly surrounded the local police station for several hours in September.

Elections in 23 urban and 10 rural municipalities in November returned the ruling *Frente da Libertação de Moçambique* (FRELIMO), Front for the Liberation of Mozambique, to power in most areas. The *RENAMO-União Eleitoral*, RENAMO-Electoral Union, which had boycotted municipal elections in 1998, gained a majority in Beira and three other areas.

In December the Assembly of the Republic passed a new family law establishing gender equality.

Steps to end impunity for corruption and organized crime
In January, six men were convicted of the murder of Carlos Cardoso, editor of a daily newspaper, in November 2000. The journalist had been investigating a US$14 million fraud at the state-run Commercial Bank. Two businessmen and a former bank manager were convicted of contracting the murder of Carlos Cardoso and the three others of carrying out the killing. Five received prison terms of 23 years and six months each, and one, Aníbal dos Santos Júnior, was sentenced *in absentia* to 28 years' imprisonment for the murder and related offences. In December the

Attorney General visited the six men in prison after hearing that they were being held in leg-cuffs or chains, apparently as a security measure. He declared such restraint illegal. A few days later, the businessmen and bank manager went on trial in connection with the bank fraud.

In September a court acquitted seven police officers who had been charged with assisting Aníbal dos Santos Júnior to escape from prison in September 2002. The judge said that the defendants had been used as scapegoats to "protect those who were untouchable".

Investigations continued into the murder of economist António Siba-Siba Macuácua in August 2001. He had been investigating corrupt practices and attempting to recover bad debts which had led to the collapse of the Austral Bank in April 2001.

The National Assembly passed an anti-corruption law in October compelling high-ranking civil servants to declare their wealth on taking up their posts.

Torture and excessive use of police force
There were further reports of torture, although 2003 saw a decrease in such reports.

▭ Paramilitary police arrested Francisco Alberto Come in Maputo in January without giving a reason. They reportedly beat him with batons and kicked and punched him, inflicting serious wounds, and then took him to a police station. He was subsequently hospitalized. The Mozambique Human Rights League (MHRL) lodged complaints with the police and the Procurator General's Office, but no criminal investigation had apparently been initiated by the end of the year.

Police shot dead criminal suspects in circumstances which suggested inadequate training in the use of force and firearms. In some cases the police announced that inquiries were being held but the results of such investigations were apparently not made public.

▭ Virgilio Amade, a former worker in the former German Democratic Republic (GDR), died after being hit by a police bullet in Maputo in September during one of the regular demonstrations in support of the GDR workers' pay claims. A ballistics investigation reportedly confirmed that the bullet came from a police weapon. A criminal investigation was ongoing at the end of the year.

▭ A police officer was detained after shooting dead 18-year-old Carlos Faruca in Beira in October. The officer reportedly claimed that he had acted in self defence when Carlos Faruca and other unarmed youths tried to steal his mobile telephone. He was detained awaiting trial at the end of the year.

People trafficking
Reports indicated that networks of traffickers took women and girls to South Africa to serve in the sex trade or in other forms of forced labour. Some victims were reportedly lured by the offer of jobs while others were said to have been taken there by force.

There were also reports of a trade in body parts, apparently for ritualistic purposes. Many of the victims were children.

⊟ A woman saved the life of a nine-year-old boy whom she found beside a road in Chimoio in October. His genitals had been removed. According to reports, a businessman had offered money to procure the genitals and an intermediary contracted a man and a woman to carry out the mutilation. After intensive pressure from the Beira office of the MHRL, all four were arrested. At the end of the year they were still awaiting trial.

NAMIBIA

REPUBLIC OF NAMIBIA
Head of state: Samuel Nujoma
Head of government: Theo-Ben Gurirab
Death penalty: abolitionist for all crimes
UN Women's Convention and its Optional Protocol: ratified

Arbitrary detention and excessive force by the police and members of the paramilitary Special Field Forces (SFF) continued to be reported. Journalists perceived to be critical of the government were harassed and threatened.

Background
In May President Nujoma announced that he would not run for a fourth term in office.

In October the Namibia Farm Workers Union (NaFwu) announced that its members would occupy white-owned commercial farms in protest at the slow pace of the government's land redistribution program. It called off plans to occupy farms after the police declared that illegal farm occupations would not be allowed and that perpetrators would be brought to justice.

Caprivi treason trial
On 20 May one of the defendants in the Caprivi treason trial made a compensation claim for alleged police assault following his arrest. The 122 defendants, charged with treason, murder and other offences in connection with the secessionist uprising in the northeast Caprivi region in August 1999, have been on trial since 2001. Similar claims made by at least five other defendants were settled out of court on 8 July.

In July charges against five defendants were withdrawn, in part because witnesses had died, and they were released. There were undue delays and numerous adjournments of the trial.

On 16 October, one of the defendants, Oscar Luphalezwi, died at the Katima Mulilo state hospital while in police custody. This brought to 12 the number of treason trial defendants who have died in police custody since 1999. No independent or impartial inquiry was carried out into this or the earlier deaths as required under Namibia's international human rights obligations.

Police abuses
Police used excessive force to disperse peaceful demonstrators. The SFF were reportedly involved in arbitrary arrests and intimidation along the border with Angola.

⊟ There was no independent investigation into allegations that police used excessive force to quell riots by refugees at the Osire refugee camp, northern Namibia, on 17 October. Seven people were shot and injured when police fired live ammunition to disperse refugees protesting about food distribution in the camp. Police later arrested and released without charge eight students at the camp.

⊟ In November, six armed members of the SFF detained and threatened to shoot journalist Paulus Sakaris of *Die Republikien* newspaper and his driver Simon Haimbodi as they drove near the Angola border. The two men were taken to an SFF base where their vehicle was confiscated and they were accused of driving without a "road authority clearance certificate". They were later released without charge.

Violence against women
Violence against women in the home remained persistent and pervasive. On 11 February police threatened to fire on women and children demonstrating peacefully in support of legislation to combat violence against women and children. On 27 March the National Assembly passed the Combating of Domestic Violence Bill, aimed at strengthening the protection offered victims by the courts and police.

Freedom of expression
President Nujoma openly attacked media professionals deemed critical of the government.

⊟ On 28 August, the President reportedly told a student audience that Hannes Smith, editor of the *Windhoek Observer* newspaper, was "looking for trouble" and would "get it" after allegations made in the President's autobiography were disputed in an article in the newspaper.

Food shortages
In August up to 400,000 people, approximately 20 per cent of the population, were in need of general food aid distributions, according to the country's Emergency Management Unit. In September the World Food Programme expressed growing concern about the food security situation. The hardest hit area was the Caprivi region, afflicted by both drought and floods.

AI country reports/ visits
Report
· Namibia: Justice delayed is justice denied — the Caprivi treason trial (AI Index: AFR 42/001/2003)

NIGER

REPUBLIC OF THE NIGER
Head of state: Mamadou Tandja
Head of government: Amadou Hama
Death penalty: abolitionist in practice
UN Women's Convention: ratified with reservations
Optional Protocol to UN Women's Convention: not signed

More than 200 soldiers, arrested following a failed mutiny in August 2002, remained in detention without trial. Three gendarmes were sentenced to prison terms for torture. Slavery, still prevalent in Niger, was made a punishable crime. As in previous years, there were attempts to restrict freedom of expression.

Background
Enacted in late 2002, the new Military Code of Justice, which established a court martial specifically to try the soldiers arrested after the 2002 mutiny, continued to raise human rights concerns. Despite protests by local human rights organizations at the Code's failure to meet international human rights standards, the Constitutional Court in February rejected a challenge by opposition parties to the constitutionality of the Code.

Detention without trial
More than 200 soldiers, arrested after the 2002 mutiny was quelled, were still in detention without trial at the end of 2003. In May police dispersed their relatives, mainly women, when they began a sit-in in the capital, Niamey. The demonstrators were complaining that most detainees had been held for months without being questioned by an investigating judge. Families did not know their place of detention in many cases. According to the authorities, 52 of the soldiers had been released in May, but no list was made public.

Torture
In April, two shepherds from the Peul community, brothers Hama and Salou Abdoulaye, were severely tortured by three gendarmes who arrested them after a bicycle theft in Dogon, western Niger. The brothers' injuries were so severe that their forearms and feet later had to be amputated. In May a court in Niamey sentenced the senior officer to two years' imprisonment and his two subordinates to 18 months. The victims lodged an appeal on the grounds that the sentences were too light.

Slavery criminalized
In May the National Assembly unanimously adopted a new Penal Code which, for the first time, made slavery a crime punishable by 10 to 30 years' imprisonment. Traditional chiefs had pledged to eradicate the practice at an International Labour Organization (ILO) forum in Niger in 2001. Local human rights organizations welcomed the measure as a move towards punishing the perpetrators of the practice.

Freedom of expression
◻ In February the government ordered the closure of *Nomade FM*, a privately-owned radio station, for "inciting rebellion". On a radio program, two former Tuareg rebels had criticized the government for not fulfilling its commitment under the peace agreements to reintegrate former rebels into society. The station was allowed to reopen two weeks later.
◻ In October Moussa Tchangari, managing editor of a private weekly newspaper, *Alternative*, was detained for two days for allegedly inciting a student protest to demand better living and working conditions. The journalist was released without charge.
◻ In November, Maman Abou, a prominent human rights defender and editor of *Le Républicain*, the leading newspaper in Niamey, was arrested and imprisoned for publishing information critical of government officials. He was a prisoner of conscience. He was sentenced to six months' imprisonment for allegedly libelling the Prime Minister and the Minister of Finance, but his trial failed to respect national or international fair trial standards. He was not questioned and could not challenge his accusers, who said he had obtained confidential documents by theft. He had no legal representation at his trial and was sentenced in his absence. His lawyer lodged an appeal but Maman Abou was still held at the end of the year.

NIGERIA

FEDERAL REPUBLIC OF NIGERIA
Head of state and government: Olusegun Obasanjo
Death penalty: retentionist
UN Women's Convention: ratified
Optional Protocol to UN Women's Convention: signed

The sentence of death by stoning passed on Amina Lawal continued to attract massive international condemnation and was quashed on appeal. However, laws still allowed the imposition of death sentences for sexually related offences, amputations for theft and floggings for consuming alcohol. Little action was taken by the federal government to end the discrimination against women and denial of fundamental freedoms under *Sharia*-inspired penal legislation in force in 12 northern states. Officials at state and local levels were accused of using vigilante forces to instigate violence for political purposes. The government failed to hold independent investigations into reports of unlawful killings by the armed forces.

Background

President Olusegun Obasanjo and the ruling People's Democratic Party (PDP) won the majority of votes in elections for the National Assembly in April and for the President and State Governors in May. Forged voter registration cards were produced on a vast scale and the elections were marred by fraud and violence (see below).

Appellate courts overturned four death sentences passed by courts in northern states under new penal legislation since 1999 inspired by *Sharia* (Islamic law) (see below). Concerns were raised in the parliamentary debate on the death penalty about the imposition of the death penalty under that legislation. The new *Sharia* penal laws continued to criminalize behaviour termed as "*zina*". In one state, *zina* was defined as sexual intercourse with any person "over whom [the perpetrator] has no sexual rights" and in circumstances "in which no doubt exists as to the illegality of the act". Offences defined in this way were used to deny both women and men their rights to privacy and to freedom of expression and association, and in practice frequently to deny women access to justice. Rules of evidence discriminating against women continued to be applied, putting women at greater risk of conviction on charges of *zina*. Trials under the new laws were grossly unfair, refusing basic rights of defence to the most poor and vulnerable individuals.

Death penalty and other cruel, inhuman and degrading punishment

No executions were carried out during the year. Death sentences were passed both by the high courts and by *Sharia* courts in northern Nigeria. The new *Sharia* penal laws have changed the punishment for Muslims convicted of *zina* crimes from flogging to a mandatory death penalty, and have extended jurisdiction in capital cases to the lowest courts in the *Sharia* judicial system.

◻ Jibrin Babaji was sentenced to death by stoning on 14 September by a *Sharia* court in Bauchi, northwest Nigeria, after being convicted under *Sharia* penal law of "sodomy" involving three minors. He was not represented by a lawyer and was convicted by a single judge. He had legal counsel at his appeal hearing in December, which had not concluded by the end of 2003.

Sentences of death by stoning passed in previous years continued to be a focus for worldwide criticism.

◻ On 25 September the Upper *Sharia* Court of Appeal of Katsina State in northern Nigeria overturned the sentence of death by stoning passed on Amina Lawal at Bakori in March 2002. The court ruled that neither her conviction nor her confession was legally valid, and that no offence had been established. She had been convicted of *zina* after bearing a child outside marriage, and the death sentence had been upheld by a lower *Sharia* court of appeal.

◻ In August the *Sharia* Court of Appeal in Dutse, Jigawa State, dismissed a sentence of death by stoning on Sarimu Mohamed Baranda, aged 54. The court allowed an appeal by his relatives on the grounds that he was suffering from a mental illness and ordered his admission to hospital. He had been sentenced to death in July 2002 after he confessed to raping a nine-year-old child, a confession he said later had been made under duress.

Others still faced the death penalty at the end of 2003 for alleged acts of *zina*.

◻ An appeal against a sentence of death by stoning passed on Fatima Usman and Ahmadu Ibrahim in May 2002 was still pending at the end of 2003 after it was indefinitely adjourned in June by the *Sharia* Court of Appeal in Minna, Niger State. The couple were initially sentenced to five years' imprisonment for *zina* by a secular lower court. A court in New Gawu imposed the death penalty in May 2002, in their absence, after Fatima Usman's father complained to the state's Islamic authorities that the first sentence was too light. The federal authorities recognized only the first sentence, however, and refused to hand the couple over to the Islamic authorities. In October 2002 they were released on humanitarian grounds to await the appeal.

President Obasanjo initiated a parliamentary debate on the death penalty in November. The National Study Group on the Death Penalty was set up to produce recommendations on the status of the death penalty in the Constitution.

AI worked with a local human rights organization to support prisoners under sentence of amputation after being convicted in Sokoto State. They were all unfairly tried, without legal representation, and were unable to lodge appeals before higher courts in the *Sharia* judicial system. Their cases will now be reviewed by the *Sharia* Court of Appeal in Sokoto State.

Women and human rights

In May a bill on violence against women was introduced in parliament. It aimed to prohibit forms of violence such as harmful traditional practices and domestic violence, including marital rape. Courts would be able to issue protective orders prohibiting abusers from approaching or threatening victims of violence. A Commission on Violence Against Women, to include representatives from religious organizations and non-governmental women's organizations, would monitor implementation of the law and provide rape crisis centres and shelters for victims.

The Nigerian government and Shell and Chevron-Texaco oil companies rejected the findings of an AI investigation into allegations of excessive use of force against women human rights activists in the Niger Delta. Soldiers and paramilitary Mobile Police officers were reported to have tear gassed, kicked and gun whipped seated women demonstrators, some of them elderly, outside oil company premises in Warri, Delta State, on 8 August 2002. Neither the government nor the oil companies carried out independent investigations into the allegations.

Women in the region continued to face harassment for demanding compensation for environmental degradation and development assistance for communities living in extreme poverty.

⌒ On 22 May Alice Ukoko, who was reportedly assaulted on 8 August 2002, was briefly detained by the Delta State security services and questioned about plans to organize women's demonstrations and interrupt the governor's swearing-in ceremony. Shortly before her arrest, she and other women had formally applied to the Inspector General of Police, head of the national police force, for permission to demonstrate about the conduct of the security forces. Permission was not granted and the demonstration did not take place.

Killings and ill-treatment by police

In other cases in which the security forces used excessive force or unlawful lethal force, the government failed to conduct independent investigations.

⌒ At least four people were reportedly killed in Lagos in clashes between the police and civilians during countrywide protests and strikes against a sharp fuel price increase. A 27-year-old man, Obot Akpan Etim, was shot dead during one reportedly peaceful protest. An eyewitness to a protest in Oshodi, Lagos, on 7 July reported that hundreds of peaceful protesters, chanting and shouting slogans, were charged and tear gassed by the police without warning. Police and city officials denied any wrongdoing by the police, blaming demonstrators for the deaths.

Detainees held by the police were routinely subjected to harsh conditions in custody and denied their constitutional rights to be promptly charged or released.

⌒ Festus Keyamo, a lawyer and leader of the Movement for the Actualization of the Future Republic of the Niger Delta, was detained without charge or trial for more than a month. He had called for wider autonomy for the Niger Delta region after President Obasanjo declined to approve allocating Niger Delta states a percentage of offshore oil revenues. He was held incommunicado and moved to various places of detention following his arrest on 28 December 2002. Held at police headquarters in the capital, Abuja, he threatened a hunger strike to protest at inadequate food, clothing and medical care. He was released on police bail on 3 February and charges were later withdrawn.

Political violence

In the months before federal and state elections in April and May, there was an increase in political assassinations and violent clashes in which party supporters died. An increasing flow of firearms into Nigeria and the creation of armed vigilante groups enabled politicians to foment political violence at local and state levels. Members of state governments and houses of assembly were reportedly implicated in the harassment and intimidation of rival candidates and their followers.

State-endorsed armed vigilante groups were responsible for large numbers of extrajudicial executions in the southeast, and suspected of involvement in a number of unsolved killings of politicians.

⌒ Marshall Harry, National Vice Chairman of the main opposition party, the All Nigeria People's Party (ANPP), was killed when armed men entered his home in Abuja on 5 March. On 10 February Ogbonaya Uche, an ANPP candidate for the Senate, died days after he had been shot by unidentified armed men at his home in Owerri, Imo State.

⌒ In November at least 12 people, including former members of a vigilante group, were charged with the murders of Barnabas Igwe, chairman of the Onitsha branch of the Nigerian Bar Association, and his wife Amaka in September 2002.

⌒ In March the trial started of 12 detainees charged in October 2002 in connection with the murder of Attorney General and Minister of Justice Bola Ige in December 2001.

Impunity

Nigeria continued to foster impunity, failing to bring to justice not only those responsible for human rights violations in Nigeria but also individuals charged with grave offences under international law. Human rights violations by the Nigerian armed forces under the present government, particularly the killing of civilians at Odi, Bayelsa State, in 1999 and in Benue State in 2001, remained uninvestigated.

The findings of the Human Rights Violations Investigation Commission, known as the Oputa Panel, were still not made public. Established in 1999 to investigate human rights violations committed between 1966 and the return to civilian rule in 1999, it reported the findings of its public hearings and investigations in May 2002 to President Obasanjo. The government had not published the report or its recommendations, and had made no public statement about plans for implementing the recommendations by the end of 2003.

Impunity for Charles Taylor

In August Liberian President Charles Taylor relinquished power and left Liberia for Nigeria with implicit guarantees from the Nigerian government that he would be neither prosecuted in Nigeria nor surrendered to the Special Court for Sierra Leone. In June an international warrant for his arrest had been issued after he was indicted by the Special Court for war crimes, crimes against humanity and other serious violations of international humanitarian law during Sierra Leone's internal armed conflict. These crimes included killings, mutilations, rapes and the use of child soldiers by Sierra Leone armed opposition forces that he had supported. President Obasanjo argued that allowing Charles Taylor to travel to Nigeria was in the interests of securing a political settlement to Liberia's conflict. In early December, Interpol allowed worldwide circulation of the arrest warrant against Charles Taylor with a view to extradition. AI protested that the Nigerian government had violated its obligations under international law, but calls for Charles Taylor to be surrendered to the Special Court or investigated with a view to criminal or extradition proceedings in Nigerian courts were ignored.

AI country reports/visits

Reports
- Nigeria: Repression of women's protests in oil-producing delta region (AI Index: AFR 44/008/2003)
- Nigeria: Legal Defence and Assistance Project (LEDAP) and AI joint statement on increasing political violence in the run-up to elections (AI Index: AFR 44/011/2003)
- Nigeria: Police use of lethal force against demonstrators must be investigated (AI Index: AFR 44/021/2003)

Visit
AI delegates visited Nigeria in March to research political violence in the context of the elections, *Sharia* penal legislation and women's human rights.

RWANDA

REPUBLIC OF RWANDA
Head of state: Paul Kagame
Head of government: Bernard Makuza
Death penalty: retentionist
UN Women's Convention: ratified
Optional Protocol to UN Women's Convention: not signed

"Disappearances", arbitrary arrests, unlawful detentions and the ill-treatment of detainees were reported. Eighteen prisoners were sentenced to death for crimes committed during the 1994 genocide; no executions were carried out. Approximately 80,000 individuals remained in detention, nearly all of them suspected of participation in the genocide. Most were held for prolonged periods without charge or trial, in harsh and overcrowded conditions. Trials of genocide suspects continued at the International Criminal Tribunal for Rwanda (ICTR) in Arusha, Tanzania. Grave human rights violations committed in previous years by state security agents remained without thorough or independent investigation. Several people were detained for peaceful opposition activities.

Background

The governments of the Democratic Republic of the Congo (DRC) and Rwanda accused each other of not honouring the July 2002 bilateral agreement, in which the Rwandese government pledged to withdraw its troops from eastern DRC and the DRC government undertook to disarm and repatriate Rwandese opposition groups. Reports of continued Rwandese involvement in eastern DRC after its forces had officially withdrawn were denied by the government. The Rwandese and Ugandan governments made accusations that the other was harbouring, sponsoring and training armed opposition movements.

The end of the government's transition program following the genocide was marked by the adoption of a new Constitution, the fifth since independence in 1960. The draft Constitution contained provisions that could restrict fundamental civil and political rights. Information provided by the government-controlled media on key provisions of the draft Constitution was limited. In May the new Constitution was overwhelmingly endorsed in a referendum.

The presidential election was held on 25 August and parliamentary elections between 29 September and 2 October. Incumbent Paul Kagame won the presidential election with 95 per cent of the vote, while his Rwandese Patriotic Front (RPF) party won 74 per cent in parliamentary elections. Opposition candidates and supporters faced severe intimidation during and after the electoral campaigns. There were consistent reports of voter intimidation before and on polling day by supporters of the governing party.

The high proportion of women elected to parliament resulted in part from government legislation and administrative practices aimed at advancing the position and status of women.

'Disappearances'

A number of "disappearances" were reported, many linked to government actions against the *Mouvement Démocratique Républicain* (MDR), Democratic Republican Movement. Others who "disappeared" were reportedly victims of criminal activities by members of the Rwandese security forces.

⌐ Several people reportedly "disappeared" in April, apparently because they were suspected of opposition to the government. They included Dr Leonard Hitimana, an MDR deputy, Lieutenant-Colonel Augustin Cyiza, former President of the Court of Cassation and Vice-President of the Supreme Court, and Eliezer Runyaruka, a university student and cantonal judge in Nyamata. According to witnesses, the vehicles in which the "disappeared" were last seen or which belonged to them were last sighted in a military detention facility or driven and subsequently abandoned by members of the security forces.

⌐ Charles Muyenzi and Aimable Nkurunziza, former armed forces officers, were forcibly returned from Burundi. They were reportedly handed over to the Rwandese security forces on 9 November, and subsequent efforts to locate them met with no response from the authorities. Aimable Nkurunziza had previously received refugee status in Uganda.

Suppression of the opposition

Opposition party members and leaders were intimidated by repeated interrogations at police stations, unlawful detentions and death threats. A number fled the country. Opposition party organizers were allegedly threatened and bribed to defect to the RPF or to make false accusations against their party's candidate. Many voters were forced or pressured to join the RPF and attend RPF political rallies. Civil society organizations were denounced as "divisionist" or "sectarian". In April a parliamentary commission accused the membership of the MDR and 46 named individuals of fomenting "division". The leading independent human rights organization was accused of financially supporting the MDR.

Abuses in the criminal justice system

Public confidence in the criminal justice system continued to erode. The police frequently detained suspects unlawfully for long periods without trial. Court decisions were not always respected by Public Prosecutors' Offices, and defendants acquitted by the courts sometimes remained in prison. One third of all arrests and preventive detentions were estimated to be in violation of the Code of Criminal Procedure. Many officials in the criminal justice system did not have the necessary legal training or experience. Draft laws before parliament proposed restructuring the judicial system and simplifying civil and criminal justice procedures to address some of these issues.

Genocide trials

More than 450 genocide suspects were tried, significantly fewer than in 2002. By the end of 2003 the Specialized Chambers had tried slightly more than 8,000 suspects since they became operational in 1996. In many cases, trials did not meet international standards of fairness. Eighteen defendants were sentenced to death. The sentences were not carried out.

The government, in an attempt to address serious prison overcrowding, provisionally released more than 20,000 detainees. Most had confessed to participation in the genocide. However, among those who did not benefit from the provisional release were detainees whose case files contained insufficient evidence to warrant their detention.

Gacaca

The long awaited start of *gacaca* trials, a community-based system of justice, did not begin as planned. Community members and elected local magistrates continued pre-trial work in the 746 tribunals, which started operating in 2002. They listed victims and suspected perpetrators, and made an inventory of civil damages claims. The remaining 8,258 tribunals were planned to be operational in 2004.

The tribunals were plagued by inaction by magistrates and community members, the unwillingness of communities to provide information and public dissatisfaction that human rights abuses by members of the former armed opposition group, the RPF, were excluded from their consideration. After the fall of the government in 1994 the RPF's political wing became the ruling party and its armed wing became the armed forces, known as the Rwandese Patriotic Army (RPA) until renamed the Rwandese Defence Forces (RDF) in June 2002.

International Criminal Tribunal for Rwanda

Trials of leading genocide suspects continued at the ICTR, which held 56 detainees at the end of 2003. Five trials involving 20 defendants continued, three of which began in 2003. The trials of seven former government ministers began in November. Judgments were given in five trials involving eight suspects. By the end of the year, the ICTR had delivered 25 judgments since its first indictments in 1995.

Two suspects were arrested in the DRC and Uganda, and transferred to the ICTR for trial. Another 16 individuals were indicted by the ICTR but not apprehended. The US Congress renewed its Rewards for Justice Program to assist in the capture of those indicted.

The ICTR had accused the Rwandese government of frustrating investigations of war crimes allegations against former RPA members. In August, human rights groups pressed the UN Security Council to ensure the independence and impartiality of the Court, despite pressure by Rwanda and other states not to prosecute RPA members for crimes against humanity that had led the court to suspend investigations against former RPA members in September 2002.

International justice

Other states continued to bring to trial or deport genocide suspects under their national jurisdiction. Despite the Belgian parliament's repeal of its legislation conferring universal jurisdiction on Belgian courts, a number of genocide cases that had already begun were pending before the courts.

⊡ In September the Canadian Federal Court of Appeal ruled in the case of Léon Mugesera, accused in Canada of crimes against humanity for making a speech inciting violence and ethnic hatred in Rwanda in 1992. The Court found that the speech did not constitute an explicit incitement to genocide or a crime against humanity, and that he could remain in Canada.

Freedom of expression

Members of the press and civil society continued to face intimidation and harassment for criticizing the government or armed forces. A number of journalists and human rights activists were interrogated by the police, detained and driven into exile. Others had to exercise self-censorship in relation to certain subjects to avoid politically motivated repression by the security forces.

⊡ Police arrested five journalists and the driver of the privately owned newspaper Umuseso on 19 November, and confiscated one edition of the paper. The journalists were interrogated and two of them reportedly beaten, allegedly because of an article that questioned the demobilization of certain senior military officers. They were released without charge after two days.

Refugees

The government continued to express its intention for all Rwandese refugees – estimated at 85,000 – to return to Rwanda. Tripartite agreements were signed between Rwanda, the UN High Commissioner for Refugees (UNHCR) and host countries: the Republic of the Congo, Malawi, Mozambique, Namibia, Uganda, Zambia and Zimbabwe. Many returning refugees expressed concern about their security and the economic situation in Rwanda. In Uganda, only 200 out of 14,000 Rwandese refugees registered for voluntary repatriation, despite attempts by the Rwandese government and UNHCR to persuade them that it was safe to return.

AI country reports/ visits
Statements
- Rwanda: Escalating repression against political opposition (AI Index: AFR 47/004/2003)
- Rwanda: End of provisional release of genocide suspects (AI Index: AFR 47/005/2003)
- Rwanda: Run-up to presidential elections marred by threats and harassment (AI Index: AFR 47/010/2003)
- Rwanda: President Kagame's inauguration – an opportunity to strengthen human rights protection (AI Index: AFR 47/013/2003)

Visits
AI delegates visited Rwanda in January, March, July and August. In October AI's Secretary General travelled to the DRC, Rwanda and Uganda to meet senior government and UN officials, survivors of human rights abuses, Congolese human rights activists and international humanitarian agencies.

SENEGAL

REPUBLIC OF SENEGAL
Head of state: Abdoulaye Wade
Head of government: Idrissa Seck
Death penalty: abolitionist in practice
UN Women's Convention and its Optional Protocol: ratified

Despite ongoing talks on implementation of the 2001 peace agreement, tension and insecurity continued to be high in the disputed region of Casamance. Several civilians were killed or arrested during military operations. Abuses against civilians by armed opposition forces continued throughout the year, notably against people with "non-Casamance" names. Several journalists were beaten or expelled in what appeared to be an attempt to challenge freedom of expression. The security forces continued to benefit from impunity.

Background

In August, President Abdoulaye Wade tried to bring opposition parties into government but failed, so retained most of the outgoing cabinet led by Prime Minister Idrissa Seck. In November thousands of people marched in the capital Dakar to protest against political violence after a brutal attack on opposition leader Talla Sylla.

In Casamance there were sporadic clashes between the security forces and armed members of the Mouvement des forces démocratiques de Casamance (MFDC – Democratic Forces of Casamance Movement), an armed opposition group claiming independence for Casamance. This was despite peace agreements signed by the government and the MFDC in 2001. In October, following an internal MFDC conference, MFDC Secretary General Jean-Marie Biagui declared that the war was over. However, members of armed MFDC factions boycotted the conference, and attacks by alleged armed members of the MFDC continued.

Killings and arrests of civilians by the army

In January the army launched several "combing" operations against the MFDC in the region of Ziguinchor, the Casamance main city. Soldiers arrested about 10 women suspected of supporting the MFDC in the region of Nyassia. All were reportedly released days later. Other civilians suspected of being members of the MFDC were tortured before being released.

⊡ In February, Sidi Diédhiou, a farmer, was killed by the army. He had been detained while working in his field and was taken to a nearby military camp apparently because he stayed out late at night. Sidi Diédhiou was reportedly shot in the back in the presence of another detainee. The soldiers claimed that he had tried to flee.

Abuses by the MFDC

Several attacks against civilians were carried out by alleged members of one of the MFDC's armed wings. The attacks mainly involved the robbery of people travelling by road in Casamance. During such attacks, unarmed civilians were beaten and some were shot after reportedly revealing their "non-Casamance" names.

⌦ In August, six vehicles were stopped by alleged armed members of the MFDC near Diegoune. After seizing belongings, the attackers ascertained the identity of the travellers and killed two of them who did not have Casamance names — Serigne Sarr and Saliou Diop. A third man, Aliou Mboup, was seriously wounded.

Threats to freedom of expression

Journalists continued to be harassed and intimidated.
⌦ In March, Fanta Badji and Mame Cira Konate, two women journalists with *Radio Manore FM*, a community radio station for women, were assaulted by riot police from the *Groupement mobile d'intervention* (GMI – Mobile Intervention Group). The women were covering a police operation involving the forcible removal of inhabitants of an illegal settlement in Dakar.

⌦ In October, Sophie Malibeaux, a correspondent with *Radio France Internationale*, was arrested and expelled from the country. She was arrested in Casamance while covering a meeting of the MFDC in Ziguinchor. She was taken by police to Dakar for questioning and expelled because of alleged "tendentious" coverage of political discussions in Casamance.

Impunity

Impact on women in Casamance

Despite formal commitments by the authorities to investigate past human rights violations, no steps were taken to institute an inquiry into the large-scale violations committed by the security forces in Casamance in the past decade. As a result of this impunity and lack of redress, dozens of women whose husbands "disappeared" after being arrested by security forces or were abducted by alleged MFDC armed members had to cope with uncertainty about the fates of their husbands and with economic hardship. In December in Dakar, AI launched a report and campaign to highlight the plight of these women and their families and to ask for justice and redress for them.

⌦ After the "disappearance" of her husband, who was arrested by security forces in Casamance in August 1999, Khady Bassène's life became much harder. Because the authorities refused to acknowledge the "disappearance", she could not obtain her husband's death certificate, which was needed to obtain his pension.

Failure to bring to justice perpetrators of violations

The justice system persistently failed to bring to justice perpetrators of human rights violations.
⌦ In September a police auxiliary arrested in October 2001 in connection with the killing of Balla Gaye was acquitted by a military court even though the State Prosecutor said that the investigation into the case had not been completed.

Hissein Habré

The repeal in July of a Belgian law which allowed the pursuit of foreign leaders for war crimes did not affect the ongoing complaint lodged in Belgium against former Chadian President Hissein Habré who lives in Senegal. In 2001 President Wade had announced his readiness to hand over Hissein Habré to stand trial in a third country for gross human rights violations.

Extradition

In July a Mauritanian military officer, Lieutenant Didi Ould M'Hamed, who had sought refuge in Senegal because he was suspected of involvement in an attempted coup in Mauritania, was extradited to Mauritania. The extradition, which was recommended by the Indictments Chamber of the Dakar Court of Appeal and endorsed by President Wade, breached Senegal's international human rights obligations that forbid any extradition to a country where the person would be at risk of torture or other serious human rights violations.

AI country reports/ visits

Report

· Senegal: Casamance women speak out (AI Index: AFR 49/002/2003)

Visit

AI visited Senegal in December to meet the authorities and investigate human rights.

SIERRA LEONE

REPUBLIC OF SIERRA LEONE
Head of state and government: Ahmad Tejan Kabbah
Death penalty: retentionist
UN Women's Convention: ratified
Optional Protocol to UN Women's Convention: signed

Further consolidation of the peace process resulted in improvements in the human rights situation. Progress was made to address impunity for past human rights abuses committed by both government and armed opposition forces during the conflict. The trial of some 90 former combatants charged with murder and other offences was repeatedly postponed and international fair trial standards were not met. Some 20 others associated with the former armed opposition remained in long-term detention without charge or trial.

Background information

Consolidation of the peace achieved in 2001 after a decade of conflict continued. Government authority was re-established throughout the country but concerns about the capacity of the army and police were heightened by instability in neighbouring Liberia. Liberian armed groups made incursions into Sierra Leone, particularly in Kailahun District. In addition, a significant number of former Sierra Leonean combatants were reported to be fighting in both Liberia and Côte d'Ivoire. Deployment of security forces, supported by the UN Mission in Sierra Leone (UNAMSIL), along the border with Liberia was increased. However, a peace agreement and subsequent deployment of a UN peace-keeping operation in Liberia in October augured a reduced threat from Liberia.

Training and restructuring of the army and police by the International Military Advisory and Training Team and UN civilian police officers continued. There was gradual withdrawal of UNAMSIL military personnel with complete withdrawal anticipated by late 2004.

Reintegration of former combatants remained a priority and, despite a shortfall in funds, was near completion at the end of the year. However, government commitments in 2002 to disband the Civil Defence Forces (CDF), which had supported the government during the conflict, remained unfulfilled.

Ninety-eight per cent of over 7,000 registered former child combatants and separated children had been reunited with their families. The Special Representative of the UN Secretary-General for Children and Armed Conflict visited Sierra Leone in February and called for continuing international support to sustain progress made so far in the protection of war-affected children.

The government made efforts to increase control of diamond-mining areas, inhibit unregulated mining and tackle potential insecurity in Kono and Kenema Districts.

On 13 January there was an unsuccessful armed attack on the armoury at Wellington barracks, on the outskirts of Freetown. Johnny Paul Koroma, an elected member of parliament and also former leader of the Armed Forces Revolutionary Council (AFRC) which came to power following a military coup in 1997 and which subsequently allied itself to the armed opposition Revolutionary United Front (RUF), was implicated in a plan to destabilize state authority but evaded arrest.

The Special Court for Sierra Leone

There was significant progress in addressing impunity for gross human rights abuses committed during the conflict. Thirteen people were indicted by the Special Court for Sierra Leone, nine of whom were in custody at the end of the year. The Special Court had been established in 2002 to try those bearing the greatest responsibility for crimes against humanity, war crimes and other serious violations of international humanitarian law committed after 30 November 1996.

The first seven indictments, against members of all parties to the conflict, were announced on 10 March. Charges included murder, rape and other forms of sexual violence, sexual slavery, conscription of children, abductions and forced labour. Those indicted included former RUF leader Foday Sankoh, RUF commander Sam Bockarie, Johnny Paul Koroma and Samuel Hinga Norman, Minister of Internal Affairs and former National Coordinator of the CDF.

All but Sam Bockarie and Johnny Paul Koroma were arrested and detained. Sam Bockarie, who was closely associated with then Liberian President Charles Taylor and was in Liberia when indicted, was killed in May. Although the Liberian government claimed that he had died in a confrontation with government forces, the circumstances remained unclear and suspicions surrounding his death were compounded by the reported murder several days later of his mother, wife and two children in the Liberian capital, Monrovia. It appeared that Sam Bockarie had been killed to prevent him giving evidence to the Special Court which would implicate President Taylor. Johnny Paul Koroma remained at large; reports that he too had been killed in Liberia remained unconfirmed. The case against Foday Sankoh was adjourned because of serious ill-health; he died in July.

On 4 June an indictment against President Taylor was announced as he attended the opening of negotiations to end Liberia's conflict in Accra, Ghana, under the auspices of the Economic Community of West African States (ECOWAS). The charges were based on his active support to the RUF and AFRC in order to destabilize Sierra Leone and gain access to diamond resources. Despite an international arrest warrant and an appeal by AI that he be arrested by the Ghanaian authorities, he was allowed to return to Liberia the same day.

President Taylor announced his willingness to relinquish power in the interests of peace. On 11 August he left Liberia for Nigeria with implicit guarantees from the Nigerian government that he would be neither prosecuted in Nigeria nor surrendered to the Special Court. Nigerian President Olusegun Obasanjo argued that he was acting in the interests of peace in Liberia. AI protested strongly that the Nigerian government had violated its obligations under international law but calls to either surrender Charles Taylor to the Special Court or open an investigation with a view to determining whether to pursue criminal or extradition proceedings in Nigerian courts were ignored. AI called for all ECOWAS and other governments to cooperate fully with the Special Court. In early December, Interpol allowed worldwide circulation of the arrest warrant against Charles Taylor with a view to extradition.

From late October the Appeals Chamber of the Special Court considered preliminary defence motions, including in relation to the denial of the right of appeal against decisions on preliminary motions challenging the jurisdiction of the Special Court, and the applicability of amnesty provisions in the 1999 Lomé peace agreement. AI urged that the right of appeal be ensured; the Appeals Chamber, however, rejected this motion. AI also argued that international law prohibited amnesties or other impunity measures for crimes against humanity, war crimes and other serious violations of international law. The indictment against Charles Taylor was challenged on grounds of "sovereign immunity" and extraterritoriality. The Prosecutor submitted motions seeking to join existing cases into two combined indictments: those of RUF and AFRC members and those of CDF members. Decisions on these motions had not been reached by the end of the year. Trials were expected to begin in March or April 2004.

A severe funding crisis, threatening the Special Court's continued operation beyond the end of 2003, was partially alleviated by additional contributions and bringing forward funds for subsequent years.

Further measures needed to end impunity
The Special Court for Sierra Leone was expected to try only a small number of people; others responsible for serious crimes throughout the conflict, which began in 1991, continued to benefit from the amnesty provided by the peace agreement and subsequently passed into law. AI called for this legislation to be repealed. It also stressed the importance of the Special Court's contribution to strengthening the national justice system so that it could in future assume responsibility for ending impunity for such grave crimes.

Truth and Reconciliation Commission
Despite a shortfall in its budget, the Truth and Reconciliation Commission (TRC) made progress towards providing a historical record of human rights abuses during the conflict and promoting reconciliation. More than 7,500 statements were collected, including from Sierra Leonean refugees in other West African countries. Public hearings throughout the country, involving victims, witnesses and perpetrators, were completed in August. Particular attention was given to the experiences of women and children. The mandate of the TRC, scheduled to end in October, was extended and its report was anticipated in early 2004.

High Court trial of former combatants
The trial of some 90 former combatants charged with murder, conspiracy to murder and other offences was repeatedly adjourned and failed to advance. The defendants included Foday Sankoh, other former RUF members and renegade soldiers known as the "West Side Boys". Most had been arrested in May 2000 following the deaths of about 20 people and injuries to many others when RUF members fired on civilians protesting outside Foday Sankoh's Freetown residence. Foday Sankoh was transferred to the Special Court's custody after his indictment.

None of the defendants benefited from legal representation, violating international fair trial standards. Concerns about lack of legal representation were exacerbated by the fact that the defendants, if convicted, could face a death sentence. They continued to be denied family visits.

Treason trial
Following the attack on Wellington barracks, more than 100 people were reported to have been arrested. While most were subsequently released, 17 people, including soldiers on active duty, former members of the "West Side Boys" and some civilians, were charged in March with treason and related offences; they included a boy believed to be 15 years old who was held with adult prisoners in the Central Prison, Pademba Road, in Freetown. One of those charged was subsequently indicted by the Special Court and transferred to its jurisdiction. The trial was continuing at the end of the year.

Political detention without charge or trial
Twenty-three detainees, all military personnel, remained held without charge or trial in Pademba Road prison. Most had been arrested in mid-2000, although one had been held since February 1999. There was no legal basis for their continued detention and they were denied all access to lawyers and family members.

Prison conditions and deaths in custody
Notwithstanding some improvements, conditions of detention in police stations and prisons frequently failed to conform to international standards as a result of overcrowding, unhealthy conditions and inadequate medical attention.

In April, prison authorities agreed to investigate the death of a prisoner held in Magburaka Prison, Tonkolili District, who was reported to have died from injuries sustained as a result of beatings by prison officials, but there was no further progress. The precise cause of death of a prisoner who died in Pademba Road prison in August 2002, officially described as "psychosis", remained unclear.

Strengthening national institutions
Despite some progress in rehabilitating the national justice system, serious problems persisted in the effective administration of justice. There were few incentives for qualified lawyers to become judges. Although magistrates' courts were restored to all 12

districts, lack of magistrates remained a major constraint. Justices of the peace were trained and deployed to help reduce lengthy backlogs of cases. Criminal suspects continued to be held in police custody beyond legal limits, often because of lack of legal representation, especially in the provinces.

There was lax implementation of international standards in respect of separation of categories of prisoners, for example juveniles and women. Serious inadequacies in the juvenile justice system remained and overall lack of access to the judicial process, including in cases of gender-based violence, continued.

There was further delay in establishing a permanent National Human Rights Commission, anticipated in the peace agreement, despite assistance in preparing draft legislation to establish the Commission from UNAMSIL and the Office of the UN High Commissioner for Human Rights, in consultation with civil society organizations. Although presented to the government in September, legislation had not been submitted to parliament by the end of the year.

Refugees and internally displaced people

Refugees continued to return from Guinea and Liberia, although lack of basic amenities in areas such as Kailahun and Kono Districts impeded voluntary return of some refugees and internally displaced people to their place of origin. Emergency repatriation of Sierra Leonean refugees by the UN High Commissioner for Refugees (UNHCR) from Monrovia was temporarily suspended as the security crisis in Liberia deepened in June and July, and humanitarian agencies were forced to withdraw. Some 14,000 Sierra Leonean refugees remained in Liberia.

As conflict in Liberia intensified, more than 9,000 Liberians, including deserting combatants, crossed into Sierra Leone during the first three months of the year. UNHCR, UNAMSIL and security forces along the border and in refugee camps attempted to identify combatants and separate them from civilians. Liberian former child soldiers benefited from an accelerated integration program in refugee camps.

UN Mission in Sierra Leone

The UNAMSIL human rights section continued to monitor the human rights situation, including in relation to police stations, prisons, the justice system and national institutions. It also continued to document human rights abuses during the conflict. Additional regional offices were opened.

The human rights section also carried out training in international human rights and humanitarian law for UNAMSIL peace-keeping troops, members of the judiciary, law enforcement officials, and civil society organizations, including human rights groups.

AI country reports/ visits
Report
- Sierra Leone: Special Court for Sierra Leone – denial of right to appeal and prohibition of amnesties for crimes under international law (AI Index: AFR 51/012/2003)

Visit
AI delegates visited Sierra Leone in May and met officials and staff of the Special Court for Sierra Leone and the TRC as well as senior government officials and members of UNAMSIL.

SOMALIA

SOMALIA
Head of Transitional National Government: Abdiqasim Salad Hassan
Head of Somaliland Republic: Dahir Riyaale Kahin
Head of Puntland Regional State: Abdullahi Yusuf Ahmed
Death penalty: retentionist
UN Women's Convention and its Optional Protocol: not signed

Peace talks continued with some progress after over 12 years of state collapse and internal conflict, but were still not concluded. There was further faction fighting in central and southern Somalia. Thousands of people fled the fighting and abuses including kidnappings and threats to human rights defenders. Rape of internally displaced women and girls, particularly from minority communities, was reported in Mogadishu. There was no effective rule of law. Journalists and human rights defenders were harassed and threatened.

Background

Throughout much of the central and southern regions, particularly in the capital, Mogadishu, and Baidoa, there was constant insecurity and intermittent faction fighting during the year, leaving the October 2002 cease-fire mostly ineffective. There had been no national government or administration, army, police or justice system since the state collapsed in 1991. In August the Transitional National Government (TNG) extended its three-year term. Although nominally recognized by the UN and part of the international community, it controlled only a small part of Mogadishu; other areas were held by various armed faction leaders. The TNG was opposed at the peace talks by the Ethiopia-backed Somalia Reconciliation and Restoration Council but supported by a new faction grouping, the Somali National Salvation Council. International humanitarian workers were generally unable to work in the south for security reasons. The Somali Medical Association reported in July after the murder of a well-known eye doctor that over 70 health professionals had been killed since 1991. The same month a non-governmental organization (NGO) in Mogadishu said over 530 civilians had been killed and 185 people kidnapped in the previous 12 months.

Somaliland

Multi-party presidential elections were held in April in the self-declared independent Somaliland Republic in the northwest. This was still the only part of the former Somali Republic with government, democratic institutions, a justice system, and peace. A Human Rights Commission was in preparation, with the support of many local NGOs. Somaliland pursued its demand for international recognition and refused to participate in the peace talks in Kenya or to consider rejoining a federal Somalia. The incumbent President Dahir Riyaale Kahin won the election by a narrow margin. Elections to parliament were postponed until 2005. New security concerns for humanitarian workers arose following the murders of three international health and education workers in October, although police arrested and charged several suspects. Relations between Somaliland and Puntland remained tense on account of conflicting claims over the eastern Sool and Sanag regions which were affected by drought and food shortages.

Puntland

The self-declared federal regional state of Puntland in the northeast participated in the peace talks and supported a federal constitution. In May a peace and reconciliation agreement was signed between Puntland President Abdullahi Yusuf Ahmed and an armed opposition group, the Puntland Salvation Council, headed by General Mahamoud Musse Hersi ("Ade") and linked to former presidential claimant Jama Ali Jama. Opposition political leaders and militias were integrated into the Puntland government and its security forces, and all captured opposition militias were released. Security improved but constitutional issues relating to the status of the Puntland government and parliament remained unclear.

Peace talks

The Somalia Peace and Reconciliation Conference moved to a new venue in Kenya at Mbagathi, near Nairobi, with a new chairperson. The talks were organized by the Intergovernmental Authority on Development, a regional grouping of states, and comprised over 430 delegates. Participants included the leaders of over 21 armed factions (so-called "warlords"), members of the TNG and representatives of civil society groups, among them some independent organizations working to promote human rights and the rights of women and minorities.

In September, the Conference proposed a transitional Charter for a four-year interim federal government. The TNG and one other faction grouping initially rejected the Charter, but returned to the talks. The selection of an interim parliament which would elect a president was not completed at the end of December.

International community

The continued threat to regional and global security resulting from over 12 years of state collapse and renewed faction fighting in southern Somalia led to calls by the UN Security Council and UN Secretary-General for an urgent conclusion to the peace talks and an end to cease-fire violations and human rights abuses. The UN condemned the use of child soldiers by the TNG and virtually all factions.

In March a panel of UN experts delivered a report to the UN Security Council on violations of the arms embargo by neighbouring states and others providing weapons to the TNG or faction leaders. The panel's mandate was extended for a further six months and in November the panel issued a further report with recommendations. The report linked the flow of weapons to transnational "terrorism".

In April, following the report of the UN Independent Expert for Somalia, the UN Commission on Human Rights called on all Somali groups to stop acts of violence and human rights abuses, comply with the arms embargo, prevent "terrorism", and protect humanitarian workers. The African Union began preparing a cease-fire monitoring group.

The UN condemned killings and kidnappings of children, including the killing of three girls in Baidoa in May in clan revenge attacks, and the brief kidnapping of a group of schoolgirls travelling on a bus in Mogadishu in June.

Violence against women

Female genital mutilation continued to be inflicted on most girls, despite educational campaigning by Somali women's organizations. Members of the Coalition of Grassroots Women's Organizations also documented rape of internally displaced women and girls, most of them members of minorities, by faction militias and gunmen in Mogadishu. A UN report noted the severe disadvantages affecting women's access to justice.

Refugees and internally displaced people

Refugee flows from the south continued as civilians fled faction fighting, kidnappings, threats to human rights defenders and other abuses. Somalis made up a considerable proportion of asylum-seekers in neighbouring countries and in the industrialized countries of the North.

In April the UN Resident Humanitarian Coordinator for Somalia appealed to Somali political and militia leaders to protect 350,000 internally displaced people, many of them members of minority communities and the majority of them women and children, in over a dozen areas. They were subjected to rape, abductions and looting by armed groups, and also suffered poor conditions in camps.

Rule of law

Throughout the south of the country there was no effective or competent system of administration of justice to uphold the rule of law and provide impartial protection of human rights. The TNG and faction leaders failed to protect citizens; abuses by faction militias were committed with impunity. A few remaining *Shari'a* (Islamic Law) courts continued to function on a local basis, but their proceedings bore little relation to international standards of fair trial.

Clan-based faction militias protected their own clan members, leaving the unarmed members of minority communities vulnerable to abuses. Conditions in the TNG's central prison in Mogadishu were harsh.

In Somaliland there were reports of arbitrary arrests. Jama Mohamed Ghalib, a former police general advocating the return of Somaliland to a federal Somalia, was detained for two days on his return to Hargeisa in June and deported. Several of his supporters were arrested after a shoot-out with Somaliland security forces and remained detained without charge or trial at the end of the year.

Courts in Puntland functioned intermittently in some areas; they did not observe international standards for fair trial.

Freedom of opinion and the media
Activists and journalists reporting on human rights abuses or critical of the political authorities were frequently at risk of arbitrary arrest or, in the south, of being killed. Political freedom with open party structures existed only in Somaliland where people had considerable freedom to express opinions, publicly criticize the government and campaign in elections.

▢ In Mogadishu in January, the *Hornafrik* television and radio station was raided by a faction leader following the broadcast of a program linking certain businesspeople to "terrorism".

▢ In Mogadishu in June, TNG police detained two radio journalists, Abdurahman Mohamed Hudeifi and Hussein Mohamed Gedi, for criticizing the authorities. They were released after two days.

▢ Four human rights NGOs were banned in Puntland in March, shortly after representatives attended an AI workshop in Somaliland for Somali human rights defenders. They were later allowed to resume activities after discussions with government officials.

▢ In Somaliland in October, a journalist from the *Jamhuuriyya* (*Republican*) newspaper, was convicted of defamation but his eight-month prison sentence was quickly commuted to a fine on appeal.

AI country reports/ visits
Reports
- Somalia: AI calls on the United Nations Commission on Human Rights to support human rights reconstruction (AI Index: AFR 52/003/2003)
- Somalia: Call for a human rights-committed interim parliament (AI Index: AFR 52/005/2003)
- Somalia and Somaliland: Supporting and strengthening the work of Somali human rights defenders – a workshop report (AI Index: AFR 52/004/2003)

Visits
In February AI held a human rights defenders' workshop in Hargeisa and met the Somaliland government. In April an AI delegate attended the Somali peace talks in Kenya and met Puntland government representatives, other political leaders and members of NGOs.

SOUTH AFRICA

REPUBLIC OF SOUTH AFRICA
Head of state and government: Thabo Mbeki
Death penalty: abolitionist for all crimes
UN Women's Convention: ratified
Optional Protocol to UN Women's Convention: not signed

Plans were announced to strengthen delivery of non-discriminatory health care for people living with HIV/AIDS, but most of the estimated 5.3 million people with HIV remained without access to appropriate care including anti-retroviral drug therapy. Despite improvements in police and prosecution responses in some areas, the number of reported rapes of women and children remained at a high level. The government began making reparation payments to victims of human rights violations in the apartheid era. Investigations revealed ill-treatment of prisoners by police and prison officials, and the misuse of lethal force by the police.

Background
A Commission of Inquiry headed by former Judge Joos Hefer was appointed in September to examine allegations that the National Director of Public Prosecutions had spied for the apartheid government and was abusing the powers of the National Prosecuting Authority. The Commission heard no evidence to support the allegations and concluded its hearings in December. It was expected to present its findings to President Mbeki early in 2004.

Right to health
On 19 November the government announced an Operational Plan for Comprehensive Treatment and Care for HIV and AIDS, "founded upon the principle of universal access to care and treatment of all, irrespective of race, colour, gender and economic status". It also announced details of the plan's budget, which included provision for anti-retroviral drug treatment, and of measures to strengthen the health care infrastructure. Of the estimated 5.3 million people living with HIV/AIDS, only a tiny proportion of those requiring anti-retroviral drug therapy had access to it through private or company medical schemes or services run by non-governmental organizations (NGOs).

The Operational Plan allocated resources for treatment to reduce the risk of HIV transmission after sexual assault. Although the government had promised such treatment in April 2002, there was still limited access to anti-retroviral drug treatment, particularly for child victims, by late 2003.

In July the government removed a clause from the draft Criminal Law (Sexual Offences) Amendment Bill which would have compelled the state to provide non-discriminatory access to care and treatment to survivors of rape. The Department of Health national guidelines on care and treatment for rape survivors had not been completed by the end of the year. In December the Medical Research Council reported that three-quarters of doctors and nurses who treated rape survivors lacked proper training and that just under half of the health centres did not have a private examination room for these patients.

The provincial minister and senior officials in the Department of Health in Mpumalanga province were removed from their positions in August. They were under investigation for corruption, including misappropriation of the province's 19 million Rand HIV/AIDS budget.

The right of access for orphaned HIV-positive children to anti-retroviral drug treatment was improved by a Johannesburg High Court ruling in December. The AIDS Law Project and paediatric doctors had challenged the law preventing doctors from providing treatment to children without parents or guardians.

Violence against women
On 13 December, 21-year-old Lorna Mlofana, a community educator for the Treatment Action Campaign in Khayelitsha, Cape Town, was raped by a group of men who then beat her to death after she disclosed that she was HIV-positive. A woman friend, Nomava Mangisa, who intervened to help her, sustained head injuries. Two men were later arrested and appeared in the Khayelitsha magistrate's court on 22 December in connection with murder and rape charges.

The police Annual Report for the period ending March 2003 recorded a decrease of 5.7 per cent in reported rapes. There were 52,425 officially reported rapes, a third of the estimated actual number. More than 40 per cent of the victims were aged 18 or younger. The conviction rate for rape remained low, at an average of seven per cent.

The police and prosecution services continued to implement programs to improve their response to rape and other sexual offences. "Victim-friendly facilities" were established at 78 police stations in the year to March 2003, including at those stations where half of all rapes were reported, according to police statistics. NGOs and the organization Business Against Crime, however, continued to provide support facilities in most cases. The National Prosecuting Authority established 40 more specialized sexual offences courts and dedicated regional courts during the year, working with NGOs to minimize the trauma for rape survivors, especially children, involved in court hearings.

The Independent Complaints Directorate (ICD), the police oversight body, criticized police management for a lack of commitment to ensuring that the police fulfilled their obligations under the Domestic Violence Act.

Reparations and redress
On 29 January, the Truth and Reconciliation Commission (TRC) settled a legal dispute with the Inkatha Freedom Party (IFP). As a result, in March the TRC was able to hand over to the President Volume 6 of its 1998 Report. The TRC agreed to include in Volume 6 a "schedule of changes and corrections" to its findings against the IFP and to publish the IFP's objections to the TRC process and findings. However, the settlement left intact the TRC's core findings that the IFP, the former KwaZulu

homeland government and the KwaZulu police were responsible for gross human rights violations.

Volume 6 also summarized the work of the Amnesty Committee. The Committee heard evidence, in amnesty applications from members of the state security forces, which substantiated allegations of state complicity in political violence in the late 1980s and early 1990s. The evidence confirmed that the police had routinely tortured government opponents.

The TRC urged the government to implement its 1998 recommendations for reparations and rehabilitation programs for victims of gross human rights violations. The government announced in April that it would pay final reparations to 22,000 such victims identified by the TRC. Victim support groups and NGOs criticized the offer as being far below the TRC's recommended amount. In October the President assented to the Promotion of National Unity and Reconciliation Amendment Act, which authorized use of the President's Fund not only for reparations to individual victims but also for "the rehabilitation of communities". In November the government began one-off payments to individual victims.

The new law also authorized the government to establish a mechanism with the power to review TRC decisions where required by court rulings. A 2001 court ruling had ordered the government to review the TRC's refusal of amnesty to former security police officer Gideon Nieuwoudt and two others convicted of four murders in Port Elizabeth in 1989. The delay in holding this review had affected the prosecution of certain other apartheid era perpetrators.

In May the Supreme Court of Appeals ruled that it could not hear the prosecution's case for reviewing certain decisions made by the judge at the trial of Dr Wouter Basson. Dr Basson, the former head of the military's covert biological and chemical warfare program in the apartheid era, had been acquitted in 2002 of 46 murder and other charges. The trial judge had ruled, among other things, that certain charges against Dr Basson relating to murders committed outside South Africa should be excluded. In November the Constitutional Court heard arguments on an appeal by the state against the Supreme Court of Appeal's ruling; a decision was pending at the end of the year. Potential prosecutions in other cases involving extra-territorial murders were delayed because of the trial court's ruling in this case.

Ill-treatment and excessive force
In November the National Assembly passed the Protection of Constitutional Democracy against Terrorism and Related Activities Bill. After criticism by NGOs, including AI, the final version of the law increased safeguards against arbitrary arrest and searches and infringements of freedoms of expression, association and assembly. The authorities would also be obliged to apply the protections under the ordinary law and the Constitution to suspects under investigation or facing extradition from South Africa at the request of a foreign state.

The Jali Commission continued its hearings into corruption and abuses in prisons. In November a warder at the C-MAX maximum security prison in Pretoria told the Commission that a medical officer and section head had failed to stop named warders stripping, punching and slapping newly arrived prisoners, and torturing them with electric shocks. He alleged that he had been threatened if he testified. The Commission requested his transfer to another prison.

In Vryheid prison more than 80 prisoners were assaulted by warders in January when they objected to a new form of body searches. Independent medical evidence corroborated prisoners' allegations that, after being stripped and forced to lie on the ground, they were beaten with batons and stamped on. Civil proceedings were launched against the Correctional Services authorities.

There were a number of reports of excessive force by the new municipal police forces. In Cape Town in December a City Police officer sprayed tear gas or pepper spray at minibus taxi drivers held in the back of a patrol van following arrest. One of the drivers became critically ill and required hospital treatment. He later laid a charge of assault against the City Police. The ICD also initiated an investigation. During disciplinary proceedings, 18 officers signed affidavits stating that they were not properly trained in the use of their weapons, including stun guns, metal batons, pepper spray and firearms.

Between April 2002 and March 2003 the ICD received 528 reports of deaths in custody and as a result of police action. The police used lethal force while conducting an arrest or stopping a suspect from fleeing in 189 cases, more than half of them in Gauteng and KwaZulu Natal provinces. The ICD reported that, despite the Constitutional Court ruling in 2002 against lethal force where there was no threat to life, it had been used without justification. At the end of the year the trial for murder was pending against a Vaalbank police officer in connection with the death of 16-year-old Edward Molokomme in September 2002. The boy and his 17-year-old friend, Duncan Phiri, had been shot at by a police officer when they fled into a forest to escape arrest for breaking bottles at the roadside. Duncan Phiri survived.

In the year to March 2003 the ICD also investigated 353 assaults with intent to commit grievous bodily harm, 23 cases of torture and 16 rapes by police officers.

Human rights defenders

Journalists with the independent *African Eye News Service* in Nelspruit were harassed by officials as a result of their investigations into alleged corruption within the provincial government. In late 2003 police officials in Pretoria instituted an investigation into the failure by local police to act on complaints lodged by the journalists in 2002 of threats and attacks by known criminals.

AI country reports/ visits
Reports
- South Africa: Truth and justice – Unfinished business in South Africa, joint publication with Human Rights Watch (AI Index: AFR 53/001/2003)

- South Africa: Submission to the Parliamentary Portfolio Committee on Justice and Constitutional Development, Parliament of South Africa, on the draft Criminal Law (Sexual Offences) Amendment Bill, 2003, from Amnesty International and Human Rights Watch (AI Index: AFR 53/006/2003)

Visit
AI delegates visited South Africa in April and May.

SUDAN

REPUBLIC OF THE SUDAN
Head of state and government: Omar Hassan Ahmad al-Bashir
Death penalty: retentionist
UN Women's Convention and its Optional Protocol: not signed

A cease-fire was in force between the government and the Sudan People's Liberation Army (SPLA) throughout the year. However, in January and February government-sponsored militias attacked and burned villages and killed scores of civilians in oil-rich areas. In Darfur, western Sudan, militias allied to the government killed hundreds of civilians and government aircraft bombed villages. Up to 600,000 people in Darfur were displaced within the region, and tens of thousands fled to Chad. Hundreds of thousands of refugees and internally displaced persons (IDPs) from the south and other areas affected by the fighting remained in camps around the borders with Sudan and in the north. In Darfur the security forces detained hundreds of people incommunicado without charge. Torture was widespread, particularly in Darfur. At least 10 people were reported to have been executed and more than 100 death sentences were imposed. Floggings were imposed for numerous offences, including public order offences, and were usually carried out immediately. Amputations, including cross-amputations, were also imposed but none was known to have been carried out. Trials of ordinary criminal offenders were frequently unfair and summary. In the states of North, South and West Darfur, special courts continued to hold summary and unfair trials. Freedom of expression continued to be restricted in the areas controlled by the government and by the SPLA.

Background
The peace process between the government and SPLA continued with an agreement on security arrangements signed in September. According to this accord government forces would withdraw from the south and

SPLA forces from the north; joint forces would be set up in Khartoum and the border areas of the Nuba Mountains and Abyei. The US-led Civilian Protection Monitoring Team (CPMT) and the Verification and Monitoring Team (VMT) helped to monitor the cease-fire.

Militia based on southern ethnic groups opposed to the SPLA attacked villages and killed civilians in the oil provinces of Western Upper Nile (Unity State) in January and February. These attacks were accompanied by forced recruitment of children and others into militia in Khartoum and in the conflict areas, and by the abduction of women. The government reportedly supported these militia with logistical help. In Darfur the conflict deepened.

In April the UN Commission on Human Rights failed to renew the mandate of the Special Rapporteur on Sudan. Between July and October all but two of the political detainees held in the political wing of Kober Prison in Khartoum North were released. Hassan al-Turabi, leader of the Popular Congress, an Islamist opposition to the ruling National Congress Party, was released in October after two years' detention without trial, most of it spent under house arrest.

Crisis in Darfur

In Darfur the conflict intensified after February as the Sudan Liberation Army (SLA) and the Justice and Equality Movement (JEM) attacked government forces and militia. In response, government-supported and reportedly funded militia (known as the *Janjawid*) based on nomadic Arab groups attacked the sedentary population, killing civilians, destroying hundreds of villages and making hundreds of thousands of people homeless.

The conflict continued despite a cease-fire agreement signed in Abéché, Chad, between the Sudanese government and the SLA in September and an extension of the cease-fire in October. Government aircraft bombed homes in Darfur, killing scores of civilians, while *Janjawid* militia attacked villages, deliberately killing civilians, burning homes and looting cattle and other possessions. As a result, hundreds of thousands of people took refuge in towns in the area or across the border in Chad.

Government authorities committed numerous human rights violations in response to the conflict. Scores of people were arrested and held in prolonged incommunicado detention by the national security, military security (*istikhbarat*) and police. Systematic torture, including the use of beatings and electric shocks, was recorded in centres of the military security in Darfur. Detainees held for offences such as theft, killing or banditry faced summary and unfair trials. Hundreds of prisoners were released by government authorities and the SLA after the September cease-fire, but arrests and detentions of those suspected of links with armed opposition groups continued. The *Janjawid* also abducted some villagers, including women and children, during raids. Some escaped often after alleged torture. Others remained unaccounted for.

The towns of al-Tina, Kornoy and Kutum in North Darfur and nearby villages were repeatedly bombed by government aircraft between June and September. In the early August bombing of Kutum, three days after the withdrawal of the armed opposition, the hospital and prison were destroyed and 42 people reportedly killed, including patients, prison guards and prisoners. Instances of indiscriminate bombings were also reported during the cease-fire period. Dozens of civilians were killed as a result, including Abdallah Issa Barday, on his way back from al-Tina to Basaw, his village. Homes and public facilities were destroyed.

The SLA and JEM endangered civilians by stationing their forces in civilian areas. There were also reports of looting and torture by the JEM.

▢ On 16 August, the *Janjawid* attacked Garaday, a village of about 400 inhabitants near Silaya town, and reportedly killed about 200 civilians, some of them in their homes, and beat or arrested others. All the survivors fled.

▢ On 20 August, the village of Murli near al-Geneina was raided by government-backed militia and 82 people were killed, either shot or burned alive in their homes. Murli was attacked again by *Janjawid* militia in September, on market day, and 72 people were killed.

▢ Raids by the *Janjawid* against villages included acts of violence against women, including sexual violence. In Murli, three girls, aged 10, 15 and 17, were reportedly raped by members of the *Janjawid* while they were fleeing the attack. Two women, aged 20 and 25, were reportedly raped by *Janjawid* members while they were collecting wood around the village.

▢ In September, six people were arrested by the JEM as spies and were beaten with gun butts. JEM members then put a mixture of acid, chilli and petrol in the mouth, nose and ears of two of them. They were released in December; the four others arrested with them had escaped in October.

Refugees and the internally displaced

Between April and December some 600,000 people fleeing attacks by armed groups took refuge in towns in Darfur or crossed over the border to Chad. The government often barred access to Darfur to representatives of humanitarian organizations, the UN and diplomats.

The population of Mukjar expanded from 8,000 to 40,000. Aid workers said that refugees were living in appalling conditions and disease was rife. Many refugees on the border with Chad lacked security.

Despite positive declarations of intent on the future resettlement of IDPs and refugees in the context of the peace process between the government and the SPLA, millions of displaced people and refugees remained in precarious humanitarian conditions in camps in Sudan and bordering countries.

Excessive use of force

On at least three occasions in March police appeared to use excessive force against student demonstrations in Bakht Er-Ruda near Dueim and in Khartoum. Police reportedly used tear gas and beat students violently with truncheons; they then used live ammunition. Three students died. No independent investigation was held into their deaths.

Sharif Hassibullah, a student of El-Nilein University in Khartoum, was shot in the head and killed in March when police fired live ammunition against stone-throwing students.

Torture

Torture appeared to be systematically practised by military and national security forces in Darfur and to be frequently used elsewhere.

Five members of the Nuba ethnic group living in Dongola were arrested by national security in May after meeting to discuss repatriation after the peace process. National security forces reportedly beat them severely and poured battery acid over them. One of them, Awad Ibrahim, died in custody. Two others were taken in June to Khartoum Hospital. They were released without charge in July. No independent investigation was carried out into the torture and death of Awad Ibrahim.

Forty-four people mostly from the Ma'aliya ethnic group were tortured in Aduma in South Darfur after their arrest by police and army in July, apparently to get information or to force them to confess to being involved in the killing of a member of the Rizayqat ethnic group. They were reportedly beaten severely with sticks, plastic hoses and gun butts. Some were allegedly tortured with electric shocks and two of them had metal truncheons inserted into the anus. A doctor confirmed that their injuries were consistent with their allegations. After their torture received wide publicity, their "confessions" were rejected by a Specialized Criminal Court in Nyala in November and 43 of them were acquitted. One of the group, Abdallah Agai Akot, a Dinka, was sentenced to death for murder.

Southern Sudan

There were reports of torture, including rape, and other ill-treatment in prisons under the control of the SPLA in southern Sudan.

Incommunicado detention without trial

National and military security forces continued to hold detainees in prolonged incommunicado detention without access to lawyers or any judicial review, using Article 31 of the National Security Forces Act of 1999 which allows incommunicado detention without charge or trial for a maximum of nine months.

Ahmad Mukwai, a 16-year-old Dinka boy arrested in Babanusa in August 2002 and held in the political section of Kober Prison, apparently as a hostage, was reportedly released in July after 11 months' detention without charge or trial.

Special Courts

Special Courts in North and West Darfur and Specialized Criminal Courts in South Darfur continued to hand down heavy sentences after unfair trials. Lawyers were often not allowed to plead except as "friends", and "confessions" extracted under duress were frequently accepted as evidence.

Thirty-eight people were tried before the Nyala Specialized Criminal Court and 26, including a child, were sentenced to death in April, convicted of killing 35

people and wounding a further 28 in a raid on the village of Singita in Darfur. The accused were all represented by three lawyers who were not allowed access to them or the case files until five days before the trial opened in March. The three judges, of whom one came from the police, one from the army, and one, the presiding judge, was a civilian, only permitted defence lawyers to ask each defendant and each witness four questions. The prosecution was allowed to ask an unlimited number of questions. The death sentence on the child was commuted to 25 lashes on appeal in May. The sentence was carried out immediately.

Death penalty

At least 10 executions were carried out. Trials in criminal cases were frequently unfair and detainees were often not represented by lawyers until the case came to appeal.

Adam Musa Beraima and Adam Al-Zain Ismail were executed in Kober Prison in September. They had been sentenced to death in March 2002 for armed robbery (*haraba*) after a trial in Nyala before a Special Court where they were not represented by lawyers.

Restrictions on freedom of expression

Despite promises in August that censorship would be lifted, freedom of expression continued to be restricted.

The *Khartoum Monitor*, an English language daily, suffered numerous penalties: it was suspended, had all its copies confiscated and faced fines on several occasions. A journalist for the newspaper spent 18 days in detention in March and the managing editor was detained for a night and badly treated in May.

Human rights defenders

Human rights defenders continued to be harassed and sometimes arrested.

Ghazi Suleiman, Chair of the Sudanese Human Rights Group (SHRG), was arrested in July and held incommunicado for two weeks in Kober Prison as the SHRG was about to organize a launch ceremony for the Khartoum Declaration which called for an end to Islamic law and one-party rule in Sudan.

Violence against women

Women continued to suffer abduction and rape by members of government-supported militia as well as displacement in the context of the conflict in the oil regions and Darfur. Women were singled out for flogging as a punishment for unlawful sexual intercourse in circumstances where men normally escaped unpunished. They also continued to be harassed and sometimes punished under the Public Order Act which restricts their freedom of movement.

In May a 14-year-old unmarried girl who was nine months pregnant was sentenced by the Criminal Court in Nyala to 100 lashes. She appealed against the sentence on the grounds of pregnancy, her age and the fact that no lawyer represented her at the earlier trial. The Darfur appeal court and the Supreme Court in El

Obeid upheld the sentence, which had not been carried out by the end of the year.

AI country reports/ visits
Reports
- Sudan: Empty promises? – Human rights violations in government-controlled areas (AI Index: AFR 54/036/2003)
- Sudan: Humanitarian crisis in Darfur caused by Sudan Government's failures (AI Index: AFR 54/101/2003)

Visits
In January AI delegates conducted research in Khartoum and Darfur, and met government officials. In November AI delegates conducted research among Sudanese refugees in Chad.

SWAZILAND

KINGDOM OF SWAZILAND
Head of state: King Mswati III
Head of government: Absalom Themba Dlamini (replaced Barnabus Sibusiso Dlamini in November)
Death penalty: retentionist
UN Women's Convention and its Optional Protocol: not signed

The independence of the judiciary and the authority of the courts continued to be seriously undermined by government officials and police. The rights of freedom of association, assembly and expression remained restricted, and security forces used excessive force to disperse demonstrators. Women continued to be denied equal rights under the law, and the incidence of reported rapes rose sharply. One death sentence was imposed by the High Court; there were no executions.

Background
In May King Mswati III released for public consultation a draft constitution. The draft contained a bill of rights but included extensive limitations to those rights. AI raised its concerns about these limitations in a submission to the Constitution Drafting Committee. In November, following public discussions on the draft, the King postponed the adoption of a constitution until 2004.

Parliamentary elections took place in October. Nearly a fifth of the members of the parliament were women. In November the King appointed a new Prime Minister, Absalom Themba Dlamini – the Chief Executive Officer of Tibiyo Taka Ngwane, a company controlled by the royal family.

Up to a quarter of the population required food aid. The government announced that the level of HIV infection among pregnant women attending ante-natal clinics was 38.6 per cent. There was extremely limited availability of appropriate drug treatment for those living with or at risk of HIV/AIDS. Prisoners at Matsapha Central Prison told the Swaziland Red Cross Society in November that prisoners suffering from HIV and AIDS-related illnesses were denied adequate medical care.

Rule of law undermined
The crisis in the rule of law remained unresolved despite the intervention of intergovernmental organizations and expert legal bodies. Prime Minister Sibusiso Dlamini would not withdraw his November 2002 statement in which he declared that the government would not obey two Appeal Court judgments. The judges of the Appeal Court resigned in protest and were not replaced. High court judges and some magistrates were subjected to intimidation, demotion or other forms of pressure as a consequence of their rulings.

Prison officials refused to release suspects charged with offences that fell under the Non-Bailable Offences Order, despite court rulings granting the suspects bail and the Appeal Court ruling in 2002 that the "non-bailable" law was invalid.

The authorities continued to prevent the families of Chief Mliba Fakhudze and Chief Mtfuso II from returning to their homes in rural Macetjeni and KaMkhweli despite an Appeal Court ruling in their favour in 2002. The families, evicted at gunpoint in 2000 for political reasons, continued to suffer harassment and violations of economic and social rights, including the right to education.

In November, AI raised its concerns on these issues in a submission to the 34th Ordinary Session of the African Commission on Human and Peoples' Rights.

Violations of freedom of assembly, association and expression
The rights of freedom of association, assembly and expression remained restricted under the King's Proclamation of April 1973.

On 13 August, when Swaziland was hosting the International Smart Partnership Dialogue, police and members of the Operational Support Services Unit used excessive force to disperse a trade union-organized demonstration in Mbabane. The security forces beat demonstrators and bystanders, including a woman with a baby on her back, with batons and gun butts. They targeted several trade unionists for systematic beatings amounting to torture. In one case, a branch official of the teachers' union, Micah Mathunjwa, fled into the Ministry of Agriculture building to escape tear gas and a police baton charge. A police officer pursued him and then beat him. When he ran into the street he was beaten by other police officers and shot with a rubber bullet. He required hospital treatment for his injuries. He lodged a complaint against the police but the police investigators appeared to have taken no action by the end of the year.

⊟ Roland Rudd, a member of the Swaziland Agricultural and Plantations Workers Union (SAPWU), was detained by the security forces during the demonstration on 13 August after he had been hit on the head and body with gun butts and batons. While in custody he was denied proper medical care despite having visible injuries when brought to court. He and three other detained SAPWU members, Alex Langwenya, Lynn Dingani Mazibuko and Samkeliso Ncongwane, were charged with offences under the Arms and Ammunitions Act. They were granted bail by Mbabane magistrate's court, but the authorities refused to release them, citing orders of Prime Minister Sibusiso Dlamini. The detainees were finally released on bail after a second ruling by the magistrate's court on 3 September. Their trial had not begun by the end of the year.

Violence against women and girls

Under the law women continued to be denied equal rights. In March Prime Minister Sibusiso Dlamini reported that the number of rape cases had increased by 20 per cent in the past year. The frequent reports of rape particularly involved young girls from poverty-stricken homes. The Swaziland Action Group Against Abuse reported 88 such cases in a three-month period from July. Some victims were infected with HIV and other sexually transmitted diseases as a result of rape. People arrested for rape included police officers, teachers, pastors and relatives of the victims. Although some victims were put under pressure to accept informal settlement of their case, there were some prosecutions of perpetrators that resulted in convictions and prison sentences.

Death penalty

In February the High Court imposed a death sentence for murder on Richard Mabaso, a South African national. An appeal was lodged but could not be heard because there was no Appeal Court.

AI country reports/ visits
Visit
AI delegates visited Swaziland in July.

TANZANIA

UNITED REPUBLIC OF TANZANIA
Head of state: Benjamin Mkapa
Head of government: Frederick Sumaye
Death penalty: retentionist
UN Women's Convention: ratified
Optional Protocol to UN Women's Convention: not signed

Police and armed forces officers responsible for unlawful killings of demonstrators and torture, including rape, in Zanzibar in January 2001 continued to benefit from impunity. Violence against women was a major human rights concern, with high levels of female genital mutilation, and continued killings of elderly women suspected of witchcraft. Police used excessive force, including by firing live ammunition to disperse demonstrators. Prison conditions were harsh. Several death sentences were imposed. There were no executions.

Zanzibar

Reconciliation (*Muafaka*) talks between the ruling *Chama Cha Mapinduzi* (CCM), Party of the Revolution, and the opposition Civic United Front (CUF) throughout 2003 continued to lower political tensions in semi-autonomous Zanzibar, headed by President Amani Abeid Karume. Many issues raised by the 2001 protests remained unresolved, however, in particular legal, judicial and electoral reform. CUF ended its boycott of the national (Union) and Zanzibar parliaments, and won 15 and 11 seats respectively in by-elections in May.

The government had made no public response by the end of 2003 to the findings of the public inquiry into the January 2001 demonstrations. The inquiry's report, made public in November 2002, found that the security forces had unlawfully killed over 31 people, tortured and ill-treated hundreds of arbitrarily detained prisoners, and raped dozens of women. However, it failed to recommend bringing the perpetrators to justice.

Violence against women

Female genital mutilation continued to be practised widely in several regions, despite campaigning by the government and non-governmental organizations against this harmful traditional practice. In October, three women were jailed for 30 years each after being convicted of involvement in the death of a teenage girl from an infection linked to female genital mutilation.

Killings of elderly women for alleged witchcraft were still being reported, but the authorities took little action to prosecute those responsible.

Freedom of association and expression

Police used live ammunition on at least three occasions against banned demonstrations: a Muslim demonstration over a religious issue in Zanzibar in February and opposition party rallies in the towns of

Mwanza and Bukoba in June and July respectively. Several demonstrators were shot and wounded in these incidents, and many were beaten and arrested.

Opposition parties, non-governmental organizations and the privately-owned media operated with greater freedom than in 2002 on the mainland, but less so in Zanzibar. There was no new use of the sedition law against government critics. Several ongoing sedition trials were halted while the law was challenged before the Constitutional Court. The Zanzibar government continued to refuse registration to the Zanzibar Association for Human Rights without providing a reason.

'Terrorism' trial
The trial continued throughout 2003 of a suspect in the 1998 bombing of the US embassy in the capital, Dar es Salaam, in which 11 Tanzanians were killed.

Two people were reportedly deported to their home countries under the 2002 Anti-Terrorism Law, which gives the government sweeping new powers.

Human rights commission
The Commission for Human Rights and Good Governance continued its investigation into harsh prison conditions but did not publish a report. It began a public hearing into human rights abuses in Serengeti district, including forced removals and deportations. It had not opened an office in Zanzibar by the end of 2003.

Death penalty
Several death sentences for murder were reported during the year, although there were no executions. The government continued to keep secret the number of people awaiting execution, which was believed to be over 100.

Refugees
Government threats to force the last remaining 2,300 Rwandese refugees to return to Rwanda were not carried out. Conditions in refugee camps for over 350,000 Burundians, including tens of thousands of new arrivals during 2003, were poor. Refugees were prevented from leaving the camps and were often subject to arrest.

TOGO

TOGOLESE REPUBLIC
Head of state: Gnassingbé Eyadéma
Head of government: Koffi Sama
Death penalty: abolitionist in practice
UN Women's Convention: ratified
Optional Protocol to UN Women's Convention: not signed

President Eyadéma, head of state since 1967, won another presidential election marred by violence and repression. There were no investigations into reports that the security forces had used excessive force when dispersing protesters, or into the apparent extrajudicial execution of an opposition activist. Arbitrary detentions and torture of critics and opponents continued, including of the supporters of opposition candidates before and after the election. Some prisoners of conscience were released after serving prison terms for criticizing the head of state. Other political prisoners suspected of opposition activities were detained without charge or trial for long periods, sometimes years.

Background
Opposition candidates called for the results of the June presidential election to be annulled on the grounds that it had been seriously marred by fraud and intimidation. Gilchrist Olympio, President of the *Union des forces du changement* (UFC), Union of Forces for Change, was barred from contesting the election. The results were confirmed by the Constitutional Court in June.

In July the European Union (EU) expressed concern about "the restrictions on the opposition in the form of disqualifications, harassment and detentions, the obstacles to freedom of expression, the refusal of access for certain people to electoral rolls and the difficulties for local electoral commissions in collecting and transmitting results".

Killings
There were no independent investigations into reports that the security forces had used excessive force in suppressing popular protests. In incidents of unrest around the country over electoral irregularities, a number of people were injured or killed when opposition supporters clashed with the security forces.

On 1 June, the day of the election, the security forces fired on people protesting at the stuffing of ballot boxes in Tsévié, 30km north of the capital, Lomé. A primary school pupil, Akama Kokou, was killed in gunfire, and another, Mawuki Adonyo, was injured.

At least two people were killed and several others wounded when the security forces fired to disperse demonstrators in Mango, northern Togo, in September. The protesters were opposing the visit of government officials and EU representatives to launch a campaign to protect the environment while the government was not protecting people's welfare and fundamental rights.

At least one opposition supporter was shot dead in an apparent extrajudicial execution.

⌕ On 1 June, Egbla Kossi Messan and another UFC activist reportedly surprised the district official at Djagblé, an area of Lomé, in the act of stuffing ballot boxes at his home. When they protested, the official called the security forces, who arrived as the two men were leaving on a motorbike. They allegedly shot and killed Egbla Kossi Messan and seriously wounded the other man.

Arbitrary detentions and torture
Arbitrary detentions and ill-treatment of suspected critics and political opponents continued, including around the election.

⌕ Marc Palanga, a UFC leader in Kara, northern Togo, was detained twice in February. He was first detained for a fortnight with five other UFC members. The second time, he was arrested on suspicion of having held a meeting in Sokodé, central Togo, and was still detained, without charge or trial, at the end of 2003. Reports indicated that he and others detained at the gendarmerie in Kara were beaten and held in harsh conditions.

Opposition activists and others were detained in the days and weeks following the election on suspicion of voting for opposition candidates or encouraging others to do so. Some were illegally detained for several weeks without charge. Most were still imprisoned at the end of the year, the charges unknown. They included members of the security forces arrested because of alleged links with former Army Chief of Staff Colonel Kouma Biteniwé, who reportedly supported an opposition candidate and had to flee the country in May. Most of the officers were detained without charge or trial.

Seven out of a group of nine refugees arrested in Ghana in December 1997 and handed over to the Togolese authorities remained in detention. They had not been charged or tried, and reports suggested that no investigating magistrate had interrogated them.

The authorities failed to improve conditions of detention. Prisoners awaiting trial and sentencing, often for prolonged periods, were held in overcrowded and insanitary conditions. In particular, conditions at Lomé prison were frequently so harsh as to amount to cruel, inhuman or degrading treatment.

Release of prisoners of conscience
In February, Claude Ameganvi, President of the *Parti des travailleurs* (PT), Workers' Party, and Julien Ayi, publisher of the weekly journal, *Nouvel Echo*, were released after serving full prison terms. They had been convicted in September 2002 of "attacking the honour" of the head of state and sentenced to four months' imprisonment, increased on appeal to six months in December 2002.

Attacks on freedom of expression
Human rights defenders, including journalists, remained at risk of arrest and intimidation, and continued to receive anonymous threats.

⌕ In February the *Action des Chrétiens pour l'abolition de la torture au Togo* (ACAT-Togo), Christian Action for Abolition of Torture-Togo, was targeted after its report on the human rights situation in Togo was widely distributed to members of the European Parliament. The report said that people in Togo did not dare to speak about political matters in public for fear of intimidation, harassment and arrest by the authorities. Yannick Bigah, President of ACAT-Togo, was summoned to meetings, first by the Ministers of Justice and the Interior and then by President Eyadéma. He was accused of writing a defamatory political document and threatened with legal proceedings.

Freedom of the press was under frequent official attack. In some instances when the government came under criticism, journalists were summoned by the Minister of Communications. In others, a radio station was ordered to stop broadcasting and another had its transmitter seized.

⌕ On 14 and 15 June, three journalists were detained on charges of "spreading false information and public disorder". Dimas Dzikodo, Chief Editor of *l'Evènement* newspaper, was arrested in a cyber café in Lomé while scanning photos of people allegedly injured by the security forces during the election. Philipe Evegno, Publishing Director of *l'Evènement*, and Colombo Kpakpabia, a journalist on the *Nouvel Echo* newspaper, were acquitted and released on 23 July. Dimas Dzikodo was convicted, fined and released on 24 July. Dimas Dzikodo and Colombo Kpakpabia, who was reportedly beaten on his back and feet, told the court that they had been ill-treated in custody.

AI country reports/visits
Reports
- Togo: Quiet, there's an election! (AI Index: AFR 57/003/2003)
- Togo: An election tainted by escalating violence (AI Index: AFR 57/005/2003)

UGANDA

REPUBLIC OF UGANDA
Head of state and government: Yoweri Kaguta Museveni
Death penalty: retentionist
UN Women's Convention: ratified
Optional Protocol to UN Women's Convention: not signed

Rulings by the Constitutional Court allowed political organizations to participate more freely in public life. Reports of torture increased against a background of government campaigns against crime and "terrorism". The 17-year conflict between the government and the Lord's Resistance Army (LRA) intensified, resulting in a sharp rise in the number of internally displaced persons to over 1,200,000. There were many cases of violence against women. Freedom of speech was subject to additional restrictions. Death sentences continued to be passed and at least three soldiers were executed.

Background

On 21 March the Constitutional Court declared Sections 18, 19 and 21 of the Political Parties and Organizations Act (2002) null and void as they contravened the Constitution. This allowed political organizations to participate more freely in public life, although political parties remained banned from such participation until they registered with the Registrar General.

In June Uganda signed a bilateral agreement with the USA providing impunity for US nationals accused by the International Criminal Court (ICC) of genocide, crimes against humanity and war crimes. US President George W. Bush visited Uganda in July.

The Sudanese government extended the military protocol allowing Uganda to carry out military operations in southern Sudan against the LRA. Senior Ugandan army officers and others were cited as responsible for pillaging resources from the Democratic Republic of the Congo (DRC) in a report by a UN panel of experts and in the report of Uganda's official Inquiry Commission headed by Judge David Porter.

In early May the Uganda People's Defence Forces (UPDF) began withdrawing troops from eastern DRC following pressure by the international community.

On 7 November the International Court of Justice postponed the hearing in a case against Uganda concerning armed activities involving violations of international humanitarian law and massive human rights violations in the DRC.

Violence against women

Violence against women prevailed in male-female relations in Uganda. Few cases of sexual violence in the home, including rape in marriage and rape of minors, were prosecuted. Children, including orphans, were frequently subjected to sexual assault and violence by relatives within the extended family system, as well as by schoolteachers, people helping in the home and other carers. According to police statistics circulated in May, 4,686 children were raped in 2002; there was no indication that this figure was decreasing.

📁 Alice, aged 12, was brought from her native village to Kampala by a maternal aunt who promised to send her to school. She was left alone with the aunt's husband, who allegedly raped her three times in one night, threatening to kill her if she talked. The girl reportedly told her aunt about the rape, but the aunt accused her of seducing the husband and beat her in the area of her genitals. The rape was reported to the police but the case was later dropped.

The absence of a law criminalizing domestic violence limited legal recourse for abuse in the home. Between January and September, 2,518 cases of family-related violence (excluding murder and rape) were reported to the Childcare and Family Protection Unit of the Uganda Police Force. However, many cases went unreported and campaigners argued that the lack of a specific law hampered efforts to fight domestic violence.

In December a Domestic Relations Bill was presented to parliament for debate. It addressed issues such as the criminalization of marital rape, property in marriage, polygamous marriages, bride price, widow inheritance and minimum age for marriage and cohabitation.

Women and girls living and travelling in areas affected by insurgencies led by the LRA in northern Uganda were raped and suffered other forms of violence, including abduction and sexual slavery.

📁 On 24 June about 100 schoolgirls were abducted by the LRA following a raid at the Lwala Girls Secondary School in Kaberamaido district in northeast Uganda. AI was concerned that at least 15 of the girls might have crossed into Sudan where they could be at risk of sexual violence.

Torture and death in custody

Throughout the year operatives from the police, various security agencies and the army, including the Violent Crime Crack Unit (VCCU), the Internal Security Organization, the Chieftaincy of Military Intelligence and the Joint Anti-Terrorism Task Force were persistently reported to have tortured people detained on suspicion of political or criminal offences. Suspects were held incommunicado at unrecognized detention centres commonly referred to as "safe houses". According to official reports, security forces frequently extracted information through torture and other cruel, inhuman or degrading treatment.

📁 On 14 June VCCU officers arrested Nsangi Murisidi, aged 29, on suspicion that he had facilitated friends to commit robbery and for alleged possession of a gun. Relatives tried in vain to visit him in detention. On 18 June the lawyer representing the family received confirmation of his death in custody while at the VCCU headquarters at Kireka, a suburb of Kampala. The death certificate established the cause of death as extensive loss of fluid and blood, severe bleeding in the brain and extensive deep burns on the buttocks. The body also bore 14 deep wounds. In October the Minister of Internal Affairs informed AI that an inquiry had been ordered, but no progress was subsequently reported.

Further restrictions on freedom of expression

Numerous official warnings and directives added to existing legislative limitations regarding the enjoyment of freedom of expression. On 28 February the Defence Ministry and army cautioned media houses and their staff that they would be prosecuted before a military court if they published classified information. On 22 August the Uganda Law Council issued a directive forbidding lawyers from writing articles, speaking to the media or making any other media appearance without the Council's permission. The Council is an official regulatory body which registers all lawyers and can suspend or deregister its members.

☐ On 22 June police closed the Soroti-based private FM radio station *Kyoga Veritas* allegedly because it defied a ministerial directive to refrain from broadcasting news about LRA attacks in the region.

☐ The trial continued of the managing editor, the news editor and a reporter with *The Monitor* newspaper. They were charged in 2002 with publishing information prejudicial to national security and false information. The charges related to an article alleging that the LRA had shot down an army helicopter in the north.

Harassment of political opponents

On 23 March riot police used tear gas and rubber bullets to disperse a peaceful rally held at Constitutional Square in Kampala by members of the Democratic Party. No casualties were reported. On 1 May police blocked a political rally at Constitutional Square called by the Conservative Party.

Insurgency in northern Uganda

The 17-year conflict in the north showed no signs of resolution despite attempted peace talks between the Presidential Peace Team (PPT) and the LRA, with the involvement of religious leaders. Joseph Kony, leader of the LRA, announced an immediate unilateral cease-fire on 1 March. President Museveni initially rejected it, reportedly after the LRA continued to commit abuses, including abductions, ambushes, lootings and killings, in breach of its own cease-fire. However, shortly afterwards, President Museveni called for a limited cease-fire in areas where the LRA could assemble to hold peace negotiations. On 18 April the PPT revoked the limited cease-fire and talks failed before formal negotiations began. A new cycle of violence started and subsequently intensified.

In mid-June the LRA expanded its activities to the districts of Katakwi, Soroti and Kaberamaido. The humanitarian crisis spread to these areas in addition to Gulu, Kitgum, Lira and Pader, increasing the number of internally displaced persons to over 1,200,000 by October. In response to the LRA's advance, bands of local vigilante youths – the "Arrow Boys" in Teso and the "Rhino Boys" in Lira – organized and armed themselves with the support of the UPDF to hunt down LRA fighters. The increased insecurity in Pader, Gulu and Kitgum gave rise to "night commuting", the practice of parents sending their children to sleep in the open in urban areas, walking up to five kilometres each way morning and evening, to avoid abduction.

The use of helicopter gunships and air bombardments to force the LRA out of hiding continued throughout the year. Civilians were killed during such attacks.

Death penalty

At least 432 people were under sentence of death. No executions of civilians took place. Government and military officials repeated their readiness to execute soldiers as a disciplinary measure to safeguard state security; at least three soldiers were executed.

In July, 398 death row inmates, including 16 women, filed a petition before the Constitutional Court challenging their death sentences on the grounds that they were unconstitutional, inhuman and degrading. The petition was based on Articles 24 and 44 of the Constitution prohibiting any form of torture or cruel, inhuman or degrading treatment and punishment. The Attorney General opposed the petition.

☐ On 3 March, three UPDF soldiers were executed by firing squad in circumstances where the swiftness of their trials, without any possibility of appeal, constituted a denial of the right to a fair trial. Private Richard Wigiri was executed in Kitgum Matidi Township, near Kitgum, after a military court found him guilty of murdering a civilian in December 2002. Privates Kambacho Ssenyonjo and Alfred Oketch were executed after a military court near Kitgum found them guilty of killing three people on 4 January 2003.

AI country reports/visits
Statements
- Uganda: Soldiers executed after unfair trial (AI Index: AFR 59/004/2003)
- Uganda: Urgent need to end torture following death in custody (AI Index: AFR 59/009/2003)
- Uganda: Open letter to all members of parliament in Uganda urging rejection of the impunity agreement with USA concerning the ICC (AI Index: AFR 59/008/2003)

Visits
AI delegates visited Uganda in March. In October AI's Secretary General travelled to the DRC, Rwanda and Uganda to meet senior government and UN officials, survivors of human rights abuses, human rights activists and international humanitarian agencies.

ZAMBIA

REPUBLIC OF ZAMBIA
Head of state and government: Levy Mwanawasa
Death penalty: retentionist
UN Women's Convention: ratified
Optional Protocol to UN Women's Convention: not signed

Journalists perceived to be critical of the government were harassed and arrested. Media outlets were closed under the pretext that they were operating illegally. Human rights violations by the police continued. More than 50 people were sentenced to death, including 44 soldiers involved in a failed coup in 1997. No executions were carried out and reports indicated that the President would not sign execution orders.

Background
In May President Mwanawasa appointed opposition leader Nevers Mumba as Vice-President, which resulted in a High Court challenge and impeachment proceedings by opposition parties who claimed the move was unconstitutional. The impeachment motion was defeated in August. President Mwanawasa still faced a Supreme Court petition over the results of the 2001 presidential elections. The President's ongoing anti-corruption drive resulted in the arrest of former President Frederick Chiluba. On 11 November Lusaka magistrates' court ruled that Frederick Chiluba should stand trial for theft of government funds.

Threats to freedom of expression
Freedom of the press faced continuing threats, despite the withdrawal of the Freedom of Information Bill in November 2002.

Journalist Chali Nondo from the *Monitor* newspaper was arrested on 5 February and charged with "publishing false news with intent to cause fear and alarm to the public" in connection with a story alleging that police used charms to catch a former minister wanted for corruption. Chali Nondo was released on bail five days later. Publishing false news is an offence under Section 67 of the Penal Code and carries a maximum prison sentence of three years.

On 24 June Masautso Phiri, editor of the *Today* newspaper, was summoned for police questioning in connection with a story commenting on President Mwanawasa's leadership style and an alleged coup plot. He was accused of publishing false news with intent to cause public alarm. After presenting himself to police a week later, he was issued with a "warn and caution" statement.

On 1 November police officers raided the privately-owned *Omega* television station in Lusaka and ordered staff to immediately cease test broadcasts. The station's closure followed a letter on 27 October by the Solicitor General Sunday Nkonde to the Minister of Information and Broadcasting Services, which said that the station was operating illegally and should be shut down by police. The Minister then cancelled the construction permit (a temporary broadcasting licence) of the television station stating that it was "in the public interest" to do so.

Violations by police
Torture of suspects in police custody continued as did the use of excessive force by police. The Police Public Complaints Authority, which allows individuals to lodge complaints against police, was launched on 7 May.

On 26 March, three men — Felix Mengo, Kalengo Kalowani and Stuart Chulu — were arrested and allegedly tortured by police at Lusaka Central Police Station. According to medical reports, Felix Mengo had swollen feet, wounds on his right leg and arms, and had difficulty urinating. Kalengo Kalowani reportedly had infected wounds on both forearms, bruises on the buttocks and a swollen head. The police's Professional Standards unit stated in April that they were taking statements from police witnesses.

Police opened investigations into the beating on 7 June of a pregnant detainee by a senior police officer and three junior officers. The woman's injuries included swollen buttocks, bruises on the left side of her body and an inflamed heel. She was later taken to hospital where doctors reportedly terminated her pregnancy as she was bleeding profusely.

In September, police fired tear gas into a crowd of striking civil servants in Ndola. The strikers were protesting against the government's failure to pay housing allowances.

ZIMBABWE

REPUBLIC OF ZIMBABWE
Head of state and government: Robert Mugabe
Death penalty: retentionist
UN Women's Convention: ratified
Optional Protocol to UN Women's Convention: not signed

There was an escalation in state-sponsored attacks on critics of the government, particularly supporters of the opposition Movement for Democratic Change (MDC). Incidents of ill-treatment and torture were reported throughout the year. Hundreds of people were detained for holding political meetings or peaceful political protests. Journalists were harassed and detained, and a leading private newspaper was shut down. Political manipulation of food aid by officials and supporters of the ruling Zimbabwe African National Union-Patriotic Front (ZANU-PF) continued. The food situation remained critical.

Background

In March the Commonwealth upheld Zimbabwe's suspension from its governing councils until the December Commonwealth Heads of Government Meeting in Abuja, Nigeria. At the December meeting, Commonwealth leaders voted to maintain the suspension and Zimbabwe withdrew from the organization. In May the heads of state of South Africa, Nigeria and Malawi visited Zimbabwe in an attempt to mediate talks between the MDC and ZANU-PF. The country's economic situation steadily deteriorated, with rampant inflation and unemployment, and critical shortages in basic food commodities, fuel and cash.

In July President Mugabe announced in Parliament plans to introduce legislation to govern non-governmental organizations (NGOs) and to amend the National Council for Higher Education Act. There were concerns that the proposed laws would further restrict the rights of freedom of expression, association and peaceful assembly.

The government reportedly established training camps throughout the country for youth militia members, increasing concerns about the use of youth militia to carry out serious human rights violations against the government's perceived political enemies.

Four men convicted of murder and sentenced to death were hanged in June.

Elections

Local council, mayoral and parliamentary by-elections were the occasion for increased intimidation and politically motivated violence by government forces and supporters, mostly against opposition supporters.

⮞ Parliamentary by-elections in March in Kuwadzana and Highfield, two suburbs in the capital, Harare, were marred by violence. State-sponsored militia, police and ruling party supporters harassed and attacked MDC candidates and supporters.

⮞ During local council, mayoral and parliamentary by-elections on 30 and 31 August, ZANU-PF supporters armed with catapults, stones and iron bars intimidated polling agents and MDC supporters by blocking approaches to the polling stations.

On 3 November the petition filed by the MDC in April 2002 challenging the results of the March 2002 presidential election was heard in the High Court. No ruling in the case had been given by the end of 2003.

Impunity

The perpetrators of human rights violations continued to enjoy impunity, and allegations against state agents remained without investigation. The majority of abuses were committed by ruling party supporters and police, security and army officers against opposition supporters.

⮞ In July, Henry Dowa, a Zimbabwean police officer serving with the UN civilian police force (Civpol) in Kosovo, was accused of committing and directing torture while working at Harare Central police station. He returned to Zimbabwe in October after a UN internal inquiry into the allegations. It was not known whether disciplinary action was taken.

Threats to the independence of the judiciary

The authorities continued to harass, intimidate and force out of office magistrates and judges who handed down judgments perceived to be in support of the political opposition.

⮞ On 17 February Justice Benjamin Paradza, a High Court judge, was arrested on charges of attempting to obstruct the course of justice and contravening the Prevention of Corruption Act in connection with a case allegedly involving a business partner. He was detained in a police cell for a night before being released on bail the next day by a magistrates' court. It appeared that he was arrested because, in January, he had ordered the release of Elias Mudzuri, the Executive Mayor of Harare and an MDC member, arrested with 21 town councillors and municipal workers and charged with holding an unauthorized political meeting. In September the Supreme Court ruled that Justice Paradza's arrest was unlawful and unconstitutional. The charges against Elias Mudzuri were later withdrawn.

Attacks on the political opposition

Police carried out widespread arrests of opposition members and supporters following MDC-led mass national protests.

⮞ MDC spokesperson Paul Themba Nyathi was arrested on 8 April and charged in connection with a nationwide stay-away organized by the MDC on 18 and 19 March. He was released on 11 April and all charges were withdrawn.

In August charges against two co-accused in the treason trial of MDC leader Morgan Tsvangirai – Welshman Ncube, MDC Secretary-General, and Renson Gasela, an MDC member of parliament – were dismissed for lack of evidence. The trial resumed for one day on 2 December after a four-month recess. The three men had been charged with treason in March 2002 for allegedly plotting to assassinate President Mugabe, charges they denied.

Torture, ill-treatment and unlawful killings

Police officers were implicated in torture, ill-treatment and unlawful killings, mostly of MDC supporters.

On 15 January the police arrested Job Sikhala, an MDC member of parliament, Gabriel Shumba, a lawyer with the Zimbabwe Human Rights NGO Forum, and MDC supporters Bishop Shumba, Taurai Magaya and Charles Mutama. All five were reportedly tortured in police custody. Medical examinations later revealed that Job Sikhala and Gabriel Shumba had injuries consistent with electric shocks to their genitals, mouth and feet. Both had reportedly been forced to drink urine. In February, charges of treason against the five were dismissed by the Harare High Court for lack of evidence.

MDC activist Tonderai Machiridza was reportedly kicked and hit with truncheons and handcuffs by police officers on 13 April. The same day police officers took him to a hospital in Harare where he was kept chained to the bed under police surveillance. On 17 April a judge ordered his release on bail and he was moved to a private hospital, where he died of his injuries on 18 April.

Repression of freedom of association and assembly

Police arrested hundreds of activists, including trade union leaders and civil society leaders, following a number of peaceful protests. Most were charged with violations under the 2002 Public Order and Security Act (POSA).

Following the national stay-away organized by the MDC in March, the police arrested hundreds of opposition supporters and human rights activists. Many were beaten and tortured in police custody. Approximately 130 people were charged with inciting violence and acts of "terrorism" and later released on bail. Gibson Sibanda, MDC Vice-President, was arrested on 31 March and charged with treason, which carries a maximum penalty of 20 years, after the authorities accused him of trying to overthrow the government by inciting people to join the stay-away. He was released on bail on 7 April. No trial date had been set by the end of 2003.

Up to 200 trade union activists were arrested throughout the country on 8 October following protests against high taxes and inflation. In Harare, Lovemore Matombo and Wellington Chibebe, President and Secretary General respectively of the Zimbabwe Congress of Trade Unions, and more than 50 union activists were arrested to prevent them organizing a protest. Some were charged with public order offences under Section 7 of the POSA and released to await trial on 9 October.

Update

In June charges against Raymond Majongwe, Secretary-General of the Progressive Teachers' Union of Zimbabwe, were withdrawn for lack of evidence. He had been arrested in October 2002 and charged under the POSA with encouraging teachers to strike.

Crack-down on the media

The 2002 Access to Information and Protection of Privacy Act (AIPPA) was used in an attempt to silence journalists. Members of the private and foreign media were subjected to harassment, arbitrary detention and attacks.

On 18 March, Philimon Bulawayo, a photographer with the *Daily News*, Zimbabwe's leading privately owned newspaper, was arrested and reportedly assaulted by police for attempting to cover the March stay-away. He was later released without charge.

On 16 May, Andrew Meldrum, a US national and journalist with the United Kingdom-based *Guardian* newspaper, was held incommunicado for several hours before being forcibly and illegally deported by the Zimbabwean authorities, despite a High Court order that he should not be deported.

In September the police shut down the Harare offices of the *Daily News* the day after the Supreme Court ruled that the newspaper was publishing illegally because it had not registered with the state-controlled Media Information Commission (MIC), a requirement of the AIPPA. Twenty journalists were arrested, charged with working without media accreditation and released on bail. After the MIC refused registration, on 24 October the Administrative Court ordered it to issue a licence. However, after the newspaper published an edition on 25 October, police again closed down its offices, arrested five of the newspaper's directors and charged them with publishing a newspaper without a licence. All were released on bail. Justice Michael Majuru, the Administrative Court judge who presided over the *Daily News* appeal against closure, was forced to step down in November after he was accused of bias by the state-owned *Herald* newspaper.

Human rights defenders

The work and safety of human rights defenders continued to be threatened as government authorities clamped down on critics.

In August the MIC was reported to have accused the non-governmental Media Institute of Southern Africa of operating illegally and to have threatened its members with jail if they continued to refuse to register.

On 12 October human rights lawyer Beatrice Mtetwa was alleged to have been severely beaten by police officers when she called for assistance after thieves tried to break into her car. She was reportedly punched and kicked all over her body, sustaining severe bruising and cuts to her face, throat, arms and legs. She had previously represented journalist Andrew Meldrum (see above) and the *Daily News*.

Food shortages

The authorities and state-sponsored militia continued to deny people access to food aid based on real or perceived political affiliation, and used food aid to buy votes during parliamentary by-elections. In July the government formally appealed for continued food aid from UN agencies. On 7 November the UN Office for the Coordination of Humanitarian Affairs said that food security remained critical in the rural and urban areas of Zimbabwe, where most people had only limited access to food. Also in November the World Food Programme warned that Zimbabwe's food crisis was set to worsen in the coming year.

AI country reports/ visits
Report
· Zimbabwe: Rights under siege (AI Index: AFR 46/012/2003)
Visit
AI delegates visited Zimbabwe in January to carry out research.

AMERICAS

Argentina
Bahamas
Belize
Bolivia
Brazil
Canada
Chile
Colombia
Cuba
Dominican Republic
Ecuador
El Salvador
Guatemala
Guyana

Haiti
Honduras
Jamaica
Mexico
Nicaragua
Paraguay
Peru
Puerto Rico
Suriname
Trinidad and Tobago
United States of America
Uruguay
Venezuela

AMERICAS REGIONAL OVERVIEW 2003

Despite the commitments made by governments at the Organization of American States (OAS) Special Conference on Hemispheric Security in October and other forums, human rights in the region continued to be sacrificed in the name of "security". Most governments interpreted the concept of security narrowly, failing to address effectively the threat to human security posed by hunger, poverty, disease, environmental degradation and other such factors.

National security and 'war on terror'

The US-led "war on terror" continued to be waged using indiscriminate and disproportionate means. Hundreds of foreign nationals remained in prolonged indefinite detention without charge or trial in US custody outside the US mainland. Most of those detained as so-called "enemy combatants" were held without any form of judicial process; for a handful, the only way out of their legal black hole appeared to be through grossly unfair trials before military commissions. Authoritative worldwide opinion condemned the blatant disregard for international and US constitutional standards by the USA. Many of the measures taken by the US authorities in the wake of the 11 September 2001 attacks undermined the fabric of international law. Other aspects of US security policy, including the threat in July to cut off military aid to 35 countries for refusing to guarantee US nationals immunity before the International Criminal Court, threatened to have a similarly corrosive effect on the international rule of law.

The security policies pursued by the Colombian government since 2002 continued to exacerbate the already severe human rights and humanitarian crises, during which thousands of civilians have been killed, have "disappeared" or been kidnapped by the armed forces, army-backed paramilitaries or armed opposition groups. New security measures sidestepped constitutional guarantees and granted broad powers to the military to deal with public order issues. Initiatives such as the creation of an army of "peasant soldiers" and a civilian informers' network risked dragging civilians further into the conflict.

"Anti-terrorism" legislation adopted in Guyana and proposed in the Bahamas extended the scope of the death penalty and included dangerously broad definitions of "terrorism". In March, the Cuban authorities detained scores of dissidents accused of conspiring with the USA and seeking to subvert the Cuban system; prior to this, the USA had named Cuba on a list of seven states accused of "sponsoring terrorism" and some US officials had accused Cuba of

researching biological weapons and providing technology to "other rogue states". Seventy-five activists were tried unfairly and sentenced to up to 28 years in prison. The Cuban government sought to justify its unprecedented crack-down as a necessary response to the threat to its national security posed by the USA. After reviewing the available trial documentation for the 75, AI considered them to be prisoners of conscience and called for their immediate and unconditional release.

Political insecurity and the rule of law

Political, economic and social crises in several countries laid bare the fragile foundations of the rule of law and the faltering process of democratic consolidation in the region. Deteriorating economic and social conditions in Bolivia prompted mass demonstrations, sparked by the signing of coca eradication agreements with the USA, and plans to export Bolivia's natural gas via Chile. Civil unrest left more than 80 people dead, many as a result of apparently excessive use of force by police, and forced the President out of office.

Haiti was on the verge of being ungovernable. An impasse between President Jean Bertrand Aristide and opposition groups stalled implementation of a framework sponsored by the OAS for elections due in 2003, threatening a void in governance as parliamentarians' mandates were set to lapse in early January 2004. Meanwhile, economic conditions in the poorest country in the continent deteriorated further and politically motivated violence escalated.

Political polarization also continued to destabilize Venezuela. A national stoppage organized by the opposition virtually shut down the country but failed to force President Hugo Chávez, who survived a coup attempt in 2002, out of office. International mediation led to a commitment to resolve the political crisis through peaceful means. However, few steps were taken to bring to justice those responsible for the killings committed during the failed coup.

In other countries, some progress was made towards restoring faith in the administration of justice. President Néstor Kirchner took office in Argentina in May and embarked on reforming state institutions such as the police and judiciary. In Brazil, newly elected President Luis Inácio Lula da Silva set out detailed and long-term plans for public security reform, including human rights standards, in an attempt to combat high levels of crime and stem systematic human rights violations. In Mexico, a human rights study carried out as part of the government's cooperation agreement with the UN High Commissioner for Human Rights included recommendations for structural reform and committed the government to drawing up a national human rights program.

Efforts across the region to combat impunity for gross human rights violations committed in previous decades gained momentum in 2003. In Argentina, some of the legal barriers to the investigation and prosecution of "disappearances" and other human rights violations were lifted and former high-ranking members of the military faced charges at home and abroad. In Chile, plans for dealing with the legacy of human rights violations under military rule were announced, including the transfer of ongoing cases from military to civilian courts, although the proposals included granting immunity to certain perpetrators of abuses.

In Mexico, the Special Prosecutor investigating abuses during the "dirty war" in the 1970s and 1980s issued at least three arrest warrants for officers implicated in "disappearances". A Paraguayan court ordered the arrest of former President Alfredo Stroessner in connection with a case of torture and killing in 1974, and a law was passed creating a Truth and Justice Commission to examine human rights violations under the Stroessner government. The Peruvian Truth and Reconciliation Commission called for justice and reparation for families of the thousands of victims of killings and "disappearances" between 1980 and 2000 by the armed forces and armed opposition groups. In Uruguay, the Peace Commission's report on "disappearances" under military rule concluded that 26 "disappeared" Uruguayans had died under torture. Killings under military rule in Suriname were also under investigation, both by the Surinamese courts and before the Inter-American Court of Human Rights.

Less progress was made, however, in tackling the legacy of more recent conflicts in Central America. El Salvador's National Assembly failed to support ongoing efforts by relatives and non-governmental organizations to uncover the fate of children who "disappeared" during the 1980-1991 conflict. In Guatemala, witnesses and human rights defenders attempting to bring to justice those responsible for the widespread abuses during the 30-year civil conflict were among the main targets of threats, attacks and killings. The recommendations of the Historical Clarification Commission, which concluded in 1999 that genocide had been committed, had still not been implemented, and General Ríos Montt, Head of State at the height of the genocide, was allowed to run for President in the November elections, despite being constitutionally barred.

Corruption, parallel power structures and the failure to assert effective civilian control over the military remained serious threats to human rights and the rule of law in Guatemala and elsewhere in the region. Military and police jurisdiction over human rights cases also remained an obstacle to justice in Colombia, the Dominican Republic, Ecuador and Mexico.

Economic insecurity

The pace of regional and sub-regional economic integration increased, in part due to vigorous efforts by the USA to pursue its trade liberalization agenda through the adoption of multilateral and bilateral free trade agreements. Disagreements over aspects such as agricultural subsidies and anti-dumping

policies led a number of governments in the region to mount an increasing challenge to the US free trade agenda.

Promoted as a vehicle for alleviating poverty and boosting development, the proposed Free Trade Agreement of the Americas (FTAA) and other similar agreements prompted sceptical and hostile responses from many sectors of civil society wary of their impact on economic, social and cultural rights, including labour rights, access to health and public services, and rights related to the environment. Large demonstrations against the FTAA and agreements with international financial institutions in countries including the Dominican Republic and the USA were met by indiscriminate use of force by police. States of emergency were declared in parts of Peru and Ecuador to contain civil unrest regarding economic policies in the region.

The economic situation in Latin America and the Caribbean remained dire, with 220 million people – 43 per cent of the population – living in poverty and one in five in extreme poverty, according to the Economic Commission for Latin America and the Caribbean. Poverty had a disproportionate impact on women and children – one in five children under the age of five was chronically malnourished.

Unequal land distribution, plunging export commodity prices and other structural causes of poverty remained to be addressed. Indigenous, environmental and peasant farmers' groups campaigning against exploitative resource extraction by transnational companies or defending their land rights faced increased risks to their safety in Bolivia, Brazil, Chile, Ecuador, Guatemala, Honduras, Mexico, Paraguay and elsewhere.

Social insecurity and discrimination

Against this backdrop, crime and social insecurity reached alarming proportions. Both rural and urban society remained riven by social exclusion and discrimination based on factors such as class, race and gender. In many countries, the insecurity generated by high levels of crime and deepening inequality resulted in increased tolerance of repressive policing by both governments and the public at large. In Brazil, entire communities of the urban poor appeared to be targeted by police as scapegoats for the failure of broader public security policies.

Torture and ill-treatment by police and prison officers remained endemic in Brazil, and a frequent tool of law enforcement in numerous countries across the region. In Jamaica, where levels of armed violence were extremely high, police brutality and unlawful killings were commonplace.

The death penalty continued to be imposed in the USA and Caribbean, and the USA stood in shameful isolation by executing child offenders. In Latin America, Cuba resumed executions and there were occasional proposals to reintroduce the death penalty in response to rising levels of crime.

Studies by UN experts on racism and indigenous peoples in 2003 highlighted the marginalization and lack of access to justice of indigenous people and others facing ethnic discrimination in countries such as Bolivia, Guyana and Mexico.

The impunity surrounding the murder and abduction of hundreds of women and girls in the state of Chihuahua, Mexico, highlighted the obstacles to justice faced by women at risk of violence in the community and home. Similar gender-based killings were reported in other parts of Mexico and Central America. Women's rights activists across the region highlighted the barriers that prevented legislation on violence against women from offering real protection in practice. Sexual violence against women, including rape and mutilation, were used as a weapon of war in Colombia's armed conflict. Cases of violence against lesbian, gay, bisexual and transgender people, including by police, were also documented in several countries.

Street children continued to be seen as easy targets of government measures to combat crime. An anti-gang law was adopted in El Salvador with apparent disregard for the requirements of national law and international standards, while in Argentina there were reports of torture and ill-treatment of minors, including street children, by police. Despite well-publicized initiatives by the Honduran authorities to halt the killing of street children, few of those responsible for the killings were brought to justice.

Refugees and migrants escaping conflict and insecurity faced further human rights abuses. Those fleeing the Colombian conflict encountered discrimination and lack of protection in neighbouring countries. Detention and ill-treatment of refugees and migrants from Haiti were reported in the USA, Canada and several Caribbean countries, while countries including Canada, Uruguay and the USA continued to return non-nationals to countries where they were at risk of torture and other violations.

Action for human rights

An element of hope in an otherwise bleak landscape was the regionalization and increasing strength of social movements and other civil society actors seeking to respond to key threats to human security in the region. Movements working for women's rights, for the rights of indigenous people, environmentalists and sexual rights activists were among those whose voice emerged with increased prominence. Like other human right defenders, they faced an array of threats and obstacles, including fabricated criminal charges. Countries where attacks on human rights defenders were widespread included Brazil, Colombia, Cuba and Guatemala.

Forums such as the World Social Forum in Porto Alegre, Brazil, in January opened up new spaces for regionally coordinated human rights activism. The regional media remained relatively free, despite concentrated ownership and sporadic attacks on media workers in some countries. The OAS provided an important forum for collective action and the

promotion of human rights throughout the region, with the Inter-American human rights system playing a crucial role in monitoring violations, challenging impunity and analysing current human rights challenges such as poverty and insecurity. At global forums such as the UN Security Council, the General Assembly, the Commission on Human Rights and the World Trade Organization, countries including Brazil and Mexico emerged as an increasingly effective counter-balance to the regional superpower on issues ranging from trade and the war on Iraq, to international justice and other human rights issues. As the year ended, there was hope that fresh leadership in the region might promote more effective action for human rights and security, based on a renewed understanding that these two concepts are not incompatible but indivisible and interdependent.

ARGENTINA

ARGENTINE REPUBLIC
Head of state and government: Néstor Kirchner
(replaced Eduardo Duhalde in May)
Death penalty: abolitionist for ordinary crimes
UN Women's Convention: ratified with reservations
Optional Protocol to UN Women's Convention: signed

Prison conditions did not meet international standards, and there were reports of torture and ill-treatment of detainees, including minors, in police stations. Human rights defenders were threatened. There were judicial and legislative decisions in Argentina and abroad to investigate past human rights violations.

Background

Néstor Kirchner, from the ruling Peronist party, was inaugurated as President in May, following the withdrawal of former President Carlos Menem from the second round of the presidential elections. The new administration faced continuing fragility in terms of the country's democratic institutions and the economy. Among the urgent challenges were a new agreement on revenue with the provinces, reform of the judiciary and the police, and addressing the severe social crisis generated by high levels of poverty and unemployment.

Prison conditions

The UN Working Group on Arbitrary Detention visited Argentina between September and October at the invitation of the government. The delegation visited detention centres in the federal capital, the provinces of Buenos Aires, Mendoza, and Salta. Public statements made by the delegation described conditions of detention in prisons and police stations as extremely severe and cruel and inhuman. Their statements also drew attention to the criminalization of poverty and stressed the direct impact on human rights of the negative economic situation.

Children

There were reports of torture and ill-treatment of minors in police stations.

▱ In Santiago del Estero there were reports that children under the age of 12 who were arbitrarily arrested by police sustained bruises and injuries consistent with allegations of police ill-treatment.

▱ In La Plata, Buenos Aires Province, there were reports that many minors who had been detained in police stations needed treatment for cuts and bruises, but did not dare to file complaints for fear of reprisals.

▱ In January, children begging in the city of Mendoza, Mendoza Province, were arrested by provincial police and detained in police stations. Up to 30 children were registered as having been taken to the Third Police Station of Mendoza. According to reports, two girls,

aged 11 and 13, stated that they had been kept in the Third Police Station in a padlocked cell in darkness with one blanket, together with their six-year-old brother, who had to urinate in the cell as he was not taken to the toilet when he requested it. A habeas corpus petition filed by human rights lawyers was initially rejected by the first court. Several hours later the children were handed over to their families or transferred to the Detention Centre for Minors on the orders of a provincial judge.

Human rights defenders

Relatives of victims of human rights violations and human rights defenders and journalists reporting on human rights issues continued to be subjected to harassment and death threats.

▱ In January, Gustavo Melmann, his wife, their four children, relatives and friends received death threats as the second anniversary of the rape and killing of his daughter, Natalia, approached and the family continued to press for the trial of two men allegedly involved in her murder. Three policemen had been sentenced to life imprisonment in September 2002 in connection with her rape and murder.

▱ Marcelino Altamirano, coordinator of a home for street children in the city of Mendoza, was harassed on several occasions. In August his car was set on fire while it was parked a few metres from a room were five children were sleeping. An unidentified caller left a message saying, "we did it". Despite support and guarantees for his safety from the provincial authorities, Marcelino Altamirano was attacked again in October near a police station close to his home in the locality of Guaymallén, Mendoza Province. An unidentified man reportedly accosted him, saying, "your time is up", before firing a gun into the air and snatching Marcelino Altamirano's rucksack containing legal documents relating to 12 street children.

Past human rights violations

In May, two judges from the Federal Court in La Plata declared that crimes against humanity are not subject to any statute of limitations. The judges revoked the dismissal of the case against a former police officer accused of destroying information from the morgue of the Buenos Aires Police Headquarters about the causes of death of people who had "disappeared". The judges stated that crimes that occurred during the military government (1976-1983) linked to crimes against humanity can be investigated and punished.

In June the Mexican Supreme Court confirmed the extradition of former Argentine naval captain Ricardo Miguel Cavallo to Spain to face charges in connection with human rights violations (see Mexico entry).

In July, President Néstor Kirchner repealed Decree 1581/01 which prohibited the extradition of individuals allegedly involved in human rights violations under military governments.

In August, the Senate declared the Full Stop and Due Obedience Laws null and void. These laws had blocked the investigation of thousands of cases of human rights abuses committed during the period of military government. In October the Supreme Court referred the issue of the constitutionality of these laws to the Appeal Court. A ruling was pending at the end of the year.

In December, the Nuremberg Prosecutor's Office in Germany issued an international arrest warrant for former Argentine President Jorge Rafael Videla and two former members of the armed forces. The three men were accused of involvement in the killing of German citizens Klaus Zieschank and Elisabeth Kasemann in 1976 and 1977 respectively.

International organizations

In October the Inter-American Court of Human Rights ruled that Argentina had to continue and complete the investigation of the case of Walter Bulacio, who died following his detention by police in April 1991, and bring to justice those found responsible. The ruling established that the statute of limitations was not applicable and ordered the payment of a compensation of US$400,000 to Walter Bulacio's relatives. The ruling also called for changes in police laws and practice to avoid similar cases in the future.

AI country reports/ visits

Reports

- Argentina: Open letter from Amnesty International to the Governor of Mendoza Province, Mr Roberto Raúl Iglesias (AI Index: AMR 13/003/2003)
- Argentina: The Full Stop and Due Obedience Laws and international law (AI Index: AMR 13/004/2003)

BAHAMAS

COMMONWEALTH OF THE BAHAMAS
Head of state: Queen Elizabeth II, represented by Ivy Dumont
Head of government: Perry Gladstone Christie
Death penalty: retentionist
UN Women's Convention: ratified with reservations
Optional Protocol to UN Women's Convention: not signed

Conditions of detention amounted to cruel, inhuman or degrading treatment; the government announced reforms in response to the report of the Prison Reform Commission. Asylum-seekers and migrants continued to be held in conditions amounting to arbitrary detention. There was continued concern that asylum-seekers were returned to their countries of origin without access to a full and fair refugee determination procedure. Instances of police brutality were reported. Death sentences continued to be imposed; no executions were carried out.

Cruel, inhuman and degrading punishment

At the end of 2003 there were at least 27 people on death row. Death sentences continued to be imposed by the courts; no executions were carried out.

The Court of Appeal had not ruled by the end of the year on whether the cat-o'-nine-tails (a whip of several knotted cords) or the rod should be used in carrying out sentences of flogging.

Prison conditions

In November the government announced reforms, including classification and employment schemes, in response to the February report of the Prison Reform Commission. Areas highlighted for urgent reform included overcrowding, training, sanitation and rehabilitation. According to the report, 478 in every 100,000 people – one in every 200 Bahamians – were imprisoned in 2003.

Conditions in some detention facilities amounted to cruel, inhuman or degrading treatment. Concerns in Fox Hill prison included severe overcrowding, medical neglect, inadequate exercise provision and "slopping-out" (detainees having to empty buckets used as toilets). Many prisoners awaiting trial continued to be detained for long periods, in many cases, over 24 months. In November the Attorney General announced a review of the Bail Act and other measures to decrease delays in hearing criminal cases.

Immigrants were reportedly arbitrarily detained and received inadequate health care. There were also allegations of beatings and sexual abuse at the Carmichael Immigrant Detention Centre. Children held at the centre were denied access to education, exercise and adequate family contact. The government stated that it would consider the recommendations put forward by AI in its report highlighting these concerns published in November.

There was no further progress in the investigation of the death in custody of a Polish national in August 2002, reportedly as a result of medical neglect.

There were reports that two detainees aged 14 and 15 died in Willamae Pratt Centre for Girls on 2 November. The girls were reportedly locked in their cells, shackled to their beds, when a fire broke out at the centre. An investigation headed by Archbishop Drexel Gomez had not reported its findings by the end of the year. An inquest into the deaths was ordered.

Asylum-seekers
Asylum-seekers from countries including Haiti and Cuba continued to be forcibly returned without access to a full and fair refugee determination procedure, in violation of international law.

Police ill-treatment and shootings
There were continuing reports of ill-treatment of detainees by police officers and several fatal shootings.

On 6 August police shot Giselle Glinton in disputed circumstances. The police alleged that they were under fire when the fatal shot was fired. However, witnesses claimed that police opened fire without provocation as Giselle Glinton rode pillion on a motorcycle. An internal investigation had not reported by the end of the year.

In October, the inquest commenced into the fatal shooting by police of Jermaine Alexander Mackey on 5 December 2002. Witnesses claimed that he was stopped by police and shot several times in the head and chest as he ran away. The inquest had not concluded by the end of 2003.

Legislative and constitutional reform
There were concerns about the draft Anti-Terrorism Act 2003 which proposed a radical extension of the scope of the death penalty to cover "terrorist acts" resulting in death. Concerns were expressed by lawyers and others that the extremely broad definition of the new offence of committing a "terrorist act" risked seriously undermining fundamental rights including freedom of expression, assembly and association and that – despite a provision to safeguard the right to demonstrate or strike – legitimate, peaceful activities of individuals or organizations could be criminalized. The bill also proposed introducing the offence of "soliciting and giving support to terrorist groups", punishable by 20 years' imprisonment.

AI country reports/ visits
Report
· Bahamas: Forgotten detainees? Human rights in detention (AI Index: AMR 14/005/2003)

BELIZE

BELIZE
Head of state: Queen Elizabeth II, represented by Colville Young
Head of government: Said Musa
Death penalty: retentionist
UN Women's Convention: ratified
Optional Protocol to UN Women's Convention: ratified

There were reports of killings in disputed circumstances by law enforcement officers. Several people were reportedly ill-treated by police. Prison conditions were reported to have improved, although an official oversight mechanism had yet to be set up. Six people remained on death row.

Background
Said Musa of the People's United Party (PUP) was sworn in as Prime Minister for a second consecutive period of office following his victory in the March general elections. The Organization of American States set up an office near the border with Guatemala to monitor compliance with "confidence-building measures" aimed at resolving the border dispute between the two countries. In December the government signed an impunity agreement with the USA not to surrender US nationals accused of genocide, crimes against humanity and war crimes to the International Criminal Court. Such agreements are in breach of states' obligations under international law.

Killings by security forces in disputed circumstances
There were several reports of unlawful killings by security forces.

On 7 June, Ruben "Pony" Alarcon was reportedly shot in the back of the head by a police constable in Caye Caulker police station. When Ruben Alarcon, who was unarmed, fell to the ground he was reportedly shot again in the back. The officer responsible was said to have been charged with manslaughter and suspended from duty pending trial. The trial had not started by the end of the year.

On 14 June, Darnell McDonald was reportedly shot and killed by police in Ladyville. The officers alleged that they opened fire in self-defence after shots were fired at them from a crowd of onlookers as they were carrying out an arrest. Darnell McDonald, who was apparently driving past, was fatally wounded in the neck. In November it was reported that a police officer had been charged with manslaughter in connection with the killing.

In September there were reports that police in Punta Negra shot and killed Frederick Espinoza, who was believed to be suffering from a mental illness. Police officers had been called to his house after an altercation with his uncle and reportedly found him armed with a machete. Witnesses reported that the officers threw stones at Frederick Espinoza and then shot him four times as he tried to run away.

Alleged ill-treatment by police

There were allegations of ill-treatment by police. Human rights defenders working on such cases were reportedly harassed.

In January, human rights lawyer Antoinette Moore and her husband, radio journalist Michael Flores, were charged with drug-related offences by police in Dangriga. Concerns were expressed that the charges may have been intended to intimidate them and stop them protesting against police brutality. The case against Antoinette Moore was dismissed by the court in April. They were released on bail and the case against them was due to be heard by the Magistrate's Court in January 2004.

In August a high-ranking police officer in Dangriga was arrested and charged with wounding Timotheo Cano and harming Lincoln Cardinez after reportedly illegally detaining and beating them. The officer was reportedly relieved of his duties pending investigation. At the first hearing, which was held in December, additional charges were filed against the officer including false imprisonment and aggravated assault.

Prison conditions

There were improvements to Belize's main penal institution, the Hattieville Rehabilitation Centre. However, a government mechanism for ensuring compliance with international and domestic human rights standards had yet to be fully established.

Death penalty

A proposed constitutional amendment bill was shelved. It would have abolished appeals to the Judicial Committee of the Privy Council (JCPC) in the United Kingdom – currently the final court of appeal for Belize – in certain murder cases, and made the Belize Court of Appeal the final appellate court in such cases.

The last execution in Belize took place in 1985. Six people were on death row at the end of 2003. No one had their death sentences commuted to life imprisonment. There was one new death sentence.

Refugees

Belize continued to fail to offer a meaningful mechanism for people fleeing persecution to apply for asylum, in violation of the 1951 UN Refugee Convention to which Belize has acceded.

BOLIVIA

REPUBLIC OF BOLIVIA
Head of state and government: Carlos Mesa Gisbert (replaced Gonzalo Sánchez de Lozada in October)
Death penalty: abolitionist for ordinary crimes
UN Women's Convention and its Optional Protocol: ratified

There were several reports of excessive use of force by law enforcement officers against demonstrators; more than 80 people were reported to have died as a result. Prison conditions fell short of international standards and there were reports of ill-treatment of detainees.

Demonstrations

The political situation was dominated by civil unrest over government economic policies. Deterioration in economic and social conditions and opposition to government plans to export national resources, including gas, triggered protests in areas of La Paz Department, the capital, La Paz, and other parts of the country.

Demonstrations and roadblocks in the El Chapare area, staged by coca leaf growers against eradication agreements signed with the US government, left five peasants dead and dozens more injured during confrontations with the security forces. Protests escalated during September and October. Human rights organizations claimed that over 80 people were killed and scores more were injured, the majority reportedly as a result of excessive use of force by the security forces. Information provided by the Ombudsman Office indicated that 59 people died while the General Attorney indicated that the number of people killed was 56. Hundreds of demonstrators were arrested; they were released in November after an amnesty was decreed. The protests resulted in the resignation of President Gonzalo Sánchez de Lozada and his replacement by the Vice-President, Carlos Mesa Gisbert.

Excessive use of force
La Paz

In February more than 33 people were killed during confrontations between the army and demonstrators in La Paz. The demonstration was staged by members of the national police protesting at the government's decision to increase income tax. Those killed were members of the police and army as well as civilians. More than a hundred people were injured. The civil unrest that followed affected other cities. Investigations into the La Paz incident were initiated within the civil justice system. In October the cases of four members of the armed forces charged with the killing of two civilians were passed to the jurisdiction of the military justice system.

Warisata

In September, five civilians, including an eight-year-old girl, and a soldier were shot and killed and more than

20 people were injured during demonstrations and roadblocks in the town of Warisata, La Paz Department. The shootings occurred when a joint army and police force attempted to remove the roadblocks. The joint security forces reportedly opened fire after forcing their way into a secondary school and private houses.

Highlands and La Paz

In October, thousands of demonstrators, including trade unionists, miners, peasants and indigenous people, staged demonstrations in the area of El Alto and La Paz to protest against the government's proposal to sell national gas resources. Demonstrations spread to other cities. At least 59 people were killed during clashes between demonstrators and the security forces. Investigations by civilian courts were announced, but there were reports that military courts were also involved in the investigations.

Prison conditions

Prisons conditions were harsh and failed to meet international standards; most prisons lacked basic facilities. The government failed to implement effective policies or allocate adequate resources to resolve the problems. In many prisons, prisoners were effectively in control, sometimes with the cooperation of prison guards. Prisoners were reportedly subjected to beatings and punishments both by other inmates and prison guards. Economic and social pressures meant that prisoners' relatives often lived with them inside the prison.

◻ San Sebastian prison, which houses both men and women, and San Antonio prison for men – both in Cochabamba, Cochabamba Department – had a poor infrastructure and suffered from severe overcrowding. In San Antonio prison wives or partners of the inmates lived inside the prison with their children up to seven years of age, in extremely harsh conditions.

◻ The Palmasola prison in Santa Cruz, Santa Cruz Department, did not have an adequate sewage system or clean drinking water. Improvements, including the construction of facilities for drinking water, were made by the prisoners themselves.

Intergovernmental organizations

In August the UN Committee on the Elimination of Racial Discrimination expressed concern about reports that human rights defenders providing assistance to members of indigenous groups in the context of land disputes continued to be threatened and harassed by police officers. It also recommended that measures be adopted with a view to ensuring that members of the Afro-Bolivian community are able to fully enjoy their economic, social and cultural rights.

In June the government signed an impunity agreement with the USA providing that Bolivia will not surrender US nationals accused of genocide, crimes against humanity and war crimes to the International Criminal Court. Such agreements are in breach of states' obligations under international law. The agreement had not been ratified at the end of the year.

AI country reports/visits
Reports
- Bolivia: The rule of law must not be weakened by social conflict (AI Index: AMR 18/002/2003)
- Bolivia: The present crisis calls for effective measures to protect human rights and the rule of law (AI Index: AMR 18/009/2003)
- Bolivia: Open letter from Amnesty International to the Bolivian authorities regarding deaths in the town of Warisata (AI Index: AMR 18/011/2003)
- Bolivia: Open letter to the President of the Republic of Bolivia Sr. Carlos Mesa Gisbert (AI Index: AMR 18/018/2003)

Visits
In February and November AI delegates visited Bolivia to meet government officials and representatives of non-governmental organizations and to gather information.

BRAZIL

FEDERATIVE REPUBLIC OF BRAZIL
Head of state and government: Luiz Inácio Lula da Silva (replaced Fernando Henrique Cardoso in January)
Death penalty: abolitionist for ordinary crimes
UN Women's Convention: ratified with reservations
Optional Protocol to UN Women's Convention: ratified

The federal government proposed a new national policy for public security, which set standards for policing, including human rights, for state governments. Nevertheless, security measures adopted by state governments to combat high levels of urban crime continued to result in increasing human rights violations. Thousands of people, predominantly young, poor, black or mixed-race males, were killed in confrontations with the police, often in situations described officially as "resistance followed by death". Few if any of these were fully investigated. Police officers were also killed in the line of duty, especially in São Paulo where several police stations were attacked. "Death squads" involved in "social cleansing" and organized crime were reportedly active in most of the country's 26 states. Officials acknowledged the continued widespread use of torture by law enforcement officers, but this did little to stem its use. Land activists and indigenous peoples continued to suffer attacks and increasing numbers were killed as a result of their fight for land rights. Land activists were detained on apparently politically motivated charges. In response to attacks against human rights defenders, the federal government set up a task force to devise a national plan for their protection.

Although several important trials took place, some leading to long awaited convictions of human rights violators, the majority of those responsible for human rights violations continued to enjoy widespread impunity.

Background

In January the newly elected government of President Luiz Inácio Lula da Silva, Brazil's first *Partido dos Trabalhadores* (PT – Workers' Party) federal government, took office. Although it made various proposals for social investment, in particular to combat hunger, economic pressures led it to adopt a stringent fiscal policy limiting its social spending, while plans for political reforms dominated its agenda in Congress. Internationally, the government came out strongly in favour of multilateralism, the rule of law and international human rights at a time when such issues were under grave threat. For example, Brazil refused to sign an impunity agreement with the USA on the International Criminal Court (ICC) that would have been in breach of its obligations under international law. However, Brazil's own process to bring its legislation in line with the requirements of the Rome Statute of the ICC was still under review.

At the World Trade Organization conference at Cancún, Mexico, in September, Brazil was one of the main forces behind the formation of a block of nations to challenge the traditional economic powers of the USA and the European Union.

In November, President Lula assured AI's Secretary General that he would support the worldwide campaign for the introduction of an international Arms Trade Treaty. AI noted with interest the government's "disarmament statute", aimed at controlling the carrying and sale of small arms, as a first step towards combating violence.

Police killings, extrajudicial executions and 'death squads'

High levels of urban violence and crime continued to generate a public outcry for stronger policing and further punitive judicial measures. The federal government set out a long-term plan for public security reform, including the implementation of human rights standards, in its Single Public Security System to be adopted by all state governments. However, some state governments, such as those of São Paulo and Rio de Janeiro, continued to defend the use of repressive policing methods. Both states recorded dramatic increases in the number of civilians killed in conflicts with the police. According to official figures, police killed 915 people in São Paulo, an increase of nearly 11 per cent on the previous year. In Rio de Janeiro, between January and November, state police forces killed 1,195 people, a rise of 32.7 per cent. Both state governments informed AI that increased killings were the result of tougher policing measures. However, many of these killings reportedly took place in situations that pointed to excessive use of force or extrajudicial execution. The killings were rarely investigated as they were often registered as "resistance followed by death". In São Paulo a number of police

stations were attacked, reportedly by criminal gangs, resulting in numerous police deaths.

On 16 April, four unarmed young men were shot dead in the community of Borel in Rio de Janeiro during an operation carried out by military police. The precise circumstances of the deaths were not clear, but forensic evidence and testimony indicated that the men were summarily executed. A civil police investigation was only initiated two months after the killings, following demonstrations by members of the community and pressure from the federal government. Five military police officers were charged with the killings and suspended from duty. However, AI had concerns about the investigation.

"Death squads" aided by police or former police officers were reportedly responsible for "social cleansing" and organized crime. During a visit to Brazil in September, the federal government told the UN Special Rapporteur on extrajudicial, summary or arbitrary executions, Asma Jahangir, that "death squads" were active in 15 of the country's 26 states. The difficulty of protecting witnesses and thus ensuring prosecutions in such cases was made evident by the killing of two witnesses in the states of Bahia and Paraíba who gave evidence to Asma Jahangir. In São Paulo state, members of civil society, the state human rights commission and the police ombudsman denounced the existence of "death squads" in the towns of Guarulhos and Ribeirão Preto, reportedly responsible for numerous killings of young men in circumstances suggesting summary executions. On 16 April a military policeman from Guarulhos stated on *Globo TV* that he had been involved in the killing of around 115 people and that around 90 per cent of alleged police shoot-outs were staged to hide executions.

Several trials took place in relation to the 1993 Vigário Geral and Candelária massacres, in which 21 shanty town residents and eight street children were killed by military police "death squads". One policeman was sentenced in February to 300 years' imprisonment for the Candelária massacre, and another to 59 years' imprisonment in September for participation in the Vigário Geral massacre. Eighteen police officers were acquitted for participation in the Vigário Geral massacre in two separate hearings. The public prosecutor's office appealed against the acquittal of nine of these men. Out of a total of at least 40 officers originally charged with involvement in the Vigário Geral massacre, only two were reported to be in prison.

Important investigations into police killings and corruption took place.

In November federal authorities in São Paulo charged two federal police commissioners and a federal judge with involvement in organized crime and the sale of judicial rulings. The prosecutions were seen as an important step in the fight against corruption within the criminal justice system which had long contributed to impunity surrounding organized crime and human rights violations.

On 4 December the São Paulo state prosecutor's office announced that it was charging 53 military police members on triple counts of homicide. The military police, mostly members of the special GRADI unit, originally created to investigate hate crimes, were accused of having summarily executed 12 suspected criminal gang members on the Castelinho motorway on 5 March 2002. The state Supreme Court continued to investigate the involvement of the State Secretary for Public Security and two judges in the same case.

Torture and ill-treatment

Torture continued to be widespread and systematic in most prisons and police stations as well as during arrest. Following the death of Chan Kim Chang, a Chinese businessman reportedly tortured to death in August by prison guards at the Ary Franco prison in Rio de Janeiro, President Lula's Chief of Staff and Rio de Janeiro's State Secretary for Public Security acknowledged publicly that torture was still prevalent in Brazil. Nevertheless, according to reports, the number of charges and convictions under the 1997 law against torture did not rise significantly. On 26 June the government launched a second campaign against torture involving training for prosecutors and judges.

Torture, rebellions, violence between detainees, escapes and industrial disputes continued to be reported at the FEBEM juvenile detention system in São Paulo. In June, AI delegates and local human rights groups visited Unit 30 of the FEBEM Franco da Rocha complex. Delegates documented dozens of cases of beatings and other forms of torture reportedly committed by warders. Minors reported being forced on arrival to run barefoot along corridors strewn with broken glass. Detainees said torture was used by a minority of warders who acted with impunity. Unit 30 and Unit 31 of Franco da Rocha were closed by the end of the year.

Conditions of detention and deaths in custody

Detainees in police stations, prisons and juvenile detention centres continued to be held in cruel, inhuman or degrading conditions. Overcrowding, poor sanitation, limited access to health services, persistent use of torture, riots and prisoner-on-prisoner violence were regularly reported. At least 285,000 inmates were held in a prison system built to accommodate 180,000.

AI continued to express concern about the Differentiated Disciplinary Regime, a proposed disciplinary measure that would allow "dangerous detainees" in high security prisons to be held in solitary confinement for up to a year. Congress formally approved the proposal, but it was widely condemned as being unconstitutional and an abuse of human rights.

In the robbery and theft police station in Belo Horizonte, over 20 detainees were killed by other inmates during the year. Some 530 detainees were held in 22 cells designed to hold a total of 67 detainees. State public prosecutors told AI that they continued to receive complaints of torture from detainees in this and other police stations in the city.

Human rights defenders

Human rights defenders, denounced by certain state officials as well as elements of the media as "defenders of criminals", faced continued threats to their lives. In June, the Special Secretariat for Human Rights of the presidency set up a task force, including state and federal authorities as well as members of civil society, to devise a national plan for the protection of human rights defenders.

In Espírito Santo, the "special mission" set up by the federal government to investigate organized crime and "death squads" in the state made several high-profile arrests, including that of the former president of the state legislative assembly and a former military police colonel. A judge involved in the case, Alexandre Martins, was killed by a gunman in March. The state public security secretary said that he believed the killing was linked to the imprisonment of the former military police colonel.

Violence against indigenous people

Killings, intimidation and harassment of indigenous people escalated. Between January and October, 23 indigenous leaders were killed. Demarcation procedures for indigenous territories were stalled in many areas, reportedly in some cases as a result of political bargaining, dramatically raising tensions. Indigenous leaders were often criminalized as a result of their activities, and attacks on them were frequently dismissed by the authorities as the result of internal tribal disputes. The Minister of Justice told AI that all indigenous killings during the year had been the result of internal conflicts.

◻ On 7 February, in Pesqueira, Pernambuco state, the leader of the Xucuru tribe, Marcos Luidson de Araújo, and his 12-year-old nephew escaped from an apparent ambush in which two other indigenous men, Adenilson Barbosa da Silva and Joséilton José da Silva, were killed. In October 2002 the Inter-American Commission on Human Rights had called on the Brazilian authorities to give Marcos Luidson protection, but this was not done. One man was charged with involvement in the attack. According to reports, federal police investigating the attack repeatedly attempted to accuse Marcos Luidson of provoking the attack. An area of 27,000 hectares demarcated in favour of the Xucuru in 1992 has been disputed by landowners ever since, and two previous Xucuru leaders have been shot dead since 1998.

Violence and land conflict

Violence, threats, intimidation and political harassment of rural activists continued to be endemic. According to the Pastoral Land Commission, 53 rural activists were killed between January and September. Only five people were in prison for 976 such killings committed between 1985 and 1996. A major flashpoint for rural conflict once again was in the south of Pará state, an area afflicted by slave labour, illegal lumber operations, drug trafficking and land disputes. By September, 31 killings had been recorded in the state, the majority of these in the south.

On 12 September, seven rural workers and a farmer were shot dead by gunmen in São Felix do Xingu, a day after they had been threatened by the security guards of a local landowner with whom they were in dispute.

In Paraná state on 4 August, Francisco Nascimento de Souza, a leader of the Landless Rural Workers' Movement (MST), was found shot dead in Mariluz. Francisco Nascimento was one of seven MST leaders whose names were reportedly on a "death list" in circulation in the state.

Land activists were imprisoned on what appeared to be politically motivated charges. In the Pontal do Parapanema region of São Paulo, state national MST leader José Rainha Júnior was sentenced to two years and eight months in prison for the illegal carrying of a weapon. The Special Secretary for Human Rights of the federal government reportedly described the sentence as "absurd". In November the Federal Supreme Court upheld José Rainha Júnior's request for habeas corpus and he was released pending appeal. According to reports, a judge in the region issued 11 arrest warrants against 40 MST activists between September 2002 and September 2003. The warrants, all of which were overturned, characterized the organization as a criminal gang, a characterization AI and others condemned.

Human rights defenders in the northeast reported that eight rural workers detained in Paraíba state were also apparently held on politically motivated charges, and that they were tortured in detention.

The convictions in two separate cases of those responsible for ordering the killing of land activists were an important victory in the fight against impunity. On 25 May in Pará state, Vantuir Gonçalves de Paula and Adilson Carvalho Laranjeira, a former mayor, were sentenced to 19 years and 10 months' imprisonment for ordering the murder of trade unionist João Canuto in Rio Maria in 1985. In Maranhão, landowner Osmar Teodoro da Silva was sentenced to 19 years' imprisonment for ordering the killing of Pastoral Land Commission worker and priest Father Josimo Moraes Tavares, shot dead by a gunman in 1986.

AI country reports/ visits
Report
- Brazil: Rio de Janeiro 2003 – Candelária and Vigário Geral 10 years on (AI Index: AMR 19/015/2003)
Visits
AI delegates visited Brazil in March and June to conduct research. In November, AI's Secretary General and delegates met the President and other senior government officials, the governors of Rio de Janeiro and São Paulo, as well as members of civil society and victims of human rights violations. An AI delegate observed the trial of Vantuir Gonçalves de Paula and Adilson Carvalho Laranjeira in May.

CANADA

CANADA
Head of state: Queen Elizabeth II, represented by Adrienne Clarkson
Head of government: Paul Martin (replaced Jean Chrétien in December)
Death penalty: abolitionist for all crimes
UN Women's Convention and its Optional Protocol: ratified

There were concerns about the protection of human rights in security-related cases, as well as about police brutality, refugee protection and the rights of indigenous peoples.

Security and human rights
At least five men alleged to pose a risk to national security remained in detention pending deportation. Three of them had been held for over two years. They were detained on the basis of a "security certificate" which denies detainees full access to evidence against them, and may result in an individual being returned to a country where they face serious human rights violations.

AI called for a public inquiry into Canada's possible role in the case of Maher Arar, a Canadian citizen of Syrian origin summarily deported in October 2002 from the USA to Syria, where he was tortured and detained without charge. He was released and returned to Canada in October 2003.

Police brutality
Several cases of alleged brutality by police were reported. At least two people died after being struck with Tasers fired by police officers.

In April, Terry Hanna died in Prince George, British Columbia, after being struck with a Taser by police officers. A coroner's inquiry was opened in November but was adjourned.

In May, police officers allegedly fired Tasers at peaceful protesters during a demonstration outside the Immigration Ministry in Ottawa. Algerian nationals who occupied the office of the Immigration Minister to protest against the deportation of several Algerian families from Canada also alleged that they were beaten by police officers and struck with Tasers despite presenting no threat.

In June, Albert Duterville, a Haitian national and prisoner at Port-Cartier Penitentiary in Quebec, was allegedly sprayed with tear gas and hit by guards. He was then reportedly left without adequate medical care for several days. AI had previously expressed concern about beatings suffered by Albert Duterville that were administered by other prisoners and allegedly by prison guards, and called for investigations into allegations that the abuse was racially motivated.

In July, Clayton Alvin Wiley died in Prince George after being struck with a Taser by police officers. An internal investigation by the Royal Canadian Mounted Police (RCMP) cleared the officers of any wrongdoing. The inquest into the death had not been held by the end of the year.

Ongoing cases

🗀 AI remained concerned about the deaths of several indigenous men over a period of years on the outskirts of the city of Saskatoon, Saskatchewan. It appeared that the men had frozen to death after being dumped in remote areas by police officers. An inquiry was opened into one case, that of Neil Stonechild, who died in 1990. In May, AI urged the government of Saskatchewan to establish an independent, civilian body to investigate such cases.

🗀 In October an interim report by the Commission for Public Complaints against the RCMP was released regarding policing at the Summit of the Americas in Quebec City in April 2001. The report concluded that the RCMP had failed to provide adequate warnings before using force, and had inappropriately used tear gas, rubber bullets and a Taser.

🗀 A public inquiry was announced in November into the 1995 killing of indigenous rights activist Dudley George by an Ontario Provincial Police officer. AI and numerous other organizations and individuals had been calling for an inquiry since his death.

🗀 In November the four Toronto city police officers accused of the manslaughter of Otto Vass in August 2000 were acquitted.

Refugees

Provisions for a refugee appeal process in the Immigration and Refugee Protection Act passed in June 2002 were not implemented. As a result, failed refugee applicants continued to be denied access to an appeal on the merits of their case following a negative decision by the Immigration and Refugee Board.

The Canada/USA "Safe Third Country Agreement" remained pending as the USA did not introduce regulations to implement the Agreement. Concerns remained that the Agreement could lead to human rights violations in the USA, including arbitrary detention and *refoulement*.

AI remained concerned that the safety of Mansour Ahani, forcibly returned to Iran from Canada in June 2002 despite a request from the UN Human Rights Committee to suspend the deportation, had not been adequately established. According to reports, he had been briefly detained on his return to Iran and his whereabouts subsequently were unknown. A newspaper reported in September that he was "safe and sound", but had relied on a local reporter to interview him.

Indigenous rights

AI called on the Canadian government to reach a fair settlement regarding the land rights of the Lubicon Cree (an indigenous nation in northern Alberta) that ensures the protection of their rights as required by international and national law.

AI country reports/visits
Reports
- Canada: "Time is wasting" – Respect for the land rights of the Lubicon Cree long overdue (AI Index: 20/001/2003)
- Canada: Why there must be a public inquiry into the police killing of Dudley George (AI Index: AMR 20/002/2003)

Visit
In May AI's Secretary General met government officials in Saskatchewan to discuss the organization's concerns.

CHILE

REPUBLIC OF CHILE
Head of state and government: Ricardo Lagos
Death penalty: abolitionist for ordinary crimes
UN Women's Convention: ratified with reservations
Optional Protocol to UN Women's Convention: signed

Prison conditions fell short of international standards and there were reports of ill-treatment of detainees. Two Mapuche leaders and a sympathizer were tried under "anti-terrorism" legislation. President Ricardo Lagos put forward proposals to deal with past human rights violations.

Background

Indigenous people continued to press for reforms related to land and the upholding of their economic, social and cultural rights. There were further incidents between Mapuche indigenous people and the *carabineros* (uniformed police) in the context of land tenure and the commercial exploitation of timber in the south of the country. In the report of his visit to Chile in July, the UN Special Rapporteur on indigenous people underlined the marginalization of indigenous communities economically and socially as well as the criminalization of indigenous social protest movements through the use of "anti-terrorism" legislation. The Special Rapporteur recommended the judicial review of the case of two Mapuche community leaders.

Ill-treatment and prison conditions

There were reports of ill-treatment of prisoners by prison guards (*gendarmeria*). Prison conditions, including overcrowding, remained a matter of concern and some prisons failed to meet international standards. Lack of external control in the allocation of benefits to prisoners by prison authorities was recorded.

🗀 In January, Jorge Espinola Robles and Marcelo Gaete Mancilla, political prisoners at the Colina II prison in the Metropolitan Region, were reported to have been severely beaten and dowsed with water by *gendarmeria* and the anti-riot unit *Grupo Especial Antimotines de Gendarmeria.* The two men were transferred to punishment cells even though they had not participated in the riot that had provoked the *gendarmeria* operation.

◻ The Former Penitentiary Prison in Santiago South was grossly overcrowded with more than 5,300 detainees held in facilities designed for 2,500. Some detainees in Block I had to sleep in the open air, and there was a lack of adequate sanitary facilities and maintenance. Although minors were housed in special blocks separated from adults, their separation was not guaranteed. In Temuco Prison in the IX Region, overcrowding led to the mixing of minors and adults in communal and services areas, and there was a lack of open spaces and facilities for children held with their mothers. In both prisons there was ineffective separation between sentenced prisoners and those awaiting trial.

Trial of Mapuche leaders

In March in the city of Angol, IX Region, the trial began of Segundo Aniceto Norín Catriman and Pascual Pichún Paillalao, both Mapuche community leaders, and of a Mapuche sympathizer, Patricia Troncoso. They were tried under an "anti-terrorism" law enacted during the military government on charges of "terrorist arson" and "threat of terrorist action". The court allowed evidence from two anonymous witnesses to be given from behind a screen with the voice distorted. All three defendants were acquitted of all charges owing to lack of evidence. However, an appeal against the verdict by the prosecution was accepted by the Supreme Court. After a retrial in September, the two men were acquitted of "terrorist arson" but were sentenced to five years and one day in prison for "terrorist threats". An appeal was lodged and rejected. Patricia Troncoso was acquitted of all charges.

Past human rights violations

The issue of past human rights violations continued to have a high political and legal profile throughout the year and legal proceedings against former members of the armed forces continued.

Government proposals

In August, President Lagos announced plans for dealing with the legacy of human rights violations committed during the military government (1973-1990). The proposals included: possible immunity from prosecution for people currently not charged or on trial who present themselves before courts to supply information on the whereabouts of victims or the circumstances of their "disappearance" or death; possible immunity from prosecution for military personnel who argued they were acting under orders; the transfer of all cases of human rights violations committed during the military government currently under trial in military courts to civil courts; and the establishment of a commission to examine cases of torture. The plans did not include the annulment of

Decree Law 2191 of 1978, known as the Amnesty Law, which has obstructed the attainment of truth, justice and full reparations for victims, but instead proposed that courts continue to decide on the Amnesty Law's application. Human rights organizations, victims and relatives rejected the plans, arguing that they would fail to bring a complete end to impunity. In October, three draft bills based on the proposals were submitted to Congress.

Exhumations

In June the judge presiding at Santiago's 5th Criminal Court began the trial of five former members of the armed forces charged with illegally exhuming the remains of 14 people who had been taken from La Moneda presidential palace following the military coup of 11 September 1973. Reportedly, the remains were removed from a grave in the north of the Metropolitan Region in December 1978 and dumped in the sea. It was the first time that the crime of unlawful exhumation was prosecuted in Chile.

AI country reports/visits

Reports
- Chile: Torture and the naval training ship the "Esmeralda" (AI Index: AMR 22/006/2003)
- Chile: Continuing failure to bring a complete end to impunity (AI Index: AMR 22/009/2003)

Visit
In March an AI delegation visited Chile and collected human rights data, raised concerns with government officials and met representatives of the human rights community. It attended the opening of the trial of two Mapuche leaders and a sympathizer.

COLOMBIA

REPUBLIC OF COLOMBIA
Head of state and government: Álvaro Uribe Vélez
Death penalty: abolitionist for all crimes
UN Women's Convention: ratified
Optional Protocol to UN Women's Convention: signed

Some key indicators of politically motivated violence, such as kidnappings and numbers of internally displaced people, fell sharply in 2003. However, this masked some significant regional variations. The human rights situation in the special security areas, known as Rehabilitation and Consolidation Zones (RCZs), which covered a number of departments, deteriorated during the period these zones were in operation, as did the situation in several conflict zones. Reports of a decline in certain human rights violations coincided with a context in which the work of human rights defenders was made increasingly difficult. In Colombia as a whole, grave violations of human rights and breaches of international humanitarian law by all parties to the long-running internal armed conflict – the armed forces, army-backed paramilitaries and armed opposition groups – remained widespread. In 2003, more than 3,000 civilians were killed for political motives and at least 600 "disappeared". Around 2,200 people were kidnapped, more than half by armed opposition groups and army-backed paramilitaries. The civilian population continued to bear the brunt of the armed conflict. The government and security forces stepped up their campaign to undermine the legitimacy of human rights defenders, peace activists and trade unionists. This coincided with paramilitary threats and attacks against these groups. Congress passed legislation granting judicial police powers to the military, thereby strengthening impunity for human rights abuses. On 15 July, the government signed an agreement on the eventual demobilization of the umbrella paramilitary organization *Autodefensas Unidas de Colombia* (AUC), United Self-Defence Forces of Colombia, following their cease-fire in December 2002. Killings by paramilitaries, however, continued unabated, and there were fears that they were being incorporated into new legal paramilitary structures. In August, the government presented a bill which could result in the release "on licence" of members of illegal armed groups implicated in war crimes and crimes against humanity. Guerrilla groups were blamed for a number of bomb attacks in urban areas.

State of Emergency and special security zones

On 29 April, the Constitutional Court ruled against the renewal of the State of Emergency and Decree 2002, under which the government set up special security zones, RCZs, in the departments of Arauca, Sucre and Bolívar. Reports from the Human Rights Ombudsman and the Procurator General concluded that the human rights and security situation in Arauca deteriorated during the RCZ period.

The army carried out raids and detained individuals in the RCZs without judicial order, despite a Constitutional Court ruling in November 2002 which declared these practices illegal. The military also carried out arrests and searches in RCZs in joint operations with agents of the Attorney General's Office, who signed search or arrest warrants *in situ* on the basis of information from army informants rather than on the basis of full and impartial judicial investigations. As a result, there were hundreds of arrests and over half of those arrested were released without charge. Some of those released were threatened or killed by paramilitaries.

Impunity

Reforms to the Constitution threatened to consolidate impunity in cases of human rights violations. There was concern that these reforms, and the failure to ensure strict application of the 1997 Constitutional Court ruling excluding all human rights violation cases from military courts, would increase the military's control over the judicial process.

In December Congress approved a law granting judicial police powers to the armed forces. This allows the military to detain individuals, raid homes and intercept communications without judicial authorization. This law could help cover up human rights violations committed by the military, particularly if it is claimed that those killed were guerrillas "killed in combat".

▭ Eight-year-old Kelly Quintero was killed on 24 February when the air force bombed the area around Culebritas in the Barí Corronkaya Indigenous Reserve, Carmen municipality, Norte de Santander department. Shortly before the bombing, her family had reportedly lodged complaints about human rights abuses in the region with the authorities. Jurisdiction for the criminal investigation into the case was claimed by the military justice system.

The Office of the Procurator General called on the Attorney General to advance criminal investigations against retired General Álvaro Hernán Velandia, implicated in the "disappearance", torture and killing of Nydia Erika Bautista in 1987, and found Rear-Admiral Rodrigo Quiñónez guilty of dereliction of duty for failing to prevent the 2001 Chengue massacre by paramilitaries.

However, little information was received to suggest that the Attorney General's Office was making progress in prosecuting high-ranking military personnel or paramilitaries implicated in human rights violations.

Government seeks accommodation with paramilitarism

On 15 July, the government and paramilitaries of the AUC signed an agreement under which the AUC would demobilize by the end of 2005. In November a first group of around 800 paramilitaries were demobilized in Medellín. This followed the declaration of a cease-fire by the AUC on 1 December 2002. In January 2003, the government issued Decree 128. This grants pardons to members of illegal armed groups who surrender to the authorities as long as they are not implicated in criminal investigations for human rights violations or abuses, or are not in prison for such crimes.

In August, the government presented a bill to Congress that would release "on licence" incarcerated combatants and members of illegal armed groups who surrender to the authorities, even if they are responsible for serious human rights abuses. The main beneficiaries would be paramilitary groups involved in talks with the government. The Bill was pending at the end of the year. These measures, if implemented, could encourage impunity for paramilitaries, security force personnel and members of guerrilla groups accused of serious abuses of human rights and breaches of international humanitarian law. There was also concern that many of the "demobilized" paramilitaries could be allowed to join private security firms, civilian informer networks and the army of "peasant soldiers".

In Medellín, around 200 private security posts were reportedly made available to demobilized paramilitaries, raising concerns that these combatants were being "recycled" in the conflict.

Paramilitaries
Despite the declared cease-fire, paramilitaries were still responsible for massacres, targeted killings, "disappearances", torture, kidnappings and threats. They were allegedly responsible for the killing or "disappearance" of at least 1,300 people in 2003, over 70 per cent of all attributable, non-combat, politically related killings and "disappearances".

There were further credible reports pointing to the ongoing consolidation of paramilitary forces in heavily militarized areas and indicating strong collusion between paramilitaries and the security forces.

⌐ On 8 February, a group of 50 gunmen, some wearing paramilitary armbands, others in military uniform, reportedly entered Corosito, Tame municipality, Arauca department. They remained for 20 minutes. During that time they allegedly killed one person and abducted eight others. Three of those abducted were released soon afterwards; the whereabouts of the remaining five was not known at the end of the year. The gunmen were able to drive through the town of Tame in the direction of the Naranjitos military base. As they left Corosito, the paramilitaries reportedly addressed each other by military rank. The paramilitary operation occurred one day after the military and police forces left the town of Tame on 7 February. On 9 February military and police units returned to the town.

⌐ On 13 March, 300 men claiming to be from the AUC, some of them hooded, entered the Nueva Vida community in Cacarica, Chocó department. The commander and some of his men were allegedly wearing the uniform of the army's XVII Brigade. The paramilitaries reportedly made death threats against some community leaders and accused the inhabitants of being drug traffickers and guerrillas.

Armed forces
The armed forces were reportedly directly responsible for serious human rights violations, including killings, "disappearances", arbitrary detention and torture. According to the 2003 Report of the Office in Colombia of the UN High Commissioner for Human Rights, there was a significant increase in reports of violations attributed directly to members of the security forces.

⌐ On 30 January troops belonging to the Manosalva Florez Battalion forced José Amancio Niasa Arce, a 15-year-old student, from the bus in which he was travelling in Bagadó municipality, Chocó department. His body, which reportedly bore signs of torture, was found several days later dressed in a military-style uniform.

⌐ On 16 May, four members of the *Asociación Campesina de Arauca* (ACA), Peasant Farmer Association of Arauca, were reportedly detained by members of the XVIII Brigade and the police in Tame municipality, Arauca department. Among those detained were brothers Eduardo Peña Chacón and Ronald Peña Chacón, who were allegedly accused by the police of being members of guerrilla militias operating in the department of Arauca. The police agents reportedly beat them, put plastic bags over their heads and forced them under water. They were released without charge after a few hours.

Armed opposition groups
Guerrilla groups were responsible for repeated and serious breaches of international humanitarian law, including hostage-taking and the abduction and killing of civilians. They carried out attacks using disproportionate and indiscriminate weapons which resulted in the death of numerous civilians.

The *Fuerzas Armadas Revolucionarias de Colombia* (FARC), Revolutionary Armed Forces of Colombia, continued to target and kill public officials following a "resign or die" threat issued to mayors, town councillors and judges in 2002. At least eight mayors were killed in 2003.

⌐ On 6 October, Orlando Hoyos, the Mayor of Bolívar, Cauca department, was killed, allegedly by the FARC, reportedly after a meeting with the armed group.

The guerrillas continued to target those they suspected of collaborating with their enemies.

⌐ On 3 January, five people, including a minor, were allegedly killed by the *Ejército de Liberación Nacional* (ELN), National Liberation Army, in El Botalón and Pesebre in Betoyes, Tame municipality, Arauca department.

⌐ On 16 January, the FARC allegedly killed 17 peasant farmers in Dosquebradas, La Tupiada and Dinamarca, San Carlos municipality, Antioquia department.

Human rights defenders, peace activists and trade unionists
Human rights defenders, peace activists and trade unionists who exposed abuses committed by the

parties to the armed conflict were themselves killed, attacked, threatened and arbitrarily detained. Scores endured ongoing surveillance as well as raids on their offices or homes. In several instances, military intelligence information gathered by the security forces resulted in spurious criminal investigations of activities in connection with their legitimate human rights activities. This heightened concerns that these attacks were part of a coordinated military-paramilitary strategy to discredit human rights and trade union activities.

◻ On 17 August, the security forces and judicial officials arrested around 150 people in the municipalities of Chalán, Colosó and Ovejas, Sucre department, including members of the *Sindicato de Pequeños y Medianos Agricultores de Sucre*, Sucre Small and Medium Farmers' Union. The arrests occurred shortly after an international human rights delegation visited the area. Some of those detained had reportedly spoken to the delegation about human rights violations committed by the military. A judge who released all the detainees in November owing to lack of evidence was being investigated by the Attorney General's Office at the end of the year.

◻ On 21 August, 42 social activists and human rights defenders in Saravena, Arauca department, were detained by the military. Among those detained were José Murillo Tobo, president of the "Joel Sierra" Regional Human Rights Committee, and Alonso Campiño Bedoya, also a member of the Committee and leader of the regional branch of the *Central Unitaria de Trabajadores* (CUT), Trade Union Congress. Their arrest came after the Committee had highlighted the presence of paramilitaries operating in collusion with the military in Saravena.

◻ In September, criminal investigations were reportedly initiated against five members of the non-governmental organization, the *Comisión Inter-eclesial Justicia y Paz*, Inter-ecclesiastical Justice and Peace Commission. The Attorney General's Office initiated judicial investigations into allegations of corruption, drug smuggling, homicide and formation of illegal armed groups. These proceedings were the latest in a string of threats and harassment against members of the Commission. They followed a Constitutional Court decision to allow the Commission to participate in judicial proceedings into over 200 human rights violations committed by paramilitaries operating in conjunction with the XVII Brigade in 1997 and 1998.

Detentions repeatedly coincided with paramilitary threats and killings of human rights defenders and trade unionists. Human rights defenders were put under further threat of attack after President Uribe described some human rights non-governmental organizations as "political manoeuverers in the service of terrorism, who cowardly wave the human rights banner" in a speech in September.

Violence against women

Women were victims of extrajudicial executions, arbitrary and deliberate killings, and "disappearances". They were often targeted because of their role as activists and leaders campaigning for human rights, peace or socio-economic alternatives or because they were members of communities in conflict zones. Sexual violence against women, including rape and genital mutilation, was also used as a weapon of war to generate fear by all parties to the conflict.

◻ Between 1 and 7 May, soldiers of the XVIII Brigade, wearing AUC armbands, reportedly entered Julieros, Velasqueros, Roqueros, Genareros and Parreros, hamlets of the indigenous reserve of Betoyes, municipality of Tame, Arauca department. In Parreros, a pregnant 16-year-old girl, Omaira Fernández, was allegedly raped and killed. Her stomach was reportedly cut open and the foetus pulled out before her body was placed in a bag, which was then thrown into the River Cravo.

Kidnappings

Guerrilla groups, especially the FARC, accounted for most of the kidnappings carried out by paramilitaries and armed opposition groups. Mass kidnappings also continued.

◻ On 12 September, eight foreign tourists were kidnapped by the ELN in the ruins of Ciudad Perdida in the Sierra Nevada. One of the hostages escaped. The remaining hostages were released by the end of the year.

Abuses against civilians

Internally displaced people, peasant farmers, and Afro-descendant and indigenous communities living in conflict or economically strategic areas were disproportionately affected by the violence. Over 175,000 Colombians were forcibly displaced in the first nine months of 2003, a 49 per cent fall on the previous year's record high.

Government policies, such as the creation of an army of peasant soldiers and the network of civilian informers, dragged civilians further into the conflict by blurring the distinction between combatants and civilians. The families of peasant soldiers, who mostly operate in their own communities, unlike regular soldiers, were threatened by guerrillas in several departments, including Caquetá and Arauca.

Members of indigenous communities continued to be targeted.

◻ On 6 March, the FARC allegedly killed five members of the Murui indigenous community in La Tagua, Puerto Leguizamo municipality, Putumayo department.

◻ On 16 October, paramilitaries reportedly killed three Kankuamo indigenous leaders in the Sierra Nevada de Santa María. At least 50 Kankuamos were allegedly killed in 2003, the majority by paramilitaries and the remainder by armed opposition groups.

There was also a spate of bombings in urban areas, some of them attributed to armed opposition groups, which killed a significant number of civilians.

◻ On 7 February, at least 35 people were killed and more than 160 injured in a bomb explosion in the "El Nogal" club in Bógota. On 15 July, the judicial investigator working on the case, Germán Camacho Roncancio, was dismissed, after failing to link the bombing to the FARC. He was killed on 4 September.

International Criminal Court

On 6 October, the US government released US$5 million in military aid to Colombia after the Colombian government entered into an impunity agreement not to surrender US nationals accused of genocide, crimes against humanity or war crimes to the International Criminal Court. Such agreements are in breach of states' obligations under international law.

Military aid

In the fiscal year 2003 the USA sent an estimated US$605 million in military and police assistance to Colombia. Most of the aid was earmarked for "counter-terrorism" and "international narcotics control" purposes. The requirement that the US State Department certify progress on human rights was retained. However, this applied to only 25 per cent of US assistance, down from 100 per cent in 2002.

Intergovernmental organizations

The UN Commission on Human Rights expressed concern about a further deterioration in respect for human rights and international humanitarian law by guerrilla and paramilitary groups. It highlighted the persistence of impunity, continuing links between paramilitaries and the security forces, and the alleged existence of a campaign to create a climate of hostility towards human rights organizations. The Commission noted continuing reports of human rights abuses attributed to the security forces and the failure of the Attorney General's Office to show sufficient willingness to investigate serious human rights cases. It called on the government not to grant permanent judicial police powers to the military.

AI country reports/ visits

Reports
- Colombia: Letter to Congress on judicial police powers (AI Index: AMR 23/039/2003)
- Colombia: Amnesty International's briefing to the UN Committee against Torture (AI Index: AMR 23/066/2003)

Visits
AI delegates visited Colombia in March, April, September and November.

CUBA

REPUBLIC OF CUBA
Head of state and government: Fidel Castro Ruz
Death penalty: retentionist
UN Women's Convention: ratified with reservations
Optional Protocol to UN Women's Convention: signed

2003 saw a severe deterioration in the human rights situation in Cuba. In mid-March the Cuban authorities carried out an unprecedented crack-down on the dissident movement. Seventy-five long-term activists were arrested, unfairly tried and sentenced to up to 28 years' imprisonment; they were prisoners of conscience. In April, three men convicted of involvement in a hijacking were executed by firing squad, ending a three-year *de facto* moratorium. Criticism from the international community, including countries and individuals previously supportive of the Cuban government, intensified. The Cuban authorities sought to justify these measures as a necessary response to the threat to national security posed by the USA. The US embargo and related measures continued to have a negative effect on the enjoyment of the full range of human rights in Cuba.

Prisoners of conscience

Eighty-four prisoners of conscience remained held, seven of whom were awaiting trial at the end of the year.

Crack-down in March

A government crack-down in March led to the imprisonment of most of the leadership of the dissident movement including teachers, librarians, journalists, medical personnel, and political and human rights activists. Only a few very well-known figures critical of the regime were not affected.

Detainees were brought to trial immediately and subjected to hasty and unfair proceedings. Most were charged under Article 91 of the Penal Code with "acts against the independence or territorial integrity of the state" or under the previously unused Law for the Protection of the National Independence and the Economy of Cuba. The latter mandates stiff prison terms for anyone found guilty of supporting US policy against Cuba. The dissidents were convicted on the basis of activities such as giving interviews to the US-funded broadcasting station for Cuba, *Radio Martí*; receiving materials or funds believed to have originated in the US government; or having contact with officials of the US Interest Section in Havana, whom Cuban authorities had accused of engaging in subversive and provocative behaviour. By the end of the year all the sentences had been ratified by the Supreme Popular Court, exhausting the possibilities for appeal under Cuban law. Following a detailed assessment of the available evidence against them, AI considered that all 75 were prisoners of conscience.

🗐 Marcelo López Bañobre, a member of the *Comisión Cubana de Derechos Humanos y Reconciliación Nacional*, Cuban Commission for Human Rights and National Reconciliation, was sentenced to 15 years in prison for, among other activities, "sending information to international organisms like Amnesty International".

Health concerns

There were continuing concerns about the health of many prisoners of conscience. Some were reportedly denied access to appropriate medical attention and held in harsh conditions. Access to family was limited, as many of the prisoners were held in facilities far from their home provinces.

🗐 Roberto de Miranda Hernández, aged 56, was believed to have suffered a heart attack, cardiac pain and a stomach ulcer in custody. The health of Oscar Manuel Espinosa Chepe, aged 63, deteriorated after his arrest, making it probable that he would need a liver transplant. The families of both claimed that prison conditions contributed to their illnesses.

Releases

A handful of prisoners of conscience were released during 2003.

🗐 Yosvany Aguilar Camejo, José Aguilar Hernández and Carlos Oquendo Rodríguez were released on 11 October after having spent 20 months in prison. The latter was the only one of the three to have been tried and sentenced.

🗐 Bernardo Arévalo Padrón was released in November after having served six years for "disrespect" towards President Fidel Castro and Vice-President Carlos Lage.

🗐 Eddy Alfredo Mena González, sentenced in 2000 to five years' imprisonment on charges including "disrespect" and "public disorder", was also released.

Executions resumed

The three-year *de facto* moratorium on the use of the death penalty ended with the execution by firing squad of Lorenzo Enrique Copello Castillo, Bárbaro Leodán Sevilla García and Jorge Luis Martínez Isaac on 11 April. They were among a group of people convicted of hijacking a Cuban ferry with several dozen passengers on board. The hijacking was resolved without violence. The three men were brought to trial, found guilty under "anti-terrorism" legislation, and had their appeals denied all within the space of one week. This raised profound concerns about the fairness of the judicial procedure to which they were subjected. President Castro said the executions were necessary to halt hijackings and stem a growing migration crisis from Cuba to the USA. Approximately 50 prisoners remained on death row at the end of the year.

International community

United Nations

In April the UN Commission on Human Rights passed a resolution asking the Cuban government to achieve similar progress in respecting civil and political rights as it had done in economic and social rights. It also called on Cuba to receive the visit of the personal representative for Cuba of the UN High Commissioner for Human Rights. The Cuban government responded that they did not accept the mandate of the resolution and would not allow the High Commissioner's representative onto the island.

In November, for the 12th consecutive year, the UN General Assembly passed a resolution calling on the USA to end its embargo.

USA

In March the US government tightened rules for travel from Florida in the USA to Cuba.

The Cuban government angrily protested against the expulsion of 14 diplomats from Florida, USA, because of alleged "inappropriate activities"; the inclusion of Cuba in the US annual report on trafficking in persons; and renewed US allegations of a Cuban biological weapons program.

In August, 12 alleged boat hijackers were forcibly returned from the USA – a step criticized by the Cuban exile community and Florida Governor Jeb Bush. In a move that was interpreted by some as a response to such criticism, the US government announced the creation of a commission for a transition to democracy in Cuba and improvements in the broadcasting and distribution of printed materials to Cuba. In October the US Agency for International Development announced that it would increase aid to dissidents in Cuba.

European Union (EU)

Days before the March crack-down the EU opened its first ever office in Cuba. The EU condemned the crack-down in Cuba in April, June and July. In June the EU announced a number of measures in response to the crack-down, such as inviting dissidents to national day celebrations and scaling back high-level diplomatic and cultural contacts while maintaining economic ties. In response, Fidel Castro and Raul Castro, First Vice-President of the Council of Ministers and Minister of the Revolutionary Armed Forces, led demonstrations outside the embassies of Spain and Italy, accused by Cuba of instigating the measures, and suspended the agreement establishing the Spanish Cultural Centre in Havana. In August, Cuba wrote to the EU saying that it would no longer accept development aid from the EU or its member states, as a rejection of the conditionality of EU aid on human rights improvements. The EU deplored this decision. However, it reiterated its commitment to supplying aid to the Cuban people and called for the embargo imposed on Cuba by the USA to be lifted immediately.

The dissident movement

The activities of the dissident movement stalled following the imprisonment of middle-ranking activists in the opposition movement. Trials in April revealed the existence of 12 state security agents who had infiltrated the dissident movement, some several years earlier. This, together with the publication of two books on alleged state security activity within the dissident movement, was seen as an attempt to promote suspicion and mistrust among those dissidents still at liberty.

In October, in the first big movement of opposition after the March crack-down, Oswaldo Payá Sardiñas, leader of the unofficial political group *Movimiento Cristiano Liberación,* Christian Liberation Movement, presented more than 14,000 new signatures for the Varela Project — a petition for a referendum on political and economic reforms — to the General Assembly. The Constitutional and Legal Affairs Committee of the Cuban Parliament had ruled the initiative unconstitutional in January. In December, Oswaldo Payá presented for public debate a national plan for transition to democracy.

Restrictions on travel outside Cuba continued to be applied to the most prominent dissidents. In June, Elizardo Sánchez Santacruz, Vladimiro Roca Antúnez, Manuel Cuesta Morúa and Oswaldo Payá Sardiñas were not allowed to travel to Italy to attend a seminar on the democratic opposition movement in Cuba organized by an Italian political party; Vladimiro Roca was denied permission to travel to Mexico in July to witness Mexico's federal elections; and Oswaldo Payá was prevented from attending a session in the European Parliament to which he had been invited.

AI country reports/ visits
Reports
- Cuba: Continued detentions following mass arrests in February and December 2002 (AI Index: AMR 25/001/2003)
- Cuba: Massive crack-down on dissent (AI Index: AMR 25/008/2003)
- Cuba: "Essential measures"? Human rights crack-down in the name of security (AI Index: AMR 25/017/2003)
- Cuba: Ongoing repercussions of the crack-down (AI Index: AMR 25/035/2003)
Visits
AI last visited Cuba in 1988. The government did not respond to AI's repeated requests to be allowed into the country.

DOMINICAN REPUBLIC

DOMINICAN REPUBLIC
Head of state and government: Hipólito Mejía
Death penalty: abolitionist for all crimes
UN Women's Convention and its Optional Protocol: ratified

The government, confronting economic fallout from a major banking scandal, reached an agreement with the International Monetary Fund (IMF), during months of violent demonstrations across the country in which people were killed or wounded. Killings by police in disputed circumstances again became frequent. Despite legal changes opening the way for trial in ordinary rather than police or military courts, little practical progress appeared to have been made in bringing perpetrators of human rights violations to justice.

Background
Presidential elections were set for May 2004. Former President Leonel Fernández won the primary election for the opposition Dominican Liberation Party.

In March, hundreds of children born in the Dominican Republic of Haitian descent marched on the Supreme Court demanding the right to Dominican nationality. On 16 October an appellate court rejected the government's appeal against an earlier decision granting citizenship rights to two children born in such circumstances. The earlier decision had effectively opened the door to citizenship rights, long denied by the authorities, to all such children. It was not known whether the government intended to appeal to the Supreme Court.

In June the US Department of State named the Dominican Republic as one of 15 countries making insufficient efforts to combat human trafficking, and threatened to cut off aid. In response, the National Police created a specialized unit to combat trafficking, and a new anti-trafficking bill was presented to parliament in August.

Violence during protests against IMF accords
Following accusations of fraud, in May the powerful Banco Intercontinental (BANINTER), or Intercontinental Bank, collapsed, costing the government a reported US$2.2 billion. The authorities began negotiating for emergency credits with the IMF and signed an agreement in August. Street protests broke out against the IMF talks and against price hikes and power blackouts. Demonstrators clashed regularly with police; in some cases, protesters were accused of setting off homemade bombs or firing on security forces, while police were often accused of unlawful killings and excessive use of force. Several people were shot dead and many wounded during the disturbances.

⮑ In the Capotillo area of Santo Domingo on 8 July, 33-year-old Juan Lin, a merchant, was reportedly shot dead by police firing on people demonstrating against the government's economic policy. He was believed to have been closing his business at the time to avoid damage during the disturbances.

⮑ On 6 August police raided the Santo Domingo office of the National Union of Unified Transport Workers where a pre-protest meeting was under way, and fired on those inside. At least three organizers were reportedly injured. The union lodged a judicial complaint.

⮑ During a general strike on 11 November, at least six people were killed and 30 wounded in clashes between protesters and police in several towns, including Santo Domingo, Santiago, Bonao, San Francisco de Macoris and Moca. The protests were about the economic situation and government policies. In an attempt to discourage the strike, police had earlier arrested several hundred activists.

Alleged unlawful killings by security forces
In spite of an initial reduction in reported unlawful killings following the 2002 naming of a new police chief, such allegations became increasingly frequent in 2003. In December the National Human Rights Commission announced that more than 200 people had been killed in alleged "exchanges of gunfire" with police since January. In such cases, victims have often been killed in disputed circumstances. Progress was made in ensuring that officers accused of human rights violations be tried in ordinary courts, through changes to the Penal Procedure Code, scheduled to come into force in 2004, and a police reform bill approved by the lower chamber in March and debated by the Senate in September. However, in practice most alleged unlawful killings continued to go unpunished. In particularly high-profile cases, security forces named their own commissions to carry out initial investigations, which suspended some officers but brought few to justice.

⮑ Jacobo Abel Grullar Ortega, aged 16, died after being shot in the back of the head by a police patrol in the Los Frailes area of Santo Domingo on 27 May. The police were reportedly pursuing two suspects and shot Jacobo Abel Grullar Ortega in error. Family members lodged a formal complaint against the patrol, and the officers involved were reportedly arrested. The police force named a commission to investigate the incident, but no further information was made available.

⮑ On 22 September, in Sabana Perdida, a police officer reportedly killed 22-year-old student José Francisco Nolasco López in front of numerous witnesses, including the victim's father, after mistaking him for a criminal suspect. Witnesses said that police prevented a doctor from assisting José Francisco Nolasco López and placed a gun in his belt in an attempt to justify the killing. An investigative commission set up by the police recommended that the officer responsible be tried in an ordinary court. He was taken into custody but later freed on orders of the investigating judge, provoking street protests. In November the Chief Justice of the Supreme Court said that the investigating judge had been suspended pending review of the release.

Freedom of expression curtailed
In May the *Listín Diario* media group was taken over by the Public Ministry following the detention of its owner on corruption charges related to the BANINTER scandal. Directors and some journalists resigned fearing attacks on their freedom of expression. In July a judge ordered that *Listín Diario* be returned to its owners; the ruling was appealed. Some journalists from other outlets were briefly detained and several programs temporarily taken off the air after publishing material critical of President Mejía.

Prison conditions
Endemic problems in prisons persisted, including severe overcrowding. At least two prisoners died and more than 20 were injured in two separate riots in Najayo prison, San Cristobal; one of the riots took place in the youth detention centre. In Moca prison in October, detainees rioted after one of their number died in custody allegedly because of inadequate medical attention.

The authorities announced that the first class of a new National Penitentiary School for training a corps of specialized prison guards would graduate in December. In the meantime, most prisoners continued to be guarded by security forces with no specific custodial responsibilities or training.

Impunity
In January an appeal court ruled that there was insufficient evidence to proceed against those accused in the 1994 "disappearance" of journalist and university lecturer Narciso González following his reported arrest on the streets of Santo Domingo by members of the army.

With regard to the 1975 killing of journalist Orlando Martinez Howley, in late 2002 relatives petitioned a court to find incompetent the judges who had overturned convictions of four men on appeal. The four men remained in prison while the family's petition was considered. Eventually, the family's petition was rejected; the Supreme Court ordered an appellate court to continue hearings in the case, and the four men remained held. At the conclusion of the hearings, the court found that the sentences handed down to the four men were excessive and reduced them by a minimum of half. The family lodged an appeal against this decision before the Supreme Court.

Violence against women
In February the Supreme Court announced the opening of a special court in Santo Domingo to try domestic violence cases.

ECUADOR

REPUBLIC OF ECUADOR
Head of state and government: Lucio Gutiérrez Borbua
Death penalty: abolitionist for all crimes
UN Women's Convention and its Optional Protocol: ratified

Police courts, which were neither independent nor impartial, continued to claim jurisdiction to investigate and try police officers accused of grave human rights violations. Torture and ill-treatment of detainees remained widespread. People who filed complaints of torture and ill-treatment were threatened, harassed and intimidated.

Background

Lucio Gutiérrez Borbua, a retired army colonel, took office as President in January with the support of the Pachakutic Movement, the political party backed by the indigenous communities. However, by August the Pachakutic Movement broke ranks with the government amid accusations that the government was continuing to implement economic policies that did not serve the interests of the majority of the population.

Throughout the year, trade unions and grassroots organizations, including those based in the indigenous communities, staged demonstrations against the growing poverty and government economic policies.

The President declared states of emergency in November in the city of Cuenca and the province of Azuay. According to the decree, this was prompted by a "wave of delinquency with loss of human life and the material damage which was unquantifiable".

Concerns remained about the effect the escalating conflict in Colombia (see Colombia entry) was having on Ecuador, in particular in the border areas. It appeared that the native population in Ecuador was blaming rising crime levels on the increasing number of Colombian migrants in the country.

Impunity and the use of police courts

The use of police courts to try members of the security forces allegedly responsible for human rights violations continued to be a concern. Police officers tried in these courts for crimes such as torture and ill-treatment usually go unpunished. In October, AI launched in the capital, Quito, a special report on this issue. The organization welcomed the commitment expressed by the authorities to make the necessary changes so that police courts do not deal with cases of human rights violations. However, the Commander in Chief of the Police disagreed with AI's concerns and insisted that human rights violations by police were a "thing of the past".

Torture and ill-treatment

Torture and ill-treatment of detainees and prisoners remained widespread. Victims and their relatives were intimidated and threatened after lodging complaints.

☐ Wilmer Lucio León Murillo told AI in October that he received death threats after he filed a complaint in July of torture and ill-treatment by five police officers in Quevedo town, Los Ríos province. Wilmer Lucio León and three others were detained in July outside Quevedo on suspicion of belonging to a well-known armed gang and were driven to an open space on the outskirts of the town. Wilmer Lucio León said that he had been tied up and made to lie on a concrete floor where two officers held him down and a third covered his mouth and poured water into his nose with a hose until he lost consciousness. The prosecution subsequently said that there was no case to answer against Wilmer Lucio León and he was released.

Abuses in the army

Torture and ill-treatment of junior army officers and conscripts in military installations were reported.

☐ Carlos Javier Paredes Rosero told AI in February that he had been tortured and ill-treated while on military service. In September 2002 he had reportedly been forced to wear a tyre around his neck for 12 days and made to fight other conscripts until he lost consciousness. After his family filed a complaint, Carlos Javier Paredes reportedly received death threats and was verbally abused by army personnel in the hospital where he was being treated.

Threats against indigenous activists in oil zones

In February, two leaders of the Sarayaku indigenous community in Pastaza province received death threats. The two men strongly opposed the extraction of oil in the region, the contract for which had been granted to an Argentine oil company. In November 2002 the community had declared a "state of alert" to mobilize against the incursion of the oil company into their territory. Since then, the community reportedly faced a campaign of intimidation and defamation. Other surrounding communities were allegedly induced to surrender part of their land by offers of financial and other benefits, such as employment and schools. Some individuals from the Sarayaku community were also approached, which allegedly created divisions within the community.

AI country reports/ visits

Report

- Ecuador: With no independent and impartial justice there can be no rule of law (AI Index: AMR 28/010/2003)

Visits

In February an AI delegation carried out research in Ecuador. In October another delegation visited the country to launch the above report and met various authorities, including representatives of the President and Minister of the Interior, the President and magistrates of the National Police Court, the Attorney General and members of Congress.

EL SALVADOR

REPUBLIC OF EL SALVADOR
Head of state and government: Francisco Flores
Death penalty: abolitionist for ordinary crimes
UN Women's Convention: ratified with reservations
Optional Protocol to UN Women's Convention: signed

The government failed to tackle impunity for human rights violations. Human rights defenders were threatened and harassed. There were persistent reports of violence against women and girls. New legislation was introduced which violated both the Constitution of El Salvador and international human rights treaties.

Background

The opposition Farabundo Martí National Liberation Front gained more seats than the ruling ARENA party in the March parliamentary elections. Several political activists were killed during the election campaign which was marred by violence. El Salvador continued to face high levels of violence to which the authorities responded by introducing repressive measures, including the so-called Get Tough Plan. The government failed to deal with the underlying causes of violence, including grave economic and social inequalities and the easy availability of firearms. Poor economic and living conditions led to chronic malnutrition among children.

A monument to the victims of human rights violations during the armed conflict was inaugurated in December as a result of the efforts of the families of the victims. The monument was a recommendation of the Truth Commission which the authorities had failed to implement.

Impunity

Those responsible for human rights violations during the 1980-1991 armed conflict and since were not brought to justice.

In January the UN Working Group on Enforced or Involuntary Disappearances reported on the lack of progress by the government in investigating "more than 2,000 [disappearance] cases pending" and noted that the Working Group had received no information from the government for some time.

The National Assembly did not support efforts by relatives of victims and non-governmental organizations to create a national committee to search for "disappeared" children. The success of the organization Pro-Búsqueda, established by the relatives of "disappeared" children, in reuniting such children with their biological families provided strong evidence both of the violations and of the fact that many of the children were still alive.

◻ Ernestina and Erlinda Serrano Cruz "disappeared" in June 1982 when they were seven and three years old respectively. The two girls were separated from their parents during an army operation in Chalatenango Department and reportedly taken in an army helicopter to an unknown destination. In February, the Inter-American Commission on Human Rights urged the government to investigate the case and establish the girls' whereabouts, provide adequate reparation, and find those responsible. The government ignored these recommendations and in June the Commission submitted the case to the Inter-American Court of Human Rights; the case was pending at the end of the year.

◻ No progress was known to have been made in bringing to justice those responsible for the rape and murder of nine-year-old Katya Miranda in April 1999 at the family home, despite statements by the Attorney General's Office that it was reopening the investigation. Evidence at the scene of the crime had been tampered with or destroyed and the judicial process had been characterized by irregularities and delays. Her father and uncle, both members of the security forces, and her grandfather, a lawyer, were charged in the case, but acquitted in October 2001. The Human Rights Procurator's Office strongly condemned the handling of the case.

Human rights defenders

Individuals, organizations and institutions working to defend human rights were threatened or harassed.

In May the office of the Human Rights Commission (CDHES), a non-governmental organization, in San Miguel Department, was broken into and office equipment, documentation relating to allegations of human rights abuses, and information about staff were taken. The CDHES believed that the raid may have been connected with the organization's actions on behalf of some 250 families facing eviction from land where the Air Force intended to build a base. The incident was reported to the police but no investigation was carried out.

In August, three death threats were made against the Human Rights Procurator, Beatrice de Carrillo. The Director of the Institute of Human Rights of the Central-American University and others involved in the defence of human rights and opposition to the Anti-*Maras* law (see below) were harassed and threatened.

Violence against women

There were numerous reports of physical and psychological violence against women and girls in the home and community. Rape of women and girls as young as seven was reported. Non-governmental organizations and women's groups sought to provide support to survivors. However, the Division of Youth and Family Services within the National Civil Police did not have sufficient resources to fulfil its mandate adequately.

In the first few months of 2003 several women were murdered, decapitated and their bodies mutilated and left in different locations. An investigation was carried out on only one of the murders but no one had been convicted by the end of the year.

Legislation

In October the National Assembly approved the Anti-*Maras* Act, to deal with the criminal activities of youth gangs. Under the law membership of a gang is considered an "illegal association". The law applied to anyone over the age of 12, and allowed children under 18 to be treated as adults at the discretion of the judge. Human rights and civil society organizations, and members of the judiciary expressed their opposition to the law on the grounds that it violates the Constitution and international treaties to which El Salvador is a party. President Francisco Flores responded by launching an attack on judges who did not apply the law and accusing them of favouring criminals rather than their victims.

AI country reports/ visits

Reports

- El Salvador: Where are the "disappeared" children? (AI Index: AMR 29/004/2003)
- El Salvador: Open Letter on the Anti-*Maras* Act (AI Index: AMR 29/009/2003)
- El Salvador: Monument to Memory and Truth – dignifying the victims of armed conflict (AI Index: AMR 29/011/2003)

Visit

An AI delegation visited El Salvador in March and April and met with government officials and non-governmental organizations.

GUATEMALA

REPUBLIC OF GUATEMALA
Head of state and government: Alfonso Portillo
Death penalty: retentionist
UN Women's Convention and its Optional Protocol: ratified

Human rights abuses in Guatemala reached levels not seen for many years. Among the principal targets were those involved in challenging the impunity enjoyed by those responsible for widespread massacres and other atrocities during Guatemala's 30-year civil conflict. Those at risk included human rights defenders, legal personnel, journalists and land activists defending the rights of indigenous communities. The run-up to the first round of elections in November 2003 saw a further steep rise in political violence. There was little progress in bringing to justice those responsible for human rights abuses or in eliminating the structures responsible for past and current abuses.

Background

It was widely believed that a major contributory factor in the upsurge in political violence and repression that characterized President Alfonso Portillo's administration (2000-2003) was the control exercised by General Efraín Ríos Montt behind the scenes. General Ríos Montt, a founder member of the *Frente Republicano Guatemalteco* (FRG), Guatemalan Republican Front, was head of state during one of the most repressive periods of the Guatemalan army's rural counter-insurgency campaign in 1982 and 1983. During 2003 he faced lawsuits both in Guatemala and abroad in connection with army-led massacres carried out while he was head of state, which the UN-sponsored *Comisión para el Esclarecimiento Histórico* (CEH), Historical Clarification Commission, judged had constituted genocide. Despite provisions in the Constitution barring those who gained office through a coup from contesting the presidency, the Guatemalan Constitutional Court ruled in July that General Ríos Montt could stand as the FRG candidate in the presidential elections. This resulted in heightened tension and sparked off further violence and abuses. There were numerous incidents of political violence in advance of the first round of presidential elections in November. General Ríos Montt failed to make it through to the second round in December, which passed off without major incident and resulted in the election of Óscar Berger of the *Gran Alianza Nacional* (GANA), Great National Alliance, as President.

Failure to tackle impunity

President Portillo failed to deliver on repeated promises to implement the human rights elements of the 1996 Peace Accords, which ended the civil conflict, or the recommendations of the CEH created under the Accords.

Little progress was made in resolving specific high-profile human rights cases. The few convictions for human rights abuses obtained in the Guatemalan courts, often after long and courageous struggles by relatives or local human rights groups, faced continuing appeals or were reversed. Witnesses and others involved in the cases remained at risk of further abuses.

In October, the *Estado Mayor Presidencial* (EMP), Presidential High Command, the military intelligence structure involved in human rights abuses during the country's armed conflict and implicated in high-profile human rights cases, was abolished, to be replaced by a civilian agency. There were continuing concerns, however, that few steps had been taken to ensure effective civilian oversight and accountability.

Civil patrols, responsible for grave abuses while serving as the army's civilian adjuncts during the conflict years, remobilized and held violent demonstrations demanding compensation for their wartime service. Human rights groups and government officials opposing their demands were threatened. Payments were subsequently made to them by President Portillo's government. However, despite the CEH recommendation, comprehensive reparations for the victims of violations by army and civil patrols had not been agreed by the end of 2003.

Agreements reached through the Inter-American system regarding reparations for specific past abuses were generally not implemented. Neither were significant steps taken to meet human rights conditions set by the May 2003 Consultative Group meeting of major donor countries and institutions.

In March, the government signed an agreement to establish a commission to investigate clandestine structures responsible for attacks on human rights defenders, lawyers, journalists and others. The *Comisión para la Investigación de Cuerpos Ilegales y Aparatos Clandestinos de Seguridad* (CICIACS), Commission to Investigate Illegal Armed Groups and Clandestine Security Apparatus, which came about as a result of lobbying by local human rights organizations, was due to be established in 2005 as soon as Congress had approved several important legal reforms.

▭ In May, the 2002 conviction of an army officer for ordering the extrajudicial execution of anthropologist Myrna Mack in 1990 was overturned. The court ruled on the institutional responsibility of the EMP, an issue not argued by either side, rather than the actions of the individual officer, and acquitted him. An appeal was pending at the end of the year.

▭ In October, the Constitutional Court rejected the 2002 reversal of guilty verdicts passed in 2001 against three military officers for the extrajudicial execution of Bishop Juan José Gerardi. The Bishop was killed in 1998, two days after presenting the Guatemalan Roman Catholic Church's findings on abuses during the conflict years. One of the three officers convicted in 2001 was murdered in prison in January 2003, allegedly as he was about to implicate other officers in the murder. In October, Erick Urízar Barillas became the 14th witness to the Bishop's death to be killed. An appeal in this case was pending at the end of the year.

▭ Suits for genocide and crimes against humanity filed in Guatemala and abroad against the former governments of General Romeo Lucas García (1978-1982) and Efraín Ríos Montt (1982-1983) continued to be accompanied by intimidation and reprisals against the human rights organizations and forensic experts involved in the cases. In March, two workers at the *Centro para la acción legal en derechos humanos*, Centre for Legal Action in Human Rights, Mario Minera and Héctor Amílcar Mollinedo Caceros, were repeatedly followed by suspicious individuals and in September, the group's legal director, Fernando López, received a written death threat. Staff of the *Fundación de Antropología Forense de Guatemala*, Guatemalan Forensic Anthropology Foundation, and their relatives were subjected to repeated intimidation.

Abuses against human rights defenders

Virtually every major Guatemalan human rights organization suffered abuses. No one, however prominent, was immune.

▭ Nobel Peace Prize winner Rigoberta Menchú was verbally harassed and manhandled by FRG supporters in October when she went to the Constitutional Court to challenge the Ríos Montt candidacy.

▭ In September, Eusebio Macario, co-founder of the indigenous rights organization *Consejo de Comunidades Étnicas: Runujel Junam* (CERJ), Council of Ethnic Communities: We are all Equal, was killed by unidentified assailants. A week earlier he had met indigenous villagers to advise them of their right to reparations for conflict-related abuses.

Abuses against lawyers and judges

Several special prosecutors assigned by the Public Prosecutor's Office to investigate abuses against human rights defenders and the judiciary, as well as national and regional staff of the *Procuraduría de Derechos Humanos* (PDH), Human Rights Procurator's Office, were threatened and attacked.

▭ In June, José Israel López López, an indigenous activist, lawyer and PDH worker in Chimaltenango Department, was shot and killed by unidentified assailants in Guatemala City. He had been investigating military abuses and attacks against other human rights defenders and indigenous survivors also working on such cases. Several other prominent members of the Mayan community have been killed in recent years.

Lawyers, judges, prosecutors and witnesses involved in high-profile human rights cases and initiatives to combat impunity continued to be subjected to abuses.

▭ In April, unidentified assailants in Zacapa Department attacked Special Prosecutor Manuel de Jesús Barquín Durán, who had been assigned to investigate abuses and corruption allegedly committed by officials in neighbouring Izabal Department. His bodyguard was seriously injured in the attack.

Journalists attacked

Journalists targeted because of their human rights reporting included *Prensa Libre* columnist Marielos Monzón, who received anonymous threats after publication of her articles on the 2002 kidnapping, killing and decapitation of indigenous leader and lawyer Antonio Pop Caal. The threats intensified at the beginning of the year following her coverage of the initiatives by Graciela Azmitia both in Guatemala and through the Inter-American human rights protection system to establish responsibility for the 1981 "disappearance" of family members, including her "disappeared" sister who was pregnant at the time. After intruders raided her home in March, Marielos Monzón fled abroad.

Abuses against environmental activists

In July, armed men forced their way into the Guatemala City home of environmental activist Norma Maldonado, threatening occupants, destroying data and taking film and other materials relating to the *Mesa Global de Guatemala*, Guatemalan Global Alliance. The Alliance works with Guatemalan and Mexican environmentalists to publicize concerns about feared adverse effects of the proposed Free Trade Area of the Americas and the Central American infrastructure development project, *Plan Puebla Panamá*.

Election campaign violence

At least 16 political leaders were killed and many others attacked in violence connected with the election campaign. Many more suffered threats and intimidation. However, the most dramatic incidents occurred in July when crowds, armed with machetes and clubs, were apparently trucked into the capital by the FRG and then led by party officials in violent attacks against individuals and institutions including the Constitutional and Supreme Courts and the Supreme Electoral Tribunal. Journalists were also targeted; radio reporter Héctor Ramírez suffered a fatal heart attack after being pursued by a mob.

Abuses arising out of land conflicts

The government's failure to implement the land-related elements of the Peace Accords and the deteriorating economic situation of Guatemala's rural poor contributed to widespread unrest in the countryside and continued violent disputes over land tenure. Numerous activists defending their communities against land claims by large landowners or agricultural corporations have been killed in recent years.

☐ Several land activists from the Lanquín II community, Morales, Izabal Department, were killed in 2003. The killings occurred in the context of a dispute between the community and cattle ranchers, apparently supported by local officials, trying to acquire banana plantation lands.

Violence against women

Many of Guatemala's foremost human rights groups were set up by women seeking "disappeared" relatives or campaigning for justice for extrajudicially executed family members. They remained prominent in combating impunity for abuses, including the widespread rape perpetrated against non-combatant indigenous women during the conflict, and campaigning for reparations for abuses and faced constant threats, intimidation, and attacks including rape, by those opposed to their activities.

In 2003 women's rights defenders drew attention to alarming levels of violence against women in the post-conflict period, including domestic violence and the deaths of hundreds of women who had been subjected to various forms of sexual violence before they were killed.

Lynchings

Numerous people died in mob lynchings. These were commonly portrayed as the result of communities' frustration at the failure of the law to deal adequately with real or perceived human rights violations and ordinary crimes. However, there were claims that villagers were being manipulated and incited to attack targeted individuals whom local politicians or the security forces wished to have eliminated. The instigators of many of these lynchings were reported to be former members of the Civil Patrols.

Death penalty

Death sentences continued to be passed for a range of common crimes. More than 30 people remained on death row at the end of the year; however, no executions took place.

International concerns

The grave human rights situation provoked increasing expressions of concern and international missions of inquiry to the country. In September the Inter-American Commission on Human Rights expressed concern at the deteriorating human rights situation, while the UN extended the mandate of its observer mission, MINUGUA, for an additional year. In September it was announced that an expanded office of the UN High Commissioner for Human Rights in Guatemala from 2004 would monitor human rights and provide targeted technical assistance.

AI country reports/ visits

Reports

- Deep cause for concern – Amnesty International's assessment of the current human rights situation in Guatemala (AI Index: AMR 34/022/2003)
- Guatemala: Accountable intelligence or recycled repression? Abolition of the EMP and effective intelligence reform (AI Index: AMR 34/031/2003)
- Guatemala: Legitimacy on the line – human rights and the 2003 Guatemalan elections (AI Index: AMR 34/051/2003)
- Guatemala: Open letter from Amnesty International to Guatemalan presidential candidates for the November 2003 elections (AI Index: 34/052/2003)

Visits

AI delegates visited the country in March and June to collect information on human rights, including on economic, social and cultural rights, and to assess the risks facing human rights defenders. Delegates raised concerns with government officials.

GUYANA

REPUBLIC OF GUYANA
Head of state: Bharrat Jagdeo
Head of government: Samuel Hinds
Death penalty: retentionist
UN Women's Convention: ratified
Optional Protocol to UN Women's Convention: not signed

Death sentences continued to be imposed. There were reports of killings in circumstances suggesting that they were extrajudicial executions. Torture, ill-treatment and severe overcrowding in detention were reported. The Disciplined Forces Commission (DFC) published interim findings of its examination of the Guyana Police Force.

Background
In a joint communiqué on 6 May, President Jagdeo and Robert Corbin, Leader of the Opposition and head of the People's National Congress/Reform party (PNC/R), pledged to continue "constructive engagement" and agreed various parliamentary and constitutional reforms. These reforms included the establishment of a Disciplined Forces Commission (DFC) to inquire into, among other things, the operations of the Guyana Police Force; legislation to strengthen human rights; the creation of an Ethnic Relations Commission; and the appointment of members to new Constitutional Committees on Human Rights, Women and Gender Equity, Children, and Indigenous Affairs. The communiqué signalled the reopening of talks between the two leaders, which had been suspended in March 2002. Following the signing of the communiqué, PNC/R members returned to the National Assembly for the first time since March 2002 and Parliament resumed operations.

There were continued reports of high levels of violent crime, although no official statistics were published. At least nine police officers were killed. Joint police-army anti-crime operations continued in some areas. In May the President attributed the crime rise to the drug and gun trade, the return of people deported from other countries, illegal migration and politically motivated interests.

Racial and ethnic tension
In July the UN Special Rapporteur on contemporary forms of racism, racial discrimination, xenophobia and related intolerance visited Guyana. In an interim report to the UN General Assembly in August, he observed that ethnic polarization between Guyanese of African and Indian descent, reflected in the composition of political parties, greatly affected the structure of state mechanisms and perpetuated economic and social underdevelopment. He expressed hope that the joint communiqué by the President and the Leader of the Opposition reflected political commitment towards finding democratic and

sustainable responses to such problems. His full report was due in January 2004.

In May and July, members of the Ethnic Relations Commission were appointed. The Commission's task was to investigate and address complaints of racial discrimination, and promote equal access to public services. Appeals against its decisions could be made to the Ethnic Relations Tribunal but this had not started work by the end of the year.

Death penalty
Death sentences for murder were imposed by the courts. At the end of 2003 there were at least 20 people on death row. There were no executions. The government did not respond to AI's request to be informed of the number of death sentences imposed following the introduction of "anti-terrorism" legislation in 2002. Amendments to the Criminal Law Offences Act had expanded the scope of the death penalty to include "terrorist acts" and threatened freedom of expression and association.

In July, journalist Mark Benschop was committed to stand trial for treason with political activist Phillip Bynoe, who remained unapprehended. They were charged with "form[ing] an intention to overthrow the lawfully elected Government of Guyana by force" and other conspiracy charges. The charges related to an attack on the Presidential Palace following a demonstration in July 2002. Both faced a death sentence if convicted. In September the Director of Prisons denied reports that Mark Benschop was being ill-treated in prison or that he was on hunger strike. The trial was due to start in October but had not begun by the end of the year.

Violations by law enforcement officials
In July the DFC started public hearings into the operations of the Guyana Police Force. The DFC was to look at a wide range of issues including pay, training, structures, the need for a police force that was ethnically balanced, and complaints relating to human rights. Between August and November it received over 100 submissions from government officials, non-governmental organizations (NGOs), members of the public and others. Its preliminary report to the National Assembly in November stated that the police needed "urgent, serious and wide-ranging reform". In addressing the problem of extrajudicial executions the DFC made several recommendations. These included the establishment of a dedicated or distinctly identifiable Coroner's Court to reduce the backlog of inquests and inquiries into police killings; the provision to coroners of independent investigative resources; greater independence in the investigation of complaints against the police; and clearer terms of reference and lines of command for specialist units likely to confront armed and dangerous criminals.

AI submitted its concerns and recommendations on police reform to the DFC. While welcoming the DFC's preliminary conclusions and recommendations, AI remained concerned at the limited extent to which its report drew on international human rights standards.

A number of police officers were charged with murder but none was convicted. There were at least 29 fatal shootings by the police, some of which appeared to be extrajudicial executions, and further reports of the unlawful use of force. Torture and ill-treatment was alleged in some cases. Conditions in police lock-ups reportedly remained severe.

📁 There were reports of ill-treatment during security force operations in Buxton, East Coast Demerara, in January. The incident prompted a meeting between the Commissioner of Police and the Leader of the Opposition in January.

📁 In March, two police officers were charged with the murder of unarmed Yohance Douglas, aged 17. On 1 March armed police fired, reportedly without provocation, on a car in which he was travelling, killing him and wounding other passengers. The killing led to a public outcry. A pathologist who observed the autopsy on behalf of AI concluded that Yohance Douglas was shot from behind and that his death was caused by a haemorrhage resulting from a gunshot wound. None of the surviving car passengers was charged with any crime. The preliminary inquiry had not been completed by the end of 2003.

📁 In September, a police officer and another man were charged with the murder of Albert Hopkinson, aged 26. The police reported that he was found unconscious in a cell at a Mabaruma police station. Eyewitnesses alleged that he was beaten after his arrest on 2 September. An autopsy reportedly revealed death from strangulation, a fractured skull and other injuries.

📁 In November jurors unanimously returned a verdict of police criminal liability for the death of Mohammed Shafeek, who died in Brickdam police station on 3 September 2000. Eyewitnesses said that he was denied medical attention after being injured by police officers.

📁 In November a police officer was charged with manslaughter in connection with the fatal shooting on 25 June of Michael Clarke, allegedly while he was trying to escape an escort during a prisoner transfer. The trial had not taken place by the end of the year.

Conditions in detention

Conditions in detention remained harsh and amounted in some cases to cruel, inhuman and degrading treatment. Severe overcrowding was aggravated by a substantial population of prisoners on remand, many of them detained for excessive periods, often for several years. However, local human rights activists reported a reduction in the prison population of Central Prison from 1,000 to 600.

Severe delays in hearing criminal cases were also reported. In October, 10 prisoners brought a legal action against the authorities, challenging the decision to bring Mark Benschop to trial within three months of committal when they had been awaiting trial for years.

Violence against women

In November, 41 NGOs, including women's rights groups, launched a three-month awareness campaign to eliminate violence against women, in conjunction with the governmental Women's Affairs Bureau.

Access to health care

Official figures released in 2003 showed that 1,500 of around 20,000 women who gave birth in Guyana in 2002 were HIV positive. In October a Memorandum of Understanding on HIV/AIDS education in the workplace was signed between the Ministry of Labour and the International Labour Organization.

AI country reports/ visits

Report

- Guyana: Human rights and crime control – not mutually exclusive (AI Index: AMR 35/003/2003)

HAITI

REPUBLIC OF HAITI
Head of state: Jean Bertrand Aristide
Head of government: Yvon Neptune
Death penalty: abolitionist for all crimes
UN Women's Convention: ratified
Optional Protocol to UN Women's Convention: not signed

The government faced growing discontent from opposition and civil society movements, and attacks by armed groups and some disaffected street gangs that had formerly repressed dissent on the government's behalf. Elections again failed to take place as some opposition parties demanded the President's departure as a pre-condition for participating in elections while the President remained committed to completing his term. Political violence increased as parties in the continuing electoral deadlock became more polarized. The police and judiciary were accused of bias in favour of the government. The police committed numerous human rights violations and frequently failed to protect demonstrators and others from abuses by pro-government activists.

Background

The Organization of American States (OAS) attempted to negotiate the holding of elections in the run-up to January 2004, when many legislative terms end. In June its General Assembly urged all parties to engage in forming a new Provisional Electoral Council to hold elections once security was ensured. This was refused by the main opposition coalition, *Convergence Démocratique* (CD – Democratic Convergence), which insisted that security could not be guaranteed until President Jean Bertrand Aristide was removed from office and a transition government set up. The

President reiterated his determination to complete his term, which expires in February 2006. The Catholic Church's Conference of Haiti condemned political leaders on both sides for failing to compromise, urging the President to form a multi-sector advisory council in the run-up to elections and calling on the opposition to participate.

Haiti's economic situation, the most precarious in the region, deteriorated further in 2003 with grave ramifications for the rights to health, work, education and development. In April the UN Development Programme appealed for emergency funds for food, security, health and other projects in Haiti, one of the poorest countries in the world. However, aid from donors such as the European Union, partially frozen because of the electoral dispute in Haiti, continued to be blocked. The International Monetary Fund launched a one-year project aimed at establishing conditions for a longer-term poverty reduction program. After the government used funds from its dwindling foreign currency reserves to pay US$30 million in arrears on earlier loans, the Inter-American Development Bank resumed lending. The World Bank's private sector lending arm, the International Finance Corporation, loaned US$20 million to the first company to set up factories in a new free trade zone near Ouanaminthe, on the Haitian border with the Dominican Republic, on the condition that it respect labour rights. Meanwhile, Haiti claimed over US$21 billion in restitution and reparation for an indemnity it paid to France in exchange for recognition of Haitian independence; a French commission visited in October to investigate the claim.

Political violence increased as rifts between opposing sides widened. Numerous abuses were allegedly committed, most frequently by supporters of the government and its party, *Fanmi Lavalas* (FL — Lavalas Family). The Haitian National Police (HNP) were accused of disproportionate use of force and pro-government bias in responding to abuses.

Demonstrations

Political demonstrations became increasingly frequent during the year.

▭ Numerous anti-government demonstrations were held in Cap Haïtien, department of the North. On 6 April pro- and anti-government activists clashed in Carrénage, an opposition area of the city. A supporter of each side was said to have been killed. On 30 August members of Group of 184, a civil society movement, the CD and other groups staged a rally in Carrénage against police advice. FL supporters reportedly set up barriers in the streets and threw bottles and stones to prevent participants from reaching the venue. During the rally, stones were allegedly thrown by both sides. Police officers reportedly used tear gas and fired shots to disperse the crowd. On 14 September, HNP officers allowed separate opposition and FL marches to converge and, after rocks and bottles were thrown by demonstrators, fired tear gas at both groups. Several people were reportedly injured. Government officials indicated that one government supporter had been killed, although the circumstances were unclear.

▭ In Port-au-Prince, several Group of 184 activities were disrupted. On 12 July, dozens of passengers in a motorcade to Cité Soleil, a Port-au-Prince slum, were reportedly injured after their cars were stoned in the presence of police. Officials accused the group of provoking residents' violent reaction and of causing four deaths, although little detailed information on this claim was made public. A Group of 184 march to the central square in Port-au-Prince on 14 November was broken up when demonstrators were surrounded by a large crowd of FL supporters throwing rocks and bottles, and police fired tear gas. The head of the OAS Special Mission for Strengthening Democracy in Haiti denounced officials' failure to prevent FL activists from repressing opponents' demonstrations. Group of 184 accused the OAS of ineffectiveness and occupied its offices to demand the release of two businessmen arrested on illegal weapons charges during the march. The Mission said that its role was to advise, not to replace, Haitian institutions. The two businessmen were released on 1 December.

▭ Confrontations became even more violent in the run-up to the celebration of Haiti's bicentennial on 1 January 2004. On 5 December, FL supporters attacked demonstrating State University of Haiti students in the presence of the police. More than 20 people, primarily students, were reportedly injured by firearms, batons or other weapons, while the University rector's kneecaps were broken by blows from an iron bar. Students and others again protested on 22 December; two people were reportedly killed and six wounded when shots were fired at demonstrators and police fired back.

Protests against deaths of former pro-government gang leaders

Two leaders of armed gangs that had formerly supported the government were killed in September and October. Their supporters accused the government of ordering the killings in response to international criticism of its links with street violence. As a result, residents of formerly pro-FL neighbourhoods in Gonaïves and Cité Soleil staged violent protests calling for President Aristide's departure.

▭ The body of Amiot "Cubain" Métayer, a former FL activist, was found on the outskirts of St Marc, department of the Artibonite, on 22 September with gunshot wounds to the eyes and chest. His home town of Gonaïves was racked by weeks of violent demonstrations as his supporters clashed repeatedly with police. On 2 October, police supported by Coast Guard units and a helicopter raided the Raboteau area of the city. At least eight people were said to have been killed and others injured. The violence continued and on 26 October a young bystander was reportedly killed and two police officers, including the Gonaïves Commissioner, were wounded when an armed anti-government group laid siege to the police station. During several days of reprisal raids on Raboteau, police were accused of injuring residents with gunfire and of setting fire to houses.

▭ On 31 October, Rodson "Kolibri" Lemaire, leader of a formerly pro-government gang that had reportedly been involved in suppressing the Group of 184 rally in July in Cité Soleil (see above), was shot dead by unidentified assailants. Days of violent clashes followed between his supporters and the police in Cité Soleil, resulting in several deaths.

Other violations by police

Other violations by the HNP continued to be reported. There were also allegations of abuses committed by unofficial groups of armed men attached to police stations and acting with police complicity. During his November visit, which focused on police behaviour, the UN Independent Expert on Haiti said that he received assurances that these unofficial groups would be investigated.

Unlawful killings

⌐ On 22 October, Fernande Jean died after reportedly being shot in the head by a police commissioner when a rock she threw during a family dispute hit his car. No investigation was known to have been initiated.

⌐ Viola Robert, whose three sons were found dead with bullet wounds to the head after they were taken into police custody in December 2002, was forced to flee Haiti in June with other members of her family after receiving numerous death threats apparently in response to her attempts to gain justice for her sons' deaths.

Torture and ill-treatment

There were frequent allegations of torture and ill-treatment by police.

⌐ Judith Roi, Jeantel Joseph, Chavanne Joseph and Adeler Reveau, all members of the opposition Patriotic Assembly for National Revival, were arrested on 14 July on charges of illegal possession of weapons and involvement in planning attacks on officials. They were reportedly beaten with iron bars and other objects in police custody. The case was under review by an investigating judge.

⌐ On 14 October, Jonathan Louisma, a street child, was reportedly beaten severely by police and bitten by a police dog at the Champs de Mars police station. He was arrested after he was accused of stealing a wallet. It appeared that no investigation was initiated.

Attacks on government supporters

Officials and FL activists were targeted by a group of unidentified armed individuals in the Pernal section of the commune of Belladère, in the lower Central Plateau. The assailants were generally referred to by the authorities as the "Armée sans maman" ("Motherless Army"), which they alleged included former soldiers of the disbanded Haitian army. The government said that the group had killed up to 25 people and accused opposition parties of supporting it. Opposition leaders denied any such ties. In response to the attacks, the HNP reportedly burned homes and beat residents suspected of anti-government sympathies.

⌐ On 6 May a group of armed men reportedly attacked the Péligre hydroelectric dam in the lower Central Plateau, the country's largest power source, killing two civilian security guards, setting fire to the control room and threatening staff. While escaping,

they allegedly identified themselves as former soldiers of the disbanded army.

⌐ A vehicle transporting an Interior Ministry delegation was reportedly ambushed in Ouasèk, near Pernal, on 25 July. Four civilian Ministry employees were killed. The Interior Minister told the press that the bodies of the four men had been mutilated and burned. Another Ministry employee was said to have been shot twice and needed hospital treatment.

Journalists under attack

The family of Jean Dominique, the Director of *Radio Haïti Inter* who was killed by unidentified assailants in April 2000, moved to have the trial documents in the case thrown out due to the absence of any information on the motives and authors of the crime. The motion was upheld by the Court of Appeal, which ordered that the investigation be reopened to address these issues. No progress was made in investigating the attack in late 2002 on Michèle Montas, a journalist and the widow of Jean Dominique, which left her bodyguard dead. *Radio Haïti Inter* closed indefinitely in February because of security concerns.

⌐ In Saint Marc on 12 November, the authorities reportedly confiscated transmitters and material from the radio station *Tête à Tête*, which broadcast views critical of the government. In an apparent reprisal attack, a group of residents reportedly set fire to *Pyramide FM* radio station after accusing its staff of not supporting their anti-government views. The station director filed a complaint against the leaders of a local opposition group.

Harassment of women's organizations

Some activities by women's organizations were repressed by FL activists or police.

⌐ On 10 March, a coalition of women's groups organized a march in Port-au-Prince to commemorate International Women's Day and to protest against the difficult conditions faced by Haitian women. The march was reported to have been forcibly broken up by the HNP, and participants were harassed and threatened by FL counter-demonstrators in the presence of police.

⌐ A sit-in by women's organizations on 29 October outside the downtown court offices to draw attention to insecurity and violence was reportedly broken up by FL activists throwing stones and bottles.

AI country reports/ visits
Reports
- Haiti: Abuse of human rights – political violence as the 200th anniversary of independence approaches (AI Index: AMR 36/007/2003)
- Haiti: Human rights and the Bicentennial – a 10-point action plan (AI Index: AMR 36/010/2003)

HONDURAS

REPUBLIC OF HONDURAS
Head of state and government: Ricardo Maduro
Death penalty: abolitionist for all crimes
UN Women's Convention: ratified
Optional Protocol to UN Women's Convention: not signed

Children and young people, including people in custody, were killed by police officers, prison personnel or unidentified individuals; some may have been the victims of extrajudicial executions. Human rights defenders were threatened, harassed and killed. Members of indigenous groups faced torture, threats and harassment. Members of the National Police were involved in alleged human rights violations.

Background
There were massive popular demonstrations to protest at poor living conditions, threats to basic public services, government policies and new laws. Various studies showed that over 60 per cent of the population lived in poverty and 36 per cent of children suffered from malnutrition.

The National Congress approved an amendment to the Penal Code which was intended to deal with crimes committed by gangs but which in fact imposed severe restrictions on the right to freedom of association, in contravention of the Constitution and of international instruments to which Honduras is a party.

Children and young people
The killing and possible extrajudicial execution of children and youths continued; over 500 new cases were reported during the year. Several well-publicized initiatives by the authorities to investigate the killings did not prove as effective as expected and only a few of those responsible for past killings were brought to justice. However, it appeared that the police were taking initial steps in at least some more recent cases. In a positive development, some steps were taken in the latter part of the year to create a national witness protection program.

In April, 69 people were killed in the El Porvenir prison in La Ceiba, Department of Atlántida. Among them were 29 young men and boys and three visitors to the prison; many others were injured. Initially, the authorities said the incident was the result of a riot and a fight between gang members and other inmates. However, 61 of the 69 dead reportedly belonged to the same gang. Some of the dead had been decapitated and a large number were found burned to death in a locked cell. Despite a flurry of promises and investigations by official bodies, no one had been detained or brought to trial in connection with the deaths by the end of the year.

Human rights defenders
One human rights defender was killed and many others were threatened and harassed. Among those targeted were members of the Centre for the Prevention, Treatment and Rehabilitation of Torture Victims and their Families investigating the deaths at the El Porvenir prison; and members of the Committee of Relatives of the Disappeared, which had opposed the Anti-Gang Law, as well as the nine-year-old daughter of the Committee's General Coordinator.

▢ In July Carlos Arturo Reyes, aged 23, an environmental activist, was shot dead in the backyard of his home in the municipality of El Rosario. Three heavily armed men were seen fleeing the scene. *Pastoral Social*, the organization he worked for, had recently relocated him because of death threats against him. Other people involved in activities to protect the environment in Olancho Department were harassed and threatened, including Gilberto Flores, Orlando Nájera and Father Osmín Flores. Father José Andrés Tamayo was warned to leave the country, allegedly by a group of powerful individuals involved in the logging industry.

▢ In November, journalist Germán Antonio Rivas was killed in Santa Rosa de Copán, Department of Copán, by an unidentified man who shot him in the head outside his office. He was the managing director of *Channel 7* of the Maya Vision Corporation. He had investigated and publicly criticized a mining company for damaging the environment and water supplies to the population of Santa Rosa de Copán by leaking cyanide from their plant. The Ministry of Natural Resources then imposed a fine on the company. Germán Antonio Rivas had survived an earlier attempt on his life in February.

Violence against women
Several, mostly young, women were murdered, decapitated and dismembered, most of them in San Pedro Sula, northern Honduras. In some cases the victims were shot in the head, in others they were killed with knives or similar weapons. The police carried out some initial investigations but these did not progress and no one was brought to justice for these killings.

Domestic violence affected hundreds of women and it cost the lives of over a hundred. However, the authorities failed to investigate appropriately and bring those responsible to justice.

There were reports that women and children were trafficked both within the country and to other Central American countries, the USA and Canada for the purpose of sexual exploitation.

Indigenous people
Indigenous people were subjected to human rights violations including torture.

▢ In January, brothers Marcelino and Leonardo Miranda, indigenous leaders in the Civic Council of Indigenous and Popular Organizations, were taken from the Lenca community in Montaña Verde, Lempira Department, by armed police officers and armed civilians who used tear gas and fired shots into the air and Marcelino Miranda's house. According to reports, their relatives, including a young girl, were threatened with firearms during the arrest. While being taken to Gracias Prison the brothers were reportedly beaten.

Leonardo Miranda was stabbed in the head and cigarettes were stubbed out on their ears. The officers reportedly threatened to kill both men. Later, Leonardo Miranda's head was repeatedly submerged in water. In April the brothers were again tortured by three officers of the Cobra unit, an elite group in the National Police force. In June a police officer reportedly put a gun to Leonardo Miranda's head, threatening to kill him if he did not admit the charges against him, and put a blank piece of paper in front of him, which he refused to sign. In September charges of torture, abuse of authority and damages against 21 police officers were dismissed despite medical evidence of physical abuse. On 16 December the two brothers were sentenced to 25 years in prison. AI was concerned that they may not have had a fair trial. Between February and September the brothers' lawyer, Marcelino Martínez Espinal, was subjected to acts of intimidation.

Lesbians, gay men and bisexual and transgender people

Lesbians, gay men and bisexual and transgender (LGBT) people faced discrimination and human rights violations.

▭ Elkyn Suárez Mejía (also known as China) – a transgender member of San Pedro Sula's Gay Community and an LGBT rights defender – was subjected to death threats by two police officers implicated in the killing in July of Erick David Yáñez (also known as Ericka). China's information about the killing led to the arrest in late July of two officers who were charged with homicide and complicity in the murder. China was provided with police protection. However, one of the accused officers escaped custody in mid-August, making China's safety more precarious. All protection was later withdrawn and China, fearing for her safety, left the country. The trial of the two police officers accused of involvement in the killing of Ericka had not started by the end of the year.

International Criminal Court

In May the government ratified an impunity agreement with the USA, providing that Honduras will not surrender US nationals accused of genocide, crimes against humanity or war crimes to the International Criminal Court. Such agreements are in breach of states' obligations under international law.

AI country reports/ visits
Reports
- Honduras: Zero tolerance... for impunity – extrajudicial executions of children and youths since 1998 (AI Index: AMR 37/001/2003)
- Honduras: Amnesty International demands an investigation by the authorities into the death of a journalist (AI Index: AMR 37/021/2003)

JAMAICA

JAMAICA
Head of state: Queen Elizabeth II, represented by Howard Felix Cooke
Head of government: Percival James Patterson
Death penalty: retentionist
UN Women's Convention: ratified with reservations
Optional Protocol to UN Women's Convention: not signed

Reports of police brutality and excessive use of force continued. At least 113 people were killed by the police, many in circumstances suggesting that they were extrajudicially executed. Detainees continued to be held for extremely long periods without being brought to trial. Conditions of detention frequently amounted to cruel, inhuman and degrading treatment. At least three people were sentenced to death; there were no executions.

Background

The economic situation remained dire, with a large number of people living below the poverty line. Jamaican society continued to suffer from an extremely high level of violence; at least 975 people were reported murdered, including 13 police officers.

Police brutality

At least 113 people were killed by the police, a significant drop on previous years. Many of these killings were suspected extrajudicial executions. There were continuing reports of ill-treatment, possibly amounting to torture, in police custody.

In February the UN Special Rapporteur on extrajudicial, summary or arbitrary executions visited Jamaica for discussions with the government and to investigate alleged unlawful killings. The authorities were not able to provide the Special Rapporteur with details of any police officer convicted of an unlawful killing between 1999 and January 2003. The Special Rapporteur concluded that the system for investigating potential extrajudicial executions by police officers appeared to be "wholly inadequate and marred by a number of institutional obstacles and by a lack of resources" and that extrajudicial executions appeared to have occurred.

▭ In January police officers assaulted and shot at members of a crowd at a dance hall event in Portmore. According to the event's organizers, the police officers had demanded money to allow the dance to continue but were unhappy with the amount offered. Video footage that showed police officers firing into and above the crowd supported allegations of police brutality.

▭ On 7 May, two women – Angela Richards and Lewena Thompson – and two men – Kirk Gordon and Matthew James – were shot dead by members of the police Crime Management Unit in disputed circumstances in Crawle. According to the police, the four were killed in an exchange of fire after officers approached a house. Local residents who said they witnessed the incident stated that the two men were killed immediately when the police opened fire on the house without provocation, and that the two women were subsequently killed inside the building. The eight-year-old daughter of one of the women was reportedly removed from the house by police officers before her mother was killed. Members of the local community reported being threatened by police officers following the killings. The government requested and received assistance with the investigation from the police forces of Canada, the United Kingdom and the USA. The police officers involved were reportedly removed from frontline duties.

On 25 July, 10-year-old Renee Lyons was shot dead in Majesty Gardens, Kingston. The police officer said he was firing on an unarmed youth who fled after being suspected of smoking a marijuana cigarette. Local demonstrations followed the killing. No one had been charged in relation to the killing by the end of the year.

In December, a coroner's court jury ruled that the police officers responsible for the fatal shooting of 15-year-old Jason Smith in July 2002 should be held criminally liable and charged with murder. No decision on charging the officers had been made by the Director of Public Prosecutions by the end of the year.

Impunity

There was a continuing failure to hold the perpetrators of human rights violations to account and to offer redress to victims. Investigations into alleged extrajudicial executions and other human rights violations were inadequate. In numerous instances, police allegedly failed to protect the scenes of crime after such killings and those investigating failed to arrive promptly or investigate thoroughly. Although police officers were occasionally charged with offences related to human rights violations, no officer was known to have been convicted of such offences.

However, in November the Director of Public Prosecutions announced that charges would be filed against six of the police officers involved in the killing of seven young men in Braeton in 2001. In March 2003, AI had released a report examining the killing of the seven and the subsequent investigation. The report concluded that the evidence overwhelmingly indicated that the seven had been extrajudicially executed. The government accused the report of being "damaging, offensive and a broadside against what Jamaica stands for" and said that AI had "consistently sought to impugn the government and the police in its reports." An AI delegation that included a firearms crime scene expert found potential new evidence at the scene of the killing, a summary of which was presented to the government.

In May, the authorities announced the disbandment of the Crime Management Unit, a police unit that had been implicated in numerous alleged extrajudicial executions, including the killings of the Braeton Seven and the four people in Crawle.

In May a judicial review of the Director of Public Prosecution's decision not to prosecute the police officers involved in the 1999 killing of Patrick Genius

ruled that there was no basis to interfere with the decision. A coroner's court had earlier found that the police should be held criminally responsible for the killing. The family of Patrick Genius lodged an appeal against the judicial review's decision.

The government announced several measures that would strengthen the investigation into police killings, including undertakings to improve the autopsies on those killed by the police and to reduce the backlog for coroner's court inquires into police killings. To AI's knowledge such proposals had not been implemented by the end of the year.

In July AI issued a report calling for a fresh inquiry in line with international standards into the killing of 27 people during an operation headed by the Crime Management Unit in Tivoli Gardens in July 2001. The government alleged that the report would give "succour and comfort" to criminals and said that the failure of witnesses to come forward to testify at the inquiry suggested that they had no credible story to tell.

In December new policies were introduced by the police force to make senior officers more accountable for the actions of those under their command and to improve the investigation of fatal shootings. This followed the announcement of new rules on the use of deadly force in September.

Detention without trial

Many detainees continued to be held for long periods without trial. Among them were detainees held for up to 28 years who had been declared unfit to plead.

Three detainees who had been declared unfit to plead and held for many years without trial were released in October – Errol Campbell, detained for 24 years on a charge of shooting with intent; Roy Williams, detained for 11 years on a charge of wounding with intent; and Gladstone Ricketts, detained for 28 years on a charge of murder. The Independent Jamaica Council for Human Rights, a non-governmental organization that submitted appeals to the courts to free the three men, estimated that there were approximately 100 other similar cases that were effectively lost in the system. Following the release of the three men, the prison authorities announced a review of the cases of all prisoners who had been declared unfit to plead and had identified 70 such cases by the end of the year.

Torture and ill-treatment in detention

Conditions in prison and other places of detention were harsh and in many cases amounted to cruel, inhuman and degrading treatment. Severe overcrowding was commonplace. The Tower Street Correctional Centre and the St Catherine Correction Centre both reportedly housed at least twice the number of prisoners for which they were originally built. Many prisoners were forced to share small cells and to defecate and urinate in buckets in their cell.

Tuberculosis was present in at least one prison, Tamarind Prison, causing it to be closed to new prisoners for several months.

In September, two prison guards were dismissed after being found guilty of beating prisoners in the

Horizon Remand Centre. To AI's knowledge no criminal charges were brought against the officers involved.

Death penalty

At least three people were sentenced to death, bringing to at least 40 the number of people on death row. No executions took place. There were numerous calls for the reintroduction of hanging from various sections of society.

In June the Court of Appeal freed Dwight Denton, who had been sentenced to death in 2001 for murder. Records from his employer showed he was at work on the day of the crime, as he had always maintained, and could not have taken part in the killings. The court ordered retrials of his two co-defendants, who had also been sentenced to death.

In September the Court of Appeal freed Randall Dixon who had been sentenced to death in 1998 for the murder of a police officer during a bank robbery. The court heard that the prosecution had withheld a videotape of the robbers escaping from the bank that showed that Randall Dixon was not among them. His co-defendant was also freed.

AI country reports/ visits

Reports

- Jamaica: The killing of the Braeton Seven – a justice system on trial (AI Index: AMR 38/005/2003)
- Jamaica: "...Until their voices are heard..." – The West Kingston Commission of Inquiry (AI Index: AMR 38/010/2003)

Visits

In March an AI delegation visited Jamaica and met the Attorney General, Minister of National Security and Minister of Foreign Affairs to discuss concerns about impunity for the police.

In May AI sent a pathologist to observe the autopsies of the four people killed in Crawle on 7 May.

MEXICO

UNITED MEXICAN STATES
Head of state and government: Vicente Fox Quesada
Death penalty: abolitionist for ordinary crimes
UN Women's Convention and its Optional Protocol: ratified

The Mexican government maintained its commitment to protect and promote human rights. However, its initiatives were insufficient to stem frequent and widespread human rights violations. Structural flaws in the criminal justice system remained a key source of human rights violations and impunity. The authorities made commitments to end the continuing murders and abductions of women in Ciudad Juárez and Chihuahua. At least one human rights defender was murdered and others received threats. Several social activists faced criminal charges that were reported to be politically motivated. A Supreme Court ruling potentially opened the way to the prosecution of officials responsible for past "disappearances". Many indigenous communities continued to suffer marginalization and violence. The UN published a diagnostic of the human rights situation in Mexico to serve as the basis for a governmental National Human Rights Programme.

Background

President Fox's administration continued to play a leading role in promoting respect for human rights in initiatives at the UN and the Organization of American States (OAS), and to engage openly with international human rights organizations.

In May the President established the Government Policy Commission on Human Rights to coordinate federal government human rights policies and initiatives. Human rights non-governmental organizations (NGOs) participated in the work of the Commission and seven sub-commissions dealing with a range of issues, including the harmonization of domestic legislation with international human rights standards and the development of measures to end the murders and abductions of women in Ciudad Juárez.

Elections for the lower chamber of Congress increased the government's dependence on opposition votes. Anti-discrimination legislation was passed in June. Limited constitutional reform to enable Mexico to ratify the Rome Statute of the International Criminal Court was awaiting approval from the lower chamber and state congresses.

Nevertheless, urgently needed structural reforms to end human rights violations, particularly at state level, by the prosecution services, police and military did not take place. Weaknesses in the judiciary and the network of Human Rights Ombudsman's Offices meant that by and large they were unable to provide effective oversight to prevent and punish abuses.

In its 10th year the North American Free Trade Agreement (NAFTA) continued to have a significant impact on Mexico's economy. The year started with demonstrations by peasant farmers against NAFTA's removal of import tariffs on certain agricultural products, but failed to change government policy. Peasant farmers and other sectors mobilized in October to protest outside World Trade Organization talks in Cancun.

Violence against women

The pattern of abductions and murders of women continued in the cities of Ciudad Juárez and Chihuahua, Chihuahua State. There were repeated reports of negligent investigations by the local authorities, of suspects being tortured, and of harassment and smear campaigns against relatives of victims and NGOs campaigning for justice. Under intense international and national pressure, the federal authorities announced a range of security and justice measures to tackle the crimes. In October the President appointed a Commissioner to coordinate these initiatives. In March the Inter-American Commission on Human Rights (IACHR) published a report on the killings. In November the National Human Rights Commission also issued a report and recommendations.

⌷ In March, 16-year-old Viviana Rayas was abducted in Chihuahua and subsequently murdered. The authorities failed to investigate adequately her abduction until the remains of a body were found in May. A man and a woman were arrested shortly afterwards, but subsequently filed complaints of torture. Witnesses also said they had been tortured to make them implicate the two suspects. The authorities denied flaws in their response to the abduction or gathering of evidence.

Arbitrary detention and torture

In May the UN Committee against Torture published its report on a five-year investigation into torture in Mexico. The report stated that incidents of torture "are not exceptional situations or occasional violations committed by a few police officers but that, on the contrary, the police commonly use torture and resort to it systematically as another method of criminal investigation".

Legal aid defence lawyers, prosecutors and judges frequently failed to prevent the admission as evidence of information obtained under torture in criminal proceedings, particularly at state level. An extensive study by Physicians for Human Rights of torture at state and federal level demonstrated that the scale of the problem continued to be much larger than official statistics presented. The federal Attorney General's Office formally adopted international standards for the documentation of medical evidence of torture, but the independence of the investigating agency in such cases was not guaranteed.

⌷ In September, four indigenous Totanac men from Huehuetla municipality, Puebla State, were detained and reportedly tortured by state judicial police to force them to confess to a murder. The authorities reportedly opened an investigation into the allegations of torture.

There were a number of reports of unlawful killings by police and at least one possible "disappearance".

⌷ Marcelino Santiago Pacheco, last seen leaving his home in Oaxaca City on 27 April, was feared to have "disappeared". He had allegedly been tortured by the security forces in 1997 and detained with scores of members of the indigenous community of Loxicha. He was reportedly to give evidence of human rights violations against members of the Loxicha community to an inquiry.

Human rights defenders

At least one human rights defender was murdered, and others received threats or were subjected to smear campaigns. Those working in local communities were most vulnerable to hostility from state authorities, although the federal authorities provided some protection in a number of cases.

⌷ Lawyer Griselda Tirado Evangelio was gunned down outside her home in Huehuetla, Puebla State, on 6 August. She was a member of the *Organización Independiente Totonaca* (OIT), Totonaca Independent Organization, which defends the rights of indigenous communities in Puebla's Sierra Norte region.

⌷ In July a Special Prosecutor assigned to investigate the death of human rights lawyer Digna Ochoa in 2001 concluded that she had committed suicide. The case was officially closed, despite the failure to correct or account for serious deficiencies in the initial investigation identified by the IACHR.

Politically motivated criminal charges

Human rights defenders and social activists continued to face politically motivated criminal charges, particularly at state level where local prosecutors and judges remained subordinate to the executive.

⌷ In March Isidro Baldenegro and Hermenegildo Rivas Carrillo, who led peaceful opposition to illegal logging within the indigenous Coloradas de la Virgen community in the Sierra Tarahumara in Chihuahua, were detained by the state police and charged with illegal possession of arms and marijuana. Numerous witnesses testified that the police had planted the evidence and that the prosecution was politically motivated. Their trial verdict was pending. The two men were prisoners of conscience.

⌷ In November a federal court ordered the release of indigenous leader Julio Sandoval Cruz, who had served two years of a five-year prison sentence in Ensenada, Baja California, for his role in a land dispute.

Impunity

The Special Prosecutor for past human rights violations, appointed in 2002, made limited progress in holding to account those responsible for human rights violations from the 1960s to the 1980s. In November Zacarías Barrientos, a key witness to cases in Guerrero, was murdered, raising fears for the safety of other witnesses. The Supreme Court made two important rulings against impunity.

⌷ In April a judge in Nuevo León refused an arrest warrant for officials accused of kidnapping Jesús Piedra

Ibarra in 1976 on the grounds that the crime had passed the statute of limitations. In November the Supreme Court reversed the decision, ruling that such crimes are continuous until the abducted person reappears, in line with international standards against "disappearances". The Special Prosecutor subsequently issued at least three arrest warrants for a number of former officials implicated in "disappearances".

◻ In June the Supreme Court confirmed the extradition to Spain of former Argentine naval captain Ricardo Miguel Cavallo, to face charges of genocide and "terrorism", setting an important precedent for universal jurisdiction. However, contrary to international law prohibiting statutes of limitation for crimes against humanity, the Supreme Court excluded charges of torture amounting to crimes against humanity, based on a Mexican statute of limitations for torture.

The civilian courts continued to forward allegations of human rights violations by military personnel to the military prosecutor and courts, ensuring impunity and denying victims the right to justice. A Supreme Court ruling was still awaited on the constitutionality of Mexico's reservation to the Inter-American Convention on Forced Disappearance of Persons.

◻ In May a federal court denied an appeal by Valentina Rozenda Cantú, an indigenous woman from the community of Barranca Bejuco, Acatepec municipality in Guerrero, who was reportedly raped by military personnel in 2002, for her case to be heard by the civilian courts. The judge's decision to recognize military jurisdiction guaranteed that the case would not be impartially investigated.

Indigenous peoples
In June the UN Special Rapporteur on the situation of the human rights and fundamental freedoms of indigenous people visited six states – including Chiapas, Oaxaca and Guerrero – where discrimination, marginalization and community conflicts continued to give rise to multiple human rights violations. The Special Rapporteur urged the resumption of negotiations with the *Ejército Zapatista de Liberación Nacional* (EZLN), Zapatista National Liberation Army, in Chiapas, and the reform of controversial 2001 indigenous rights legislation which failed to fulfil commitments made in the 1996 peace negotiations. There was continued concern that the regional development plan, *Plan Puebla Panamá*, threatened indigenous communities in southern Mexico as infrastructure and development projects risked undermining their economic, social and cultural rights.

◻ In June local human rights organizations opposed the threatened eviction of up to 42 indigenous settlements in the Montes Azules Biodiversity Reserve in Chiapas, on the grounds that communities had not been adequately consulted and the measures were intended to encourage private investment, not protect the environment.

National Human Rights Programme
In December the Office of the UN High Commissioner for Human Rights presented President Fox with an extensive diagnostic on the human rights situation, including specific legislative and non-legislative recommendations for structurally reforming the state to effectively guarantee human rights. The unprecedented diagnostic, which was carried out by four national experts in consultation with civil society, was part of the second phase of the Technical Cooperation Agreement with the UN. This committed the government to drawing up and implementing a National Human Rights Programme in the following months on the basis of the diagnostic.

AI country reports/visits
Reports
- Mexico: Unfair trials – unsafe convictions (AI Index: AMR 41/007/2003)
- Mexico: Intolerable killings – 10 years of abductions and murders of women in Ciudad Juárez and Chihuahua (AI Index: AMR 41/026/2003)
- Mexico: Prisoners of conscience – indigenous environmental activists (AI Index: AMR 41/051/2003)

Visits
In August AI Secretary General Irene Khan visited Mexico and met President Fox and senior government officials. Also in August, AI held its biennial International Council Meeting and a Youth Conference in Cocoyoc, Morelos State.

NICARAGUA

REPUBLIC OF NICARAGUA
Head of state and government: Enrique Bolaños
Death penalty: abolitionist for all crimes
UN Women's Convention: ratified
Optional Protocol to UN Women's Convention: not signed

Members of the National Police were responsible for ill-treatment. Children were victims of human rights violations, including sexual abuse and trafficking. A member of the judiciary was threatened as a result of her professional activities.

Background
Economic conditions did not improve generally for the mass of Nicaraguans who live in extreme poverty. Peasants and other sectors of society organized marches towards the capital, Managua, to call attention to their living conditions. There were several deaths as a result of long marches and lack of food; children were among the dead.

In June the government signed an impunity agreement with the USA providing that Nicaragua will not surrender US nationals accused of genocide, crimes against humanity or war crimes to the International Criminal Court (ICC). The agreement, which breaches Nicaragua's obligations under international law, had not been ratified at the end of the year. Nicaragua has not signed the Rome Statute of the ICC.

Human rights violations by National Police members

Members of the National Police were involved in the ill-treatment of people in their custody. The image of the National Police was also tarnished by the involvement of some officers in illegal activities including drug trafficking.

⛶ In May, Saturnino Varela Escalante died as a result of being kicked by a police officer who had arrested him. The victim, who was reportedly disorderly at the time of arrest, was kicked in a police vehicle. By the time he arrived at the police station he was having difficulty breathing. He was taken to hospital but was pronounced dead on arrival. A post-mortem found that the cause of death was rupture of the heart's right auricle. The police officer who kicked Saturnino Varela Escalante went into hiding.

Children

The rape and subsequent pregnancy of a nine-year-old girl provoked national debate about violence against girls and reproductive rights. Sexual violence and trafficking of children were widely reported. Children, as well as women, were victims of domestic violence.

⛶ In February a nine-year-old Nicaraguan girl was raped in Costa Rica where her parents were working in the agricultural sector. She became pregnant. The family returned to Nicaragua where the case generated heated debates about abortion, which was being advocated in her case in view of her age and the danger for her physical and psychological well-being but strongly opposed by the Church. The abortion was eventually carried out. A 22-year-old man was arrested in Costa Rica but later conditionally released.

Other girls, some as young as seven, were raped by family members or others.

Update: threats against judge

Judge Juana Méndez, in charge of the case against former President Arnoldo Alemán, reportedly received further threats following her decision that he should be transferred from house arrest to prison. Death threats against her seven brothers were made by unidentified men in August. Judge Méndez had been under police protection because of previous threats against her and her family. Arnoldo Alemán was on trial on charges including fraud, embezzlement and electoral crimes. He persisted unsuccessfully with attempts to claim immunity from prosecution. In August he was moved from house arrest to a cell in the headquarters of the National Police in Managua but later sent back to house arrest because of health problems. In December he was found guilty and sentenced to 20 years in prison and a heavy fine. He submitted an appeal against the conviction.

PARAGUAY

REPUBLIC OF PARAGUAY
Head of state and government: Nicanor Duarte Frutos (replaced Luis Angel González Macchi in August)
Death penalty: abolitionist for all crimes
UN Women's Convention and its Optional Protocol: ratified

There were continued reports of torture and ill-treatment of criminal suspects and army conscripts and of excessive use of force by the security forces during demonstrations. There were limited advances in criminal investigations into cases of torture committed by the security forces. A law was passed to set up a Truth and Justice Commission to document human rights violations committed under the government of General Alfredo Stroessner (1954-1989).

Background

Attempts to impeach outgoing President Luis Angel González Macchi, accused of corruption, failed when Congress voted against the measure. The government of President Nicanor Duarte Frutos took office in August.

In April, former Vice-President Angel Roberto Seifart and 18 others were cleared of involvement in the killing of at least seven students during anti-government demonstrations in March 1999; eight other people, including two senators, were sentenced to prison terms ranging from six months to five years. In October, charges against 68 members of the armed forces accused of involvement in the March 1999 killings and an attempted coup in May 2000 were reportedly dropped after the time period stipulated by the statute of limitations expired.

Excessive use of force by the security forces

According to reports, peasant farmer and trade union demonstrations continued to be met with excessive use of force by the police.

⛶ In August, Cástulo Manuel Riveros Garay was reportedly shot dead by police agents during a strike by municipal workers in the Zeballos Cué district of Asunción. Police denied responsibility in the killing.

⛶ In October, Miguel Peralta, a landless peasant farmer, was killed and several other peasant farmers injured, reportedly by the security forces, during an attempt to evict landless peasant farmers from the Santa Bárbara farm in Hernandarias. Several members of the security forces were also injured in the operation.

Torture and ill-treatment

There were continued reports of torture and ill-treatment of criminal suspects.

⛶ In May, police agents in Santa Lucía de Villarica, Guairá Department, reportedly forced entry into

Pascual Trinidad's home, accused him of theft, placed a plastic bag over his head and beat him. No information had been received by the end of the year regarding criminal investigations into this case.

⬠ In July, two police agents accused former Interior Minister Walter Bower, police commanders Humberto Núñez Aguero and Merardo Palacios, and police officer Osvaldo Vera of being involved in their torture following the May 2000 coup attempt. In November criminal proceedings against the accused reportedly stalled.

Prisons

Prison conditions continued to be of concern with reports of serious overcrowding. In September, Justice and Labour Minister Juan Darío Monges made commitments to reform the prison system. Several detainees died, reportedly as a result of excessive use of force by prison guards.

⬠ On 26 April, 18-year-old Víctor Javier Lugo died and another youth was injured when prison guards at the Itaguá juvenile detention centre allegedly opened fire on the youths as they tried to escape. No information had been received by the end of the year regarding investigations into the killing.

Torture and ill-treatment of conscripts

There were continued reports of ill-treatment of army conscripts.

⬠ Four conscripts belonging to the First Cavalry Division based in Pozo Colorado, Chaco Department, alleged in May that they had been ill-treated. Another soldier belonging to the Cuguaty First Army Corps testified before a judge that he had been tortured and raped by an officer. Judicial authorities were reportedly investigating both cases at the end of the year.

No significant advances were reported in investigations into the deaths of the more than 100 young conscripts who had died since 1989. In October, the Inter-American Commission on Human Rights accepted a request to investigate the "disappearance" of two underage conscripts, Marcelino Gómez and Cristian Ariel Núñez, in 1998 in Chaco Department.

Impunity

The Office of the Attorney General failed to press charges against members of the armed forces in relation to the killing of José "Coco" Villar on 2 July 1999. The reason given was lack of evidence, although the officer in command of the security operation during which José Villar was killed was known to the authorities and had been implicated in the killing of Vice-President Luis María Argaña earlier that year.

Few advances were made in criminal investigations into the alleged torture of Anuncio Martí and Juan Arrom in 2002. In November, legal proceedings against two police officers and a judicial investigator were suspended.

On 16 October, a court in Asunción reissued a judicial order for the arrest of the former President, General Stroessner, in exile in Brazil, and former Interior Minister Sabino Augusto Montanaro, in exile in

Honduras, to face charges for their alleged involvement in the torture and killing of Celestina Pérez in 1974 while in police detention.

In October, a law was passed creating a Truth and Justice Commission to examine human rights violations under the Stroessner government. The Commission had not been established by the end of the year.

Also in October, the government informed the US authorities that it would not sign an impunity agreement not to surrender US nationals accused of genocide, crimes against humanity and war crimes to the International Criminal Court. Such agreements are in breach of states' obligations under international law.

Concerns continued to be expressed over the failure of the state to pay compensation to victims of human rights violations committed under the Stroessner government. In August, the new Procurator General declared that he would appeal to the Supreme Court to make payments possible.

PERU

REPUBLIC OF PERU
Head of state and government: Alejandro Toledo Manrique
Death penalty: abolitionist for ordinary crimes
UN Women's Convention and its Optional Protocol: ratified

The Truth and Reconciliation Commission presented its final report to the President. "Anti-terrorism" legislation, which had rendered all trials unfair since 1992, was ruled unconstitutional and reforms were introduced. Scores of prisoners of conscience remained in jail. Prison conditions remained harsh.

Background

Opinion polls continued to reveal widespread public discontent with government economic policies. According to the Peruvian Institute of Statistics, over half the population was living in poverty.

A 30-day state of emergency was declared in May in response to nationwide strikes and protests by the teachers' union and other unions demanding higher salaries. The state of emergency restricted the rights to personal security and freedom of movement and assembly, and allowed the authorities to enter a home without a search warrant. In the department of Puno scores of protesters against the state of emergency clashed with security forces. One student died and scores were injured reportedly in circumstances suggesting that the security forces used excessive force to disperse protesters.

The post of Ombudsman was not permanently filled; an interim Ombudsman had been in place since February 2001. Critics said there was an apparent lack of political will to establish a strong Office of the Ombudsman.

Truth and Reconciliation Commission

The Truth and Reconciliation Commission, set up in 2001 to establish the circumstances surrounding human rights abuses committed by the state and by armed opposition groups between May 1980 and November 2000, delivered its final report in August. The Commission concluded that of the estimated 69,000 people who were killed or had "disappeared" during the 20 years, 54 per cent of the cases were the responsibility of the armed opposition group Shining Path and 46 per cent were the responsibility of armed forces. The Commission also concluded that three quarters of the victims were Quechua native speakers, reflecting "the discrimination and marginalization against the Andean rural population which is impregnated in Peruvian society".

The Commission stated that justice was an essential element of reconciliation, and said that it had submitted to the Public Ministry the identity of 24,000 victims in order that justice could be achieved. The Commission also stated that "an ethically healthy and politically viable country cannot be built on the foundations of impunity". Its recommendations included proposals for institutional reform, an integrated plan for reparations, and a national plan for forensic anthropological interventions in light of the 4,644 burial sites the Commission had recorded, as well as measures to ensure that its recommendations were implemented.

In response, President Alejandro Toledo apologized in the name of the state to "all those who suffered". He announced that he would spend approximately US$800 million on a Peace and Development Plan which would improve public works in the areas most affected and strengthen state institutions and civil society. He did not, however, offer the individual reparations that victims and their relatives had sought. On the issue of impunity the President was criticized for stating that "some members of the security forces had committed painful excesses" and for not accepting that human rights violations committed by the security forces were widespread and systematic, as the Truth and Reconciliation Commission had concluded. The President did insist that it was now the task of the Public Ministry and the judiciary to implement justice in these cases "without protecting either impunity or abuse".

'Anti-terrorism' legislation

In January the Constitutional Tribunal ruled that life imprisonment and the use of military courts to try civilians were unconstitutional. The executive then issued a series of decree laws to conform with this ruling. The decree laws annulled the sentences handed down by military courts for the crime of "treason" and ordered that all those tried before military courts be retried in civilian courts. The decree laws also ordered the retrial of all those tried between 1992 and 1997 by "faceless judges" (judges whose identities were kept secret) and modified the length of sentences applied under the "anti-terrorism" legislation. After this ruling some political prisoners were retried in public hearings before ordinary courts. There were still serious concerns that the definition of the crime of "terrorism" in the legislation remained too wide and vague, and that although life imprisonment was reduced to 30 years, the possibility of release after 30 years was subject to review.

Prisoners of conscience

Scores of prisoners of conscience and possible prisoners of conscience falsely charged with "terrorism-related" offences remained in jail. A special commission within the Ministry of Justice that was established to review these cases was effectively suspended after it was announced that all those tried before military courts and "faceless judges" would be retried. There were serious concerns that instead of immediately and unconditionally releasing these prisoners, they would be retried within a judicial system that was slow and inefficient and were therefore likely to spend many more years in prison.

Harsh prison conditions

Conditions in maximum security prisons, where those charged with "terrorism-related" offences were held, continued to be harsh and in some cases amounted to cruel, inhuman and degrading treatment. In February the Inter-American Commission on Human Rights again called on the authorities to close Challapalca prison, which is at more than 4,600 metres above sea level and is extremely cold. The inaccessibility of the prison seriously limits prisoners' rights to maintain contact with the outside world, including with relatives, lawyers and doctors. The Inter-American Commission also called for the high security prison of Yanamayo in Puno department to be closed; the prison was reopened in January after undergoing building works.

Human rights defenders and journalists under attack

There were reports of threats and intimidation against human rights defenders in Lima, the capital, and against journalists who opposed the local government in the province of Canchis.

Torture

Torture and ill-treatment by security officials remained a concern, and there continued to be few investigations into alleged incidents.

◻ In November a public prosecutor invoked the statute of limitations to close the investigation into the case of Luis Alberto Cantoral Benavides, who was tortured in 1993. He argued that the time limit under the statute of limitations for prosecution of the crimes of grave bodily harm and abuse of authority had expired. The Penal Code was not amended to include torture as a specific crime until 1998. In December the Inter-American Court of Human Rights ruled that Peru could not invoke the statute of limitations to avoid complying with the Court's rulings in this case. The Court had ruled in 2000 that Peru had violated, among other things, the right to humane treatment and the right to personal liberty. It had also ruled in 2000 and 2001 that the authorities should investigate the case, bring the perpetrators to justice and offer reparation to the victim and his relatives. The Inter-American Court ordered Peru to present by April 2004 a report detailing the steps it has taken to implement the Court's 2000 and 2001 rulings.

Update on 1996 alleged extrajudicial executions

The military court that heard the case of 15 military officers charged with extrajudicially executing members of the armed opposition group *Movimiento Revolucionario Túpac Amaru* (MRTA – Túpac Amaru Revolutionary Movement) ruled that there was no case to answer. There were serious concerns that military courts were neither independent nor impartial. Relatives of the victims appealed against the court's ruling. The MRTA members had broken into the residence of the Japanese Ambassador in December 1996 and taken hostages. The hostage crisis ended in April 1997 when the then President, Alberto Fujimori, ordered a military assault. All 14 MRTA hostage-takers were killed, leading to allegations that some may have been extrajudicially executed.

Abuses by the armed opposition

Small groups of Shining Path reportedly continued to operate in some areas. In June members of Shining Path kidnapped more than 60 workers of the Argentine firm Techint near the town of Toccate, some 350 kilometres southeast of the capital, where they were building a natural gas pipeline. The workers were released 36 hours later.

There were reports of Shining Path members threatening human rights defenders in Tabalosos, Requena province.

Tambogrande: social and economic rights under threat

The local population of the district of Tambogrande in the northern department of Piura continued to express fears that the possible mining activities in the area by a Canadian mining company would result in contamination of the water and soil and endanger crops, fears the mining company said had been disproved in an environmental impact study it had carried out. The area produces 40 per cent of Peru's mango and citrus crops. Local human rights organizations urged the authorities not to approve the company's impact study on the grounds that the project would endanger the environment and therefore threaten the social and economic rights of the local population. The authorities had not made a decision by the end of the year. In 2002 a neighbourhood poll organized by the municipality and the population of

Tambogrande resulted in an overwhelming rejection of the mining plans.

Former President Fujimori: extradition request

In July, the government submitted an extradition request to the Japanese authorities for former President Alberto Fujimori on charges of human rights violations and corruption. The Japanese authorities had not made a decision by the end of the year.

AI country reports/visits
Reports
- Peru: The "anti-terrorism" legislation and its effects – an unfinished business in the transition to democracy (AI Index: AMR 46/001/03)
- Peru: Letter to the President in support of the work of the Truth and Reconciliation Commission (AI Index: AMR 46/011/2003)

PUERTO RICO

COMMONWEALTH OF PUERTO RICO
Head of state: George W. Bush
Head of government: Sila María Calderón Serra
Death penalty: abolitionist for all crimes

The USA stopped using the island of Vieques as a military training ground, thereby ending three years of protest outside the US naval base there. Puerto Rico's sodomy law was effectively voided by a US Supreme Court ruling.

Background

The US government stopped using Vieques (an island off the east coast of Puerto Rico) as a military training area on 1 May. Vieques had been used as a US naval base and training ground for more than 50 years but had been dogged by protests since 1999 when naval bombing exercises accidentally killed a civilian security guard.

No information was available regarding the outcome of a complaint filed with the US Justice Department alleging that the navy used excessive force against demonstrators at the Vieques base in April 2002. It was alleged that US marines had bombarded peaceful demonstrators with tear gas and pepper spray, causing several injuries. The navy had denied using excessive force.

Legal reform

A Puerto Rico law which criminalizes consensual sexual relationships between men was effectively voided by a US Supreme Court ruling in June. The ruling – given in a Texas case but applying to all state and commonwealth laws – held that anti-sodomy laws which made private sexual conduct a crime violated gay men's rights to privacy and liberty under the US Constitution.

Federal death penalty
In July the first death penalty trial in Puerto Rico for more than 75 years ended in acquittal for the two defendants. Héctor Oscar Acosta Martínez and Joel Rivera Alejandro had been charged under the 1994 Federal Death Penalty Act with the 1998 abduction and murder of Jorge Hernández Díaz, a grocer. The US government's pursuit of the death penalty in the case had sparked protests in Puerto Rico which has been abolitionist since 1929.

Puerto Rico's 1952 Constitution defines the island as a self-governing commonwealth and also enshrines the abolitionist statement: "the death penalty shall not exist." Lawyers for Héctor Oscar Acosta Martínez and Joel Rivera Alejandro challenged the federal government's decision to seek death sentences against their clients. In 2000, a US District Court judge ruled that the death penalty could not be an option in the case, noting that Puerto Ricans have no vote in US presidential elections and have only a single non-voting representative in Congress. However, in June 2001 the US Court of Appeals for the First Circuit overturned the District Court's decision. It held that the federal death penalty could apply in Puerto Rico, and that the US government could pursue death sentences against Héctor Oscar Acosta Martínez and Joel Rivera Alejandro.

SURINAME

REPUBLIC OF SURINAME
Head of state: Ronald Venetiaan
Head of government: Jules Ajodhia
Death penalty: abolitionist in practice
UN Women's Convention: ratified
Optional Protocol to UN Women's Convention: not signed

Impunity for killings committed under military rule in the 1980s continued to be a major issue. Also of concern were reports of police brutality.

Background
President Ronald Venetiaan reportedly put the government and security forces on a security alert in the run-up to the 25 February anniversary of the military coup in 1980 which brought Desi Bouterse to power. In July, the National Democratic Party (NDP) formally nominated Desi Bouterse as its presidential candidate for the 2005 elections. Meanwhile, Desi

Bouterse's son was accused of leading a raid on a weapons depot in July 2002 in which assault rifles and other equipment were said to have been stolen. When the case was brought to trial, the robbery charges against him were dropped, and he was released pending trial on weapons charges.

In March the UN Committee on the Elimination of Racial Discrimination noted a number of violations of the rights of indigenous communities including discrimination, lack of recognition of their rights to land and resources, and failure to consult them about forestry and mining concessions affecting their environment.

In June the USA included Suriname on a list of countries accused of insufficient efforts to comply with minimum standards for combating human trafficking. The report described trafficking of women and children, primarily for prostitution. In July, the Minister of Justice and Police announced the formation of a commission to study the question.

Impunity
1982 'December murders'
The investigation continued into the 1982 "December murders" in which 15 journalists, academics and labour leaders were extrajudicially executed at Fort Zeelandia, an army centre in Paramaribo. The homes of the Minister of Justice and Police and of the investigating judge were broken into in early 2003 and documents relating to the case were reportedly taken from their respective houses. A suspect was arrested, although no information on the motive for the burglaries or their possible relation to the investigation was known to have been made public.
1986 Moiwana massacre
The Inter-American Court of Human Rights review of the 1986 Moiwana massacre case, submitted to the Court's jurisdiction by the Inter-American Commission on Human Rights in December 2002, began. The petition regarding the November 1986 massacre, in which 35 people, mostly women and children, were killed during an attack by a specialized military unit, was brought by the non-governmental organization Moiwana '86.

Allegation of police brutality
Three men, reportedly suspected of embezzlement, were allegedly beaten with batons in the Nieuwe Haven police station on 18 May. Several days later, the public prosecutor announced that the case would be investigated; it is not known whether an investigation had been initiated at the end of the year.

AI country reports/ visits
Report
• Suriname: Government commitments and human rights (AI Index: AMR 48/001/2003)

TRINIDAD AND TOBAGO

REPUBLIC OF TRINIDAD AND TOBAGO
Head of state: George Maxwell Richards (replaced Arthur Napoleon Raymond Robinson in March)
Head of government: Patrick Manning
Death penalty: retentionist
UN Women's Convention: ratified with reservations
Optional Protocol to UN Women's Convention: not signed

There were continuing reports of torture and ill-treatment by the police and army, sometimes resulting in death. Death sentences continued to be imposed; no executions were carried out. Conditions in places of detention continued to cause concern.

Abuses by police

Torture and ill-treatment by police continued to be reported.

In February, Varune Matthew was awarded TT$30,000 (approximately US$5,000) in compensation; he had been beaten by police officers and left bleeding and semi-conscious in November 2000.

In June, Aldryn Noel was shot by police officers and died of his injuries. Relatives who stated that they witnessed the incident alleged that two plainclothes police officers ran towards Aldryn Noel without identifying themselves and with guns drawn. The officers fired as Aldryn Noel fled and he was hit in the buttocks. The relatives further alleged that the police officers refused to allow Aldryn Noel to be taken to hospital or to call an ambulance and left him without medical attention for over 30 minutes before a neighbour was allowed to take him to hospital, where he later died.

In September, Shaun McLeod died shortly after being taken into custody by police officers. An autopsy reportedly found that he died from bleeding in the brain caused by a blow to the head with a blunt object. Junior St Clair, an eyewitness to the incident, alleged that he too was assaulted and threatened by police in an attempt to prevent him from making a statement in connection with the death of Shaun McLeod. A police officer was charged with manslaughter in connection with Shaun McLeod's death, but had not been tried by the end of the year.

Death penalty

Courts continued to impose death sentences during 2003; at least six men were sentenced to death during the year. More than 80 men and four women remained on death row at the end of 2003. No executions were carried out. In January, the government announced it was drafting new legislation to facilitate the resumption of executions, but no new laws relating to the death penalty had been passed by the end of the year.

In November, the Judicial Committee of the Privy Council in the United Kingdom, the highest court of appeal for Trinidad and Tobago, ruled in the case of Balkissoon Roodal that the mandatory death penalty was in violation of the Constitution. Prior to the ruling, the death penalty was the only available sentence for those convicted of murder. Following the ruling, judges will be required to consider further evidence on whether execution is the appropriate sentence and all those under sentence of death will be granted new sentencing hearings.

Abuses in detention

Conditions in places of detention continued to cause grave concern and in some cases amounted to cruel, inhuman and degrading treatment. Many prisoners lacked the most basic facilities to ensure hygiene. Reports of inmate-upon-inmate violence continued, including some of a sexual nature. A new maximum security prison designed to alleviate prison overcrowding was opened, although security and sewage problems delayed the transfer of some 1,600 prisoners to the facility.

In June, Michael Bullock, a prisoner at the maximum security prison, alleged that he was severely beaten by prison guards, resulting in severe injuries including a broken jaw. He claimed he was initially denied adequate medical treatment and was kept in solitary confinement.

The trial of the prison officers charged with the murder of detainee Anton Cooper in 2002 had not begun by the end of 2003.

Corporal punishment

Sentences of corporal punishment continued to be imposed by the courts. It was not known if any sentences of corporal punishment were carried out during the year.

In December, brothers Winty and Keith Roberts were sentenced to terms of imprisonment and 15 and 10 strokes with a birch respectively for rape and other offences.

Violence against women

Violence against women in the home and community was reported to be widespread. There were numerous reports of women being beaten, raped and killed in the home and incest continued to be a major area of concern. More cases were brought before the courts. However, the system of evidence taking and the court system remained hostile to victims, resulting in fewer perpetrators being brought to justice. The disbanding of the Community Policing Division was reported to be a major contributor to this problem. The authorities responded to the situation by collaborating with non-governmental organizations, but this was constrained by limited funding and a continued lack of coordination between services. Services such as shelters, counselling and support for victims and perpetrators remained inadequate. Mediation centres closed and magistrates and judges remained insufficiently aware of and unresponsive to issues related to violence against women.

AI country reports/ visits
Visit
In November an AI delegation met with the minister responsible for prisons and the Attorney General.

UNITED STATES OF AMERICA

UNITED STATES OF AMERICA
Head of state and government: George W. Bush
Death penalty: retentionist
UN Women's Convention: signed
Optional Protocol to UN Women's Convention: not signed

More than 600 foreign nationals were detained indefinitely without charge or trial or access to family members or legal counsel in the US naval base in Guantánamo, Cuba, on grounds of possible links with *al-Qa'ida*; others were held in undisclosed locations. There were allegations of torture or ill-treatment of detainees held at a US base in Afghanistan and of detainees held by US forces in Iraq following the US-led invasion and occupation. Three people were held incommunicado without charge or trial in the USA as "enemy combatants". Death sentences continued to be imposed and carried out under federal and state law. There were reports of police brutality, deaths in custody and ill-treatment of prisoners.

Background
Thousands of people were detained in the context of the US-led war against Iraq and subsequent occupation of Iraq by the Coalition Provisional Authority (see Iraq entry). Others were held in US bases in Afghanistan, Cuba and elsewhere as part of the ongoing "war against terrorism". While calling for those responsible for the 11 September 2001 attacks on the World Trade Center and other crimes to be brought to justice, AI condemned the US denial of basic rights to many of those detained.

International Criminal Court
In July the USA announced that it was cutting military aid to 35 countries which had refused to enter into an impunity agreement not to surrender US nationals accused of genocide, crimes against humanity or war crimes to the International Criminal Court. Such agreements are in breach of states' obligations under international law.

Detentions outside the USA
Hundreds of detainees from around 40 countries remained in legal limbo in the US naval base in Guantánamo Bay. In April, the US authorities revealed that children as young as 13 years old were among those held at the base. None of the detainees were charged, tried, or given access to lawyers, relatives or the courts. In October, the US Supreme Court said that it would decide whether the US courts "lack jurisdiction to consider challenges to the legality" of the Guantánamo detentions, as lower federal courts had earlier held. The Supreme Court ruling was expected to be handed down in 2004. Meanwhile, in December, the Court of Appeals for the Ninth Circuit ruled that foreign nationals held as "enemy combatants" in Guantánamo Bay had a right to seek court review of the legality of their detention. The appeal judges concluded that the government position was "inconsistent with the fundamental tenets of American jurisprudence and raises serious concerns under international law". This ruling may also form part of the Supreme Court's review.

During 2003, concern continued to grow about the psychological impact on the detainees of the indefinite and isolating detention regime in Guantánamo. The International Committee of the Red Cross (ICRC), the only international non-governmental organization with access to the detainees, took the unusual step of publicly criticizing the lack of legal process and spoke of the deterioration in mental health that the organization had witnessed among large numbers of the detainees. There were numerous suicide attempts among the detainees during the year.

The US air base in Bagram, Afghanistan, continued to be used as a detention facility. There, too, detainees were denied any sort of legal process. The ICRC did not have access to all those held there. During the year, allegations were made that detainees had been tortured or ill-treated in Bagram. Former detainees interviewed by AI in Afghanistan alleged that they were subjected to prolonged enforced standing and kneeling, sleep deprivation and the cruel use of shackles. By the end of the year, the US authorities had not announced any results of the military investigation into the deaths of two Afghan men in US custody in Bagram in December 2002. Their autopsies had revealed "blunt force injuries" in both cases and gave the cause of death as "homicide". Another man died in custody in a US holding facility in Asadabad in Kunar province, Afghanistan, in June.

There were also allegations of torture and ill-treatment by US forces in Iraq (see Iraq entry). Twelve US soldiers charged with ill-treating Iraqi detainees were awaiting court martial at the end of the year.

An unknown number of prisoners continued to be held incommunicado in undisclosed locations without access to the ICRC or any sort of legal process.

There were continuing concerns about the possible transfer of prisoners to countries where it was feared they might face torture during interrogation.

Military commissions

On 3 July, the Pentagon announced that President Bush had selected six foreign detainees to be subject to the provisions of the Military Order he signed in November 2001. The Order provides for non-US nationals suspected of involvement in "international terrorism" to be held indefinitely without trial or to be tried by military commissions. The names of the six were not made public by the US authorities, but it emerged that two were United Kingdom (UK) nationals, Moazzam Begg and Feroz Abbasi, and one, David Hicks, was an Australian national. The UK and Australian authorities pursued discussions with their US counterparts over the detainees' future. In December, the Pentagon revealed that Guantánamo detainee Salim Ahmed Samdan, a Yemeni national, was among the six. By the end of the year, no detainee had been brought to trial before a military commission.

Detentions in the USA following attacks of 11 September 2001

A government watchdog agency reported in June that there had been "significant problems" in the treatment of hundreds of foreign nationals detained in the aftermath of the 11 September attacks on the Pentagon and World Trade Center. The investigation, by the Justice Department's Office of Inspector General (OIG), confirmed many of the concerns raised by AI and other groups that detainees' basic rights had been violated. Violations included denying detainees prompt access to lawyers and family members and failing to charge detainees promptly or to "clear" them for release or removal from the USA, leaving many to languish for months in detention centres despite having no connection with the attacks. The report found evidence of a "pattern of physical and verbal abuse" by some correctional officers towards some 11 September detainees.

Although most of those detained – many for minor immigration violations – in the original sweeps had been released or deported by the time of the report, the OIG made 21 recommendations to the US government to improve procedures during any similar arrests, including speedier reviews and more objective criteria in detention decisions.

US nationals Yaser Esam Hamdi and José Padilla continued to be held in military custody without charge or trial as "enemy combatants", despite their detentions being criticized as "arbitrary" by the UN Working Group on Arbitrary Detention. In January, a three-judge panel of the Fourth Circuit Court of Appeals upheld the right of the US government to detain Yaser Esam Hamdi without trial or access to an attorney. However, in December the Pentagon announced that it had decided to allow Yaser Esam Hamdi to meet with his lawyer, while stressing that this "is not required by domestic or international law and should not be treated as a precedent". The announcement came one day before the government was scheduled to file a response to an appeal to the US Supreme Court in the case.

In December the Second Circuit Court of Appeals ruled that the President did not have the power,

without authorization by Congress, "to detain as an enemy combatant an American citizen seized on American soil outside a zone of combat", and ordered José Padilla's release from military custody within 30 days. The judges said the government could then bring criminal charges against him in civilian courts or seek to have him held as a material witness, stating that "under any scenario" he would be entitled to his constitutional rights. However, José Padilla remained in incommunicado military detention at the end of the year, pending a government appeal against the court's decision. A government appeal also continued to place on hold a 2002 federal court order granting José Padilla access to a lawyer.

In July Ali-Saleh Kahlah Al-Marri, a Qatari national facing trial on criminal charges, was removed from the judicial system on the order of President Bush and designated an "enemy combatant" for alleged links to al-Qa'ida. He remained held incommunicado in military custody at the end of the year.

Some people detained for alleged links to al-Qa'ida were deported to countries where they were at risk of torture or ill-treatment. In October, AI called on the US government to hold a full inquiry into its treatment of Maher Arar, a Canadian citizen deported from the USA in October 2002 to his native Syria, where he was allegedly tortured and held for months in cruel conditions before being returned without charge to Canada.

A "special registration" program introduced in late 2002 which required boys and men aged 16 and over from 25 countries, mostly in the Middle East, to register annually with the authorities to be questioned, photographed and fingerprinted, ended in December 2003, although exit and entry registration requirements remained. The measure had been criticized by human rights groups as discriminatory. Many people who had complied with the order were detained, often for minor visa irregularities, and many continued to face deportation even though they had proceedings under way to regularize their status.

Refugees, migrants and asylum-seekers

In April the Attorney General ruled that Haitian asylum-seekers must be kept in detention, stating that the policy was necessary as a deterrent and on national security grounds. The ruling was given in the case of 18-year-old David Joseph, whose release on bail had been ordered by an immigration judge and upheld by the Board of Immigration Appeals. David Joseph was one of some 200 Haitian asylum-seekers detained in October 2002 after their boat ran aground off the Florida coast. AI urged the government to rescind the blanket detention policy, which the Attorney General said in his ruling could be applied to other groups on similar grounds, in line with international human rights and refugee standards.

There were continuing concerns about between 5,000 and 6,000 unaccompanied migrant children who, contrary to the USA's own guidelines and international standards, were detained in some cases for months. Many were held in punitive conditions alongside juvenile offenders, and subjected to humiliating treatment such as shackling and strip searches.

Ill-treatment and excessive use of force by law enforcement officials

There were reports of ill-treatment, excessive use of force by police and prison officers, and deaths in custody. Incidents included misuse of stun weapons and chemical spray. Nine people died after being struck by police Tasers. Although the cause of death was attributed to other factors or autopsy results were still pending, questions remained about the health risks of such equipment. There were continued reports of cruel conditions in prison isolation units.

▱ In September a police officer from Bayton, Texas, was charged with using unnecessary force against a disabled 59-year-old Latina woman. The officer struck Naomi Autin three times with a Taser as she knocked on her brother's door with a brick after getting no answer. The trial was pending at the end of the year.

▱ John Allen Muhammad was given an electric shock twice with a stun belt in August while in hospital in the custody of the Prince William County Sheriff Department, Virginia. The belt, which was wrapped round his arm, was activated after he refused to submit to a head X-ray by moving his head and trying to sit up while strapped to a stretcher. He allegedly suffered welts on his arm from the 50-70,000-volt shock.

▱ In October the state of Virginia paid out an undisclosed sum to the family of Larry Frazier, who died in prison in July 2000 after being repeatedly shocked with a stun gun. The Corrections Department suspended the use of the Ultron II stun gun shortly after the incident when an autopsy found it could have contributed to Larry Frazier's death.

▱ Fort Lauderdale Police Department, Florida, tightened its procedures after the Medical Examiner ruled that police use of pepper spray had contributed to the death in April of 21-year-old Raymond Sterling who suffered from sickle cell trait. The new procedures provided that anyone pepper sprayed or injured by police must be taken to hospital instead of jail.

▱ A lawsuit was filed against the Florida prison authorities alleging that prisoners were repeatedly sprayed with pepper spray and tear gas while trapped in their cells, causing breathing difficulties, burning and skin blisters. According to the lawsuit, chemical agents had become the most common force used in Florida prisons.

Conditions in prison isolation units, including "supermaximum security" facilities, remained extremely harsh in many states.

▱ In Unit 32 of Parchman Prison, Mississippi, nearly 1,000 prisoners, many severely mentally ill, were reportedly confined to insect-infested, insanitary cells for between 23 and 24 hours a day and were not allowed fans or sufficient water despite extreme summer heat. Litigation to improve conditions for death row prisoners in Unit 32 was being pursued at the end of the year.

There were allegations of police brutality and excessive use of force against anti-war protesters in several US cities, including Chicago, Illinois and Oakland, California. In November, police in Miami were alleged to have fired rubber bullets, pepper spray, Tasers, gas canisters and concussion grenades at crowds demonstrating against the Free Trade Area of the Americas negotiations. Several protesters required hospitalization as a result of police action and dozens more were treated for injuries.

Women prisoners

In October AI called on the California prison authorities to rescind a policy allowing male guards to conduct "pat down" (clothed body) searches of women prisoners which included touching intimate parts of the inmate's body. Contrary to international standards, California and other US states continued to allow male guards unsupervised access to women prisoners. In several states, including New York, prisoners alleged they were sexually abused by male guards.

Supreme Court overturns sodomy laws

In June the Supreme Court issued a far-reaching decision overruling a Texas sodomy law on the ground that adults had a constitutional right to private sexual conduct (*Lawrence v Texas*). The ruling invalidated laws in Texas and three other states – Kansas, Oklahoma and Missouri – which criminalized sodomy between same-sex partners, as well as laws in nine other states – Alabama, Florida, Idaho, Louisiana, Mississippi, North Carolina, South Carolina, Utah and Virginia – which made sodomy a crime in all cases.

Death penalty

In 2003, 65 people were executed, bringing to 885 the total number of prisoners put to death since the US Supreme Court lifted a moratorium on executions in 1976. The USA continued to violate international standards in its use of the death penalty, including by executing people who were under 18 at the time the crime was committed. The US government carried out its third federal execution since 1963 – all three were carried out under the current administration. Texas carried out its 300th execution since 1976 and accounted for 24 of the USA's executions during 2003.

In January, Mexico brought a case in the International Court of Justice (ICJ) on behalf of more than 50 of its nationals on death row in the USA. The case concerned alleged violations of the UN Vienna Convention on Consular Relations which requires states to inform foreign nationals upon arrest of their right to seek consular assistance. There were more than 100 foreign nationals on death row in the USA in 2003, the majority of whom were denied this right. The ICJ was expected to make its judgment in 2004.

▱ On 11 January 2003, the outgoing governor of Illinois, George Ryan, emptied the state's death row. He pardoned four condemned prisoners whom he believed had been tortured into confessing to crimes they did not commit, and commuted the death sentences of 167 others on the grounds that the system that sentenced them was flawed.

▱ In July, Joseph Amrine was released after more than 16 years on Missouri's death row for the murder of a fellow prisoner. He had been convicted on the basis of testimony from other inmates which was later retracted. Joseph Amrine became the 111th person to be released from death row in the USA since 1973 on the grounds of innocence. The 112th such case occurred in December, when a Pennsylvania prosecutor announced that he would not retry Nicholas Yarris who had been on the state's death row for two decades. A federal judge had ordered a new trial after DNA testing supported Nicholas Yarris' claim of innocence.

On 3 April, Scott Hain was executed in Oklahoma for a crime committed when he was 17 years old. On 8 December, the outgoing governor of Kentucky, Paul Patton, commuted the death sentence of Kevin Stanford, on death row for a crime committed in 1981 when he was 17. Governor Patton had described the death sentence as an "injustice" because of Kevin Stanford's age at the time of the crime.

James Colburn was executed in Texas on 26 March and James Willie Brown was put to death in Georgia on 4 November. Both men had long histories of mental illness, including diagnoses of schizophrenia.

In October the US Supreme Court refused to take Arkansas death row prisoner Charles Singleton's appeal against a lower federal court ruling that the state could forcibly medicate him for his mental illness even if that rendered him competent for execution.

In November, two years after Mexican national Gerardo Valdez came within days of his execution in Oklahoma, a jury resentenced him to life imprisonment. In 2001, the state parole board had recommended clemency after reviewing evidence that Gerardo Valdez had been denied his right to seek consular assistance. The Governor denied clemency, despite the board's recommendation and a personal appeal from President Vicente Fox of Mexico. A state court subsequently granted Gerardo Valdez a new sentencing hearing.

AI country reports/ visits
Reports
- USA: Special registration process must be reviewed (AI Index: AMR 51/004/2003)
- USA: Texas – in a world of its own as 300th execution looms (AI Index: AMR 51/010/2003)
- USA: Another planned killing by the US government – the imminent federal execution of Louis Jones (AI Index: AMR 51/020/2003)
- USA: Death by discrimination – the continuing role of race in capital cases (AI Index: AMR 51/046/2003)
- USA: Not in the jury's name – the imminent execution of Abu-Ali Abdur'Rahman (AI Index: AMR 51/075/2003)
- USA: One year in detention without charge (AI Index: AMR 51/085/2003)
- USA: Shameful isolation – US leads worldwide execution of child offenders (AI Index: AMR 51/102/2003)
- USA: Urgent Action appeal in case of Ali-Saleh Kahlah Al-Marri (AI Index: AMR 51/112/2003)
- USA: The threat of a bad example – undermining international standards as "war on terror" detentions continue (AI Index: AMR 51/114/2003)
- USA: Degrading treatment for women at Valley State Prison (AI Index: AMR 51/135/2003)
- USA: Deporting for torture? (AI Index: AMR 51/139/2003)
- USA: A lethal ideology – more state killing on Human Rights Day as 900th execution looms (AI Index: AMR 51/149/2003)
- USA: Death and the President (AI Index: AMR 51/158/2003)
- USA: Holding human rights hostage (AI Index: AMR 51/164/2003)
- "Why am I here?" Children in immigration detention (published by AIUSA, June 2003)

Visits
An AI delegate visited the USA in October. An AI delegation visited Afghanistan in July to interview former US detainees.

URUGUAY

EASTERN REPUBLIC OF URUGUAY
Head of state and government: Jorge Batlle Ibáñez
Death penalty: abolitionist for all crimes
UN Women's Convention and its Optional Protocol: ratified

The Peace Commission stated in its final report that 26 Uruguayans had died as a result of being tortured during military rule. Nobody was brought to justice for these grave human rights violations.

Past human rights violations
In April the Peace Commission, established by President Jorge Batlle in August 2000 to clarify the fate of Uruguayans who "disappeared" between 1973 and 1985, published its final report. The Commission concluded that 26 Uruguayans who "disappeared" during that period had died as a result of being tortured. According to the information received by the Commission from military sources, the victims were first buried in military barracks, but in 1984 their bodies were exhumed, burned and the ashes thrown in the waters of the Rio de la Plata. The Commission also concluded that five Argentine nationals were detained in Uruguay during those years and transferred to secret detention centres in Argentina. In addition the Commission stated that 182 Uruguayans were detained during the military dictatorship in Argentina.

The Commission recommended that the relatives of all those detained in Uruguay receive "integral and complete" reparation and that crimes such as forced disappearances and torture should be codified in Uruguay's penal code. Relatives as well as human rights organizations welcomed the progress made by the Commission towards establishing the truth about human rights violations during the period of military rule. However, they insisted that uncovering the truth was not enough and that without justice reconciliation was not possible.

Impunity

In April there were signs that the authorities wanted to extend the 1986 Expiry Law which grants exemption from punishment to police and military personnel responsible for human rights violations committed before 1 March 1985. Moves to extend the Expiry Law to cover civilians were believed to be connected with the detention of a former Minister of Foreign Affairs charged with the unlawful imprisonment of Elena Quinteros Almeida who "disappeared" in 1976 after being forcibly taken from the Venezuelan Embassy in Uruguay were she had taken refuge. This was the first time anyone had been detained for human rights violations committed during military rule. The Minister was granted conditional release and was at liberty awaiting trial at the end of the year.

There were serious concerns that the government was interfering with the judiciary after a judge was asked to stop investigating the possibility that the bodies of "disappeared" people were buried in military compounds.

Extradition

Al-Sayid Hassan Mukhlis, an Egyptian national, was extradited to Egypt in July despite concerns that he would be at grave risk of human rights violations, including torture and unfair trial. The Egyptian authorities had sought his extradition for his alleged involvement in human rights abuses by the armed Islamist opposition group, *al-Gama 'a al-Islamiya*. Uruguay's Supreme Court approved Al-Sayid Hassan Mukhlis' extradition in May despite strong evidence that several alleged members of armed Islamist groups had been tortured after being forcibly returned to Egypt.

Torture and ill-treatment

There were reports of torture and ill-treatment of detainees. Investigations into these allegations were initiated but none had been completed by the end of the year.

VENEZUELA

BOLIVARIAN REPUBLIC OF VENEZUELA
Head of state and government: Hugo Chávez Frías
Death penalty: abolitionist for all crimes
UN Women's Convention: ratified with reservations
Optional Protocol to UN Women's Convention: ratified

Political polarization continued to destabilize Venezuela. Those responsible for killings and injuries during the failed coup of 11 April 2002 were not brought to justice. There were continued reports of widespread unlawful killings and torture of criminal suspects by the police. Poor and overcrowded prison conditions resulted in repeated protests by inmates. A human rights defender was killed and a number of others received threats. There were reports of harassment of journalists. Political killings were reported in the border region with Colombia and many of those fleeing the Colombian conflict continued to be at risk.

Background

The national stoppage called by the opposition at the end of 2002 to try to force President Chávez from office continued until February 2003, but failed in its objective. The stoppage had a crippling impact on the economy, lowering the standard of living for many. Internationally sponsored negotiations led to an agreement in May committing both sides to seek a "constitutional, peaceful, democratic and electoral solution" to the crisis. The National Electoral Commission's decision on a referendum on Hugo Chávez' presidency remained pending at the end of the year.

Over the year, the number of reports of political violence fell against a background of continuing negotiations between the government and opposition. However, a number of bombs exploded in various locations, including outside some embassies, raising concerns of further destabilization. There were a number of arrests in November in connection with these attacks; investigations were continuing at the end of the year.

Police brutality

The National Guard and police were accused on a number of occasions of using excessive force in the context of the political crisis.

☐ In January, during the national stoppage, strikers and protesters at a bottling plant in Valencia, Carabobo State, were reportedly beaten and intimidated by the National Guard.

☐ In September the National Guard reportedly used excessive force and threats during the eviction of sacked national oil industry employees and their families from a company-owned housing development.

Media

The mutual hostility between private media organizations and the government continued. A number of journalists were reportedly threatened and attacked, but the authorities apparently failed to conduct effective investigations. The media accused the authorities of seeking to use administrative powers to curtail press freedoms.

In July the Supreme Court ruled against the implementation of a general recommendation by the Inter-American Commission on Human Rights to abolish antiquated laws on disrespect for authority. The laws violated international standards on freedom of expression by potentially criminalizing the publication of allegations against public officials.

Access to justice

Elements of draft legislation to regulate the composition and functions of the Supreme Court threatened to give unprecedented powers to the National Assembly and potentially undermined the Court's independence.

Insufficient numbers of prosecutors, investigative police and judges contributed to serious deficiencies, including long delays, in the justice system. Almost half of all prisoners were held on remand. Prison overcrowding led to repeated protests against judicial delays and conditions of detention. There were also continuing concerns about the independence and impartiality of the judiciary, the Public Prosecutor's Office and the Human Rights Ombudsman.

Impunity

Those responsible for the deaths of at least 50 people and the wounding of many others during the failed coup between 11 and 14 April 2002 were not brought to justice. Despite considerable evidence, only a small number of those implicated were identified and prosecuted. The quality of the prosecutions and the role of the judiciary raised serious doubt about the willingness or ability of the state to ensure justice. Four suspects accused of firing on police and protesters from the Puente Llaguno in central Caracas were acquitted on the grounds that they had acted in self-defence. Eight Metropolitan Police officers remained in custody pending trial at the end of the year in connection with the deaths of the protesters.

Killings and torture by police

There were continuing reports of unlawful killings of criminal suspects by police. The victims were routinely accused of resisting arrest, although in many cases witnesses challenged the police version of events. Victims, witnesses or family members who reported such abuses were frequently threatened or attacked. No effective witness protection program was made available.

The use of torture also remained common in many police forces. Investigations into allegations of human rights violations by police were often ineffectual and helped create a climate of impunity for the officers responsible.

In May, Enmary Cava was shot and killed by a gunman in the streets of Cagua, Aragua State. She and her family had been repeatedly threatened after they called for an investigation into the killing of two of their brothers and their father by Aragua State police in January. Threats against the family continued throughout the year despite the detention of a number of police officers in connection with the killings.

Human rights defenders

At least one human rights activist was killed in the border region with Colombia. Other human rights defenders were threatened and harassed. The response of the authorities to threats against defenders was inadequate.

In August, José Luis Castillo was shot and killed by two gunmen in Machiques, Zulia State. He was a member of the church-based organization, *Vicariato Apostólico de Machiques*, Apostolic Vicariate of Machiques, working with local communities and Colombian refugees. His wife and child were also injured. A few days later the *Vicariato Apostólico de Machiques* received an anonymous call threatening other staff for their human rights work.

The border and refugees

The conflict in Colombia continued to spill over into Venezuela's border states where the reported presence of paramilitary and guerrilla forces gave rise to scores of political murders. Civilians continued to flee the conflict in Colombia, but conditions in the border states were frequently precarious. In July the government established a National Refugee Commission to assess asylum applications, but the Commission was still not operational at the end of the year.

In April Jorge Nieves, leader of the political party *Patria para Todos*, was shot and killed in Guasdualito, Apure State. Throughout the 1990s Jorge Nieves had been a leading human rights activist working in the border area.

Inter-American Commission on Human Rights

President Chávez' administration appeared increasingly averse to scrutiny by international human rights bodies, such as the Inter-American Commission on Human Rights. There was concern at the authorities' failure to comply fully with the recommendations issued by the Commission and by the Inter-American Court of Human Rights. However, in November the government committed itself to comply with the Court ruling to pay compensation to relatives of the victims of the widespread civil disturbances of 1989, known as the Caracazo.

AI country reports/visits
Report
- Venezuela: A human rights agenda for the current crisis (AI Index: AMR 53/001/2003)

ASIA/PACIFIC

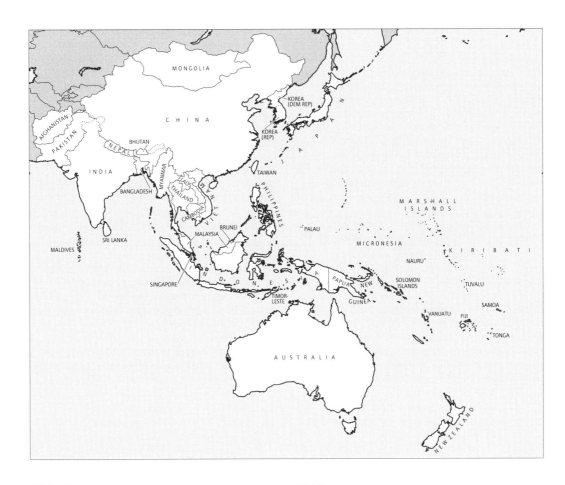

Afghanistan
Australia
Bangladesh
Bhutan
Brunei Darussalam
Cambodia
China
Fiji
India
Indonesia
Japan
Korea, Democratic People's Republic of
Korea, Republic of
Laos
Malaysia

Maldives
Mongolia
Myanmar
Nepal
Pakistan
Papua New Guinea
Philippines
Singapore
Solomon Islands
Sri Lanka
Taiwan
Thailand
Timor-Leste
Tonga
Viet Nam

ASIA/PACIFIC REGIONAL OVERVIEW 2003

The war on Iraq and issues of national security dominated much of the political debate in the Asia-Pacific region during 2003, and several governments used the "war on terror" to curtail human rights. Poverty and discrimination continued to dominate the lives of millions of people, adversely affecting in particular women and indigenous people. Human rights protection remained inadequate across the region and in some countries human rights violations increased as a result of renewed or ongoing armed conflicts.

National security and the 'war on terror'

Security firmly established itself as the prime concern of most governments in the region, often informed by a US-led approach. At the civil society level, however, there was mounting resentment at growing US power and influence both globally and more specifically in Asia. A "strategic partnership" agreement signed between China and the Association of Southeast Asian Nations (ASEAN) in October in Bali, Indonesia, was seen by many as part of China's strategy to counter US unilateralism as well as to build closer economic and security ties within Southeast Asia. In East Asia, tension increased between Taiwan and China after Taiwan adopted legislation in November allowing its people to vote on sovereignty and other issues.

The belief of several governments that human rights could be curtailed under the "war on terror" umbrella was particularly apparent in China, India, Malaysia, Pakistan and Thailand. Hundreds of people suspected of "terrorism" found themselves condemned to legal black holes as the authorities ignored national and international legal frameworks. In Pakistan, more than 500 people, including Arabs and Afghans, were arbitrarily arrested and handed over to the US authorities on suspicion of membership of *al-Qa'ida* and the *Taleban* in violation of Pakistan's Extradition Act of 1974. Others were believed to be held at undisclosed locations in Pakistan, but the authorities refused to provide any information about them. In Gujarat, India, hundreds of members of the Muslim community were held in illegal detention against a background of investigations into a range of conspiracies against the state. In China, thousands of members of the predominantly Muslim Uighur community were detained or imprisoned as "separatists, terrorists and religious extremists" and the Uighur culture came under attack through the closure of mosques, restrictions on the use of the Uighur language and the banning of certain Uighur-language publications.

Protests by half a million people in Hong Kong in July prompted the authorities to withdraw controversial proposals prohibiting acts of treason, secession, sedition and subversion.

Economic, social and political rights

A growth in economic inequality was particularly marked in the region's most populous state, China, as a consequence of economic liberalization. In some countries that were hit hard by the Asian financial crisis of 1997, including South Korea and Thailand, the economies continued to recover. However, life for the large majority of the region's rural population remained largely unchanged. The dominant reality for the most vulnerable, including women and indigenous people, continued to be widespread poverty and discrimination. Farmers' organizations and others defending the rights of poor rural populations expressed alarm at the impact on human rights of the failure to reach agreement on tariff barriers and agricultural subsidies at the World Trade Organization summit in Cancun, Mexico, in September. Under the pressure of economic hardship in the countryside, more and more people migrated to nearby cities or other countries in the region. Among them were many women looking for work in garment and export assembly plants where they could earn higher wages than in their villages. They were exposed to widespread abuse, including poor working conditions and sexual violence at work.

Many governments, including those in China, Laos and Viet Nam, did not match their apparent support for increased economic freedom with a commitment to political freedom as they continued to hold on to political power in an absolute way. In China, the Maldives, Myanmar and Viet Nam, many prisoners of conscience remained in jail for the peaceful expression of their political beliefs. In China and Viet Nam in particular, there were crack-downs on people using the Internet to download or circulate information on human rights and democracy. After substantial levels of media attention, several of these prisoners were released.

While widespread violations of the right to health continued to be reported, the outbreak of Severe Acute Respiratory Syndrome (SARS) in February pushed some governments to act with greater transparency and accountability. In October the Chinese authorities officially acknowledged for the first time that there were 840,000 people with HIV and 80,000 AIDS patients in the country. The true figures were thought to be considerably higher.

Armed conflict

Armed conflict continued to ravage parts of the region. The seven-year conflict in Nepal resumed after a six-month cease-fire collapsed in August. Both sides to the conflict missed an opportunity to strengthen human rights protection when the National Human Rights Commission presented them with a draft Human Rights Accord in May. Although both sides agreed in principle to the Accord, neither had signed up to it by the time the cease-fire collapsed, and efforts by civil society and the international community to put in place an effective framework for human rights protection remained unsuccessful. In the meantime, there were fears that the continued delivery of weapons from India, the United Kingdom, Belgium, Israel and the USA to the Royal Nepal Army would contribute to an escalation of the conflict.

A cease-fire also collapsed in Nanggroe Aceh Darussalam (NAD) province, Indonesia, with disastrous consequences. After the imposition of a military state of emergency in May, there were allegations of grave human rights violations, including extrajudicial executions, "disappearances", arbitrary detention and torture. Verification of such reports was virtually impossible because the province was effectively closed to independent human rights monitors, humanitarian workers and journalists.

In Laos a decades-old internal armed conflict largely forgotten by the international community was highlighted during the year by reports from journalists. This apparently led to an intensification of military operations by government forces and reports of scores of civilian deaths.

In Afghanistan, there were concerns about the lack of commitment of resources by the international community to the reconstruction of the country, particularly after the focus shifted to Iraq. The Constitutional *Loya Jirga* took place in late December amid a deteriorating security situation. Factional fighting continued and Taleban forces gained strength. Instability was compounded by a lack of substantial progress in the disarmament, demobilization and reintegration of former combatants. As the year drew to an end, the Constitutional *Loya Jirga* was reaching agreement on a new Constitution. Despite being hailed as a step forward on the country's road to stability, the *Loya Jirga* was marred by intimidation of delegates and lack of transparency, and highlighted the continued fractured nature of Afghan society.

Five years of conflict and lawlessness ended in the Solomon Islands when the government invited an Australian-led regional intervention force to restore law and order and to rebuild public services, including police posts, prisons and courts. The operation, which was continuing at the end of the year, had a regional assistance mandate outside a UN framework. From July, around 2,500 South Pacific troops and police worked with local police officers to arrest more than 400 key suspects, including senior police and rebel commanders, many for crimes relating to serious abuses of human rights. Intervention forces uncovered graves of torture victims and secured the evidence, and ensured the safe return of internally displaced people.

Nuclear weapons
The issue of nuclear weapons continued to cause concern across the region, although for much of the year it was overshadowed by the "war on terror". In February, the International Atomic Energy Agency found North Korea in breach of nuclear safeguards and

referred the matter to the UN Security Council. In April, the Security Council expressed concern about North Korea's nuclear program. China acted as the main broker of six-nation talks to resolve the threat of North Korea's nuclear program, also involving Japan, North and South Korea, the Russian Federation and the USA. Tension around the issue dissipated somewhat when in November North Korea stated that it was ready to abandon its nuclear program if the USA dropped its "hostile policy". The North Korean government agreed to consider a US offer of a written security guarantee from the USA and North Korea's neighbours.

Tension between Pakistan and India – both nuclear powers – began to ease towards the end of the year when confidence-building measures, including the resumption of transport links between the countries, were taken by both sides in preparation for the possible resumption of dialogue.

Lack of human rights protection
Against a background of massive political, economic and security challenges, the legal framework for the protection of human rights remained very weak. Asia continued to be the only region without a regional human rights mechanism and governments remained reluctant to ratify key international human rights instruments. For instance, Asia remained the region with the lowest ratification rate for the International Covenant on Civil and Political Rights. The fact that 18 countries in the region were known to have signed immunity agreements with the USA that they would not surrender US nationals accused of genocide, crimes against humanity or war crimes to the International Criminal Court was also an indication of the lack of commitment to combat impunity.

Weak and corrupt criminal justice systems in countries such as Bangladesh, Cambodia and Indonesia continued to impact negatively on human rights. Torture, "disappearances" and extrajudicial executions continued to be widespread across the region.

As in previous years, respect for the right to life was lacking in many Asia-Pacific countries. The region bucked the worldwide trend towards abolition of the death penalty. More people were executed in 2003 in the region than in the rest of the world combined, thanks largely, but not exclusively, to China and Singapore. There was a sharp increase in death sentences and executions in Viet Nam. Singapore was believed to have carried out the highest number of executions per capita in the world since 1994.

According to the UN Office on Drugs and Crime, Asia was the largest producer of illicit drugs – opium and increasingly methamphetamine. The death penalty was frequently used in countries such as China, Malaysia, Singapore, Thailand and Viet Nam as a policy response to drug trafficking, despite evidence of its ineffectiveness. The Thai government appeared to condone killings of drug suspects as one method of fighting drug trafficking and use in the country. According to official statements, 2,245 people suspected of trafficking or using drugs were killed during a three-month campaign starting in February.

Child offenders in three countries were known to be at risk of execution. In Pakistan, children continued to be sentenced to death, especially in tribal areas, reflecting the government's failure to implement nationally the laws that forbid the imposition of the death penalty on children in most areas of the country. However, no children were executed during the year. In China, it was reported that a young man was executed in January for a murder committed when he was 16 years old. China's criminal law forbids the execution of minors. In the Philippines, at least seven children held in adult facilities remained under sentence of death.

US-led forces continued military operations in parts of Afghanistan and persisted with arbitrary arrests and detentions. There were grave concerns about detention conditions at the US airbase at Bagram in Afghanistan where approximately 100 detainees were believed to be held outside any legal framework. In March, US military officials reportedly confirmed reports that "homicide" was the cause of death of two detainees in Bagram in December 2002. The Pentagon opened investigations into their deaths, but the results of these were not made public. Bombings by the US-led coalition forces continued to cause civilian casualties, including two incidents in December that resulted in the deaths of 15 children.

Campaigning for human rights

Human rights defenders across the Asia-Pacific region continued to strengthen their cooperation in response to threats to human rights. In doing so, they faced a wide range of abuses, including killing, "disappearance", torture, arbitrary arrest and detention, and harassment.

Human rights defenders in Indonesia, particularly in areas of armed conflict, were prevented from carrying out their legitimate activities because of the risk of human rights violations. Five activists "disappeared" or were killed in NAD province in Indonesia. Elsewhere in the country, human rights defenders were charged with defamation for publishing information about human rights violations. In various states in India, including Gujarat and Andhra Pradesh, the legitimate activities of human rights defenders continued to be branded as "anti-national", and activists were harassed and threatened by government forces and other agents. In Malaysia, in what was a serious blow for human rights defenders, Irene Fernandez, Director of *Tenaganita*, a non-governmental organization working with migrant women, was sentenced to 12 months in prison in October for "maliciously publishing false news". The charge related to a report released by *Tenaganita* documenting patterns of ill-treatment, abuse and deaths from preventable diseases in camps for detained migrant workers.

AFGHANISTAN

AFGHANISTAN

President of the Transitional Administration: Hamid Karzai
Death penalty: retentionist
UN Women's Convention: ratified
Optional Protocol to UN Women's Convention: not signed

A deteriorating security situation undermined human rights. Serious human rights abuses and armed conflict continued in many areas. The criminal justice system remained ineffective and was a source of violations rather than a mechanism for providing justice. Women and girls in particular faced discrimination in the justice system. Police lacked pay, training and control structures. Prison conditions were poor. Detainees were held for excessive periods before appearing before a judge. Women and girls faced a high level of violence. Rape and sexual violence by armed groups was reportedly common. Violence in the family, and forced and underage marriage, were widespread. Past human rights abuses were not addressed and the international community did not provide the necessary support to ensure progress in this area. The US-led coalition was responsible for arbitrary detentions as the "war on terror" continued. Refugees continued to return from neighbouring states but in much reduced numbers, owing largely to concerns about the security situation, employment opportunities and housing. There were serious concerns about the voluntariness of returns from Iran and Pakistan.

Background

The security situation continued to deteriorate throughout the country and was particularly serious in the north, south and southeast. The central government – the Afghan Transitional Authority (ATA) – had virtually no control outside Kabul. Local armed groups and regional commanders, some of whom continued to receive US support, consolidated their regional power bases and acted with impunity in these areas. Several pilot projects on disarmament, demobilization and reintegration began in October but had made little progress by the end of the year.

Various armed factions engaged in sporadic fighting throughout the country. Armed groups in some regions perpetrated serious human rights abuses in areas they controlled: reported abuses included abductions and kidnapping; arbitrary detention in private prisons; confiscation of land and property; rape; abduction of women, girls and boys; and forced conscription of boys and men.

In October the UN Security Council authorized the expansion of the International Security Assistance Force (ISAF) outside Kabul after repeated calls by the ATA, the UN Secretary-General and international and national non-governmental organizations. However, NATO, which took over the ISAF command in August, had trouble securing commitments for the extra troops required. A delegation of Security Council ambassadors visited Afghanistan in November. The UN Assistance Mission in Afghanistan (UNAMA), established in March 2002, continued to have mixed results in its efforts to support the implementation of the December 2001 Bonn Agreement and was criticized for its failure to fully integrate human rights into its activities. The Afghan Independent Human Rights Commission (AIHRC), formed in June 2002, made considerable progress, although its work was sometimes obstructed by government officials.

There was no significant improvement in the economy or infrastructure of the country. Child labour continued to be unchecked and widespread. Drug production increased, orchestrated and controlled by regional commanders and armed groups, and led to a further rise in organized crime and related human rights abuses.

Constitution building

The Constitutional *Loya Jirga*, which met to decide on a new Constitution, was delayed until December. The delay threatened the electoral process, which was due to be completed by June 2004. There were concerns that the draft constitution was not consistent with international standards. There were reports of intimidation and threats during the selection of delegates for the Constitutional *Loya Jirga*.

Ineffective administration of justice

The criminal justice system remained ineffective. Wealth and connections to those with power gave individuals impunity, whereas those without such access faced arbitrary justice. The international community's promised program of judicial assistance lacked strategic direction and its start was delayed.

Police failed to protect human rights and often committed violations themselves. Lack of pay, training, proper command and control structures and effective oversight mechanisms contributed to a situation in which violations continued to be perpetrated with impunity. Detainees were held for prolonged periods, sometimes for over a year, before being brought before a judge. Torture and arbitrary detention were commonly used by police to extract confessions or money.

Where courts had been established, they were fragile and lacked the basic facilities such as premises, furniture and necessary legal texts. Violations of fair trial procedures were routine – access to defence counsel was virtually non-existent, there was no presumption of innocence, and convictions based on little or no evidence were common. Many judges lacked proper training or professional skills and the justice system remained highly politicized. Judges and independent prosecutors could not function impartially in many areas because of local politics or threats by armed groups. In many rural areas, *jirgas* or *shuras* (informal justice mechanisms) were used to resolve most disputes, including crimes such as murder. Women's rights were particularly violated in both the formal and informal justice system.

AI welcomed the transfer of responsibility for the administration of prisons from the Interior Ministry to the Justice Ministry. However, prison conditions remained poor across the country. In some places private houses were used to hold detainees. Detainees and convicted prisoners were held together, and in many areas there were no separate facilities for juveniles and women, placing them at greater risk of sexual and other abuse. Prison staff received little or no training and went for months without pay.

Limited women's legal and social rights

A major step forward for women's legal rights was achieved in March when the Afghan authorities ratified the UN Women's Convention without reservations. However, inequality between men and women remained enshrined in national laws, particularly those relating to marriage and divorce. In certain regions of Afghanistan, women accused of adultery were routinely detained, as were those who attempted to marry a spouse of their choice.

Women's access to healthcare, education and economic resources, particularly in rural areas, remained extremely limited, exacerbated by cultural restrictions on women's movement and interaction with men outside their family.

Violence against women

Women and girls continued to face a high level of violence. Rape and sexual violence by members of armed factions and former combatants were reportedly common. Forced marriage, particularly of girls, domestic violence and other crimes of violence against women remained widespread and had the active support or passive complicity of state agents, armed groups, families and communities.

In some parts of the country tradition continued to be used to legitimize violent deaths of women. Women and girls alleged to have eloped or committed adultery were reportedly killed by the family. Adultery, "running away from home" and unlawful sexual activity (sexual intercourse by unmarried men and women) – known as *zina* crimes – remained subject to criminal prosecution. Some women accused of *zina* were at risk of being killed by their families if released. Women victims of rape remained at risk of prosecution for *zina* if they could not prove the act was against their will, and had little hope of seeing justice done. Divorce on grounds of physical violence was virtually impossible for women to obtain, even with evidence of severe domestic violence.

In many rural communities, women and girls continued to be exchanged as a mechanism for addressing community disputes or criminal issues including murder or elopement. Women and girls exchanged in this way are married to a man or boy from the victim's family.

The criminal justice system remained too weak to offer effective protection of women's rights to life and physical security, and itself subjected them to discrimination and abuse. Prosecutions for violence against women, and protection for women at acute risk of violence, were virtually absent. The few women who overcame powerful barriers to seek redress rarely had their complaints considered or their rights defended. No safeguards were in place to protect women from sexual abuse while in police custody and detention. There were unconfirmed reports of sexual abuse of women prisoners in official detention centres in Herat, Mazar-e-Sharif and Kabul.

Harassment of journalists

Many independent newspapers, periodicals and radio stations were operating, although journalists regularly received threats for criticizing the authorities.

◻ Two journalists, Sayed Mirhassan Mahdavi, editor of *Aftab* newspaper, and Ali Payam Sistani, the newspaper's designer, were arrested on 17 June and accused of "insulting Islam" for publishing an article criticizing the involvement of religion in politics. They were released after just over a week, but President Karzai stated that both men would be tried. After their release the men went to live in exile.

Impunity for past human rights violations

Despite the ratification in February by the Afghan authorities of the Rome Statute of the International Criminal Court, little action was taken to bring to justice perpetrators of serious abuses in the past. Many of those holding central and regional government posts were allegedly responsible for human rights and humanitarian law violations committed during 23 years of armed conflict. Many also allegedly had connections with armed groups responsible for ongoing violations.

The international community proved unwilling to take concrete steps to ensure accountability for past human rights violations and UNAMA shied away from the issue. In February the UN Special Rapporteur on extrajudicial executions proposed the establishment of an international commission of inquiry into abuses in Afghanistan since 1978, a proposal supported by the AIHRC. However, the proposal was opposed by a majority of governments and the UN Commission on Human Rights then failed to endorse the proposal. Despite this setback, the AIHRC continued to try to map past abuses, and requested training and technical expertise specifically on investigation and monitoring to undertake this work.

Abuses by US-led military forces

US-led forces, which continued military operations in various parts of the country, made arbitrary detentions. Men and boys were arrested, detained and transferred without charge and without any formal legal process through which they could challenge the legality of their detention. There were reports of ill-treatment in US detention facilities in Afghanistan. Findings from internal military investigations into two deaths in custody in December 2002 allegedly caused by ill-treatment were not published.

Bombings by US-led forces reportedly caused civilian casualties. In April AI called for an immediate investigation into the deaths of four men and seven women who were killed when a bomb hit their house on the outskirts of Shkin, Paktika province. In December, a total of 15 children were killed in two separate bombings by US forces.

Refugees and internally displaced people

Refugees continued to return to Afghanistan from neighbouring states but in greatly reduced numbers, largely because of the security situation and lack of access to employment and adequate housing. There were serious concerns about the voluntariness of returns from Iran and Pakistan because of official strategies of deportation and police harassment respectively. On 28 April 2003 the United Kingdom (UK) deported 21 rejected asylum-seekers to Kabul. This was followed by a second chartered flight on 20 May carrying 34 asylum-seekers from the UK and four from France. There were concerns about the sustainability of these and other returns to Afghanistan.

AI country reports/ visits

Reports

- Afghanistan: Police reconstruction essential for the protection of human rights (AI Index: ASA 11/003/2003)
- Afghanistan: Out of sight, out of mind – the fate of the Afghan returnees (AI Index: ASA 11/014/2003)
- Afghanistan: Crumbling prison system desperately in need of repair (AI Index: ASA 11/017/2003)
- Afghanistan: Re-establishing the rule of law (AI Index: ASA 11/021/2003)
- Afghanistan: "No one listens to us and no one treats us as human beings" – Justice denied to women (AI Index: ASA 11/023/2003)

Visits

In July, AI's Secretary General visited Afghanistan and met President Karzai and other senior government officials, UNAMA officials, representatives of non-governmental organizations, and human rights defenders. The delegation also visited a women's prison in Kabul. Other AI delegates visited the country throughout the year, working alongside an AI field presence that ended in August. In December, AI delegates attended the Constitutional *Loya Jirga*.

AUSTRALIA

AUSTRALIA
Head of state: Queen Elizabeth II, represented by Michael Jeffery (replaced Peter Hollingworth in August)
Head of government: John Howard
Death penalty: abolitionist for all crimes
UN Women's Convention: ratified with reservations
Optional Protocol to UN Women's Convention: not signed

National security was invoked to justify the erosion of human rights safeguards in draft laws on "anti-terrorism" measures and refugee rights. Domestic violence against Aboriginal women and children and indefinite detention of child asylum-seekers were prominent themes in the domestic human rights debate.

Background

Australia took over the vice-chair at the UN Commission on Human Rights, but failed to take a strong stand on fair trial and death penalty issues. National security dominated foreign policy and aspects of domestic policy. Australia led a military-backed regional intervention in the Solomon Islands and participated in the war against Iraq.

In March, new legislation was proposed to reduce the powers of the national Human Rights and Equal Opportunity Commission (HREOC), including its freedom to seek leave to intervene in legal proceedings on international human rights concerns.

'Anti-terrorism' legislation

In June, a new law gave the authorities powers to detain people suspected of having information about "terrorist" offences for seven days before being brought before a court. There was no requirement that relatives be informed of the whereabouts of detainees during this time. In November, newly appointed Attorney-General Philip Ruddock moved to extend these powers further.

Violence against women

According to a 20-year study conducted by Australian universities, one in four women aged between 18 and 23 reported some experience of domestic violence. In October, public concern about even higher rates of indigenous victims of domestic violence led the Prime Minister to initiate a consultation process with Aboriginal women's leaders.

In February, a Northern Territory coroner's inquest report criticized police for releasing an Aboriginal victim of domestic violence into the care of her *de facto* husband in October 2001. The woman died from her injuries after the husband beat her again as soon as the officers had left.

Indigenous social justice

In October, the Prime Minister publicly accepted that policies on indigenous social welfare were failing. That month, a Senate inquiry found that reconciliation with Aborigines was "off the track", mainly as a result of inadequate measures to boost their enjoyment of economic, social and cultural rights. The inquiry reported that life expectancy for Aborigines was on average 20 years less than for other Australians and that Aborigines were 15 times more likely to be imprisoned. Reports by the Australian Institute of Criminology and the HREOC found that for indigenous women, life expectancy was declining while imprisonment rates had increased by 262 per cent during the 1990s. HREOC's Indigenous Social Justice Commissioner said he felt "a mounting sense of despair and urgency among Indigenous people and communities relating to [...] violence, abuse, unemployment, poor health, contact with criminal law processes, removal of children through care and protection and so on."

Deaths in custody

Deaths in custody of indigenous and non-indigenous prisoners fell to the lowest level for 10 years, with the exception of Western Australia. In April, the Western Australia government directed the state's independent prison inspector to review its largest prison because of concerns over deaths in custody, including suicides by teenage Aboriginal prisoners awaiting trial.

In February, the family of Stephen Wardle, who died in 1988 aged 18 in a police cell in disputed circumstances, accepted an apology by a police officer during a Royal Commission inquiry into the Western Australia Police Service which investigated Stephen Wardle's death.

Legal proceedings on child asylum-seekers

In August, the Family Court of Australia ordered the release of five Pakistani child asylum-seekers from Baxter Detention Centre on the grounds that their detention was harmful. They had been in detention since January 2001. An appeal by the government was due to be heard in February 2004. The decision did not affect another 108 asylum-seeker children detained on Nauru under agreements with the Australian authorities, because the transfer to Nauru removed them from Australian jurisdiction.

Refugees

In July, the government announced the departure of the last detainee from its immigration detention centre on Manus Island, Papua New Guinea, run by the International Organization for Migration on behalf of the Australian government. However, Aladdin Sisalem remained detained on his own on Manus by the end of the year. A similar detention centre on Nauru remained open.

▭ In August, almost 30 organizations joined AI Australia in campaigning for nine women and 14 children held on Nauru to be reunited with their husbands and fathers, already recognized as refugees in Australia.

▭ In November, the UN Human Rights Committee urged the release from immigration detention of Roqia

Bakhtiyari and found that she and her children, released by the Family Court after 32 months' detention (see above), had been arbitrarily detained. The Committee said Australia was under an obligation to pay compensation to her and to the children, who "suffered demonstrable, documented and ongoing adverse effects of detention."

BANGLADESH

PEOPLE'S REPUBLIC OF BANGLADESH
Head of state: Iajuddin Ahmed
Head of government: Begum Khaleda Zia
Death penalty: retentionist
UN Women's Convention: ratified with reservations
Optional Protocol to UN Women's Convention: ratified

Torture remained widespread. At least 13 detainees died in police custody. Police used unnecessary or disproportionate force against demonstrators, injuring hundreds of people, some critically. Over 130 people were sentenced to death. Two men were executed. Harassment of human rights defenders continued. Rape and other violence against women was widely reported.

Background

Dozens of people died in violence during and after local elections in the first quarter of the year. Several opposition politicians were assassinated. Corruption and poor governance remained key factors blocking economic prosperity. The government reportedly pressured judges to dismiss criminal charges against ruling Bangladesh Nationalist Party supporters. Most sessions of parliament were boycotted by the main opposition party, the Awami League.

Torture

The government failed to implement safeguards against torture. Victims included suspected criminals, children and people detained on politically motivated grounds. At least 13 people died in police custody. The police reportedly denied allegations that their deaths were the result of torture.

▭ Following his release from police custody on 5 January, senior journalist Enamul Haque Chowdhury said that he was beaten, tortured with electric shocks, and threatened with death at gunpoint. Arrested on 13 December 2002, he was accused of misquoting the Home Minister in a news agency report. No official investigation was initiated into his allegations of torture.

▭ Abdul Gaffar, 45, a day labourer from Ekbarpur village in Mougachhi area of Rajshahi, died on 6 May in police custody. He had reportedly been beaten with batons and rifle butts to compel him to reveal the whereabouts of a suspect. A three-member police committee, formed following protests by villagers, failed to hold responsible any of the officers involved in his death.

Police brutality

Police continued to use excessive force during opposition or trade union demonstrations. Hundreds of protesters were injured, some critically. No officers were known to have been brought to justice for these attacks.

▭ On 10 October officers attacked and beat unemployed and student nurses from 38 government nursing institutions who were protesting against changes in their terms and conditions of employment. When demonstrators tried to enter the Directorate of Nursing Services, police officers beat them. Over 50 nurses were reportedly injured, most of them women, and 23 were admitted to hospital, three of them in a critical condition.

Death penalty

Courts sentenced to death more than 130 men and women. Most death sentences were passed by Speedy Trial Tribunals, which were required to conclude trials within 135 days, increasing the risk of convictions based on flawed evidence. Two men were hanged on 10 July.

Arbitrary detention

Following repeated High Court orders and international appeals, some prominent political detainees were released in January. They included human rights defenders Shahriar Kabir, Professor Muntasir Mamun and Saleem Samad, as well as Awami League leaders Bahauddin Nasim, Saber Hossain Chowdhury and Tofael Ahmed. However, they continued to suffer harassment and threats of detention.

▭ In June, warrants of arrests were issued against Mahfuz Anam, editor and publisher of the *Daily Star* newspaper; Matiur Rahman, editor of the *Daily Prothom Alo* newspaper; and Abdul Jalil, Secretary General of the Awami League. A senior government official had brought a criminal defamation case against them after publication of a letter in which Abdul Jalil criticized the nomination of the official to an executive post in an international organization. They were not detained but the arrest warrants remained pending.

Violence against women

Reports of rape were widespread, including of young children. There were frequent reports of women being beaten by their husbands, sometimes with fatal results. The perpetrators were often husbands whose demands for dowry had not been met. Scores of women were victims of acid attacks, usually by rejected partners or people settling scores with the victims' families. Some 20,000 women and children were reportedly trafficked to other countries, usually after abduction from rural areas.

Women's rights groups blamed the low rate of convictions for violence against women on a lack of government institutions to support the victims and a lack of trained police officers to investigate the cases.

▭ On 26 August, nine women from tribal communities in the Chittagong Hill Tracts were reported to have been sexually assaulted by Bengali settlers who attacked Jumma villages and set fire to hundreds of homes. One of them was reportedly gang-raped. Army connivance in the attacks was suspected. Attempts by the tribal people to file a complaint with the police against the attacks were not successful, while police filed a complaint on behalf of Bengali settlers against 4,000 tribal people, accusing them of attacking the settlers.

Attacks against Hindus

In an apparently planned arson attack on a Hindu family in Banskhali Upazila near Chittagong around midnight on 19 November, 11 members of the family were burned to death. The government called it an act of banditry, but evidence suggested it was a motivated attack against the family because of their identity as Hindus. Police filed a case but despite repeated demands from civil society groups, no independent inquiry was set up.

Attacks against Ahmadis

From October onwards, Islamist groups embarked on a campaign of hate speech against members of the Ahmadiyya community and marched on their places of worship in Dhaka and other parts of the country, calling on the government to declare them non-Muslim. The government deployed security personnel to protect Ahmadis against attacks but took no action against those using hate speech.

▭ On 31 October, Shah Alam, the Imam of the Ahmadi mosque in the village of Raghanathpur Bank in Jessore District, was beaten to death in front of his family. Some 90 men led by a local Islamist leader attacked him because he refused their demand to recant his Ahmadiyya faith. No one was charged in connection with the killing even though the assailants' identities were known.

Impunity

Immunity from prosecution was granted to officials and army personnel associated with human rights violations during the anti-crime "Operation Clean Heart" from 17 October 2002 to 9 January 2003. At least 40 men died, reportedly as a result of torture, after being detained by soldiers.

AI country reports/ visits
Reports
- Bangladesh: Urgent need for legal and other reforms to protect human rights (AI Index: ASA 13/012/2003)
- Bangladesh: Harassment of news editors must stop (AI Index: ASA 13/015/2003)

Visit
AI delegates visited Bangladesh in November and December to conduct research.

BHUTAN

KINGDOM OF BHUTAN
Head of state: King Jigme Singye Wangchuck
Head of government: Jigme Thinley (replaced Kinzang Dorji in August)
Death penalty: abolitionist in practice
UN Women's Convention: ratified
Optional Protocol to UN Women's Convention: not signed

A durable solution remained remote for over 100,000 refugees from southern Bhutan who have lived in refugee camps in eastern Nepal for more than 10 years. Ministerial-level meetings between Bhutan and Nepal and the announcement of results from a process to "verify" refugees produced little visible progress. The UN High Commissioner for Refugees (UNHCR) announced the gradual withdrawal of his office from the camps.

Background
A further draft of the Constitution was produced by mid-year. A National Judicial Commission was established to strengthen the system of appointing and removing judges. The first professional woman judge was appointed to Zhemgang district court.

The activities of the United Liberation Front of Assam, the National Democratic Front of Bodoland and the Kamtapur Liberation Front, armed separatist groups from northeast India, increased tensions in southern areas. They ignored a 30 June government deadline to vacate their 20 camps or face military action. In December nearly 600 militia volunteers, including 20 women, were deployed in southern Bhutan alongside the regular armed forces. This was followed on 15 December by the launch of a military offensive to expel the armed separatist groups from the country. Sixty women and children who had been living in the camps were arrested and handed over to the Indian authorities.

A European Parliament mission to Bhutan in November discussed the refugee issue with government officials and expressed their concerns.

Nepali-speaking refugees
At a UNHCR meeting in September, the High Commissioner announced that his office would phase out its direct involvement in the refugee camps, and would promote local integration and resettlement of refugees instead of repatriation.

In February and March the governments of Bhutan and Nepal agreed the categorization by a Joint Verification Team (JVT) of the refugees in Khudunabari camp. Refugees had been categorized as "*bona fide* Bhutanese who would be eligible for repatriation to Bhutan", Bhutanese who had "voluntarily" emigrated, non-Bhutanese, and refugees who had committed criminal acts.

In May the two governments agreed that some of the refugees would be allowed to return to Bhutan under certain conditions. Those who were deemed to have "voluntarily" emigrated would have to reapply for citizenship. The JVT report, published in June, recognized only 2.4 per cent of refugees as "*bona fide* Bhutanese", and categorized 70.55 per cent as having emigrated voluntarily.

In October it was announced that refugees from Khudunabari camp who applied to return would be repatriated, except those categorized as non-Bhutanese, whose cases would be reviewed.

Tensions among refugees about their uncertain future increased after members of the Communist Party of Nepal (Maoist) shot dead a police officer in an attack on a police post in September.

Women
The UN Committee on the Elimination of Discrimination against Women, in its report published in January, concluded that women in Bhutan enjoyed a high status compared to other developing countries but that sexual harassment of women remained a major concern.

Children
Children in southern Bhutan continued to suffer discrimination because of the requirement to produce a Security Clearance Certificate to be admitted to schools. In the case of southern Bhutanese children, decisions were often arbitrary and protracted.

The World Bank approved a credit of US$31 million to fund an education program. Non-governmental organizations lobbied for a proportion to go to refugee children in the camps in eastern Nepal on the grounds that they constituted a quarter of all Bhutanese children.

Possible prisoners of conscience
Eleven possible prisoners of conscience from eastern Bhutan continued serving long prison sentences. Four of them were not released despite completing their sentences. An estimated 50 political prisoners from southern Bhutan remained in prison.

🗁 Sangla Dukpa, a member of the Sharchhop ethnic community originally from Mongar district, was arrested in India in January and handed over to the Bhutanese authorities. He was charged with theft and reportedly sentenced to life imprisonment. He was reported to be a political prisoner, victimized because he was formerly a member of the Druk National Congress, a banned political party.

AI country reports/ visits
Statement
- Bhutan: International observers should be given access to Indo-Bhutan border (AI Index: ASA 14/002/2003)

BRUNEI DARUSSALAM

BRUNEI DARUSSALAM
Head of state and government: Sultan Haji Hassanal Bolkiah
Death penalty: abolitionist in practice
UN Women's Convention and its Optional Protocol: not signed

Six members of a banned religious group were reportedly detained without charge or trial. Criminal suspects were sentenced to caning. The UN Committee on the Rights of the Child considered Brunei's initial report and made recommendations.

Background
The monarch, Sultan Haji Hassanal Bolkiah, continued to exercise a wide range of executive powers, holding the offices of Prime Minister, Defence Minister, Finance Minister and head of the police. Under the state of emergency declared in 1962 constitutional provisions safeguarding fundamental liberties remained suspended. The sole opposition party remained inactive.

Arrests under the Internal Security Act
The Internal Security Act (ISA) allows the Minister of Home Affairs, with the approval of the Sultan, to detain any person deemed to be a threat to national security or public order. The Minister is empowered to sign two-year detention orders renewable indefinitely. ISA detainees are denied the rights to a trial, to legal counsel and to be presumed innocent. During prolonged interrogation, while held in isolation and denied access to lawyers, family members and independent medical attention, ISA detainees were at risk of ill-treatment or torture.

▭ Six alleged former members of the *Al-Arqam* Islamic religious group were detained under the ISA in September. The six were alleged to have been involved in attempts to revive the group and to have been in contact with the group's former leader in Malaysia. *Al-Arqam*, which had maintained a wide membership and extensive business interests in the region, was banned in 1991 for religious teachings that "deviated" from the officially recognized Shafeite School of Islam.

Death penalty and corporal punishment
The trials of four Malaysian nationals facing the death penalty for alleged drugs offences continued. Although death sentences have been imposed for drugs and other serious criminal offences in recent years, no executions were known to have been carried out since 1957. Caning continued to be carried out as a mandatory punishment for a range of criminal offences.

Rights of the child and juvenile justice
Pursuant to reporting obligations under the UN Children's Convention – the sole international human rights treaty ratified by Brunei – government representatives presented an initial report before the Committee on the Rights of the Child in September. While welcoming high standards of health care and school enrolment, the Committee expressed concern about a number of issues including the absence of a juvenile justice system; the detention of children together with adults; and the use of caning as a form of punishment for boys. It urged that juvenile offenders under the age of 18 be held separately from adults and that non-discriminatory legislative measures be taken to prohibit all forms of physical and mental violence against children, including corporal punishment, in state institutions and within the family. The Committee also recommended the establishment of a national human rights institution and systematic cooperation with civil society to better ensure the monitoring and implementation of the Convention.

CAMBODIA

KINGDOM OF CAMBODIA
Head of state: King Norodom Sihanouk
Head of government: Hun Sen
Death penalty: abolitionist for all crimes
UN Women's Convention: ratified
Optional Protocol to UN Women's Convention: signed

Impunity and a weak and corrupt judicial system that is neither fair nor independent continued to seriously undermine any progress on human rights. At least 18 politically motivated killings were reported, as well as harassment and intimidation of political party activists and voters in the context of the July national elections and the aftermath. Cambodia's willingness to respect its obligations under international treaties that it has signed was in doubt as a result of its weak implementation of legal safeguards against torture, its failure to bring perpetrators of human rights violations to justice and its policies towards asylum-seekers. Hundreds of Vietnamese (Montagnard) asylum-seekers were forcibly returned to Viet Nam. A revised agreement for the establishment of a criminal tribunal to bring to justice Khmer Rouge leaders was endorsed by the UN General Assembly, but was not formally ratified by the Cambodian legislature.

Background

In Phnom Penh in January, one woman was shot dead and dozens injured as mobs attacked and looted Thai-owned property, including the Thai embassy, after inflammatory anti-Thai newspaper articles and remarks by senior politicians. Dozens of people who were arrested, tried and sentenced in connection with the riots were released in September and October. The riots provoked serious international concern about stability and security in Cambodia and a sharp deterioration in relations with neighbouring Thailand.

National elections were held in July. The Cambodian People's Party (CPP) led by Prime Minister Hun Sen won the largest number of votes but not sufficient to form a government. This led to increased tensions and a political crisis when the two opposition parties, the National United Front for an Independent, Neutral, Peaceful and Cooperative Cambodia (FUNCINPEC) and the Sam Rainsy Party (SRP) formed an Alliance of Democrats and refused to join a government with Hun Sen as prime minister. The stalemate had not been resolved by the end of the year.

In September Cambodia became one of the first countries with Least Developed Country status to join the World Trade Organization (WTO), pending ratification by the Cambodian legislature by March 2004. Some concerns were expressed about the possible social and economic impact on the population.

Drafts of a Criminal Code, a Criminal Procedure Code and other much needed legislation were not completed. A draft Law against Domestic Violence was debated but, along with other legislation, was still awaiting the formation of a new government before it could be further debated and approved.

Refugees

The Cambodian authorities failed to respect their international obligations under the 1951 UN Refugee Convention and the UN Convention against Torture. Hundreds of Vietnamese asylum-seekers from the Central Highlands (Montagnards) were forcibly returned to Viet Nam despite mounting evidence of ill-treatment amounting to torture and the imposition of long prison sentences after unfair trials upon their return (see Viet Nam entry). Many asylum-seekers – women, children and men – spent long periods hiding in jungle areas with little access to food and medical care. There were numerous reports of interference by Vietnamese border police and other security officials on the Cambodian side of the border in the rounding up and deportation of asylum-seekers, including payment of "bounties". Despite negotiations between the UN High Commissioner for Refugees (UNHCR) and the authorities, the UNHCR continued to be denied access to border areas and was unable to provide full protection to asylum-seekers.

▭ Information emerged in July confirming concerns that Thich Tri Luc, a Vietnamese Buddhist monk recognized as a refugee by UNHCR, had been forcibly returned to Viet Nam in July 2002, despite previous government denials. On his return he was detained pending trial (see Viet Nam entry).

Khmer Rouge tribunal

The UN resumed negotiations with the Cambodian government on the establishment of a criminal tribunal to bring to justice suspected perpetrators of gross human rights violations during the period of Khmer Rouge rule (1975-1979). After a series of meetings, a revised draft agreement was put to the UN General Assembly, which was endorsed in May. The draft agreement, not yet ratified by the Cambodian legislature, provided for the establishment of Extraordinary Chambers in Cambodian courts with international assistance. While this agreement was an improvement on earlier versions, serious flaws remained which threatened the integrity of the legal process and set a dangerous precedent for other future international or mixed tribunals. Concerns included the feasibility and inherent weakness of the proposed "mixed" tribunal consisting of Cambodian and international judicial officials, and inadequate provision for victim and witness protection.

Political violence and intimidation

Political violence and intimidation took place mainly in the context of the July national elections. At least 14 people were believed to have been unlawfully killed before and during the election process, and a further four during the political crisis over the formation of a government after the election. In most instances the immediate government reaction was to deny any political motivation in the killings.

▭ Om Radsady, a senior and well-respected FUNCINPEC politician, was shot and killed in Phnom Penh in February. Although the authorities quickly claimed that he was killed in an armed robbery and two men were arrested, tried and sentenced to 20 years' imprisonment in October, it was widely believed that the killing was politically motivated.

▭ In August Khuon Dina, the 16-year-old daughter of an SRP activist, was shot dead in Kampong Cham. Local human rights organizations condemned the killing and the subsequent release of the convicted murderer, a village chief, after he was given a suspended sentence and probation.

▭ On 18 October Chuor Chetharith, the deputy editor of *Ta Prohm* radio station owned by FUNCINPEC, was shot dead in the street in Phnom Penh. It was reported that a joint CPP/FUNCINPEC committee had been established to investigate this incident, but had not made its findings public by the end of the year.

▭ On 21 October popular singer Touch Sunith was shot and critically injured. Her mother was shot trying to protect her and died. Touch Sunith had recorded many pro-FUNCINPEC songs which were played extensively on *Ta Prohm* radio during the election period.

Human rights defenders

In January Uch Kim Nary, the Director of Peaceful Women for the Environment, a Cambodian non-governmental organization (NGO), was threatened with arrest by the police. She had been accused by government officials of helping to organize a gathering in Phnom Penh of representatives of forest communities in December 2002 who wished to make representations to the Department of Forestry and Wildlife. Police violently broke up the peaceful gathering, beating people and using electric batons. At the same time the authorities threatened to sue Eva Galabru, the local representative of the environmental NGO Global Witness, for "disinformation", a charge carrying a maximum three-year prison sentence. Global Witness had issued a statement detailing the excessive force used by police in breaking up the December gathering. The case was later dropped by the authorities. The Cambodian authorities subsequently terminated their agreement with Global Witness to monitor logging activities in the country.

Torture

As in previous years, there were no successful prosecutions of alleged perpetrators of torture. The long overdue initial report on implementation of the UN Convention against Torture, which was examined by the Committee against Torture in April, showed weak implementation of legal safeguards to prevent torture and lack of effective sanctions against perpetrators. The government did not send a delegation to attend the Committee's hearing.

AI country reports/visits

Reports
· Cambodia: Amnesty International's position and concerns regarding the proposed "Khmer Rouge" tribunal (AI Index: ASA 23/005/2003)
· Cambodia: A human rights review based on the Convention against Torture (AI Index: ASA 23/007/2003)

Visit
An AI delegation visited Cambodia in January.

CHINA

PEOPLE'S REPUBLIC OF CHINA
Head of state: Hu Jintao (replaced Jiang Zemin in March)
Head of government: Wen Jiabao (replaced Zhu Rongji in March)
Death penalty: retentionist
UN Women's Convention: ratified with reservations
Optional Protocol to UN Women's Convention: not signed

Despite a few positive steps, no attempt was made to introduce the fundamental legal and institutional reforms necessary to bring an end to serious human rights violations. Tens of thousands of people continued to be detained or imprisoned in violation of their rights to freedom of expression and association, and were at serious risk of torture or ill-treatment. Thousands of people were sentenced to death or executed. Restrictions increased on the cultural and religious rights of the mainly Muslim Uighur community in Xinjiang, where thousands of people have been detained or imprisoned for so-called "separatist" or "terrorist" offences. In Tibet and other ethnic Tibetan areas, freedom of expression and religion continued to be severely restricted. China continued to use the international "war against terrorism" as a pretext for cracking down on peaceful dissent.

Background

A new administration headed by President Hu Jintao and Premier Wen Jiabao took office in March and introduced a few positive reforms, including the abolition of the "custody and repatriation" system of administrative detention (see below). However, no significant attempt was made to address underlying legal and institutional weaknesses that allow human rights violations to be perpetrated with impunity.

The outbreak of Severe Acute Respiratory Syndrome (SARS) in February became the first major test for the new leadership. After months of attempting to conceal vital information about the spread of the disease, the authorities eventually began to respond to international pressure for greater accountability and transparency. The World Health Organization announced that the outbreak was under control in June.

In July, a senior Chinese leader, Luo Gan, called for a continuation of the "strike hard" campaign against crime, which led to a rapid rise in the number of death sentences and executions after its initiation in April 2001, raising fears that this would continue to result in curtailed trial procedures, the use of torture and ill-treatment to obtain "confessions" and imposition of the death penalty without due process.

In August delegates to the Ninth National Women's Congress reportedly discussed a survey that showed that domestic violence had occurred in a third of all

Chinese families. Increased media reporting on this issue appeared to indicate a growing willingness to tackle this entrenched and widespread abuse.

China strengthened its ties with neighbouring countries, including Central Asian countries under the auspices of the Shanghai Cooperation Organization, as well as India, Nepal and Pakistan. One motive appeared to be the forcible return of Chinese nationals, particularly Uighur asylum-seekers and refugees branded as "separatists" or "terrorists" by the Chinese authorities.

There were concerns that the international community was taking a "softer" line on China by confining its human rights concerns to private dialogue sessions rather than public scrutiny. These were borne out when for the second year running the UN Commission on Human Rights failed to propose a motion criticizing China's human rights record. Nevertheless, the UN Special Rapporteur on education delivered a highly critical assessment of China's education policies following her visit to Beijing in September.

Violations in the context of economic reform

The authorities took an increasingly hard line against people protesting against house demolitions and evictions, particularly in large cities such as Shanghai and Beijing, where demolitions of old homes were accelerated by Beijing's preparations for hosting the Olympics in 2008. Scores of peaceful protesters were detained and lawyers assisting in such cases were at risk of arrest or intimidation.

The rights of freedom of expression and association of workers' representatives continued to be severely curtailed and independent trade unions remained illegal. Many of those involved in protests against mass lay-offs, low wages, corrupt management and other issues were detained or imprisoned.

☐ In October, Zheng Enchong, a defence lawyer in Shanghai, was sentenced to three years in prison after he had assisted hundreds of displaced families to contest their evictions through the courts. He was convicted of the vaguely defined offence of "illegally providing state secrets to entities outside China" following a prosecution which appeared to be politically motivated.

☐ In May workers' representatives Yao Fuxin and Xiao Yunliang were sentenced to seven and four years in prison respectively after participating in protests in Liaoyang in northeast China where state-owned companies had laid off millions of men and women. They were transferred in October to Lingyuan Prison, notorious for its poor conditions and brutal regime, despite concerns that they were suffering from serious health problems.

Violations in the context of the spread of HIV/AIDS

Increasing openness on health issues after the outbreak of SARS appeared to result in greater official concern for those affected by HIV/AIDS, but the authorities failed to meet demands for full transparency and accountability in the context of the spread of the virus. Official figures of 840,000 people infected with HIV and 80,000 AIDS patients were considered to be serious underestimates.

The authorities continued to resist calls from non-governmental organizations (NGOs) and others to conduct an independent inquiry into the operation of state-sanctioned blood collection stations in Henan and other central provinces which reportedly resulted in up to one million HIV infections. Vaguely defined "state secrets" legislation continued to be used to detain those suspected of publicizing statistics about the spread of the disease. Medical specialists and others who attempted to raise public awareness of the issue were arrested or intimidated.

People living with HIV/AIDS continued to suffer because of a lack of specialized medical treatment and some were detained and beaten after participating in protests relating to lack of access to medical care.

☐ In September Gao Yaojie, a gynaecologist in her seventies, was tried for libel in connection with her accusation that untrained Henan "folk doctors" had made false claims about their AIDS remedies to make huge profits. She was acquitted in November. There were serious concerns that the case had been brought for political reasons to disrupt her work. Gao Yaojie had reportedly been placed under surveillance by local police and warned against speaking to journalists since she began to draw attention to the spread of HIV/AIDS in Henan in the mid-1990s.

Repression of spiritual and religious groups

Members of unofficial spiritual or religious groups, including some Qi Gong groups and unregistered Christian groups, continued to be arbitrarily detained, tortured and ill-treated.

Rhetoric intensified in the official media against the Falun Gong spiritual movement, which was banned as a "heretical organization" in July 1999, apparently exacerbating the climate of violence and intolerance against the Falun Gong. Detained Falun Gong practitioners, including large numbers of women, were at risk of torture, including sexual abuse, particularly if they refused to renounce their beliefs. According to overseas Falun Gong sources, more than 800 people detained in connection with the Falun Gong had died since 1999, mostly as a result of torture or ill-treatment.

☐ Deng Shiying reportedly died on 19 July, the day after her release from Jilin Women's Prison in Changchun City, Jilin Province, where she was serving a seven-year prison sentence in connection with producing and distributing information describing human rights violations against Falun Gong practitioners in China. According to Falun Gong sources, she was beaten by other inmates, apparently prompted by prison officials, shortly before her release.

Political activists and Internet users

Political activists and Internet users continued to be arrested after peacefully exercising their rights to freedom of expression and association. Many were imprisoned after unfair trials, often on vaguely defined charges relating to "state secrets" or "subversion". One dissident, Wang Bingzhang, was sentenced to life imprisonment on "terrorist" charges (see below).

By the end of the year, at least 50 people had been detained or imprisoned after accessing or circulating politically sensitive information on the Internet. Sentences ranged from two to 12 years. Over 100 others were detained for "spreading rumours" or "false information" by Internet and text message about the outbreak of SARS in March. It was unclear how many were still detained at the end of the year.

⌂ In May, Huang Qi, a computer engineer from Sichuan province, was sentenced to five years' imprisonment for "inciting subversion of the state" after he published articles on his website about human rights and political issues. Huang Qi had been detained without access to his family for almost three years before his sentence was announced. His sentence was upheld on appeal in August. In November, Liu Di, a psychology student from Beijing, who had appealed for the release of Huang Qi in an Internet chatroom under the pseudonym "Stainless Steel Mouse", was released on bail after being detained for over a year. In December it was announced that she would not face formal indictment.

⌂ Veteran dissident Kang Yuchun was released from prison five years before the end of his sentence on the eve of the European Union (EU)-China human rights dialogue in October.

Torture, administrative detention and unfair trials

Torture and ill-treatment remained widespread in many state institutions. Common methods included kicking, beating, electric shocks, suspension by the arms, shackling in painful positions, and sleep and food deprivation. Women in detention were vulnerable to rape and sexual abuse.

"Custody and repatriation", a system of administrative detention which had allowed for the arbitrary detention and abuse of millions of migrant workers, vagrants, homeless children and others in urban areas, was formally abolished when new rules for dealing with vagrancy came into effect in August. Its abolition was prompted by a public outcry about the brutal murder of migrant worker Sun Zhigang in March while he was being held unlawfully in a "custody and repatriation" centre in Guangzhou city.

However, another system, "re-education through labour", continued to allow for the detention of hundreds of thousands of people for up to three years without charge or trial. In September the Ministry of Public Security announced new regulations aimed at preventing the police from using torture in administrative cases, but it remained unclear how well they would be enforced in practice.

People accused of both political and criminal offences continued to be denied due process. Detainees' access to lawyers and family members continued to be severely restricted. Political trials fell far short of international fair trial standards. Those charged with offences related to "state secrets" or "terrorism" had their legal rights restricted and were tried *in camera*.

⌂ In February US-based dissident Wang Bingzhang became the first democracy activist known to have been convicted of "terrorist" offences. He was sentenced to life imprisonment in connection with various charges, including passing military secrets to Taiwan and leading a "terrorist" group. There were serious violations of Chinese and international law during his trial and pre-trial detention. In May the UN Working Group on Arbitrary Detention ruled that his arrest and detention were arbitrary and called on the authorities to remedy the situation.

Death penalty

The death penalty continued to be used extensively and arbitrarily as a result of political interference. People were executed for non-violent crimes such as tax fraud and pimping as well as drug offences and violent crimes. The authorities continued to keep national statistics on death sentences and executions secret. By the end of the year, with the limited records available, AI had recorded 1,639 death sentences and 726 executions, although the true figures were believed to be much higher.

Execution was by shooting and increasingly by lethal injection. In March it was reported that the authorities in Yunnan province had purchased 18 mobile execution chambers for execution by lethal injection to improve the "efficiency" and "cost-effectiveness" of executions.

Judicial interpretations issued by the Supreme Court in May and September respectively extended the potential application of the death penalty to people suffering from SARS who deliberately spread the disease, and to those involved in the illegal production, trade and storage of defined quantities of toxic chemicals.

⌂ In January Lobsang Dhondup, a Tibetan from Sichuan province, was executed after being convicted after an unfair trial of "causing explosions" and other offences. The authorities stated that his trial was held in secret because it involved "state secrets" without providing further clarification. He was executed hours after his sentence was passed, without his case being referred to the Supreme Court for review as required under Chinese law, and despite official assurances to the USA and the EU that his case would receive a "lengthy" review.

North Korean asylum-seekers

Hundreds, possibly thousands, of North Korean asylum-seekers in northeast China were arrested and forcibly returned during the year. China continued to deny North Koreans access to any refugee determination procedures despite evidence that many had a genuine claim to asylum and in breach of the UN Refugee Convention to which China is a state party. Reports suggested that the majority of those crossing the border were women who were at risk of being sold as brides or forced into prostitution. In August China reportedly increased its military presence along the border in an apparent attempt to curb the flow of North Koreans into China.

The crack-down extended to people suspected of helping North Koreans, including members of foreign aid and religious organizations, ethnic Korean Chinese nationals, and journalists attempting to raise awareness of their plight, many of whom were detained for interrogation.

⌷ In May, Seok Jae-hyun, a South Korean journalist, was sentenced to two years in prison for "trafficking in human beings" after he photographed a group of refugees boarding boats bound for South Korea and Japan. It was not known what became of the several dozen North Koreans boarding the boats who were detained at the same time.

Xinjiang Uighur Autonomous Region

The authorities continued to use the international "war against terrorism" to justify harsh repression in Xinjiang, which continued to result in serious human rights violations against the ethnic Uighur community. The authorities continued to make little distinction between acts of violence and acts of passive resistance. Repression was often manifested through assaults on Uighur culture, such as the closure of several mosques, restrictions on the use of the Uighur language and the banning of certain Uighur books and journals.

The crack-down against suspected "separatists, terrorists and religious extremists" intensified following the start of a renewed 100-day security crack-down in October. Arrests continued and thousands of political prisoners, including prisoners of conscience, remained in prison. Concerns increased that China was putting pressure on neighbouring countries to forcibly return Uighurs suspected of "separatist" activities, including asylum-seekers and refugees.

⌷ Officials confirmed in October that Shaheer Ali, who had been forcibly returned to China from Nepal in 2002, had been executed after being found guilty of "terrorist" offences in a closed trial. He had been recognized as a refugee by the UN High Commissioner for Refugees in Nepal. Shaheer Ali had secretly left behind a detailed testimony in which he described being beaten, given electric shocks and kicked unconscious during a previous period of detention in 1994.

Tibet Autonomous Region and other ethnic Tibetan areas

A series of releases of high-profile Tibetan prisoners of conscience during 2002 was not maintained in 2003, and freedom of religion, association and expression continued to be severely restricted. Contacts between the Chinese authorities and representatives of the Tibetan government in exile apparently failed to result in any significant policy changes. Over 100 Tibetans, mainly Buddhist monks and nuns, continued to be imprisoned in violation of their fundamental human rights, and arbitrary arrests and unfair trials continued.

⌷ Choedar Dargye, Gedun Thogphel and Jampa Choephel, three monks from Khangmar monastery, Ngaba prefecture, Sichuan province, were tried in August. They had been arrested for distributing material calling for independence for Tibet, painting a Tibetan flag and possessing photographs of the Dalai Lama. They were sentenced to 12 years in prison. Three others were arrested in connection with the same case. Some sources indicated that they had been sentenced to between one and eight years in prison. One of the three, Jamyang Oezer, was reported to be seriously ill in hospital.

Hong Kong Special Administrative Region

In the wake of protests involving half a million people in July, the Hong Kong authorities eventually withdrew proposed legislation under Article 23 of the Basic Law, which stipulates that Hong Kong is to enact its own laws to prohibit acts of treason, secession, sedition and subversion. There were serious concerns that such legislation could be used to suppress rights to freedom of expression and association as well as legitimate activities of NGOs and the media. The authorities promised further public consultation on revised proposals, but made no commitment on a timescale for their reintroduction.

AI country reports/ visits
Reports
- People's Republic of China: Miscarriage of justice? The trial of Tenzin Deleg Rinpoche and related arrests (AI Index: ASA 17/029/2003)
- People's Republic of China: Continuing abuses under a new leadership – summary of human rights concerns (AI Index: ASA 17/035/2003)

Visit
In December, an AI delegate attended an EU-China experts' seminar in Venice, Italy, on judicial guarantees of human rights and capacity-building of NGOs.

FIJI

REPUBLIC OF THE FIJI ISLANDS
Head of state: Ratu Josefa Iloilovatu Uluivuda
Head of government: Laisenia Qarase
Death penalty: abolitionist for ordinary crimes
UN Women's Convention: ratified
Optional Protocol to UN Women's Convention: not signed

The government pursued a policy of encouraging indigenous Fijian dominance over the mainly Indo-Fijian non-indigenous community. Many supporters of the coup in 2000 and rebel soldiers were convicted and imprisoned but others continued to enjoy impunity. The police, military and civilian justice systems struggled in their investigation and prosecution of coup-related criminal cases, including those involving human rights violations. Legal reforms incorporated international standards on women's and children's rights into domestic legislation.

Background
Political and economic stability improved. Prime Minister Laisenia Qarase continued his policy of favouring indigenous Fijians, who made up 51 per cent of the population, over other citizens. The policy, which was intended to increase economic and educational opportunities for indigenous Fijians, was criticized for exacerbating racial differences and creating inequalities both between and within racial groups. Racial intolerance was linked to an attack on a Hindu temple, the 44th Hindu temple reported to have been burned down, damaged or desecrated since the 2000 coup. Indigenous Fijian students were granted new benefits, provided they attend predominantly indigenous schools.

In July the Supreme Court confirmed that the composition of Cabinet was unconstitutional because it failed to ensure power-sharing between ethnic communities through a multi-party Cabinet. The Constitution obliges the Prime Minister to offer Cabinet posts to all parties with at least 10 per cent of seats in parliament, in proportion to their numbers in the House. The Court's ruling forced the government to negotiate with the mainly Indo-Fijian Labour Party which held 39 per cent of the seats in parliament. The government sought a ruling from the Supreme Court on the issue, which was expected in 2004.

Post-coup legal developments
Criminal investigations, some involving influential political leaders, highlighted the continuing indigenous power struggle which had given rise to the coup in 2000 and the ongoing problem of impunity for human rights abuses.

Dozens of people were charged, tried or sentenced for human rights-related crimes and other offences linked to the 2000 coup and army mutiny. In October, the newly appointed Police Commissioner announced that of 3,521 people investigated since 2000 for coup-related crimes, 704 were found guilty and nearly 200 sentenced to prison terms; 461 had been acquitted or conditionally released.

Among prominent indigenous leaders charged in 2003 for their role in the coup were Vice-President Ratu Jope Seniloli, Cabinet Minister Isireli Leweniqila, and Deputy Speaker of Parliament Ratu Rakuita Vakalalabure. They were key politicians in the governing coalition. A provincial leader, Ratu Inoke Takiveikata, was charged with inciting a post-coup mutiny at military headquarters. Court proceedings were continuing at the end of the year.

In June, former politician Timoci Silatolu and journalist Jo Nata were sentenced to life imprisonment for treason in connection with their role in the coup.

Others responsible for crimes committed during the coup effectively continued to enjoy impunity.

In February, a magistrate acquitted nine indigenous villagers from the Muaniweni area. They had been charged in connection with some of the most violent and well-documented racist attacks against Indo-Fijian families during the coup. They were reportedly acquitted for lack of evidence following earlier allegations of witness intimidation.

Ten indigenous Fijian coup suspects were acquitted on human rights grounds because a military prosecution witness failed to appear in court.

Renewed police investigations into former Police Commissioner Isikia Savua's role in the coup did not result in any further legal action. He took up his post as Fiji's representative at the UN in New York in January.

The police made little progress investigating the beating to death by soldiers of four suspected rebel prisoners following a post-coup mutiny. This was in part because several soldiers were unavailable for interrogation owing to their participation in UN peace-keeping operations. In November, in a related case, the High Court acquitted a soldier of the manslaughter of Alifereti Nimacere, an escaped prisoner who had joined the rebels during the mutiny.

No one was charged or disciplined after a military witness admitted in court that a group of coup supporters being tried had been ill-treated during their arrest at Kalabu school in July 2000.

Law reform, human rights legislation and education
A new Family Law Bill was passed in October and was due to come into effect in 2005. It brings some key women's and children's rights into line with national and international human rights law. The Bill prioritizes the best interests of children in government decision-making.

The Cabinet approved a Fiji Law Reform Commission program to modernize legislation on prisons, criminal procedure, sentencing and domestic violence.

Parliament raised Penal Code penalties for sexual violence, particularly against children.

In April, school principals agreed to a National Plan of Action, developed by the Fiji Human Rights Commission, to introduce human rights education formally into school curricula.

Violence against women

Following a major campaign on violence against women in 2002, the non-governmental Fiji Women's Crisis Centre found that more women were prepared to report such crimes, including apparently increasing racist violence. Cases reported to police had increased by 24 per cent since 1997. The Centre highlighted concerns at the rise in reported cases of sexual violence over the previous year and stated that in May alone 96 cases were reported.

International scrutiny

The UN Committee on the Elimination of Racial Discrimination expressed concern in June about reservations to the UN Convention against Racism which Fiji inherited from colonial times and which the government refused to withdraw. The Committee requested detailed information on prosecutions for racist violence and religious intolerance against Indo-Fijians, and any preventive measures undertaken. The Committee urged that no "affirmative action" measures for disadvantaged indigenous Fijians "should abrogate or diminish the enjoyment of human rights for all". It strongly recommended that poverty alleviation programs benefit all poor citizens, irrespective of race, "to avoid undue stress on already strained ethnic relations."

INDIA

REPUBLIC OF INDIA
Head of state: A.P.J. Abdul Kalam
Head of government: Atal Bihari Vajpayee
Death penalty: retentionist
UN Women's Convention: ratified with reservations
Optional Protocol to UN Women's Convention: not signed

There was increasing concern at the erosion of human rights protections in the context of "anti-terrorism" measures against armed political groups, and continuing communal tensions. Systemic discrimination against vulnerable groups – including women, religious minorities, *dalits* and *adivasis* (tribal people) – was exacerbated by widespread use of security legislation, political interference with the criminal justice system and slow judicial proceedings in a continuing climate of impunity. Tensions remained high in the state of Gujarat in the aftermath of widespread communal violence in 2002. Witnesses to the violence and human rights defenders were threatened and concerns grew about the impartiality of institutions of the criminal justice system in the state, including the police, prosecution service and elements of the judiciary. A committee constituted by the Ministry of Home Affairs suggested recommendations for the reform of the criminal justice system which could potentially undermine human rights protections even further.

Background

The National Democratic Alliance, led by the Bharatiya Janata Party (BJP), remained in government. Some state elections were marred by political campaigns that fuelled inter-caste or inter-communal tensions.

Bomb attacks targeting civilians were reported during the year. On 25 August, 52 people were killed and around 150 injured by two car bombs in Mumbai, Maharashtra state. No group claimed responsibility. However, at least six Muslims accused of involvement in the attacks were arrested and charged; they remained in custody at the end of the year awaiting trial. Human rights protections were further eroded, ostensibly in response to security considerations.

Relations between India and Pakistan improved in some respects, although underlying tensions remained. Security concerns continued to dominate foreign policy discussions, including in the context of the US-led "war on terrorism" which continued to be supported by the Indian government.

In the northeast, a cease-fire between the National Socialist Council of Nagaland (Isaac-Muivah) and the central government was extended in July for one year.

There were reports of collective expulsions by the Indian authorities of Bangladeshi nationals accused of being illegal immigrants. However, the Bangladeshi authorities were reluctant to allow them to return. The incident resulted in a stalemate where 213 people were trapped between the two borders.

Heightened tensions in Gujarat

Following widespread communal violence in the state of Gujarat in February and March 2002, the state continued to witness sporadic incidents of communal violence. More than 2,000 people had been killed in early 2002 in the wave of violence targeting the Muslim community. These killings followed an attack on a train in Godhra in February 2002 in which 59 Hindus were killed by a mob. Reports implicated police officers and members of Hindu nationalist groups, including the Vishwa Hindu Parishad (VHP) and the ruling BJP in the violence against Muslims.

There was increasing concern about the failure of the state government of Gujarat to ensure that those responsible for widespread communal violence in early 2002 were brought to justice. In many cases, attempts to hold the perpetrators accountable were hampered by the highly defective manner in which police recorded complaints. Victims complained that police failed to register complaints, or recorded details in such a way as to lead to lesser charges, omitted the names of prominent people who were pivotal in the attacks, and did not take appropriate action to arrest suspects, particularly where they were supporters of the BJP. Reports indicated that out of 4,252 complaints filed by individuals regarding the communal violence, 2,032 were closed even though the alleged abuses were found to have occurred. One of the reasons given by the police for closing the cases was that they were unable to identify the individual perpetrators.

Concerns about the impartiality of institutions in the state and the government's commitment to ensure justice for the victims of communal violence were brought to the fore in June when 21 people accused of the murder of 14 people burned to death in the Best Bakery in Baroda on 1 March 2002 were acquitted. Following the acquittal, key witnesses indicated that they lied in court because they had been threatened with death unless they did so. Following a public outcry, the National Human Rights Commission (NHRC) carried out an investigation and subsequently filed a petition in the Supreme Court. The petition asked the court to provide protection to witnesses, to ensure a retrial of the case in a court outside Gujarat state, and to order the transfer of other ongoing key cases to courts outside Gujarat to ensure fair proceedings. During the proceedings the Supreme Court severely criticized the state government of Gujarat for failing to provide justice to victims of the communal violence and pointed to the possible collusion between the state government and the prosecution in subverting the cause of justice. Following the criticism, the Gujarat government amended its original appeal, this time seeking a retrial of the Best Bakery case. This was dismissed by the Gujarat High Court in December.

Following the investigation into the killing on 26 March of Haren Pandya, the former Home Minister of Gujarat, police reported that they had unearthed a series of conspiracies to target Hindus and prominent officials held responsible for the communal violence. From March onwards, scores of Muslims were reported to have been illegally detained in Gayakwad Haveli Police Station in Ahmedabad by Crime Branch police, reinforcing concerns about the break-down in the rule of law in relation to the Muslim minority in the state. Many of those formally arrested were charged under the Prevention of Terrorism Act. Police routinely resorted to arbitrary and incommunicado detention, denied detainees access to lawyers and medical attention, and used torture or ill-treatment to extract confessions. There were concerns that patterns of illegal detention may have been replicated in other areas of the state following a statement by a senior police officer which endorsed such actions. The widespread use of incommunicado detention by police against members of the Muslim minority in Ahmedabad is reported to have intimidated members of the Muslim community who were too scared to make official complaints.

Following comments in which the Chief Minister alleged that foreign-funded "five star activists" were maligning Gujarat and attacking India's democratic system for the sake of their vested interests, there were reports that a committee had been set up to monitor the activities of those foreign funded non-governmental organizations which were active in the reconstruction of the state after the January 2000 earthquake.

Violence against women in Gujarat

The specific targeting of Muslim women in the communal violence of early 2002 remained unacknowledged by the state government and criminal justice system. Witnesses reported that a large number of women were beaten, stripped naked, gang raped and stabbed. Many of the victims were mutilated before being burned alive by mobs, allegedly led by Hindu nationalist groups. The stigma associated with sexual violence impeded many women from making formal complaints. Those who did lodge complaints were often faced with wholly inadequate responses from the police and the health, rehabilitation and justice systems. In some cases victims were asked to file their complaints with officers who had allegedly colluded with the attackers. Nearly two years after the attacks, the survivors still had no access to rehabilitation packages or procedures geared to their needs.

Discrimination

Socially and economically marginalized groups, such as *dalits*, *adivasis*, women and religious minorities, including Muslims, continued to face discrimination at the hands of the police, the criminal justice system and non-state actors.

In April a government-appointed committee under the direction of Justice Malimath published its recommendations for reforms of the criminal justice system in India. There were concerns that the Committee's recommendations threatened to weaken protection of women's rights in law. For example the Committee recommended that in cases where the offence of cruelty is committed against a woman by her husband or his relatives, it should be possible to settle the case out of court and bail should be available to the accused. The Committee's reasoning for this proposal was that it would facilitate forgiveness of the husband and the return of the woman to the matrimonial home.

The Malimath Committee was silent on issues related to protecting the rights of the poor, *dalits*, ethnic and religious minorities and other disadvantaged communities who face daily abuse and violence. The criminalization of poverty coupled with the complete inability of the poor to negotiate the criminal justice system and retain competent legal counsel, remained a major human rights problem as such individuals were at risk of mistreatment without redress.

There were continuing reports of police inflicting cruel, inhuman or degrading treatment on members of *adivasi* communities in the context of land disputes and evictions. Other abuses reported included arbitrary detentions and the destruction of homes and livelihoods.

⌷ On 21 July, members of an *adivasi* community were forcibly evicted from their homes in Puntamba village and surrounding areas in the Ahmednagar district of Maharashtra. Around 50 huts and several acres of crops were destroyed by officials of the Maharashtra State Farming Corporation (MSFC), accompanied by up to 100 police officials. An appeal regarding their rights to the land, which was pending, was ignored by the officials carrying out the evictions. During the action at least one activist of the *Adivasi Bhoomi Hakka Andolan* (Tribal Land Rights Movement) was placed in preventive detention by police. The findings of a police investigation into the complaints filed by *adivasis* concerning the destruction of their homes remained unknown at the end of the year. In recent years a number of incidents have been reported where *adivasis* and activists working with them have faced harassment from local landowners and officials of the MSFC, including destruction of their property, verbal and physical abuse, arbitrary arrest and beating in police custody. While police have registered complaints against *adivasis* by officials and landowners, they have regularly refused to register complaints made by *adivasis* or to investigate their allegations of harassment.

Security legislation
The Prevention of Terrorism Act (POTA) continued to be used to detain political opponents and members of minority populations. The lapsed Terrorist and Disruptive Activities Act continued to be used to arrest people in Jammu and Kashmir by linking them to cases filed before 1995. Preventive arrest and detention provisions contained in other security laws as well as in the Code of Criminal Procedure were also misused against political and human rights activists.

There were grave concerns about recommendations of the Malimath Committee to incorporate into criminal law several provisions of the POTA which violate international human rights standards or which, if implemented, would lead to a heightened risk of human rights violations. For example, the Committee recommended that confessions recorded by a

Superintendent of Police (or higher rank) which was also audio or video recorded should be admissible as evidence. Concerns that the provisions of the POTA could encourage the use of torture and ill-treatment by admitting such confessions appeared to have been realized in practice. In Gujarat several detainees alleged in court that their confessions were extracted under duress. Preventive arrests and detention continued to be used against political opponents using state legislation similar to the POTA in a number of states including Jammu and Kashmir, Andhra Pradesh, Arunachal Pradesh, Karnataka and New Delhi Union Territory. Only a handful of high-profile releases had been made by the end of the year despite a promise to review all cases of detainees held without trial for long periods under security legislation made under the Common Minimum Programme adopted by the new state government in Jammu and Kashmir.

Human rights commissions
The government failed to consider the recommendations made by the NHRC in 2002 for amendments to the Protection of Human Rights Act 1993 under which the NHRC operates. These amendments would have permitted the NHRC to investigate allegations of human rights violations committed by the army or paramilitary forces, as well as those committed by the police, and incidents that took place more than a year before the complaint was made. The government's failure to deal with these amendments served to strengthen impunity for human rights violations. State human rights commissions, established in 13 of the 28 states, continued to suffer from lack of resources and expertise.

Impunity
Members of the security services continued to enjoy virtual impunity for human rights violations.

In Punjab a culture of impunity, developed within the criminal justice system during the period of widespread armed political opposition in the mid-1990s, continued to prevail. This was strengthened by provisions contained in special security laws and the Protection of Human Rights Act, and by the frequent failure to implement recommendations issued by various commissions of inquiry.

⌷ In 1996 the Supreme Court had ordered the NHRC to examine the findings of the Central Bureau of Investigations that 2,097 people had been illegally cremated by police officials in Amritsar district. The cremations took place following widespread "disappearances" in police custody and possible extrajudicial executions in the mid-1990s. Seven years after this decision, the state of Punjab had only just begun to file its affidavits on cases under examination by the NHRC.

In Jammu and Kashmir the state government kept its promise made in the Common Minimum Programme to assimilate the Special Operations Group (SOG), a paramilitary division of the police accused of human rights violations, into the regular police. However, the SOG continued to operate as a cohesive unit and despite disciplinary action being taken against a few of its members, there continued to be regular reports of human rights violations being committed by the SOG. In May, the NHRC asked the Chief Secretary of Jammu and Kashmir for specific information on the systems used by the state authorities to record and investigate allegations of "disappearances" and on measures taken to prevent further "disappearances". A substantive response to the Commission's request remained outstanding at the end of 2003.

Civilians continued to be targeted for gross human rights violations in Jammu and Kashmir and scores of allegations of human rights violations were made against the security forces, paramilitaries and "renegades" (former members of armed opposition groups working with the security forces).

Abuses by opposition groups

There were continuing reports of human rights abuses by armed opposition groups against civilians. In Jammu and Kashmir human rights abuses by militants persisted at a high level with a reported 344 civilians killed in targeted or indiscriminate violence by armed groups in the period from January to the end of November. On 24 March armed men shot dead 24 Kashmiri Pandits, including 11 women and two children, in the village of Nadimarg. In the states of the northeast, abuses included the torture and killings of non-combatants and attacks on civilians by *naxalites* (armed left-wing groups) in areas of Andhra Pradesh, Bihar, Madhya Pradesh, Orissa and West Bengal.

Human rights defenders

Human rights defenders continued to face accusations of "anti-national" activities, harassment by state agents, political groups and private individuals, including threats, preventive arrest and detention, and violence.

There were reports that following an assassination attempt on the Chief Minister of Andhra Pradesh in October, allegedly by *naxalites*, retaliatory harassment was initiated against human rights defenders. At least six members of the Andhra Pradesh Civil Liberties Committee (APCLC) were detained for questioning in October in connection with the assassination attempt and APCLC activists were put under constant surveillance and were repeatedly detained for questioning. In November there were growing concerns the APCLC could face a ban following statements by the Director General of Police indicating that the organization was sympathetic to the *naxalites*.

Death penalty

At least 33 people were sentenced to death in 2003. No executions were reported. India's highest courts have ruled that the death penalty can only be applied in the "rarest of rare" cases. In the absence of any more detailed definition, the interpretation of this phrase by judges varied greatly. The majority of those sentenced to death are poor and illiterate. The government of India does not publish statistical information about the implementation of the death penalty. Politicians continued to make statements favouring the extension of the death penalty. In mid-2003 the Law Commission issued a questionnaire asking citizens to indicate which mode of execution should be used when executing those on death row.

AI country reports/visits

Reports

- India: Break the cycle of impunity and torture in Punjab (AI Index: ASA 20/002/2003)
- India: Report of the Malimath Committee on Reforms of the Criminal Justice System – Some observations (AI Index: ASA 20/025/2003)
- India: Abuse of the law in Gujarat – Muslims detained illegally in Ahmedabad (AI Index: ASA 20/029/2003)
- India: Open letter to the Chief Minister of Jammu and Kashmir on the failed promises of the Common Minimum Programme (AI Index: ASA 20/033/2003)

Visits

In 2003 AI continued to have an ongoing dialogue with the government of India about access to India for AI representatives.

INDONESIA

REPUBLIC OF INDONESIA
Head of state and government: Megawati Sukarnoputri
Death penalty: retentionist
UN Women's Convention: ratified with reservations
Optional Protocol to UN Women's Convention: signed

The human rights situation deteriorated in some areas as the government resorted to increasingly repressive methods against independence movements. Increases in the number of cases of extrajudicial executions, "disappearances", arbitrary detention, torture, sexual violence, forced displacement and destruction of property were reported following the declaration of a military emergency to combat the armed independence movement in Nanggroe Aceh Darussalam (NAD) in May. Military operations against both armed and peaceful independence activists in Papua also resulted in human rights violations, including arbitrary detention and torture. Elsewhere, the police employed excessive force against protesters. At least 30 prisoners of conscience were sentenced to terms of imprisonment. Trials of prisoners of conscience and political prisoners did not meet international standards for fair trial and there were reports that some detainees were tortured. Efforts to hold perpetrators to account for human rights violations suffered a major setback as the trials of individuals charged with committing crimes against humanity in the Democratic Republic of Timor-Leste (formerly known as East Timor) ended without having delivered either truth or justice.

Background

Indonesia enjoyed a year of relative political and economic stability, but a lack of political will and pervasive corruption inhibited progress in key areas, including reform of the law and the judiciary. The decision to resort to military operations in NAD was regarded as a reflection of the growing confidence of the military and its renewed influence on government policy.

Security legislation

Legislation on Combating Criminal Acts of Terrorism was adopted. AI was concerned that the act of "terrorism" was not adequately defined and that the rights of suspects were not fully guaranteed under the law.

Over 100 people were arrested under the legislation. The majority were alleged members of *Jemaah Islamiyah* (Islamic Community), an organization which has pledged to use violent means to set up a pan-Islamic state in Southeast Asia and has allegedly been responsible for a number of bomb attacks in Indonesia, including at the Marriot Hotel in Jakarta in August 2003. Those arrested included three men who were sentenced to death for involvement in the bombings in Bali in October 2002 in which over 200 people died.

Others arrested included five senior members of the armed group, the Free Aceh Movement (GAM). The five represented GAM in peace negotiations with the government and were arrested in May on their way to talks with the government. All were found guilty of rebellion and acts of "terrorism" and sentenced to between 12 and 15 years' imprisonment. One complained of receiving death threats and suffering ill-treatment in police custody. AI was concerned that their trials may not have been fair.

Other concerns about lack of protection for suspects under this legislation were raised after reports emerged that a number of Islamist activists held under the security legislation had been tortured or ill-treated and that their families were not initially informed of their whereabouts.

Repression of pro-independence movements

A marked deterioration in the human rights situation in NAD followed the imposition of a military state of emergency on 19 May after the collapse of a peace process between the government and GAM. Tight restrictions on access to NAD by international human rights monitors, humanitarian workers and international journalists, as well as intimidation and harassment of local human rights activists and journalists, effectively prevented independent monitoring of the situation. According to official sources, over 1,100 people had been killed by the end of the year, including some 470 civilians. Local human rights organizations claimed that many more civilians were among the dead. Members of the National Commission on Human Rights (Komnas HAM) publicly stated that both government security forces and GAM were responsible for human rights abuses and that they had documented cases of extrajudicial execution – including of children – arbitrary detention, torture, sexual violence and "disappearances".

Tens of thousands of people were displaced by the military operations, some by force. There were serious concerns for the security and well-being of internally displaced persons, including those in government-established camps where there were unconfirmed reports of sexual violence by the security forces.

The government claimed that 2,000 members of GAM had surrendered or been captured by the end of the year and several hundred brought to trial. Detainees were denied access to lawyers. There was concern that they were at risk of torture or ill-treatment, apparently routine in military and police custody.

GAM was responsible for human rights abuses, including kidnapping. Over 150 people were alleged to have been abducted by GAM after May, including local government officials and journalists.

Peaceful expressions of support for independence in Papua were prohibited. Several trials of individuals involved in flag-raising ceremonies or other symbolic actions took place. Three people were sentenced to imprisonment for up to two years for participating in a peaceful pro-independence ceremony in Abepura in December 2002. Nine others who participated in a similar ceremony in Manokwari in late 2002 were also sentenced to terms of imprisonment of up to 15 months. Other ceremonies in late 2003 resulted in the arrest of over 40 people, seven of whom were subsequently charged with rebellion.

Komnas HAM reported that seven people were killed during a military operation in Jayawijaya District in April to recover weapons and ammunition allegedly stolen from the military by members of the armed opposition group, the Free Papua Movement (OPM). Two soldiers were killed in the raid. Villagers were allegedly tortured and ill-treated, and houses and other property were destroyed or damaged during the operation. At least 30 people were detained, including human rights activists. One person died in custody, allegedly as a result of torture; others were reported to have suffered injuries. No one was held to account for these human rights violations, but 16 people were found guilty of offences related to the raid and were reportedly sentenced to up to life imprisonment. AI was concerned that their trials may not have been fair.

Prisoners of conscience and unfair trials

Thirty prisoners of conscience were sentenced to terms of imprisonment during the year. Nineteen people were charged under provisions in the Criminal Code that forbid insulting the President or government. The provisions contravene the right to freedom of expression.

Prisoners of conscience included labour and political activists and peaceful supporters of independence in NAD and Papua. Journalists were also put on trial. AI was concerned that trials of journalists represented a serious threat to press freedom in Indonesia.

Prisoners of conscience and political prisoners were convicted after unfair trials. Irregularities included incommunicado detention and denial or restriction of access to lawyers and family members. Cases of torture or ill-treatment of suspects were also reported.

⊐ Six members of the Governing Front of the Poor were arrested after participating in a demonstration in Kendari town, South Sulawesi, in January during which portraits of the President and Vice-President were burned. The six were reported to have been beaten, punched and slapped and had objects thrown at them while in police custody in Kendari. Access to legal representation was restricted. All were found guilty of insulting the President. They were sentenced to four months and 15 days' imprisonment, the time already spent in pre-trial detention. It appeared that there was no investigation into the allegations of torture and ill-treatment, although one police officer allegedly involved in the beatings was reportedly transferred to another police station.

⊐ Two editors of the daily tabloid *Rakyat Merdeka* were sentenced to suspended prison terms for publishing material deemed insulting to political leaders. Karim Paputungan was found guilty of defamation and sentenced to five months in jail for printing a cartoon considered insulting to a leading politician. Supratman was sentenced to six months' imprisonment for "insulting the President" after printing headlines critical of the government's plans to increase fuel and basic commodity prices.

Human rights defenders at risk

Human rights defenders continued to be at risk, particularly in NAD where human rights organizations were among those publicly accused by the security forces of links to GAM. Two members of human rights organizations in NAD were believed to have been extrajudicially executed and three others "disappeared" during the year. At least 11 human rights activists were briefly detained under the military emergency. A workshop on human rights monitoring organized by Komnas HAM in NAD was broken up by the security forces in October. There was no progress on resolving the cases of 18 other human rights defenders believed to have been extrajudicially executed or who had "disappeared" in NAD since 2000.

Elsewhere charges of defamation were brought against several human rights defenders apparently to discourage them from carrying out their legitimate work.

⊐ Mukhlis Ishak, 27, and Zulfikar, 24, "disappeared" after they were arrested in March by plainclothed men believed to be from a military intelligence unit. The arrest, which was photographed, took place as the men were accompanying villagers demonstrating outside the office of the head of Bireuen District, NAD. Both are members of the Link for Community Development, which assists internally displaced people.

⊐ A defamation suit against Inda Fatinaware, Director of the Indonesian Forum for the Environment (Wahli), was filed by the Police Commander of South Sulawesi Province in October after three farmers were shot dead during land protests against a plantation company in Bulukumba District in July and October. Wahli had issued a press statement which accused the police of responsibility for the killings and called on the local police commander to resign.

Accountability for human rights violations

The verdict in the last of 12 trials relating to the violence in Timor-Leste around the ballot on independence in 1999 was delivered in August. Major General Adam Damiri, former Regional Military Commander for Timor-Leste, was sentenced to three years' imprisonment. He was one of six people found guilty of crimes against humanity but, like the others, he remained free pending the outcome of an appeal against the conviction. He also continued in active service in the military. Twelve others were acquitted in trials that began in 2002. Problems with the earlier trials were not resolved and later trials were also characterized by weak prosecutions that failed to present credible cases in court. The failure to provide effective protection meant that many victims and witnesses from Timor-Leste were unwilling to appear before the court.

Indonesia's reluctance to bring to justice those responsible for the violence in Timor-Leste in 1999 was reinforced by its continued refusal to transfer to Timor-Leste some 280 suspects who live in Indonesia against whom there were indictments issued by the Timor-Leste Prosecutor General. Among them were individuals charged with committing crimes against humanity.

Other landmark trials began in September when 13 military officials, including the current commander of the Special Forces Command (Kopassus), appeared before a Human Rights Court charged in relation to the killing of Muslim protesters in Tanjung Priok, North Jakarta, in 1984. The trials were ongoing at the end of the year, but shortcomings similar to those that undermined the effectiveness and credibility of the Timor-Leste trials had already emerged, including allegations of intimidation of victims and witnesses.

Seven members of Kopassus were sentenced to between one year's and 42 months' imprisonment by a military tribunal after being found guilty of causing the death of the leader of the Papuan civilian independence movement, Theys H. Eluay, in 2001. The trials were criticized because command responsibility for the killing was not established and because of the light sentences. After the verdict the Army Chief of Staff publicly described the seven as "heroes".

There were a few investigations by the military into alleged human rights violations under the military emergency in NAD. However, these represented a tiny fraction of the total reported cases and the investigations were not considered sufficiently independent or impartial. Ten soldiers were known to have been convicted in military courts, including three soldiers who were sentenced to up to three and a half years' imprisonment for the rape of four women in North Aceh District in June.

The majority of alleged human rights violations were not investigated or, when they were, prosecutions did not follow. In October the US Senate voted to maintain a ban on training Indonesian armed forces because of lack of progress in the investigation into the killing of one Indonesian and two US teachers near the US-owned Freeport Indonesia mine in Mimika District, Papua, in August 2002. It was alleged that the military were involved in the attack.

Death penalty
At least 61 people were believed to be on death row, nine of whom were sentenced during the year. No executions took place.

Lack of judicial independence: report of UN Special Rapporteur
The report of the UN Special Rapporteur on the independence of judges and lawyers' visit to Indonesia in July 2002 was published. The report expressed extreme concern about the lack of a culture of judicial independence and of widespread corruption in the judiciary, police, prosecutors' offices and the Office of the Attorney General.

AI country reports/visits
Reports
- Indonesia & Timor-Leste: International responsibility for justice (AI Index: ASA 03/001/2003)
- Indonesia: Protecting rights in Nanggroe Aceh Darussalam during the military emergency (AI Index: ASA 21/020/2003)
- Indonesia: Protecting the protectors – Human rights defenders and humanitarian workers in Nanggroe Aceh Darussalam (AI Index: ASA 21/024/2003)
- Indonesia: Old laws – new prisoners of conscience (AI Index: ASA 21/027/2003)
- Indonesia: Press freedom under threat (AI Index: ASA 21/044/2003)

JAPAN

JAPAN
Head of government: Koizumi Junichiro
Death penalty: retentionist
UN Women's Convention: ratified
Optional Protocol to UN Women's Convention: not signed

A man reportedly suffering from a mental health condition was executed. An 86-year-old prisoner died after spending more than 36 years on death row. More than 55 prisoners had their death sentences confirmed by the Supreme Court and were at risk of execution. Reports of ill-treatment in prisons continued to be received. There were reports that prisoners were held in isolation for prolonged periods.

Background
The 9 November election saw Prime Minister Koizumi re-elected.

Peru formally requested the extradition of former Peruvian president Alberto Fujimori in connection with the murder of 15 people in 1991 at Barrios Altos, Lima, and the "disappearance" and murder of nine students and a university professor in Lima in 1992. The Japanese Foreign Ministry stated that Alberto Fujimori, in exile in Japan since 2000, is a Japanese citizen and so his extradition was prohibited under the Extradition Law, raising criticism that Japan was complicit in Alberto Fujimori's impunity.

Japan warned North Korea it could not expect substantial Japanese aid until the sensitive issue involving the alleged abduction of several hundred Japanese citizens by North Korean secret agents in the 1970s and 1980s was resolved. During a visit by Prime Minister Koizumi to Pyongyang in 2002, North Korea admitted to abducting 13 Japanese nationals.

A bill to extend the term of a special "anti-terrorism" law was passed in October.

Death penalty
One man was known to have been executed. Many prisoners under sentence of death spent years on death row, in solitary confinement for prolonged periods. Execution is by hanging and is carried out in secret and with little notification to prisoners and none to their families.

▢ Shinji Mukai was executed by hanging in Osaka detention centre in September. He was informed of his impending execution just a few hours before it was carried out; his family and lawyer received no warning. He was reportedly suffering from mental health problems and his lawyer was preparing an appeal for retrial at the time of the execution.

▢ In September, Tomiyama Tsuneki, an 86-year-old prisoner under sentence of death, died of kidney failure after spending 39 years in detention, 36 of them on death row.

In July, nine Diet members were allowed to tour an execution chamber. The last time any Diet members were given permission to visit such a facility was reportedly in 1973.

Asylum-seekers

Asylum determination procedures were subject to long delays. The authorities continued to forcibly return asylum-seekers to countries where they could be at risk of human rights violations. Many repatriations were carried out in secret. Reports of ill-treatment of asylum-seekers continued to be received. On 17 October there was a joint declaration by the Immigration Bureau of the Ministry of Justice, the Immigration Office of the Tokyo Metropolitan government and the Metropolitan Police department to strengthen measures against illegal migrants in Tokyo by calling for speedier deportation procedures.

◻ A 31-year-old Pakistani woman whose application for refugee status was refused by the Immigration Bureau was deported to Pakistan in October. The deportation came as lawyers were preparing to appeal against the decision. She had been detained since June 2002. While in detention she was separated from her two children, who were reportedly placed in a children's institution; they were also deported to Pakistan.

In March the Cabinet approved a bill proposing to abolish the 60-day deadline for applicants to file for refugee status. The bill was presented to the Diet but was abandoned when parliament was dissolved in October. There was concern that the bill did not give adequate protection to asylum-seekers.

Torture and ill-treatment

Reports of torture and ill-treatment in custody continued to be received. In March it was reported that over half of the 91 complaints that the Japan Federation of Bar Associations received during special consultations on prisons were about violence and cruelty by warders. The Federation reported that warders assaulted inmates in almost all prisons across the country.

A Prison Reform Committee was established on 31 March to consider reforms of prison conditions and the creation of a prison conditions monitoring body, and to look into health care and transparency in prisons. AI was invited to brief the Committee whose recommendations were issued in December.

◻ In February a deputy chief guard at Nagoya Prison was accused of fatally assaulting an inmate with a fire hose in December 2001. The guard reportedly aimed water from the hose at the 43-year-old inmate's bare buttocks as punishment for dirtying his cell. As a result, the inmate suffered serious injuries and died of an infection the next afternoon. Nagoya Prison initially reported to the Ministry of Justice that the man had inflicted the injuries on himself and died from peritonitis.

The Ministry of Justice stated in May that it would stop the use of leather restraining devices, and by 1 October they were no longer being used. In previous years the use of leather restraining devices, which can be tightened around a prisoner's abdomen and cause internal injury, had resulted in the deaths of prisoners in Nagoya Prison.

Torture and ill-treatment during pre-trial detention continued to be reported. In a system where convictions are heavily dependent on confessions, there was concern that many confessions were extracted during long interrogations often without a lawyer present. Suspects who did not understand Japanese were denied adequate interpretation facilities and were forced to sign transcripts of their interrogation in Japanese without translation.

Violence against women

In April the Supreme Court dismissed an appeal filed by a group of South Korean "comfort women" demanding compensation from the Japanese government for being forced to provide sex for Japanese troops during World War II. The Court upheld the decision of the Hiroshima High Court in March 2001, which overturned a lower-court ruling ordering the Japanese government to pay compensation to some of the women.

A Cabinet Office report released in April revealed that one in five Japanese women suffered physical or mental violence from their partners and that victims wanted police and other public bodies to take a more active role in combating the abuse.

The UN Committee on the Elimination of Discrimination against Women expressed concern that the "Law for the Prevention of Spousal Violence and the Protection of Victims currently does not cover forms of violence other than physical violence" and that the penalty for rape was relatively lenient. The Committee also recommended that Japan increase efforts to combat trafficking in women and girls.

AI country reports/ visits
Visit
An AI delegation visited Japan in November.

KOREA
(DEMOCRATIC PEOPLE'S REPUBLIC OF)

DEMOCRATIC PEOPLE'S REPUBLIC OF KOREA
Head of State: Kim Jong-Il
Head of government: Pak Pong-ju (replaced Hong Song-nam in September)
Death penalty: retentionist
UN Women's Convention: ratified
Optional Protocol to UN Women's Convention: not signed

Systemic food shortages continued; more than 40 per cent of children were reported to suffer from chronic malnutrition. Concerns about the nuclear capability of the Democratic People's Republic of Korea (North Korea) continued to prevail in the international arena. The North Korean government continued to deny its people fundamental human rights, including freedom of movement and expression. Hundreds of people fled to China, and those forcibly returned were at risk of detention, prolonged interrogation and imprisonment in poor conditions. Independent human rights monitors were not allowed access to the country.

Background
In April, the UN Commission on Human Rights passed its first ever resolution on North Korea. The Commission expressed "its deep concern about reports of systemic, widespread and grave violations of human rights".

In November the UN Committee on Economic, Social and Cultural Rights raised a series of questions on measures to deal with the food shortage; to introduce positive discrimination for women; to ensure trade union rights, including the right to strike; and to end the practice of forced labour.

North Korea's nuclear capability continued to affect its relationship with neighbouring countries and the USA, although efforts to find a diplomatic solution gathered momentum towards the end of the year. In January the International Atomic Energy Agency (IAEA) issued a resolution demanding North Korea readmit UN inspectors, who had been expelled in December 2002, and abandon its secret nuclear weapons program. Missile tests were carried out in February, March and October. In February, the IAEA found North Korea in breach of the Nuclear Non-Proliferation Treaty and referred the matter to the UN Security Council. In April, the Security Council expressed concern about North Korea's nuclear program, but failed to condemn it for pulling out of the IAEA. The US-led consortium in charge of building nuclear power plants in North Korea, the Korean Peninsula Energy Development Organization (KEDO), announced in November that it was suspending the project for one year; KEDO stated that North Korea had failed to meet the necessary conditions for continuing the project.

In April, China hosted talks in Beijing between the USA and North Korea, which ended a day early when the North Korean delegation reportedly admitted to the US delegation that North Korea possessed nuclear weapons. In August, North Korea attended six-nation talks in Beijing on its nuclear program. No concrete decisions were reportedly made, although delegates agreed to meet again. In November, North Korea stated that it was ready to abandon its nuclear program if the USA dropped its "hostile policy". The North Korean government agreed to consider US President George W. Bush's offer of a written security guarantee from the USA.

China continued to assist North Korea in addressing the widespread economic crisis. It reportedly provided a million tons of fuel and 150,000 to 200,000 tons of food. China reportedly stopped fuel supplies for a few days in early 2003 after North Korea pulled out of the IAEA and conducted missile tests.

South Korea was also a major food supplier to North Korea. Family reunions between North and South Korea continued.

Relations between Japan and North Korea continued to be tense. This was attributed in large part to the abduction of Japanese nationals by North Korean government agents in the 1970s and 1980s and reports that a substantial part of North Korea's nuclear program was built using materials from Japan. Normalization talks planned in 2002 did not take place and North Korea called for the withdrawal of Japan from the six nation talks in Beijing.

Freedom from hunger and malnutrition
According to a special report by the UN Food and Agriculture Organization and the World Food Programme (WFP) in October 2003, despite improved harvests, North Korea faced another substantial food deficit in 2004. The report stated that a combination of insufficient domestic production, the narrow and inadequate diet of much of the population and growing disparities in access to food as the purchasing power of many households declines meant that about 6.5 million vulnerable North Koreans out of a total population of 23 million were estimated to be dependent on international food aid. The situation remained particularly precarious for vulnerable sections of the population including young children, pregnant and nursing women and elderly people.

An economic policy adjustment process, initiated in July 2002, led to further decreases in the already inadequate purchasing power of many urban households. Rations from the Public Distribution System (PDS) – the primary source of food for over 60 per cent of the population living in urban areas – were reportedly set to decline from the already insufficient 319g per person per day in 2003 to 300g in 2004. Despite the very low level of PDS rations, industrial workers and elderly people were believed to spend more than half of their income on these rations alone.

On 19 November, UN agencies and non-governmental organizations issued a new appeal for more aid to North Korea and warned of a continuing "emergency" because of a lack of pledges from the international community. Officials of the 15-member Consolidated Inter-Agency Appeal sought US$221 million for food, health, water and education. Relief agencies said that while they sought US$225 million for aid in 2003, they received pledges for only 57 per cent of that amount. Some countries appeared to have cut off aid to North Korea after a worsening of relations over the country's nuclear weapons program.

In October, the WFP announced that it would have to cut food rations to 680,000 people beginning in November because of funding shortfalls. The North Korean authorities continued to deny access to humanitarian organizations to nearly 15 per cent of the country. Reports that food aid was being diverted to the black market and the military could not be investigated as the authorities prevented independent monitoring of the final delivery of food aid.

Denial of access

Access to North Korea remained severely restricted. The denial of access to independent human rights observers, including AI representatives, and to other independent observers, including UN Special Rapporteurs and thematic experts, severely hampered investigation of the human rights situation.

Among the concerns expressed by the UN Committee on Economic, Social and Cultural Rights were lack of impartiality and independence of the judiciary, women's rights and lack of domestic legislation to combat discrimination and domestic violence. It also expressed concern about the repression faced by people who had fled the country when they returned, and the particularly severe effect of the famine on certain sectors of society. The Committee made a series of recommendations to the North Korean government. These included the adoption of legislation to give full effect to the principle of non-discrimination against women and of specific measures to promote their rights; the ending of penalties against people for travelling abroad; a review of legislation to ensure trade union rights, including the right to form independent trade unions and the right to strike; and a guarantee that the more vulnerable sectors of society would be given equal access to international food aid and priority in relation to food programs.

Freedom of expression and movement

Political opposition of any kind was not tolerated. Any person who expressed an opinion contrary to the position of the ruling Korean Workers' Party reportedly faced severe punishment, as did their family in many cases. The domestic news media continued to be severely censored and access to international media broadcasts was restricted. Religious freedom, although guaranteed by the Constitution, was in practice sharply curtailed. There were reports of severe repression – including imprisonment, torture and execution – of people involved in public and private religious activities. Many Christians were reportedly being held in labour camps, where they faced torture and were denied food because of their religious beliefs. There were reports of severe restrictions on internal travel.

North Koreans faced punishment if they left their country without permission, even if they had gone in pursuit of food.

Returned asylum-seekers from China

Hundreds of North Koreans continued to cross the border into China. In October, the South Korean consulate in Beijing was reportedly occupied by some 300 North Koreans seeking asylum. Many were allowed to leave China for South Korea via a third country.

Thousands of North Koreans were reportedly apprehended in China and forcibly returned to North Korea. A number of sources reported that on their return they often faced prolonged detention, interrogation and torture. Some were reportedly sent to prison or labour camps, where conditions were cruel, inhuman or degrading.

Executions

Reports of public executions continued to be received. Executions were by firing squad or hanging. In April, the UN Commission on Human Rights passed a resolution on North Korea expressing concern at public executions and imposition of the death penalty for political reasons. Reports suggested a decline in the trend of public executions, although it was feared that extrajudicial executions and secret executions may have taken place in detention facilities.

Violence against women

There were reports indicating that women detainees were subjected to degrading prison conditions. For example North Korean women detained after being forcibly returned from China were reportedly compelled to remove all clothes and subjected to intimate body searches. Women stated that during pre-trial detention the male guards humiliated them and touched their sexual organs and breasts. Women who attempted to speak up about these conditions were reportedly beaten. All women, including those who were pregnant or elderly, were forced to work from early morning to late at night in fields or prison factories. Prisons lacked basic facilities for women's needs. There were unconfirmed reports that pregnant women were forced to undergo abortions after being forcibly returned from China.

KOREA
(REPUBLIC OF)

REPUBLIC OF KOREA
Head of state: Roh Moo-hyun (replaced Kim Dae-jung in February)
Head of government: Goh Kun (replaced Kim Suk-soo in February)
Death penalty: retentionist
UN Women's Convention: ratified with reservations
Optional Protocol to UN Women's Convention: not signed

Long-term prisoners of conscience convicted under the National Security Law were released. Over 800 conscientious objectors, mainly Jehovah's Witnesses, continued to be detained. A revised Terrorism Prevention Bill was under consideration by the National Assembly at the end of the year. No executions were carried out.

Background

In February, a new president Roh Moo-hyun was sworn in. The new government included three human rights lawyers: the President; Kang Kum-sil, who was appointed Minister of Justice; and Ko Young-koo, the Director of the National Intelligence Service.

Corruption scandals dogged the *de facto* ruling Uri Party, the Millennium Democratic Party and the main opposition Grand National Party, leading to the resignations of close associates of President Roh. In December, under pressure and following a Supreme Court decision overriding a presidential veto, President Roh signed into legislation a bill approved by parliament calling for a special counsel to investigate corruption allegations.

Improvements in links between the Republic of Korea (South Korea) and the Democratic People's Republic of Korea (North Korea) continued. Rail and road connections between the two countries were established for the first time since the Korean War ended in 1953. Aid to North Korea continued in the form of food and fertilizers; some was distributed by the World Food Programme, some was given to South Korean non-governmental organizations implementing agricultural projects, and a substantial portion was given to North Korea as bilateral aid or in the form of food loans. Family reunions took place in February, June and September, and groups from South Korea were able to visit North Korea by road for the first time.

The South Korean government participated in talks in Beijing, China, to defuse security tensions in the Korean peninsula. Internationally, the government committed itself to send thousands of troops to Iraq. These troops had not been deployed by the end of the year.

Death penalty

No executions have been carried out since former President Kim Dae-jung took office in February 1998. It was believed that at least 56 prisoners remained under sentence of death at the end of 2003. According to reports, death row prisoners continued to be handcuffed at all times for the first year after sentencing.

A bill calling for the abolition of the death penalty which had been submitted to the National Assembly in November 2001 made no further progress. It appeared to have stalled in deliberations by the Standing Committee for Judiciary and Legislation, despite bipartisan support from 155 members of the 273-member National Assembly.

National security legislation

Five long-term prisoners of conscience imprisoned under the National Security Law (NSL) were released in April. The National Human Rights Commission reportedly began a review of the NSL.

◻ Park Kyung-soon, who had been serving a seven-year sentence imposed in 1998 for "formation and membership of an enemy-benefiting organization", was released in April. AI had repeatedly expressed concern at reports of his deteriorating health.

◻ Ha Young-ok, a graduate student at Seoul University, was released in April. He had been arrested in August 1999 and sentenced to eight years' imprisonment for organizing an "anti-state revolutionary group" and "communicating with a North Korean spy".

However, no changes were made to the NSL. This provides for long sentences or the death penalty for "anti-state" activities and "espionage" which are very loosely defined. The NSL has often been used arbitrarily against people for exercising the rights to freedom of expression and association. In October, at least 17 prisoners were reportedly being held under the NSL.

◻ Song Du-yol, a 59-year-old German citizen and a professor at Muenster University in Germany, was reportedly interrogated for several hours by up to 10 agents without access to a lawyer after his arrival in Seoul on 22 September. He was detained, allegedly to prevent him fleeing the country and destroying evidence, and charged under the NSL with "praising the enemy" (North Korea), a charge which carries a minimum sentence of five years' imprisonment and is punishable by death. He had not been sentenced by the end of the year.

In October a revised Terrorism Prevention Bill was introduced to the National Assembly. The revised Bill contained provisions that would further empower the National Intelligence Service, a secretive agency that reportedly has been responsible for serious human rights violations. It also contained vaguely worded clauses such as Article 13 (false reports or spreading wrong information regarding "terrorism") that could be used to increase surveillance on political activists and allow greater government monitoring of the means of communication used by activists and civil society in general, increasing the potential for human rights abuses.

Conscientious objectors

About 800 conscientious objectors, mostly Jehovah's Witnesses, remained in prison at the end of the year for their refusal on religious grounds to perform military service. Every year, about 600 men refuse to accept military conscription orders and are detained for periods ranging from 18 months to three years. By the end of the year the Constitutional Court had still not ruled on proposals for an alternative to military service. Although there appeared to be a reduction in the length of detention, conscientious objectors continued to be given a criminal record which negatively affected their chances of employment. At least four people claimed conscientious objector status for reasons other than religious beliefs in 2003.

Trade unionists

Trade union leaders who organized strikes and demonstrations to protect their basic rights were harassed and arrested. Trade unionists were protesting against the government's economic policies, including restructuring which had led to mass redundancies; inadequate social welfare provision; and the failure of the authorities to prosecute employers engaging in illegal termination of employment contracts.

At least 63 trade unionists were arrested. All were awaiting trial at the end of the year. Six trade union leaders committed suicide to highlight the precarious situation of Korean workers.

Migrant workers

New legislation came into force during the year which introduced a new employment permit system. This requires migrant workers to renew their employment contracts annually and obliges those staying for over three years to leave Korea and reapply after a year. The act is not applicable to foreign workers who had stayed for more than four years as of 31 March. There were concerns about possible government action including mass deportations to implement the new policy.

Women's rights

There was a high incidence of domestic violence and studies showed that a significant factor in the increase was the economic crisis of the late 1990s.
Discrimination against women and sexual harassment in the workplace were reported and there was a large gap between the average salaries paid to women and to men. An Anti-Prostitution and Sex Trafficking Bill submitted to the National Assembly in 2001 appeared to have been stalled during deliberations by the Standing Committee for Judiciary and Legislation. Legislation to prevent domestic violence and discrimination against women had been strengthened by the passage of laws and special acts in 2001, but implementation remained a matter of concern.

LAOS

LAO PEOPLE'S DEMOCRATIC REPUBLIC
Head of state: Khamtay Siphandone
Head of government: Bounyang Vorachit
Death penalty: retentionist
UN Women's Convention: ratified
Optional Protocol to UN Women's Convention: not signed

The long-running armed conflict between government and ethnic Hmong forces, hidden from international scrutiny largely by restricted access, gained increased international attention following a visit to a rebel group hiding in the jungle by two foreign journalists. The subsequent publicity and embarrassment for the Lao authorities appeared to prompt a military crack-down, resulting in scores of reported civilian casualties. At the same time, armed opposition forces increased deliberate or indiscriminate bombings in areas crowded with civilians and on civilian buses. Responsibility for these attacks was unclear as several armed opposition groups appeared to be active including ethnic Hmong insurgents. The UN Committee on the Elimination of Racial Discrimination (CERD) comprehensively criticized the country's civil and political human rights record in August. Lack of freedom of expression, the administration of justice and corruption in the judicial sector remained of serious concern.

Background

Laos continued to delay ratification of the International Covenant on Civil and Political Rights and the International Covenant on Economic, Social and Cultural Rights, which it signed in December 2000. It is ranked as one of the world's poorest countries and is reported to be the third largest producer of opium in the world. Tourism is a mainstay of economic activity. Major infrastructure projects receiving international assistance included a large dam project to provide hydro-electric power to neighbouring Thailand, and the construction through Laos of a highway linking China with Thailand.

Bilateral meetings and assistance projects, including on defence and security, continued with Viet Nam and increased with China. The powerful Hmong lobby in the USA raised human rights concerns and issues of religious freedom when the US government moved towards normalizing trade relations to underpin its policy of engagement with Laos.

New ministers and provincial governors were appointed in a government reshuffle in January. In October, Bouasone Bouphavanh was made Deputy Prime Minister, responsible for internal affairs. He was reportedly also in charge of security, at a time of mounting tension over insurgencies.

Arrests and harassment of members of unauthorized Christian churches reportedly continued. Verifiable information about religious persecution and other human rights violations was extremely difficult to obtain because of official restrictions on freedom of expression and lack of access by independent human rights monitors.

The Lao authorities continued to seek the extradition from Thailand of 16 Lao nationals alleged to be members of an opposition group involved in an armed attack in Champassak province in 2000, despite a surprising Thai court decision in June turning down the extradition request on unclear grounds.

Ethnic Hmong conflict

In January two Australian journalists visited an ethnic Hmong rebel group that had fought the authorities since the fall of the previous Lao government in 1975. Their reports brought the long-running insurgency by ethnic Hmong and other minority groups into the international spotlight. The Lao authorities appeared to react by increasing military pressure on isolated rebel groups that included large numbers of children, women, people with disabilities and the chronically sick. Such groups rely on foraging for food, and the military stranglehold reportedly led to scores of civilian deaths from starvation and disease, including at least 200 women and children.

In August, Laos came up for periodic examination by CERD. The Committee called for the office of the UN Secretary-General to take further measures including the despatch of a mission "to assist [Laos] in honouring its obligations to protect human rights and to eliminate all forms of racial discrimination". In response to the recommendations and reports of increasing civilian casualties, UN agencies in Laos reportedly tried to gain access to rebel groups to provide desperately needed humanitarian assistance, including food and medicines.

Detention conditions

There was no indication that appalling conditions of detention reported in previous years had improved significantly. Widespread torture and ill-treatment continued to be reported. In one case, prison guards reportedly burned a detainee's testicles. In general, detainees, particularly those without family support, lacked medical care and sufficient food. Detainees suffering from mental illness were particularly harshly treated. Much of the violence between detainees in detention facilities was said to be instigated by guards. In one reported case, the dates of birth of two ethnic Hmong minors were falsified so that they could be detained as adults. Evidence continued to suggest that ethnic Hmong prisoners received harsher treatment than other inmates.

▭ Pa Fue Khang and Thao Moua were driver and guide respectively to two European journalists and their US interpreter who, with a number of Lao nationals, were arrested in early June after they visited an encampment of ethnic Hmong rebels and their families in Xieng Khouang province. International pressure secured the swift release of the foreign nationals after they were sentenced to 15 years' imprisonment following a grossly unfair two-hour trial that appeared to be politically motivated. They were convicted of obstructing an official, collaboration in the commission of an offence, possession of firearms and explosives, possession of drugs, destruction of evidence and attempting to flee. At the same trial Pa Fue Khang and Thao Moua were sentenced to 15 and 12 years' imprisonment respectively after being convicted on the same charges. Unlike the foreign nationals, they were not allowed legal representation. They were still imprisoned at the end of 2003. The Lao nationals among the group were reportedly shackled in leg irons after their arrest, beaten with sticks and bicycle chains by the police and one of them was knocked unconscious. The fate of at least one other Hmong detainee reportedly arrested at the same time was unclear.

Political prisoners

Official secrecy about political imprisonment continued. The collection of independent and impartial information remained hampered by lack of access to the country and restrictions on freedom of expression.

▭ Khamtanh Phousy, a prisoner of conscience, was released in April after completing a seven-year prison sentence imposed following his conversion to Christianity and because of his contacts with people abroad.

▭ During the course of the year conflicting information emerged regarding the fate of five prisoners of conscience imprisoned since 1999. All members of the Lao Students' Movement for Democracy, they were arrested after attempting to hold a peaceful demonstration in Vientiane in October 1999 to call for respect for human rights, the release of political prisoners, a multi-party political system and elections for a new National Assembly. In reply to appeals from AI members, the authorities said that three of them – Thongpaseuth Keuakoun, Khamphouvieng Sisaath and Seng-Aloun Phengphanh – had been convicted of treason and sentenced to 10 years' imprisonment, and that two others, Phavanh Chittiphong and Khamlane Kanhot, had been convicted of a "subversive attempt against the nation" and sentenced to five years' imprisonment each. Unofficial sources reported that the five had been sentenced to life imprisonment, or, alternatively, that some of the group had died in custody. The authorities disputed the identity of Bouavanh Chanhmanivong and Keochay, two others reportedly detained with the group in 1999.

▭ Prisoners of conscience Feng Sakchittaphong and Latsami Khamphoui, both 62-year-old former government officials, remained in Prison Camp 7 in a remote area of Houa Phan province. They had been arrested in 1990 after advocating peaceful political and economic change and were sentenced to 14 years' imprisonment in 1992 under national security legislation after an unfair trial. Their conditions of detention remained extremely harsh, with access to their families severely restricted.

▭ Sing Chanthakoummane and Pangtong Chokbengboun continued to be imprisoned at Prison Camp 7. They had been arrested in 1975 and detained without charge or trial for 17 years, for "re-education", before they were sentenced to life imprisonment after an unfair trial in 1992.

Death penalty
Twenty-seven people were reportedly sentenced to death during the year, at least four for drug-related offences. No executions were reported. A number of offences remained punishable by the death penalty, but no executions are known to have been carried out for over 10 years.

AI country reports/ visits
Statements
- Laos: Charges and whereabouts of the detained Laotians must be made public (AI Index: ASA 26/006/2003)
- Laos: 15-year prison sentence – following a two-hour trial (AI Index: ASA 26/008/2003)
- Laos: Three foreigners released but Lao nationals are tortured and remain in detention (AI Index: ASA 26/010/2003)
- Laos: Use of starvation as a weapon of war against civilians (AI Index: ASA 26/013/2003)

MALAYSIA

MALAYSIA
Head of state: Raja Tuanku Syed Sirajuddin
Head of government: Abdullah Ahmad Badawi
(replaced Mahathir Mohamad in October)
Death penalty: retentionist
UN Women's Convention: ratified with reservations
Optional Protocol to UN Women's Convention: not signed

Six opposition activists were released after two years in detention without trial under the Internal Security Act (ISA). Scores of suspected Islamist activists were arrested under the ISA. Attempts to legally challenge the alleged grounds for ISA detentions remained ineffective. Opposition figures, journalists, students and other members of civil society had their rights to freedom of expression, association and assembly curtailed through the selective application of an array of restrictive laws. Reports of unlawful killings, torture and ill-treatment of criminal suspects by police continued. Undocumented migrant workers, asylum-seekers and others were at risk of ill-treatment and poor conditions while detained in camps prior to deportation. At least seven people were sentenced to death. Hundreds of convicted prisoners, including undocumented migrant workers and asylum-seekers, were caned.

Background
The United Malay National Organization (UMNO)-led *Barisan Nasional* (National Front) ruling coalition continued to dominate a stable political scene. In October Prime Minister Mahathir Mohamad retired after 22 years in office. He was replaced by his deputy, Abdullah Ahmad Badawi.

The government continued to justify detention without trial under the ISA as a means to counter the threat of "terrorism". It also put before parliament additional "anti-terrorism" measures, including amendments to the Anti-Money Laundering Act, which were passed in November, and amendments to the Criminal Procedure Code giving public prosecutors additional investigative powers in "terrorism"-related cases. In November the Penal Code was amended to impose criminal penalties, including imprisonment of up to 30 years, on lawyers, accountants and others aiding or facilitating "terrorist" activities. There were concerns about the broad definition of "terrorist" acts in the amendments, and about the extension of capital punishment to "terrorist" acts resulting in deaths.

Detention without trial under the ISA
The ISA allows detention without trial for up to two years, renewable indefinitely, of any person considered by the authorities to be a potential threat to national security or public order. Those arrested are at risk of aggressive interrogation methods, at times amounting to ill-treatment or torture, particularly during an initial

60-day incommunicado investigation period. In April the National Human Rights Commission (*Suhakam*) issued a report recommending the repeal of the ISA and its replacement by a comprehensive law balancing national security concerns and respect for human rights. Legal safeguards proposed by *Suhakam* included the provision of precisely defined offences, limited periods of custodial investigation, the right of effective judicial review, and a guarantee that detainees be charged or released after a maximum detention period of three months. The government had not responded to the recommendations by the end of the year.

Opposition activists

In June the Minister of Home Affairs chose not to renew the two-year ISA detention orders of six *reformasi* (reform) activists, most of them leading members of the opposition *Parti Keadilan Nasional* (PKN), National Justice Party. They were detained in 2001 for allegedly planning to overthrow the government by "militant" means, including by organizing mass demonstrations. No evidence to support the allegations was made public. The detainees – Saari Sungib, Tian Chua, Hishamuddin Rais, Mohamad Ezam Mohamad Nor, Badrul Amin Baharom and Lokman Noor Adam – who were all prisoners of conscience, were released without ISA orders restricting their freedom of expression or movement. However, most of them continued to face criminal proceedings related to charges filed previously under other restrictive laws.

Alleged Islamist activists

Scores of people were reportedly arrested under the ISA for alleged involvement in domestic or regional Islamist "extremist" groups including *Kumpulan Mujahidin Malaysia* (KMM), Malaysia Mujahidin Group, and a southeast Asian network *Jemaah Islamiah* (JI) reportedly linked to the 2002 Bali bombings and *al-Qa'ida*. A total of at least 90 alleged members of these groups had reportedly been issued ISA detention orders since 2000.

Attempts by ISA detainees to challenge the lawfulness and alleged reasons for their arrest continued to prove ineffective. In July, Ahmad Yani Ismail and Abdul Samad Shukri Mohamad, arrested in 2001 for alleged membership of JI, filed habeas corpus applications before the Kuala Lumpur High Court on the grounds that their arrest and detention had been illegal and conducted in bad faith. Hopes for their release were undermined in August by a ruling of the Federal Court (Malaysia's highest court) in a similar ISA habeas corpus petition. The Federal Court, on the basis that the courts should not review the decisions of the executive in matters of national security, upheld an appeal by the Attorney General against a High Court order in 2002 to release ISA detainee Nasharuddin Nasir. The High Court had found that the police had failed to provide any evidence to support claims that he was a member of the KMM. On his release Nasharuddin Nasir was immediately rearrested under the ISA.

▭ Thirteen students, aged between 17 and 21, were detained under the ISA in September immediately after

being deported from Pakistan where they attended universities. Police stated they wished to investigate suspected links with JI or *al-Qa'ida*. In December, five of those detained were given two-year ISA detention orders. The remainder were released, four of them with restriction orders curtailing their freedom of movement.

Selective application of restrictive legislation

Opposition figures, journalists and other members of civil society remained at risk of politically motivated prosecutions and application of legislation imposing unjustified restrictions on their rights to freedom of expression, association and assembly. In August *Suhakam* recommended a review and repeal of sections of the Official Secrets Act (OSA) and the Printing Presses and Publications Act (PPPA) to ensure greater protection of freedom of expression and information. The government had not responded by the end of the year.

▭ In a blow to the work of human rights defenders, Irene Fernandez, the director of the women's non-governmental organization (NGO) *Tenaganita*, was convicted in October under the PPPA for "maliciously publishing false news". Sentenced to 12 months' imprisonment, she remained free on bail pending the outcome of an appeal. The charges against her were filed in 1996 following *Tenaganita*'s release of a report highlighting alleged patterns of ill-treatment, abuse and deaths from preventable diseases in camps for detained migrant workers.

▭ The granting of police permits for public assemblies, and the policing of demonstrations, remained inconsistent. In March, two separate rallies opposing war in Iraq took place in Kuala Lumpur. The larger demonstration, organized by government-backed groups, was facilitated by police. A smaller demonstration, organized by opposition parties, was blocked by police, who ordered participants to disperse. When the demonstrators refused, police fired tear gas and arrested 12 people. In August the NGO All Women's Action Society lodged a complaint with *Suhakam* against the rejection by the police, for "security reasons", of their application to hold a rally in July to protest against an increased incidence of rape.

▭ In July the trial resumed of seven students arrested in 2001 and charged with illegal assembly for allegedly participating in a peaceful anti-ISA demonstration. Under the Police Act, assemblies of more than three people without police permission are prohibited. The students faced up to a year's imprisonment and remained suspended from their colleges.

▭ An ISA detention order against PKN youth leader Mohamad Ezam Mohamad Nor expired in June. However, he was not immediately released because of his 2002 conviction under the OSA for reading out at a 1999 press conference documents regarding investigations by the Anti-Corruption Agency into senior government ministers. He was subsequently released on bail, pending his appeal against the OSA conviction.

◻ In January police searched the offices of the independent on-line news service *Malaysiakini* and confiscated computers. The raid followed a complaint lodged by UMNO's youth branch that a letter carried on the website that questioned affirmative action in favour of Malays was seditious. Publication of the news service was disrupted, but no charges under the Sedition Act had been filed by the end of the year.

◻ In April the Court of Appeal rejected the appeal of former Deputy Prime Minister Anwar Ibrahim against a nine-year prison sentence for sodomy imposed in 2000, and turned down his bail application. The Court also rejected the appeal of Anwar Ibrahim's co-accused, Sukma Darmawan Sasmitaat Madja, revoked his bail and ordered him to begin serving a six-year prison sentence and receive four strokes of the cane. AI believes that these prosecutions were politically motivated and that the trials failed to meet international standards of fairness. The organization considers that Sukma Darmawan was prosecuted solely to secure a conviction against Anwar Ibrahim, and is gravely concerned that Sukma Darmawan's complaints of ill-treatment, threats and sexual humiliation by police to force a confession have not been fully and independently investigated, and that the suspected perpetrators have not been held to account. Both men are prisoners of conscience.

Treatment of migrant workers and asylum-seekers

Reports of ill-treatment in detention camps for undocumented migrant workers and asylum-seekers continued. There were concerns that conditions, including provision of adequate medical care, failed to meet international standards. Asylum-seekers and refugees remained at risk of detention and forced deportation. In August police erected roadblocks around the Kuala Lumpur office of the UN High Commissioner for Refugees (UNHCR) and arrested individuals, mostly from Myanmar and Nanggroe Aceh Darussalam in Indonesia, seeking to lodge asylum claims. They detained over 235 people and transferred them to detention camps. UNHCR expressed alarm at this "unprecedented action" and urged the authorities to release those who were detained and to respect the principle of *non-refoulement*. However, at least 170 of those detained were reported to have been deported by the end of the year. In November, eight detained asylum-seekers were reportedly ill-treated physically and psychologically after refusing to return "voluntarily".

Police brutality and deaths in custody

There were repeated reports of excessive use of force and unlawful killings during arrests of ordinary criminal suspects by police, and of assaults, ill-treatment and lack of adequate medical care by police and prison staff in police cells and jails. In October, the Home Ministry announced an increase in the average number of deaths in custody from 19 to 26 per month in the first half of the year.

◻ In July, Ho Kwai See, a coconut trader arrested on suspicion of drugs offences, died in prison a week after his arrest. He had been held for most of the week in police cells. Attempts by his family to challenge initial post-mortem findings after seeing bruises on his body were unsuccessful.

In October, the Home Ministry revealed that 27 people had been shot dead by police since January. Human rights groups said that many of the killings were unlawful.

◻ In October police shot dead three men whom they claimed were known robbers who had opened fire after reportedly refusing to surrender. The family of 19-year-old V. Vikenes, one of those killed, disputed this version of events and claimed that bruises suggested that he had been assaulted before being shot. They lodged a complaint against police for allegedly suppressing evidence.

Death penalty and corporal punishment

At least seven people were sentenced to death, mostly for drug trafficking offences. Caning, a cruel, inhuman or degrading punishment, was carried out throughout the year as an additional punishment to imprisonment. Hundreds of migrant workers, including asylum-seekers, found guilty of breaches of the Immigration Act were also caned. In January *Suhakam* recommended that the mandatory penalty of caning for illegal immigrants be reviewed.

AI country reports/visits
Visits

AI delegates visited Malaysia in May and September.

MALDIVES

REPUBLIC OF MALDIVES
Head of state and government: Maumoon Abdul Gayoom
Death penalty: abolitionist in practice
UN Women's Convention: ratified with reservations
Optional Protocol to UN Women's Convention: not signed

Repression of peaceful political opposition continued. Government opponents, including prisoners of conscience, continued to be detained and imprisoned after unfair trials. Fundamental flaws in the criminal justice system were partially addressed.

Background
There were severe restrictions on freedom of the press, and political parties were unable to function. The government refused to acknowledge responsibility for wide-ranging human rights violations. Unprecedented civil protests in late September gave voice to increasing anger at the lack of human rights protection. Maumoon Abdul Gayoom was elected President for a sixth consecutive five-year term in a referendum in October. In December, in response to the September protests, the Human Rights Commission of the Maldives was established under a presidential decree with a mandate to protect and promote human rights in the country.

Prisoners of conscience and mass arrests
At least six prisoners of conscience continued to serve long sentences after grossly unfair trials. Among them were Fathimath Nisreen, whose 10-year sentence was reduced to five years and who was transferred to a remote island in December to serve the remainder of this sentence in "banishment"; Mohamed Zaki and Ahmed Ibrahim Didi, whose sentences of life imprisonment were reduced in December to 15 years; Naushad Waheed, who was serving a 15-year sentence; and Ibrahim Fareed whose whereabouts remained unknown to AI at the end of the year.

Following unprecedented civil protests in Malé, the capital, in September, scores of people were arbitrarily detained and interrogated. The protests were sparked off by a prisoner's death at the hands of National Security Service (NSS) personnel in Maafushi prison and an attempt to bury him secretly. On 20 October, police officials claimed they had released 95 of the 121 people arrested in the wake of the September protests. However, some sources put the number of people arrested at more than 300, including children. Among those detained was prisoner of conscience Jennifer Latheef, an artist and film-maker whose work focuses on the prevalence of sexual abuse and who had been critical of government policy and censorship. Jennifer Latheef and the remaining detainees from the September protests were released on 9 December, but she was prevented from travelling abroad.

Torture, ill-treatment and killings by the security forces
Torture or ill-treatment of prisoners at Malé police headquarters, Dhoonidhoo detention centre, and Maafushi prison continued to be reported. At least two prisoners were beaten to death by NSS personnel in Maafushi prison. Most prisoners suffered from a lack of adequate food or access to medical facilities, but were reportedly afraid of being beaten if they complained. Some prisoners were subjected to severe beatings or held in chains for days at a time. Others were deprived of medication despite their deteriorating health.

⊟ Hassan Evan Naseem died on 19 September after being beaten by NSS personnel following an altercation with a prison guard. The news of his death triggered unrest in Maafushi prison and protests in Malé.

⊟ Abdulla Amin died in Maafushi prison after NSS forces opened fire on protesting prison inmates on 20 September. Dozens of other prisoners received gunshot wounds. Over a dozen of the injured were flown to Sri Lanka for medical treatment. Three subsequently died of their injuries. The rest of the injured were reportedly not given adequate medical treatment. Several were held at Malé airport and others at Maafushi prison rather than being transferred to hospital.

President Gayoom ordered an investigation into the death of Hassan Evan Naseem and the shootings at Maafushi prison. Subsequently, a number of NSS personnel were arrested. On 29 December, President Gayoom announced that he had received the report of the investigating commission which, he said, would be published by the end of January 2004. He said he would "study the report and implement the necessary steps".

Violence against women
The government appeared to have acknowledged the need for the adoption of legislation to protect women from domestic and other violence. A project to draft a bill to this effect was reportedly under way at the end of 2003.

AI country reports/visits
Report
- Maldives: Repression of peaceful political opposition (AI Index: ASA 29/002/2003)

MONGOLIA

MONGOLIA
Head of state: Bagabandi Natsagiin
Head of government: Enkhbayar Nambariin
Death penalty: retentionist
UN Women's Convention and its Optional Protocol: ratified

Political opponents of the government suffered human rights violations, including arbitrary detention and ill-treatment. Torture was common in detention centres and allegations of torture and ill-treatment were rarely investigated adequately. Conditions in detention continued to improve, but serious inadequacies persisted.

Background

The Mongolian People's Revolutionary Party, which governed from 1921 until 1996 and returned to government in 2000, remained in power.

Abuses of political opponents

Human rights violations against political opponents were reported, including during attempts to solve the 1998 assassination of Zorig Sanjasuuren, leader and co-founder of the opposition National Democratic Party, who helped to bring about the transition to democracy in Mongolia in 1989.

In May, Enkhbat Damiran, a Mongolian citizen resident in France, was allegedly detained by the Mongolian General Intelligence Agency (GIA) in Le Havre, France. He was reportedly beaten and drugged before being forcibly returned to Mongolia. The GIA suspected him of involvement in the assassination of Zorig Sanjasuuren, but he was not charged and no evidence against him was made public. In November the State General Prosecutor stated that his office had not seen any evidence pointing to a suspect in Zorig Sanjasuuren's murder. Enkhbat Damiran was reportedly taken in May to Abdarabt Prison to serve a previous sentence for assault. He had been released on parole while serving this sentence in 1998 because of poor health. Enkhbat Damiran's health deteriorated after his return to Mongolia. He suffered severe trauma to his liver and pancreas, and was reportedly denied the necessary hospital treatment.

Lanjar Gundalai, a member of parliament for the opposition Democratic Coalition and vocal opponent of the government, was detained by plainclothes police officers as he attempted to leave the country to attend a regional conference on democracy in Singapore. Witnesses said the police showed no arrest warrants or identity cards. A videotape of the incident allegedly showed Lanjar Gundalai's driver, who was also arrested, being choked, and his assistant being beaten. Lanjar Gundalai was released the next day without charge. No further information was available about the driver.

Torture and ill-treatment

The authorities acknowledged that torture in detention was a problem, but the culture of impunity persisted.

In April police allegedly beat four people at a sit-in protest by farmers in the capital Ulaanbaatar. Two of the men reportedly needed hospital treatment for injuries to their head and legs. No investigation was known to have been carried out.

Conditions in detention

In September 2002 responsibility for the authorization of pre-trial detention was transferred from the Public Prosecutor's office to the courts. As a result, according to information gathered by the Centre for Human Rights and Development, the number of detainees in pre-trial detention had halved by early 2003, leading to a reduction in overcrowding. Anecdotal evidence from across the country suggested that the transfer in 2002 of supervision of pre-trial detention facilities from the police to the Judicial Decision Execution Agency had also led to an improvement in conditions. The quantity and quality of food provided was reportedly better, as was guards' treatment of detainees.

However, conditions in detention continued to cause concern. Detainees in Gants Hudag detention centre continued to have little or no access to lawyers, insufficient access to toilets and inadequate lighting. In addition, detainees were grouped together without regard to age or the nature of their offence.

Death penalty

The death penalty continued to be applied and executions were carried out in secret. No official statistics were available and the number of executions was unknown.

Violence against women

A survey conducted by the National Anti-Violence Centre found that one in three women in Mongolia said they had suffered some kind of violence, and one in 10 reported harassment by their husbands. Several organizations, along with members of parliament and the government, continued drafting a bill on domestic violence.

AI country reports/ visits
Visit
AI Mongolia delegates visited Gants Hudag detention centre in March.

MYANMAR

UNION OF MYANMAR
Head of state: Senior General Than Shwe
Head of government: General Khin Nyunt (from August)
Death penalty: retentionist
UN Women's Convention: ratified with reservations
Optional Protocol to UN Women's Convention: not signed

On 30 May, while travelling in Upper Myanmar, leaders and supporters of the National League for Democracy (NLD), the main opposition party, including General Secretary Daw Aung San Suu Kyi, were attacked by pro-government supporters. At least four people were killed and scores of government critics were arrested. Many of those arrested after 30 May were sentenced to long terms of imprisonment. Discussions between the State Peace and Development Council (SPDC), the military government, and Daw Aung San Suu Kyi did not progress during the year. Ethnic minority civilians continued to suffer extensive human rights violations, including forced labour, in SPDC counter-insurgency operations in parts of the Shan, Kayin, Kayah, and Mon States.

Background
During the early part of the year Daw Aung San Suu Kyi and other NLD leaders travelled to many areas of the country to meet supporters and reopen NLD offices. After the 30 May attack, all NLD offices were shut by the SPDC and remained closed at the end of the year.

In August, in a cabinet reshuffle, General Soe Win was appointed to the post of SPDC Secretary I. Also in August General Khin Nyunt announced a seven-point "roadmap" for transition from military rule to democracy.

In August the SPDC announced that the National Convention, which had not met since March 1996, would be reconvened. The SPDC had established the National Convention in 1992 to draft principles for a new Constitution, to replace the 1974 Constitution abrogated when the military reasserted power in September 1988. The SPDC established two committees to organize the National Convention but, by the end of 2003, the list of participants in the Convention itself had not been made public. Some ethnic minority cease-fire groups agreed to participate, but it was unclear whether the NLD, which won over 82 per cent of the seats in the 1990 general election, would participate in the National Convention.

In February parts of the private banking sector collapsed, increasing economic hardship in the country.

As in previous years, the army was involved in skirmishes with the Karen National Union (KNU), the Karenni National Progressive Party (KNPP), and the Shan State Army-South (SSA-South), and small armed opposition groups in the Mon State. In December the SPDC held cease-fire discussions with the KNU and the KNPP. The SPDC also agreed a truce with the KNU in December, but low-level fighting was still reported.

Death penalty
In August the Supreme Court upheld the death sentences against three grandsons and the son-in-law of General Ne Win, who headed the military government from 1962 to 1988. Nine others, including journalists and political activists, were sentenced to death in November for high treason after unfair political trials. No executions were reported.

30 May events and aftermath
The 30 May attack on NLD leaders and supporters occurred at night near Depeyin in a remote part of Sagaing Division. The SPDC stated that four people were killed and 50 injured. Opposition sources reported much higher casualties. As the SPDC did not permit an independent investigation, it was not possible to establish the numbers of casualties.

The assailants beat NLD supporters with iron bars and bamboo staves, in some cases with fatal results. Several women were badly beaten and had their clothes ripped.

Of the scores of NLD supporters arrested the same night, 24 were still detained in Kalay Prison at the end of 2003, including NLD Vice-Chairman U Tin Oo, aged in his late 70s. Daw Aung San Suu Kyi, under effective house arrest, was permitted to see only her physician and personnel from the UN and the International Committee for the Red Cross (ICRC). She told the UN Special Rapporteur on Myanmar that she refused to be released until others detained during or after the 30 May attack were also released.

Political arrests and imprisonment
Over 1,350 political prisoners, scores of whom were prisoners of conscience, remained imprisoned.

▭ At least 24 people remained in administrative detention under the 1975 State Protection Act, which provides for up to five years' detention without charge, trial or recourse to judicial review. Elderly prisoner of conscience U Kyaw San, elected as a member of parliament for the NLD in the 1990 elections but never allowed to take up office, had his detention order extended by one year in September. In December Democracy Party leaders and prisoners of conscience U Htwe Myint and U Thu Wai, both elderly and in frail health, had their detention orders extended for another year.

▭ Buddhist nuns Ma Than Than Htay and Ma Thin Thin Oo were arrested in January for staging a peaceful demonstration in Yangon. In June they were sentenced to 15 years' imprisonment under the 1950 Emergency Provisions Act, most frequently used to criminalize peaceful dissent, and under the Burma Immigration (Emergency Provisions) Act for illegally leaving and entering Myanmar.

Before the 30 May events, the SPDC released only 30 political prisoners, a much lower number of releases than in the previous three years.

⊟ Dr Salai Tun Than, a 75-year-old academic and prisoner of conscience from the Chin ethnic minority, was released in May.

Some of those arrested during the 30 May violence and then released were rearrested in December. Arbitrary arrests by Military Intelligence of peaceful political opposition activists accelerated after 30 May. At least 52 people arrested after 30 May remained in prison; many of them were subsequently sentenced to long prison terms.

⊟ Maung Maung Lay and Ne Win, two NLD members from Yangon, were arrested in June and received a seven-year prison sentence in October for distributing information about the 30 May violence.

⊟ Daw Tin Tin Nyo, an NLD member from Dallah, Yangon Division, was arrested in June and sentenced to seven years' imprisonment in September for writing a letter to Daw Aung San Suu Kyi about the poor quality of education.

⊟ Phone Aung, an NLD member and former soldier, was arrested in September for a solitary demonstration at Yangon City Hall calling for the release of all political prisoners. In December he was sentenced to five years' imprisonment under the 1950 Emergency Provisions Act.

More than 30 members of parliament-elect were held at the year's end, including 13 arrested in the context of the 30 May violence.

⊟ Prisoner of conscience and NLD member of parliament-elect U Saw Naing Naing continued to serve a 21-year sentence for condemning arrests and restrictions on the NLD in September 2000.

The ICRC continued to visit prisons and labour camps throughout the country. Food and medical care for political prisoners were inadequate, and those injured and arrested on 30 May were not given proper medical treatment. The military continued the widespread use of criminal convicts from prisons and labour camps as porters and to clear landmines by walking across suspected minefields.

Pre-trial political detainees were held incommunicado in solitary confinement, which facilitated torture and ill-treatment during interrogation. Political trials fell far short of international fair trial standards: detainees were often denied legal counsel, and long sentences were handed down solely on the basis of statements by Military Intelligence or police personnel.

Ethnic and religious minorities

The army reportedly continued to confiscate, without adequate compensation, large tracts of land owned by civilians and to take civilians for forced labour. The use of forced labour was reported in Ye Township, Mon State; Yebyu township, Tanintharyi Division; parts of the Rakhine, Kayin, Kachin and Shan States; and cease-fire zones or locations where there was no armed conflict.

⊟ Members of the Rohingya Muslim ethnic minority in northwestern Rakhine State were reportedly used as forced labour on road works between Rathedaung and Maungdaw township. Rohingya civilians continued to be subjected to severe restrictions on freedom of movement and denied citizenship. Some 3,000 Rohingya refugees were repatriated from Bangladesh to the Rakhine State amid widespread reports that many of them were coerced into leaving refugee camps.

During October and November communal violence by Buddhists against Muslims was reported in Mandalay and Yangon Divisions. Muslims were killed and their property destroyed.

International initiatives

The UN Secretary-General's Special Envoy visited the country twice in attempts to renew dialogue between the NLD and the SPDC and to facilitate the release of political prisoners. The UN Special Rapporteur on Myanmar visited the country in March and November. He cut short his March visit after he discovered a covert listening device when he was interviewing prisoners.

In April the UN Commission on Human Rights adopted by consensus its 12th resolution extending the mandate of the Special Rapporteur on Myanmar for another year. In December the UN General Assembly adopted by consensus a resolution deploring the 30 May violence, subsequent arrests and continuing human rights violations against ethnic minorities. It called for "enhance[d] cooperation with the UN Secretary-General's Special Envoy and the UN Special Rapporteur" by the SPDC.

In July the Association of Southeast Asian Nations (ASEAN) publicly criticized a fellow ASEAN member, for the first time in its history, when it issued a statement calling on the Myanmar government to release Daw Aung San Suu Kyi. The European Union (EU) Common Position, which provided for some sanctions on Myanmar, was renewed in April and strengthened after the 30 May violence. The USA increased economic sanctions in August.

In May the International Labour Office (ILO) Liaison Office in Yangon agreed a Plan of Action with the SPDC, providing for the appointment of an independent facilitator to assist victims of forced labour to obtain redress. However, after the 30 May violence, the ILO decided not to implement the Plan because a climate of "uncertainty and intimidation" did not provide an environment for victims to safely approach the facilitator.

AI country reports/visits
Reports
- Myanmar: Justice on trial (AI Index: ASA 16/019/2003)
- Myanmar: Violent attack on political party members — Independent investigation must take place (AI Index: ASA 16/028/2003)
- Myanmar: Amnesty International's second visit to Myanmar — Official statement (AI Index: ASA 16/037/2003)

Visits
During AI's first ever visits to Myanmar in January and February, delegates met government officials, political prisoners and members of civil society. During a longer visit in December, AI delegates carried out research into political imprisonment and the administration of justice, interviewing 35 political prisoners in three prisons.

NEPAL

KINGDOM OF NEPAL

Head of state: King Gyanendra Bir Bikram Shah Dev
Head of government: Surya Bahadur Thapa (replaced Lokendra Bahadur Chand in June)
Death penalty: abolitionist for all crimes
UN Women's Convention: ratified
Optional Protocol to UN Women's Convention: signed

An escalation in arbitrary arrests, "disappearances", extrajudicial executions and torture by the security forces was reported following the breakdown of peace talks in August. This was in contrast to a marked improvement in the human rights situation in the first seven months of the year after the government and the Communist Party of Nepal (CPN) (Maoist) declared a cease-fire. Increasing human rights abuses by both sides contributed to the breakdown of the cease-fire. Despite repeated appeals for an effective human rights monitoring mechanism, including from the UN and the National Human Rights Commission (NHRC), no such mechanism was established.

Background

A cease-fire between the government and the CPN (Maoist) was declared on 29 January. In March both sides agreed to observe a "Code of Conduct" that contained several human rights provisions, but no monitoring mechanism was put in place to enforce them. Three rounds of peace talks between the government and the CPN (Maoist) took place in April, May and August. Prime Minister Chand resigned on 30 May, following criticism by the main political parties, and was replaced by Surya Bahadur Thapa, also from the monarchist Rastriya Prajatantra Party (RPP). In May, five main political parties began a campaign for the restoration of parliament. The peace process broke down on 27 August when the CPN (Maoist) declared it was withdrawing from the talks because the government had failed to implement agreements reached during the second round of talks and would not agree to setting up a constituent assembly.

The Women's Commission and the Dalit Commission, set up as governmental departments in 2002, prepared draft legislation for their formal establishment which was left pending. Eighty cases of women's rights violations, including property and inheritance rights and domestic violence, were registered with the Women's Commission. In February the Dalit Commission published a strategy paper aimed at promoting greater interaction with public bodies to eliminate racial discrimination and "untouchability" in the country. The Commission said that *dalits* were victims of human rights abuses by both sides in the conflict.

Extrajudicial executions

Reports of extrajudicial executions by the security forces were received during the cease-fire and increased following the resumption of hostilities. On 17 August the army surrounded a house in Doramba, Ramechhap district, where a Maoist meeting was taking place. They shot one person dead and took 19 others, including five women, into custody. The 19 were marched with their hands tied to Dandakateri, where they were alleged to have been summarily executed. An investigation team appointed by the NHRC found that the majority had been shot in the head at close range. The Royal Nepal Army (RNA), which initially claimed that the victims were rebels who had been killed during an ambush, said they would conduct an investigation but had not made public any conclusions by the end of the year.

The NHRC also investigated and corroborated reports that the army had fired indiscriminately at a group of students attending a cultural program organized by the Maoists at the Sharada Higher Secondary School, Mudabhara Village Development Committee, Doti district, on 13 October. Four students, including three minors, were shot dead.

'Disappearances'

Following the breakdown of the cease-fire in August, more than 150 people were reported to have "disappeared" after arrest during counter-insurgency operations by the security forces in Kathmandu and other districts. Among them were seven women. Many were believed to be held incommunicado at army barracks throughout the country.

One woman, Nirmala Bhandari, and six men — Krishna Katri Chhetri, Min Kumar Koirala, Lokendra Dhwaj Kand, Prakash Chandra Lohani, Pradeep Adhikari and Amrit Kadel — were among several students who "disappeared" after arrest by security forces in Kathmandu in September. Some were alleged to belong to student unions affiliated to the CPN (Maoist).

Teachers and journalists were also targeted. Madhab Ghemere and Udaya Raj Gautam, members of the Nepal Teachers' Organization, which is close to the leftist political parties, "disappeared" after they were arrested in Kathmandu in late September. Tej Narayan Sapkota, an employee of the Sarbottam printing press, was arrested in late November and "disappeared".

Fifty-eight habeas corpus petitions were filed before the Supreme Court on behalf of people who "disappeared" after arrest following the resumption of hostilities. However, as in previous years, the security forces did not cooperate with the courts in cases involving Maoist suspects.

During the year AI submitted 42 "disappearance" cases to the UN Working Group on Enforced or Involuntary Disappearances, which were forwarded to the government for clarification.

Torture and ill-treatment

Torture and ill-treatment of detainees in the custody of the RNA, Armed Police Force (APF) and civilian police continued to be reported regularly.

▭ In April, seven men believed by police to be homosexuals were reportedly beaten with batons and gun butts, kicked and whipped with belts after they were taken into custody in Kathmandu.

⬜ Deepak Thapa was arrested after a fight with a taxi driver on 20 September by two policemen who beat him with a gun butt and kicked him to the ground. In custody at Hanuman Dhoka district police office, police allegedly beat him on the thighs and arms, the soles of the feet (*falanga*) and rolled a weighted stick across his thighs (*belana*). He was not provided with any medical treatment.

⬜ Om Bahadur Thapa was arrested on 11 September at his watch repair shop on suspicion of being a Maoist sympathizer. He was reportedly held at Singha Durbar army barracks, where he was blindfolded, beaten and denied food for several days.

⬜ Seven members of the civilian police from Kohalpur police station, Banke district, allegedly raped two girls aged 16 and 14 on 27 September. The police officers involved were arrested and remanded in custody, but there were concerns for the safety of the two girls who were threatened in order to induce them to retract their statements.

The UN Special Rapporteur on torture, the Special Rapporteur on the promotion and protection of the right to freedom of opinion and expression and the Chairperson-Rapporteur of the Working Group on Arbitrary Detention issued a joint statement in November expressing their profound concern over reports that dozens of people were being detained secretly and were at risk of torture and ill-treatment.

Arbitrary arrests

More than 1,000 members and leaders of the five main political parties were arrested during demonstrations in Kathmandu between May and August. Most were released within 24 hours. The demonstrations were part of a campaign for the restoration of democracy. Those detained were prisoners of conscience. Following the breakdown of the cease-fire in August, several hundred people were arrested and held under the Terrorist and Disruptive Activities (Control and Punishment) Act, which allows for preventive detention for up to 90 days.

Action on human rights violations and continuing impunity

A military court sentenced two soldiers to periods of imprisonment for human rights violations committed during 2002 and 2003 in Kathmandu and Bardiya districts. A further 10 cases were reported to be under investigation by the RNA human rights cell but details were not made public. The NHRC investigated allegations of extrajudicial executions by the army in Ramechhap and Doti districts and concluded that the army had committed serious human rights violations. Army investigations into the incidents were continuing.

An investigation by the RNA human rights cell into the alleged rape of two young Muslim women, Tabsum, aged 16, and Tarnum Maniyar, aged 18, concluded that the allegations of rape were unfounded but that one of the army officers involved was guilty of unlawful arrest. It was not clear what departmental action, if any, was taken against him.

Investigations by the army, APF and police human rights cells were criticized by observers as not being transparent and unlikely to address the impunity enjoyed by the security forces.

In September the Acting UN High Commissioner for Human Rights called on the government to act swiftly on the findings of the NHRC on the reported extrajudicial executions in Ramechhap district and urged both sides to abide by international humanitarian law.

Maoist abuses

Maoist abuses were reported during the cease-fire and escalated following the resumption of hostilities. Following the breakdown of the cease-fire, there were reports that 30 civilians had been killed by the Maoists. Maoists were also responsible for over 40 abductions and several reports of torture of abductees.

⬜ In June, four members of the Communist Party of Nepal-United Marxist Leninist were abducted by the Maoists from Jubithan village, Kalikot district, allegedly because they were "under investigation" by the local Maoist leadership. They were reportedly tortured by the Maoists who broke their arms and legs.

⬜ On 1 September Maoists responded to the alleged extrajudicial executions by the army in Ramechhap district by killing Reli Maya Muktan, a senior rural health worker in Doramba. The Maoists accused her of being an informant.

⬜ In late September and early October, 21 people from Bijuli, Pyuthan district, including several members of the *Jana Morcha Nepal* (People's Front, Nepal), were abducted by the Maoists. Most were released immediately, but six were held captive for 74 days.

Child soldiers

There were reports that the CPN (Maoist) continued to abduct and recruit children between the ages of 15 and 18. Reports were received that scores of secondary-school children were abducted from schools in mid-western and far west regions and held for short periods for "re-education". It was alleged that the CPN (Maoist) used the cease-fire to recruit more children into their ranks. The CPN (Maoist) denied that children aged under 16 were recruited into its army or trained in the use of guns.

Refugees

Eighteen Tibetan asylum-seekers, including eight children, were forcibly returned to China on 31 May, despite international appeals. They were among a group of 21 Tibetans detained by police in April and given prison sentences of up to 10 months for entering the country illegally.

Human Rights Watch issued a report in September which exposed how the registration policy in the refugee camps for Nepali-speaking refugees from Bhutan discriminated against women by denying them independent access to food, shelter and supplies and imposed particular hardship on women trying to escape domestic violence.

Human rights monitoring

No monitoring mechanism was put in place to implement the human rights provisions in the Code of Conduct governing the cease-fire. A Human Rights Accord drafted by the NHRC in May, mandating it to set up five regional offices to monitor human rights with technical assistance provided by the UN, was presented to the government and CPN (Maoist). Both sides agreed in principle to the Accord, although neither had signed up to it by the end of the year. The NHRC investigated cease-fire violations, including those in Ramechhap, Panchthar, Siraha and Doti districts, and concluded that serious abuses of international human rights and humanitarian law had occurred. In December the government established a Human Rights Promotion Centre to ensure that fundamental rights were adhered to. There were concerns that the centre might jeopardize the independence of the NHRC.

AI country reports/ visits

Report
· Nepal: Widespread "disappearances" in the context of armed conflict (AI Index: ASA 31/045/2003)

Visit
AI delegates visited Nepal in July. They met government ministers and facilitators involved in the peace process, and senior APF and police officers. The delegation regretted that the chief of the RNA and the leadership of the CPN (Maoist) failed to meet them.

PAKISTAN

ISLAMIC REPUBLIC OF PAKISTAN
Head of state: Pervez Musharraf
Head of government: Mir Zafarullah Khan Jamali
Death penalty: retentionist
UN Women's Convention: ratified with reservations
Optional Protocol to UN Women's Convention: not signed

There was a sharp increase in sectarian violence in the second half of the year particularly in the provinces of Sindh and Balochistan. Hundreds of people were arbitrarily detained in the context of the US-led "war on terror". Human rights abuses against women, children and religious minorities continued to be ignored by the government. There were severe restrictions on freedom of expression in the North West Frontier Province (NWFP) particularly targeting musicians and artists. At least 278 people were sentenced to death and at least eight were executed.

Background

There was serious concern about constitutional amendments introduced under the Legal Framework Order (LFO) in 2002. President Pervez Musharraf as head of state and chief of army staff retained sweeping powers. The government sidelined the main opposition parties and only held talks on the LFO with an alliance of religious opposition parties, the *Muttahida Majlis-e-Amal* (MMA). The talks, which had been initiated in July, did not produce any agreement as the government failed to set a firm date by which President Musharraf would resign as chief of army staff.

The judiciary, especially at the lower level, remained ineffective and prone to political interference and corruption.

In June, the MMA implemented *Shari'a* law in NWFP, introducing a conservative criminal code reminiscent of that enforced during the *Taleban*'s control of neighbouring Afghanistan. During demonstrations, MMA supporters destroyed billboards displaying images of women in Peshawar and surrounding areas, saying they were "un-Islamic". The national and international media criticized the MMA and some multinationals initially threatened to withdraw their investment from the NWFP unless such actions were stopped.

Having become a nuclear state in May 1998, Pakistan continued test firing its nuclear-capable short and medium range missiles. In June a Foreign Office spokesman stated that Pakistan's nuclear program would not be rolled back. A series of nuclear tests was carried out in October.

Sectarian violence

At least 76 people were killed during sectarian violence, mostly carried out by unidentified gunmen who were believed to belong to organized sectarian groups.

In June unidentified attackers fired at a vehicle and killed 12 Shi'a Hazara police cadets in Quetta. Several investigations were initiated; however by the end of the year they had stalled.

In July at least 50 Shi'a worshippers were killed and over 80 injured during an attack on their mosque in Quetta. A series of Shi'a and Sunni murders followed, mainly in Karachi. Between August and September, six Sunnis and seven Shi'a were killed in targeted killings in Karachi.

In October tensions ran high after the killing of Azam Tariq, a senior Sunni religious leader. Azam Tariq was shot dead in Islamabad with his driver and three bodyguards as he drove to parliament. No one claimed responsibility for the killings.

Arbitrary detention

The government's continuing support for the US-led "war on terrorism" resulted in a further undermining of human rights protections. Hundreds of people were arrested and deported, in violation of Pakistan's Extradition Act of 1974. More than 500 people including Pakistani and foreign nationals, among them Arabs and Afghans, were arbitrarily detained and handed over to US officials on suspicion of being members of *al-Qa'ida* or the *Taleban*.

▭ Khalid Sheikh Mohammad was arrested in February and handed over to the US authorities in early March. His two young sons, nine-year-old Yousaf Al-Khalid and seven-year-old Abed Al-Khalid, who were taken into custody in September 2002 in an apparent attempt to force their father to give himself up, were also reportedly flown to the USA in March. The US Central Intelligence Agency (CIA) and the government of Pakistan denied these reports. The whereabouts of the children remained unknown at the end of 2003.

Violence against women

Women and girls in Pakistan continued to be subjected to abuses in the home, the community and in the custody of the state. Impunity for such abuses persisted. Very poor women and women from religious minorities were particularly vulnerable to violence in the community and home. According to the local human rights organization, Lawyers for Human Rights and Legal Aid, at least 631 women and six girls died in "honour killings" in the first eight months of the year. About half of these deaths were reported in Sindh province. Many more killings went unreported in Balochistan and NWFP.

▭ In September, Riasat Bibi was killed in Peshawar. Her father accused her former fiancé of the killing. However, neighbours believed that she was killed by her own family for choosing her marriage partner. No one had been arrested for her murder by the end of the year.

The review of discriminatory laws by the National Commission on the Status of Women announced in 2002 had not been published by the end of 2003.

Abuses against children

The government failed to ensure that officials in the criminal justice system were made aware of the

Juvenile Justice System Ordinance (JJSO) of July 2000. Children continued to be brought to court in chains and tried before judges not empowered to hear their cases, in breach of the JJSO. Children were also sentenced to death in violation of both the JJSO and international law. President Musharraf had announced in December 2001 that all children sentenced to death before the JJSO came into force would have their sentences commuted. Despite this, several of those juvenile offenders remained under sentence of death.

In October the UN Committee on the Rights of the Child expressed concern at the poor implementation and awareness of the JJSO. There was widespread failure on the part of the authorities to implement the provisions of the JJSO during the arrest, trial and imprisonment of children.

In September, a sexual abuse scandal which stretched back over two decades surfaced at a government school in Peshawar. Several teachers and other employees were accused of involvement in supplying students as child prostitutes to guests in a local hotel. Five employees of the school including two teachers were suspended by the education authorities but no action was taken by police.

Restrictions on freedom of expression

The MMA government in NWFP introduced a series of measures to curtail freedom of expression, effectively banning musicians and artists from performing in public. Local police reportedly instructed all music shops to keep their shutters down so that musical instruments could not be seen from the streets. *Balakhanas* (gathering places for musicians) in Dabgari bazaar, Peshawar, were closed down by local police without any legal basis. Dozens of musicians who had shops in the area were directly affected. Several artists alleged that they were harassed, arrested and fined by local police for playing music.

▭ Fazal Wahab Wahab, a resident of Mingora, Swat district, NWFP, was shot dead by unidentified individuals in January allegedly because of his writings on political issues. Local observers believe that Fazal Wahab Wahab was killed because he had written several books in which he was critical of the role of clerics in Pakistan. There were reports that those responsible were known to the police, but no action was taken against them.

Religious discrimination

Pakistan's blasphemy law continued to be abused to imprison people on grounds of religious belief, contributing to a climate in which religiously motivated violence flourished. President Musharraf had announced in 2001 that the law would be amended to make it less open to abuse. This move had been fiercely resisted by religious political parties and groups and the amendment was hastily shelved. The law continued to be abused to settle all kinds of personal scores.

▭ In February, Mushtaq Zafar was shot dead by two unidentified gunmen. He was on his way home from the High Court while on bail in a blasphemy case brought against him by his neighbours. In November 2001, a dispute between Mushtaq Zafar and his neighbours apparently resulted in his house being set alight and shots being fired at him, killing a friend of his. The neighbours were arrested for the murder; court proceedings in the case were continuing at the end of the year. However, according to Mushtaq Zafar's son, the neighbours' family put pressure on his father to withdraw the murder case and the accusation of blasphemy against him was part of an attempt to intimidate him. Friends and relatives of the neighbours allegedly wrote to religious leaders, demanding Mushtaq Zafar's death.

Torture and ill-treatment and deaths in custody

Torture and ill-treatment by the police and prison officers remained routine and the perpetrators were rarely held to account. Several people died in custody. ✉ In May, Nasim Bibi was accused under the blasphemy law of desecrating the Holy Qur'an. She had initially been granted bail by the Lahore High Court but was later taken back into judicial custody. In August she died in the Kot Lakhpat Jail, Lahore, the same prison where Yousuf Ali, also accused of blasphemy and held in solitary confinement, died in 2002. Nasim Bibi, who suffered from asthma, was allegedly denied medical treatment while in prison. The Human Rights Commission of Pakistan called for an investigation into her death. The Deputy Superintendent of the prison claimed Nasim Bibi had a pre-existing heart condition and died of heart failure.

Death penalty

At least 278 people were sentenced to death, bringing the total number of people under sentence of death by the end of the year to over 5,700. At least eight people were executed. Difficulties in determining the ages of those detained made it impossible to establish the exact number of children under sentence of death. In Punjab Province alone, it was believed that the age of detainees held on death row had been challenged in more than 300 cases.

AI country reports/visits
Report
- Pakistan: Denial of basic rights for child prisoners (AI Index: ASA 33/011/2003)

Visits
AI delegates visited Pakistan in June and July.

PAPUA NEW GUINEA

PAPUA NEW GUINEA
Head of state: Queen Elizabeth II, represented by Pato Kakaraya (replaced Silas Atopare in December)
Head of government: Michael Somare
Death penalty: abolitionist in practice
UN Women's Convention: ratified
Optional Protocol to UN Women's Convention: not signed

Ethnic violence left more than 500 people dead. Agreement was reached to deploy Australian police in Papua New Guinea in 2004 to improve the security situation. The government took steps towards the resumption of executions. Proposed legislation on refugee status determination was drafted.

Background

Local power struggles and reprisal killings fuelled provincial violence. A report prepared for a Law and Order Summit in Enga Province in October found that 501 people had been killed during armed clashes between ethnic groups in the province during the 12 months to August 2003.

In March the Australian Centre for Independent Studies published a study that found that law and order had broken down, and that the country showed "every sign of following its Melanesian neighbour, the Solomon Islands, down the path to economic paralysis, government collapse and social despair". Prime Minister Michael Somare summoned Mike Manning, co-author of the study, to a parliamentary committee for questioning, saying the committee had powers to jail him without the right of appeal. The committee questioned Mike Manning and proposed new legislation to "deter critics who persistently and knowingly publish damaging articles".

In December, the government signed an agreement with Australia on the deployment of up to 230 Australian police and 100 civilian advisers from June 2004 to help restore law and order.

Bougainville

In March, the UN Committee on the Elimination of Racial Discrimination repeated its request for information on the situation on Bougainville island and for renewed dialogue with Papua New Guinea.

In June, the international Peace Monitoring Group left Bougainville. A new Bougainville Transition Team took over some of its functions.

In August, the UN delegate's report on implementation of the UN Security Council's mandate on Bougainville cleared the way for elections for a Bougainville autonomous government expected in 2004. In December, three districts destroyed weapons collected under a UN program.

Death penalty

Violent crime fuelled public debate on the death penalty. Government ministers called for a resumption of executions; the last execution was carried out in 1954. In November the government announced that it would research execution methods in Southeast Asia in preparation for a possible resumption of executions.

◻ In January and September, two men were sentenced to death for murder, taking to seven the number of people sentenced to death by hanging since capital punishment was reintroduced in 1991.

Police brutality

Allegations of police brutality increased. Little information was given as to whether investigations led to anyone being held accountable. The government announced a major review of police operations and discipline to be completed by mid-2004.

◻ In January, Gabby Kutali, a 17-year-old schoolboy, was shot dead in Mount Hagen as he watched police mobile squad officers firing at suspects escaping police custody. The Social Welfare Minister urged parliament in March to establish a national human rights commission to investigate "summary executions and brutality" by police mobile squad units.

◻ In November, Ekar Keapu, a newspaper photographer covering a violent confrontation between police and vendors in Port Moresby, was punched in the face by police and had his camera destroyed.

Crisis in prisons

Conditions in detention facilities deteriorated. In February, police in West New Britain Province complained that they lacked the resources to provide adequate food and healthcare for more than 60 prisoners held in overcrowded police cells following the closure of the province's only prison a year earlier. In March, a health inspector condemned the failure to close Bomana Prison, which had sewage problems, because Correctional Services reportedly lacked funds to transfer the 650 prisoners elsewhere. In September, a court ordered Buimo Prison in Morobe Province to be closed for refurbishment after seven prisoners died and 63 were admitted to hospital during 2002 due to infections linked to overcrowding and unhygienic conditions.

Asylum-seekers

In March, the government announced it would grant 100 families from Indonesia's Papua Province, who had sought refuge near Vanimo, the opportunity to apply for protection under a new refugee status determination system developed with the UN High Commissioner for Refugees.

From August, only one asylum-seeker remained arbitrarily detained at a facility funded by Australia on Manus Island after the others held there had been resettled in Australia and elsewhere.

PHILIPPINES

REPUBLIC OF THE PHILIPPINES
Head of state and government: Gloria Macapagal Arroyo
Death penalty: retentionist
UN Women's Convention and its Optional Protocol: ratified

Attempts to revive peace talks with Muslim separatists in Mindanao made little progress following a military offensive, which sparked mass displacement of civilians and increased tension related to alleged Islamist "terrorist" bombings. Arbitrary arrests, torture, extrajudicial executions and "disappearances" were reported in the context of operations against suspected Islamist "terrorists", Muslim separatists and communist insurgents. Weaknesses in the criminal justice system made criminal suspects, including women and children, vulnerable to ill-treatment or torture and denial of fair trial safeguards. A moratorium on executions for convicted kidnappers and drug traffickers was lifted. Armed opposition groups were responsible for abuses, including killings and hostage-taking.

Background

Following bomb attacks by suspected Islamist "terrorists" in Mindanao in March and April, the government pledged to step up the "war on terror" through legislative "counter-terrorist" measures and military action. In July a mutiny by over 300 soldiers who occupied part of Manila's business district, allegedly as a prelude to a coup attempt, heightened concerns over wider political and economic instability. The soldiers surrendered and were charged with rebellion. Growing public unease over rising crime rates, especially high-profile kidnappings for ransom, and an abortive attempt by an opposition group in Congress to impeach the Chief Justice for alleged corruption, further exacerbated political tensions. Political manoeuvring in advance of the 2004 presidential elections accelerated as President Arroyo announced in October that she would seek re-election.

Armed conflict in Mindanao

Attempts to revive peace talks with the separatist Moro Islamic Liberation Front (MILF) faltered throughout the year. Following clashes between the Armed Forces of the Philippines (AFP) and MILF forces around Pikit (central Mindanao) in February, and amid accusations that the MILF were harbouring criminals responsible for kidnappings, the AFP launched an offensive against nearby MILF camps and communities. Over 200 people were reported to have been killed in the fighting and over 40,000 civilians were displaced. Following the offensive the MILF launched sporadic attacks on communities and infrastructure. Scores of civilians were reportedly killed. In July the two sides agreed cease-fire arrangements, but progress towards a resumption of peace talks, to be mediated by Malaysia, was slowed by periodic armed clashes. Government concerns that the MILF maintained links with a regional "terrorist" network, *Jemaah Islamiyah* (JI), believed responsible for the 2002 Bali bombings, also impeded progress.

Bombings and the arrests of Muslim suspects

At least 38 civilians were killed in two bombings in Davao city, eastern Mindanao, in March and April. Officials announced that the MILF and JI may have been responsible, and President Arroyo declared a "state of lawlessness" in the city. In subsequent police sweeps, at least 12 Muslim suspects were reportedly arrested without warrants in Davao and Cotabato and held incommunicado for extended periods. There were fears that some were tortured or ill-treated by the Philippine National Police (PNP) seeking confessions and information.

◻ In separate incidents in April following the Davao bombings, Muslim community leader Datu Abdullah Sabudura and Islamic teacher Zulkifle Alimmudin were abducted by unidentified armed men. Relatives believed their abductors were members of the PNP. Their fate and whereabouts remained unknown.

◻ In October a court ordered the release of 14 Muslim civilians who had been arrested on Basilan island, southern Mindanao, in 2001, charged with kidnapping, and subsequently transferred to a jail near Manila. The detainees were among at least 28 men arrested during AFP sweeps against Muslim communities on Basilan suspected of sympathizing with the *Abu Sayyaf*, a Muslim separatist group responsible for kidnappings and killings. Many of the detainees alleged they were tortured during incommunicado detention, including by being beaten, burned with cigarettes and assaulted with pliers. Complaints of torture failed to result in charges being filed against the alleged AFP perpetrators.

Communist insurgency

Peace negotiations between the government and the National Democratic Front representing the Communist Party of the Philippines (CPP) and its armed wing, the New People's Army (NPA), remained largely stalled. Progress was impeded by the 2002 designation of the CPP-NPA as a "terrorist" organization by the Philippine, US and some European Union governments. However, informal talks on restarting formal negotiations took place in Norway in October and November.

Scattered clashes between AFP and NPA units continued throughout the year. Alleged NPA members were vulnerable to human rights violations, including arbitrary arrest, "disappearance", torture and extrajudicial execution. Also at risk were members of legal leftist organizations suspected by the AFP of being sympathetic to the NPA.

◻ In April, leftist activists Eden Marcellena, a local leader of the human rights group Karapatan, and Eddie Gumaloy, a peasant leader, were abducted and killed in Mindoro Oriental by alleged members of a vigilante group reportedly linked to the AFP. A senior AFP officer was transferred pending investigations of AFP suspects. Amid reports of witness intimidation, no charges were reported to have been filed by the end of the year.

◻ In November human rights groups welcomed the decision by Davao city prosecutors to file murder charges against AFP and militia personnel accused of killing Karapatan activist Benjaline Hernandez and three peasant activists in 2002. AFP officials had claimed that the activists were killed during an armed clash with the NPA.

The CPP-NPA committed human rights abuses. In January the CPP-NPA claimed responsibility for killing former senior CPP-NPA leader Romulo Kintanar in Manila for "criminal and counter-revolutionary" activities. In November NPA forces reportedly abducted and killed two villagers near Bananga (Mindanao) whom they suspected of assisting the AFP.

Torture and the administration of justice

Procedural weaknesses in the administration of criminal justice, including unlawful arrests without warrants by the PNP, and lack of access to lawyers and doctors during extended periods of "custodial investigation" before the filing of charges, continued to facilitate the use of torture or ill-treatment to coerce confessions. Intimidation and torture continued to undermine complaints procedures and fair trial safeguards. Those vulnerable after arrest included alleged members of armed opposition groups and ordinary criminal suspects, including women and children. Campaigning by a coalition of non-governmental organizations (NGOs) focused attention on legislative initiatives criminalizing acts of torture and further safeguarding the rights of detainees. However, the legal reforms had not been passed by Congress by the end of the year.

◻ In August the Philippine Commission on Human Rights (PCHR) upheld the complaint of construction worker Paterno Pitulan. He was arrested in June during a criminal investigation by PNP officers and reportedly tortured, including by suffocation with plastic bags and electric shocks. The PCHR recommended that public prosecutors file charges against four PNP officers related to causing physical injuries.

Defective juvenile justice system

Despite an array of laws and safeguards specifically designed to protect children in custody, defects in the juvenile justice system continued to facilitate abuses, including torture and ill-treatment. Children were detained with adults in overcrowded facilities, exposing child detainees to abuse by other prisoners. Children were also denied prompt access to social workers, lawyers and families following arrest, and suffered lengthy delays before being brought before a judge and before their trials were concluded. The lack of a requirement to establish the age of a child on arrest continued to lead to inappropriate sentencing and treatment.

Violence against women

Despite plans by government agencies to improve the protection of women in detention, women continued to be at risk of rape, sexual assault and other forms of torture and ill-treatment. Investigations into such violations were inadequate and rarely resulted in prosecutions. Domestic violence continued to be widespread: the lack of a law criminalizing domestic violence continued to limit legal recourse for violence in the home. A bill criminalizing domestic violence remained pending before Congress.

Death penalty

In November, President Arroyo declared that a moratorium against executions (announced in 2002 pending congressional consideration of bills abolishing the death penalty) would be lifted with regard to convicted kidnappers and drug traffickers. More than 1,916 people had been sentenced to death since capital punishment was restored in 1993 and seven men executed. The President had previously rejected calls for executions to resume as a response to public concerns over increased criminality, especially kidnappings for ransom. She said that broad-based institutional reform of the PNP and the criminal justice system offered a more effective means to confront and deter criminality.

At least seven young offenders remained under sentence of death for offences committed when they were under the age of 18, even though the law makes clear that child offenders cannot be sentenced to death or executed. They were transferred off death row in 2002, but their cases had yet to be reviewed by the lower courts or their death sentences commuted.

 In November the UN Human Rights Committee (HRC) found that the denial of fair trial safeguards and the treatment in detention of Albert Wilson, who had been sentenced to death for rape in 1998 and detained on death row before being acquitted by the Supreme Court in 1999, amounted to violations of the International Covenant on Civil and Political Rights (ICCPR), including the prohibition on torture and cruel, inhuman or degrading treatment or punishment.

UN Human Rights Committee concerns

In October the Philippines presented its consolidated second and third periodic reports to the HRC on its implementation of the ICCPR. The Committee expressed concern at reports of cases of grave human rights violations that had not been investigated or prosecuted, thus encouraging a culture of impunity, and of threats and intimidation impeding the right to an effective remedy. In relation to persistent reports of torture, the Committee called for an effective system of monitoring of all detainees; prompt investigations of complaints by an independent authority; and for the guarantee in practice of free access to lawyers and doctors immediately after arrest and at all stages of detention. Other recommendations included more effective laws and measures to protect children, especially in detention, and to prevent trafficking of women and children. The Committee expressed

concern at the vague definitions and broad scope of "counter-terrorism" legislative proposals. It also called for greater protection for indigenous peoples.

Killings of journalists

Within the context of a vibrant free press, seven journalists were killed during the year. Most of the killings were believed to be related to broadcasts or articles seen as exposing alleged corruption or criticizing local political, business or criminal interests. Despite government offers of rewards for information leading to the arrest of suspects, investigations into the killings had not made significant progress by the end of the year.

AI country reports/visits
Reports
- Philippines: Torture persists – appearance and reality within the criminal justice system (AI Index: ASA 35/001/2003)
- Philippines: A different childhood – the apprehension and detention of child suspects and offenders (AI Index: ASA 35/007/2003)
- Philippines: Something hanging over me – child offenders under sentence of death (AI Index: ASA 35/014/2003)

Visit
AI delegates visited the Philippines in May, liaising with the NGO coalition against torture and conducting research.

SINGAPORE

REPUBLIC OF SINGAPORE
Head of state: S.R. Nathan
Head of government: Goh Chok Tong
Death penalty: retentionist
UN Women's Convention: ratified with reservations
Optional Protocol to UN Women's Convention: not signed

In September the government confirmed that 86 people had been executed since 2000. Freedom of expression continued to be curbed by restrictive legislation and by the threat of civil defamation suits against political opponents. Thirty-seven men were held without charge or trial under the Internal Security Act (ISA). Jehovah's Witnesses continued to be imprisoned for their conscientious objection to military service. Caning remained mandatory for certain criminal offences.

Background
The ruling People's Action Party (PAP), in power since 1959, continued to dominate the political scene, occupying 82 of 84 seats in parliament. Although the government showed tentative signs of allowing more freedom of expression, tight controls remained in place. In July the authorities announced that homosexuals would be allowed to hold certain government posts, although homosexual acts continued to be illegal. The same month, an opposition party held a youth conference on democracy and human rights. It was reportedly the first time the police had granted a permit for such a conference.

Death penalty
The death penalty remained mandatory for drug trafficking, murder, treason and certain firearms offences. In September the authorities made a rare statement on executions, announcing that 10 people had been executed so far during the year, and that 86 executions had taken place since 2000. The figures were revealed after the Prime Minister stated during a television interview that he believed that up to 80 people had been executed in 2003. When asked for the precise number he said he had "more important things to worry about".

Singapore has one of the highest execution rates in the world relative to its population of just over four million. More than 400 people are known to have been executed since 1991, the majority believed to have been convicted of drug trafficking offences.

▭ Vignes s/o Mourthi, a Malaysian national arrested in 2001, was hanged in September despite serious concerns that he had not received a fair trial and may have been innocent. His lawyer's applications for a retrial on account of a miscarriage of justice were rejected. Under Singapore law, anyone found in possession of specified quantities of drugs is automatically presumed to be trafficking in the drug unless the contrary can be proved. This presumption conflicts with the right to be presumed innocent until proven guilty.

Curbs on freedom of expression and assembly
Strict government controls on civil society organizations and the press curbed freedom of expression and were an obstacle to the independent monitoring of human rights. A range of restrictive laws remained in place, undermining the rights to freedom of expression and assembly.

The threat of potentially ruinous civil defamation suits against opponents of the PAP continued to inhibit political life and engendered a climate of self-censorship. While the government maintained its stance that PAP leaders had a legitimate right to defend their reputation, there were continuing concerns that its real motive was to silence selected opposition figures and remove them from public life.

Chee Soon Juan, leader of the opposition Singapore Democratic Party, continued to face a defamation suit lodged against him by PAP leaders in 2001. In April he lost his appeal against a court order to pay damages to the Prime Minister and Senior Minister. The amount of damages had not been fixed by the end of the year.

Detention without trial
Thirty-seven men accused of plotting to carry out bomb attacks continued to be held without charge or trial under the ISA. The authorities claimed the men, who were arrested in 2001 and 2002, were members or supporters of an Islamist group, *Jemaah Islamiyah*. In January the government published a White Paper justifying the arrests. The authorities rejected criticism that the ISA violates the right to a fair and public trial and the right to be presumed innocent until proven guilty according to law.

Conscientious objectors
At least five conscientious objectors to military service were imprisoned, while 19 others continued to serve their sentences during 2003. All were members of the banned Jehovah's Witnesses religious group. There is no alternative civilian service in practice for conscientious objectors to military service in Singapore.

Violence against female migrant workers
Foreign domestic workers were reportedly subjected to violence by employers and employment agents. In July the Indonesian embassy in Singapore stated that 89 Indonesian domestic workers had died in Singapore in the previous four and a half years. The statistics were said to include accidental deaths and suicides.

Cruel judicial punishment
Caning, which constitutes torture or cruel, inhuman or degrading punishment, remained mandatory for some 30 crimes, including attempted murder, rape, armed robbery, drug trafficking, illegal immigration offences and vandalism. A 17-year-old boy was reportedly

sentenced in September to 24 strokes of the cane and a jail term for a series of sexual offences.

UN Committee on the Rights of the Child

In October the UN Committee on the Rights of the Child urged the authorities to "prohibit the use of corporal punishment, including whipping and caning, and solitary confinement in all detention institutions for juvenile offenders, including police stations". The Committee also recommended that law enforcement officials and those working in places of detention receive training about the principles and provisions of the UN Children's Convention, and that human rights education be included in the school curriculum. The authorities were urged to amend legislation in order to prohibit discrimination on the basis of gender or disability, and to combat discrimination through public education and awareness campaigns.

SOLOMON ISLANDS

SOLOMON ISLANDS

Head of state: Queen Elizabeth II, represented by John Ini Lapli
Head of government: Allan Kemakeza
Death penalty: abolitionist for all crimes
UN Women's Convention and its Optional Protocol: ratified

Five years of conflict and lawlessness ended after a military-backed regional police force began a major operation in July to restore law and order, the economy and basic government services . Australian-led intervention forces facilitated the surrender of at least 3,700 weapons and the arrest of more than 400 people – the most significant steps towards ending violence and impunity since armed conflict began in 1998. Police officers and former rebels were charged with deliberate killings, torture, rape and other crimes. However, witnesses were reluctant to come forward while other suspected perpetrators remained at liberty. Prisons and police posts resumed operations and courts were overwhelmed with cases. Thousands of internally displaced people received assistance, and some began to return home to rebuild their lives and villages.

Escalating violence

Prior to the armed intervention by the Regional Assistance Mission to Solomon Islands (RAMSI) in July, civilians, public servants and officials including the Prime Minister and Police Minister suffered frequent violence and threats of extortion by police and former rebels.

In January, civilian leaders from the Weathercoast of Guadalcanal, the main island, publicly reported incidents of torture, rape, forced displacement and the burning of up to 175 village homes by both supporters and opponents of a police operation against rebel leader Harold Keke. The *Solomon Star* newspaper stopped reporting on the issue after delegates who had been quoted in the paper were threatened and ill-treated. Harold Keke's Guadalcanal Liberation Front (GLF), which together with other rebel groups had initiated civil conflict in 1998, was well-known for terrorizing settlers and villagers on Guadalcanal.

Senior police blamed special constables – former rebels recruited into the police force – for the abuses but made no arrests.

In February, retired Police Commissioner Fred Soaki, a highly respected member of the National Peace Council (NPC), a national body of community leaders which facilitates the peace process, was shot dead opposite the police station of Auki, capital of Malaita province. At the time of the shooting he was preparing to take part in a workshop on demobilization of special constables organized by the UN Development Programme (UNDP). Fred Soaki was an outspoken critic of police abusing their powers. In April, the Malaitan police sergeant charged with his murder escaped from custody; he had not been rearrested by the end of the year. The Auki police station had been a base for the paramilitary Malaita Eagle Force (MEF) which, like its Guadalcanal rebel opponents, was well known for torture and deliberate killings.

Meanwhile, armed violence and serious human rights abuses intensified on Guadalcanal's Weathercoast, where the GLF killed at least 19 people in March and April. Nathaniel Sado, a peace delegate sent by an (Anglican) Church of Melanesia Brotherhood, died from injuries apparently suffered after days of torture. Fellow Melanesian Brothers, including experienced and respected human rights defenders, were sent to investigate his death in April. The GLF took seven of them hostage and killed six of them – Robin Lindsay, Francis Tofi, Alfred Hilly, Patteson Gatu, Ini Partabatu and Tony Sirihi. The bodies of three of them, found in September, showed signs of beatings and torture.

At Marasa in June, GLF fighters reportedly forced scores of terrified villagers to watch a student and a young man being tortured with sticks and stones. One was beheaded and the other reportedly died of his injuries. More than 50 village homes were burned down and food gardens were destroyed.

By July, reports of such violence had displaced around 1,000 people along the Weathercoast, in addition to those displaced in previous years. Another 1,300, nearly half of them children, fled to live in makeshift camps and villages on Guadalcanal's north coast, straining local food resources. By the end of the year, hundreds of people remained in camps which lacked basic sanitation facilities.

Days before the arrival of the first RAMSI officers in July, Harold Keke declared a cease-fire and released the first three of seven Melanesian Brotherhood delegates taken hostage in June. In August, he was the first among prominent rebel and police leaders to surrender to RAMSI. Court proceedings were continuing at the end of the year. Harold Keke remained detained, initially at an undisclosed location because of fears for his safety.

Operation 'Helping a Friend'

International perceptions of the Solomon Islands as a weak or "failing state" which threatened regional security led Australia in April to accede to requests by the Solomon Islands government for armed forces to be sent to help restore law and order. The Australian authorities had previously rejected such requests.

From April, Australia used the intervention mandate under the regional Biketawa Declaration of 2000 to engage the Cook Islands, Fiji, Kiribati, New Zealand, Papua New Guinea, Tonga and Vanuatu in forming RAMSI. RAMSI's Operation "Helpem Fren" (Helping a Friend) was the first regional intervention in the Pacific and regarded as a possible blueprint for future armed operations in the region outside a UN mandate.

From July, around 2,500 military, police and civilian personnel, supported by warships and aircraft, were deployed on the Solomon Islands. As RAMSI prepared its deployment, church and community leaders called for a truth and reconciliation commission to investigate the roots of the conflict and unresolved human rights abuses. At the end of the year, international donors and non-governmental organizations were discussing resuming assistance programs stalled by the conflict, and improvements in the security situation were facilitating the restoration of basic public services such as courts, clinics and schools.

The struggle against impunity

In January, newly appointed Police Commissioner William Morell pledged to make human rights one of his top priorities. He took over a police service paralysed by a widespread fear of influential criminals in leading positions, including within the police. By March, some 800 special constables — mostly former rebels — had been demobilized under a UNDP-assisted program. Another 300 special constables were stood down in October.

Working with the Royal Solomon Islands Police (RSIP), RAMSI arrested more than 400 people and set up or reopened police posts and prisons. At least 110 police officers were sacked, stood down or retired. Another 33, including a Chief Superintendent, were arrested for serious human rights violations and charged with murder, assault, intimidation and other crimes including sexual violence against women. Most MEF leaders who signed the 2000 Townsville Peace Accord and who had since controlled the government were arrested. More than 660 illegally held military-style weapons and 3,100 other firearms were surrendered and destroyed. RAMSI also started a capacity-building program for prosecution, court and prison services which were struggling to cope with a rapidly increasing caseload.

The most senior politician to be brought to justice was Communications Minister Daniel Fa'afunua. He allegedly kicked a RAMSI policewoman in the face after she arrested him for causing bodily harm to his former wife. The Minister, who had close links with the MEF, was remanded in custody.

Despite RAMSI's initial success in restoring basic law and order, fears remained that witnesses or their relatives could face intimidation for assisting police investigations into human rights abuses or fraud, as prominent politicians and businessmen associated with such crimes were not charged.

SRI LANKA

DEMOCRATIC SOCIALIST REPUBLIC OF SRI LANKA
Head of state: Chandrika Bandaranaike Kumaratunga
Death penalty: abolitionist in practice
UN Women's Convention and its Optional Protocol: ratified

The cease-fire and peace talks between the government and the Liberation Tigers of Tamil Eelam (LTTE) continued to contribute to an improved human rights situation, despite the LTTE suspending negotiations in April. LTTE breaches of the cease-fire included the killing and abduction of members of other Tamil political groups and the recruitment of children. Torture in police custody continued to be widely reported, although steps to address the problem were announced in September. Measures aimed at holding the security forces to account for past human rights violations failed to show significant progress. The long-standing practice of automatically commuting all death sentences continued despite pressure to reopen debate on a resumption of executions.

Background

The government and the LTTE, during talks in Japan in March, made commitments to adopt a Declaration of Human Rights and Humanitarian Principles. The Principles had not been adopted by the end of the year. After the LTTE was excluded from an international aid conference, peace talks stalled in April. According to the LTTE, the peace talks failed because of lack of progress in dismantling army High Security Zones and in resettling Tamils internally displaced by the conflict, and because of the failure to address poverty in the north and east.

According to the office of the UN High Commissioner for Refugees, since the cease-fire, over one third of the estimated 800,000 internally displaced people had returned home by August. Uncleared mines and lack of basic infrastructure continued to impede resettlement. In October, the LTTE published its proposal for the establishment of an Interim Self-Governing Authority, which differed substantially from an earlier government proposal in July for an interim authority to govern the north and east. In November a disagreement between the government and the President saw the sacking of three ministers and the suspension of parliament. The Norwegian government responded to the political uncertainty by suspending its involvement in the peace negotiations. However, the cease-fire agreement remained in place and the Sri Lanka Monitoring Mission, an international monitoring mechanism consisting of representatives from Nordic countries, continued to monitor its implementation.

The National Human Rights Commission (NHRC) launched a three-year plan to improve its effectiveness. Proposals to amend the Human Rights Commission Act were still before parliament at the end of 2003.

The UN Human Rights Committee considered the combined fourth and fifth reports of Sri Lanka and presented its findings in November.

LTTE abuses

LTTE abductions and killings of members of Tamil political parties and their relatives were reported, particularly between April and August.

▢ Sivapunniam Rathirani Varatharjah was abducted and briefly detained by the LTTE in July. Her abductors beat and threatened to kill her if her husband did not renounce membership of the Eelam People's Revolutionary Liberation Front-Varathar. She went into hiding with her two children.

Reports of child recruitment continued throughout the year, despite commitments by the LTTE to end the practice. In August the government and the LTTE agreed an Action Plan for the demobilization and rehabilitation of children. Three transit camps would be established, managed by the Tamil Rehabilitation Organization and UNICEF (the UN Children's Fund), to assess the children's needs before returning them to their communities and to provide them with education, health care, vocational training and micro-credit facilities.

The first camp opened in Kilinochchi in October, housing 49 children. There were reports that, the next day, the LTTE forcibly recruited up to 23 children, and that child recruitment continued but on a smaller scale. UNICEF said it was informed that, of 1,155 children with the LTTE, 385 had been released.

Prevention of Terrorism Act

In December, 65 people were still held under the Prevention of Terrorism Act (PTA). Since the cease-fire agreement in February 2002 over 1,000 prisoners held for prolonged periods under the PTA, many of them Tamil political prisoners, have been released. The government continued its review of PTA cases, but in September the Attorney General suspended the withdrawal of indictments under the PTA where the

prosecution was solely based on the confession of the accused. Government plans to review or repeal the PTA had not progressed by the end of 2003.

'Disappearances'

A commission of inquiry, appointed by the NHRC to investigate complaints of "disappearances" in Jaffna, Kilinochchi and Vavuniya districts from 1990 to 1998, published its findings in October. The commission investigated the cases of 281 "disappeared" people, 245 of whom had been detained by the army, 25 by the LTTE. Neither the army nor the LTTE cooperated fully with the inquiry. The commission found no evidence that "disappearances" occurred in police custody, but it did find that the police had systematically hindered investigations into complaints by relatives of the "disappeared". It made recommendations on procedures for the arrest, transfer or release of detainees, including keeping the next of kin, the NHRC and the local magistrate informed. It also recommended that officers with command responsibility be held criminally liable in "disappearance" cases and that the government consider compensating relatives of the "disappeared".

Torture, including rape

Torture in custody continued to be reported. In September the Police Commission and the NHRC agreed to produce guidelines on action to be taken against police officers named in complaints of torture or ill-treatment by the police that were upheld by the Supreme Court. They also announced that officers with command responsibility would be held responsible for torture in police stations, that families and lawyers would be given access to detainees in police custody, and that the rights of those arrested would be displayed on posters in all police stations.

According to the Secretariat for Coordinating the Peace Process, at least 10 members of the security forces had been indicted under the Convention Against Torture Act of 1997. However, no successful prosecutions had been reported.

In July, five officers from Wariyapola police station were charged under the Torture Act of 1994 with the sexual assault of Nandini Herat. She was arrested in March 2002 and was reported to have been sexually tortured, including by the Officer in Charge of the police station. All five officers were suspended from active duty. Their trial started in November. Nandini Herat's family complained of harassment and intimidation aimed at making them withdraw the charges. The police failed to investigate these allegations.

Sinnathamby Sivamany and Ehamparam Wijikala filed a fundamental rights petition against security forces personnel they accused of rape and other torture while they were detained at the Mannar Police Special Investigation Unit Camp in March 2001. The Attorney General's Office informed the court that the perpetrators would be indicted under the Torture Act. Charges under the PTA brought by police against the two women were withdrawn.

Impunity

Despite progress in a small number of cases, there was still widespread impunity for human rights violations. According to the government, criminal action had been instituted against 597 security forces personnel, of whom 262 had been indicted in the High Court. Little or no progress was reported in these cases.

◻ In July, five people, including two police officers, were convicted in the Colombo High Court of involvement in the killing in October 2000 of 27 young Tamil men and boys detained for "rehabilitation" at Bindunuwewa. The five were sentenced to death, and their sentences immediately commuted to life imprisonment. The case went to appeal.

◻ The UN Human Rights Committee concluded that Sri Lanka was responsible for the "disappearance" of Thevarajah Sarma in the first case to be brought before the Committee since Sri Lanka acceded to the Optional Protocol to the International Covenant on Civil and Political Rights. Thevarajah Sarma was detained by the army in June 1990, with three other young Tamil men, during an operation in Anpuvalipuram, Trincomalee district.

Death penalty

Parliament debated reintroducing executions, amid public concerns over a rise in violent crime, but no vote was taken. In September the Interior Minister assured a delegation of European parliamentarians that the government had no plans to resume executions.

AI country reports/visits
Statement
- Open letter to Liberation Tigers of Tamil Eelam (LTTE), Sri Lanka Monitoring Mission (SLMM), and Sri Lankan police concerning recent politically motivated killings and abductions in Sri Lanka (AI Index: ASA 37/004/2003)

TAIWAN

TAIWAN
President: Chen Shui-bian
Head of government: Yu Shyi-kun
Death penalty: retentionist

At least seven people were executed during 2003. Proposals for a National Human Rights Commission and an "anti-terrorism" bill were under consideration by the Legislative *Yuan*.

Background

Relations between Taiwan and China were strained after the Legislative *Yuan* approved a bill to hold a referendum on constitutional amendments dealing with sovereignty.

Death penalty

At least seven people were executed in 2003; executions were carried out by shooting, although lethal injection is legally permitted. A further six death sentences were approved by the Supreme Court.

Debate continued within the government and the Legislative *Yuan* about the introduction of life imprisonment without parole as one of the measures towards the eventual abolition of the death penalty. However, no moves were made to introduce a moratorium on executions during 2003.

◻ Hsu Tzu-chiang remained in danger of imminent execution. He had been convicted of kidnapping and murder and sentenced to death by the Supreme Court in April 2000 on the basis of testimony from two alleged accomplices, one of whom provided a signed statement retracting his testimony and stating that Hsu Tzu-chiang had not been involved with the crime.

◻ In October, Liu Bing-lang, Su Chien-ho and Chuang Lin-hsun returned to the High Court for their 10th trial on the same charges. The case against the three was based almost entirely on their confessions which were allegedly extracted under torture.

There were also allegations of extensive irregularities in the investigative process, including unlawful detentions. The three men all described being beaten and having water or urine forced into their mouths. Su Chien-ho and Chuan Lin-hsun also alleged that they were subjected to electric shocks to their genitals.

The three men were acquitted by the High Court in January, but in August the Supreme Court overturned the acquittal and ordered the case to be returned to the High Court yet again. At the time of their successful appeal in January the three men had already spent more than seven years on death row.

Legislative developments

In November, the Cabinet proposed a draft "anti-terrorism" law which provides for the death penalty for "terrorist" acts causing loss of life, and establishes penalties for participation in or assistance to "terrorist" groups or activities, which are reportedly vaguely defined.

In September the Cabinet began drafting a Human Rights Law, in order to incorporate the International Covenant on Civil and Political Rights and the International Covenant on Economic, Social and Cultural Rights into domestic law. In November, an expert mission from the International Commission of Jurists (ICJ) visited Taiwan and commended articles in the draft law which go beyond the requirement of the two Covenants, including those on protecting and promoting the rights of indigenous peoples; same-sex marriages; the right to asylum, nationality and property; and the right of access to the media. The ICJ strongly recommended that the law be given constitutional or quasi-constitutional status.

The draft law included provisions for the gradual abolition of the death penalty but did not call for the complete, immediate and unconditional abolition of the death penalty.

In January, Legislative *Yuan* members adopted 136 amendments to the Code of Criminal Procedure. Among the changes which were adopted were requirements that law enforcement officers clearly inform suspects at the time of their arrest that they have the rights to remain silent and to a lawyer of their choice and that at least two law enforcement officers, including a prosecutor or police officer, be present during interviews of suspects.

Refugees

Taiwan lacked any legal framework for accepting or processing applications for asylum. A draft law on refugees was announced in August, but had not been approved by the Cabinet by the end of the year.

THAILAND

KINGDOM OF THAILAND
Head of state: King Bhumibol Adulyadej
Head of government: Thaksin Shinawatra
Death penalty: retentionist
UN Women's Convention: ratified with reservations
Optional Protocol to UN Women's Convention: ratified

The government launched a three-month anti-drugs campaign in February, during which 2,245 people were killed, according to police reports. The authorities claimed that the vast majority of deaths were as a result of drug traffickers killing one another, rather than killings by the police. Four people were executed during the year, all by lethal injection, which replaced the firing squad as a method of execution in October. Groups such as land rights activists, people opposing infrastructure projects, tribal people and migrant workers continued to face abuses and were not adequately protected by the government.

Background

The coalition government led by Prime Minister Thaksin Shinawatra's *Thai Rak Thai* party launched a three-month anti-drugs campaign from February to April. Police reported that 2,245 people were killed in this context. The campaign's stated intent was to drastically reduce trafficking in methamphetamines, which are reportedly used by almost five per cent of the population. Other government campaigns during the year included attempts to wipe out organized crime, corruption, and illegal weapons.

Government critics, including human rights defenders and non-governmental organizations (NGOs) continued to face threats, covert surveillance, attacks, and other forms of harassment. In May reports emerged that the government had planned to restrict some NGOs from receiving foreign funding, but the plan was dropped.

In October press reports stated that the level of violence against women in the home in Thailand was among the top 10 in the world.

Abuses during the anti-drugs campaign

Almost 42,000 people were placed on government "blacklists" as suspected drug traffickers or users. Many of the 2,245 killings took place after "blacklisted" suspects had left police stations where they had gone either to turn themselves in or to clarify their status. Officials claimed that the vast majority of these deaths were the result of drug traders shooting one another, which the authorities appeared to condone.

In February, a husband and wife were shot dead in Petchburi Province on their way back from the local police station after having been summoned by police because of their alleged involvement in drugs.

A Thai National Human Rights Commissioner received repeated anonymous death threats after he publicly criticized the government's conduct of the anti-drugs campaign.

Two government-appointed committees were designated in February to receive complaints about abuses during the campaign, but effective investigations into the killings were not known to have been initiated. In December, during his annual birthday address to the nation, His Majesty the King called on the government to initiate an investigation into the killings of 2,245 people during the "drugs war" earlier in the year. In response, the government stated that 200 people had been arrested for the killings, and it also set up two committees to investigate the murders.

Death penalty

In October lethal injection replaced the firing squad as the method of execution. Four executions took place during the year, all by lethal injection. The number of people under sentence of death had reportedly nearly tripled between January 2001 and December 2003 to nearly 1,000. The majority of those sentenced in recent years had been convicted of drug offences. Sixty-eight men and women under sentence of death had exhausted all legal appeals. A further 905 people on death row had appeals pending at the end of the year.

Rights of rural and tribal people

Land rights activists, rural people opposing infrastructure projects, and tribal people continued to come into conflict with the government about control over their local resources. Hundreds of thousands of tribal people reportedly continued to be denied full Thai citizenship. The government continued to pursue court cases against 26 farmers in Lamphun Province for trespassing, claiming they had illegally occupied vacant land. If convicted, the farmers, who had been arbitrarily detained in 2002, could be prisoners of conscience.

The government also continued to prosecute 20 leaders of the protest against the Thai-Malaysian natural gas pipeline project in Songkla Province. Local fishing communities opposed the offshore pipeline construction on the grounds that it would adversely affect their livelihoods and damage the environment. The 20, charged on six counts including disturbing the peace, were released on bail and awaiting trial at the end of the year. They had been arrested after a December 2002 demonstration was violently suppressed by local police. Other anti-pipeline leaders have received anonymous threats and have been kept under surveillance.

◻ Kham Pan Suksai, a farmer and village headman, was shot dead in Chiang Dao District, Chiang Mai Province, in February after a dispute with local forestry officials who were attempting to fell trees in a community forest. A junior forestry employee confessed to the murder, but was later released without charge. No one was known to have been brought to justice for the crime by the end of the year.

Migrant workers, asylum-seekers and refugees

There were frequent reports of violence and harassment against migrant workers.

◻ In May, six migrant workers from Myanmar were killed in Tak Province allegedly on the orders of a village headman; the case was still being pursued in the courts at the end of the year.

◻ No one had been brought to justice for the murders of more than 20 migrant workers from Myanmar whose bodies were found in a river on the Thai-Lao border in February 2002. The case was reportedly not being actively pursued by the government at the end of the year.

◻ On at least two occasions during the year migrant workers from Myanmar protesting against the denial of their labour rights were arrested and at least 446 were deported to Myanmar.

◻ In June over 400 male and female migrant workers at the King Body Concept Company factory in Tak Province were arrested and deported after they protested at being paid less than half the minimum wage and against very poor working and living conditions.

Refugees from Myanmar continued to arrive in significant numbers and stayed in camps with a population of over 140,000 along the Myanmar border. Refugees from the Shan community, who also continued to enter the country in large numbers, were still denied access to refugee camps. Asylum-seekers outside refugee camps continued to be at risk of arrest and detention for prolonged periods for "illegal immigration".

In June, 11 Myanmar asylum-seekers were arrested during a peaceful demonstration in front of the Myanmar embassy in Bangkok. They remained in detention at the end of the year. In September, 15 asylum-seekers from Myanmar were also arrested in front of the Myanmar embassy and remained in detention at the Special Detention Centre in Bangkok at the end of the year.

Prisoner of conscience

Sok Yoeun, a Cambodian refugee and prisoner of conscience in poor health, continued to be detained and remained at risk of being extradited to Cambodia.

AI country reports/visits

Reports

- Thailand: Executions must stop (AI Index: ASA 39/007/2003)
- Thailand: Grave developments – killings and other abuses (AI Index: ASA 39/008/2003)

Visit

AI delegates visited Thailand in June.

TIMOR-LESTE

DEMOCRATIC REPUBLIC OF TIMOR-LESTE
Head of state: Kay Rala Xanana Gusmão
Head of government: Dr Marí Bim Amude Alkatiri
Death penalty: abolitionist for all crimes
UN Women's Convention and its Optional Protocol: ratified

Limited progress was made in developing a legal framework that would protect human rights and strengthen the nascent judiciary, police force and other key institutions. In this context, human rights could not be guaranteed, including the right to a fair trial within a reasonable time. Allegations of excessive use of force, misuse of firearms and other violations by the police were not always adequately or consistently addressed. The findings of a UN police investigation into two fatal shootings, allegedly by the police, in late 2002, was made public; no one was held to account for the killings.

Background
2003 marked the first full year of independence for Timor-Leste. Building and strengthening new institutions and developing policy in all areas continued to present a considerable challenge to the new nation. The UN peace-keeping mission, the UN Mission of Support in East Timor (UNMISET), continued to assist in the development of the National Police Service of Timor-Leste (PNTL) and the provision of interim law enforcement.

Human rights law
In April Timor-Leste acceded to a number of core international human rights treaties and instruments, including those relating to economic, social and cultural rights, the rights of women and children, and protection against torture.

Some progress was made in drafting national legislation on human rights, such as the law establishing an Office of the Provedor for Human Rights to provide oversight of government activities, the police and military, and the prison service. The Provedor's Office had not been set up by the end of the year.

However, some new laws were not fully consistent with the Constitution or with international human rights standards. The Immigration and Asylum Law was adopted by Parliament in September despite a Court of Appeal decision that provisions restricting the rights to freedom of assembly and association were unconstitutional. It had not been promulgated by the President by the end of 2003.

Justice system
Weaknesses within the justice system, particularly lack of human resources, training and oversight of officials, continued to undermine the rule of law, security and human rights. The Court of Appeal began sitting in July for the first time in 18 months. Of the four courts of first instance, only one functioned regularly. Women and children faced particular difficulties in accessing the formal justice system. Police and prosecutors frequently referred criminal cases, including of assault and rape, to "traditional" or alternative justice mechanisms.

Suspects were held in pre-trial detention for extended periods, often for minor offences. In the first week of December at least one third of the 223 pre-trial detainees were held illegally after their detention orders had expired. Officials exceeded their authority and investigating judges failed to exercise their role in protecting detainees' rights. Legal representation for detainees remained severely limited.

▭ Some 90 people, including women and children, were arrested by the armed forces after five people were killed in an armed attack on civilians in Ermera District in January. Many of those arrested were thought to have no connection with the attack, but were singled out because of their membership of a religious sect. Thirty-nine people who were subsequently transferred to prison custody were held illegally, initially without detention orders and later with orders issued by a prosecutor, not a judge as required by law. All were held beyond the legal limit of 72 hours before being brought before a judge. The detainees did not have access to legal representation until they first appeared in court.

▭ Carlos Ena, who was charged with two counts of crimes against humanity, including in connection with two murders in 1999, was released in September after 17 months in pre-trial detention. The Court of Appeal ruled his detention illegal because pre-trial detention should not exceed six months, except in exceptional circumstances not present in this case.

Police
The UN retained executive control of the police but had transferred command for all 13 districts to the PNTL by the end of 2003. The absence of a legal and procedural framework, inadequate training and lack of oversight hampered the PNTL's development. Officers misused firearms in a number of incidents and were alleged to have assaulted suspects on more than 20 occasions.

Efforts to improve accountability resulted in the dismissal of several police officers. In one case, an officer was dismissed after beating and breaking the arm of an armed forces officer detained for assaulting him a few days earlier. However, investigations into, and sanctions for, police misconduct were generally not consistent or transparent.

A UN police investigation into the fatal shooting of two people, allegedly by police, in disturbances in the capital, Dili, on 4 December 2002 failed to identify those directly responsible. No one was held to account for the fatal shooting of another person, also allegedly by the police, one month earlier in the town of Baucau.

Past human rights violations

By December, indictments had been served against 369 individuals for serious crimes, including crimes against humanity, in connection with the independence ballot in 1999. Among those indicted were 281 people residing in Indonesia, including senior Indonesian military officials. Indonesia refused to transfer suspects for trial to Timor-Leste (see Indonesia entry).

Human rights violations during and immediately before the Indonesian invasion in 1975 were the subject of an ongoing inquiry by the Commission for Reception, Truth and Reconciliation.

AI country reports/visits

Report
· Democratic Republic of Timor-Leste: A new police service – a new beginning (AI Index: ASA 57/002/2003)

Visit
AI delegates visited Timor-Leste in October to facilitate a workshop for human rights activists and PNTL officers on "Civil society and the police working together to protect human rights".

TONGA

KINGDOM OF TONGA

Head of state: King Taufa'ahau Tupou IV
Head of government: Prince 'Ulukalala-Lavaka-Ata
Death penalty: abolitionist in practice
UN Women's Convention and its Optional Protocol: not signed

The government adopted measures to restrict media freedom and the powers of the courts to review government decisions.

Freedom of speech threatened

In February the authorities banned the *Taimi 'o Tonga* (Times of Tonga), a privately owned newspaper, on the grounds that it was a "foreign concern with a political agenda". The Supreme Court overturned the first ban and, when a second was issued, overturned it in May. Publisher Kalafi Moala had moved the newspaper's production to New Zealand after repeated government efforts to prevent its publication in Tonga. The ban followed awards of compensation by the Supreme Court in December 2002 to three journalists, including Kalafi Moala and Member of Parliament 'Akilisi Pohiva, for unlawful imprisonment in 1996. They were prisoners of conscience.

In May 'Akilisi Pohiva, his son Po'oi Pohiva, and Member of Parliament 'Iseleli Pulu were acquitted of sedition and forgery. The charges were brought after

Kele'a, a magazine linked to the Tonga Human Rights and Democracy Movement, published an article about the King's offshore assets in January 2002.

In June the government announced plans to amend constitutional guarantees of freedom of speech and to curb the power of the Supreme Court to review decisions made by Parliament and the Tonga Privy Council. Despite unprecedented public opposition, in October Parliament passed constitutional amendments allowing the media to be regulated and its freedoms restricted – including on grounds of national security and of cultural and religious concerns – and preventing claims for damages when publications were banned.

In July legislation was introduced prohibiting foreign nationals from owning media in Tonga, which was perceived as an attack on Kalafi Moala, who holds US citizenship. In October the Newspaper Act, which further regulated newspapers and controlled their content, was passed into law.

VIET NAM

SOCIALIST REPUBLIC OF VIET NAM

Head of state: Tran Duc Luong
Head of government: Phan Van Khai
Death penalty: retentionist
UN Women's Convention: ratified with reservations
Optional Protocol to UN Women's Convention: not signed

The civil and political rights situation did not improve in 2003. Attacks on freedom of expression and association continued throughout the year. Members of a "democracy group" faced arrest, unfair trial and lengthy prison sentences. In several cases, sentences were reduced on appeal in a rare move by the authorities, widely interpreted as a reaction to growing international criticism of Viet Nam's stifling of dissent. The number of death sentences and executions reported increased alarmingly. Trials of those accused of involvement in the 2001 Central Highlands uprising also continued throughout the year as did reports of targeted repression of members of religious denominations not sanctioned by the authorities. The Central Highlands remained under tight government control; no independent monitors were allowed access to verify the government's assertion that the situation had returned to normal.

Background

An agreement was reached in June between the UN Children's Fund (UNICEF), the UN Office for Drugs and Crimes (UNODC) and the Vietnamese authorities to bolster law enforcement and assess current anti-trafficking legislation. Provision was also made to offer improved assistance to victims of trafficking and help them to reintegrate into their communities.

Government concern that widespread corruption was corroding support for the Communist Party was exemplified by the prosecution of two former ministers and the two-month show trial which began in June in Ho Chi Minh City of Nam Cam (also known as Truong Van Cam) and over 150 co-defendants, including high-level figures in the judiciary. The group was accused of murder and bribery and being part of a vast underworld network with connections throughout the government and Party apparatus. The trial was widely publicized in Viet Nam, and Nam Cam and five others were sentenced to death. Five of the death sentences were upheld on appeal. Many others involved were given lengthy prison sentences; their appeals were still pending at the end of the year.

An amended Criminal Procedure Code was debated and approved by members of the National Assembly. Revisions to the controversial draft Land Law dealing with issues of ownership and disputes were approved by the National Assembly in November. Disputes over land management and use have been the flash-points for considerable rural unrest in recent years and have led to many arrests.

Viet Nam continued to deny access to independent human rights monitors.

Detention and trial of government critics

The trials continued of a group of vocal government critics made up of former military officers, Communist Party members, leading intellectuals and their families.

The loosely formed "democracy group" used the Internet to circulate information critical of the government and used e-mail and mobile phones to contact overseas Vietnamese groups regarded as "reactionary" by the Ha Noi authorities.

⊡ In June, Dr Pham Hong Son was sentenced to 13 years' imprisonment, reduced to five years on appeal, on charges of espionage.

⊡ Tran Dung Tien, aged 74, was sentenced in November to 10 months' imprisonment – the length of time for which he had been held in pre-trial detention – for "abusing democratic freedoms to infringe upon the interests of the State". He was released immediately.

⊡ In December, Nguyen Vu Binh was sentenced to seven years' imprisonment on charges of espionage relating to his open criticism of government policies over several years.

Many of those awaiting sentence or already in prison were elderly men. AI's criticism of Viet Nam's treatment of elderly prisoners of conscience provoked a furious and defensive public response from the government. More high-profile prisoners were awaiting trial at the end of the year.

⊡ Dr Nguyen Dan Que, aged 61 and in poor health, was rearrested by the authorities in March after using the Internet to criticize the lack of freedom of information in Viet Nam. Dr Que, a former prisoner of conscience and leading human rights advocate, had

previously spent 18 years in prison. He refused government offers to leave the country and go into exile on his release. He was still held in incommunicado detention at the end of the year.

Death penalty

Despite a small reduction in the number of capital offences on the statute books in recent years and the commutations by the President of several death sentences, 2003 witnessed a dramatic rise in the reported imposition of the death penalty in Viet Nam, particularly for drugs-related offences and economic crimes. Twenty-nine offences in the Criminal Code still carry the death penalty.

According to information collated from official sources, 103 people were sentenced to death in 2003; 63 were convicted of drugs-related charges and four women of fraud. There were reports that 64 were executed, many in public; the true figures were believed to be much higher.

⊡ Two women – 43-year-old Hoang Tu Lien and 30-year-old Tran Thi My Ha – were sentenced to death after a four-day trial by Quang Nam People's Court in August. They were found guilty of running a large network trafficking counterfeit money worth nearly US$90,000.

⊡ Four men and one woman were executed on 5 November in front of nearly a thousand onlookers at Thu Duc execution ground on the outskirts of Ho Chi Minh City. Nguyen Ngu Dung, Nguyen Thi Loan and Nguyen Anh Tuan had been sentenced to death in July 2001 for trafficking 13.5kg of heroin. Duong Ho Vu and Luu Kim Hien had been sentenced to death in 2002 for murder.

Suppression of religious freedom

Unprecedented talks between the authorities and the outlawed Unified Buddhist Church of Viet Nam (UBCV) – epitomized by the televised meeting between the UBCV's senior monk Thich Huyen Quang and the Prime Minister in April – reinforced earlier optimism that Viet Nam would experience greater religious freedom.

However, these hopes were dashed in October when comprehensive repression of the Buddhist church resumed. Thich Huyen Quang, who had been under house arrest almost continuously since 1977, and Thich Quang Do, his deputy, who was released early from a two-year house arrest order in June, were placed under *de facto* house arrest at different locations, along with at least 30 other senior UBCV monks.

In a move reflecting the improving relationship between Viet Nam and the Vatican, the Vietnamese authorities supported the election of a new Vietnamese Roman Catholic Cardinal in October. This positive development was tempered by the continued detention of Father Thadeus Nguyen Van Ly and the initial sentencing to long terms of imprisonment of his two nephews and niece for passing information about their uncle and religious freedom in Viet Nam to overseas Vietnamese groups. However, their sentences were reduced on appeal. His niece was released and the two nephews were due for release in February 2004. Father

Ly's prison sentence was also reduced from 15 to 10 years in response to international criticism of the case.

Allegations of repression, including forced renunciations of faith in village meetings, against members of unauthorized evangelical Protestant churches, particularly in the Central Highlands, continued to emerge, despite government attempts to prevent the free flow of information.

▭ Thich Tri Luc, a Buddhist monk recognized as a refugee by the Office of the UN High Commissioner for Refugees (UNHCR) in Cambodia in 2002 and believed to have been abducted from Cambodia by Vietnamese agents, was finally located after one year, when his family in Ho Chi Minh City were informed by the authorities of his impending trial. He was charged under Article 91 of the Criminal Code with fleeing abroad in order to oppose the Vietnamese government. This was the first indication that he was still alive and had indeed been forcibly returned to Viet Nam. His trial date was postponed and news of his case caused an international outcry. If found guilty, he could face between three years' and life imprisonment.

Central Highlands

Arrests and trials continued of those linked to the 2001 unrest and the resulting flight of hundreds of ethnic minority (Montagnard) asylum-seekers to neighbouring Cambodia. Allegations of torture and deaths in custody were also reported by overseas Montagnard groups.

Thirty-three men were sentenced to between 18 months' and 13 years' imprisonment for their involvement in the unrest or for helping those trying to flee the country, bringing to 76 the total number of people known to have been tried since 2001. No outside monitoring was permitted of the trials, and detainees' access to family members and lawyers was limited. Not all such cases were made public and the number of those arrested and detained was believed to be much higher. Access to the Central Highlands remained strictly controlled; several groups of diplomats and journalists were permitted to visit the region under close supervision.

▭ Y Kuo Bya, Ye He E Ban, Y Jon Enuol and Y Bri Enuol were sentenced to between 10 and 13 years' imprisonment and between three and four years' house arrest on release by the People's Court of Dak Lak province in the Central Highlands on 16 October. They were charged with inciting unrest in 2000-2001 and "sabotaging the policy of national unity".

AI country reports/visits
Reports
- Socialist Republic of Viet Nam: The espionage case against the nephews and niece of Father Thadeus Nguyen Van Ly (AI Index: ASA 41/004/2003)
- Socialist Republic of Viet Nam: Dr Pham Hong Son — prisoner of conscience (AI Index: ASA 41/017/2003)
- Socialist Republic of Viet Nam: Two official Directives relating to anti-government activities (AI Index: ASA 41/018/2003)
- Socialist Republic of Viet Nam: The death penalty — inhumane and ineffective (AI Index: ASA 41/023/2003)
- Socialist Republic of Viet Nam: In place of veneration, incarceration — elderly prisoners of conscience (AI Index: ASA 41/032/2003)
- Socialist Republic of Viet Nam: Freedom of expression under threat in cyberspace (AI Index: ASA 41/037/2003)

EUROPE/CENTRAL ASIA

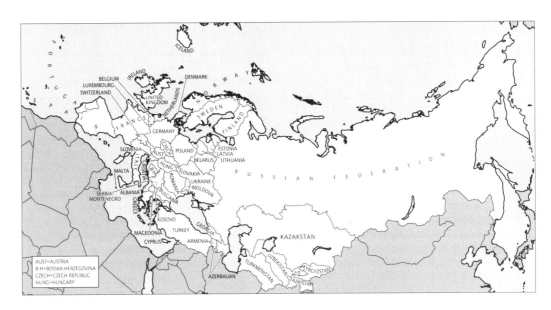

Albania	Latvia
Armenia	Lithuania
Austria	Macedonia
Azerbaijan	Malta
Belarus	Moldova
Belgium	Poland
Bosnia-Herzegovina	Portugal
Bulgaria	Romania
Croatia	Russian Federation
Czech Republic	Serbia and Montenegro
Estonia	Slovakia
Finland	Slovenia
France	Spain
Georgia	Sweden
Germany	Switzerland
Greece	Tajikistan
Hungary	Turkey
Ireland	Turkmenistan
Italy	Ukraine
Kazakstan	United Kingdom
Kyrgyzstan	Uzbekistan

EUROPE/ CENTRAL ASIA REGIONAL OVERVIEW 2003

Governments across Europe and Central Asia continued to use the so-called "war on terror" to undermine human rights in the name of security. Among the steps taken by governments were regressive moves on "anti-terrorist" legislation, attacks on refugee protection, and restrictions on freedom of association and expression. Simplistic rhetoric about security, immigration and asylum, together with an upsurge in populism, bolstered racism and discriminatory practices towards minorities across the region. The lack of political will shown by the European Union (EU) to confront human rights violations within its own borders was increasingly disturbing, particularly in light of the planned accession of 10 new member states in 2004. Those responsible for violations, including torture or ill-treatment, continued to enjoy impunity.

'War on terror'

Under the auspices of combating "terrorism" governments continued to undermine human rights in law and practice. By the end of the year, 14 foreign nationals who could not be deported remained interned in the United Kingdom (UK) under legislation that allowed for indefinite detention without charge or trial, principally on the basis of secret evidence. Those detained in the UK under "anti-terrorism" legislation were held in high-security facilities under severely restricted regimes.

Spain continued to ignore long-standing recommendations by various international bodies to introduce greater safeguards for suspects held under "anti-terrorist" legislation, and indeed planned to more than double the time which certain people could be held incommunicado. The authorities also closed the only entirely Basque-language newspaper and 10 people associated with it were held under "anti-terrorist" legislation in moves that appeared to be injurious to the right to freedom of expression.

The authorities in Uzbekistan used the "war on terror" to justify a continuing clampdown on religious and political dissent. At least 6,000 political prisoners remained in jail there and members of independent Islamic congregations were among those who faced detention and intimidation. In Turkmenistan, a wave of repression continued, following an alleged assassination attempt in November 2002 on the President, with scores of people convicted after blatantly unfair trials amid credible allegations of torture and ill-treatment.

Government efforts to limit asylum provisions and immigration benefited from the new language of "national security" and "counter-terrorism", with an emphasis on control rather than protection. In Italy, for example, there were fears that some asylum-seekers were forced to return to countries where they risked grave human rights violations and that some individuals, expelled on grounds that they posed a danger to national security and public order, had no opportunity to challenge the decision in fair proceedings. The human rights perspective remained lacking from the thinking of the EU on asylum, which continued to promote a further sealing off of the EU at the expense of international protection obligations.

Racism

Racism, discrimination and intolerance, including anti-Semitism and Islamophobia, continued to be a major concern across the region. Manifestations included institutional racism in the spheres of economic, social and cultural rights.

Discrimination against Roma was widespread in many states in the region, often affecting virtually all areas of life including access to education, housing, employment and social services.

Many people seeking to return home after being displaced by war in the western Balkans faced discrimination on ethnic grounds, particularly with regard to accessing employment, education and health care. This acted as a barrier against the return and reintegration of minorities.

Racist application of citizenship laws in the Russian Federation meant that certain ethnic minority groups – including members of the Meskhetian population in one region – remained effectively stateless, and as such were denied access to pensions, child benefits and higher education.

Racism continued as a backdrop to human rights abuses by law enforcement officials in the administration of justice. Reports of race-related ill-treatment by law enforcement officials came from a distressingly wide range of states, including Belgium, Bulgaria, France, Greece, Italy, Poland, the Russian Federation, Slovakia, Slovenia and Spain. There was also a lack of due diligence by some states in investigating and prosecuting assaults by private actors on minorities, ethnic as well as religious. In Georgia, for example, religious minorities continued to face harassment, intimidation and violent attacks, while the police failed to provide adequate protection for those targeted or show vigour in prosecuting those allegedly responsible.

Lack of human rights protection

Torture and ill-treatment were reported from across the region, including in Albania, Moldova, Romania and Serbia and Montenegro, where reports of such treatment were common and credible. In Turkey, torture and ill-treatment in police detention remained a matter of grave concern, despite some positive legislative reforms. In Germany, an intense public debate on the permissible use of torture occurred after it emerged that a senior police officer had ordered a subordinate to use force against a criminal suspect. Some states, such as Belgium, Italy and Switzerland, lacked fundamental safeguards against ill-treatment in police custody.

In other states, such as Greece, Macedonia, Portugal and Spain, there were reports of reckless or excessive use of firearms, sometimes resulting in deaths. In several countries, conditions in prisons as well as in detention facilities holding asylum-seekers and unauthorized immigrants, were cruel and degrading. In some states, people with mental disabilities were treated inhumanely – in social care homes in Bulgaria, and through the use of cage beds in the Czech Republic, Hungary and Slovakia. Many states lacked independent scrutiny mechanisms to address such violations, a problem compounded by the continued failure to accept accountability at EU level for human rights observance by member states.

In some states impunity for human rights violations continued. In Turkey, the ratio of prosecutions of members of the security forces to complaints of torture and ill-treatment filed by members of the public continued to be pitifully low. Russian Federation security forces continued to act with virtual impunity in the conflict in the Chechen Republic, amid ongoing reports of their involvement in torture and "disappearances". Continued impunity for wartime violations remained a concern in the western Balkans. Although some people suspected of war crimes were transferred to the custody of the International Criminal Tribunal for the former Yugoslavia, others continued to evade arrest, some apparently protected by authorities in Bosnia-Herzegovina, Croatia and Serbia and Montenegro. Thousands of "disappearances" that occurred during the 1992-1995 war remained unresolved. Although there were some domestic prosecutions for war crimes, lack of political will and deficiencies in the domestic justice systems led to continued widespread impunity.

In Belarus, Turkmenistan and Uzbekistan, dissent from official policies in civic, religious and political life was systematically and often brutally repressed. Human rights defenders in a number of countries faced threats and detention, including in Turkey where a range of laws and regulations was used to frustrate their activity, and in Azerbaijan where a campaign by the state-sponsored media against several prominent human rights defenders culminated in violent attacks on their offices and raised fears for their safety and that of their families. In both these countries, as well as in other states such as Italy, Greece and Switzerland, police were reported to have used excessive force against demonstrators.

The lack of effective redress for human rights violations in countries in Europe compounded concerns about proposals under consideration which would have the effect of curtailing redress available at the regional level in the European Court of Human Rights. Member states of the Council of Europe proposed adding new admissibility criteria to the only international human rights court where individuals enjoy the right of direct petition.

Violence against women

Human rights violations against women and girls continued across the region. In the context of trafficking and forced prostitution, there were concerns that victims were being failed by the judicial systems in source, transit and destination countries. Domestic violence was also an entrenched problem across Europe and Central Asia, from Belgium to the Russian Federation. Contributory factors included states regarding domestic violence as belonging to the "private sphere"; a lack of legal provisions in some states specifically prohibiting or criminalizing domestic violence; a lack of specialist police units and training; insufficient provisions to provide protection to victims; and court decisions which did not always reflect the gravity of such offences.

Death penalty

There were some positive moves on the death penalty during the year. Armenia abolished capital punishment in peacetime, Kazakstan announced a moratorium on executions pending legislation on abolition, and Kyrgyzstan maintained its moratorium on executions. Tajikistan, while retaining the death penalty, reduced its scope. However, in recent years Tajikistan and the two other retentionist states in the region, Belarus and Uzbekistan, have continued to carry out executions. The level of executions was believed to be particularly high in Uzbekistan, where scores of people have been executed in recent years after unfair trials, frequently amid allegations of torture, and with corruption an integral part of the investigation, trial and appeal in such cases. In Belarus, Tajikistan and Uzbekistan, the clemency process and executions themselves were shrouded in secrecy, compounding the punishment inflicted not only on the prisoners but also on their families. Executions took place in secret, with family members and friends denied the chance to say goodbye; in many cases families were not told for months whether their relative was alive or had been executed. They were also not told where their loved one was buried. None of these three countries published comprehensive statistics on their use of the death penalty.

Action for human rights

Although human rights remained under attack across the region, action to promote and protect fundamental rights continued. Many voices highlighted that human rights and security are not incompatible, but indivisible and interdependent. Human rights defenders continued their work despite harassment, intimidation and detention. Social movements responded to a range of human rights concerns in the region, bringing together activists across borders, with forums such as the Second European Social Forum in Paris, France, in November providing opportunities for regional coordination of popular activism. Strong regional intergovernmental bodies, including the Council of Europe and the Organization for Security and Co-operation in Europe, continued to play key roles in promoting and protecting human rights.

ALBANIA

REPUBLIC OF ALBANIA
Head of state: Alfred Moisiu
Head of government: Fatos Nano
Death penalty: abolitionist for ordinary crimes
UN Women's Convention and its Optional Protocol:
ratified

Detainees continued to be ill-treated following arrest and in police custody, usually to obtain confessions. Several police officers accused of ill-treating detainees were tried, but many incidents of ill-treatment were not investigated. Detention conditions were harsh, especially for remand prisoners, who were generally held in overcrowded and often dirty cells in police stations. Women and children were frequently victims of domestic violence and continued to be trafficked for forced prostitution or as cheap labour.

Background
One of the poorest countries in Europe, Albania continued to suffer from weak government, widespread corruption, high unemployment rates and little public confidence in the independence of the judiciary – all factors contributing to the persistence of violent and organized crime.

In October Albania became the second country to ratify the Optional Protocol to the UN Convention against Torture.

Torture and ill-treatment
Ill-treatment of detainees at the time of arrest and in police custody continued to be common.

⌑ In May Ndoc Vuksani, aged 37, was alleged to have been brutally beaten at Shkodër police station while being questioned in connection with a crime. He was released six hours later for lack of evidence. A medical forensic expert found he had a fractured left arm and bruising on his left shoulder.

Convicted prisoners reported ill-treatment less frequently, in part because of their relative isolation in prisons.

⌑ In November the Ombudsperson visited a high security prison in Burrel after receiving a telephone call from an injured prisoner. The Ombudsperson concluded that a senior prison official had beaten and ill-treated 10 prisoners, and requested the local prosecutor to start criminal proceedings against him.

Impunity for ill-treatment
Victims of police ill-treatment often did not file complaints. In the absence of a complaint, prosecutors and judges generally failed to initiate an investigation when a detainee brought before them bore visible injuries. Even when a complaint was made, prosecutors did not always investigate or did so only after a lengthy delay.

⌑ In July, 18-year-old Artan Llango from Çorovodë attempted to file a complaint with the prosecutor of Skrapar district. He alleged that two police officers had beaten him after he intervened when they evicted a friend from a school graduation party. Although there were numerous witnesses, and photographs of the alleged victim appeared to show bruising, the prosecutor reportedly declined to investigate.

Trials of police officers
In general, police officers enjoyed considerable impunity. Nonetheless, several officers were prosecuted and brought to trial, sometimes after considerable delay, on charges of ill-treating detainees, in one case with fatal results.

⌑ On 3 January Gazmend Tahirllari, aged 37, from a village near Korça, was arrested for allegedly threatening a taxi driver. Later that day the police took him to hospital, apparently claiming they had found him drunk on the road. The next day he died. A local doctor initially attributed his death to excessive alcohol. His family, supported by the Ombudsperson, insisted on his body being exhumed. A forensic examination by experts from the capital, Tirana, found that death had been caused by kicks or punches to his head. In March Korça district court sentenced police officer Lorenc Balliu, in his absence, to 16 years' imprisonment for murder. Five other officers, co-defendants who were present in court, were sentenced to between four months' and three years' imprisonment.

⌑ In April an investigation by the Tirana Prosecutor's Office of a charge of torture against Edmond Koseni, a former police chief of Elbasan district, was stopped. Several previous investigations into complaints of ill-treatment brought against him had been similarly suspended. However, the Prosecutor General ordered the latest investigation to be re-opened. In May Edmond Koseni and his brother-in-law, Xhaferr Elezi, also a police officer, were tried before Elbasan district court. They were accused of beating and injuring a taxi-driver, Naim Pulaku, in December 2001, and attacking him the following day in hospital. In November Xhaferr Elezi was convicted of torture and of possessing an unlicensed weapon, and was sentenced to 10 years' imprisonment, which included four years imposed by an Italian court for pimping. Edmond Koseni, charged with torture, was acquitted. The prosecutor appealed against the acquittal.

Conditions of detention
Over 1,000 prisoners, mostly detainees held on remand, were held in often severely overcrowded and insanitary conditions in police cells. They had inadequate food and no access to reading or writing materials or radio or television. The conditions often amounted to inhuman and degrading treatment, provoking protests by inmates. Children aged between 14 and 17 years frequently shared cells with adults, although this was illegal. Several hundred convicted prisoners, who could not be transferred to congested prisons, were also detained illegally in police stations.

From late November onwards some of these prisoners were moved to a new prison in Peqin, built with Italian funding and mainly for the accommodation of repatriated Albanians convicted in Italy.

◻ In June, 80 per cent of detainees held in Vlora police station were reportedly infected with scabies. Up to 125 were held in cells with capacity for 45. In August responsibility for the detention facilities at Vlora police station passed to the Ministry of Justice, the first step in a delayed government plan to improve conditions and transfer responsibility for all preventive detention facilities from the Ministry of Public Order to the Justice Ministry.

◻ Mirdita district court set a precedent in August when it ordered Mirdita police station and the General Directorate of Prisons to pay Artan Beleshi 700,000 Albanian leks (about US$6,000) in compensation for detaining him in degrading conditions for over three years and for failing to transfer him to prison within the legal time limit following his conviction.

Domestic violence and trafficking

Traditional attitudes contributed to a high incidence of violence against women and children, particularly in rural areas. In September the UN Children's Fund (UNICEF) published findings that 40 per cent of women in 11 districts were regularly subjected to violence in the home. No legal provisions specifically prohibited domestic violence, and court decisions did not always reflect the gravity of the offence.

◻ In October the National Council of Albanian Women protested at the leniency of a 16-month prison sentence imposed by Tirana District Court on Ruzhdi Qinami for the "honour killing" of his 17-year-old daughter. The court ruled that he had committed the murder in a state of severe psychological shock, after his daughter, betrothed by the family to one man, returned home late one night from a meeting with another.

Poverty, lack of education and family breakdown had a major role in the continued trafficking of women and children, primarily to Italy and Greece, for forced prostitution and cheap labour. The authorities increased efforts to arrest and prosecute offenders, but by the end of 2003 had brought only a small number of cases to court. In July, analysis reportedly showed that 80 per cent of prosecutions for trafficking for prostitution in the previous six months had failed because victims feared reprisals. An office providing free legal aid to victims was opened in Tirana. In June the government signed an agreement on witness protection with a number of international agencies, and in November approved a draft law on witness protection.

AI country reports/ visits
Report
· Concerns in Europe and Central Asia, January-June 2003: Albania (AI Index: EUR 01/016/2003)
Visit
In April AI representatives visited Albania to conduct research.

ARMENIA

REPUBLIC OF ARMENIA
Head of state: Robert Kocharian
Head of government: Andranik Markarian
Death penalty: abolitionist for ordinary crimes
UN Women's Convention: ratified
Optional Protocol to UN Women's Convention: not signed

In line with its human rights commitments to the Council of Europe, Armenia abolished capital punishment in peacetime. However, it failed to meet its commitments to the Council of Europe on conscientious objectors to compulsory military service, who continued to be imprisoned. The authorities detained hundreds of protesters who took part in peaceful opposition rallies to contest the outcome of the presidential elections.

Background

In March incumbent President Kocharian won presidential elections that were marred by widespread voting irregularities, including ballot box stuffing, and intimidation and violence towards independent and opposition election monitors. Mass opposition rallies protested at illegal election practices. Following international criticism, the President acknowledged that the elections had not met international standards and set up a commission of inquiry to investigate reported irregularities. Nevertheless, parliamentary elections in May were likewise flawed by reported ballot box stuffing and intimidation of international observers. Parties that supported the President won a large majority in parliament.

Administrative arrests

Some 100 protesters who participated in peaceful demonstrations after the presidential elections were reportedly sentenced to short prison terms after being convicted of disrupting public order. Reportedly denied access to lawyers, they were sentenced in closed trials without legal representation. In April the Armenian Constitutional Court declared the arrests unlawful.

◻ Prisoner of conscience Artur Sakunts, Chairman of the Vanadzor branch of the Helsinki Citizens Assembly (HCA), was released from prison on 25 March after serving a 10-day sentence. He was arrested after he attempted to organize a public meeting on 15 March on the findings of HCA election monitoring. He was tried the same day and convicted of "disobeying the authorities" (Article 182 of the Armenian Administrative Code). He was not permitted access to a lawyer before or during his trial. His arrest and the firebombing of the Vanadzor HCA office in the early hours of 14 March raised fears of a campaign to prevent the HCA from carrying out legitimate human rights work.

Unfair trial concerns

In December Nairi Unanyan and five co-accused were sentenced to life imprisonment by a court in Yerevan for their part in the October 1999 attack on the Armenian parliament in which eight deputies and government officials, including Prime Minister Vazgen Sarkisian and parliamentary Speaker Karen Demirchian, were killed. There were concerns about the fairness of the trial and the widespread support for imposing the death penalty in the case.

Proceedings in the case had been accompanied since the 1999 arrests by concerns about due process and the detention conditions of those detained in connection with the arrests. These included allegations of torture and ill-treatment, difficulties in access to defence lawyers, lack of access to families, and denial of access to independent medical practitioners. Widespread public and political support for the death penalty in this case had led to the Council of Europe warning Armenia that it would face suspension from the organization if any of the defendants were executed.

Death penalty

In May parliament adopted a new criminal code, which abolished the death penalty in peacetime but contained a provision that could have allowed use of the death penalty in the parliamentary shootings trial. In July President Kocharian commuted all outstanding death sentences to life in prison.

In September the newly elected parliament voted to abolish the death penalty in peacetime and to ratify Protocol No. 6 to the European Convention on Human Rights, one of the commitments Armenia undertook when it joined the Council of Europe in 2001. However, in November deputies voted unanimously to amend the new criminal code to deny the right of parole to prisoners serving life sentences for grave crimes including murder and assassination of a state or public figure. It was widely believed that the amendment was intended to ensure that those convicted in the parliamentary shootings case were never released.

Conscientious objection

Parliament adopted a law in December that provided for unarmed military service of three years or alternative civilian service under the Ministry of Defence for three and a half years – almost double the length of ordinary military service.

Conscientious objectors continued to be sentenced to prison terms despite Council of Europe requirements that all those imprisoned for conscientious objection should be freed. By December, prison sentences of between one and two years had been imposed on at least 27 men, all Jehovah's Witnesses, for conscientious objection. Five more had been arrested and were awaiting trial. A further two had been released on parole.

AUSTRIA

REPUBLIC OF AUSTRIA
Head of state: Thomas Klestil
Head of government: Wolfgang Schüssel
Death penalty: abolitionist for all crimes
UN Women's Convention and its Optional Protocol: ratified

A man died in police custody after reportedly being ill-treated and dangerously restrained by public officials. The investigation into the fatal shooting of a man in 2002 was ongoing. Allegations of police ill-treatment and excessive use of force continued. Parliament adopted the controversial new Asylum Law. The European Court of Human Rights ruled against Austria in the case of three convicted gay men.

Deaths in police custody

Thirty-three-year-old Cheibani Wague from Mauritania died in police custody in Vienna in the night of 15-16 July. Police were called to Cheibani Wague's workplace at around 11pm on 15 July after a dispute between him and a colleague had been reported. Cheibani Wague, who had initially reacted calmly to the presence of the police and medical personnel, was reportedly violently restrained by police officers after he suddenly leapt out of an ambulance.

Video footage of the incident depicted six police and medical officials surrounding Cheibani Wague as he lay handcuffed, face-down on the ground, apparently unconscious. While one police officer could be seen standing on the detainee's leg with one foot, a medical attendant stood on him with both feet. Cheibani Wague was subsequently taken to Vienna's General Hospital, where he reportedly died at around 6am on 16 July. An autopsy report published in November indicated lack of oxygen to the brain and irreversible failure of the circulatory system as the causes of death. The official investigation into the incident was ongoing at the end of the year.

In December, however, Vienna's Independent Administrative Tribunal examined whether the police officers had acted unlawfully during the incident. However, during the hearings the police officers refused to cooperate with the Tribunal and declined to make any statements, even though such non-cooperation was illegal.

Police shootings: update

The investigation into the fatal shooting of 28-year-old Binali Ilter was still ongoing at the end of the year. Binali Ilter, an Austrian national of Turkish origin was shot dead by police in Vienna's city centre on 31 August 2002. At the time of the shooting he was unarmed and suffering from schizophrenia.

Allegations of police ill-treatment

There were continued allegations that police officers ill-treated and used excessive force, including against detainees.

⬜ On 24 April, Vienna's Independent Administrative Tribunal found that police officers had ill-treated a man during a demonstration in Vienna on 13 April 2002. The man had taken part in a counter-demonstration to a far right-wing meeting on Vienna's Heldenplatz. The Tribunal found that, without apparent necessity, the police officers knocked the man to the ground by using their batons and kicking his legs away from under him and then kicked and hit the man as he lay on the ground. As a result of the incident the man sustained large bruising to his left upper arm, left thigh and pelvis and various abrasions and swelling on other parts of his body.

⬜ On 3 June Klagenfurt District Court ordered Austria to pay Ewald Stattmann 30,000 euros in compensation for the extensive injuries he suffered as a result of being ill-treated in police custody in Villach in 1996. Ewald Stattmann was repeatedly kicked by two police officers in a holding cell at Villach police headquarters in the early hours of 29 December 1996. He was found unconscious at around 6am and was later taken to hospital where he underwent a life-saving operation and spent 10 days in intensive care. He suffered various injuries, including multiple bruising, a fractured skull and a cerebral haemorrhage. Despite the serious injuries no charges were ever brought against the police officers.

⬜ In early September, Lower Austria's Independent Administrative Tribunal ruled in favour of 32 foreign nationals of African origin who had lodged multiple complaints about their cruel, inhuman and degrading treatment by police in January 2000. Around 130 police officers raided a building used to house asylum-seekers in Traiskirchen, Lower Austria on the evening of 17 January 2000, searching for drugs. The Tribunal found that the police had violated Article 3 of the European Convention on Human Rights (ECHR) by binding the residents' hands in plastic restraints for several hours without good reason, thereby causing them physical and mental suffering, and not allowing them to use the toilet or giving them access to water. The Tribunal also ruled that the overall operation was illegal owing to the absence of a search warrant.

Racism

⬜ In May Linz District Court ruled that a police officer who had verbally abused a black motorist on 31 July 2002, calling him a "shit negro", had not violated his human dignity under Austria's Criminal Code. The Court argued that, although the police officer had insulted the man, the insult was directed at the complainant as an individual, "who 'by chance' belongs to the black race and not against the black race as such". An earlier court decision had also rejected the man's complaint.

Refugees

A new Asylum Law, adopted by parliament in October, was heavily criticized by refugee and human rights organizations. The new law, among other things, eliminates the suspensive effect of appeals, introduces a list of safe countries of origin and effectively prevents asylum-seekers bringing at a later date new facts and evidence to the attention of the asylum authorities. It is feared that cases of *refoulement* (forcible return) may result from these new procedures.

Unequal age of consent

On 9 January the European Court of Human Rights ruled in favour of three gay men who had filed complaints against Austria after being convicted under Article 209 of the Austrian Criminal Code in the period 1996-1997. The article, which was repealed in July 2002, set the age of consent for gay men at 18 years of age as opposed to 14 for heterosexuals and lesbians. Gay men convicted of violating Article 209 faced up to five years' imprisonment. In the cases of *L. and V. v. Austria* and *S.L. v. Austria* the European Court of Human Rights ruled that in convicting all three men under Article 209 Austria had violated Articles 14 and 8 of the ECHR, namely the prohibition of discrimination and the right to respect for private life.

AI country reports

Report
· Concerns in Europe and Central Asia, January-June 2003: Austria (AI Index: EUR 01/016/2003)

AZERBAIJAN

REPUBLIC OF AZERBAIJAN
Head of state: Ilham Aliyev (replaced Heydar Aliyev in December)
Head of government: Artur Rasizade
Death penalty: abolitionist for all crimes
UN Women's Convention and its Optional Protocol: ratified

Hundreds of opposition supporters were detained following police clashes with demonstrators protesting at presidential election results. Human rights defenders were intimidated and their offices attacked. Police reportedly used excessive force to detain villagers involved in peaceful protests. Political prisoners were among 160 prisoners released in December.

Background

In August President Heydar Aliyev appointed his son, Ilham Aliyev, as Prime Minister. Two weeks before presidential elections in October, he withdrew his candidacy in favour of his son, who was subsequently elected with a large majority as candidate for the ruling *Yeni Azerbaijan* (New Azerbaijan) party. Heydar Aliyev died, aged 80, in December.

Election-related abuses

The pre-election campaign was marked by intimidation of opposition supporters and use of excessive force by the police in breaking up peaceful opposition rallies. Widespread voting irregularities during the election included ballot box stuffing, multiple voting and intimidation of voters and election observers. Scores of election officials who refused to sign flawed election protocols during the count were reportedly threatened and detained. International observers were barred from monitoring the activities of the Central Electoral Commission as they compiled the results at the final count.

Hundreds of protesters and dozens of police officers were injured, many seriously, in clashes between opposition activists protesting at election irregularities and officers from the police and the Ministry of Internal Affairs (MVD) Special Forces in the capital, Baku, on 16 October. At least one person was reported killed. Over 50 journalists were allegedly beaten by the police, and several were among the scores of protesters detained.

Many opposition supporters and their relatives were reportedly intimidated and dismissed from their jobs following the election. The state-run printing house refused to print opposition newspapers, and the authorities closed down the opposition *Yeni Musavat* newspaper.

Politically motivated arrests

After the post-election clashes, more than 600 opposition activists – mainly from the *Musavat* (Equality) party – were detained throughout the country. Most were convicted of "organizing or participating in violent activities" and sentenced to short-term administrative detention. More than 100 were still awaiting trial at the end of 2003. MVD officers allegedly used torture to coerce some opposition leaders into denouncing Isa Gambar, *Musavat* Chairman, who was subsequently placed under house arrest.

▭ On 27 October a court in Baku ordered the three-month pre-trial detention of Rauf Arifoglu, *Musavat* Deputy Chairman and editor-in-chief of *Yeni Musavat*. He faced charges of organizing violence and storing weapons in the *Yeni Musavat* offices. He was reportedly held in solitary confinement for 32 days and forced to sleep on the floor of an unheated cell for 18 days. He was among dozens of opposition detainees who went on hunger strike on 1 December in protest at their arrests.

Excessive use of force – update

In February police raided Nardaran, a village near Baku where in June 2002 they had arrested 15 community leaders, clashed with inhabitants protesting about local socio-economic conditions and shot dead one villager. In the early hours dozens of masked officers in

camouflage uniforms, armed with automatic weapons and batons, reportedly stormed a tent in the central square, erected in protest at the June 2002 arrests and where some 50 villagers were sleeping. The officers were said to have fired at the tent and assaulted the occupants, injuring about 20. Eight men were arrested, charged with resisting arrest and illegal possession of weapons, and in March sentenced to suspended prison terms.

In April the 15 villagers arrested in June 2002 were convicted. Alikram Aliyev, Chairman of the Islamic Party of Azerbaijan, and Dzhebrail Alizade, Chairman of the Union of Baku and Baku Villages, were sentenced to nine and eight years' imprisonment respectively for allegedly participating in the clashes. Other defendants received suspended sentences. In June an appeal court reduced Alikram Aliyev's sentence to six years. In November the Supreme Court reduced his and Dzhebrail Alizade's sentences to suspended four-year terms.

Attacks on human rights defenders

A campaign in the state-sponsored media against prominent human rights defenders was followed by orchestrated attacks and threats.

▭ In February and March pro-government newspapers accused Eldar Zeynalov, head of the non-governmental Human Rights Centre of Azerbaijan, of supporting Armenia. In February Ilham Aliyev reportedly said Leyla Yunus, Director of the non-governmental Institute for Peace and Democracy, and others were assisting Armenia and threatening Azerbaijan's interests by opposing construction of the Baku-Tbilisi-Ceyhan oil pipeline. On 22 April pro-government organizations denounced Eldar Zeynalov and Leyla Yunus as "enemies of the people" on state-run television. Between 23 and 25 April a mob broke the windows and locks of the Human Rights Centre, burned a wooden cross bearing the effigy of Eldar Zeynalov, called on him to leave Azerbaijan and shouted death threats. The police did not interfere. On 28 April, when neighbours assaulted his sister-in-law and father-in-law, the police reportedly refused to respond to a call for protection. Also on 28 April, 40 *Yeni Azerbaijan* supporters outside the Institute of Peace and Democracy called for Leyla Yunus to leave the country.

Political prisoners – update

On 30 December President Ilham Aliyev decreed a pardon for 160 prisoners, including 65 political prisoners, all of whom were subsequently released, and a reduction in the sentences of five other prisoners. Those released included a number of political prisoners whom the Council of Europe had required Azerbaijan to release or retry as one of its obligations on joining the organization.

BELARUS

REPUBLIC OF BELARUS
Head of state: Alyaksandr Lukashenka
Head of government: Sergey Sidorsky (replaced
Gennady Novitsky in July)
Death penalty: retentionist
UN Women's Convention: ratified
Optional Protocol to UN Women's Convention: signed

Investigations into a number of high-profile
"disappearances" were halted without adequate
explanation. The authorities closed down human
rights organizations and other non-governmental
organizations (NGOs), and suspended several
privately owned newspapers. The independent trade
union movement was targeted and its leaders were
imprisoned. Numerous protesters were detained for
non-violent opposition activities. There remained
several long-term prisoners of conscience. Domestic
violence was widespread. The courts continued to
pass death sentences.

Background
Relations remained strained with the international
community, which repeatedly criticized Belarus for
violations of human rights and fundamental freedoms.
In April the UN Commission on Human Rights expressed
deep concern about human rights violations in Belarus,
including "disappearances", arbitrary arrest and
detention, and the harassment of individuals engaged
in opposition activities. A range of intergovernmental
bodies echoed similar concerns throughout 2003.

'Disappearances'
There was no progress in determining who was
responsible for the "disappearances" of leading
opposition figures Yury Zakharenko and Viktor
Gonchar, businessman Anatoly Krasovsky and
journalist Dmitry Zavadsky. Criminal investigations
were halted in January and February, reportedly
without substantive reasons for the decisions being
provided to the families concerned. After campaigning
by the families, investigations into the
"disappearances" were reopened – in June for the case
of Yury Zakharenko; in July for Viktor Gonchar and
Anatoly Krasovsky; and in December for Dmitry
Zavadsky.

Human rights defenders
Throughout 2003 human rights defenders faced a
heightened campaign of harassment and intimidation
by the authorities. Several prominent human rights
organizations were closed after receiving two or more
official warnings from the Ministry of Justice. Warnings
were issued for spurious violations of a controversial
law that tightly regulated the activities of civil society. A
large number of other NGOs were refused registration
or had their registration annulled for equally

questionable reasons. The spate of closures elicited
considerable international condemnation.
⬚ On 8 September the prominent human rights
organization, Legal Assistance to the Population, was
closed by Minsk City Court. The organization had
received two official warnings in the previous year, for
providing free legal assistance to members of the public
who were not members of the organization and for
using a different organizational symbol from that
submitted at registration.
⬚ On 28 October the Belarusian Supreme Court ruled
to close the influential human rights organization
Spring-96. The Court cited various alleged violations of
the law including, among other things, the legal
representation of persons not members of the
organization, not charging membership fees and
irregularities in registration documents.

Freedom of the press
The Ministry of Information regularly employed a
similar system of official warnings and suspensions to
keep in check the privately owned press. Several
influential newspapers were suspended. Others were
burdened by crippling defamation suits brought by
state officials.
⬚ On 29 May *Belaruskaya Delovaya Gazeta* was
closed for three months by the authorities after three
warnings for alleged violations of the press law. In June
it reappeared for two editions under the mastheads of
newspapers *Ekho* and *Salidarnasts* before the
authorities again stopped it going to print. *Ekho* was
then suspended for three months, *Salidarnasts* fined
the equivalent of US$2,000, and the director of their
publishing house dismissed. Another privately owned
newspaper, *Predprinimatelskaya Gazeta*, was
suspended for three months in June after publishing an
article about the case.

Detention of protesters
Numerous peaceful protesters were detained as
prisoners of conscience solely for exercising their
rights to freedom of expression and assembly. They
risked ill-treatment by the police at the time of arrest,
and frequently received prison sentences of up to 15
days or fines.
⬚ At least 24 protesters received short prison
sentences when the authorities enforced a concerted
clampdown on peaceful protests in March. On 12 March
former Deputy Foreign Minister Andrei Sannikov,
Charter-97 human rights activists Ludmila Gryaznova
and Dmitry Bondarenko, and small business leader
Leonid Malakhov were sentenced to 15 days'
imprisonment for their role in organizing a
demonstration in Minsk the same day. Two further
participants were later convicted and sentenced to
prison terms for similar offences.

Violations of trade union rights
The International Labour Organization criticized
repeated violations of workers' rights throughout the
year. On 19 November it announced the establishment
of a Commission of Inquiry into allegations of abuses of

workers' rights in Belarus, a procedure used only in the most serious cases. Independent trade unionists complained that they were imprisoned, harassed and dismissed, that their right of association was severely restricted, and that the state interfered in the internal affairs of several trade unions and of the national trade union federation.

⬚ On 18 September Leninsky District Court in Minsk sentenced the President of the Belarusian Congress of Democratic Trade Unions, Alyaksandr Yaroshuk, to 10 days' imprisonment for contempt of court. He had criticized the decision of the Belarusian Supreme Court to close down the Trade Union of Air Traffic Controllers of Belarus in a newspaper article in August. On 17 October the union's lawyer, Vladimir Odynets, was sentenced by a court in Minsk to five days' imprisonment, also for contempt of court and reportedly in connection with his representation of Alyaksandr Yaroshuk.

⬚ On 30 October the President of the Belarusian Automobile and Agricultural Machinery Workers' Union, Alyaksandr Bukhvostov, was detained by police in central Minsk for staging an unauthorized but peaceful protest against alleged government interference in the union's internal affairs. A court in Minsk sentenced him to 10 days' imprisonment later the same day.

Long-term prisoners of conscience

⬚ In March Nikolai Markevich and Pavel Mozheiko, editor and staff writer of the privately owned newspaper *Pagonia*, were released early from respective 18- and 12-month sentences of "restricted freedom". They had been convicted by a court in the town of Grodno in June 2002 of libelling President Lukashenka in an unpublished newspaper article in which they raised widely held concerns about government involvement in "disappearances".

⬚ In June Viktor Ivashkevich, editor of the influential trade union newspaper *Rabochy*, had his two-year sentence of "restricted freedom" reduced on appeal to one year. In September 2002 a court in Minsk had convicted him of libelling President Lukashenka in a newspaper article. He was released in mid-December.

⬚ The health of imprisoned scientist Professor Yury Bandazhevsky reportedly deteriorated during the year. Family members who visited him in the UZ-15 labour colony in Minsk said that he was suffering from depression. He had been sentenced to eight years' imprisonment for alleged bribe-taking in June 2001, but it was widely believed that he was convicted because he had criticized official responses to the Chernobyl nuclear reactor catastrophe of 1986.

Violence against women

Domestic violence remained prevalent and women seeking justice continued to face numerous obstacles. Belarus submitted a report combining its fourth, fifth and sixth periodic reports to the UN Committee on the Elimination of Discrimination against Women in anticipation of examination of the report by the Committee in January 2004. The report described the various measures taken to implement recommendations made by the Committee in 2000 to prevent and eliminate violence against women, particularly domestic violence. Belarus outlined its National Plan for Gender Equality 2001-2005, which contained measures to address the issue. These included research, the establishment of crisis and advice centres for victims of domestic violence, and public awareness campaigns.

Death penalty

At least one prisoner was believed to have been executed in 2003, although accurate information on the death penalty was difficult to obtain. The Deputy Chairman of the Supreme Court said in October that two men were sentenced to death in 2003, although other sources suggested the number could have been five.

⬚ On 13 May the UN Human Rights Committee ruled that the secrecy surrounding the death penalty in Belarus amounted to inhuman treatment of the families. Prisoners are executed in secret and the families are not provided with information about the time of the execution or the location of the burial sites of the deceased. In the cases *Bondarenko v. Belarus* and *Lyashkevich v. Belarus*, the Committee ruled that these practices "had the effect of intimidating or punishing families intentionally leaving them in a state of uncertainty and mental distress".

AI country reports/ visits
Reports
- Concerns in Europe and Central Asia, January-June 2003: Belarus (AI Index: EUR 01/016/2003)
- Belarus: And then there were none (AI Index: EUR 49/006/2003)

BELGIUM

KINGDOM OF BELGIUM
Head of state: King Albert II
Head of government: Guy Verhofstadt
Death penalty: abolitionist for all crimes
UN Women's Convention: ratified
Optional Protocol to UN Women's Convention: signed

There were allegations that criminal suspects, demonstrators, asylum-seekers and unauthorized immigrants were subjected to ill-treatment, excessive force and racist abuse by police officers. Fundamental safeguards against ill-treatment in police custody were lacking and there were deficiencies in relevant monitoring, complaints and investigation mechanisms. Four law enforcement officers were given suspended sentences in connection with the death of an asylum-seeker during a forcible deportation operation in 1998. Organizations working for refugees' human rights criticized asylum procedures for excessive complexity, delays, lack of transparency and restrictive interpretation of the definition of a refugee. The treatment of child asylum-seekers continued to fall short of international standards on the treatment of children. New legislation severely restricted the former wide scope of Belgium's universal jurisdiction legislation, increasing the possibility of impunity for the perpetrators. There were continuing concerns about prison conditions, including overcrowding, inter-prisoner violence, under-staffing, inadequate staff training and insufficient external monitoring. There were racist incidents directed against Jewish, Arab and other Muslim communities. Despite numerous initiatives undertaken by the authorities to address violence against women in the family, the majority of women's formal complaints of domestic violence did not result in prosecutions. Measures undertaken to combat human trafficking appeared insufficient in view of reports of a continuing increase in trafficking in women and children for sexual exploitation.

UN Committee against Torture

In May the UN Committee against Torture examined Belgium's initial report and expressed a number of concerns relating to the treatment of criminal suspects and demonstrators by police; the detention and treatment of asylum-seekers and unauthorized immigrants, including children; the prison system, including the treatment of juvenile offenders; and amendments to universal jurisdiction legislation. It issued detailed recommendations to address the concerns raised.

Police ill-treatment

There were further reports of police ill-treatment of criminal suspects on the streets and in police stations: many of the alleged victims were foreign and non-Caucasian Belgian nationals and racist abuse was frequently reported in such cases. The reports of domestic monitoring bodies, including the Standing Police Monitoring Committee, the General Inspectorate of Police Services and the Centre for Equal Opportunities and Opposition to Racism also reflected continuing allegations of police misconduct, including violence and verbal abuse. None of the internationally recognized fundamental safeguards against ill-treatment in police custody was in place. The UN Committee against Torture recommended that national legislation expressly guarantee the right of all people, whether under judicial or administrative arrest, to have immediate access to a lawyer and a doctor of their own choice, to be informed of their rights in a language understood by them and to inform their relatives of their detention. The government announced the establishment of an inter-ministerial working group to examine aspects of police arrest, including the rights of detainees in police custody. The Committee also expressed concern about excessive use of force during demonstrations and asked the government to ensure that guidelines on the use of force and their implementation were brought fully into line with the Convention against Torture.

Some criminal investigations into alleged ill-treatment by police officers did not appear to be conducted with due diligence: some were unduly protracted and eventual sentences, where issued, were frequently nominal.

Update

◻ In June, following criminal proceedings lasting some 10 years, the Brussels appeal court found a law enforcement officer guilty of assaulting and racially insulting Rachid N., a Tunisian national, and sentenced the officer to eight months' suspended imprisonment and to pay damages. A first instance court had acquitted the officer in 2002. Rachid N. said he was ordered to strip naked in the presence of 10 officers and assaulted and insulted when he tried to refuse. The first instance court, while not disputing that he had suffered injuries in detention, had said that there was insufficient evidence that the one officer committed for trial was a perpetrator.

Human rights violations during the deportation process

There were reports that people were subjected to physical as well as psychological ill-treatment at various stages of the deportation process. It was alleged that during police raids to search for unauthorized immigrants and rejected asylum-seekers under specific deportation orders, people, including children, were subjected to traumatizing and intimidating treatment. Several asylum-seekers released from detention by court order were immediately transferred and confined to the transit zone of the national airport by police officers and left there for several days or weeks without the basic means of survival.

Allegations continued of police officers subjecting some foreign nationals resisting deportation to threats, racist abuse, physical assault and dangerous methods of restraint, including restraining deportees in positions which could restrict breathing and lead to death from positional asphyxia, despite a specific ban on such methods. There were also reports that in some cases medical treatment for injuries incurred during aborted deportation operations was inadequate and delayed.

The UN Committee against Torture expressed concern about such reports as well as about "the possibility of placing unaccompanied minors in detention for lengthy periods" and of prolonging the detention of foreigners "for as long as they do not cooperate in their repatriation". It was also concerned that people could be deported while awaiting the outcome of final appeals against the rejection of asylum applications and against deportation orders.

Individuals wishing to lodge official complaints about ill-treatment in the context of a deportation operation often faced obstacles, including limited access to appropriate legal advice for those held in detention centres for aliens; fear of reprisals during future deportation operations as a result of threats made by police officers during aborted deportations; very limited time in which to make a complaint before being successfully deported or obeying an order to leave the country; and removal from the country, which effectively closed the option of pursuing a complaint through the criminal justice system.

AI urged the authorities to ensure that, following every aborted deportation, the individual in question should automatically and immediately undergo a medical examination on return to detention. AI called for an independent inspection body to be mandated to make, and carry out in practice, regular, unannounced and unrestricted visits to airport detention cells and transit zones and the so-called INADs centre at the national airport, holding passengers refused access to Belgian territory. AI also called for a review of procedures for complaints concerning ill-treatment during deportation operations, so as to ensure that complainants have recourse to at least one accessible, effective and impartial channel of complaint.

◻ Parmananda Sapkota said that, on a second attempt to deport him in January, he was taken from Merksplas detention centre to the airport where he told police officers he was not willing to depart for Nepal where he feared he would be killed. He alleged that officers hit him both before and after binding him painfully hand and foot. He was transferred to a waiting plane by van but the pilot apparently refused to carry him and the deportation was aborted. He said the police officers threw him into the van and assaulted him there, and again in an airport room. He claimed that he received inadequate medical treatment for the injuries he incurred. An individual who saw him in detention in February observed that he had a swelling to his face, where he claimed to have been struck, swollen hands, wrists which still bore traces of where handcuffs had been secured, and that he was visibly

trembling when describing his treatment. He was deported to Nepal in March, without having lodged any formal complaint about his treatment.

Update – death during deportation

◻ In December a Brussels court found four law enforcement officers guilty of unconsciously causing grievous bodily harm resulting unintentionally in the death of Semira Adamu, a 20-year-old Nigerian asylum-seeker who died within hours of an attempt to forcibly deport her by air in 1998. Before take-off the officers employed the so-called "cushion technique", a restraint method authorized by the Ministry of the Interior at the time but subsequently banned, which allowed officers, practising caution, to press a cushion against the mouth, but not the nose, of a recalcitrant deportee to prevent biting and shouting. Semira Adamu's face was pressed into a cushion for over 10 minutes and she fell into a coma as her brain became starved of oxygen. She died of a brain haemorrhage hours later. The court sentenced the three escorting officers to one year's suspended imprisonment and the supervising officer to 14 months' suspended imprisonment. All were sentenced to fines, to be paid by the state, which was itself ordered to pay substantial damages to Semira Adamu's relatives. A fifth officer was acquitted. Following the verdict, the Minister of the Interior asked an independent commission, first mandated to evaluate instructions and techniques relating to forcible deportations immediately after the death, to reconvene and carry out a re-evaluation.

Universal jurisdiction

Legislation enacted in 1993 and amended in 1999 made provision for Belgian courts to exercise universal jurisdiction over genocide, crimes against humanity and war crimes in international and non-international armed conflict, wherever the crimes were committed and whatever the nationality of the accused and victims. By early 2003 criminal complaints had been lodged directly with investigating magistrates against people from over 20 countries, all residing outside Belgium, in addition to complaints against people found in Belgium. Those facing complaints included past and present heads of state and lower level officials.

Amendments made to the law in April allowed victims to lodge complaints directly with an investigating magistrate only if the case had a direct connection with Belgium, through the victim or the accused, otherwise complaints were to be presented to the federal prosecutor for consideration and possible further action. It also allowed the government to refer certain cases to other countries, if those countries were deemed to offer a fair and effective avenue to justice.

In July, apparently responding to political pressure exercised predominantly by the US authorities, the government proposed legislation, approved by parliament in August, allowing Belgium to pursue complaints of genocide, crimes against humanity and war crimes only in cases presenting a direct connection with Belgium through the accused or victims. This meant that further action on many criminal complaints lodged in Belgium was effectively blocked. The government gave specific assurances that criminal proceedings relating to crimes committed in Rwanda, Guatemala and Chad, all of which included Belgian victims, would continue in Belgium.

AI country reports/ visits
Reports
- Belgium before the UN Committee against Torture: alleged police ill-treatment (AI Index: EUR 14/001/2003)
- Belgium: Alleged ill-treatment and verbal, including racist, abuse of Bernardin Mbuku and Odette Ibanda by Brussels police officers (AI Index: EUR 14/002/2003)
- Belgium: The death of Semira Adamu – Responsibilities past and present (AI Index: EUR 14/005/2003)

Visit
An AI delegate visited Belgium in March.

BOSNIA-HERZEGOVINA

BOSNIA AND HERZEGOVINA
Head of state: rotating presidency – Dragan Čović, Sulejman Tihić and Borislav Paravac (replaced Mirko Šarović in April)
President of the Muslim/ Croat Federation of Bosnia and Herzegovina: Niko Ložančić (replaced Safet Halilović in February)
President of the Republika Srpska: Dragan Čavić
Head of state government: Adnan Terzić
Death penalty: abolitionist for all crimes
UN Women's Convention and its Optional Protocol: ratified

Impunity for human rights violations remained endemic. Thousands of "disappearances" which occurred during the 1992-1995 war remained unresolved and lack of cooperation continued to hinder the efforts of international and domestic courts to bring the perpetrators to justice. People displaced by the war continued to return to their homes. Around a million people had returned by the end of the year, almost half of those displaced by the conflict. However, many returns were not sustainable and returnees continued to face discrimination and violence. Some progress was made in prosecuting those responsible for serious human rights violations in the context of the

trafficking of women and girls. However, the agencies responsible for addressing these abuses received inadequate state support.

Background
Bosnia-Herzegovina comprises two semi-autonomous entities, the Federation of Bosnia and Herzegovina (Federation) and the Republika Srpska (RS), as well as the autonomous district of Brčko. The country continued to be largely under the authority of the international community, in particular the High Representative nominated by the Steering Board of the Peace Implementation Council (PIC), an intergovernmental body responsible for monitoring the implementation of the Dayton Peace Agreement. The High Representative has far-reaching powers allowing him to dismiss public officials, including government and judicial officials.

New and multi-ethnic state and RS governments were appointed in mid-January and in February a new Federation government was sworn in. In April Mirko Šarović, the Bosnian Serb member of the state Presidency, resigned after a judicial investigation discovered evidence of his involvement in an illegal arms trade arrangement with the government of Iraq.

In May the state government entered into an impunity agreement with the USA not to surrender US nationals accused of genocide, crimes against humanity or war crimes to the International Criminal Court. Such agreements breach states' obligations under international law.

Legal reform
The State Court of Bosnia and Herzegovina – which has jurisdiction over organized crime and corruption, "international terrorism" and other crimes under international law – was officially opened in January.

In mid-June the PIC endorsed a proposal by the High Representative to abolish the Human Rights Chamber and transfer its caseload to the Constitutional Court, which has a narrower mandate. Implementation of this proposal was completed at the end of 2003. There were concerns about the large outstanding caseload of the Chamber and the lack of an accessible and adequate legal mechanism to take over this work. There were further fears that the domestic court system – currently undergoing far-reaching reforms and restructuring – may not prove capable or willing to provide redress in the near future.

In June the PIC endorsed a proposal by the Office of the High Representative to establish a special chamber for war crimes in the new State Court, to be operational from 2004. It was envisaged that the War Crimes Chamber would include international judges and prosecutors for a period of three to five years, after which it would be entirely staffed by local officials. However, AI remained concerned that the proposed solution would prove inadequate to address the vast legacy of outstanding cases of war crimes and other crimes under international humanitarian law. The proposal did not take into account the regional nature of the war and the fact that many perpetrators, as well as material evidence relating to these crimes, remained in neighbouring states, beyond the reach of the Bosnian criminal justice system. Another issue of crucial importance, the protection of vulnerable witnesses from attacks and intimidation, was not adequately addressed. The rushed and unrealistic timeline envisaged for the War Crimes Chamber to become fully and independently operational suggested an insufficiently detailed plan. Limited resources heightened the risk that the War Crimes Chamber would only be able to prosecute a small number of the thousands of suspects, selected on the basis of vague and contradictory criteria, and so undermine the battle against impunity – including efforts by the International Criminal Tribunal for the former Yugoslavia (the Tribunal) itself – and adversely affect the process of reconciliation.

The comprehensive overhaul of the country's intelligence services continued, under the supervision of the international community. The integrity and professionalism of the existing Federation and RS security and intelligence services had been challenged by repeated reports that they were operating outside the law and civilian control mechanisms.

Impunity for wartime human rights violations
International prosecutions
The Tribunal continued to try alleged perpetrators of serious violations of international humanitarian law, including Slobodan Milošević, former President of the Federal Republic of Yugoslavia.

In late March, two Bosnian Croats, Vinko Martinović and Mladen Naletilić, were found guilty of crimes against humanity and war crimes and sentenced to 18 and 20 years' imprisonment respectively, for their command and individual responsibility for crimes against the non-Croat population in the Mostar region in 1993.

In May, the trial commenced of four former commanders in the Bosnian Serb Army, for their criminal involvement in the executions of thousands of Bosniak men and boys after the fall of Srebrenica in July 1995. This trial was one of six separate proceedings initiated so far, which focused solely on the massive violations committed in the former "protected area" of Srebrenica. Two of the accused, Momir Nikolić and Dragan Obrenović, pleaded guilty to crimes against humanity and were sentenced in December to 27 and 17 years' imprisonment respectively.

Cooperation between the RS authorities and the Tribunal remained unsatisfactory. The RS police failed to arrest those indicted by the Tribunal. A total of 17 publicly indicted suspects remained at large at the end of the year, the majority of them Bosnian Serbs.

Domestic prosecutions
Several trials for war crimes opened or continued before local courts, mainly in the Federation.

⊏ The Zenica Cantonal Court continued the trial of Bosnian Croat military commander Dominik Ilijašević for war crimes committed against Bosniak civilians in Stupni Do in central Bosnia, amid concerns that prosecution witnesses were not sufficiently protected from intimidating and offensive treatment by the accused and their families in court.

⊏ The Banja Luka District Court continued criminal proceedings for war crimes against 11 former police officers from Prijedor in connection with the 1995 abduction and murder of Father Tomislav Matanović and his parents. In late January, the public prosecutor charged the suspects with war crimes against the civilian population.

Time and again the domestic criminal justice system failed to take steps to actively prosecute alleged perpetrators. A major factor in fostering this continuing impunity was the lack of cooperation between Federation and RS judiciary and police forces, in particular in enforcing arrest warrants.

⊏ In April the Višegrad police in the RS failed to arrest two serving Bosnian Serb police officers charged with war crimes by the Goražde Cantonal Court in the Federation. The Višegrad chief of police denied having received an arrest warrant, despite the fact that it was reportedly handed over in the presence of police monitors from the European Union Police Mission (EUPM). The two suspects remained at large at the end of the year.

Unresolved 'disappearances'
Thousands of "disappearances" remained unresolved amid pervading impunity for the perpetrators.

⊏ In March, the Human Rights Chamber of Bosnia-Herzegovina issued a decision in the case of 49 relatives of the "disappeared" from Srebrenica who had brought an application against the RS authorities. The Chamber expressly recognized the continuing pain of the relatives of the "disappeared" and concluded that the RS had done almost nothing to relieve their agony. The Chamber held that this inaction by the RS authorities amounted to a violation of the relatives' fundamental human rights. The Chamber ordered the RS to immediately disclose all information relevant to establishing the fate and whereabouts of the "disappeared". The RS was instructed to conduct a full and thorough investigation into the human rights violations at Srebrenica, to bring those responsible to justice and to pay 2 million euros in compensation for the collective benefit of all applicants and families of Srebrenica victims. Subsequently the Chamber struck out over 1,800 further applications filed by other Srebrenica relatives, as it was decided that the March decision would apply to all victims collectively.

In early June, the RS submitted a brief report to the Chamber which failed to address adequately the various parts of the decision which the government was obliged to implement. In September the RS authorities sent a second much more detailed reply to the Chamber which proposed, among other things, the establishment of an independent commission of inquiry into the events which took place in and around Srebrenica between 10 and 19 July 1995.

Right to return in safety and with dignity

According to the UN High Commissioner for Refugees (UNHCR) field mission in Bosnia-Herzegovina, some 54,000 people had returned to their pre-war homes by the end of December. This brought the total number of returnees to nearly a million. However, the UNHCR expressed concerns about the estimated 350,000 people who remained internally displaced, and who had little or no prospects for a durable solution through either return to their pre-war homes or effective resettlement. It stressed the need for donor funding for the reconstruction of housing, infrastructure, schools and health facilities to continue and to be more targeted to the needs of vulnerable displaced individuals.

Lack of access to employment was a major factor in people's decision not to remain in their pre-war community. Employment opportunities were scarce in general, reflecting the weak economic situation and the forced transition to a market-led economy through mass privatization. However, members of ethnic minorities in addition faced discrimination when trying to find work.

According to the UNHCR, in the period from January to May there were over 100 violent incidents against returnees and displaced people and their property, memorials or religious objects. In at least two cases these resulted in death. Rabija Ćaušević, an 80-year-old Bosniak woman who had returned to Bosanska Dubica in the northern part of the RS, was killed inside her home on 1 January 2003. In March, a Bosniak man, Smail Hrnjičić, who was renovating another Bosniak returnee's flat in west Mostar, was killed by an explosive device planted in the flat. Although police investigations were immediately launched into both incidents, the perpetrators of both attacks remained at large at the end of the year.

'Anti-terrorism' measures

In April the Chamber ruled that the state and Federation authorities had violated the fundamental rights of two Algerian nationals, Bensayah Belkacem and Mustafa Ait Idir, who had been unlawfully transferred to US custody in January 2002. In October 2002 the Chamber had made a similar ruling in the case of four other Algerian nationals unlawfully transferred to US custody at the same time. The Chamber had ordered the Bosnian authorities to use diplomatic means to protect the men from the death penalty and unfair trial while they remained in US custody, and to pay them compensation. The Chamber's decision was implemented only to the extent that the Bosnian authorities, in December 2003, agreed to pay compensation to the families of those being held by the US authorities in Guantánamo Bay, Cuba.

◻ In July, Amgad Fath Allah Yusuf 'Amir, an Egyptian national whose Bosnian citizenship was withdrawn in 2001, was taken into custody in the Federation on the grounds that he was carrying forged documents. Following his arrest, the Egyptian authorities requested his extradition, claiming that he was a member of an armed Islamist group. Pending a final decision on his citizenship – Bosnian law forbids the extradition of Bosnian citizens – he remained in detention at the end of the year.

Trafficking in women and girls

Some positive developments were noted in the prosecution of those responsible for serious human rights abuses against women and girls in the context of trafficking and forced prostitution.

◻ In March the Tuzla Cantonal Court found the owner of a local nightclub guilty of enslavement and sentenced him to three and a half years' imprisonment. The case marked the first conviction in the Federation for enslavement; those tried in trafficking cases had previously always been charged with the lesser offence of procurement.

◻ In May, five Bosnian Serb men were handed over to the custody of the State Court, which started an investigation into their alleged involvement in the trafficking of women and girls who had been forced to engage in prostitution in a chain of nightclubs in Prijedor.

In June the Office of the UN High Commissioner for Human Rights in Bosnia-Herzegovina issued a report which found that the State Commission, a special law enforcement body charged with implementation of a National Action Plan against trafficking, and law enforcement agencies were not given adequate support by the state government and that there were severe shortcomings in the provision of shelter to vulnerable victims. These concerns were shared by local human rights and women's organizations.

Gaps and ambiguities in the domestic legal framework hampered effective prosecutions. For example, the delayed adoption of the new Law on Asylum and amendments to the Law on the Movement and Stay of Foreigners further restricted the prevention of trafficking and protection for victims who continued to be treated largely as illegal migrants.

AI country reports/visits

Reports

- Bosnia-Herzegovina: Honouring the ghosts – challenging impunity for "disappearances" (AI Index: EUR 63/004/2003)
- Bosnia-Herzegovina: Unlawful detention of six men from Bosnia-Herzegovina in Guantánamo Bay (AI Index: EUR 63/013/2003)
- Bosnia-Herzegovina: Shelving justice – war crimes prosecutions in paralysis (AI Index: EUR 63/18/2003)

Visits

AI delegates visited Bosnia-Herzegovina in May and August.

BULGARIA

REPUBLIC OF BULGARIA
Head of state: Georgi Parvanov
Head of government: Simeon Saxe-Coburg-Gotha
Death penalty: abolitionist for all crimes
UN Women's Convention: ratified
Optional Protocol to UN Women's Convention: signed

Conditions for people with mental disabilities living in social care homes were frequently inhuman and degrading. Many residents were abused by staff, who in some institutions imposed unacceptable practices of restraint and seclusion, or by other residents. Police ill-treatment and torture of detainees were widely reported, and at least one person died in custody in suspicious circumstances. The victims were often members of the Roma community, some of them children. The officers responsible were rarely brought to justice. At least three people were shot dead and others injured by police officers using firearms in breach of international standards on the use of force.

Background

There were no significant improvements in respect of basic human rights. However, two important new laws offered future safeguards. In May the National Assembly adopted the legal framework, to enter into force in January 2004, for establishing the Office of an Ombudsman. The Office will investigate complaints about violations of human rights by state and municipal bodies and by individuals providing public services. In September a comprehensive anti-discrimination law was adopted, which established an independent Commission to provide protection against discrimination and a system of sanctions.

People with mental disabilities

Children and adults with mental disabilities still suffered inappropriate treatment and poor living conditions in social care homes. New practices were introduced and additional resources provided in some institutions, but the government failed to propose systematic reforms, implement effective measures or demonstrate its political will to combat the stigma of mental disability.

In January an amendment to the Law on Social Support gave government greater responsibility for funding social care homes. Officials acknowledged, however, that allocated resources were usually sufficient for only basic food and heating.

An April amendment to the Law on Child Protection required the placement of children in specialized institutions to be decided by the courts, once all other possibilities for keeping them at home were exhausted. Regulations revised in May for the placement for adults, however, failed to provide safeguards against arbitrary detention and to ensure due process. Placements are decided by government officials and there is no provision for scrutiny by an independent or judicial body, for the person concerned to be legally represented or for periodic review.

The government closed a number of institutions where conditions were particularly harsh. Their residents were transferred to other facilities that were only marginally if at all better and were in similarly remote and inappropriate locations.

◻ In April representatives of AI and the Bulgarian Helsinki Committee (BHC), a local human rights organization, visited four of the five institutions where 70 men were transferred in September 2002 from a social care home in Dragash Voyvoda. Their living conditions were only marginally improved. All remained without therapy other than drugs or rehabilitation. At least 18 of the men had mental health disorders, yet they had been sent to homes for people with intellectual disabilities.

The placement of people with different needs in the same institution, without sufficient safeguards or trained staff to ensure their protection from abuse, including sexual violence, by other residents, reportedly resulted in the deaths of at least two men. The Ministry of Labour and Social Policy were said to have conducted inquiries into some of these incidents but failed to take effective measures to protect the victims or prevent further abuse.

◻ Vasil Malinov, a 32-year-old man with intellectual disabilities at a care home in Batoshevo, shared a room with four other men, some reportedly suffering serious mental illness. Around 100 residents were locked in two buildings at night, allegedly with only a nurse and an orderly on duty. On 18 March staff found Vasil Malinov bruised and battered. After medical treatment he was returned to the same room, where three days later he was found dead.

Restraint and seclusion practices led to abuses.

◻ In June a three-year-old boy with cerebral palsy, living in a social care home in the capital, Sofia, had to have his right hand amputated after it had been roped to the bed to stop him putting it in his mouth. Four nurses and orderlies were reportedly suspended from duty and five other staff members faced disciplinary sanctions.

◻ In September, after 29 women with mental disabilities were found in a seclusion ward of a social care home, some of them in cages, the Ministry of Labour and Social Policy reportedly prohibited establishments under its authority from using such practices.

Torture and ill-treatment

Numerous incidents of ill-treatment by the police, sometimes amounting to torture, were reported. In most cases, suspects were not allowed to contact a lawyer or family member. Officers reportedly punched and kicked them, or beat them with cables or electric truncheons, to obtain confessions. Injured detainees often alleged that they were denied access to a doctor or adequate medical care. Officers reportedly beat some suspects in the presence of investigators. In some instances reported by the BHC, police impunity was apparently facilitated by the failure to properly register the arrest and arraignment of the alleged victim of torture or ill-treatment. Investigations into complaints were often not independent or impartial. Prosecutors sometimes questioned suspected perpetrators only and not witnesses.

In May, 19-year-old A.K. (full name withheld) was reportedly beaten with truncheons, punched and kicked all over the body by four police officers while detained for questioning for two days at police headquarters in Blagoevgrad. After he was transferred to an Investigation Detention Facility, a doctor noted injuries to his chest and face but failed to record A.K.'s statement on how they came about.

At least one person died in suspicious circumstances. In October, 21-year-old Iliya Yordanov died in custody in Plovdiv five days after he was arrested for alleged possession of heroin. Information was not available on the cause of death; however, an investigation was initiated by the military prosecutor, who has jurisdiction to investigate police misconduct. The day before he died, doctors reportedly examined him twice, established that he was suffering from drug withdrawal and diabetes, but did not record the treatment they prescribed or its administration.

The government continued to allow the BHC and other non-governmental organizations (NGOs) access, with few restrictions, to detention facilities and to documentation.

Ill-treatment of Roma

Members of the Roma community were reported to have been ill-treated by the police, including with resort to firearms in circumstances not permitted by international standards on the use of force.

In March, two Romani men (names withheld), gathering firewood in the forest near Lukovit, were stopped by two police officers and several forest guards. One man was reportedly knocked unconscious with a rifle butt, handcuffed, beaten, and prodded with an electric baton, while the second was made to dig a pit as "a grave for the two of [them]", then beaten, according to reports. Three more Romani men, arriving on the scene in cars, were allegedly shot and injured with rubber bullets and assaulted. Four of the men obtained forensic medical certificates, which described injuries consistent with their allegations, and a complaint was filed with the military prosecutor in Pleven.

Unlawful use of firearms

The police shot dead at least three people and injured several others in circumstances that did not meet the requirements of international human rights standards on the use of force and firearms. The authorities failed to revise legal provisions on the use of firearms or to ensure that investigations into the incidents were carried out independently and impartially.

Violence against women

No legislation provided specific protection to women from domestic violence, a serious abuse that was officially perceived as belonging to the "private sphere" and thus not requiring state intervention. An inter-ministerial working group set up in 2002 made little progress in drafting new legislation. There were no official statistics on the number of reported incidents of domestic violence but research conducted by local NGOs indicated that the problem was widespread.

AI country reports/visits
Reports
- Bulgaria: Where are the men of Dragash Voyvoda? (AI Index: EUR 15/005/2003)
- Concerns in Europe and Central Asia, January-June 2003: Bulgaria (AI Index: EUR 01/016/2003)
Visits
Representatives of AI visited Bulgaria in April and June and visited seven social care homes for children and adults with mental disabilities. In April AI and the BHC organized a training program for staff in social care homes in Rusokastro and Fakia in the Burgas region, and facilitated a meeting between managers of the homes and regional and local government officials.

CROATIA

REPUBLIC OF CROATIA
Head of state: Stipe Mesić
Head of government: Ivo Sanader (replaced Ivica Račan in December)
Death penalty: abolitionist for all crimes
UN Women's Convention and its Optional Protocol: ratified

Both Serb and Croat war crimes suspects were transferred to the custody of the International Criminal Tribunal for the former Yugoslavia (the Tribunal). Other suspects continued to evade arrest, some apparently protected by the Croatian authorities. The Tribunal rejected a proposal for a former army general to be surrendered in exchange for a revision of the indictment against him. Increasingly, Croats as well as Serbs were brought to trial on war crimes charges before national courts. However, witnesses remained at risk of intimidation and harassment. The perpetrators responsible for as many as 1,200 unsolved "disappearances" remained unidentified. Thousands of members of the pre-war Croatian Serb population were obstructed from returning to Croatia by discriminatory treatment.

Background

In February Croatia formally applied to join the European Union (EU) as a full member in 2008. In March the EU Commission welcomed developments in strengthening democracy and regional relations, but criticized the lack of cooperation with the Tribunal, continuing problems with the return and reintegration of Croatian Serb refugees and the slow pace of judicial reform.

In May AI reminded the government of Croatia's obligations under international law and as a state party to the Rome Statute establishing the ICC. In June AI urged the government to consult civil society groups on legislation to implement the Rome Statute. Its adoption was postponed to allow comments by local and international experts.

Despite sustained US pressure, Croatia refused to sign an impunity agreement not to surrender US nationals accused of genocide, crimes against humanity or war crimes to the International Criminal Court (ICC).

In the general election in November the *Hrvatska Demokratska Zajednica* (HDZ), Croatian Democratic Union, became the strongest party in parliament and its leader, Ivo Sanader, became Prime Minister in December.

Impunity for wartime violations
International prosecutions

▢ The remaining two suspects of the so-called "Vukovar Three" were transferred to the Tribunal's custody after remaining at large in Serbia for years. In April Miroslav Radić, a former Yugoslav People's Army (JNA) officer, gave himself up to the Serbian authorities. In June Serb police arrested Veselin Šljivančanin, a former officer in the JNA and its successor, the Yugoslav Army. They had been indicted for crimes against humanity and war crimes by the Tribunal in connection with the mass executions of about 200 mainly Croat people taken from Vukovar hospital in November 1991 after the town fell to the former JNA and Serb paramilitaries.

▢ In April Croatian police arrested Ivica Rajić, who had been publicly indicted by the Tribunal for war crimes against the non-Croat population in Bosnia-Herzegovina. After extradition proceedings, he was transferred to the Tribunal in June. The Ministry of the Interior reportedly investigated reports that he had been in hiding in the Split area for years, shielded from arrest and provided with false identity papers by contacts in the military.

▢ The Tribunal Prosecutor repeatedly criticized Croatia's failure to arrest and transfer retired Croatian army General Ante Gotovina, charged with command responsibility for crimes against humanity and war crimes against the Krajina Serb population in 1995. In June NATO troops failed to arrest him in a raid in central Bosnia-Herzegovina. The Tribunal subsequently rejected a proposal, reportedly made by President Mesić, for Ante Gotovina to be transferred to the Tribunal provided his indictment was revised and he was allowed to make a statement to Tribunal investigators.

Domestic prosecutions

Scores of trials for war crimes continued or started before local courts, increasingly of Croat as well as Serb defendants. According to the Organization for Security and Co-operation in Europe (OSCE), 30 out of 38 arrests in 2003 were of Serbs. In the same period, local courts convicted 31 Serbs and four Croats of war crimes.

Some proceedings did not meet internationally recognized standards of fairness.

▢ In April, Mirko Graorac, a Bosnian Serb serving a 15-year prison sentence in Croatia for war crimes, was transferred to the Republika Srpska entity in Bosnia-Herzegovina where the crimes were committed. His trial before the Split County Court had been seriously flawed and he requested a retrial by a Bosnian court.

One of the few trials of senior Croat officers resulted in a conviction.

▢ In March the Rijeka County Court sentenced three Croatian army officers, including retired General Mirko Norac, to prison terms of up to 15 years for war crimes against Serb civilians in 1991. Two other defendants were acquitted.

Local human rights groups presented further evidence of wartime human rights violations to the public prosecutor, including scores of killings and "disappearances" of Croats and Serbs in Osijek in 1991 and 1992.

▢ In March, two former Croatian soldiers were indicted for war crimes against Serb civilians in Paulin Dvor near Osijek in December 1991. The bodies of 18 victims, exhumed by Tribunal investigators in 2002, were reported to have been positively identified in June. The trial started in June, after the Tribunal Prosecutor had forwarded extensive documentation to the Osijek court.

In June a court in Serbia opened an investigation into the alleged responsibility of six former commanders and members of Serb paramilitary forces for the mass executions of non-Serb prisoners after the fall of Vukovar (see above). Four of the suspects had been arrested by Serb police in a crack-down on former members of the security services with connections to organized crime networks following the murder of Serb Prime Minister Zoran Djindjić in March.

Witness protection

Victims and witnesses testifying in war crimes proceedings remained without adequate state protection from harassment, intimidation and threats in the absence of a comprehensive witness protection program.

▢ Former police and armed forces officers who testified for the prosecution in criminal proceedings for war crimes in the Šibenik and Split areas were reported to have been particular targets for intimidation and harassment.

In no cases were those responsible for intimidation or attacks against witnesses identified and brought to justice.

▢ In May the family of former Croatian army officer Mile Levar filed a civil case for damages because of inaction by state authorities. Mile Levar's murder in

2000, after he provided information on war crimes against Serbs in Gospić to Tribunal investigators, remained unsolved.

'Disappearances'

The Croatian Government Commission on Missing Persons was in February still searching for over 1,200 missing people, many of whom had "disappeared". Those responsible remained unidentified. Cooperation continued between the Croatian government and neighbouring Serbia and Montenegro in exhuming bodies buried in Serbia and returning them to Croatia for identification and final burial. In June the Government Commission said that a total of 200 bodies of Croats had been exhumed.

In March a mass grave was exhumed in Cetingrad containing the bodies of Bosniak victims of the conflict between the Bosnian army and forces loyal to political leader Fikret Abdić. The Bosnian Commission for Missing Persons was reportedly still searching for dozens of people missing in Croatia.

Right to return

According to the government, about 9,000 members of minority communities who returned to the country were registered as returnees by November. However, many returns were not sustainable. UN High Commissioner for Refugees (UNHCR) research around Knin in southern Croatia revealed that only about 60 per cent of returnees remained. Returnees continued to face difficulties in repossessing private property because legislation was enforced slowly and inconsistently by the authorities.

Tens of thousands of Serb refugees were unable to return. Most had lost pre-war tenancy rights in unfair legal proceedings in their absence. The government promised to provide social housing but failed to offer redress for the loss of their legal rights as tenancy holders, reinforcing discrimination against Serb returnees.

Asylum procedures

In June parliament adopted a new Asylum Law, to come into force in July 2004 after construction of a reception centre for asylum-seekers. The previous system for determining refugee status did not constitute a full and fair asylum procedure. Asylum-seekers and undocumented migrants were often arbitrarily detained without recourse to judicial redress.

AI country reports/ visits

Report
- Concerns in Europe and Central Asia, January-June 2003: Croatia (AI Index: EUR 01/016/2003)

Visit

AI delegates visited Croatia in February.

CZECH REPUBLIC

CZECH REPUBLIC
Head of state: Václav Klaus (replaced Václav Havel in February)
Head of government: Vladimir Spidla
Death penalty: abolitionist for all crimes
UN Women's Convention and its Optional Protocol: ratified

There were reports of ill-treatment of members of the Romani community. Police officers convicted of assault in one case received a light sentence. "Cage beds" were used to restrain patients in psychiatric hospitals and residents of social care homes for people with mental disabilities.

Discrimination against Roma

Roma continued to suffer discrimination in several areas of life in spite of some positive government measures. In January the UN Committee on the Rights of the Child expressed regret that some of its recommendations had not been sufficiently addressed. These included the development of awareness-raising campaigns aimed at reducing discriminatory practices against the Roma and the implementation of special programs to improve the standard of living, education and health of Romani children. The Committee was also concerned that Romani children continued to be over-represented in schools for children with learning difficulties, the so-called "special schools", and that illegal migrants and some refugees suffered discrimination in access to education.

In August the UN Committee on the Elimination of Racial Discrimination expressed concern "at continuing acts of racially motivated violence, incitement to hatred, the persistence of intolerance and *de facto* discrimination, in particular with regard to the Roma minority" and at the disproportionately high unemployment rate among the Roma. It recommended that existing legislation be implemented more effectively.

There were several reports that Roma had been ill-treated by the police. Very few such incidents were investigated independently and impartially. The system for investigating complaints against police officers did not meet international human rights standards for independence and impartiality, or fulfil recommendations by the UN Committee against Torture and the UN Human Rights Committee. Even when officers were convicted of serious offences, they received light sentences.

In June a court in Cheb, west Bohemia, gave three police officers a suspended prison term for severely beating Karel Billy, a Romani man. Two other officers were acquitted. The officers had reportedly stopped him for an identity check, then taken him to a nearby forest where they beat him severely, urinated on him and racially abused him. Only when the doctors who

treated him intervened did the Police Inspectorate investigate. Even then, the officers were initially charged only with "abusing the authority of a public official". The Commissioner of the Government of the Czech Republic for Human Rights was reported as describing the court's verdict as "truly sad", particularly as the offence had been committed by police officers.
🗁 On 12 May in Popovice u Jičin, northeast Bohemia, five officers from the special riot police allegedly broke into the home of the Romani Daniš family shouting racist insults. They reportedly beat Lubica Danišova, her 17-year-old son Marcel and her pregnant daughter, and accused the family of stealing from a restaurant owned by one of the officers. On 20 May the Police Inspectorate opened an investigation into a "violation of freedom of the home" without any reference to the racial motivation of the offence.

Cage beds as a method of restraint

Cage beds were used in psychiatric hospitals and social care institutions as a method of restraint, according to reports by local non-governmental organizations. The Centre for Mental Health Care Development found that 60 out of 600 beds in Jihlava Psychiatric Hospital were caged and that 416 patients had been restrained in them in 2002. In another institution, the Mental Disability Advocacy Center found around 17 cage beds and two cots "with netting, to prevent children from falling out". A cot with metal bars and a padlock contained a seven- or eight-year-old boy with severe intellectual and physical disabilities, apparently unsupervised and receiving no therapy.

The use of cage beds and the denial of appropriate rehabilitation and care to children with disabilities amount to cruel, inhuman and degrading treatment, in breach of international law and best professional practice. The Czech Ministry of Social Affairs acknowledged that cage beds are used, also noting that no legislation explicitly forbids this form of restraint and citing budgetary constraints on hiring enough qualified staff.

AI country reports/ visits

Report

- Concerns in Europe and Central Asia, January-June 2003: Czech Republic (AI Index: EUR 01/016/2003)

ESTONIA

REPUBLIC OF ESTONIA
Head of state: Arnold Rüütel
Head of government: Juhan Parts (replaced Siim Kallas in April)
Death penalty: abolitionist for all crimes
UN Women's Convention: ratified
Optional Protocol to UN Women's Convention: not signed

Estonia came under the scrutiny of various international human rights bodies, which examined a number of human rights concerns. These included ill-treatment and excessive use of force by the police, poor conditions in places of detention, and violence against women and children.

Police ill-treatment

In March the UN Human Rights Committee identified several areas of concern during its examination of Estonia's second periodic report on its implementation of the International Covenant on Civil and Political Rights. The Committee was particularly concerned that acts of ill-treatment by police officers were prosecuted as minor offences. It recommended that police officers be prosecuted effectively and on the basis of charges that reflected the seriousness of the offences.

The Committee was also concerned that Estonia's legislation on the use of firearms allowed the use of lethal force by the police in circumstances in which lives were not at risk. It recommended that Estonia revise the legislation to ensure that the use of firearms is restricted by the principles of necessity and proportionality.

Conditions of detention

The third visit to Estonia of the European Committee for the Prevention of Torture took place in September. During its visit the Committee conducted a number of follow-up inspections of places of detention visited in 1997 and 1999, in some of which there had been significant concerns about poor conditions of detention.

The Council of Europe's Commissioner for Human Rights visited Estonia in October. He called on the Estonian authorities to step up efforts to improve conditions in prisons and detention centres.

Violence against women

Violence against women in the home continued despite several positive measures to address the issue. In March the UN Human Rights Committee welcomed the inclusion of domestic violence and marital rape as specific criminal offences in the new Penal Code, which came into force in September 2002. The criminalization of these offences followed specific recommendations made in 2002 by the UN Committee on the Elimination of Discrimination against Women and the UN Committee on Economic, Social and Cultural Rights.

Ill-treatment of children

The ill-treatment and neglect of children were among the concerns raised by the UN Committee on the Rights of the Child, which examined Estonia's initial report on its implementation of the UN Convention on the Rights of the Child in January. The Committee was concerned about "the insufficient information on and awareness of ill-treatment and abuse of children within the family, in schools and in institutions, as well as of domestic violence and its impact on children". The Committee's recommendations included an explicit prohibition of corporal punishment, the implementation of measures to prevent physical and mental violence, and the establishment of effective mechanisms to receive, monitor and investigate complaints.

AI country reports

Report
- Concerns in Europe and Central Asia, January-June 2003: Estonia (AI Index: EUR 01/016/2003)

FINLAND

REPUBLIC OF FINLAND
Head of state: Tarja Halonen
Head of government: Matti Vanhanen (replaced Anneli Jäätteenmäki in June who replaced Paavo Lipponen in April)
Death penalty: abolitionist for all crimes
UN Women's Convention and its Optional Protocol: ratified

Eleven conscientious objectors to military service were prisoners of conscience. International monitoring bodies expressed concern about some aspects of Finland's human rights record.

Conscientious objectors to military service imprisoned

The length of alternative civilian service remained punitive: all conscientious objectors were required to perform 395 days of alternative service, 215 days longer than the majority of recruits who perform military service. AI continued to urge the authorities to reduce the length of alternative civilian service in line with internationally recognized standards and recommendations on conscientious objection to military service. In August AI wrote to the newly appointed government urging a review of existing legislation at the earliest opportunity.
⌂ Eleven conscientious objectors were prisoners of conscience during 2003. Most of them received prison sentences of between 175 and 197 days for refusing to perform alternative civilian service. The majority gave the discriminatory length of service as a reason for their refusal to perform alternative civilian service.

International scrutiny of human rights record

In August the UN Committee on the Elimination of Racial Discrimination considered Finland's 16th periodic report on its implementation of the International Convention on the Elimination of All Forms of Racial Discrimination. In its Concluding Observations, the Committee welcomed the approval in January of a bill revising the Penal Code and including "racist motives" as aggravating circumstances of a crime, and the introduction of a provision punishing participation in organizations which promote or incite racial discrimination. However, it expressed concern about the number of allegations brought to its attention reflecting racist and xenophobic attitudes among some sectors of the population, notably the young. It also noted that one reason for the reluctance of victims of racial discrimination to lodge a complaint was the assumption that the complaint would not lead to any result. It recommended that the authorities disseminate as widely as possible information on the available domestic remedies against acts of racial discrimination and the legal avenues to obtain compensation in such cases.

In October the Council of Europe's Committee for the Prevention of Torture (CPT) published the preliminary observations of its third periodic visit in September to various places of detention in Finland. The CPT noted that it had not received any allegations of ill-treatment by the police, by prison staff in the three prisons visited, or by staff at the psychiatric establishment visited. However, it noted that there was an urgent need to draw up detailed instructions on the use of force and means of restraint authorized in the context of deportation of foreign nationals. The CPT had obtained information about a case involving several members of the same family, including two minors, who had been forcibly injected with sedating and neuroleptic medication without proper examination by a doctor, a practice which, in the CPT's opinion, was totally unacceptable.

AI country reports/visits
Report
- Concerns in Europe and Central Asia, January-June 2003: Finland (AI Index: EUR 01/016/2003)

FRANCE

FRENCH REPUBLIC
Head of state: Jacques Chirac
Head of government: Jean-Pierre Raffarin
Death penalty: abolitionist for all crimes
UN Women's Convention: ratified with reservations
Optional Protocol to UN Women's Convention: ratified

An Ethiopian national died during forcible deportation. There were frequent reports of ill-treatment of foreign nationals in holding areas within airports. Complaints about race-related police ill-treatment rose, notably in Paris. Police officers were under investigation for the collective rape of sex workers. In a landmark decision, France's highest court, the Court of Cassation, restricted the use of weapons by the national gendarmerie. Detainees continued to face lengthy provisional detention, and seriously ill detainees or convicted prisoners continued to be held in conditions that raised fears for their physical or mental integrity. Prison conditions were aggravated by serious overcrowding. There were acts of racist violence against members of Jewish and Arab communities, as well as other Muslim groups.

New legislation
A new law on internal security came into force in March. It aggravated concerns about an increase in the number of abusive identity checks carried out by police officers. The law covered a range of new offences. These included gatherings in public spaces within residential apartment blocks, public soliciting, "aggressive" collective begging, swearing at or insulting public officials, and insulting the national flag and national anthem at certain public events. A controversial draft law on organized crime went through a second reading in November. The law aimed, among other measures, to extend the 96-hour special custody regime to a wider range of offences, including "organized crime". This would increase the numbers of people, including minors between 16 and 18, likely to be denied access to a lawyer for the first 36 hours of police custody. In December a government-appointed commission on the application of secular principles recommended a law banning conspicuous religious symbols or uniforms from state schools. The proposed law was widely seen to be targeting the Muslim headscarf.

Deaths during forcible deportation
In January AI called on the authorities to fully and impartially investigate the deaths of two foreign nationals, which had occurred in close succession during forcible deportation attempts. Both deaths occurred after the deportees were placed at the rear of the aircraft, their hands cuffed behind their backs. AI stated that existing expert advice on postural asphyxia had shown that handcuffing a person behind their back could restrict their ability to breathe, while any weight applied to the back in that position could further increase breathing difficulty. AI urged that the conclusions of all inquiries be made public, and asked the authorities for clarification of the procedures in place for forcible deportation.

☐ In June, in a letter about the death of Argentine national Ricardo Barrientos in December 2002, the Ministry of the Interior, Internal Security and Local Freedoms, informed AI that no restraint techniques involving asphyxiation had been applied and that the members of the police National Escort, Support and Intervention Unit (UNESI) had received adequate training. However, the Ministry did not clarify exactly what techniques had been used.

☐ Mariame Geto Hagos, an Ethiopian national, died in January after being taken ill on board an aircraft awaiting departure to Johannesburg from Roissy-Charles de Gaulle Airport. He had reportedly arrived in France five days earlier and was held in the waiting area at Roissy. After his asylum application was rejected he resisted attempts to deport him and apparently became ill on two separate occasions. He was, nonetheless, deemed medically fit to leave. He was escorted onto the aircraft by three frontier police officers. Before take-off he reportedly again made efforts to resist departure and was, according to reports, restrained by the "customary techniques". Three police officers were suspended pending further inquiries.

Ill-treatment in border areas
In March, two separate reports from groups which assist refugees and asylum-seekers at border areas described frequent police ill-treatment — such as blows, beatings with batons, tight handcuffing, racist insults — at the holding area at Roissy-Charles de Gaulle Airport. A group of 54 Senegalese and Côte d'Ivoire nationals subsequently complained that they had been subjected to inhuman and degrading treatment during a charter flight from France to Dakar and Abidjan in March. They alleged they had been held under restraint throughout the flight with hard rubber cable wound round wrists and ankles. Tape had also allegedly been placed round faces and legs and some individuals had been beaten. The allegations were rejected by the Ministry of the Interior and the frontier police.

In December the European Committee for the Prevention of Torture and Inhuman or Degrading Treatment or Punishment published its report of a visit to Roissy-Charles de Gaulle Airport in June 2002, to examine the situation of foreign nationals. It referred to "allegations of ill-treatment of foreign nationals (slaps, kicks, baton blows, tight handcuffing, threats and insults) by police officers during passport controls, requests for asylum and attempts to force detainees to board aircraft". The Committee recommended that procedures concerning forcible removal by air be clarified and updated. It found an improvement in conditions in two holding areas.

Police ill-treatment in Paris

In February statistics released by the General Inspection Services (IGS), which investigates complaints against police officers in the Paris area, showed that complaints about police ill-treatment had doubled between 1997 (216 complaints) and 2002 (432). According to a new human rights committee set up at Saint-Denis following established cases of police brutality, many incidents in the Department of Seine-Saint-Denis continued to arise out of identity checks and to be race-related. A report published in April by the National Commission of Deontology and Security (CNDS), a police oversight body, examined a number of cases of police ill-treatment and expressed concern about the operation of Paris police patrols at night and the lack of supervision of officers in Seine-Saint-Denis.

In March new instructions governing police custody were issued. The Interior Minister ruled that body searches should be exceptional, and called, among other things, for improved access for detainees to telephones and confidential communication with lawyers.

◻ In February the Correctional Court of Paris threw out charges brought in December 2002 by National Police officers against Omar Baha, a French national of Algerian origin, who had been held in extended custody on charges of "incitement to riot", "insulting behaviour" and "resisting arrest". Omar Baha had allegedly been ill-treated by police officers – sustaining a broken nose – during an identity check which he had witnessed and in which he had intervened. He was reportedly struck on the nose with the end of a gas canister and beaten by three officers after he reminded them of a recent public statement by the Minister of the Interior that police abuses would not be tolerated. He was detained for an extended period on the grounds that he faced a charge of incitement to riot. However, all charges were thrown out after the court found that such a charge did not exist in French law and appeared to have been invented for the purpose of holding him. Omar Baha, who received no medical treatment while in custody, lodged a complaint for ill-treatment, which was still pending at the end of the year.

Violence against foreign women

An investigation was opened by the IGS in December into complaints lodged by human rights associations about the alleged collective rape of foreign sex workers, reportedly a widespread practice among a section of police officers.

◻ Three police officers of the 7th section of the *Compagnie républicaine de sécurité* (CRS), a special police unit, in Deuil-la-Barre (Val-d'Oise) were detained after being placed by the IGS under investigation for the collective rape of several women in April. One woman was reportedly abducted by officers who ordered her to accompany them to the police station because her papers were not in order, but instead took her to a parking lot near the *Stade de France* sports stadium where she was allegedly raped. Two other women, Albanian and Lithuanian nationals,

were then allegedly raped by the same officers. One woman noted the registration number of the patrol car. It was anticipated that other officers would be drawn into the investigation.

Restrictions on gendarmes' right to shoot

An important decision restricting the use of weapons by the national gendarmerie was made in February, when the Court of Cassation, the country's highest court, ruled that gendarmes should use their weapons only when "absolutely necessary". One of AI's most long-standing and serious concerns, the continued use of a 1903 decree, had until then allowed gendarmes to fire weapons to immobilize suspects in circumstances not permitted in law to other law enforcement officers and prohibited under international standards. According to the decree, gendarmes could fire to stop a person fleeing from them if they were wearing uniform and had given a warning.

◻ In October Nadjib Naceri fell into a coma after a gendarme reportedly shot him in the head at Moissac (Tarn-et-Garonne). Gendarmes asked the driver of the vehicle in which Nadjib Naceri was travelling to park in a different position. As the vehicle moved away, one officer allegedly fired several shots at it. He said he was attempting to prevent it escaping. A judicial inquiry was opened and the gendarme was detained.

Ill prisoners

In February the Court of Cassation confirmed the suspension of a 10-year prison term being served by Maurice Papon, a former high-ranking government official and Paris police chief, in view of his age and state of health. Maurice Papon was released from prison in September 2002 under the provisions of a law of March 2002 on the rights of ill people. Under the law, prisoners' sentences can be suspended if they are critically ill or suffering from a chronic condition incompatible with their detention. In March AI retransmitted its request to the Minister of Justice, made the previous December, for information about the number of people who had been released under the law and its concern about the current circumstances of a number of individual detainees and prisoners suffering from serious and chronic medical conditions. To date AI has received no reply from the government.

◻ In November the Regional Commission on Conditional Liberty of Douai (Nord) rejected a plea for release from Nathalie Ménigon, a member of the former armed group *Action Directe*. In AI's view, the serious health condition of Nathalie Ménigon, and of other members of the group, such as Georges Cipriani, was related to long periods the prisoners had previously spent in rigorous isolation. Nathalie Ménigon, sentenced to life imprisonment in 1988, is partially hemiplegic as a result of two cerebral vascular accidents while in prison.

◻ Alain Solé, arrested in 1999 in connection with alleged illegal activities by Emgann, the Breton nationalist group, entered a fifth year of provisional detention. In June he underwent a triple bypass operation at a Paris hospital. He reportedly became insulin-dependent in prison. Several applications for provisional release have been rejected by the Paris Appeal Court.

Prison conditions

Rising tension was reported in many prisons, where serious overcrowding reportedly contributed to a high and rising suicide rate, to acts of violence against prisoners by guards and by other prisoners, and to reduced access to visits or medical attention. In April a group of prisoners at Moulins-Yzeure (Allier) complained about a series of restrictive surveillance measures. In November some inmates of the same prison, reportedly demanding an improvement in conditions, held four prison officers hostage for several hours. In November the CNDS, which had been investigating acts of violence and cruel, inhuman and degrading treatment at the prison in Maubeuge (Nord), requested an inspection of its services, which was granted in December.

Racist attacks

Acts of violence were reported against members of Muslim and Jewish communities. A consultative human rights body, the *Commission nationale consultative des droits de l'homme* (CNCDH), recorded an increase in violence towards Muslims. It referred, among other things, to desecration of Muslim places of worship and the dissemination of tracts vilifying Islam, and identified the difficulty in distinguishing anti-Muslim attacks from anti-Arab attacks in general. Government figures for the first half of 2003 showed a decrease in anti-Jewish acts compared to the previous year. However, fresh government measures were taken against all forms of racism and, after an arson attack on a Jewish school in Paris destroyed a section of the building, police surveillance of synagogues and Jewish schools was stepped up.

AI country reports/ visits

Reports
- France: The alleged ill-treatment of Omar Baha by police officers in Paris (AI Index: EUR 21/002/2003)
- France: Allegations of physical assault and racial abuse by Paris police — The case of Karim Latifi (AI Index: EUR 21/004/2003)
- Concerns in Europe and Central Asia, January-June 2003: France (AI Index: EUR 01/016/2003)

Visits
AI delegates visited France in February and November for research.

GEORGIA

GEORGIA
Head of state and government: Nino Burdzhanadze (interim President – replaced Eduard Amvrosiyevich Shevardnadze in November)
Death penalty: abolitionist for all crimes
UN Women's Convention and its Optional Protocol: ratified

Members of minority faiths continued to be attacked. The first successful prosecutions for a series of such attacks over four years resulted in five suspended prison sentences. Torture and ill-treatment continued to be reported. Chechens sought by the authorities of the Russian Federation continued to be in danger of extradition. President Shevardnadze was forced to resign in November after days of mass demonstrations.

Background

The 2 November parliamentary elections "fell short of a number of international standards", reported the Organization for Security and Co-operation in Europe (OSCE). The flawed elections triggered mass demonstrations, culminating in a peaceful mass protest at parliament on 22 November. President Shevardnadze declared a state of emergency, but on 23 November resigned, to avoid bloodshed he said. The same day Nino Burdzhanadze, Speaker of the outgoing parliament, was declared interim President. Presidential elections were scheduled for January 2004 and new parliamentary elections for later in 2004.

Following the change of power, unidentified assailants carried out attacks allegedly directed at critics of the so-called "Rose Revolution". In late November the autonomous republic of Ajaria declared a state of emergency and the unrecognized breakaway republics of Abkhazia and South Ossetia stated that they were stepping up security measures.

In September Georgia became a party to the Rome Statute of the International Criminal Court (ICC). However, it entered into an impunity agreement with the USA not to surrender US nationals accused of genocide, crimes against humanity or war crimes to the ICC. Such agreements are in breach of states' obligations under international law.

Public Defender (Ombudsperson)

During 2003 the Public Defender of Georgia published a report on human rights. Among other issues, the report deplored violent attacks on religious minorities and described the lack of prompt or appropriate action by the courts as "testimony of moral support for the perpetrators". It also highlighted numerous incidents of physical coercion exerted on detainees and of discrimination against women. The Public Defender criticized protracted and inconclusive investigation of human rights violations, and the Procurator General's "inappropriate" consideration of her recommendations.

Attacks on religious minorities

Religious minorities continued to face harassment, intimidation and violent attacks by supporters of the Georgian Orthodox Church. In many cases, the police failed to provide adequate protection for those targeted. The first prosecution of the perpetrators in a series of attacks resulted in suspended prison sentences for five men. Hundreds of other attackers remained unpunished. In his December report, the UN Special Rapporteur on freedom of religion or belief urged the authorities to "put those responsible for violence or religious intolerance on trial and to take them into custody if the courts order a term of imprisonment or pre-trial detention."

On 24 January defrocked Georgian Orthodox priest Basil Mkalavishvili and a group of his supporters allegedly attacked religious believers gathering before an inter-denominational service in a Baptist church in the capital, Tbilisi. The attackers reportedly smashed church windows and physically and verbally abused the congregation. Baptist minister Otar Kalatozishvili and his two sons, Guram and Zaza, were reportedly beaten.

On 4 November Rustavi City Court handed down suspended sentences of between two and four years' imprisonment on Paata Bluashvili, a radical supporter of the Orthodox church and member of the radical *Jvari* (Cross) group, and four supporters. They were convicted of involvement in two attacks on Jehovah's Witnesses. Reports suggested they had been involved in a series of such attacks.

Extraditions

Chechens accused of "terrorism" continued to face extradition to the Russian Federation where they risked serious human rights violations.

On 16 May the Supreme Court refused to permit the extradition to the Russian Federation of three men reportedly detained by border guards near the village of Girevi in the Akhmeta district in August 2002. On 16 September the European Court of Human Rights declared admissible an application lodged in October 2002 against the extradition – believed imminent – of the three men, as well as 10 others arrested at the same time. The Court announced that it would take evidence from the 13 applicants and from witnesses in the Russian Federation and Georgia. Five of the 13 applicants had already been extradited to the Russian Federation in October 2002, and on 19 September the trial of four of them opened in Stavropol on charges including "terrorism" and "participation in an armed group".

On 16 April, another man reportedly detained by Georgian law enforcement officers in August 2002, 22-year-old Amirkhan Lidigov, was handed over to Russian troops at the Lars border post. The Russian authorities reportedly accused him of fighting under Chechen commander Ruslan Gelayev.

Ajaria

Activists critical of the local authorities were reportedly harassed and intimidated, in particular in connection with the November parliamentary elections.

Giorgi Mshevenieradze of the non-governmental Georgian Young Lawyers Association was held in custody in Batumi from 2 November to 7 December. He was detained by police after he had observed election fraud in the parliamentary elections in a polling station in the town of Kobuleti.

Abkhazia

In the disputed region of Abkhazia, a *de facto* moratorium on executions remained in force. At least 25 death sentences had been passed since it declared independence from Georgia. Nine death row prisoners escaped from the investigation-isolation prison in Sukhumi in April. Some were recaptured; one died in his cell on 15 June.

AI country reports/visits
Reports
- Georgia: Open Letter to the President of Georgia urging rejection of the impunity agreement with the United States of America on the International Criminal Court (AI Index: EUR 56/001/2003)
- Georgia: Treatment of opponents is litmus test for commitment to human rights (AI Index: EUR 56/004/2003)

GERMANY

FEDERAL REPUBLIC OF GERMANY
Head of state: Johannes Rau
Head of government: Gerhard Schröder
Death penalty: abolitionist for all crimes
UN Women's Convention and its Optional Protocol: ratified

There was intense public debate about the circumstances in which torture was permissible in Germany. Six police officers were convicted of beating a detainee to death. There were continuing allegations that police officers had ill-treated and used excessive force against detainees. Germany informed the UN Committee on the Elimination of Discrimination against Women of measures it had taken to combat domestic violence. Refugees facing persecution by private individuals were not given adequate protection. It was unclear when criminal proceedings would take place in relation to the death in 1999 of Sudanese asylum-seeker Aamir Ageeb. One man was sentenced to imprisonment after being convicted of involvement in the 11 September 2001 attacks in the USA, and the trial of another suspect collapsed.

Torture debate

A passionate debate about whether torture was acceptable in any circumstances followed a report that a senior police officer had ordered the use of force on a suspect to elicit information from him. In February it emerged that the Vice-President of Frankfurt am Main police, Wolfgang Daschner, had ordered a subordinate officer to use force in an investigation into the kidnap and ransom of an 11-year-old boy. Before the order was given, senior officers reportedly discussed and rejected moral objections to the use of force on the detainee. An officer then threatened the detainee with force during questioning on 1 October 2002 and elicited information about the location of the dead child.

The incident provoked a nationwide discussion on torture. Wolfgang Daschner publicly defended his actions and called for the use of force to be legally permitted during police interrogations as a "last resort" to save human life. A number of leading public figures expressed sympathy with Wolfgang Daschner and stated publicly that they could envisage exceptions to Germany's ban on torture. Such sentiments attracted considerable domestic and international condemnation, including by the Secretary General of the Council of Europe who stated on 21 February: "The European Convention on Human Rights completely outlaws torture, under any circumstances. If we are to build a Europe that truly respects human rights, we must fiercely defend this principle. I shall be asking the Council of Europe's Anti-Torture Committee to examine this incident."

Frankfurt am Main District Court, which tried and convicted the suspect on charges of abduction and murder in July, unequivocally rejected as evidence the "confession" made to the Frankfurt am Main police. The presiding judge stated that the police actions had caused great harm to Germany's culture of rights. Wolfgang Daschner remained in office at the end of 2003, pending a decision on whether to prosecute him.

Death in police custody

Six police officers were given suspended prison sentences after being convicted of beating a detainee to death. They were alleged to have repeatedly hit and kicked 31-year-old Stephan Neisius at Cologne's First Police Inspectorate on 11 May 2002. Later the same evening he was admitted to hospital where he died after 13 days on a life-support system. The six officers were charged with "bodily harm resulting in death" and convicted by Cologne District Court on 25 July. The suspension of their prison sentences of between 12 and 16 months provoked accusations of leniency.

Allegations of police ill-treatment

There were continuing allegations of police ill-treatment and excessive use of force, usually at the time of arrest and in police custody. Most complainants said that they had been kicked and punched, in some instances sustaining serious injuries.

⌂ A 30-year-old partially disabled man was allegedly ill-treated in police custody in Frankfurt am Main. Andre Heech and a friend were arrested for alleged drunken behaviour on 14 February and detained at the Fourth District Police Station. A police officer reportedly hit Andre Heech's right thigh three times with a long metal object, fracturing the thigh bone of his partially amputated leg. He was in considerable pain and required an operation as a result of the assault. To date no response has been received by AI from the German authorities about the incident.

⌂ An investigation was initiated into the reported ill-treatment of a 19-year-old man at Cologne's police headquarters on 28 February. It was alleged that at around 4am an official supervising the detention area hit the detainee in the face after the detainee activated the alarm in his cell, breaking his nose and damaging one of his teeth.

⌂ On 15 July three police officers from the state of Thuringia were given suspended prison sentences for seriously injuring two undercover police officers from the state of Schleswig-Holstein. A court in Hamburg convicted them of "dangerous bodily harm" for repeatedly hitting the undercover officers with their batons during a protest against squat clearances in Hamburg on 16 November 2002. The presiding judge was reported to have said that, had the victims been ordinary demonstrators and not police officers, they would never have been able to identify the officers who attacked them. Thuringia's police leadership was also heavily criticized during the trial for attempting to cover up the incident.

Violence against women

In February Germany submitted its fifth periodic report to the UN Committee on the Elimination of Discrimination against Women. The report described the various measures taken to implement Germany's National Plan of Action to Combat Violence against Women, originally adopted in December 1999. Domestic violence remained a significant problem. More than 40,000 women are estimated to seek refuge in women's shelters each year.

A development highlighted in the report was the enactment of a law in 2002 to prevent violent or threatening men from contacting partners they have abused. The law also provided the legal basis for excluding violent men from the home, by allocating the home to the victims of abuse, albeit only temporarily. The law was accompanied by awareness-raising activities for professionals involved in responding to cases of domestic violence. It was supplemented several months later by a law allowing the removal of a person from the home if they are violent towards children, primarily to protect children but also in acknowledgement that such violence harms women psychologically and serves to intimidate them.

Refugees

Refugees facing persecution by private individuals were still at risk of being denied protection. German courts continued to rule that refugees fearing persecution by non-state actors were excluded from the protection of the 1951 Refugee Convention and the European Convention on Human Rights. Germany's definition of persecution in these cases was contrary to international law. People who fled human rights violations affecting the whole population in their country of origin without discrimination were also not protected from forcible return.

⬜ Despite the danger of grave human rights violations for Chechens in the Russian Federation, most claims for asylum by Chechens were rejected. Chechens were therefore denied effective and durable protection in Germany.

⬜ With the exception of Roma and Serbs, Germany began to forcibly return a number of members of other ethnic minorities to Kosovo. In doing so, the authorities did not take into account the human rights violations they might face on their return.

11 September 'terrorist' trials

The trial of Abdelghani Mzoudi unexpectedly collapsed on 11 December after evidence emerged that he had not knowingly participated in the 11 September 2001 attacks in the USA. The 31-year-old Moroccan, detained in October 2002 on suspicion of being an accessory to 3,066 murders, was immediately released from pre-trial detention by a court in Hamburg. The court made the ruling on the basis of the testimony of an unidentified witness, believed to be Ramzi bin al-Shibh, the alleged architect of the 11 September attacks imprisoned in the USA. Ramzi bin al-Shibh had reportedly informed the US authorities during interrogation that only he and the three hijackers who piloted the aircraft knew of the attacks, and that Abdelghani Mzoudi had not knowingly taken part in them. Despite the vital nature of the information, the US authorities reportedly provided it to Germany's Federal Crime Office on condition that it should not be disseminated.

Following the court's decision, an application was lodged for the immediate release of Mounir el-Motassadeq, the only person to be convicted in Germany for their role in the 11 September attacks. In February a court in Hamburg had sentenced the Moroccan student to 15 years' imprisonment for being an accessory to 3,066 murders.

Death during deportation

By the end of 2003, no date had been set for the trial of three police officers charged in connection with the death during deportation of Sudanese asylum-seeker Aamir Ageeb in May 1999. He died while being forcibly sent back from Frankfurt am Main airport to Sudan. Charges of negligent homicide were filed with Frankfurt am Main District Court in January 2002 against the officers who enforced the deportation.

AI country reports/ visits
Report
· Concerns in Europe and Central Asia, January-June 2003: Germany (AI Index: EUR 01/016/2003)
Visit
An AI delegation visited Germany in May to conduct research.

GREECE

HELLENIC REPUBLIC
Head of state: Constantinos Stephanopoulos
Head of government: Constantinos Simitis
Death penalty: abolitionist for ordinary crimes
UN Women's Convention and its Optional Protocol: ratified

There were concerns about police ill-treatment of demonstrators during the June European Union (EU) summit. One person was shot dead in an apparently unlawful killing by guards on the border with Albania. A foreign human rights activist was threatened with expulsion. Discriminatory treatment of Roma by the authorities continued, and the conditions of detention for undocumented immigrants were poor. Conscientious objectors continued to face the threat of imprisonment.

Background

Greece held the Presidency of the EU for the first half of 2003. During the EU summit in Thessaloniki in June, when the Presidency passed to Italy, anti-globalization demonstrations took place and the police arrested a number of protesters.

In July, parliament passed new legislation relating to "the possession, training and use of firearms by policemen" which limited the circumstances in which law enforcement officials could resort to arms and provided for police training in handling firearms.

In October, Greece ratified the Optional Protocol to the UN Convention on the Rights of the Child on the involvement of children in armed conflict, declaring that "the minimum age at which voluntary recruitment in the Greek armed forces is permitted by national law is 18 years".

In December the trial of 19 people on charges including carrying out bomb explosions and murder ended. Fifteen members of the "November 17" (17N) group were convicted and received prison sentences ranging from eight years to 21 life terms. Four of the defendants were acquitted. One of the accused claimed that he had been ill-treated while in custody.

Border policing

Further instances of alleged unlawful shootings and ill-treatment by police and border guards were reported, particularly on the northwest border with Albania, crossed by many Albanian migrants. The victims included authorized and unauthorized migrants. Concerns raised with the Greek authorities about a killing in September met no response. The Ombudsman in Albania subsequently took up the cases with the UN Committee against Torture and the Commissioner for Human Rights of the Council of Europe.

⬜ In September one person was shot dead while trying to cross the border into Greece with five other

Albanians. One of three border guards fired at Vullnet Bytyci and at another of the group who tried to flee. Vullnet Bytyci was pronounced dead on admission to hospital in Kastoria. The border guard was arrested shortly afterwards but later released pending investigation for "reckless homicide".

🖾 Also in September, three Albanian nationals – brothers Gori and Mili Halili and Rahman Pashollari – were allegedly detained, beaten, kicked and robbed by guards on the Albanian border near Krystallopigi. They were forcibly returned to Albania where medical examination at the hospital in the town of Elbasan found that Gori Halili had "bruising of the abdomen, rupture of the spleen and bleeding in the abdominal area", which required surgery to remove his spleen. Rahman Pashollari was found to have sustained a fractured rib.

🖾 In November Albanian national Shpëtim Shabani alleged that three Greek police officers beat him with their guns, kicked and punched him, leaving him covered in bruises and with an injured shoulder. He said they were dressed in camouflage uniforms, asked to see his papers as he drank coffee in a bar in Agrinio, and assaulted him in full public view. He was reportedly detained at a police station for two days before being forcibly returned to Albania.

Greece ratified the Ottawa Convention prohibiting anti-personnel landmines in 2002. However, the destruction of mines in border areas is still to be carried out and, in September, seven undocumented immigrants were killed when they walked into a minefield in northeastern Greece.

Impunity and independence of the judiciary

A high-profile case of alleged rape highlighted concerns about the impunity enjoyed by police officers and the independence of the judiciary in handling complaints against officers.

The judicial authorities failed to call as a prosecution witness a Ukrainian national, Olga B., who was reportedly raped by a police officer in Amaliada in February 1998. The trial of the police officer, the bar owner and three co-defendants took place before Patras Mixed Jury Criminal Court on 23 May. The bar owner was convicted of trafficking for the purposes of prostitution and sentenced to three years' imprisonment. The three co-defendants were convicted of procuring or assisting in trafficking women and received two-year prison sentences. In the absence of the victim at the trial, the court concluded that she had consented to sexual intercourse with the police officer and acquitted him of rape. He was sentenced to two years' imprisonment for breach of duty. All of the defendants' sentences were suspended.

The court bailiffs said that they delivered two summonses to Olga B. to appear in court to give evidence at the first trial. She said that she had never lived at the address where they were allegedly delivered, and the people who lived at the address testified on oath that they had never seen any bailiffs. Olga B.'s complaint that the two bailiffs had falsely

claimed to serve her the summonses was filed in Patras on 11 September, but by October had not been forwarded by the Patras prosecutor to the competent Amaliada prosecutor. Witnesses who had testified for the prosecution at preliminary hearings were also not summoned to give evidence. Olga B. reportedly received threats not to testify but was not offered any state protection.

After protests at the failure to call Olga B. as a witness in the first trial, a retrial was held in October. However, the court reportedly again failed to call her to testify.

Excessive force against protesters

Police reportedly used excessive force during a demonstration about the EU summit on 21 June – beating protesters with batons, and kicking and verbally abusing them. Of 100 demonstrators arrested between 21 and 23 June, 29 were charged, including three children under the age of 18. Three Greek nationals and four nationals of Spain, Syria and the United Kingdom (UK) were charged with possession of weapons (hammers and explosives) and detained to await trial until 26 November. Four of the detainees were allegedly ill-treated at the time of their arrest and later in police custody, and there were fears that at least one of them, UK national Simon Chapman, was charged on the basis of fabricated evidence. After international protests, the seven were released on bail.

Freedom of expression curtailed for human rights activist

🖾 Gazmend Kapllani, an Albanian journalist and human rights activist, was threatened with expulsion from Greece after his residence application was rejected in March on the grounds that he presented a "threat to Public Order and National Security". Living in Greece since 1991 and prominent on racism and migrant issues as President of the Albanian Migrants Forum, he was studying for a doctorate at Athens Panteion University on a state scholarship at the time. After public protests by human rights organizations, he was granted a residence permit.

Roma and refugees

Local and European human rights organizations filed a series of complaints to the police, judicial authorities and the government, and to international human rights bodies, about human rights violations against Roma in Greece.

🖾 In September, the police in Argostoli were accused by human rights organizations in Greece of repeated violations against Roma in the last four years. These included arbitrary and discriminatory arrests, ill-treatment in police custody, extraction of statements under duress, and falsification and corruption of evidence.

🖾 Also in September, complaints were made that the government had failed to provide adequate water and electricity supplies to a Roma settlement in Spata, where 22 families had been forcibly relocated three years earlier. The local authorities had also failed to implement an agreement to provide a bus to transport Roma children to school.

In May the UN High Commissioner for Refugees expressed concern about the authorities' implementation of legislation on matters relating to asylum and immigration. In particular, it noted difficulties in accessing the processes for claiming asylum and refugee status; inadequate facilities to accommodate asylum-seekers; the low number of claimants given refugee status; and the inability of the welfare system to satisfy the needs or assist the social integration of refugees. Another concern was the Protocol signed between Greece and Turkey in 2002 agreeing to the mutual forced return of migrants from third countries.

Overcrowding in reception facilities for asylum-seekers, which include former prison buildings, was reported in several instances.

🗁 In July, 24 asylum-seekers, among them a seven-month-old girl, were detained for five days in a secure open-air area on the seafront at the port on the island of Mytilini. They were moved from a detention centre for migrants, converted from a former prison, following complaints by local inhabitants. For the first few days, the authorities failed to provide them with adequate supplies of water or medical treatment. Local human rights organizations were refused access to them.

Conscientious objection

Twenty-six individuals lost their right to conscientious objection to military service. At least 10 of them had their right to perform alternative civilian service on religious grounds denied or revoked. Four Jehovah's Witnesses had their applications rejected because they had been unable to submit the required documents in time because of lack of cooperation from the authorities or on grounds of other procedural errors. Three Jehovah's Witnesses had their previously recognized status as conscientious objectors revoked on grounds of insubordination or breach of discipline. The applications of two other Jehovah's Witnesses were turned down on the grounds that they had carried out military service in other countries before their religious conversion and immigration to Greece. A Christian Evangelist was told that his religion was not incompatible with performing full military service and his application was also refused.

In September charges of "disobedience", brought against Jehovah's Witness Alexandros Evtousenko for refusing to carry out military service, were withdrawn after a court in Thessaloniki ruled that he could not be tried twice for the same offence. In another case, Lazaros Petromelidis was convicted and sentenced to 20 months' imprisonment by an Athens court, also for "disobedience".

The alternative civilian service available to conscientious objectors in Greece is of a punitive nature. A planned law, that would make civilian service double the length of military service, therefore still of a punitive length, had not been drafted by the end of 2003.

AI country reports/visits
Report
- Greece: To be in the army or choosing not to be – The continuous harassment of conscientious objectors (AI Index: EUR 25/003/2003)

HUNGARY

REPUBLIC OF HUNGARY
Head of state: Ferenc Mádl
Head of government: Péter Medgyessy
Death penalty: abolitionist for all crimes
UN Women's Convention and its Optional Protocol: ratified

There was continued concern about the ill-treatment of Roma by police. The detention policy concerning asylum-seekers undermined their rights and protection. Some institutions for people with mental disabilities used "cage beds" to restrain residents.

Discrimination against Roma

Despite government efforts to combat discrimination, particularly in the field of education, the Roma continued to face widespread discrimination in all walks of life, including the health services, employment and housing.

In May a newspaper using a hidden camera revealed that a hospital in Eger, Heves county, provided separate accommodation for Romani women in the maternity ward. In June, according to the Roma Press Centre, around 20 homeless families squatting in an old industrial plant in Budapest were ordered to leave the premises and threatened that if they did not their children, who were reportedly at risk at this site, would be taken into community care. In October the deputy director of the municipal office of Piliscsaba, Pest county, after being presented with data on the number of Roma in the community, reportedly stated, "Oh Lord, there are so many of them here, I wish Hitler had started his project with Gypsies". She was suspended and a disciplinary procedure was initiated.

Anti-Roma prejudices remained strong among law enforcement officials. According to the Roma Press Centre, negative stereotypes were reinforced by some photographs in *Zsaru Magazin* (*Cop Magazine*) published by the National Police Headquarters. In July, three young Romani women, one of them a minor, filed a suit against the magazine after it published without their consent a photograph of them with a caption that referred to them as prostitutes. Warrants posted on the

Internet site of the National Police Headquarters described some criminal suspects as speaking "similarly to the Roma, indicating that they are uneducated men" and others as being "gipsy in appearance... typically dark skinned".

Very few of the police officers who were suspected of ill-treatment of Roma were successfully prosecuted and those convicted were lightly punished. This discouraged victims from reporting abuses or filing complaints. AI urged the General Prosecutor to investigate two incidents of police ill-treatment which appeared to be racially motivated.

⌒ On 13 June Cs.V., a Romani man, was stopped in his van by a police vehicle in Valkó, Pest county. He stated that as he was slowing down he heard what sounded like a gunshot. Cs.V. approached the police car and a police officer reportedly pushed him face down onto the hood and handcuffed him. Another Romani man who had observed the incident was reportedly told by an officer: "Get out, you dirty gipsy!" The man and his 12-year-old daughter fled into the courtyard of their house pursued by the officer who shouted: "All gypsies should be killed". He then allegedly pointed his gun at the girl who, as a result, fainted. Before leaving, the officers reportedly stated that Cs.V. would not be charged if no complaint was filed against them. In November the authorities informed AI that they were still investigating the case.

Detention of asylum-seekers

Some improvements were reported in the conditions in detention facilities as well as in access of asylum-seekers to the lawyers of the Hungarian Helsinki Committee (HHC), a local human rights organization. However, there was continued concern about the detention policy applied to asylum-seekers, the lack of a regular monitoring mechanism concerning the fate of asylum-seekers at point of entry, and conditions in community shelters.

Because of inconsistent interpretation of regulations concerning asylum-seekers and other foreign nationals, asylum-seekers in very similar situations were treated differently — some were detained, some were not. Apart from Iraqi and Afghan nationals, single male asylum applicants and stateless people who had entered the country illegally were detained for 12 months although the spirit of the law envisages detention only as a means to implement an expulsion decision. According to HHC, no person who had been detained while their application was being reviewed had been recognized as a refugee and only a few were given permission to temporarily remain in the country. In a report issued in August, the UN High Commissioner for Refugees described this situation as "an attitude or presumption that asylum-seekers kept in detention do not deserve international protection or alternative forms of protection".

The conditions of detention varied. Those detained in Nagykanizsa centre were confined to locked dormitories day and night. In some facilities pay telephones were outside the perimeter of the detention area.

Although not recognized as refugees, people given temporary stay permits were accommodated with many other categories of people, including convicted offenders awaiting deportation, in community shelters located within military bases and providing sub-standard conditions. Better services and conditions prevailed in open reception centres used by recognized refugees. These centres, unlike community shelters, reportedly had significant spare capacity in the course of the year.

Cage beds in institutions for people with mental disabilities

A report published in June by Mental Disability Advocacy Centre, a regional non-governmental organization, claimed that in a number of social care homes for people with mental disabilities cage beds were used as a method of restraint. This is considered to be cruel, inhuman and degrading treatment and in violation of international human rights law as well as best professional practice. The Ministry of Health, Social and Family Affairs confirmed that cage beds were still in use and stated that this was not explicitly forbidden by law, although their use was forbidden by professional guidelines for psychiatric hospitals.

AI country reports/ visits
Report
· Concerns in Europe and Central Asia, January-June 2002: Hungary (AI Index: EUR 01/016/2003)
Visit
In June in Budapest, AI representatives met László Teleki, State Secretary in the Office of the Prime Minister for Romani Affairs.

IRELAND

IRELAND
Head of state: Mary McAleese
Head of government: Bertie Ahern
Death penalty: abolitionist for all crimes
UN Women's Convention: ratified with reservations
Optional Protocol to UN Women's Convention: ratified

In September the European Committee for the Prevention of Torture and Inhuman or Degrading Treatment or Punishment (CPT) published the report of its May 2002 visit and the government's response. The CPT found inhuman conditions for prisoners suffering from mental illness, and received reports of ill-treatment by prison and police officers. A new government inspector of prisons reported "appalling" sanitary facilities in some prisons. Mental health policy and service provision did not comply with international best practice and human rights standards. Legislation to incorporate the European Convention on Human Rights into domestic law was introduced. Human rights groups urged a review of its effectiveness in five years' time. Legislation to implement the Rome Statute of the International Criminal Court (ICC) was published, and AI recommended that national courts be empowered to investigate and prosecute individuals accused of crimes under the Rome Statute.

Prisons

During its 2002 visit the CPT found prisoners who needed psychiatric care and in-patient hospital treatment being held in unfurnished, padded cells, treatment it described as "anti-therapeutic", "inhuman and degrading". The delegation called for an end to the practice and for the prisoners to be transferred to appropriate institutions. In its response in August 2002, the government provided information about measures it had taken to remedy the situation.

The CPT heard reports of ill-treatment by prison officers, violence between prisoners and bullying. It reiterated its concerns about prison complaints procedures; procedural safeguards for prisoners involved in disciplinary proceedings; and the use of segregation for disciplinary reasons for periods of up to two months. The CPT found that the authorities had failed to guarantee prisoners adequate access to proper sanitary facilities.

The CPT welcomed the creation of a Prison and Places of Detention Inspectorate, and recommended that it be given the powers and resources to fulfil its functions effectively and independently.

New prison rules under preparation were expected to address some of the CPT's concerns. However, the government rejected the finding that segregation for disciplinary reasons was widespread, and refused to end its use.

In July the first report of the Inspector of Prisons and Places of Detention was published, following its submission to the government. He described sanitary facilities in a number of prisons as "appalling". Among his recommendations were that juvenile prisoners should be separated from adult prisoners wherever possible; that asylum-seekers should not be held in a prison while awaiting a decision on their application; and that prisoners should receive the same level of psychiatric care as that provided in the general community.

Policing

In its report, the CPT expressed concern about reports of ill-treatment by members of the *Garda Síochána* (police force), whose number and consistency, in addition to medical evidence in some cases, lent them credibility. The CPT found that the police complaints mechanism enjoyed little confidence, and recommended prioritizing the establishment of an independent and impartial police inspection and complaints mechanism. In June a proposal for an inspectorate to investigate complaints against Garda officers was published. The Irish Human Rights Commission expressed concern about some provisions of the draft legislation, for example the proposed transfer of staff to the new inspectorate from the existing Garda Síochána Complaints Board.

Criminal proceedings against six police officers under the Non Fatal Offences Against the Person Act 1997 were continuing at the end of the year. Summary charges against a seventh officer were dismissed in June. Proceedings arose in connection with allegations of excessive use of force during a "Reclaim the Streets" demonstration in Dublin in May 2002.

The internal inquiry established in May 2002 to probe allegations that the Garda had prior knowledge of the 1998 Omagh bombing in Northern Ireland continued at the end of 2003. In October allegations emerged that vital intelligence from a Garda officer that could have prevented the bombing was disregarded to protect an informant.

Judicial inquiries into alleged police misconduct were still hearing evidence at the end of 2003. They were the Tribunal of Inquiry (the Morris Tribunal) into complaints against members of the police Donegal Division, and the Tribunal of Inquiry (the Barr Tribunal) into the fatal shooting of John Carthy in April 2000.

Dublin/Monaghan bombings

In December the report of Justice Henry Barron on the 1974 Dublin and Monaghan bombings was published after its submission to the authorities. The judge found that the bombings had been carried out by Loyalist paramilitaries from Northern Ireland. Although unable to conclude that collusion had taken place, he did not rule out the possibility that members of the British security forces had aided them. He found defects in the Garda investigation and that numerous files were missing at the Department of Justice. He commented adversely on the indifference of the Irish authorities and the need for an effective investigation.

Special Criminal Court

In August, Michael McKevitt was sentenced to 20 years' imprisonment following his conviction at the Special Criminal Court in Dublin for "directing terrorism" in connection with his leadership role in the Real IRA, a dissident Republican group opposed to the Good Friday Agreement. At the end of the year, a number of people were awaiting trial before the Special Criminal Court in connection with charges under the Offences Against the State (Amendment) Act 1998. AI continued to be concerned about the operation of the Special Criminal Court and provisions in the Act that violated international human rights law and standards.

Mental health

In its September report, the CPT expressed concern about material conditions in the Central Mental Hospital, the only forensic psychiatric hospital in Ireland, and its limited provision of occupational therapy and rehabilitative activities. Other concerns included the absence of: a clear legal or administrative framework for involuntary admission; review procedures in relation to continued placement; and supervision of mental health institutions by an independent authority. The Mental Health Act 2001, which included provisions to address inadequate involuntary admission procedures, was not in force. The Inspector of Mental Health Services, due to begin work in January 2004, lacked the necessary statutory powers in relation to complaints.

Arms trade

A government-commissioned report by the Irish Export Control System provided for the first time firm figures on the value of exports of military and dual-use goods. AI reiterated concerns about the lack of legislation on arms brokering and licensed production; of any system of post-export checks; or of any mechanism for effective monitoring by parliament.

Racism

The review of the ineffective Prohibition on Incitement to Hatred Act 1989, announced in 2000, was not completed. According to the National Consultative Committee on Racism and Interculturalism, migrant workers were not reporting racism and discrimination in the workplace for fear of losing their work permits. Concerns about the adequacy of the system for reporting, recording and prosecuting racist crimes persisted.

Asylum-seekers

The Immigration Act 2003, which came into force in July, introduced carriers' liability for transporting inadequately documented passengers, raising concern that the right to seek asylum might be unduly obstructed. The new legislation also introduced accelerated procedures for determining asylum claims, on the basis of "safe country of origin" lists, that failed to recognize the individual character of persecution. Asylum-seekers from "safe" countries may have to overcome an unreasonable and discriminatory presumption against their claim in a process that may lack procedural safeguards. Refugee organizations voiced concerns about some aspects of the treatment of unaccompanied children. In January the Supreme Court ruled that non-national parents of children born on Irish territory – who are entitled to citizenship – do not have an automatic right of residency. The Irish Human Rights Commission expressed concern that families had abandoned asylum claims in the belief that they could obtain residency on this basis.

ITALY

ITALIAN REPUBLIC
Head of state: Carlo Azeglio Ciampi
Head of government: Silvio Berlusconi
Death penalty: abolitionist for all crimes
UN Women's Convention and its Optional Protocol: ratified

The functioning of the justice system fell short of international standards. There were further allegations of excessive use of force and ill-treatment by law enforcement and prison officers, as well as reports of detainee and prisoner deaths in disputed circumstances. Detention conditions in some facilities, including temporary holding centres for aliens, fell below international standards. The lack of a comprehensive law on asylum combined with certain provisions of the immigration law meant that many asylum-seekers faced obstacles in exercising their right to asylum. There were fears that some asylum-seekers were forced to return to countries where they risked grave human rights violations and that some individuals expelled to their countries of origin on grounds that they posed a danger to national security and public order had no opportunity to challenge the decision in fair proceedings, resulting in possible breaches of the principle of *non-refoulement*. Roma and a number of other ethnic minorities suffered discrimination in many areas, including policing, housing and employment. Women's rights organizations reported a high incidence of violence against women in the family, usually at the hands of the husband or partner. Trafficking in people for sexual purposes and forced labour was a problem.

International scrutiny of the justice system

In January the Special Rapporteur on the independence of judges and lawyers reported to the UN Commission on Human Rights on his November 2002 mission to Italy. He stated that tension between magistrates and the government was continuing, to "the detriment of the due administration of justice", including by delaying urgently needed judicial reforms; that court cases against the Prime Minister and a close associate on criminal charges involving corruption and false accounting were contributing to the tension, aggravated by them exploiting "weaknesses" in judicial procedures to delay their own cases and using parliamentary and legislative processes for their own benefit. He said the practice of magistrates seeking election to parliament without resigning from judicial office and "expressing opinions publicly on controversial political issues" was incompatible with judicial independence.

In February the Committee of Ministers of the Council of Europe, after examining measures taken to reduce the excessive length of judicial proceedings, noted "significant progress was yet to be achieved in order for Italian justice fully to comply with the European Convention on Human Rights and Fundamental Freedoms".

Asylum and immigration

Thousands of migrants continued to arrive on southern shores by boat and hundreds of others died in the attempt. There were reports of boats being turned back by Italian military vessels, thereby denying any asylum-seekers on board access to a fair and impartial individual asylum determination. Such interception of boats was allowed by a law on immigration introduced in 2002 and partly implemented through enabling legislation in 2003. There was concern that certain provisions in the law also allowed many asylum-seekers to be detained or restricted in their liberty in circumstances beyond those allowed under international standards, and permitted asylum-seekers to be expelled during appeal procedures relating to rejected asylum applications. Some asylum-seekers were left destitute while awaiting the outcome of initial asylum applications.

Temporary holding centres for aliens

Inmates of such centres, where unauthorized immigrants and rejected asylum-seekers could be detained for up to 60 days before expulsion from the country or release, often experienced difficulties in gaining access to the legal advice necessary to challenge the legality of their detention and expulsion. In January the UN Committee on the Rights of the Child expressed concern about the detention of unaccompanied minors in such centres, the lack of adequate structures to receive them, and "an increase in repatriations without adequate follow-up". It recommended increased efforts to establish special reception centres, with stays "for the shortest time possible".

There was increasing tension in the centres, which were often overcrowded and unhygienic and provided unsatisfactory diets and inadequate medical care. An increasing number of allegations emerged of physical assaults on inmates.

⊟ In October, the public prosecutor's office in Lecce concluded an investigation into a complaint lodged by 17 young North African men. The men alleged that after attempting to escape from Regina Pacis holding centre in Puglia province in November 2002, they and dozens of fellow inmates were racially abused and physically assaulted by a Roman Catholic priest acting as the centre's director, as well as by around six members of the administrative personnel and 11 *carabinieri* providing the centre's security service. The prosecutor requested the relevant judge to commit all the accused for trial.

⊟ A criminal investigation began into allegations that, following an escape attempt by two North African inmates of the Via Mattei holding centre, Bologna, in March, some 11 police officers, one *carabiniere* and a member of the Red Cross administration were involved in a physical assault on them and some 10 other inmates.

Ill-treatment by police

Allegations of ill-treatment and use of excessive force by police often concerned members of ethnic minorities and demonstrators. In January the UN Committee on the Rights of the Child expressed deep concern at "alleged ill-treatment by law enforcement officers against children and at the prevalence of abuse, in particular against foreign and Roma children".

In January the Council of Europe's Committee for the Prevention of Torture (CPT) issued its report on a February 2000 visit to Italy. The CPT noted continuing allegations of ill-treatment by state police and *carabinieri* and that fundamental guarantees against ill-treatment in the custody of law enforcement officers were still missing. It called for detainees to have the right, in practice as well as in law, to consult a lawyer without delay and in private, and for the introduction of a legal right of access to a doctor.

⊟ Investigations were opened into allegations that, during a mass anti-war demonstration in Turin in March, police and *carabinieri,* using batons and tear gas, subjected some demonstrators, in particular peaceful demonstrators from the city's Muslim community, including about 50 women and children, to unwarranted and excessive use of force.

Updates: policing of 2001 demonstrations

Among ongoing criminal investigations were some relating to policing operations surrounding mass demonstrations during the Third Global Forum in Naples in March 2001 and the G8 Summit in Genoa in July 2001.

⊟ In June the Naples public prosecutor's office requested the judge of preliminary investigation to commit 31 police officers for trial on various charges, ranging from abduction to bodily harm and coercion. Some officers were additionally accused of abusing their position and of falsifying records. The judge's decision was still pending at the end of the year.

The inquiry into the fatal shooting of a G8 demonstrator, Carlo Giuliani, by a law enforcement officer then performing his military service in the *carabiniere* force, ended in May. The judge of preliminary investigation ruled that the officer had acted in self-defence, making legitimate use of his firearm, and should not be charged. She also decided that no charges should be pursued against the officer driving the vehicle, who had run over then reversed over Carlo Giuliani's body after he was shot. She stated that he had driven over the body unwittingly and that forensic evidence indicated that the resulting injuries were superficial and played no role in the death. She concluded that a pistol was the only means which the first officer had at his disposal to confront the demonstrators' violent attack; that, after waving his pistol in warning, he had fired the fatal shot but had not aimed at Carlo Giuliani but into the air, and that the shot's trajectory was deflected by a chunk of plaster thrown by a demonstrator. Carlo Giuliani's parents subsequently announced their intention to file an application against Italy with the European Court of Human Rights.

In September, Genoa public prosecutor's office concluded its investigations into the conduct of law enforcement officers during a raid on a building legally occupied by the Genoa Social Forum, the main demonstration organizer. The prosecutors presented their findings to 30 members of the state police, including high-ranking officers, allowing them the legal right to respond, before requesting their committal for trial. The prosecutors' accusations included abuse of authority, assault and battery, slander and falsifying evidence against the 93 people detained during the raid, apparently in order to justify the raid, the arrest of the 93 and the degree of force used by officers. A criminal investigation into accusations that the 93 had violently resisted state officers, committed theft and carried offensive weapons had ended in May when a judge ruled that there was no evidence of resistance. In December prosecutors concluded a separate criminal investigation into an accusation that they belonged to a criminal association intent on looting and destroying property and requested the relevant judge to close the proceedings without any charges being brought.

The public prosecutor's office concluded investigations into events inside Bolzaneto temporary detention facility, through which over 200 detainees held during the G8 summit passed. The findings were presented to 47 individuals, including members of the state police, *carabinieri*, penitentiary and medical personnel. The accusations included abuse of authority, assault and battery, falsifying records, and failing to certify injuries.

Ill-treatment and poor conditions in prisons

Reports persisted of chronic overcrowding and understaffing, poor sanitary provisions, inadequate medical assistance and high levels of self-harm in prisons. There was concern that the so-called "41-bis" high-security regime, allowing a severe degree of isolation from the outside world and applicable to prisoners held in connection with organized crime and crimes committed "for the purposes of terrorism or subversion of the state", could in certain circumstances amount to cruel, inhuman and degrading treatment. In its report on its February 2000 visit, the CPT stated that the regime had led to an increase in anxiety problems as well as in sleep and personality disorders. Numerous criminal proceedings, some of them marked by excessive delays, were under way into alleged ill-treatment in prisons, in some cases amounting to torture.

Update

In February a judge of preliminary hearing considering the cases of defendants who had chosen to be tried via a fast-track trial procedure, allowing leniency in sentencing, concluded that inmates of San Sebastiano prison, Sardinia, had been subjected to unpremeditated ill-treatment by prison personnel in April 2000. Sentences ranging from fines to 18 months' imprisonment were handed down to nine prison officers, the former chief prison guard, a prison doctor, the former director of San Sebastiano prison and the former regional director of prisons. The judge concluded that there were no grounds to prosecute a further 20 prison officers. The public prosecutor appealed against the judge's decision, and proceedings against nine prison officers who had chosen to be tried under the ordinary criminal process were still open at the end of the year.

Update: the case of Adriano Sofri

Adriano Sofri, one of three men convicted in 1995 of participating in a politically motivated murder in 1972, following criminal proceedings whose fairness had repeatedly been called into question, remained in prison, serving a 22-year sentence. In June the European Court of Human Rights declared inadmissible an application complaining of unfairness in the criminal proceedings. Over 300 members of parliament, from both government and opposition parties, subsequently called for Adriano Sofri to be granted a presidential pardon. Although the President and Prime Minister indicated their support for a pardon, the Minister of Justice blocked it, as well as a pardon application submitted by Ovidio Bompressi, previously released from prison on health grounds. The third man convicted of involvement in the murder, Giorgio Pietrostefani, remained in hiding.

AI country reports/visits
Report
- Concerns in Europe and Central Asia, January-June 2003: Italy (AI Index: EUR 01/016/2003)

KAZAKSTAN

REPUBLIC OF KAZAKSTAN
Head of state: Nursultan Nazarbayev
Head of government: Danyal Akhmetov (replaced Imangali Tasmagambetov in June)
Death penalty: retentionist
UN Women's Convention and its Optional Protocol: ratified

A moratorium on executions was introduced pending abolition of the death penalty. One opposition leader was pardoned and released from prison; another continued to serve a long prison sentence. An independent journalist was imprisoned on allegedly fabricated criminal charges.

Background
In March a US businessman and former adviser to President Nazarbayev was arrested in the USA and charged with "making unlawful payments to Kazak government officials" under the Foreign Corrupt Practices Act. The authorities in Kazakstan allegedly tried to prevent the press from reporting the so-called "Kazakgate" affair.

Death penalty
In his annual address to the nation in April, President Nazarbayev urged the government to create the necessary conditions for introducing a moratorium on the death penalty and called for the introduction of life imprisonment. Officials in Kazakstan were unable to confirm whether a *de facto* moratorium on executions was in place after a press release issued in July on behalf of President Nazarbayev by an international consultancy group in France claimed that no executions would be carried out in Kazakstan until January 2004 when a moratorium would enter into force. In October President Nazarbayev was quoted by Kazak media as saying that Kazakstan was not ready for a moratorium on the death penalty. In November AI learned that four men were executed. In December, President Nazarbayev signed into law a moratorium on executions.

Political prisoners
Supporters of the secular opposition and members of independent media continued to report harassment by the authorities.
☐ In April Mukhtar Ablyazov, one of two imprisoned leaders of the main opposition Democratic Choice of Kazakstan (DVK) movement, appealed to President Nazarbayev for clemency. He was released under a presidential amnesty in May; he had allegedly been beaten and ill-treated in detention to force him to abandon opposition political activities. In October the presidential clemency commission said that it could not consider a petition for clemency submitted by the other imprisoned DVK leader, Galymzhan Zhakiyanov, because the National Security Committee (KNB) had brought new criminal charges against him. Concerns by his family and supporters over his deteriorating health had reportedly prompted him to appeal for pardon on humanitarian grounds. Mukhtar Ablyazov and Galymzhan Zhakiyanov were sentenced to prison in 2002 for "abuse of office" and financial crimes. They were apparently targeted because of their peaceful opposition activities.
☐ Sergey Duvanov, an independent journalist, was sentenced to three and a half years in prison in January after he was convicted of raping an underage girl. His trial, according to international observers, fell far short of international fair trial standards and may have been politically motivated. Since his arrest in October 2002 Sergey Duvanov had maintained his innocence and said that his conviction was an attempt to punish him for articles implicating government officials and the President in the "Kazakgate" affair. The appeal court refused to admit two independent experts commissioned by the Organization for Security and Co-operation in Europe (OSCE) to attend the hearing and upheld the original verdict. In November the Supreme Court turned down an appeal filed by Sergey Duvanov's legal team for a review of his case.

KYRGYZSTAN

KYRGYZ REPUBLIC
Head of state: Askar Akayev
Head of government: Nikolay Tanayev
Death penalty: retentionist
UN Women's Convention and its Optional Protocol: ratified

Police detained and reportedly ill-treated women demonstrating for justice for their relatives who had been victims of excessive use of force by law enforcement officials in 2002. Courts continued to award punitive criminal libel damages against independent newspapers critical of the government. A journalist investigating corruption allegations died in suspicious circumstances.

Background
In January the President replaced the Council for Constitutional Reforms with a group of experts to expedite the drafting of amendments to the Constitution. A national referendum on these amendments took place just two weeks later in early February amid claims of serious voting irregularities, including intimidation of election observers.

In November the President signed into law amendments to the criminal code criminalizing torture.

A moratorium on the death penalty, which had been in place since 1998, was extended until the end of 2003.

In November the Supreme Court formally banned the Islamist *Hizb-ut-Tahrir* political party, which it designated as "extremist".

Excessive use of force by police
In May police in Bishkek broke up a peaceful demonstration by members of the recently formed Committee of Mothers and Wives of the Aksy Victims. The women were protesting against the acquittal on appeal of three law enforcement officials sentenced in December 2002 to prison terms for their part in the fatal shooting of protesters in Aksy in March that year; a State Commission had found that the use of force by law enforcement agencies was "erroneous". The women, most of whom were elderly, were detained for 10 hours and reportedly threatened and humiliated by police officers. At least one woman was reportedly beaten. Following their release 18 of the women began a hunger strike, demanding to see President Akayev to appeal directly to him for justice. They ended the hunger strike after they received assurances by the presidential chief of staff that he would submit their appeal to the President.

Attacks on the press
Courts continued to award punitive criminal libel damages against independent newspapers publishing articles critical of the government or disclosing allegations of corruption and abuse of office. The state-run printing press reportedly refused to print several independent newspapers because of their perceived opposition to the government. A journalist investigating allegations of corruption died in mysterious circumstances.

In June the independent newspaper *Moya Stolitsa Novosti* was forced to close down after criminal libel damages awarded against the newspaper pushed it into bankruptcy. Over 30 libel lawsuits were filed against *Moya Stolitsa Novosti* as a result of articles critical of senior government officials or alleging corruption and fraud by state officials and in the private sector. In January Aleksandra Chernykh, the daughter of the political editor Rina Prizhivoit and a journalist herself, was assaulted and badly beaten. In June the car of Aleksandr Kim, the paper's publisher and editor-in-chief, was set on fire.

On 15 September the body of 27-year-old Ernis Nazalov, a correspondent for the *Kyrgyz Rukhu* newspaper, was reportedly found in a canal in the Kara-suu region. According to the Ministry of Internal Affairs (MVD) the original autopsy revealed no sign of a violent death and a verdict of accidental death by drowning was recorded. Ernis Nazalov's father, however, alleged that one of his son's hands was broken and bore knife wounds. According to colleagues, Ernis Nazalov had been investigating allegations of high-level corruption and was about to publish his findings. There was concern that his death could have been linked to his investigative work. The MVD confirmed that he had been attacked two weeks prior to his death by unknown assailants who had stolen some of his research materials.

LATVIA

REPUBLIC OF LATVIA
Head of state: Vaira Vike-Freiberga
Head of government: Einars Repše
Death penalty: abolitionist for ordinary crimes
UN Women's Convention: ratified
Optional Protocol to UN Women's Convention: not signed

There were concerns about alleged police ill-treatment, conditions in places of detention and imprisonment, domestic violence and conscientious objection to military service.

Alleged police ill-treatment
Both the UN Human Rights Committee and the UN Committee against Torture expressed concern about allegations of police ill-treatment of detainees, which in some cases could be considered to amount to torture. The Human Rights Committee urged Latvia to take firm measures to eradicate all forms of ill-treatment, including prompt investigations, prosecution of perpetrators and the provision of effective remedies to the victims. It urged Latvia to establish an independent body with the authority to receive and investigate all complaints of excessive use of force and other abuse of power by police officers.

The Committee against Torture additionally drew attention to alleged violations of the basic rights of detainees, including their access to a lawyer and doctor of their choice, and to existing legislation which does not provide for the right of a detainee to contact family members. Various recommendations were made to address these issues.

Prison conditions
There were persisting concerns about conditions of detention and imprisonment. Both the Human Rights Committee and Committee against Torture expressed concern about the excessive length of pre-trial detention, particularly with regard to juvenile offenders, and the deleterious effect of overcrowding on conditions in places of detention. The Committee against Torture also expressed concern about the material conditions of detention, particularly in police stations and short-term detention isolators. Both committees recommended action to deal with these concerns.

Violence against women
Further measures were needed to combat violence against women in the home. The Human Rights Committee, while recognizing positive developments made by Latvia, remained concerned that reports of domestic violence persist. It recommended that Latvia adopt a policy and legal framework to counter domestic violence, establish advice and victim support centres and raise awareness about the issue through the media.

233

Conscientious objection

AI remained concerned about the punitive length of the civilian alternative to military service stipulated in the Law on Alternative Service, which came into effect on 1 July 2002. Conscientious objectors to military service in Latvia are forced to undertake an alternative service of two years, twice the length of military service.

LITHUANIA

REPUBLIC OF LITHUANIA
Head of state: Rolandas Paksas
Head of government: Algirdas Mikolas Brazauskas
Death penalty: abolitionist for all crimes
UN Women's Convention: ratified
Optional Protocol to UN Women's Convention: signed

Human rights concerns were raised by the UN Committee against Torture and the European Commission against Racism and Intolerance (ECRI) after examination of Lithuania's human rights obligations.

Torture and ill-treatment

In November the Committee against Torture, which examined the initial report of Lithuania on the measures it had taken to implement the UN Convention against Torture, raised concerns about the lack of a specific criminal offence of torture in law and the large increase in complaints of ill-treatment by police, almost half of which were reportedly upheld by the authorities. The Committee stated that in certain instances the allegations of ill-treatment of detainees may have amounted to torture. Investigations into allegations of torture and ill-treatment were not conducted by a body independent of the police.

The Committee made various recommendations to ensure that the basic rights of detainees are guaranteed in practice. These included immediate access to a lawyer and a doctor, and contact with family members. It also appealed for urgent and effective steps to be taken to "establish a fully independent complaints mechanism, to ensure prompt, impartial and full investigations into the many allegations of torture reported to the authorities and the prosecutions and punishments, as appropriate, of the alleged perpetrators". The Committee urged Lithuania to implement similar investigative measures to examine reports of brutality against conscripts in the army.

Refugees

The April report on Lithuania of ECRI highlighted several concerns relating to refugees. In particular, it drew attention to the apparent practice of the authorities of granting asylum-seekers temporary residence permits on humanitarian grounds instead of refugee status under the UN Refugee Convention. It stated that in 2001, out of approximately 250 applications examined by the Migration Department, there were no first instance decisions recognizing refugee status and 192 decisions granting temporary residence permits on humanitarian grounds. ECRI called on the authorities to ensure that everyone entitled to refugee status under the Refugee Convention be given such status.

There was also concern about legislation containing the possibility of refusing subsidiary protection on national security and public order grounds. ECRI stated that such exclusion may result in *refoulement* of people needing protection.

MACEDONIA

THE FORMER YUGOSLAV REPUBLIC OF MACEDONIA
Head of state: Boris Trajkovski
Head of government: Branko Crvenkovski
Death penalty: abolitionist for all crimes
UN Women's Convention and its Optional Protocol: ratified

The human rights situation continued to improve, but there were continuing allegations of torture and ill-treatment by security officials, and reckless use of firearms by border guards that sometimes had fatal results. The trafficking of women and girls for forced sexual exploitation continued, although there were arrests and convictions of some perpetrators. New legislation strengthened the Office of the Ombudsperson.

Background

The international community continued to support the peace process following the conflict in 2001 in the north and west of the country between an ethnic Albanian armed opposition group and the Macedonian security forces. In March, EUFOR – a European Union (EU) armed force of between 300 and 400 soldiers from different countries – took over NATO's military functions of protecting monitors from the EU and the Organization for Security and Co-operation in Europe (OSCE). EUFOR was in turn replaced in December by an EU police force.

Despite some violent incidents and the appearance of the so-called Albanian National Army – an armed ethnic Albanian group purportedly seeking the union with neighbouring Kosovo and Albania of areas in Macedonia inhabited predominantly by ethnic Albanians – the security situation remained relatively stable. However, underlying tensions between the

Macedonian and Albanian communities at times became apparent in violent inter-ethnic incidents.

In January it was announced that the "Lions", an ethnic Macedonian paramilitary police force set up following the 2001 insurgency and allegedly responsible for many human rights violations, would be disbanded. It was subsequently agreed that half the force would be incorporated into police or army units.

In June the government bowed to pressure from the USA and entered into an impunity agreement not to surrender US nationals accused of genocide, crimes against humanity or war crimes to the International Criminal Court. The agreement was passed by parliament in October. Such agreements are in breach of states' obligations under international law.

In July parliament passed an amnesty law for those who had avoided compulsory military service since 1992. This affected 12,369 people, of whom 3,260 were ethnic Macedonians, 7,730 ethnic Albanians and the remainder from Macedonia's other ethnic groups.

In September parliament enacted a law that significantly extended the powers of the Ombudsperson Office in relation to state authorities, and proposed setting up six decentralized units throughout the country.

Killings by border patrols

In some instances, guards on the border with Albania, where smuggling was rife, used excessive force, in some cases resulting in loss of life.

◻ On 18 June, Agron Sherif Skënderi, an Albanian citizen, was shot in the head twice and killed by Macedonian border guards while trying to cross the border. The authorities said that he and another Albanian citizen, Arben Qamil Kaja – who was shot and wounded but escaped arrest – were smuggling arms and ignored orders to stop. Arben Qamil Kaja said that the border patrol opened fire without warning. No evidence of arms smuggling was known to have been produced, and reports suggested that the two men were engaged in illegal but small-scale trading in everyday goods.

Police torture and ill-treatment

Police continued to ill-treat people during arrest and detention. On 16 January the authorities authorized publication of reports by the Council of Europe's Committee for the Prevention of Torture and Inhuman or Degrading Treatment or Punishment, but failed to carry out thorough and impartial investigations into the reports' serious allegations of torture.

◻ On 7 February, two Roma, Skender Sadiković and Memet Dalipovski, were allegedly beaten by police in Kumanovo. Skender Sadiković said that he was beaten at his home and in Kumanovo police station by six officers wielding an axe handle, to try to force him to confess to a theft. Memet Dalipovski said that five officers beat him at the station. Unusually, the Minister of the Interior ordered an investigation, which confirmed that the police had ill-treated him. The police officers involved were reportedly disciplined by a 15 per cent salary reduction for six months.

Failure to address past abuses

Inadequate investigation continued in the "Rashtanski Lozja" case, in which the authorities were suspected of extrajudicially executing one Indian and six Pakistani nationals on 2 March 2002. In March 2003 the authorities announced a special inquiry, to finish by mid-April. However, no results were forthcoming by the end of 2003.

Similarly, there appeared to be no progress on ascertaining the fate of 20 people who either "disappeared" or were abducted during the 2001 fighting, despite promises by the authorities that concrete information on the cases would be produced.

Trafficking of women and girls

A number of people were arrested and charged with trafficking women and girls for forced sexual exploitation. In June the US State Department reported that, in the period from April 2002 to March 2003, 70 charges were brought against 100 alleged perpetrators, and that there were 11 convictions with sentences ranging from six months to seven years' imprisonment.

◻ In February the authorities rescued at least 40 women trafficked for forced sexual exploitation, mainly foreign nationals, in raids in Skopje, Tetovo, Gostivar, Struga and Bitola, and arrested a purported main trafficker. He was sentenced in March to the minimum sentence of six months' imprisonment for involvement in prostitution, and escaped from custody on 19 June. The Struga prison director and other officials were sacked over his escape and the court criticized for the leniency of the sentence. He was rearrested on 2 July in Montenegro and transferred back to Macedonia. A new trial of him and others on charges of trafficking and forced prostitution began in October with the evidence of protected witnesses from Moldova and Romania and in December he was sentenced to three years and eight months' imprisonment.

◻ In October, five people in Skopje were sentenced to between five and eight years' imprisonment for trafficking women and girls from Moldova for forced prostitution.

◻ Also in October, six people in Gostivar, including two Albanian citizens and a Bulgarian woman, received sentences of between seven and 12 years' imprisonment. They were convicted of trafficking and other crimes in connection with an armed incident between rival traffickers in January in which three trafficked women – two from Bulgaria and one from Moldova – were shot dead.

Refugees and the displaced

Over 2,500 people displaced by the 2001 fighting were still unable to return to their homes. In May over 600 Roma from Kosovo, including women and children, made an unsuccessful attempt to leave Macedonia – where they had temporary asylum – to seek asylum in Greece. They had fled to Macedonia, fearing attacks on them by Kosovo Albanians after the 1999 NATO operation over Kosovo. They camped on the border until August, when they were persuaded to leave and were all offered asylum status under the terms of the new asylum law which was passed by parliament on 16 July. However, most refused, hoping instead to gain entry to the EU, and thus faced the threat of forcible deportation back to Kosovo.

AI country reports/visits
Reports
- Former Yugoslav Republic of Macedonia: Police allegedly ill-treat members of ethnic minorities (AI Index: EUR 65/001/2003)
- Former Yugoslav Republic of Macedonia: Continuing failure by the Macedonian authorities to confront police ill-treatment and torture (AI Index: EUR 65/008/2003)

Visits
An AI delegate visited Macedonia in November and December.

MALTA

REPUBLIC OF MALTA
Head of state: Guido de Marco
Head of government: Edward Fenech Adami
Death penalty: abolitionist for all crimes
UN Women's Convention: ratified with reservations
Optional Protocol to UN Women's Convention: not signed

The automatic and excessively lengthy detention of asylum-seekers was criticized by national and international bodies. Conditions of detention in facilities holding asylum-seekers and migrants fell short of international standards. New information emerged reinforcing concern that a number of individuals among a group of some 220 Eritreans deported from Malta to Eritrea in 2002 were detained and tortured on return (see Eritrea entry).

Asylum and immigration
Hundreds of asylum-seekers and unauthorized migrants, including pregnant women, nursing mothers and children, were held in detention centres for aliens on grounds beyond those allowed by international standards and for periods often ranging between one and two years. The situation was the result of the unauthorized arrival of an unprecedented number of asylum-seekers and migrants between November 2001 and the end of 2003; the automatic detention of all those arriving irregularly until the conclusion of refugee determination procedures or return to the country of origin; and severe delays in the processing of asylum applications. The delays appeared to be largely the result of acute understaffing in the Refugee Commissioner's Office, the first instance decision-making body.

Some 265 people remained in detention even after being granted refugee status or temporary humanitarian protection, apparently because of a shortage of accommodation in the community. They were transferred to two newly established open centres in June.

There were claims that detainees in the closed centres were frequently unable to exercise their rights as they were not fully and regularly informed of asylum determination proceedings and their progress and lacked access to timely legal advice. The Refugee Appeals Board systematically confirmed first instance decisions rejecting asylum applications, resulting in calls for greater transparency and diligence in the appeals process.

In November the Minister for Justice and Home Affairs stated that the detention of asylum-seekers and migrants "should not exceed a reasonable period" and that the government planned to guarantee this via several reforms. These included "accelerating the procedures for processing asylum applications, increasing human resources and drafting an internal policy of not detaining irregular immigrants beyond a reasonable period of time". He said that reducing the number of detainees would improve detention conditions. In December over 65 Eritrean and Ethiopian asylum-seekers who had been detained for periods ranging between 17 and 22 months, none of whom had been granted refugee status or, apparently, temporary humanitarian protection, were transferred to an open centre.

Detention conditions
There were numerous complaints of people in some centres suffering severe overcrowding and very inadequate sanitary arrangements. In one centre people were housed in tents for months during the winter season, suffering cold temperatures and flooding with rainwater. Some inmates, including children, had little or no regular access to exercise in the open air, and no recreational facilities. During the year efforts were made to allow detained school-age children to leave the centres during the day to attend local schools.

Local non-governmental organizations providing basic social and medical services, often on a voluntary basis, reported a sharp deterioration in the mental health of many of the inmates as the time they had spent detained in poor conditions lengthened, without any apparent progress in the processing of their asylum claims.

Intergovernmental bodies
In June the UN High Commissioner for Refugees (UNHCR) stated that, in order to comply fully with international standards, Malta's asylum legislation needed improvements in several areas. UNHCR strongly recommended that the automatic detention of asylum-seekers be discontinued.

In October, in public statements made at the end of a visit to Malta the Council of Europe's Commissioner for Human Rights said that living conditions in detention centres for aliens were "shocking", that asylum-seekers were detained for unacceptable periods of time, and that the Office of the Commissioner for Refugees was seriously understaffed. He underlined that urgent action was needed to address the situation.

AI country reports/ visits
Report
· Concerns in Europe and Central Asia, January-June 2003: Malta (AI Index: EUR 01/016/2003)

MOLDOVA

REPUBLIC OF MOLDOVA
Head of state: Vladimir Voronin
Head of government: Vasile Tarlev
Death penalty: abolitionist for all crimes
UN Women's Convention: ratified
Optional Protocol to UN Women's Convention: not signed

There were numerous reports of torture and ill-treatment by police; victims included children under the age of 18. Police officers were not held to account. Prison conditions amounted to cruel and degrading treatment. In the self-proclaimed Dnestr Moldavian Republic at least three political prisoners remained held and prison conditions were inhuman and degrading. Large numbers of Moldovan women continued to be trafficked abroad for sexual exploitation.

Torture and ill-treatment
There were numerous reports of torture and ill-treatment in police custody. In most cases detainees were refused access to a lawyer and to an independent medical examination. Minors were questioned without the presence of a parent, lawyer or responsible adult. Most of the victims were criminal suspects. However, in some cases people were apprehended by police without any apparent motive before being beaten and then charged with assaulting a police officer, to pre-empt investigation of allegations of torture. The authorities were often unwilling to conduct prompt and impartial investigations into allegations of ill-treatment.
In July, two men were stopped by police in Leova as they made their way home after a party. The police officers reportedly accused them of being drunk and, when the men refused to get into the police car, beat them with a baseball bat and a gun. The men were then taken to the city police station, where the beatings allegedly continued for several hours. They were taken to a hospital to check the amount of alcohol in their blood and were then returned to police custody, reportedly without receiving medical treatment. After a visit by the local prosecutor, who took an official

statement, the two men were released. However, on the same day a criminal investigation was opened against the two men for assaulting the police officers. After the two men lodged a complaint, a criminal investigation was initiated against two police officers for abuse of police powers. Both investigations were continuing at the end of the year.
In July, a 14-year-old boy was reportedly ill-treated by three police officers in Cojuşna. The boy was detained on suspicion of theft; no one was informed of his detention. Officers tried to coerce the boy into signing a confession, but he refused to sign any papers without his mother or a lawyer being present. The boy was taken into a windowless room by an officer and beaten with a rubber stick on his head and body. The boy was released at 6pm on the day of his arrest and returned home. He was subsequently admitted to hospital where he remained for several days receiving treatment for his injuries. In November the Străşeni Prosecutor's Office decided not to initiate a criminal investigation into the alleged ill-treatment of the boy, apparently on the grounds that "he is a thief".

In May the UN Committee against Torture expressed concern about the "numerous and consistent allegations of acts of torture and other cruel, inhuman or degrading treatment or punishment of detainees in police custody" and "[t]he reported lack of prompt and adequate access of persons in police custody to legal and medical assistance, and to family members". The Committee criticized the reported failure to ensure prompt, impartial and full investigations into the numerous allegations of torture and ill-treatment, contributing to a culture of impunity among law enforcement officials. It also raised concerns about allegations of a dysfunctional criminal justice system, apparently caused in part by a lack of independence of the procuracy and the judiciary.

Prison conditions
Prison conditions did not improve and often amounted to cruel, inhuman and degrading treatment. Overcrowding, lack of sanitation and inadequate food provision and medical treatment, as well as ill-treatment by prison guards and inter-prisoner violence, were reported. Prison authorities used excessive force to quell protests by prisoners.
In March a raid by prison guards resulted in the death of one detainee, Vadim Fanin, and injuries to a large number of other inmates at prison colony 29/4 in Cricova. According to reports, 40 officers taking part in a cell search fired directly at inmates protesting against the confiscation of personal items, ill-treatment and inhuman and degrading conditions in the facility.

Self-proclaimed Dnestr Moldavian Republic (DMR)
A Russian proposal for resolution of the status of the breakaway region was rejected in November by President Voronin. Initially, he had hailed the plan as a "realistic compromise", but subsequently withdrew his support. The Organization for Security and Co-operation in Europe had expressed concern about the

lack of clarity in the proposed agreement, particularly concerning the division of powers between the central and regional authorities.

Political prisoners

In March a delegation from the European Court of Human Rights (Grand Chamber) took evidence from 43 witnesses in Chișinău and Tiraspol in the case of the so-called "Tiraspol Six". Alexandru Leșco, Andrei Ivanțoc and Tudor Petrov-Popova, who remained in prison at the end of the year, had been convicted in 1993 of "terrorist acts". There were concerns that the six men had not received a fair trial before a court in the DMR.

Death penalty

The Supreme Court of the DMR confirmed the death sentence of F.I. Negrya on 25 June. However, in September the Ministry of Justice stated that the moratorium on executions, in place since July 1999, remained in force.

Prison conditions

In November a delegation of the European Committee for the Prevention of Torture and Inhuman or Degrading Treatment or Punishment (CPT) examined the situation at prison colony 29/8 in Bender, which functions as a medical institution specifically equipped for detainees with tuberculosis. According to the CPT the penitentiary was cut off from running water and electricity supplies in July by decision of the Bender municipal authorities. The institution forms part of the penitentiary system of the Republic of Moldova, but is located in an area under the control of the DMR. Having visited the prison colony in February and July the Helsinki Committee for Human Rights in Moldova reported that the conditions of detention for the over 650 detainees amounted to cruel, inhuman and degrading treatment; in particular it noted the lack of sanitation, inadequate food provision and harsh living conditions, which could be considered "a sentence to a slow death".

Violence against women

In its 2003 reply to the UN Economic and Social Council the Moldovan government indicated that it did not envisage separate legislation to criminalize domestic violence.

According to a 2003 UN Development Programme study, a significant and growing part of the population of Moldova was stricken by poverty. More than half the population were believed to receive an income lower than the minimum subsistence level. Low salaries and high unemployment were the main reasons behind the growth in trafficking of human beings from the country. Trafficking networks were reportedly targeting Moldova as a source for women and girls who could be trafficked for sexual exploitation, as well as for human organs for use in transplants.

AI country reports/visits

Report

- Concerns in Europe and Central Asia, January-June 2003: Moldova (AI Index: EUR 01/016/2003)

POLAND

REPUBLIC OF POLAND

Head of state: Aleksander Kwaśniewski
Head of government: Leszek Miller
Death penalty: abolitionist for all crimes
UN Women's Convention and its Optional Protocol: ratified

Incidents of police ill-treatment were reported. Domestic violence was not effectively investigated or prosecuted and victims were inadequately protected from further violence and other forms of pressure by the perpetrators.

Police ill-treatment

In March the Council of Europe's Commissioner for Human Rights published the report on his November 2002 visit to Poland. Noting the genuine willingness of the authorities to combat many of the problems raised in his report, the Commissioner expressed concern that cases of ill-treatment and deaths in police custody had been reported. He stated that it appeared that prostitutes, Roma and victims of trafficking were the most frequent victims. It appeared that many incidents of police violence went unreported as victims were said to fear that they would themselves be prosecuted. The Commissioner was also concerned that incidents of police violence were not always impartially investigated and rarely reached the courts. He called on the authorities to intensify efforts to eradicate cases of police brutality through training, effective investigation and prosecution of such cases.

Domestic violence

Although there were no comprehensive statistics concerning domestic violence, the problem was believed to be serious, widespread and affecting women from all backgrounds. According to *Centrum Praw Kobiet* (Women's Rights Centre), a non-governmental organization that offers women a wide range of assistance programs, one in eight women polled in 2002 stated that they had been beaten by their partner. A poll in 1996 showed that the incidence was much higher among divorced women – 41 per cent had allegedly been beaten by their husbands. The enforcement of the Penal Code provisions regarding domestic violence and effective support for the victims was inadequate.

In August the government adopted the National Plan of Action for the Advancement of Women 2003-2005 and pledged to introduce legislation ensuring effective protection of women and children who are subjected to violence.

Domestic violence, defined as a criminal offence in Polish law only if it occurs repeatedly, is prosecuted even without the permission of the victim. However, the complaints are frequently not treated as sufficiently serious or credible. In the vast majority of cases the police do not effectively collect the evidence and the women are required to obtain and pay for forensic medical certificates for injuries that they may have suffered. A single act of violence is privately prosecuted, which for most women is difficult and expensive. Statistical data on police investigations and prosecutions is not well collected. Even if brought to justice, perpetrators are usually lightly sentenced.

There were insufficient places where women could seek refuge or assistance. In a number of shelters managed by men, there were reports of sexual harassment and assault of the women by the staff.

Racism and discrimination

In March the UN Committee on the Elimination of Racial Discrimination (CERD) expressed concern about reports of racially motivated harassment and discrimination against Jews, Roma and people of African and Asian origin that had not been properly investigated by law enforcement agencies. The Committee urged Poland to intensify its efforts to combat and punish all such cases, especially through the strict application of relevant legislation and regulations providing for sanctions. It further recommended that law enforcement bodies be given adequate training and instructions on how to address complaints of racially motivated crimes, and that similar training be provided to the judiciary

Similar concerns were raised by the Council of Europe's Commissioner for Human Rights. Both the Commissioner and the CERD expressed concern about discrimination against Roma in other areas, especially education and employment. The Commissioner considered that the practice of so-called "Roma classes" tended to further isolate Romani children and that education in these classes was reportedly often of lower quality. Both recommended that Romani children should be integrated into mainstream schools as far as possible, and that the authorities should urgently address the problems of the Roma population throughout the country. They urged that sufficient resources be allocated to achieve full participation of Roma and equal levels of development in areas such as education, employment, health, hygiene and accommodation.

AI country reports/ visits
Report
- Concerns in Europe and Central Asia, January-June 2003: Poland (AI Index: EUR 01/016/2003)

PORTUGAL

PORTUGUESE REPUBLIC
Head of state: Jorge Fernando Branco de Sampaio
Head of government: José Manuel Durão Barroso
Death penalty: abolitionist for all crimes
UN Women's Convention and its Optional Protocol: ratified

Fatal shootings by police officers highlighted failures to ensure that firearms were used only in exceptional circumstances. International human rights bodies expressed concern about police use of firearms; reports of disproportionate use of force and ill-treatment by the police; the slow functioning of the justice system; and the excessive use and length of pre-trial detention. The safety of detainees in some prisons remained under threat, including from self-harm and inter-prisoner violence. Overcrowding and inadequate medical care and sanitary facilities were of particular concern in many prisons where conditions failed to comply with international standards. Roma and other ethnic minority communities continued to experience racism and other discrimination.

Background

The Commissioner for Human Rights of the Council of Europe visited Portugal in May and expressed several concerns, including about the functioning of the criminal justice system, prison conditions, and lack of respect for human rights by law enforcement officials.

In July the UN Human Rights Committee considered Portugal's third periodic report under the International Covenant on Civil and Political Rights. The Committee criticized the failure to submit a report for more than 10 years, and the lack of information on the work of the Ombudsperson. It recommended legislative amendments to require that anyone held in pre-trial detention be charged and tried within a reasonable time, and that magistrates authorize pre-trial detention only as a last resort.

In October, Portugal ratified Protocol No. 13 to the European Convention on Human Rights, concerning the abolition of the death penalty in all circumstances.

AI submitted its recommendations for the implementation of the Rome Statute of the International Criminal Court to the parliamentary Commission on Constitutional Affairs, Rights, Freedoms and Guarantees, which was drafting the relevant legislation at the end of 2003.

A public debate – at times confrontational – about the criminal justice system, involving judges, lawyers, politicians and the media, was generated by the arrest and pre-trial detention of some public figures, including a prominent opposition politician. The arrests were in connection with allegations of sexual abuse at a state-run school for orphans and deprived children.

Policing concerns

Police use of firearms continued to be of concern. In November the General Inspectorate of the Internal Administration drew attention to six fatal shootings by the police since the beginning of 2003, and reportedly stated that police authorities were failing to ensure that firearms were used only in exceptional circumstances.

At the international level, the Human Rights Committee expressed concern about recent police killings in disputed circumstances, reports of disproportionate use of force and ill-treatment by officers, and recurrent police violence towards members of ethnic minorities. The Committee was also concerned by reported failures of the judicial and disciplinary systems to deal promptly and effectively with allegations of grave police misconduct. It suggested the establishment of "a police oversight service, independent from the Ministry of the Interior". The Commissioner for Human Rights regretted the practice of suspending disciplinary proceedings pending a criminal investigation into allegations of grave police misconduct, and of discontinuing them if no criminal charges were brought.

🗁 The trial started in November of a police officer charged with homicide in connection with the death of António Pereira in June 2002 in the town of Setúbal.

Prison concerns

Safeguards to prevent self-harm and inter-prisoner violence, and to identify vulnerable detainees, were inadequate, causing concern that the authorities were failing to protect the right to life of people in prison. There were some new reports of ill-treatment and harassment of detainees by prison officers. The authorities failed to ensure that convicted prisoners were held separately from detainees in pre-trial detention and that prisoners received adequate medical care. Reports persisted of widespread infectious diseases, and drug trafficking and use inside prisons. Conditions and sanitary facilities in some prisons remained below international standards: the latest available figures showed that 17 per cent of detainees were still using buckets as toilets in February 2002. Overcrowding aggravated all other problems in the prison system.

The Human Rights Committee expressed concern about reports of ill-treatment and abuse of authority by prison staff and of violence, in some cases lethal, among prisoners. It recommended increased efforts to eliminate violence in prisons; ensure the separation of convicted prisoners and pre-trial detainees; make appropriate and timely medical care available to all detainees; and reduce overcrowding.

In November the Ombudsperson published his first report on prisons since 1998. It drew attention to inadequate medical care and factors threatening the safety of detainees and prison staff. These included malfunctioning cell doors and inadequate systems to enable prisoners in solitary confinement to call for help, coupled in some cases with only sporadic checks by prison staff. He also stressed the potential for abuse in the lack of clear separation between disciplinary measures, security measures and measures pertaining to the regime of detainees regarded as dangerous. The Ombudsperson recommended that detainees must have legal assistance of their choice in proceedings for the application of security and disciplinary measures. Full reasons should be given for any decision to subject a detainee to a security or disciplinary measure, and all prisons should implement the requirement that the governor or a deputy must always hear a detainee before imposing the measure.

Concern regarding the situation in prisons was also voiced by the Human Rights Commission of the national Bar Association.

🗁 Three self-inflicted deaths and one killing, allegedly as a result of violence between prisoners, were reported at the Vale de Judeus prison. The criminal investigation into the killings of two prisoners at the same prison in October 2001 was in the final stage. Some reports had implicated custodial staff in the killings. However, no charges had been brought at the end of the year.

Racism and discrimination

Despite measures to integrate people of Roma origin, discrimination continued, particularly in education, housing and access to employment and social services. There were reports of harassment and discriminatory treatment of Roma people by some local police authorities. Occasional attempts by some local councils to harass Roma groups and induce them to leave the area were also reported.

The Human Rights Committee expressed concern about prejudice against Roma people. The authorities failed to provide the Committee with information, including statistical data, on the situation of the Roma, on the work of institutions responsible for their advancement and welfare or on complaints – and their outcomes – filed by members of ethnic minorities, including Roma, with those institutions.

Asylum-seekers and refugees

The Commissioner for Human Rights expressed concern about the requirement that asylum applications must be lodged within eight days of entry into the country and procedures that allowed for removals while decisions on appeals against initial rejections of asylum claims were pending. The Office of the National Commissioner for Refugees was reportedly reluctant to hear applicants before ruling on their appeals against rejection of their asylum claims, raising concern about its independence from the immigration service.

The Human Rights Committee expressed concern that domestic law did not provide effective remedies against forcible return, in violation of the state's international human rights obligations not to return people to countries where they would be at risk of grave human rights abuses.

Violence against women

According to data of the national Commission for Equality and the Rights of Women, an average of five women a month die in Portugal as a result of domestic violence.

Despite praising national legislation on domestic violence, the Commissioner for Human Rights expressed concern about failure to make use of available protection measures, for example to prevent perpetrators from having access to the home of their victims. Despite 1991 legislation providing for specialized police units to tackle domestic violence, they had not been established by the end of 2003. However, according to the Commissioner for Human Rights, a number of programs, including training for officers, were improving police responsiveness to domestic violence. Legislation passed in 1999 in connection with the First National Plan against Domestic Violence, which provided for the creation of reception and assistance centres in all districts for women affected by domestic violence, had not been fully implemented. The Second National Plan against Domestic Violence, for the period 2003-2006, was adopted in June. It provided for, among other things, the training of judges and a revision of procedures to obtain compensation for people affected by domestic violence.

AI country reports/ visits

Reports

- Portugal before the Human Rights Committee: summary of Amnesty International's concerns regarding the protection of human rights under the International Covenant on Civil and Political Rights (AI Index: EUR 38/001/2003)
- Concerns in Europe and Central Asia, January-June 2003: Portugal (AI Index: EUR 01/016/2003)

ROMANIA

ROMANIA
Head of state: Ion Iliescu
Head of government: Adrian Năstase
Death penalty: abolitionist for all crimes
UN Women's Convention and its Optional Protocol: ratified

There were numerous reports of police torture and ill-treatment. At least one man died in suspicious circumstances. Police resorted to firearms in circumstances prohibited by international standards. Many of the victims were Roma. Conditions in prisons were sometimes inhuman and degrading, and there were reports of ill-treatment of detainees.

Background

Widespread corruption, affecting all aspects of society, undermined the government's ability to promote respect for basic rights and improve the economy. Relatively few public officials were held to account, politically or criminally, for alleged abuse of power. Most people saw no improvement in their living standard, particularly their access to vital services such as health care and social support benefits.

In a report published in November, the European Union (EU) made clear that Romania could not accede to the EU before it consolidated its economy and implemented judicial and administrative reforms.

A constitutional revision came into force following a referendum in October. The way the referendum was conducted was criticized by independent observers and the main opposition parties who also claimed that there were indications that less than the required 50 per cent of the electorate had voted. The amendments to the Constitution were aimed at making the legislative process more effective and the judiciary more independent. However, the adopted revisions may not be sufficient to guarantee that the legislative process is more open to public scrutiny or that the judiciary is less susceptible to influence by the Ministry of Justice.

Trafficking of women and children for sexual exploitation remained a serious problem. The Law for Combating Trafficking adopted in 2001 did not lead to any noticeable improvement in the situation. In the reported cases, law enforcement officers failed to take effective action to protect victims.

Torture and ill-treatment

Numerous reported incidents of ill-treatment by law enforcement officials, which in some cases amounted to torture, indicated that the authorities had not made any progress in this area. At least one case resulted in death.

⬜ In October in Bucharest, 20-year-old Marian Predică, who was held in pre-trial detention in Rahova penitentiary, was taken unconscious to a hospital where he died five days later of a brain haemorrhage.

An autopsy concluded that the primary cause of death had been a head injury resulting from violence three or four days prior to the hospitalization. An authoritative medical expert stated that Marian Predică would probably not have died had he been promptly treated. Shortly before he died, Marian Predică had reportedly been beaten by officers of the penitentiary intervention unit.

In May, Mircea Iustian, Chairman of the Senate Committee for Human Rights, wrote to the Chief Military Prosecutors asking for information about cases of deaths in detention described in *Amnesty International Report 2003*. It was not known whether he received a response. However, information received by AI from the government indicated that the authorities had yet again failed to make progress in ensuring that investigations into reported incidents were independent and impartial as required by international law. Only one case resulted in a prosecution and conviction — two officers were found responsible for the death of Dumitru Grigoraş in July 2001. In fact, the government appeared to be taking measures that would make investigations even less transparent. In August an order of the Ministry of Justice and the Ministry of Health regarding investigations into deaths in penitentiaries stipulated that "conclusions concerning the provision of services and medical treatment are a state secret".

As in the past, the majority of victims of reported police ill-treatment were suspected of a petty offence or happened to be present at a scene of a police action. Some were people with a mental disability. In other reported cases women suffered sexual violence, including rape.

▢ In August, a 45-year-old woman from the municipality of Laslea complained that she had been raped by the chief of a local police station after he had come to her house to investigate a neighbour's complaint. Although she obtained a forensic medical certificate the same day she was unable to file her complaint with the County Police Inspectorate until four days later. A police commission established to investigate the case reportedly questioned the victim and the suspected perpetrator face to face and persuaded the victim to withdraw her complaint in consideration for the officer's family.

Roma were frequently targeted for police ill-treatment, apparently to intimidate all members of their marginalized communities. Some victims were afraid to make statements to non-governmental organizations or to file complaints because of fear of further harassment. Some Roma were ill-treated by police-licensed private security guards.

▢ In November, in Petroşani, 41-year-old Olga David, a Romani woman, died from injuries reportedly suffered 10 days earlier when she was severely beaten by three security guards at a coal mine. Together with her 12-year-old niece, Olga David had been collecting coal to heat her home, a single room without electricity or running water.

Children were also victims of police ill-treatment. In January the UN Committee on the Rights of the Child expressed concern at the number of allegations of children being ill-treated and tortured and the lack of effective investigations into such incidents by an independent authority. The Committee recommended that Romania "take immediate measures to stop police violence against all children and challenge the prevailing culture of impunity for such acts".

▢ In October in Urlaţi, around 20 masked officers came to search the house of Ion Catrinescu whose eldest son had allegedly stolen some corn. After the officers broke into her courtyard they hit Niculina Catrinescu in the chest with a gun making her fall to the ground, then kicked her all over her body. They also assaulted her sons, 17-year-old Cristian and 14-year-old Bujor Julian. Ion Catrinescu, who was holding their 16-month-old daughter, was beaten and shot at close range in the right foot, causing a serious injury.

Some patterns of police ill-treatment were confirmed in April by the Council of Europe's Committee for the Prevention of Torture (CPT) report concerning its second visit to Romania in early 1999. The CPT received many allegations of physical ill-treatment, some of them extremely serious, from men, including minors, and some women. The assaults took place during interrogation and were aimed at forcing confessions. Detainees were subjected to slaps, punches, kicks, truncheon blows, beatings to the soles of the feet while the victim was kneeling on a chair or suspended from a bar, and beatings with a stick to the body while rolled in a carpet. The CPT returned to Romania in each of the following three years but the government had yet to allow the publication of these reports.

A positive change to the Penal Procedure Code reduced the period the prosecutor can hold a suspect from 30 to three days. Significant improvements with respect to pre-trial detention also came into force or were due to in January 2004, including the right to remain silent. These changes were prompted by a European Court of Human Rights judgment delivered in June.

Unlawful use of firearms by the police

The authorities continued to fail to address effectively the use of firearms by law enforcement officers in circumstances that breach international standards. Investigations into almost all of the reported incidents were not impartial, independent and thorough. No official statistics were available, but dozens of people suffered injuries in reported incidents.

▢ In April, in Iaşi, two police officers in plain clothes shot and injured 24-year-old Leonard Drugu and 32-year-old Aurel Gândac, both Roma, who were in the company of three minors. All five were reportedly suspected of a theft from a car. None of the suspects was armed or seriously threatened the lives of the officers or anyone else. The victims told the Resource Centre for Roma Communities, a local human rights organization, that the police officers had not ordered them to halt, nor told them their identity nor fired a warning shot, as the officers claimed. Leonard Drugu was hit in the left leg and Aurel Gândac in the back. After falling to the ground Leonard Drugu was handcuffed and reportedly kicked and beaten by the officers who then took him to hospital. Aurel Gândac was taken to hospital by his wife in a taxi. They were reportedly prevented from entering it by about 50 masked officers who also reportedly beat two Romani women trying to enter the hospital. A doctor eventually took Aurel Gândac into the building. The minors involved in the incident, Florin Lăcustă and Florin Drugu, both aged 13, and Nelu Hristache, aged 12, were taken into custody and reportedly beaten and threatened with guns.

Prison conditions

Poor living conditions, serious overcrowding and lack of activities in some prisons amounted to inhuman and degrading treatment. Medical services throughout the penitentiary system were poor and often inadequate. Detainees allowed to receive medical treatment in hospitals were frequently handcuffed to the bed even though they were under guard. Detainees with physical or mental disabilities faced particular difficulties. In one prison hospital, handcuffs were used to restrain patients with mental health problems. In some prisons detainees were not allowed to speak to their lawyers in private; other prisons did not have facilities where visits could take place.

⬚ According to APADOR-CH (the Romanian Helsinki Committee), in May the Bacău penitentiary with 1,031 beds held 1,604 detainees. Because of overcrowding detainees were allowed on average 30 to 45 minutes in the open air. In one room 30 women shared 18 beds, without any activity. In another room 78 men shared 30 beds. A detainee who had an infected wound on his leg had asked unsuccessfully every day for a week to be taken to the medical room. Another man complained that he had been beaten by five detainees at the instigation of guards and that his complaint had not been investigated.

Domestic violence

In May parliament adopted the Law on Preventing and Combating Domestic Violence. However, regulations for its implementation were not put in place. Partnership for Equality Centre, a local non-governmental organization, published in December a comprehensive study on the effects of domestic violence. Its nationwide survey of 1,806 individuals indicated that approximately one in five women suffer violence from their husbands or partners. Prevailing social attitudes considered domestic violence as "normal".

AI country reports/ visits
Reports
- Romania: Further deaths in custody in suspicious circumstances (AI Index: EUR 39/003/2003)
- Romania: Further reports of unlawful use of firearms by law enforcement officials (AI Index: EUR 39/006/2003)
- Concerns in Europe and Central Asia, January-June 2003: Romania (AI Index: EUR 01/016/2003)
Visit
An AI delegate visited Romania in November to conduct research.

RUSSIAN FEDERATION

RUSSIAN FEDERATION
Head of state: Vladimir Putin
Head of government: Mikhail Kasyanov
Death penalty: abolitionist in practice
UN Women's Convention: ratified
Optional Protocol to UN Women's Convention: signed

Russian security forces continued to enjoy almost total impunity for serious violations of human rights and international humanitarian law committed in the ongoing conflict in the Chechen Republic (Chechnya). Chechen forces loyal to the pro-Moscow administration of Akhmad Kadyrov also committed serious human rights abuses as did Chechen fighters opposed to Russian rule. An increasing number of bomb attacks took place, not only in Chechnya itself, but in other parts of the Russian Federation. There were reports that the military raids which spread so much fear in the civilian population of Chechnya were now taking place in neighbouring Ingushetia, with the participation of Russian federal troops as well as pro-Moscow Chechen security forces. Tens of thousands of internally displaced Chechens remained in Ingushetia and were reportedly subjected to intense pressure from the authorities to return home. Elsewhere in the Russian Federation there were continuing reports of torture and ill-treatment. Conditions in pre-trial detention centres and prisons were often cruel, inhuman and degrading. Members of ethnic minorities faced widespread discrimination. Those responsible for racist attacks were rarely brought to justice. Violence in the home continued to claim the lives of thousands of women.

Background

The elections to the State Duma on 7 December were criticized by international observers as failing to meet international standards. There were allegations of vote rigging, and the state-controlled media heavily favoured the pro-Kremlin United Russia party during the campaign. The Organization for Security and Co-operation in Europe (OSCE) expressed serious concerns regarding the lack of media independence and stated that "considerable pressure was exerted on journalists, which restricted information available to voters." It also criticized some politicians for making racist and xenophobic statements.

On 25 October, business magnate Mikhail Khodorkovskii was arrested on charges of fraud and tax evasion. The Russian human rights community alleged that his case was politically motivated, as Mikhail Khodorkovskii supported political parties that were in opposition to the Kremlin and reportedly considered running for President in 2008.

In March, a new Constitution was approved by referendum in Chechnya amid allegations of voting irregularities. In October, Akhmad Kadyrov was elected president of the Chechen Republic in an election criticized by human rights campaigners and foreign governments.

On 6 June, the State Duma approved a draft decree declaring an amnesty for crimes committed in Chechnya. Critics, including AI, warned that the amnesty decree was seriously flawed.

Chechen conflict

Both Russian armed forces and Chechen fighters continued to commit serious abuses and in some respects the situation deteriorated in the aftermath of the referendum. There were reports that violations committed by federal troops and local police against Chechen civilians had spread across the border to neighbouring Ingushetia where tens of thousands of Chechens had sought refuge.

Violations by federal forces and Chechen police

Large-scale military raids (*zachistki*) appeared to decrease in 2003. However, targeted operations in which specific houses or individuals were singled out by Russian federal troops and pro-Moscow Chechen police were reported. Such operations were routinely accompanied by serious human rights violations, and large numbers of Chechens – particularly men and boys – were killed or "disappeared". Abuses reported included extrajudicial executions, "disappearances" and torture, including rape; such abuses can constitute war crimes.

▭ Rizvan Yaragevich Appazov was detained by Russian federal soldiers in the Vedeno region of Chechnya on 5 May. Russian soldiers stopped the bus in which he was travelling at a military checkpoint near his home village, Elistanzhi. The soldiers began checking passengers' passports. As soon as they found Rizvan Yaragevich Appazov, they stopped their checks and forced him off the bus. He was reportedly taken to a Russian army barracks on the site of a former asphalt factory. His whereabouts remained unknown at the end of the year. No reason was given for his detention. In 2001, Rizvan Yaragevich Appazov's brother had also been detained by Russian federal soldiers as he herded cattle. His fate also remained unknown at the end of 2003.

▭ On 21 May, six people were reportedly killed in an early morning raid on a number of houses in the Kalinovskaya settlement near one of the main military bases in Chechnya. According to eyewitnesses, a group of 15 armed men in camouflage uniforms entered a house where they shot and killed Zura Bitieva; her husband, Ramzan Iduyev; their son, Idris Iduyev; and Zura Bitieva's brother, Abubakar Bitiev. Only a one-year-old child survived the attack. Zura Bitieva had been an outspoken critic of the behaviour of federal troops and had submitted an application to the European Court of Human Rights.

Military raids spread to Ingushetia

About 70,000 internally displaced Chechens remained in Ingushetia, either in tent camps, spontaneous settlements or private homes. The situation continued to be tense. Local and federal authorities put pressure on displaced people to return to Chechnya and there were reports of raids across the border into Ingushetia, where Chechen settlements as well as Ingush villages were targeted. There were reports of arbitrary arrest and detention, ill-treatment and looting during such operations.

▭ On the evening of 10 June, a car carrying three members of the Zabiev family came under heavy fire. They were on their way home from their potato field to Ghalashki village, Ingushetia. Tamara Zabieva, aged 65, was seriously wounded, and her son Ali Zabiev ran for help, leaving his brother, Umar Zabiev, with their mother. When Ali Zabiev returned later with other relatives and representatives of the local police, they managed to find Tamara Zabieva and take her to a hospital, but Umar Zabiev could not be found. Two days later, his body was found; among the injuries he had sustained were fractures, bruises and gunshot wounds. There were reports of evidence suggesting the involvement of federal troops in the attack.

Impunity

Prosecutions for serious human rights violations by federal troops remained few and far between. The majority of investigations appeared to be superficial and inconclusive.

▭ On 25 July, Colonel Yuri Budanov was found guilty of kidnapping and murdering Kheda Kungaeva and sentenced to 10 years' imprisonment. Eighteen-year-old Kheda Kungaeva had been abducted from her home in Chechnya in March 2000. The conviction followed an appeal against a previous decision on 31 December 2002 by the North Caucasus Military Court that Yuri Budanov was not criminally responsible for the murder. He had confessed to killing Kheda Kungaeva, but his lawyers claimed that he did so in a state of "temporary insanity".

Chechnya and the international community

During its January session the Parliamentary Assembly of the Council of Europe (PACE) deplored the climate of impunity in Chechnya.

In January, the European Court of Human Rights registered and declared admissible six cases related to alleged human rights violations in the Chechen Republic.

In a major blow to the protection of human rights in the Russian Federation, a draft resolution on the Chechen Republic was defeated at the UN Commission for Human Rights for the second year in a row.

The two summits between the European Union and Russia on 31 May and 7 November failed to produce any positive developments on the question of human rights in the Chechen Republic.

In June the Russian government authorized the publication of one of the reports of the European Committee for the Prevention of Torture on its visit to the Russian Federation. In July the Committee issued a second public statement highlighting the continued resort to torture and other forms of ill-treatment by members of law enforcement agencies and federal forces and the largely unproductive action taken to bring to justice those responsible. The Committee identified measures which the Russian Federation authorities should take, including a formal statement from the highest political level denouncing ill-treatment by members of the federal forces and law enforcement agencies in the Chechen Republic. The measures had not been implemented by the end of the year.

On 7 November, the UN Human Rights Committee expressed its deep concern about "continuing substantiated reports of human rights violations in the Chechen Republic, including extrajudicial killings, disappearances and torture, including rape".

Akhmed Zakayev

On 13 November, a British court declined the request of the Russian authorities for the extradition of Chechen envoy Akhmed Zakayev on the grounds that his ethnicity and political beliefs made it likely that he would be tortured if returned to the Russian Federation. During the court hearings, experts and witnesses for the defence gave evidence of widespread torture of inmates in Russian pre-trial detention centres and prisons.

Human rights abuses by Chechen fighters

Chechen fighters continued to commit serious human rights abuses. They reportedly targeted civilian members of the pro-Moscow administration, and were allegedly responsible for a number of bombings that caused indiscriminate harm to civilians.

On 14 May, a woman blew herself up in the middle of a crowd of several thousand people attending a Muslim religious celebration in the village of Ilishkan-Yurt, east of Grozny. At least 18 people were killed and 145 wounded. The attack was apparently aimed at the leader of the pro-Moscow Chechen administration, Akhmad Kadyrov. The following week, the leader of a Chechen armed group, Shamil Basaev, claimed responsibility on a website for this and other bombings and warned that more attacks would follow.

Bomb attacks

Bomb attacks took place throughout the Russian Federation with increasing frequency during 2003. They were often indiscriminate and resulted in a large number of civilian casualties. Such attacks included a car bomb explosion in Znamenskoye, Chechnya, in May; two suicide bomb attacks at the Tushino airfield rock concert in Moscow in July; a car bomb blast at the military hospital in Mozdok, Republic of Dagestan, in August; and an explosion on a commuter train near Yessentuki, Stavropol Territory, in December. It was alleged that these attacks were related to the conflict in Chechnya.

Racially and ethnically motivated discrimination and violence

As part of its worldwide campaign against human rights abuses in the Russian Federation, AI continued to highlight abuses faced by members of ethnic minorities. These included arbitrary detention and ill-treatment; the denial of citizenship, and therefore associated rights and benefits, on grounds of race; and racist attacks against asylum-seekers and refugees.

Thousands of Meskhetians living in Krasnodar Territory continued to be refused Russian citizenship on grounds of ethnicity. Meskhetians, most of whom are Muslims, were forcibly relocated from southwest Georgia in 1944 by the former Soviet regime. As Soviet citizens residing in the Russian Federation at the time the Law of Citizenship came into force in 1992, they are entitled to Russian Federation citizenship. The result of the authorities' failure to enforce this right was discrimination in almost every aspect of daily life including education, employment and health care.

Ethnically motivated violence

Racist attacks were widespread, although many were not reported to the police. Victims feared further abuse and police generally failed to pursue allegations of racist violence adequately.

Atish Ramgoolam, an 18-year-old medical student from Mauritius, died in February from injuries sustained during a vicious assault by a group of young "skinheads" in St Petersburg. His death shocked and frightened the hundreds of other foreign students at the Mechnikov Medical Academy who were routinely subjected to racist abuse by local youths. Prior to the attack on Atish Ramgoolam, the authorities had reportedly failed to address allegations of such abuse. Three youths were arrested in connection with the killing.

On 8 April a group of between 10 and 15 young men were reported to have viciously attacked Kelvin Benson Sinkala, a student from Zambia, in the city of Vladimir. He received a large number of stab wounds and spent two and a half weeks in hospital. On the day of the attack, three suspects were arrested, but they were subsequently released.

The anniversary of the birth of Adolf Hitler was again marked by an escalation of racially motivated harassment and violence in a number of Russian cities, although levels were down on previous years.

On 25 April a group of 50-60 youths, some of them reportedly armed with chains, knuckle-dusters and other weapons, carried out a series of racially motivated attacks in Krasnodar Territory. They attacked nightclubs in the villages of Kholmskii and Akhtyrskii where they singled out people who appeared to originate from the Caucasus. Some of the victims were beaten unconscious. In total, 30 people were reported to have been injured during the attacks and six were hospitalized. Following pressure from AI and local non-governmental organizations, news of the incident reached the national press, and on 29 April a criminal investigation was opened into the Kholmskii attack. The investigation was continuing at the end of the year.

Human rights defenders

The School of Peace, a prominent Russian non-governmental organization, was threatened with imminent closure by the authorities of Krasnodar Territory in August as a result of its activities in defence of ethnic minority rights. In recent years the School of

Peace has come under considerable pressure from the authorities to stop its campaigning on behalf of the Meskhetian minority. Three other non-governmental organizations in Krasnodar Territory were also subjected to harassment from the regional authorities and through the state-controlled media.

Parliamentarian assassinated

Member of Parliament Sergei Yushenkov was shot dead in April. He had been an outspoken opponent of both conflicts in Chechnya and had consistently demanded an independent investigation into the apartment bombings in September 1999 that served as one of the grounds for Russian Federation forces to re-enter Chechnya. He was the 10th Russian parliamentarian to be murdered during the past decade; none of the murders had been solved by the end of 2003.

Torture and ill-treatment

The use of torture and ill-treatment by police to extract confessions from detainees was virtually routine. The failure to investigate allegations of torture thoroughly and to bring the perpetrators to justice contributed to a climate of impunity.

On 27 January the official investigation into the alleged torture and ill-treatment of Andrei Osenchugov and Aleksei Shishkin, two 17-year-old youths serving eight-year sentences for robbery, was closed. Both alleged that they were tortured while in pre-trial detention in early 2002. Although there was evidence that the teenagers were ill-treated by officers at the pre-trial detention centre, the case was closed because both boys withdrew their statements. Andrei Osenchugov and Aleksei Shishkin were reportedly both put under severe pressure by prison staff to retract their accusations. Following international pressure from AI and other human rights groups, the investigation was reportedly reopened in August 2003. At around the same time, AI received information that the teenagers were being intimidated in order to force the closure of the case.

Although the overall number of prisoners in the Russian Federation decreased in 2003, prisons continued to be overcrowded, creating conditions which facilitated the spread of HIV/AIDS, tuberculosis and other infectious diseases. Conditions in many pre-trial detention facilities were so poor that they amounted to cruel, inhuman or degrading treatment.

Conditions for prisoners serving life sentences remained so harsh that they amounted to cruel, inhuman or degrading treatment or punishment, and in some cases possibly torture. Every aspect of their imprisonment was designed to ensure their isolation from the outside world and other prisoners. Parliamentarians and human rights activists described some of these prison colonies as needlessly restrictive and others as downright humiliating.

Violence against women

Violence in the home continued to claim the lives of thousands of women and to result in serious injuries to tens of thousands more. Perpetrators were rarely brought to justice, in part as a result of the reluctance of the police to intervene in what they perceived as a private matter. The fact that the Russian Federation had no law specifically addressing domestic violence further reinforced this tendency. In some regions improvements were reported following initiatives by local women's organizations to establish cooperation with local government structures.

In the armed conflict in the Chechen Republic women continued to suffer a wide range of abuses.

Every year, thousands of Russian women are reportedly trafficked to as many as 50 countries around the world for the purpose of sexual exploitation. Insufficient legislation makes it difficult to prosecute traffickers effectively. The Russian government acknowledged this problem and the State Duma was working on a draft law on trafficking at the end of the year.

Prisoner of conscience released

Journalist and environmentalist Grigory Pasko was released on parole in January. He had been sentenced in December 2001 to four years' imprisonment on charges of misuse of office. While welcoming his release, AI continued to insist that his conviction must be quashed. Grigory Pasko had filmed a Russian navy tanker dumping radioactive waste and ammunition into the Sea of Japan. He also reported on corruption in the navy. A decision by the European Court of Human Rights on Grigory Pasko's case was not expected until 2005.

AI country reports/visits
Reports

- "*Dokumenty!*" Discrimination on grounds of race in the Russian Federation (AI Index: EUR 46/001/2003)
- Russian Federation: Amnesty International is concerned about the climate of impunity prevailing in the Russian judicial system (AI Index: EUR 46/002/2003)
- Russian Federation: Open Letter from a coalition of non-governmental organizations to Vladimir Vladimirovich Putin, President of the Russian Federation (AI Index: EUR 46/051/2003)
- Russian Federation: Violence against women – time to act! Joint Public Statement with the Russian Association of Crisis Centres "Stop Violence" (AI Index: EUR 46/019/2003)
- Rough Justice: The law and human rights in the Russian Federation (AI Index: EUR 46/054/2003)
- Russian Federation: "School of Peace", non-governmental minority rights organization (AI Index: EUR 46/069/2003)

Visits

AI delegates visited the Russian Federation in January, March, April, May, September, October and December. Two reports were launched in Moscow – on 19 March and 2 October respectively – as part of AI's worldwide campaign on human rights in the Russian Federation.

SERBIA AND MONTENEGRO

SERBIA AND MONTENEGRO (UNTIL FEBRUARY, FEDERAL REPUBLIC OF YUGOSLAVIA)
Head of state: Svetozar Marović (replaced Vojislav Koštunica in March)
Head of government: Zoran Živković (Serbia, replaced Zoran Đinđić in March), Milo Đjukanović (Montenegro)
Death penalty: abolitionist for all crimes
UN Women's Convention and its Optional Protocol: ratified

War crimes trials started in some cases, but impunity for war crimes and other crimes against humanity continued. There were continuing allegations of torture and ill-treatment by security officials. The trafficking of women and girls for forced sexual exploitation continued. Domestic violence against women remained widespread. Roma continued to suffer racist attacks and discrimination. In Kosovo, attacks on minorities and returnees persisted, deterring the return of refugees and people internally displaced from their homes, and witnesses in war crimes trials were intimidated and even killed.

Background
Following an agreement in November 2002 on a new Constitutional Charter and acceptance by the respective parliaments, the name of the country was changed in February from the Federal Republic of Yugoslavia (FRY) to Serbia and Montenegro (SCG). The constituent republics became semi-independent states running their own economies, currencies and customs systems. The joint entity controlled defence, foreign policy and UN membership, and was responsible for human and minority rights. The agreement allowed either republic to secede after three years.

In April, SCG joined the Council of Europe and signed the European Convention for the Protection of Human Rights and Fundamental Freedoms.

The UN Mission in Kosovo (UNMIK) continued to administer Kosovo. The Special Representative of the UN Secretary-General held governmental powers. In August, Harri Holkeri took over the post from Michael Steiner who left office in June. In October the first talks between the Serbian government and Kosovo Albanian leaders on the future of Kosovo took place in Vienna.

Legal developments
In April the Serbian Assembly approved amendments to the Law on Organization and Jurisdiction of Government Authorities in Suppression of Organized Crime, some of which clearly breached international human rights standards. The amendments allowed the Interior Ministry to order detention of up to 60 days

without judicial authorization. In June the Constitutional Court of Serbia ruled such amendments unconstitutional and suspended them.

In April the widely criticized Law on Cooperation with the International Criminal Tribunal for the former Yugoslavia (Tribunal) was amended to allow immediate extradition of indicted suspects. Before the repeal of Article 39, suspects could be transferred to the Tribunal only if they had already been indicted when the law entered into force.

In May the Serbian Assembly passed a law prohibiting individuals who had violated human rights from holding public office. However, no one subsequently seemed to be removed from office.

In July, Montenegro adopted a law creating an Ombudsperson's Office.

In August, SCG enacted legislation to provide a civilian alternative to military service. It took effect in October.

State of emergency
In March, Prime Minister of Serbia Zoran Đinđić was assassinated. The government declared a state of emergency. Under emergency legislation in force until 22 April, the Ministry of the Interior had powers to detain people incommunicado for up to 30 days. Thousands were arrested, including serving or former high state officials, in "Operation Sabre", a clampdown on organized crime elements suspected of the assassination.

The authorities claimed to have solved a number of murders and "disappearances", including that of former Serbian President Ivan Stambolić who was extrajudicially executed and buried in a pre-dug lime pit after "disappearing" in August 2000. Murder charges were filed against former Yugoslav President Slobodan Milošević and others, including members of a special police force said to have carried out the kidnapping and killing.

War crimes
The trial of Slobodan Milošević, accused of responsibility for war crimes committed in Croatia, Bosnia-Herzegovina and Kosovo, continued before the Tribunal. Witnesses testified that his government controlled Serb "paramilitaries" responsible for atrocities. In August former Vice-Admiral Miodrag Jokić pleaded guilty to war crimes in connection with events in Dubrovnik in Croatia in 1991, and in December the trial began of similarly accused former General Pavle Strugar.

A number of suspects were transferred to the Tribunal. Former Serbian President Milan Milutinović, who had enjoyed immunity while in office, voluntarily went before the Tribunal in January to face charges of crimes against humanity in Kosovo. Vojislav Šešelj, leader of the Serbian Radical Party, was indicted in February for crimes against humanity in connection with events in Croatia, Bosnia-Herzegovina and the Vojvodina, and flown to the Tribunal.

However, the Tribunal Prosecutor complained that in some cases official documents were not made available or those indicted remained at large in Serbia. In October, Serbian Deputy Interior Minister and former Kosovo police chief Sreten Lukić, former FRY army chief Nebojša Pavković and two other generals were indicted for war crimes and crimes against humanity in Kosovo, but the Serbian authorities refused to transfer them.

In February the International Court of Justice in the Hague agreed to hear a case brought by Bosnia-Herzegovina against SCG for genocide and aggression in connection with the 1992-95 war.

Domestic war crimes trials

Of four domestic war crimes trials in 2003, three were completed in the year.

▢ In September, Dragutin Dragićević, a Bosnian Serb, and Djordje Sević were sentenced to 20 and 15 years' imprisonment respectively for the abduction and murder in October 1992 of 17 Muslims, 16 of them taken from a bus in Bosnia-Herzegovina. Milan Lukić and Oliver Krsmanović, also Bosnian Serbs, received 20-year sentences *in absentia*.

▢ In October the Supreme Military Court sentenced Major Dragiša Petrović and reservist Nenad Stamenković to nine and seven years' imprisonment respectively for killing an elderly Albanian couple in Kosovo in 1999.

In May the Tribunal transferred the case concerning a massacre near Vukovar in Croatia in 1991 to Serbian courts — the first such transferral — while retaining jurisdiction over the three main accused. In June, Serbia and Croatia agreed that each would try its own nationals for war crimes. In July, Serbia approved legislation authorizing a special war crimes prosecutor, and in October opened a special war crimes court.

Exhumations and returns

In June and July, 65 bodies previously found in a mass grave in Serbia were returned to Kosovo. This brought to 110 the total repatriated out of about 850 bodies of ethnic Albanians from Kosovo exhumed from mass graves in Serbia. No suspects were indicted.

Trafficking in women and girls

Women and girls continued to be trafficked in and through SCG for the purposes of forced prostitution. Anti-trafficking legislation was passed by Serbia in April and subsequently 75 criminal charges were filed under the new legislation but no trials completed. There was concern that victims of forced trafficking in Montenegro were being failed by the judicial system.

▢ In May a high-profile trial of the Montenegrin deputy state prosecutor and three other men for involvement in sex slavery collapsed. The authorities agreed to an investigation by the Organization for Security and Co-operation in Europe (OSCE) and the Council of Europe, which in September submitted a report highly critical of the authorities' handling of the case.

Domestic violence

Domestic violence against women remained widespread but prosecutions were rare. In March a poll of 500 married women in Montenegro reported that one in four was beaten and one in three slapped by their husbands.

Police abuses and impunity

Torture and ill-treatment by police officers continued to be widespread, especially in connection with "Operation Sabre".

▢ Goran Petrović and Igor Gajić, arrested in Kruševac in Serbia on 14 March and detained incommunicado until 13 May, were allegedly tortured to extract confessions of extortion. Officers reportedly taped bags over their heads and severely beat them both, and doused Igor Galić with water before subjecting him to electric shocks.

▢ In June, three police officers in Pljevlja in Montenegro were alleged to have tortured Admir Durutlić, Dragoljub Džuver, Jovo Ćosović and Mirko Gazdić in an attempt to force them to confess to dealing in narcotics. They were reported to have hit and kicked Admir Durutlić, including in the genitals, knocked him to the ground and shoved his head down the toilet, and hit Dragoljub Džuver repeatedly in the stomach and ribs. The four men were detained overnight at the police station where all were allegedly beaten. After their release, medical examination found they had numerous bruises and welts.

Roma

Widespread discrimination against Roma continued. A memorandum in April by the European Roma Rights Center, an international non-governmental organization, and the UN High Commissioner for Human Rights, reported discrimination in almost every aspect of life. The authorities appeared to afford little protection against attacks on Roma by racist groups. In February an attack by groups of youths armed with baseball bats on Roma in a settlement in Belgrade reportedly met no official response.

In May an unofficial Roma site in Belgrade was destroyed and its inhabitants — some 250 mostly Kosovo Roma, the majority children — forcibly evicted without provision for alternative housing.

Kosovo (Kosova)
War crimes

Arrests and trials continued of ethnic Albanians accused of war crimes.

▢ In January the Tribunal secretly indicted four former Kosovo Liberation Army (KLA) members including Fatmir Limaj, a senior aide to leading Kosovo politician Hashim Thaci. The indictment was for crimes against humanity and violations of the laws or customs of war in connection with the murder and torture in 1998 of Serbs and of Kosovo Albanians perceived as Serb collaborators. It was made public after three of the accused were arrested in February and transferred to the Hague.

▢ In July former KLA commander Rustem Mustafa and three others were convicted in Priština (Prishtinë) of war crimes connected with the illegal confinement, torture and murder of suspected ethnic Albanian "collaborators". They received sentences of up to 17 years' imprisonment.

The arrests, transferrals and trials provoked mass protests by tens of thousands of Kosovo Albanians, who regarded the detainees as "freedom fighters", and attacks on UNMIK vehicles and property.

Trials and retrials continued of Serbs previously convicted of war crimes or genocide by panels with a majority of ethnic Albanian judges.

Witnesses killed and intimidated
In January gunmen murdered Tahir Zemaj in his car, along with his son and cousin. He was a key witness in the trial of four former KLA members – one of them the brother of a leading politician – who were convicted in December 2002 for unlawful detention and murder. In April gunmen shot dead another witness, Ilir Selmanaj, and a relative. In September the Tribunal's chief prosecutor said that witnesses in KLA trials had been too intimidated to testify.

'Disappearances' and abduction
There was limited progress in identifying those who had "disappeared" or been abducted. Further exhumations of burial sites took place. In March the International Commission for Missing Persons announced that DNA analysis had identified 209 bodies. In May, UNMIK announced the formation of a special police unit to investigate the hundreds and possibly thousands of unsolved killings in 1999 and 2000.

Minorities and returns
Attacks against minorities and their properties continued. In January the NATO-led peace-keeping Kosovo Force (KFOR) reversed a decision from late 2002 and reinstated protection for Orthodox churches and monasteries against attacks by ethnic Albanians. In October the UN Security Council reported a deterioration in the security situation as minorities were victims of shootings and grenade and bomb attacks. Few of the internally displaced or refugees returned. In September UNMIK reported that 1,000 Serbs, out of the 180,000 who had fled since the 1999 war, had returned since January.

▢ In June a Serb family – 80-year-old Slobodan Stolić, his 78-year-old wife Radmila and 55-year-old son Ljubinko – were brutally murdered in Obilić (Obiliq) and their house was burned in an apparently racist attack aimed at driving out remaining Serbs in the area.

Trafficking in women and girls
The trafficking of women and girls for forced prostitution remained widespread in and through Kosovo, despite measures by UNMIK. In October, UNMIK announced that, since its formation in October 2000, the Police Trafficking and Prostitution Unit had made over 2,000 raids, rescued 300 trafficked victims and brought 140 charges.

▢ In June UNMIK police arrested three Kosovo Albanians and a Pakistani member of the international civilian police force (CIVPOL) whose immunity from prosecution – granted to all UNMIK personnel – was waived. The three Kosovars were charged with obscene behaviour, rape and other sex crimes, and neglecting and injuring minors. The CIVPOL officer was charged with obscene behaviour and failure to perform official duties.

AI country reports/ visits
Reports
- Federal Republic of Yugoslavia (Serbia and Montenegro): Continuing police torture and ill-treatment (AI Index: EUR 70/001/2003)
- Serbia and Montenegro (Kosovo/Kosova): "Prisoners in our own homes" – Amnesty International's concerns for the human rights of minorities in Kosovo/Kosova (AI Index: EUR 70/010/2003)
- Serbia and Montenegro: Alleged torture during "Operation Sabre" (AI Index: EUR 70/019/2003)

Visits
AI delegates visited Serbia and Montenegro in July, November and December, and Kosovo from January to March, and in September and October.

SLOVAKIA

SLOVAK REPUBLIC
Head of state: Rudolf Schuster
Head of government: Mikuláš Dzurinda
Death penalty: abolitionist for all crimes
UN Women's Convention and its Optional Protocol: ratified

An investigation into reports that Romani women had been illegally sterilized was not independent and impartial. Many of the victims were subjected to harassment and intimidation. There were reports that the police ill-treated members of the Roma community in custody. People with mental disabilities in psychiatric hospitals and social care homes were restrained in "cage beds".

Alleged illegal sterilization
Allegations of illegal, and in some cases forcible, sterilization of Romani women were brought to public notice in a report in January by two non-governmental organizations (NGOs), the US-based Center for Reproductive Rights and *Poradna pre obcianske a lucske prava*, Center for Civil and Human Rights. Pál Csáky, Deputy Prime Minister responsible for Human and Minority Rights, initiated a criminal investigation but also threatened the report's authors with prosecution for "spreading false rumours" or, should the allegations prove true, failing to report a criminal offence.

The criminal investigation did not comply with international standards. In February, 21 Romani women were taken from their homes without prior warning, for questioning at the police station in Krompachy. The names of 19 of them had apparently been given to the police by the Krompachy hospital. Most were not aware of their right not to comply with an orally presented summons. Some thought they were criminal suspects. The police conduct was perceived as threatening and degrading, and questioning by male police officers demonstrated insensitivity. At least two women who claimed that they had been forcibly sterilized said that officers threatened them and implied that they were induced to make the claim by promises of financial and other gain. The women were reportedly advised to sign criminal complaints of genocide, without advice on the significance of this charge, and told that they could be imprisoned for up to three years for "false accusation" if their complaint proved untrue. After a new investigative team was put in place, some victims were still questioned without prior notice or summons and threatened with prosecution.

Police investigators examined only the existence and authenticity of the women's signatures on the consent forms and whether the sterilization had been medically necessary according to Slovak professional standards. They did not ask whether the women had freely requested sterilization, received appropriate counselling about its risks and irreversibility, understood the information provided, or were given appropriate time to consider the information and include others in the decision. According to international human rights and professional standards, a signature alone is not sufficient evidence of full and informed consent, and sterilization should never be carried out without that consent.

In October the Deputy Prime Minister stated that the investigation had been closed for lack of evidence of any crime, noting also that there would be changes in regulations concerning certain medical procedures. The Council of Europe's Commissioner for Human Rights, in a report in October, concluded that "it can reasonably be assumed that sterilizations have taken place, particularly in eastern Slovakia, without informed consent". He recommended that the government accept its responsibilities, offer swift and just redress to the victims, and enact new legislation on patients' consent to medical procedures and right of access to their medical files.

Cage beds as a method of restraint
Cage beds were still in use as a method of restraint in psychiatric hospitals and a number of social care homes for people with mental disabilities, according to a report in June by a regional NGO, the Mental Disability Advocacy Center. This method of restraint is cruel, inhuman and degrading, and violates international law and best professional practice. Cage beds appeared to remain widely in use despite recommendations to discontinue them by the European Committee for the Prevention of Torture, which described such confinement as "execrable" after a visit to Slovakia in 2000.

Discrimination against Roma
Government efforts failed to have a significant impact in reducing widespread prejudice and discrimination against the Roma. Measures aimed at improving their access to employment, health care, housing and education were largely ineffective. A Council of Europe study noted that the mortality rate among Romani children in eastern Slovakia was three times higher than the country's average and that Romani women in general died 17 years earlier than other women in Slovakia.

The ruling coalition failed to agree comprehensive anti-discrimination legislation, reportedly because of opposition within the Christian Democratic Party to equal rights regardless of sexual identity.

In April the Slovak police said that 109 cases of racially and ethnically motivated crimes reported in 2002 were more than double the number of reported cases in 2001, attributing the rise to greater police awareness of racially motivated offences.

The official investigations into allegations that police officers ill-treated Roma in a number of instances were not independent and impartial as required by international law.

◻ In May, three police officers stopped Juroslav Cipkes for an identity check in the town of Jelsava. After being handcuffed for allegedly raising his voice, he was reportedly beaten severely at the police station, lost consciousness and needed hospital treatment. In August the League of Human Rights Advocates, a local NGO, filed a complaint with the General Prosecutor, who initiated an investigation.

UN Human Rights Committee review
In August the Human Rights Committee, reviewing Slovakia's compliance with the International Covenant on Civil and Political Rights, expressed concern at reports of high rates of domestic violence. The Committee noted positive legislative measures and recommended the establishment of "crisis centre hotlines and victim support centres equipped with medical, psychological, legal and emotional support". The Committee also expressed concern about the persistent allegations of ill-treatment during police investigations, particularly of the Roma minority, reports of forcible sterilization of Romani women and the continued use of cage beds as a measure of restraint in social care homes and psychiatric institutions.

AI country reports/ visits
Reports
- Slovakia: Failing to ensure an impartial and thorough investigation into allegations of illegal sterilization of Romani women (AI Index: EUR 72/002/2003)
- Concerns in Europe and Central Asia, January-June 2003: Slovakia (AI Index: EUR 01/016/2003)

SLOVENIA

REPUBLIC OF SLOVENIA
Head of state: Janez Drnovšek
Head of government: Anton Rop
Death penalty: abolitionist for all crimes
UN Women's Convention: ratified
Optional Protocol to UN Women's Convention: signed

In May the UN Committee against Torture examined a report by the Slovenian authorities on the measures taken to give effect to the rights enshrined in the UN Convention against Torture. Before the examination of this report AI submitted a briefing to the Committee, highlighting in particular Slovenia's failure to establish an independent mechanism to address complaints of ill-treatment brought against the police.

Ill-treatment and excessive force
In its briefing to the Committee, AI documented reports of ill-treatment and excessive force by police officers.
◻ AI reported the assault on a 23-year-old man in Šentjur-pri-Celju in November 2002 by a police officer who reportedly kicked him to the ground and jumped on his back with such force that he broke his collarbone. The man's 19-year-old girlfriend was also reportedly beaten and threatened at the police station.

Members of ethnic and racial minorities, often children, were targeted for ill-treatment, which usually occurred during routine police arrests and detentions. Police detainees were frequently denied their rights to call their family or a lawyer, or to receive medical assistance.

Failures of investigation
AI reported on the failure to investigate promptly and impartially all allegations of ill-treatment as required under the Convention against Torture and Slovenian domestic law. In virtually every case, this was despite formal complaints lodged with the relevant police station or local public prosecutor. Even where victims provided medical evidence of their injuries, their complaints were rejected after apparently summary investigations. The mechanism for investigating complaints of police misconduct did not meet international standards of independence and effectiveness. The authorities also failed to ensure that victims of torture and ill-treatment obtained redress and had the right to fair and adequate compensation.
◻ In its briefing, AI reported the case of a 36-year-old man who died during a house search in Ljubljana in early 2000, allegedly after ill-treatment by special police officers who also refused him timely access to vital medical equipment. More than three years later, a thorough and impartial investigation had still not been initiated.

The Slovenian authorities have repeatedly failed to publish or make accessible up-to-date data on the total number of complaints of ill-treatment against the police and other law enforcement officials, the number of complaints that result in disciplinary or criminal proceedings, and the outcome of such proceedings.

UN Committee against Torture recommendations
In May the Committee against Torture examined Slovenia's second periodic report on measures taken to implement the Convention against Torture. The Committee recommended that Slovenia establish an "effective, reliable and independent complaints system to undertake prompt and impartial investigations into allegations of ill-treatment or torture by police and other public officials and to punish the offenders". It also urged Slovenia to introduce a broad definition of torture as required under the Convention against Torture, an outstanding obligation since May 2000 when the Committee examined Slovenia's initial report. Slovenia was requested to repeal the statute of limitation for torture, to increase the limitation period for other types of ill-treatment and to provide up-to-date statistics on cases of ill-treatment.

AI country reports/ visits
Reports
- Republic of Slovenia before the UN Committee against Torture (AI Index: EUR 68/003/2003)
- Open letter to the Prime Minister of Slovenia urging rejection of the impunity agreement with the USA concerning the International Criminal Court (AI Index: EUR 68/004/2003)
- Concerns in Europe and Central Asia, January-June 2003: Slovenia (AI Index: EUR 01/016/2003)

SPAIN

KINGDOM OF SPAIN
Head of state: King Juan Carlos I de Borbón
Head of government: José María Aznar López
Death penalty: abolitionist for all crimes
UN Women's Convention and its Optional Protocol: ratified

A constitutional crisis loomed between the Basque autonomous and Spanish governments. The armed Basque group *Euskadi Ta Askatasuna* (ETA), Basque Homeland and Freedom, carried out shootings and bombings, some of them fatal. There were a number of apparently reckless shootings by Civil Guard or police officers. Many immigrants drowned attempting to reach Spain by sea from North Africa. Detainees made allegations of torture and ill-treatment. The European Committee for the Prevention of Torture and Inhuman and Degrading Treatment or Punishment (CPT) was strongly critical of the continuing lack of fundamental safeguards against ill-treatment of detainees held under "anti-terrorist" legislation. However, a new law more than doubled the maximum period that suspects could be held incommunicado. The government continued to categorically deny the existence of torture. Unaccompanied foreign children aged 16 or over faced expulsion in circumstances that could contravene international law. There were continuing allegations of ill-treatment or cruel, inhuman and degrading treatment in reception centres for children. Almost 100 women were killed in incidents of gender-based violence.

Crisis in the Basque Country

A number of incidents, mainly related to the Basque Country, increased the threats to freedom of expression and assembly. The fatal shooting by ETA of a Socialist Party activist, Joseba Pagazaurtundua, in the run-up to the municipal elections in February, was a clear attack on such freedoms and the right to life. Continuing tensions during the elections resulted in part from the annulment of 249 candidate lists by the government and the public prosecutor, on the grounds that they contained candidates linked to ETA and the Basque nationalist coalition, *Batasuna*. The latter was formally banned in March, because of alleged integral links to ETA that *Batasuna* members have always denied. The Basque parliamentary grouping *Sozialista Abertzaleak* (SA) was also declared illegal by the Supreme Court on the grounds that it served the interests of *Batasuna* in Parliament. The Spanish government accused the Basque Nationalist Party (PNV) of "sponsoring" ETA.

In February a National Court judge ordered the precautionary closure of the only entirely Basque language newspaper, *Euskaldunon Egunkaria*, and the detention of 10 people associated with the newspaper under "anti-terrorist" legislation – a move which appeared to have injurious consequences for the right to freedom of expression.

Throughout the year there was confusion about the legitimacy of political demonstrations and concern about attempts to stifle the expression of nationalist sentiments on the grounds that these were synonymous with support for armed groups such as ETA. Tension between the Basque and Spanish authorities rose steadily after the Basque Parliament failed, for various reasons, to dissolve SA. A new plan for Basque self-determination, launched by the Basque President (the *Lehendakari*), was described by the Spanish authorities as a deliberate attack on the sovereignty of the Spanish people and was challenged by them in the courts.

ETA killings

ETA attempted to stifle freedom of expression with shootings, bombings and campaigns of intimidation, including of civilians.

▭ Joseba Pagazaurtundea was shot dead in February. He was a member of the *Basta Ya* movement, which is vigorously critical of ETA violence, and a former member of the ETA *Politico-Militar* wing. He was on sick leave from his post as commander of the Municipal Police of Andoain following persistent death threats.

▭ In July at least 13 people, including tourists, were injured in bomb explosions in the resorts of Alicante and Benidorm.

Torture allegations

Detainees held incommunicado, mainly ETA suspects, said they were tortured or ill-treated by Civil Guards or police officers.

▭ In November the European Court of Human Rights set out the details of a case it was examining of 15 Catalans suspected of being sympathizers of a Catalan independence movement. The Catalans alleged they had been subjected to physical and mental torture and inhuman and degrading treatment on their arrest and in custody in Catalonia and at the Civil Guard headquarters in Madrid in mid-1992.

▭ In February, following the closure of *Euskaldunon Egunkaria*, a group of directors and journalists were arrested and held incommunicado. After being released, Martxelo Otamendi Egiguren and several fellow detainees said they had been tortured by asphyxiation with a plastic bag (*bolsa*), exhausting physical exercises, threats and simulated execution. The government lodged a complaint against them with the National Court, accusing them of "collaborating with an armed band [ETA]" by making torture claims as part of an ETA-inspired strategy to undermine democratic institutions. AI responded that the best way to guard against false complaints was to introduce greater safeguards and was concerned that the government's reaction, before thorough examination of the detainees' accusations, risked fostering a climate of impunity in which detainees or prisoners were afraid to report torture or ill-treatment. No reply was received to AI appeals for a thorough investigation of the journalists' complaints, irrespective of whether formal complaints had been lodged with the courts.

Impasse on torture

In March the European Committee for the Prevention of Torture and Inhuman or Degrading Treatment or Punishment (CPT) published the findings of a visit in July 2001. The report criticized the failure of the authorities, despite earlier reassurances, to implement previous CPT recommendations. These included the right of access to lawyers at the outset of detention for suspects held under "anti-terrorist" legislation. The CPT called for concrete action to implement two other fundamental safeguards – the right to communicate the fact of detention to a third party and the right to medical examination by a doctor of choice as well as by an officially appointed doctor. It also urged the creation of a fully independent investigating agency to process complaints against law enforcement agencies. It reminded Spain of its obligations to cooperate with the CPT, stating that "the current impasse... on a subject as important as the safeguards against ill-treatment... cannot be allowed to continue".

However, far from examining how to implement long-standing recommendations by the CPT and other international bodies to strengthen safeguards for detainees, the authorities more than doubled the maximum period for which certain people could be held incommunicado. In October a reform of the Code of Criminal Procedure with regard to provisional imprisonment entered into force. It allowed a suspect to be held incommunicado for a total of 13 days: a maximum of five days in police or Civil Guard custody, followed by a further eight days in prison if ordered by a judge.

In November the Spanish parliament approved a reform of the Penal Code that widened the definition of torture to include among the motives of torture "discrimination of any kind".

Reckless shootings

There were reports of reckless shootings by Civil Guards in response to stone-throwing incidents in frontier areas between Spain and Morocco. The shootings had fatal consequences in at least one case and resulted in severe injuries to Moroccan nationals in others. Over 200 stoning incidents were reported, in which Civil Guards also sustained injuries. AI expressed concern in November at the number of reportedly "accidental" shootings in the last two years and underlined the dangers of firing warning shots in the air.

▱ In July an inquiry was opened into the case of a Civil Guard officer who was filmed firing with apparent recklessness at several Moroccans attempting to reach the beach in the autonomous city of Ceuta.

▱ In October a Civil Guard officer reportedly shot dead Moroccan national Mustafa Labrach, one of a group suspected of attempting to smuggle goods to Morocco from Ceuta. According to disputed reports, a Civil Guard patrol, which had come under a hail of stones at the frontier fence, at first responded with anti-riot equipment. One officer then fired a warning shot in the air, but slipped on the wet and rocky ground and fatally shot Mustafa Labrach in the mouth. An internal investigation was opened, followed by a judicial investigation after initial uncertainties over judicial competence, because the death had occurred in "No man's land" between national borders.

Racism

In July the European Commission against Racism and Intolerance (ECRI) published a report on the steps taken by Spain towards combating racism and intolerance. The report noted that racism and xenophobia persisted and that there was widespread use in public debate of arguments and imagery that created a negative climate around immigration and immigrants. Racism particularly concerned non-EU nationals and Roma. ECRI commented that the racist dimension of offences tended to be overlooked, and stressed the urgent need for improvement of control mechanisms in complaints of race-related ill-treatment against law enforcement officers.

Immigrant drownings

Thousands of immigrants risked the sea crossing from Morocco, including an increased proportion of unaccompanied children. New arrivals faced a serious lack of resources and infrastructure for receiving or detaining them. Over 150 immigrants drowned before reaching Spanish shores. The national Ombudsperson opened an investigation into the drowning of 36 undocumented immigrants when their boat sank in the Bay of Cádiz within close proximity of the US-Spanish naval base at Rota. There were allegations that the base had ignored a warning that the boat was in danger and that the authorities had shown negligence by taking an unreasonably long time to launch a rescue bid.

Expulsions and ill-treatment of children

In October the Attorney General issued an instruction establishing criteria for the expulsion of unaccompanied foreign children aged 16 or over. The guidelines did not provide for examination of each case on an individual basis and appeared to violate the UN Convention on the Rights of the Child as well as Spain's own laws on protection of minors and on discrimination.

The authorities failed to meet their obligation to abide by international standards on the care and protection of unaccompanied children. Allegations were made of ill-treatment or inhuman and degrading conditions in reception centres for children.

▱ Ill-treatment, overcrowding, abusive distribution of sedatives, lack of supervision and racist attitudes were reported in the secure reception centre in Gáldar, Gran Canaria. In July, four prosecutors attached to the juvenile section of the High Court of Canarias claimed that the 42 children held there were receiving "humiliating" treatment. In one case an African child had allegedly been beaten and held naked and in chains for a whole night by one of the centre's teachers.

'Disappearances'

The UN Working Group on Enforced or Involuntary Disappearances added Spain to its list of countries where people "disappeared". It was concerned about the period under the government of General Franco (1939-75) and asked the government to investigate two cases dating from after 1945, the date of the UN's foundation. Efforts continued to locate the bodies of some of the thousands shot during or after the 1936-39 Civil War. However, families continued to suffer difficulties in their search for lost relatives, owing to lack of funds or of a common and internationally recognized policy for locating, accessing and exhuming the burial sites.

Violence against women

According to official figures, 98 women were killed as a result of gender-based violence: 72 at the hands of partners, 10 by other relatives, and 16 in other incidents of violence directed particularly at women, including rape or trafficking for prostitution. Although judges were accorded greater powers to accelerate complaints procedures and increase sentences, some courts continued to show a disturbing lack of due diligence with regard to victims.

◻ In September the General Council of the Judiciary opened an investigation into the conduct of a Barcelona judge who had allegedly ignored 13 attempts by Ana María Fábregas to lodge a complaint against her husband for violence. She was killed with a hammer on the doorstep of her house in June.

AI country reports/ visits
Report
- Concerns in Europe and Central Asia, January-June 2003: Spain (AI Index: EUR 01/016/2003)

SWEDEN

KINGDOM OF SWEDEN
Head of state: King Carl XVI Gustaf
Head of government: Göran Persson
Death penalty: abolitionist for all crimes
UN Women's Convention and its Optional Protocol: ratified

International monitoring bodies expressed concern about some aspects of Sweden's human rights record. The Gothenburg Committee published its investigation report into the policing of two events in 2001.

International scrutiny

A delegation of the European Committee for the Prevention of Torture and Inhuman or Degrading Treatment or Punishment (CPT) visited Sweden from 27 January to 5 February. It reviewed a significant number of complaints of assault by police in the county of Västra Götaland and found that in a number of well-documented cases the system for investigating suspected police ill-treatment had been ineffective, and that some complaints had not been expeditiously investigated. The CPT delegation also found that its 1998 recommendations to prevent police ill-treatment had not been implemented. In particular, the rights to inform a relative or other third party of one's custody, to have access to a lawyer from the outset of one's custody, and to have access to a doctor were still to be fully guaranteed by national laws; and a form setting out the rights of people in police custody had yet to be produced.

The CPT found that detainees kept in prolonged isolation at Tidaholm prison suffered from "deleterious mental health consequences" and were offered an extremely poor regime; and that all remand detainees at the Västberga section of Kronoberg remand prison and remand prisoners subjected to restrictions at Umeå and Gothenburg remand prisons were locked in their cells for 23 hours per day, in some cases for weeks. The CPT reiterated its concerns regarding the legal procedures to impose and maintain restrictions on remand prisoners, which do not allow for an effective review by the courts of the grounds on which the prosecutor's request is based, and about the type of restrictions requested.

In April the European Commission against Racism and Intolerance (ECRI) published its second report on Sweden. It welcomed recent legislative and policy measures to combat racism and discrimination, but noted an increase in racial violence and harassment, including against immigrants, Jews, Roma, and – since the attacks in the USA on 11 September 2001 – in the number of Islamophobic incidents. ECRI noted a significant incidence of discrimination in employment, housing, education and access to public places, coupled with a scarce use of anti-discrimination legislation; and a risk of segregation of society along ethnic lines, affecting in particular women and children of immigrant and Roma origin. ECRI recommended that steps should be taken to ensure that non-citizen women wishing to leave abusive relationships are not prevented from doing so for fear of losing permission to reside in the country.

Policing of 2001 protests in Gothenburg and Malmö

In January the Gothenburg Committee investigating police activities at demonstrations during the meeting of the European Union (EU) Council for Economic and Financial Affairs (Ecofin) in Malmö in April 2001 and at the EU summit in Gothenburg in June 2001 published its findings. In relation to the Malmö meeting, the Committee found that police actions had severely restricted the freedom to demonstrate of some 300 people, and that some officers had used excessive force against demonstrators taken into custody, and abusive language, in particular directed at young women. With respect to the Gothenburg summit, the Committee criticized the police for flaws in the planning of the operation and handling of police reinforcements. It also found serious deficiencies in crowd management training of officers and a lack of background knowledge among the police officers on duty about the groups involved in the protests and the social issues that they raised. The Committee was particularly critical of the planning, preparation and implementation of the police operation at Hvitfeldtska school, and found that it disproportionately obstructed the freedom of movement and assembly of the people on the school's premises. The Committee found that police had violated various legal provisions in connection with the treatment of people arrested. The Committee noted that many demonstrators reported police use of abusive language during the operation at the school.

☐ In June, following an investigation initiated by the parliamentary Ombudsman into the mass arrests at Hvitfeldtska school, the chief police commissioner in charge of the operation was charged with "unlawful detention" and misconduct in public duty. His trial was due to start in January 2004.

☐ In May the prosecutor in charge of the third investigation into the shooting of Hannes Westberg, one of the demonstrators seriously injured by police at the time of the EU Summit, decided that no charges should be brought against the police officers involved.

Refugees and asylum-seekers

During the year a broader range of asylum applications was considered to be "manifestly unfounded" even though the legislation was unchanged and the profile of arriving asylum-seekers remained largely the same. AI believed that the accelerated procedure used to determine these claims fell short of the requirements international standards demand of a fair asylum procedure. The claimants were, among other things, denied access to legal aid and were not protected against being forcibly returned to their home countries or a third country pending appeal against an initial rejection of their claim.

AI also expressed concern that the Swedish government on several occasions referred to the changed situation after 11 September 2001 as a reason to introduce carrier sanctions (penalties against carriers who transport inadequately documented passengers, including asylum-seekers).

☐ AI continued to express concern about the case of two Egyptian asylum-seekers, Muhammad Muhammad Suleiman Ibrahim El-Zari and Ahmed Hussein Mustafa Kamil Agiza, who were forcibly returned to Egypt in 2001 despite a serious risk that upon their return they would face grave human rights violations. AI had been concerned that the Swedish authorities accepted assurances given by the Egyptian authorities, even though the two asylum-seekers concerned and their lawyer had not been notified of the assurances or been given an opportunity to comment on them. Furthermore, their deportation had taken place on the day of the final decision on their asylum application, thus preventing the submission of an individual communication to international human rights monitoring bodies that could have scrutinized the decision of the Swedish authorities prior to their removal. In January AI expressed concern that the so-called assurances had not been fulfilled, and that the Swedish authorities had been unable to provide detailed information about the charges brought against the two men, the dates of the trial and the nature of the court that would hear the trial.

Swedish national held in US custody in Cuba

In February the head of the legal division at the Ministry of Foreign Affairs requested the immediate release of the Swedish national held in US custody at Guantánamo Bay, Cuba, on grounds that there was no legitimate basis in international law to hold him. The Swedish authorities also expressed concern that the US practice might lead to the evolution of a norm of customary international law.

SWITZERLAND

SWISS CONFEDERATION
Head of state and government: Pascal Couchepin
Death penalty: abolitionist for all crimes
UN Women's Convention: ratified with reservations
Optional Protocol to UN Women's Convention: not signed

Police officers allegedly ill-treated detainees, particularly non-Caucasian Swiss and foreign nationals, and used excessive force against demonstrators. There was concern that new measures relating to social assistance and a draft law on asylum might result in hardship for people in need of international protection and impede the effective exercise of the right to seek asylum. Domestic violence against women continued to be a serious problem, despite a number of initiatives by the authorities to address it.

Background

In October, the right-wing Swiss People's Party (SVP/UDC) won the largest share of the vote in parliamentary elections. As a result, it obtained a second seat in the seven-member federal government thus changing the balance of power in the four-party coalition government for the first time since 1959. There was widespread concern about the deeply xenophobic tone of the SVP/UDC's election campaign. A spokesperson for the UN High Commissioner for Refugees commented that it included "some of the most nakedly anti-asylum advertisements by a major political party which we've seen to date in Europe". Ministerial responsibility for the federal department of justice and police, which covers asylum matters, was subsequently assigned to the SVP/UDC leader for the duration of 2004.

Police ill-treatment and use of excessive force

There were regular reports of ill-treatment, often accompanied by racist abuse, during identity checks, at the moment of arrest and in police stations, as well as persistent reports of the use by police of inherently dangerous restraint techniques. Such acts were apparently often committed with impunity. Tasers (dart-firing, high-voltage stun guns) were acquired by several cantonal police forces. There was concern about the health risks associated with such weapons, as well as their potential for abuse. Many detainees were denied fundamental safeguards against ill-treatment in police custody, such as the right to have immediate access to a lawyer and to have relatives informed of their arrest.

Further progress was made towards the eventual unification of the 26 cantonal codes of penal procedure, as recommended by intergovernmental bodies to ensure, in particular, legal guarantees of fundamental safeguards for detainees in all cantons.

There were sporadic allegations of ill-treatment and racial abuse of foreign nationals by police at Zurich-Kloten Airport. In October, the Council of Europe's Committee for the Prevention of Torture and Inhuman or Degrading Treatment or Punishment visited the airport, principally to assess implementation of measures it had recommended concerning procedures and restraint methods applied in the context of forcible deportation operations. In 2001 it had found that the manner of such operations presented a manifest risk of inhuman and degrading treatment. The Committee also reviewed in October the treatment of foreign nationals detained in the airport's transit zone and Prison No. 2 pending deportation.

There were reports of ill-treatment by police during raids on two transit centres for asylum-seekers in Glarus Canton in July. Police officers forced their way into the rooms of the sleeping asylum-seekers in the early hours of the morning. They bound them hand and foot, covered their heads and photographed them while some were almost or completely naked. They then held them in the centres' common rooms for around five hours. One man was gagged with adhesive tape. Neither search resulted in any criminal proceedings against those detained. In November, an examining magistrate issued the findings of his investigation into police conduct during the raids. He concluded that some of the measures used by the police went beyond "acceptable and proportionate bounds", that the gagging was dangerous, and the manner in which the asylum-seekers were photographed was "degrading". He stated that there was an obvious need for relevant police training, but could not discern deliberate intent by the police to abuse their authority or wrongfully detain the asylum-seekers. He ordered the destruction of the photographs. He also ordered the state and the commanding officer to share the costs of the proceedings, and the officer also to compensate four asylum-seekers who had lodged a criminal complaint.

Demonstrations

Police allegedly used excessive and unwarranted force in the context of several demonstrations, and inappropriately used police equipment designed to temporarily disable or incapacitate people.

In March, after violent confrontations had developed between demonstrators and police, Denise Chervet was injured at Geneva's central railway station. After Denise Chervet threw a bottle at the police following an altercation between her son and a police officer, she was hit on the forehead and body by two projectiles, which left fragments permanently embedded. It subsequently emerged that a weapon firing plastic capsules, containing paint and covered with bismuth, had recently been tested by the Geneva police and that an officer had used the weapon against Denise Chervet. The weapon's manufacturers indicate that the projectile is intended to bring a targeted person to a halt, while the paint marks them for arrest, but warn that police officers should never aim towards the face, throat or neck. The Geneva authorities subsequently withdrew the weapon. An independent commission of inquiry conducted several investigations, some ongoing at the end of the year, into the behaviour of the cantonal police, who had initially denied responsibility for injuring Denise Chervet. In December, a criminal investigation concluded that the officer who fired the weapon had acted according to his instructions and no charges were brought against him. The police captain who had authorized the use of the weapon during the demonstration was charged with causing bodily harm through negligence.

◻ In June, there were extensive violent confrontations between protesters and police, as well as peaceful demonstrations and protest actions in Switzerland, in connection with the G8 Summit in neighbouring France. Geneva police were alleged to have indiscriminately and abusively used batons, stun grenades and rubber bullets. The Geneva Cantonal Parliament established an extra-parliamentary commission of inquiry to investigate, among other things, the conduct of the relevant Geneva authorities during G8 policing operations. A number of criminal proceedings were opened into individual incidents.

Investigations: updates

◻ In May, a Bern court acquitted four police officers of the attempted grievous bodily harm of Cemal Gömeç, a Turkish-Kurd refugee, in July 2001. Two of the officers were also acquitted of causing his death through negligence. The judge ruled that his death was attributable to intense stress combined with the restraint methods used to subdue him while he lay on the ground, resulting in positional asphyxia. The police officers indicated that they were unaware of the dangers of positional asphyxia associated with the restraint methods they had used. Noting this, the judge ruled that they had used no more force than necessary in subduing Cemal Gömeç. The Bern Attorney General lodged an appeal against the verdict.

◻ In April, a Geneva court rejected an appeal against the Attorney General's decision to dismiss a criminal complaint lodged against police officers by a Cameroonian woman following her detention in August 2002. The woman alleged that police officers had physically and racially abused her, strip-searched her in the presence of male officers, and separated her from her five-week-old baby. Her lawyers announced their intention of lodging an appeal with the Federal Court. They said the criminal investigation had been closed without their client being questioned and without any attempt to obtain statements from relevant witnesses.

◻ In June it was announced that an independent complaints body established by Zurich City Council in 2002, following revelations about a series of cases of alleged misconduct and ill-treatment by Zurich Municipal Police, had dealt with over 100 complaints and inquiries over a 12-month period and that 46 complaints concerned "real or putative" physical and/or verbal infringements of rights by the police. The lawyer heading the complaints body indicated that he had found no evidence of systematic physical assault by the municipal police but stressed that "no police force is immune to error". He proposed a range of measures to ensure all appropriate steps were taken to minimize the use of force and, in order to reduce "possible discrimination against foreigners", recommended increased levels of advice to police on inter-cultural matters. The Council stated that the proposals were under consideration by the police and that the work of the independent body would fall under the auspices of the city's Ombudsman's Office in future. In July, the City Council's Audit Commission issued a report following its examination of 10 controversial incidents involving the police, mostly occurring in the first half of 2002. It made a series of recommendations aimed at improving the conduct and functioning of the police.

Violence against women

In January the UN Committee on the Elimination of Discrimination against Women examined Switzerland's combined first and second reports. The Committee listed violence against women among its principal areas of concern in Switzerland. While recognizing legal and other efforts to address the issue, the Committee expressed concern about the prevalence of domestic violence, trafficking in women and girls and "a significant number of cases of female genital mutilation among migrant women of African descent". It called on Switzerland to intensify its efforts to address these problems as infringements of human rights. A series of legislative and other measures to combat violence against women were subsequently taken at cantonal and federal level.

AI country reports/ visits

Reports

- Switzerland: Alleged cruel, inhuman and degrading treatment of asylum-seekers in the Canton of Glarus (AI Index: EUR 43/005/2003)
- Concerns in Europe and Central Asia, January-June 2003: Switzerland (AI Index: EUR 01/016/2003)

TAJIKISTAN

REPUBLIC OF TAJIKISTAN
Head of state: Imomali Rakhmonov
Head of government: Akil Akilov
Death penalty: retentionist
UN Women's Convention: ratified
Optional Protocol to UN Women's Convention:
signed

Significant steps were taken to reduce the scope and application of the death penalty, although death sentences continued to be handed down.

Background

In June the Organization for Security and Co-operation in Europe (OSCE) expressed concern at the results of a nationwide referendum to amend the Tajik Constitution. Over 93 per cent of voters had reportedly approved 56 amendments, including a proposal to allow the President to serve two seven-year terms, which could potentially extend incumbent President Rakhmonov's term in office until 2020.

Two senior members of the opposition Islamic Renaissance Party (IRP) were charged with serious criminal offences amid claims that their arrests were politically motivated. IRP deputy head Shamsuddin Shamsiddinov was formally charged in October with treason, the formation of an armed criminal group and other offences. He had reportedly been held incommunicado for several days following his detention in June. In August Kasym Rakhimov, a senior IRP member, was among 14 men charged with the rape of 11 underage girls. He could face the death penalty.

The Tajik general procuracy asked the Russian authorities for the arrest and extradition of two senior secular opposition figures – Yakub Salimov and Habib Nasrulloyev – on charges of attempting to overthrow the state in connection with their alleged participation in coup attempts in 1997 and 1998.

Labour migration

Labour migration from Tajikistan involves around 600,000 Tajik citizens and affects one in four households in Tajikistan, according to a report published in October by the International Organization for Migration. Widespread poverty and unemployment were believed to be behind this rising trend, with 80 per cent of the population estimated by the UN to be living below the poverty line.

The government continued to negotiate bilateral agreements with the Russian authorities to establish safeguards to protect the basic human rights of Tajik labour migrants in the Russian Federation. More than 200 Tajik migrant workers were reported to have died in the Russian Federation in suspicious circumstances during the first half of the year; unofficial sources put the number at over 800.

Death penalty legislative reforms

In July parliament approved a draft law, proposed by President Rakhmonov, amending the Criminal Code. Among the amendments were the abolition of the death penalty for all women and for men aged under 18, and a reduction from 15 to five in the number of articles in the Criminal Code carrying a possible death sentence. The amendments became law in August. Unofficial sources reported that the President had instructed the Clemency Commission to recommend more prisoners on death row for pardon. At least two death sentences were overturned on appeal.

The authorities continued to treat information on death sentences and executions as a state secret and consequently it was difficult to obtain precise figures. At least 34 men were believed to have been sentenced to death. AI did not learn of any executions during the year.

▭ In November the UN Human Rights Committee called for death row prisoner Abduali Kurbanov to be given a new, open and fair trial or released. The Committee found that Tajikistan had violated Abduali Kurbanov's rights under six articles of the International Covenant on Civil and Political Rights, including the right to a fair trial and the right not to be tortured. Abduali Kurbanov was sentenced to death for "aggravated murder" in March 2002 without effective right of appeal. He was detained in May 2001 on allegations of fraud, and was subsequently convicted and sentenced to a term of imprisonment. While in prison he was allegedly tortured to force him to confess to three murders.

TURKEY

REPUBLIC OF TURKEY
Head of state: Ahmet Necdet Sezer
Head of government: Recep Tayyip Erdoğan (replaced
Abdullah Gül in March)
Death penalty: abolitionist for ordinary crimes
UN Women's Convention: ratified with reservations
Optional Protocol to UN Women's Convention: ratified

Important legal reform packages (known as the
"harmonization laws") relating to human rights
protection and aimed at meeting the criteria for
accession to the European Union continued to be
introduced by the Justice and Development Party
(AKP) government. Implementation of the reforms
was uneven and it was too early to gauge significant
progress on human rights as a result of the
legislation. Reports of torture and ill-treatment in
police detention and disproportionate use of force
against demonstrators continued to be matters of
grave concern, although the use of some torture
methods appeared to diminish. Those who
attempted to exercise their right to demonstrate
peacefully or express dissent on some issues
continued to face criminal prosecution.

Background

On 1 March parliament refused to authorize US troop
deployment on Turkish soil, signalling that Turkey
would not be closely involved with the war in Iraq.

A change in the Constitution brought in by the new
AKP government paved the way for AKP Chair Recep
Tayyip Erdoğan to stand for parliament in a by-election
in Siirt province, and on 14 March he replaced Abdullah
Gül as Prime Minister.

Four "harmonization" reform packages entered into
law on 11 January, 4 February, 19 July and 7 August.
Among the notable elements were: provisions aimed at
removing certain regulations and practices that had
contributed to impunity for torture and ill-treatment;
the possibility of retrial for those whom the European
Court of Human Rights ruled had suffered a violation of
the European Convention on Human Rights as a result
of a court ruling in Turkey; abolition of Article 8 of the
Anti-Terror Law (the crime of spreading separatist
propaganda); lifting of restrictions on non-Turkish
language broadcasting on private television and radio
stations; the end of incommunicado detention and the
right to immediate legal counsel for State Security
Court detainees; and changes in the organization and
status of the National Security Council.

Changes were also made to other laws, including the
Law on Associations, the Press Law, the Law on Political
Parties, the Law on Meetings and Demonstrations, and
the Law on Foundations. However, the reforms
consisted of amendments to articles of these laws
rather than the fundamental redrafting of the laws that
human rights lawyers and defenders had called for.

There was concern that despite amendments to and
repeal of certain articles of the Turkish Penal Code
(TPC) and Anti-Terror Law, the lack of an holistic
approach meant that similar articles to those altered or
repealed were retained in other laws. AI feared that
these could be used by prosecutors in place of the
earlier articles.

As a result of the new law on retrial, four former
Democracy Party (DEP) deputies – Leyla Zana, Hatip
Dicle, Orhan Doğan and Selim Sadak – attended the
first hearing of their retrial on 28 March. AI believed
that the four prisoners of conscience, imprisoned since
1994, were punitively punished for their non-violent
political activities relating to the Kurdish question.
One-day hearings of the retrial were subsequently held
once a month; AI and other international observers
voiced serious concerns about the fairness of the trial
procedures and the continued imprisonment of the
four former deputies.

The pro-Kurdish political party HADEP (People's
Democracy Party) was banned by a Constitutional
Court ruling on 13 March.

On 23 September Turkey ratified the International
Covenant on Civil and Political Rights and the
International Covenant on Economic, Social and
Cultural Rights.

On 25 September Turkey signed the Ottawa
Convention (Law on Prohibition of the Use, Stockpiling,
Production and Transfer of Anti-personnel Mines and
their Destruction). During the year at least 15 people,
several of them minors, were killed by landmines or
abandoned explosives in the southeastern and eastern
provinces. Many others were injured.

On 15 November the Neve Şalom and Beth İsrail
synagogues in Istanbul were bombed, allegedly by
militant Islamists, killing 26 people and injuring
hundreds. On 20 November the British Consulate and
the HSBC bank headquarters in Istanbul were bombed,
killing 31 people and again injuring hundreds.

Torture and ill-treatment

Torture and ill-treatment in police detention remained
a grave concern. Although there were far fewer reports
of the use of torture methods such as electric shocks,
falaka (beatings on the soles of the feet) and suspension
by the arms, there were regular reports of detainees
being beaten, stripped naked, sexually harassed and
denied adequate sleep, food, drink and use of the toilet.

One reason for the persistence of torture and ill-
treatment in detention was the failure of law
enforcement officials to follow prescribed procedures,
including the duty to inform detainees of their rights
and to allow access to legal counsel. Lawyers said that
in some cases they were told by police officers that a
detainee did not wish to see them without providing
any evidence of this. Other contributing factors
included inadequate documenting of torture and ill-
treatment in medical reports, and the acceptance as
evidence by courts of statements extracted under
torture.

Disproportionate use of force by police during
demonstrations was widespread. Television news

programs regularly broadcast scenes of demonstrators being beaten, kicked and ill-treated by law enforcement officials. Groups particularly targeted during demonstrations included supporters of the political party DEHAP (Democratic People's Party), leftist parties, trade unionists, students and anti-war activists.

Of particular concern were the many allegations of people being abducted by plainclothes police and then tortured or ill-treated. These incidents of unrecorded detention were almost impossible to investigate and the perpetrators continued to enjoy impunity.

⊡ Sixteen-year-old S.T. reported that on 26 November in the town of Siirt, southeast Turkey, he was abducted in the street by plainclothes police, had a sack put over his head and was pushed into a car. He said that his hands and feet were bound and he was beaten over the head and knocked unconscious. He stated that he was beaten severely and threatened with a gun held to his head for information about the whereabouts of his brother. He was later left in a cemetery outside the town.

⊡ Gülbahar Gündüz, active in the women's section of the Istanbul branch of DEHAP, reported that on 14 June she was abducted in the street in Istanbul by plainclothes police officers, blindfolded, taken in a car to an unknown building, raped and otherwise tortured. Although a report from the Forensic Institute documenting the evidence of torture was pending, an internal police investigation was dropped.

Impunity for police abuses

The 11 January reform package ended the possibility of prison sentences handed down for torture and ill-treatment by police being suspended or converted to fines. The new law was not applied retrospectively. As a result, trials and sentences in such cases continued to be suspended, sometimes on the basis of previous laws.

⊡ On 18 February the trial of Süleyman Ulusoy (known as "the Hose"), a police superintendent, was suspended under the terms of the December 2000 "amnesty law" (Law No. 4616 on Conditional Suspension of Trials and Sentences for Offences Committed up until April 1999). A videotape showing him beating transvestites with a hosepipe in the Beyoğlu police headquarters in Istanbul had been broadcast on television in 2000. He remained on duty in Istanbul.

⊡ Two police officers convicted of ill-treating Veli Kaya, a student taking part in a demonstration on 6 November 2002, received a six-month suspended prison sentence in June. The rescue of Veli Kaya by members of the public from a depot beneath a branch of the Şeker Bank in Ankara where he was beaten by police had been broadcast on television. The case was referred to the Supreme Court.

The 11 January reforms also removed the requirement to secure permission from a senior official to investigate allegations of torture or ill-treatment by police. This reform was sometimes ignored.

⊡ Ali Ulvi Uludoğan and his brother İlhan Uludoğan were detained on 25 May for driving through a red traffic light in the Kulu district of Konya province. They were reportedly beaten, kicked and subjected to verbal

sexual harassment in detention in Kulu police station. In contravention of the 11 January reforms, the Kulu *kaymakam* (local state official) on 8 August decided not to allow an investigation of the alleged torture and ill-treatment.

The 7 August reform package stipulated that trials relating to cases of torture and ill-treatment should be prioritized. Despite this, the ratio of prosecutions of members of the security forces in relation to the number of reports of torture and ill-treatment remained extremely low.

⊡ The trial of the police officers charged with torturing two women – Fatma Deniz Polattaş and 16-year-old N.C.S. – in İskenderun police headquarters in March 1999 was repeatedly delayed because of the Forensic Institute's two-year failure to supply medical reports detailing their torture.

In a few cases, steps were taken to hold to account perpetrators of human rights violations.

⊡ In the final stage of the "Manisa Youths" case, the Court of Appeal on 4 April approved the prison sentences ranging from five to 11 years of 10 police officers found guilty of torturing 16 young people in December 1995. The high-profile case almost exceeded the statute of limitations, grounds on which less well-known cases faced collapse.

⊡ On 22 September, Adil Serdar Saçan, former head of the Istanbul Organized Crime Branch, was reportedly discharged from the police force by the Interior Ministry for ignoring torture committed under his authority. The prosecutor's indictment also detailed incidents of torture committed by him personally. This was a landmark ruling.

Harassment of human rights defenders

A range of laws and regulations was used to restrict freedom of expression and obstruct the activities of human rights defenders. Peaceful statements and activities were prosecuted on grounds of "insulting" various state institutions (Article 159 of the TPC), "aiding and abetting an illegal organization" (Article 169) or "inciting the people to enmity" (Article 312). Other activities were prohibited or punished under Law No. 2911 on Meetings and Demonstrations, the Law on Associations, press laws and public order legislation. In some cases human rights defenders were imprisoned. However, most of the investigations and trials resulting from such prosecutions ended in acquittals or with sentences being suspended or commuted to fines, highlighting what AI regarded as a pattern of judicial harassment of human rights activists.

Some individuals – including Alp Ayan, a psychiatrist at the Human Rights Foundation of Turkey (TİHV) in İzmir; Rıdvan Kızgın, Head of the Bingöl branch of the Human Rights Association (İHD); and Eren Keskin, a lawyer who co-runs a legal aid project for women survivors of sexual assault in custody – appeared to have been particularly targeted. Punitive fines were a heavy burden on branches of associations and their members.

⊡ On 12 November, the first hearing of a trial against TİHV took place in Ankara. Seeking the suspension of nine executive board members of the foundation, the prosecutor alleged that in 2001 TİHV had violated the Law on Foundations by "cooperating" with international organizations without securing the permission of the Council of Ministers, and by raising funds via the Internet. The alleged "cooperation" took the form of translating reports and distributing them to the UN Special Rapporteur on extrajudicial, summary or arbitrary executions, the European Parliament Rapporteur for Turkey, and the Council of Europe Commissioner for Human Rights.

▢ Özkan Hoşhanli began serving a 15-month prison sentence on 28 October. He had attempted to observe demonstrations in April and May 1999 in his capacity as the then Chair of the human rights group *Mazlum Der* (Organization of Human Rights and Solidarity for Oppressed People) in Malatya, and was sentenced to prison and fined in May 2003 under Law No. 2911 for "participating in an illegal demonstration and not dispersing after orders and warnings, and having to be dispersed by government forces with force". He was a prisoner of conscience.

▢ According to the İHD, 450 prosecutions had been brought against it since 2000 compared to 300 in the previous 14 years. On 6 May police searched the headquarters and local offices of the İHD in Ankara and confiscated books, reports on human rights violations, files, cassettes and computers. The Ministry of Justice informed AI that the search had been carried out on the orders of Ankara State Security Court under Article 169 of the TPC because the İHD was suspected of "coordinating a campaign to voice support for the terrorist organization PKK/KADEK [Kurdistan Freedom and Democracy Congress]".

Teachers and health workers were often posted away from their home as a disciplinary measure for involvement in human rights or trade union activities, and some student activists were expelled or suspended from university.

Violence against women

Sexual assault and harassment of women in police custody continued to be a grave concern, and in February AI published a report on the subject.

Family violence, including so-called "honour killings", was also a grave concern. AI supported the campaign of women's groups in Turkey to remove gender-discriminatory articles in the revised draft of the TPC, work on which was started by a parliamentary sub-committee in October.

Killings in disputed circumstances

A few dozen civilians were shot dead by the security forces and village guards, most of them in the southeastern and eastern provinces. Many may have been victims of extrajudicial executions or the use of excessive force.

▢ On 8 July, five people in the village of Pul, Bingöl province, were killed by unknown assailants. There were conflicting allegations as to whether the perpetrators belonged to the state security forces or the PKK/KADEK.

AI country reports/ visits
Reports
- Turkey: End sexual violence against women in custody! (AI Index: EUR 44/006/2003)
- Concerns in Europe and Central Asia, January-June 2003: Turkey (AI Index: EUR 01/016/2003)

Visits
AI delegates visited Turkey in March, June and November to conduct research on human rights and observe trials.

TURKMENISTAN

TURKMENISTAN
Head of state and government: Saparmurad Niyazov
Death penalty: abolitionist for all crimes
UN Women's Convention: ratified
Optional Protocol to UN Women's Convention: not signed

The government failed to implement recommendations for improving its human rights record made by intergovernmental bodies including the UN Commission on Human Rights and the Organization for Security and Co-operation in Europe (OSCE). A resolution adopted by the UN General Assembly in December expressed "grave concern" about the country's human rights record. At least 55 people were convicted in further trials in connection with an alleged assassination attempt on President Niyazov in November 2002. Their trials were unfair. The courts failed to investigate credible allegations of torture. A number of prisoners were said to have died in unexplained circumstances following the trials. Religious minorities, civil society activists and others exercising their right to freedom of expression continued to face persecution. Conscientious objectors continued to be imprisoned.

Background

The human rights situation in Turkmenistan remained appalling. Key to the failure to address impunity or counter the widespread abuse of human rights was the domination by President Niyazov of all aspects of life in the country and the personality cult he has developed.

In August the Khalk Maslakhaty (People's Council), which consists of representatives of the legislative, executive and judicial branches of government, authorized itself to amend the Constitution and to define certain illegal acts as treasonable in law and certain life prisoners as "traitors". The Council appointed President Niyazov as its Chairman, a specially created post.

In continuation of an apparent purge of government critics or alleged critics, senior government officials were demoted, dismissed and imprisoned. In September the four main opposition groups in exile, barred from operating inside the country, formed the Union of Democratic Forces of Turkmenistan.

Freedom of movement inside Turkmenistan was severely curtailed. In April President Niyazov imposed a ban on dual citizenship and strict exit visa requirements for those affected, further limiting civil and political rights.

International response to violations

In January, 10 OSCE member states appointed French international law professor Emmanuel Decaux to examine the Turkmen authorities' investigation into the November 2002 attack. He was denied access to Turkmenistan for a fact-finding mission. In March he published a report condemning Turkmenistan's human rights record and calling for an urgent international response. In April, in its first resolution on Turkmenistan, the UN Commission on Human Rights expressed "grave concern" at the human rights situation in the country. The European Parliament, in a resolution in October, said that Turkmenistan had "acquired one of the worst totalitarian systems in the world." In December the UN General Assembly adopted a resolution on the human rights situation in Turkmenistan with an overwhelming majority.

The recommendations of these bodies, that Turkmenistan failed to implement, included the unconditional release of prisoners of conscience and retrial of those convicted after unfair trials in connection with the November 2002 attack; the investigation of suspicious deaths in custody and allegations of torture and ill-treatment; prisoners' access to independent bodies including the International Committee of the Red Cross; and the restoration of civil and political freedoms to civil society activists, opposition parties, religious communities and others in Turkmenistan.

Coup plot trial conducted unfairly

In January at least 55 men and women were sentenced to prison terms ranging from five years to life for involvement in the attack on President Niyazov's motorcade in the capital, Ashgabat, in November 2002. They were convicted in a series of closed trials before the Ashgabat City Court and the Supreme Court.

The authorities refused to disclose comprehensive information about the defendants, including their whereabouts. Only on 31 January was an official list of names, charges and sentences published in the *Adalat* (Justice) newspaper. Most had been convicted on charges including "conspiracy to violently overthrow the government and/or change the constitutional order" and "attempting to assassinate the President".

The defendants were not represented by lawyers of their own choice, and some lawyers appointed to defend them reportedly began their pleas in court with the words, "I am ashamed to defend a person like you". The defendants were allegedly forced to sign a statement that they were familiar with the indictment and other documentation in their case, although they had not been

given an opportunity to study their dossier. Members of the public, including diplomatic representatives, were refused access to the trials. The courts failed to investigate allegations that many defendants were tortured and ill-treated in pre-trial detention.

Relatives were harassed and ill-treated, including by eviction from their homes and severe limitations on their freedom of movement.

⊡ It was impossible to confirm reports in August that Amanmukhammet Yklymov died in custody in March. In January he was sentenced to 20 years' imprisonment after a trial in which the court reportedly ignored allegations that he had been tortured in pre-trial detention at police headquarters in Ashgabat. He allegedly had a plastic bag or gas mask put over his head and the air supply cut off, was suspended by his arms, and suffered a broken arm, loss of sight in one eye and hearing in one ear. Already ill at the time of his arrest, he was said to have been denied medical treatment in detention.

In March and April, seven men arrested in connection with the November 2002 attack were handed over to the authorities in their countries of origin – one to the USA, six to Turkey. The six were put on trial in Turkey, charged with attempting to assassinate the President of Turkmenistan.

Freedom of expression curtailed

The relatives of exiled dissidents were targeted in an attempt to stop exiles from criticizing government policies and speaking out about human rights violations in Turkmenistan.

Civil society activists had their actions severely controlled. They were routinely summoned to the security services. Many were threatened with "serious repercussions" by the security services if they met senior UN and OSCE representatives during their visits to Turkmenistan.

After a new law curtailing the rights of civil society organizations came into force in November, pressure on such groups increased and the Dashoguz Ecological Club (DEC) was deregistered in a court ruling.

⊡ DEC Co-Chair Farid Tukhbatullin was sentenced to three years' imprisonment as a prisoner of conscience after an unfair trial in Ashgabat in March. Arrested in December 2002, he was convicted on the basis of fabricated charges; he was accused of concealing a serious criminal act for allegedly not disclosing a coup plot by opposition supporters after attending an international human rights conference. He was also convicted of illegally crossing the border from Uzbekistan into Turkmenistan after border guards had failed to stamp his passport. Before the trial, his lawyer was denied access to him several times, on one occasion on the pretext that repair work was being carried out at the detention facility. Farid Tukhbatullin was released in April, following massive international pressure, but only after he signed a "confession" and promised not to commit further "criminal activities", under oath.

⊡ Saparmurad Ovezberdiyev, a 63-year-old correspondent for the US *Radio Liberty* based in

Ashgabat, was reportedly abducted by secret service officers and held incommunicado for two days in September. He was said to have been threatened with long-term imprisonment unless he gave up his work. In November he was reportedly abducted, beaten and abandoned at a cemetery in Ashgabat by two unidentified assailants.

◻ In August Sazak Begmedov, a 77-year-old former prosecutor, was reportedly abducted by four police officers in Ashgabat and forcibly resettled in the northern town of Dashoguz. Shortly before the abduction, his daughter Tadzhigul Begmedova had announced the formation of a human rights group in exile in Bulgaria and the group had alleged that two political prisoners had died in prison as a result of torture.

Religious groups harassed

A new law on religion that came into force in November criminalized all activities of unregistered religious organizations. Members of unregistered religious groups continued to face harassment and intimidation by the authorities. The only two registered religious communities – the Russian Orthodox Church and Sunni Islam – remained under strict state control.

◻ At least five Jehovah's Witnesses were sentenced to prison terms of up to two years for their conscientious objection to military service. They were held in Seydi prison colony in eastern Turkmenistan.

AI country reports/ visits
Reports
- Turkmenistan: Turkmen leader should mark birthday by introducing rule of law (joint statement with other non-governmental organizations) (AI Index: EUR 61/005/2003)
- Turkmenistan: Clampdown on dissent – a background briefing (AI Index: EUR 61/015/2003)

UKRAINE

UKRAINE
Head of state: Leonid Kuchma
Head of government: Viktor Yanukovych
Death penalty: abolitionist for all crimes
UN Women's Convention and its Optional Protocol: ratified

Torture and ill-treatment remained widespread in Ukraine. The European Court of Human Rights ruled against Ukraine in favour of six former death row prisoners. Domestic violence was a serious problem. Serious concerns about freedom of the media persisted. There was little apparent progress in determining who was responsible for the "disappearance" of journalist Georgiy Gongadze.

Torture and ill-treatment

There were numerous allegations of torture and ill-treatment by police and prison officials. In April the National Human Rights Ombudsperson, Nina Karpachova, stated in her annual report to the Ukrainian parliament that in the previous two years around 12,000 individuals had alleged that they had been tortured or ill-treated, most commonly in the context of interrogation for the purpose of extracting a confession. Detainees had been beaten by police officers, painfully suspended by their handcuffed hands, suffocated using plastic bags or gas masks, and subjected to electro-shock torture. As a result many detainees had suffered serious injury; some had died as a result. Detainees were frequently denied their rights to a lawyer or a doctor of their choice, and to notify relatives of their detention.

◻ The UN Human Rights Committee ruled in September that former death row prisoner Azer Garyverdy ogly Aliev had not received a fair trial. He had been denied access to a lawyer for the first five months of his detention. He had been arrested in Makeevka on suspicion of murder in August 1996 and sentenced to death in April 1997. Azer Garyverdy ogly Aliev had alleged that he and his pregnant wife were ill-treated and tortured by police officers during four days of interrogation shortly after their arrest.

◻ In mid-October, public prosecutors in the region of Donetsk reportedly launched an investigation into an incident of alleged torture at correctional facility No. 120. Prison officers allegedly tortured a 25-year-old prisoner, as a result of which he sustained serious injuries to both feet, necessitating their amputation. It was alleged that the incident took place after the prisoner refused to follow the orders of prison officials.

◻ In November, 20-year-old Sergei Berdyugin died in hospital in Odessa after reportedly being ill-treated in pre-trial custody.

European Court of Human Rights

In April the European Court of Human Rights ruled in favour of six men held on death row in various Ukrainian prisons in the 1990s who had lodged complaints about the cruel, inhuman and degrading conditions of their detention. In the case of Borislav Poltoratskiy, the Court ruled that the conditions of his detention caused him "considerable mental suffering, diminishing his human dignity". The Court found that he, in common with other death row prisoners imprisoned at Ivano-Frankivsk Prison, "was locked up for 24 hours a day in cells which offered only a very restricted living space, that the windows of the cells were covered with the consequence that there was no access to natural light, that there was no provision for outdoor exercise and that there was little or no opportunity for activities to occupy himself or for human contact".

Violence against women
Domestic violence continued to be common in Ukraine, although no official statistics were available. In late 2002 Ukraine informed the UN Human Rights Committee of the various measures it was implementing to combat domestic violence. These included the enactment of the Prevention of Domestic Violence Law, which identified the public bodies and institutions responsible for taking preventative action; new procedures to investigate acts of domestic violence; and the establishment of a network of specialized institutions for victims of domestic violence such as crisis centres, shelters and social rehabilitation centres. Despite these positive measures, there remained significant obstacles to women seeking justice.

Freedom of expression
Widespread concerns about freedom of the media persisted. In February the Council of Europe published its experts' report on freedom of expression and information in Ukraine, following a visit to the country in November 2002. The report concluded: "[W]e feel compelled to repeat the conclusion made in our report of 2000 that Ukraine gives rise to very serious concern in terms of expression and information". The report highlighted a whole series of concerns including: the high incidence of defamation suits against media outlets and the level of damages awarded; controversial disputes over the licensing of radio and television stations; attempts by the authorities to guide media content; and crimes committed against journalists.

▭ Although several present and former officials of the Ministry of the Interior were reportedly arrested in connection with the "disappearance" of the independent journalist Georgiy Gongadze in September 2000, the investigation appeared to come to a standstill in late October when Prosecutor General Svyataslav Piskun, who was heading the investigation, was dismissed from his post by President Kuchma. It was suggested in certain quarters that his dismissal may have been connected to the arrests.

AI country reports/ visits
Report
· Concerns in Europe and Central Asia, January-June 2003: Ukraine (AI Index: EUR 01/016/2003)

UNITED KINGDOM

UNITED KINGDOM OF GREAT BRITAIN AND NORTHERN IRELAND
Head of state: Queen Elizabeth II
Head of government: Tony Blair
Death penalty: abolitionist for all crimes
UN Women's Convention: ratified with reservations
Optional Protocol to UN Women's Convention: not signed

Serious human rights violations continued to take place in the context of the United Kingdom (UK) authorities' response to the 11 September 2001 attacks in the USA. Detention conditions in some facilities were inhuman and degrading. In Northern Ireland there were 10 paramilitary killings, the majority of which were committed by Loyalists. Members of armed groups were also responsible for "punishment" shootings and beatings and sectarian attacks. The European Court of Human Rights ruled that the UK authorities had violated the right to life. Draft legislation threatened to withdraw legal safeguards from asylum-seekers and potentially breached international standards.

Background
AI expressed concern about violations of international human rights and humanitarian law by the UK military during the war on Iraq and in the context of the occupation of the country which was ongoing at the end of the year (see Iraq entry).

In June the UK ratified the Optional Protocol to the Convention on the Rights of the Child on the involvement of children in armed conflict with a reservation which AI considered "incompatible with the object and purpose" of the Protocol because it allows the deployment of under-18s in hostilities in certain circumstances.

In October, the UK ratified Protocol No. 13 to the European Convention on Human Rights, concerning the abolition of the death penalty in all circumstances.

Response to 11 September 2001
By the end of the year, 14 foreign nationals who could not be deported continued to be interned under the Anti-terrorism, Crime and Security Act 2001 (ATCSA). They were held in high-security facilities under severely restricted regimes.

In February, the European Committee for the Prevention of Torture and Inhuman or Degrading Treatment or Punishment (CPT) published the report of its February 2002 visit to the UK to review the detention conditions of those held under the ATCSA in two high-security prisons. The CPT noted allegations of verbal abuse; expressed concern about the detainees' access to legal counsel; and remarked that the detention regime and conditions of ATCSA detainees should take into account the fact that they had not been accused or convicted of any crime and the indefinite nature of their detention. The CPT expressed concern about the fact that secret evidence may be considered in hearings under the ATCSA and that detainees and their legal representatives of choice can be excluded from such hearings.

In May, June and July, appeals brought by 10 individuals against their certification as "suspected international terrorists" under the ATCSA were heard in both open and closed sessions; all were dismissed in October. Proceedings under the ATCSA fell far short of international fair trial standards, including the right to the presumption of innocence, the right to a defence and the right to counsel. There was also grave concern at the reliance on secret evidence and at the executive's and judiciary's willingness to rely on evidence extracted under torture. Since only non-UK nationals could be interned, AI also considered the ATCSA discriminatory.

In December, the Committee of Privy Counsellors, who had been charged with reviewing the ATCSA, recommended the urgent repeal of ATCSA powers allowing non-UK nationals to be detained potentially indefinitely.

⌒ In October an appeal by Mahmoud Abu Rideh, a Palestinian refugee and torture victim, against his internment under the ATCSA was rejected by the Special Immigration Appeals Commission. At the end of the year he continued to be held at a high-security psychiatric hospital.

In August the UN Committee on the Elimination of Racial Discrimination expressed concern about increasing racial prejudice against ethnic minorities, asylum-seekers and immigrants; reported cases of "Islamophobia" following the 11 September attacks; discrimination faced by Roma and Travellers; and reports of attacks on asylum-seekers. The Committee also expressed deep concern about provisions of the ATCSA targeting exclusively foreign nationals.

During the year, nine UK nationals, including Asif Iqbal, Shafiq Rasul, Moazzam Begg and Feroz Abbasi, who continued to be held indefinitely — without charge or trial or access to courts, lawyers or relatives — in US custody at Guantánamo Bay, Cuba, were "visited" and interviewed on a number of occasions by UK officials, including members of the security services. AI remained deeply concerned that UK authorities were taking advantage of the legal limbo and the coercive detention conditions in which their nationals were held at Guantánamo Bay in US custody to interrogate them and extract information to use in proceedings under the ATCSA.

⌒ By the end of the year, Bisher al-Rawi, an Iraqi national legally resident in the UK, and Jamil Al-Banna, a Jordanian national with refugee status in the UK, remained in US custody at Guantánamo Bay. AI expressed concern about the role that the UK government may have played in their unlawful rendering to US custody, and about its refusal to make representations on their behalf to the US authorities.

Northern Ireland

At the end of the year, the Northern Ireland Assembly remained suspended and direct rule continued.

Collusion and political killings

In April, the Metropolitan Police Commissioner, John Stevens, delivered his long-awaited report into collusion in Northern Ireland, only a short summary of which was published. Among other things, it confirmed widespread collusion between state agents and Loyalist paramilitaries, including state agents being involved in murder such as the killing of human rights lawyer Patrick Finucane in 1989. It also confirmed the existence of the British Army's secret intelligence unit known as the Force Research Unit which had actively colluded with Loyalist paramilitaries in targeting people, including Patrick Finucane, for assassination.

In May, one person was charged with the killing of Patrick Finucane. At the end of 2003, decisions were awaited on whether to instigate criminal proceedings arising from more than 50 individual files prepared by the Stevens team relating to serving and retired army personnel and police officers.

In July the European Court of Human Rights found that the UK authorities had violated Patrick Finucane's right to life, including by failing to provide a prompt and effective investigation into the allegations of security personnel collusion in his murder.

By the end of the year, the UK authorities had failed to publish the reports submitted to them in October by Justice Peter Cory, a retired Canadian Supreme Court judge, on alleged collusion by security forces in the killings of Patrick Finucane, Rosemary Nelson, Robert Hamill and Billy Wright.

In October, at an inquest into a number of cases, including that of Roseanne Mallon, where there were serious allegations of collusion between state forces and Loyalists in killings, the Police Service of Northern Ireland (PSNI) and the Ministry of Defence refused to comply with a document disclosure order issued by the Coroner.

In December Peter McBride's family was granted leave for a full judicial review of the Ministry of Defence's decision allowing the two Scots Guards convicted of his murder in 1992 to continue to serve in the army.

Abuses by non-state actors

There were 10 killings by members of armed groups during 2003, of which eight were attributed to Loyalists and two to Republican dissidents. The majority of the killings were reportedly carried out as a result of feuds among and within Loyalist paramilitary organizations.

⌒ In November James McMahon, a 21-year-old Catholic, was attacked, reportedly by a Loyalist gang armed with baseball bats, as he walked home with friends. He died in hospital the following day.

⌒ No armed group claimed responsibility for the killing in March of Keith Rogers. His death was reportedly attributed by the PSNI to a fall-out between two factions within the Irish Republican Army.

According to police figures, there were 203 shootings and assaults by Loyalist paramilitaries and 101 shootings and assaults by Republican paramilitaries. Many of the victims were children;

some reports indicated that attacks on children had increased almost fivefold since the Good Friday Agreement was signed in 1998.

⌁ Two boys aged 14 and 15 were allegedly chained to a lamppost and covered in tar in April. Members of the Irish National Liberation Army – a dissident Republican group – were reportedly accused of this so-called "punishment".

Deaths in custody

⌁ In June Christopher Alder's family announced that they were applying to the European Court of Human Rights following the outcome of a disciplinary inquiry which had cleared five police officers of responsibility for his death at Hull police station in 1998.

⌁ In October an inquest jury returned a unanimous verdict of unlawful killing at the inquest into the death of Roger Sylvester in January 1999 after he was restrained by police officers. At the end of the year, a decision by the Crown Prosecution Service on whether to prosecute the officers involved was awaited.

Police shootings

In April the "open" verdict returned by an inquest jury in June 2002 at the conclusion of an inquest into the fatal police shooting of Harry Stanley was quashed, and a fresh inquest was ordered.

Prisons

Suicides in prisons were on the rise, totalling 94 by the end of the year. The Chief Inspector of Prisons for England and Wales issued damning reports following her visits to a number of institutions. She raised concern about abuses against inmates, serious risk to their safety, and inhuman and degrading detention conditions.

The Chief Inspector of Prisons for Scotland continued to highlight inhuman and degrading detention conditions in some facilities, made worse by overcrowding.

In December settlements for compensation were reached in cases brought by victims who alleged that they had been subjected to ill-treatment, including torture such as rape, mock executions and brutal beatings while incarcerated at Wormwood Scrubs Prison in London in the mid to late 1990s.

⌁ In October, in a landmark judgment, the House of Lords ruled that a public inquiry must be held into the circumstances of the death of Zahid Mubarek. He was killed by his cellmate in Feltham Young Offenders Institution in March 2000. Despite prior knowledge of the latter's violent behaviour and strong racial prejudices, the prison authorities had placed the two men in the same cell.

Violence against women

According to government statistics, two women each week on average were killed by a partner or former partner. Draft legislation was introduced to tackle this most hidden, yet pervasive of human rights abuses. AI urged that this legislation on domestic violence be supplemented by a broad, comprehensive and fully resourced national strategy to eliminate all forms of violence against women.

During the year allegations emerged that hundreds of Kenyan women had been raped by UK army personnel posted to Kenya for training. The allegations spanned a period of more than 35 years. More than half of the cases reportedly involved allegations of gang rape. Several rapes appeared to have been reported at the time to either or both the UK and Kenyan authorities who had failed to take effective action. An investigation by the UK Royal Military Police started in April and was ongoing at the end of the year.

Army deaths in disputed circumstances

There was continuing concern about deaths in disputed circumstances of army personnel, including under-18s, in non-combat situations in and around army barracks in the UK. There were allegations that some of these deaths may have involved unlawful killings, either intentional or as a result of negligence, through, for example, the misuse of lethal weapons; deaths during strenuous training exercises; and self-inflicted deaths, at times following bullying and other ill-treatment, including sexual harassment, by other soldiers and superior officers.

Serious questions were raised about the authorities' systematic failure to address a range of concerns.

Freedom of expression

In March AI expressed concern that the police use of special powers granted by "anti-terrorist" legislation to stop, search and seize in the context of peaceful anti-war demonstrations was hampering the lawful exercise of the rights to freedom of expression and assembly.

At the end of the year, criminal proceedings were pending against Katharine Gun, a former government employee. She was being prosecuted under the Official Secrets Act 1989 for leaking an e-mail which reportedly exposed the US plan to eavesdrop on members of the UN Security Council during intensive negotiations in the run-up to the war on Iraq. She argued that her actions were necessary to prevent what she believed to be an unlawful war and to save the lives of UK servicemen and women and Iraqi civilians. AI reiterated its concern that the Act does not allow for a public interest defence.

Refugees and asylum-seekers

A significant number of asylum-seekers faced destitution because of Section 55 of the Nationality, Immigration and Asylum Act 2002. This withdraws welfare benefit entitlement from those who do not apply for asylum as soon as reasonably practicable after entering the UK.

AI country reports/visits
Reports
- United Kingdom: Army barracks deaths – families demand justice (AI Index: EUR 45/004/2003)
- United Kingdom: Decades of impunity – serious allegations of rape of Kenyan women by UK army personnel (AI Index: EUR 45/014/2003)

- United Kingdom: Justice perverted under the Anti-terrorism, Crime and Security Act 2001 (AI Index: EUR 45/029/2003)

Visits
AI delegates visited Kenya in June to investigate allegations of rape of Kenyan women by UK army personnel. An AI delegate observed judicial hearings pertaining to internment proceedings under the ATCSA and to the prosecution of Katharine Gun. An AI delegate visited Northern Ireland in June.

UZBEKISTAN

REPUBLIC OF UZBEKISTAN
Head of state: Islam Karimov
Head of government: Otkir Sultanov
Death penalty: retentionist
UN Women's Convention: ratified
Optional Protocol to UN Women's Convention: not signed

At least 6,000 political prisoners, who included dozens of women, continued to be held in cruel, inhuman and degrading conditions. Human rights defenders and hundreds of people suspected of political or religious dissent were harassed, beaten and detained without trial, or sentenced to prison terms after unfair trials and frequently tortured or ill-treated. The UN Special Rapporteur on torture reported on a visit to Uzbekistan in 2002 in which he received numerous testimonies of systematic torture and ill-treatment. Torture was reported to have resulted in the death of at least three men in custody. At least 18 death sentences were passed after unfair trials marred by uninvestigated allegations of torture and corruption. The Special Rapporteur on torture called the secrecy surrounding the death penalty "malicious and amounting to cruel and inhuman treatment" of prisoners' families.

Background
Despite limited legislative and judicial reforms, the Uzbek authorities continued to flout their international and national obligations on human rights, failing to address an appalling human rights situation which included official repression of dissent in civil, religious and political life. President Karimov failed to fulfil a commitment to publicly condemn torture in his speech to the annual meeting of the European Bank for Reconstruction and Development in the capital, Tashkent, in May.

The International Committee of the Red Cross (ICRC) resumed prison visits during 2003. After the Special Rapporteur on torture reported on his 2002 visit to Uzbekistan, the authorities granted journalists access to certain prisons and penal colonies.

In October the banned opposition *Erk* (Freedom) party held a general meeting despite official attempts to obstruct it, including the brief detention of members and confiscation of party materials. The unregistered *Birlik* (Unity) opposition movement was refused registration as a political party by the Ministry of Justice.

Human rights defenders under attack
The non-governmental human rights organization *Ezgulik* (Good Deeds) was allowed to register in March. Five members of the unregistered Human Rights Society of Uzbekistan (OPCHU) were released from imprisonment: Yuldash Rasulov in January; Musulmonkul Khamraev, Norpulat Radzhapov and Dzhura Muradov in August; and Tursinbay Utamuratov in October. However, human rights defenders continued to face intimidation, ill-treatment and imprisonment.

▢ Elena Urlaeva and Larisa Vdovina were released in December 2002 and January 2003 respectively after being forcibly confined in a psychiatric hospital in August 2002, reportedly because of their human rights activities. In June the Mirzo Ulugbek district civil court in Tashkent declared Larisa Vdovina mentally unsound, but she remained at liberty, despite failing to have the decision reversed on appeal. An independent psychiatric assessment in the Russian Federation in March found Elena Urlaeva not in need of psychiatric treatment. She was briefly detained by police on her way to a demonstration in April and again in August, when officers from the National Security Service (SNB) dragged her from her car and kicked her.

▢ Ruslan Sharipov, a 25-year-old correspondent for the Russian news agency PRIMA and Chairman of the unregistered human rights organization *Grazhdanskoe sodeystvye* (Civic Assistance), was arrested in May. In August he was convicted on charges of homosexuality, punishable by up to three years' imprisonment, "encouraging minors to commit antisocial behaviour" and having sex with minors. He was sentenced to five-and-a-half years' imprisonment. In September his sentence was reduced on appeal to four years. In October he was reportedly transferred to a penal colony. He insisted that the charges were fabricated because of his critical reporting and human rights work, and that the court had ignored forensic medical tests that exonerated him. He alleged that he was tortured into changing his plea to guilty, dismissing his lawyers and writing a suicide note. He said he was threatened with rape and suffocation, had a gas mask put over his head and the air supply turned off, and was injected with an unknown substance. In August his legal representative, Surat Ikramov, Chairman of the unregistered Initiative Group of Independent Human Rights Defenders, was dragged from his car by masked men, bound hand and foot, and driven to the outskirts of Tashkent where he was dumped. On the journey, he was beaten severely and had a plastic bag tied tightly over his head.

Rights of political prisoners violated
Supporters of the banned Islamic party *Hizb-ut-Tahrir* and members of independent Islamic congregations and their families continued to face imprisonment,

detention and intimidation. Dozens, sometimes hundreds, of women and children organized peaceful protests against the harsh conditions and torture of their imprisoned relatives. Most were forcibly dispersed or detained by the police.

Political prisoners were reportedly subjected to cruel, inhuman and degrading treatment.

⌐ In June Malika Raimova was sentenced by Chilanzar District Court in Tashkent to eight years' imprisonment, deferred for one year because she was pregnant. She had been convicted on charges of "attempting to overthrow the constitutional order of Uzbekistan" and "being a member of a religious, extremist, separatist, fundamentalist or other prohibited organization" after she allegedly smuggled *Hizb-ut-Tahrir* leaflets to a prisoner. Three other women convicted in the same trial received suspended sentences of two and three years' imprisonment. According to reports, they had no defence lawyers and the court ignored allegations that Malika Raimova had been held for four days in an unheated cell in sub-zero temperatures and that co-accused Mukaddam Nigmanova was deprived of sleep and threatened with rape.

Torture and deaths in custody
In February the UN Special Rapporteur on torture, reporting on a visit to Uzbekistan in 2002, concluded that torture and ill-treatment were systematic and condoned by the authorities. Among his recommendations, he urged the authorities to close Jaslik penal colony where conditions were cruel, inhuman and degrading. In March the Uzbek authorities responded by denying that torture was systematic and criticizing the report. In October a hunger strike by political prisoners at Jaslik, in protest at their conditions and the persecution of their relatives, was reported to have been violently suppressed by special forces.

At least three men died in custody in suspicious circumstances during 2003, reportedly as a result of torture.

⌐ The body of Orif Ershanov, a 37-year-old father of four from Tashkent, was returned to his family in May. He had reportedly been detained on suspicion of being a member of *Hizb-ut-Tahrir*. Eyewitnesses said that his body had bruising on the arms, shoulders, upper chest, legs and soles of the feet, open wounds on the back and an arm, and several broken ribs. The authorities reportedly told the family that he became ill while in SNB custody and died of natural causes in hospital, but provided no death certificate.

The death penalty in a flawed judicial system
At least 18 death sentences were passed and at least six executions were carried out. The true figures were believed to be considerably higher, but the authorities again failed to disclose comprehensive statistics, in violation of their international obligations. Death sentences continued to be passed within a criminal justice system seriously flawed by widespread corruption and the failure of the courts to investigate allegations of torture.

In December parliament passed a law reducing the number of articles in the Criminal Code punishable by death from four to two. However, the law reportedly did not come into force during the period under review. The two dropped Articles – "genocide" and "initiating or waging an aggressive war" – had not been in use.

At least four men were executed while their cases were under consideration by the UN Human Rights Committee, despite Uzbekistan's commitment to allow appeals by individuals to the Committee under the Optional Protocol to the International Covenant on Civil and Political Rights.

The authorities reportedly ignored signs of mental disturbance in prisoners under sentence of death.

⌐ Abror Isayev, aged 19, was sentenced to death for murder in December 2002. He had surrendered himself to the police in May 2002 as a potential witness, but was reportedly beaten for a week and coerced into confessing to the crime. In April 2003 he reportedly tried to kill himself and was extremely distressed. His mother repeatedly pressed for treatment but a prison doctor said her son was feigning illness. In June a Ministry of Interior official told her that he was receiving medical treatment and was in satisfactory health. However, in July she found him still severely disturbed and reported seeing senior officials making fun of him.

The clemency process and the executions themselves were shrouded in secrecy. In many cases, prisoners' relatives or anti-death penalty activists were harassed if they complained or protested publicly.

⌐ Tamara Chikunova, Director of the human rights organization Mothers against the Death Penalty and Torture, received silent phone calls at night and death threats. SNB officers openly threatened that the group risked "elimination" after its contributions to the May meeting of the European Bank for Reconstruction and Development. For several weeks, armed police came to Tamara Chikunova's flat every few days to "check her documents", once to search for weapons. She was accused by police of running a brothel and that she sympathized with Islamist "extremists".

The authorities stopped a death penalty conference organized by Mothers against the Death Penalty and Torture due to be held in Tashkent in December on the grounds that the group was not registered. The group had repeatedly been denied registration.

AI country reports/visits
Reports
- "Justice only in heaven" – the death penalty in Uzbekistan (AI Index: EUR 62/011/2003)
- Uzbekistan: Unfair trials and secret executions (summary report) (AI Index: EUR 62/012/2003)
- Uzbekistan: Authorities stop death penalty conference (AI Index: EUR 62/020/2003)
- Concerns in Europe and Central Asia, January-June 2003: Uzbekistan (AI Index: EUR 01/016/2003)
Visits
AI delegates visited Uzbekistan in June to conduct research on the death penalty and in December to attend a conference on the death penalty that was then stopped by the authorities.

MIDDLE EAST/ NORTH AFRICA

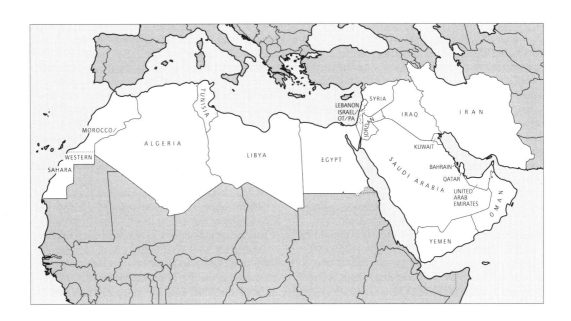

Algeria

Bahrain

Egypt

Iran

Iraq

Israel and the Occupied Territories

Jordan

Kuwait

Lebanon

Libya

Morocco/Western Sahara

Palestinian Authority

Qatar

Saudi Arabia

Syria

Tunisia

United Arab Emirates

Yemen

MIDDLE EAST / NORTH AFRICA REGIONAL OVERVIEW 2003

The death toll in the region's armed conflicts continued to rise in 2003 with the war on Iraq and the ongoing conflicts in Israel and the Occupied Territories and in Algeria. In these and other countries, including Morocco and Saudi Arabia, attacks by armed groups – often unidentified – escalated against civilian and government/military targets.

Political, judicial and legal reforms were increasingly debated in the region, with growing pressure from civil society for greater freedom of expression and association, for more representation and participation in government, and against discriminatory treatment of women in law and practice. At the end of the year the Gulf Cooperation Council announced the creation of a committee for women's affairs to consider women's role as "partners in development" in Gulf states. At the regional level there were moves by the League of Arab States to review the Arab Charter on Human Rights, adopted in 1994, in a process that would consider contributions by non-governmental organizations for the first time.

Despite government promises of reform, grave human rights violations continued across the region. While most governments have ratified major international human rights treaties, these standards were rarely incorporated into law and practice. The absence of basic safeguards facilitated patterns of arbitrary political arrest and detention, prolonged incommunicado detention, torture and ill-treatment. Minimum standards for fair trial were disregarded, resulting in the incarceration of prisoners of conscience, long-term political imprisonment and executions following unfair trials. There were few independent systems or mechanisms to carry out thorough and impartial investigations into human rights abuses, and alleged perpetrators were rarely brought to justice.

Armed conflict

The US-led military intervention in Iraq in March marked the start of a protracted occupation of the country by US, United Kingdom (UK) and other forces under the Coalition Provisional Authority (CPA). In the months leading up to the war, AI called on the US and UK authorities as well as the UN Security Council to consider seriously the human rights and humanitarian

impact of war on the people of Iraq, drawing attention to the needs of the civilian population. The post-war period was marked from the outset by the absence of basic security for ordinary Iraqis, as witnessed by AI delegates who entered the country for the first time in 20 years in April.

AI called on the occupying powers to abide by their obligations under international humanitarian law as a pattern of arbitrary and incommunicado detention, ill-treatment and excessive use of force by the occupying armed forces became more and more entrenched. As many had feared, the absence of basic security led to a sharp upturn in acts of violence by armed groups hitting military targets and, increasingly, international humanitarian operations. In its call for justice for the people of Iraq, AI urged the CPA, the Iraqi Governing Council and the international community to place human rights at the core of the ongoing reconstruction efforts, to bring laws and practice into harmony with international standards, to ensure accountability for all past and present breaches of human rights and humanitarian law, irrespective of the perpetrators, and to guarantee the protection of human rights for all Iraqis.

Armed conflict continued in Israel and the Occupied Territories as the *intifada* (uprising by Palestinians) entered its third year and the grim toll of killings, including of many children, continued to rise. Efforts by the "quartet" (the UN, USA, European Union and Russian Federation) to broker a peace agreement, known as "the road map", between Israel and the Palestinian Authority, were a dead letter by the end of the year, despite the UN Security Council's endorsement of the plan in November. As with previous peace agreements there was scant reference to human rights safeguards and no recognition that durable peace cannot be achieved in the absence of fundamental human rights for all. In December the UN General Assembly adopted a resolution by majority vote to seek an advisory opinion from the International Court of Justice on the legal consequences of the "security wall". The fence/wall is part of a policy of maintaining closures and curfews on Palestinian areas and people on the grounds of maintaining security for Israel. This policy has drastically curtailed freedom of movement and many other rights of Palestinians in the West Bank, and paralysed the Palestinian economy.

The conflict in Algeria continued while the international community and media scrutiny focused on other conflicts in the region. Although there was some reduction in the number of casualties, hundreds of civilians were killed by armed groups, hundreds of members of security forces and state-armed militias were killed in attacks and ambushes, and hundreds of suspected members of armed groups were killed during security force operations.

'War on terror'

The so-called "war on terror" continued to erode fundamental human rights in the region. Members of the League of Arab States continued to implement the

Arab Convention on the Suppression of Terrorism which contained few human rights safeguards. This, as well as a range of bilateral security arrangements, facilitated the transfer of individuals between states in and outside the region without judicial proceedings, legal counsel or recourse to asylum procedures. While some states, such as Egypt and Syria, had long-standing states of emergency in place, the "war on terror" was used as a pretext to legitimize existing practices, such as long-term administrative detention and unfair trials by special courts whose procedures fall far short of international standards. Other states, such as Morocco and Tunisia, introduced new "anti-terrorism" laws during the year, which posed a further threat to basic human rights.

Women's rights

Women's rights were increasingly debated in the region, particularly focusing on violence against women. Women in the region stepped up their campaigning for increased rights. In Kuwait they protested against their continuing exclusion from the electoral process, and in Bahrain they called for personal status laws to protect women's rights.

However, there were few concrete reforms. A series of proposed reforms to the Personal Status Code announced by King Mohamed VI of Morocco in October were intended to improve women's rights. The proposed reforms included raising the legal age of marriage for women from 15 to 18 years and according husband and wife equal and joint responsibility for the family. Other rights, however, such as inheritance rights, which discriminate against women in Morocco as elsewhere in the region, remained largely untouched. In Jordan, proposals to amend Article 340 of the Penal Code (which relates to family killings) to make it more favourable to women were rejected by the Lower House of Parliament. The more frequently used Article 98, which allows for a reduced sentence for perpetrators whose crime was committed in a "fit of rage", remained on the statute books. In Iran, parliament's attempts to press for further reforms relating to women's rights as well as the state's accession to the UN Women's Convention were repeatedly blocked by the Guardian Council, the highest legislative body in Iran. The legislation was referred to an arbitration authority in December because of irreconcilable differences between the two legislative bodies. In Saudi Arabia, despite much vaunted promises by the authorities to address women's rights in response to more vocal demands by women during the year, there were still no substantive measures to assure women their most basic human rights.

Refugees, migrants and the internally displaced

Refugees and asylum-seekers continued to suffer from a lack of protection mechanisms across the region. Only Algeria, Egypt, Iran, Israel, Morocco and Yemen were party to the 1951 UN Refugee Convention or its 1967 Protocol. For North African countries, the African system for human rights protection remained widely under-used. Most countries in the region, even those that are party to the UN Refugee Convention, lacked national asylum legislation, which further diminished the protection accorded to asylum-seekers and refugees. The UN High Commissioner for Refugees (UNHCR) continued to undertake the bulk of refugee status determination in most countries, even in those that have signed the UN Refugee Convention. Asylum-seekers continued to have no access to national judicial review procedures of their asylum claims, which in turn contributed to the growing practice of detaining refugees and asylum-seekers, including in Egypt, a party to the UN Convention, as well as in Lebanon and Libya which have not ratified the Convention.

Palestinian refugees continued to suffer from a lack of a protection mechanism in the areas of operation of the UN Relief and Works Agency for the Near East (UNRWA). UNRWA's overstretched resources also meant that the assistance received by many Palestinian refugees did not meet their needs. Palestinian refugees endured particularly severe hardship in several areas, including in Iraq where hundreds of families found themselves homeless after the fall of the government in March, and in Lebanon where the livelihood of hundreds of thousands of Palestinian refugees was undermined by policies discriminating against them and effectively restricting their economic and social rights.

Internal displacement continued to be a major issue in Iraq, affecting Kurdish, Marsh Arab, Shi'a and Sunni populations. The number of Iraqis seeking asylum decreased significantly as a result of the war. By the end of 2003, several European countries, as well as Iran, were developing plans to return Iraqi refugees and asylum-seekers, contrary to UNHCR's advice, to the precarious security conditions in Iraq and the general unsuitability of conditions there for return.

People-smuggling from North Africa to southern Europe and from the Horn of Africa to Yemen remained a concern. Restrictive immigration policies in many countries meant that for migrants and asylum-seekers alike there was no option but to use criminal groups of people-smugglers. Boat accidents continued and numerous would-be immigrants and asylum-seekers died at sea.

Human rights defenders

The human rights debate continued to flourish, although those engaged in "front line" work in defence of human rights often found themselves at risk. In Algeria, Egypt, Lebanon, Morocco/Western Sahara, Syria and Tunisia, women and men were detained or threatened because of their human rights work. In several countries human rights organizations faced severe obstacles to gaining legal status under restrictive laws governing non-governmental organizations which effectively curtailed their human rights work as well as their funding. Meanwhile the Israeli authorities denied entry into the country to many international human rights workers and restricted the movement of human rights and peace and solidarity activists within the Occupied Territories. However, the award of the Nobel Peace Prize in December to Iranian lawyer Shirin Ebadi helped to promote the cause of human rights defenders within Iran and the region as a whole.

ALGERIA

PEOPLE'S DEMOCRATIC REPUBLIC OF ALGERIA
Head of state: Abdelaziz Bouteflika
Head of government: Ahmed Ouyahia (replaced Ali Benflis in May)
Death penalty: abolitionist in practice
UN Women's Convention: ratified with reservations
Optional Protocol to UN Women's Convention: not signed

Hundreds of people were killed in the internal conflict that had been raging since 1992. Hundreds of civilians were killed in attacks by armed groups. Hundreds of members of the security forces and state-armed militias were killed in attacks and ambushes. Hundreds of suspected members of armed groups were killed during security force operations. Torture continued to be widespread, particularly during secret and unacknowledged detention, and was systematic in nearly all cases involving alleged links to what the government described as "terrorist" activities. Human rights defenders continued to be subjected to restrictions by the authorities and journalists were targeted after exposing high-level corruption. Despite increased debate on human rights issues, impunity persisted as a key obstacle in addressing the legacy of past human rights abuses, including thousands of cases of torture, "disappearances" and killings committed by security forces, state-armed militias and armed groups since 1992. The state of emergency imposed in 1992 remained in place. Several death sentences were passed against suspected members of armed groups. A moratorium on executions remained in force.

Background

The political situation was unstable in the context of open power struggles ahead of presidential elections scheduled for April 2004. Demonstrations, strikes and public protests were widespread, with some protests leading to violent clashes between protesters and security forces. Algerians voiced their discontent mainly about domestic social, economic and political problems, in addition to the war on Iraq. A ban on demonstrations in the capital Algiers, in force since October 2001, remained in in place.

Algerian women's organizations continued to campaign to reform Algeria's Family Code and to provide legal equality between men and women.

In the predominantly Amazigh (Berber) region of Kabylia, northeastern Algeria, negotiations continued between the government and part of the protest movement demanding greater independence for the region and recognition of Amazigh language and culture. During 2003 most Kabyle activists who had previously been imprisoned were conditionally released, but some continued to face trial on charges of disrupting public order or membership of unauthorized organizations.

Thirty-two European tourists were abducted in the Algerian Sahara near the town of Illizi in February and March. Seventeen were freed in May and a second group of 14 was released in August in northern Mali after one hostage had died, reportedly as a result of heat exhaustion. The abductions were believed to have been carried out by the armed group *Groupe salafiste pour la prédication et le combat* (GSPC), Salafist Group for Preaching and Combat.

The USA and several member states of the European Union repeated their public declarations of support for Algeria's "counter-terrorism" policy and paved the way to resume military transfers to Algeria following years of a *de facto* embargo.

Killings

The conflict that began in 1992 continued. According to figures published by official sources, some 900 people were killed during 2003. There was no independent confirmation of this figure. Those killed included hundreds of civilians killed in attacks by armed groups. The perpetrators of these killings were generally not identified. In addition to this, hundreds of members of the security forces and state-armed militias were killed in attacks and ambushes, and hundreds of members of armed groups were killed during security force operations. Little or no information was available on attempts made to arrest them, raising concerns that some of these killings may constitute extrajudicial executions. Based on reports issued by security sources, Algerian newspapers also reported that women and girls were sporadically abducted by armed groups.

Torture and secret detention

Torture remained widespread and was facilitated by the continuing practice of secret and unacknowledged detention. People suspected of crimes categorized as "acts of terrorism or subversion" were systematically tortured. Legal safeguards against torture and secret detention were not respected by law enforcement agents. In no case were allegations of torture fully, independently and impartially investigated.

In March, 42-year-old restaurant manager Mohamed Belkheir was arrested and reportedly tortured during a period of 10 days in the custody of Military Security in Ben Aknoun, Algiers. He stated that he had been tied down and forced to swallow large quantities of dirty water, beaten and given electric shocks. He was apparently forced to sign a "confession" without being allowed to read it and then charged with belonging to a "terrorist" group and withholding information from the police. Mohamed Belkheir denied the charges. Although he was examined by a doctor when he was remanded in pre-trial detention, the likely causes of injuries found on his body were not established, nor were the allegations of torture investigated.

Impunity

No full, independent and impartial investigations were carried out into crimes against humanity committed since 1992, including thousands of cases of extrajudicial execution, deliberate and arbitrary killings of civilians, torture and ill-treatment and "disappearances". In the overwhelming majority of cases, no concrete measures were known to have been taken to bring to justice those responsible for human rights abuses committed by the security forces, state-armed militias or armed groups in 2003 or previous years.

'Disappearances'

There was increased public debate on the issue of "disappearances" throughout 2003. Farouk Ksentini, head of the national human rights body, the *Commission nationale consultative de promotion et de protection des droits de l'homme* (CNCPPDH), National Advisory Commission for the Promotion and Protection of Human Rights, repeated earlier pledges that the problem of "disappearances" would be resolved, and met with organizations representing families of the "disappeared". In September President Bouteflika set up a temporary body, headed by Farouk Ksentini and composed of six appointed members of the CNCPPDH. Families of the "disappeared" and organizations working on the issue had not been consulted on the establishment of the new mechanism. The body is intended to serve as an interface between families of the "disappeared" and the authorities, but does not have the power to investigate cases of "disappearance".

No other measures were taken and, consequently, there was no move towards investigating the thousands of cases of "disappearance", most of which occurred between 1994 and 1998. The authorities continued to deny that state agents had been responsible for a pattern of "disappearances".

Kabylia

Although an official inquiry carried out in 2001 into the deaths of dozens of anti-government protesters in Kabylia that year had concluded that agents of the gendarmerie had used excessive lethal force during the policing of the protests, there was no follow-up to these findings in 2003. The authorities stated that they had begun to compensate victims and their families, but no investigations were known to have been opened into the more than 100 deaths and hundreds of injuries by firearms. The authorities also stated that some 20 gendarmes had been tried for abuse of firearms. However, no information was available to confirm that any gendarmes had been brought to trial for human rights violations committed during the policing of demonstrations in Kabylia.

Human rights defenders

Human rights defenders continued to face restrictions in carrying out human rights work. Some faced arrest and judicial proceedings. Freedom of association and assembly remained restricted.

Organizations working on behalf of victims of "disappearance" continued to be unsuccessful in obtaining official registration for their organizations. Although their demonstrations were largely tolerated, incidents of harassment and intimidation continued to occur.

⬜ In Oran several relatives of the "disappeared" were arrested in July during one of their weekly demonstrations outside the court and fined for public order offences.

⬜ A positive development was the acquittal and release of Salaheddine Sidhoum, a doctor and human rights defender, who had been living in hiding for nine years. His 20-year sentence, handed down *in absentia* in 1997 on charges related to "acts of terrorism or subversion", was quashed by a criminal court in Algiers in October after he turned himself in.

Freedom of expression

Restrictions on freedom of expression were stepped up in the context of heightened political tension ahead of the 2004 presidential elections. In August, six privately owned Algerian newspapers were barred from publication, officially because they owed money to the state-run printing firm. All of them had published reports in previous months alleging the involvement of senior government officials in corruption and other financial scandals. Several journalists and a newspaper director were sentenced to suspended prison terms or fines on charges of defamation, including of the Head of State, in connection with articles or cartoons.

⬜ Hasan Bouras, a journalist with a local newspaper in El-Bayadh province who had exposed corruption among local officials, was arrested in November and detained for nearly a month. He was charged with defamation and sentenced to two years' imprisonment, a fine and a five-year ban from exercising his profession as a journalist. In December an appeal court reduced the sentence to a fine and damages.

⬜ Several foreign journalists were expelled from Algeria in July. This followed the release of the two former leaders of the banned Islamist party *Front Islamique du Salut* (FIS), Islamic Salvation Front – Abassi Madani and Ali Benhadj. The expulsions were intended to curb international media reporting of the releases. Abassi Madani and Ali Benhadj had been sentenced to 12 years' imprisonment in 1992 following an unfair trial. Their arrest followed the cancellation of Algeria's first multi-party elections and the banning of the FIS which had looked set to win the elections. On their release, the military prosecutor imposed restrictions on their civil and political rights, apparently without a court order.

Prison conditions

As part of ongoing justice reform, improvements were reported in conditions of detention. In spite of this, prison conditions remained a cause for serious concern. No results were published of an inquiry opened by the Minister of Justice into the deaths of some 50 prisoners following fires in several prisons in 2002. Hunger strikes by groups of detainees were reported in different prisons throughout 2003. Dozens protested against the fact that they had been detained for more than a year without trial. Under Algerian law, those accused of "crimes considered to be terrorist or subversive acts" may be held in pre-trial detention for up to 36 months.

The International Committee of the Red Cross (ICRC) continued prison visits, resumed in 1999. The ICRC was also able to visit a number of police stations and places of detention run by the gendarmerie. No independent organization was given access to military prisons or detention centres run by Military Security; many allegations of torture, ill-treatment and inhumane conditions continued to be reported from these facilities.

UN human rights mechanisms

The UN Working Group on Enforced or Involuntary Disappearances, the UN Special Rapporteur on extrajudicial, summary or arbitrary executions and the UN Special Rapporteur on torture were not granted access to Algeria in 2003. In his 2003 report, the Special Rapporteur on torture indicated that he continued to receive information according to which a large number of people were subjected to torture and other forms of ill-treatment. The Rapporteur went on to say that he noted "the denial [by the Government] of most allegations on the basis of the absence of complaint. In view of the nature of the allegations brought to [the Rapporteur's] attention, it is unreasonable to expect alleged victims to formally file any complaint". He reminded the government "of its obligation to thoroughly investigate all torture cases even in the absence of a formal complaint."

AI country reports/ visits

Reports

- Algeria: Steps towards change or empty promises? (AI Index: MDE 28/005/2003)
- Algeria: Asylum-seekers fleeing a continuing human rights crisis (AI Index: MDE 28/007/2003)

Visits

AI delegates were able to visit Algeria in February and March, for the first time in more than two years, and in October to observe the trial of Salaheddine Sidhoum.

BAHRAIN

KINGDOM OF BAHRAIN

Head of state: King Hamad bin 'Issa Al Khalifa
Head of government: Shaikh Khalifa bin Salman Al Khalifa
Death penalty: retentionist
UN Women's Convention: ratified with reservations
Optional Protocol to UN Women's Convention: not signed

In the wake of the wide-ranging reforms of 2001, concrete safeguards for human rights continued to be implemented. Nevertheless, several journalists were prosecuted in connection with articles published. Prisoners went on hunger-strike in Jaw Prison, reportedly against ill-treatment and lack of access to lawyers. One hunger striker died. Protests were organized calling for a 2002 decree relating to impunity to be repealed and for past human rights violators to be brought to justice.

Background

Several demonstrations took place during the year. Demonstrators and police clashed in March when thousands of people protested against the US-led war in Iraq. Scores of people were reportedly injured. In May workers marched to celebrate International Labour Day and to protest against unemployment. In September unemployed teachers demonstrated outside the Ministry of Education to protest against the lack of teaching jobs. Six political groups organized a seminar in July, reportedly attended by thousands of people, to debate a royal decree issued in 2002 granting Bahraini citizenship to nationals of Gulf Cooperation Council countries residing in Bahrain. Many of those present expressed concern that the decree was aimed at shifting the demographic balance against the majority Shi'a Muslim population.

In February the authorities announced the arrest of five men on suspicion of planning "terrorist" attacks in Bahrain and of having links with *al-Qa'ida*. Three of the five were released in March and the case against them was dropped in June for "lack of evidence". In July the Supreme Court found Jamal al-Balushi guilty of possessing weapons and sentenced him to five years' imprisonment and a fine. The fifth man, 'Issa al-Balushi, a member of the armed forces, was awaiting trial before a military court. In another case, 'Uday 'Abdul Amir Hassun, an Iraqi national, was sentenced to three years' imprisonment by the Supreme Court in October after he was found guilty of a bomb attack in March near a US Navy base in al-Jufayr.

Women human rights activists repeatedly called for the enactment of personal status laws to protect women's rights, and took part in street protests and other campaigning activities.

Freedom of expression

The Press and Publications Law, which was issued in 2002 and appeared to violate international standards on freedom of expression, remained withdrawn pending amendments. However, several journalists were prosecuted in connection with articles that appeared in the national press.

🗁 In May, 11 *Shari'a* (Islamic law) judges brought a case before a criminal court against four women – Badriya Rabi'a, Ghada Jamsheer and Fatima al-Hawaj, all human rights activists; and Mariam Ahmad, a journalist – and three men – Anwar 'Abdul Rahman, editor of the daily newspaper *Akhbar al-Khaleej*; Mohammed al-Mutawa', a lawyer; and Mohammed Sa'eed al-'Aradi, a religious scholar. The seven were accused of defaming the judges in an article in *Akhbar al-Khaleej* in April that reported a hunger strike by Badriya Rabi'a which she began after a *Shari'a* court granted her former husband custody of their two children. In October the criminal court referred the case to the Constitutional Court.

🗁 Mansur al-Jamri and Hussain Khalaf, respectively the editor and a journalist of the daily newspaper *al-Wasat*, appeared in court in June for publishing an article in March about the release of three men arrested on suspicion of planning "terrorist" attacks (see above).

The authorities said the article violated the press law and "state security". At the request of the lawyers the case was postponed until 2004.

✉ Radhi al-Mousawi, editor of the monthly magazine *Aldemokrati* of the political group National Democratic Action Society, was summoned by the public prosecutor in September after an article in the magazine alleged that a government official was involved in corruption.

Prison hunger strikes

In August more than 200 prisoners went on hunger strike for about two weeks in Jaw Prison, southern Bahrain, and barricaded themselves in parts of the building, reportedly to protest against ill-treatment and lack of access to lawyers and human rights activists. The strike ended after negotiations involving the Interior Ministry, human rights groups and members of parliament. One prisoner, Yassir Jasim Makki, died in March following an earlier hunger strike at the same prison in February, allegedly as a result of not receiving timely medical treatment for his deteriorating health. The authorities indicated in a letter to AI that an investigation had concluded that his death was the result of natural causes involving a blood disease. No details of the investigation were made known.

Impunity

More than 30,000 people were reported to have petitioned the King in May to repeal Decree No. 56 of October 2002. The decree effectively grants impunity to anyone who had committed or been involved in human rights violations before February 2001. The petition also called on past allegations of torture to be investigated and for victims to be compensated. A former colonel in the Security and Intelligence Service (SIS), 'Adel Jassem Fleifel, who returned to the country in November 2002 and was arrested to face allegations of corruption, was released immediately after his arrest. Hundreds of people demonstrated in the capital al-Manama calling for him to be brought to justice for his alleged involvement in torture of political detainees. In September, two lawyers filed a complaint on behalf of three former political prisoners against several security officers, including 'Adel Jassem Fleifel and Major-General Ian Henderson, a United Kingdom national and former head of the SIS, for their alleged part in the torture of the prisoners. It was not known whether the complaint was taken up in court.

EGYPT

ARAB REPUBLIC OF EGYPT
Head of state: Muhammad Hosni Mubarak
Head of government: 'Atif Muhammad 'Ubayd
Death penalty: retentionist
UN Women's Convention: ratified with reservations
Optional Protocol to UN Women's Convention: not signed

Prisoners of conscience continued to be sentenced to prison terms. Thousands of suspected supporters of banned Islamist groups, including possible prisoners of conscience, remained in detention without charge or trial; some had been held for years. Others were serving sentences imposed after grossly unfair trials before exceptional courts. Torture and ill-treatment of detainees continued to be systematic. Death sentences continued to be passed and carried out.

Background

In February, the state of emergency was extended for a further three years despite a campaign led by human rights organizations, political parties and civil society activists calling for it to be ended.

In April, Egypt ratified the Euro-Mediterranean Association Agreement with the European Union (EU). The accord focuses on trade, economic integration, security and political relations, but also contains a legally binding clause obliging the contracting parties to promote and protect human rights.

In June, two new laws were passed. The first was to establish a national council for human rights. At the end of the year, the 27 members of the council had not been appointed by the Shura Council, Egypt's Upper House, but they were expected to include representatives from human rights organizations. The second law restricted the scope of cases to be examined by state security courts and abolished the penalty of hard labour.

Between 1,000 and 2,000 alleged members of armed Islamist groups were reportedly released during the year. The Interior Minister presented the releases in the context of the public renunciation of past and present acts of violence, particularly by leading members of *al-Gama'a al-Islamiya* (Islamic Group).

Dozens of alleged members of the banned Muslim Brothers organization were detained in so-called preventive detention. By the end of the year, the majority had been released without being tried.

In the first half of the year, hundreds of people, including lawyers, journalists, members of parliament, academics and students, associated with the movement protesting against the war on Iraq were detained, the majority for participating in unauthorized demonstrations. Some were held for several weeks in administrative detention under emergency legislation. Many alleged that they were tortured or ill-treated in detention.

Freedom of expression and association restricted

Legal restrictions and government controls continued to limit the activities of political parties, non-governmental organizations (NGOs), professional associations, trade unions and the news media. The authorities maintained bans on several political parties imposed in previous years and party newspapers remained suspended.

People continued to be detained, tried and imprisoned in violation of their rights to freedom of expression and association. Prisoners of conscience included civil society activists and members of religious groups.

▢ A verdict scheduled to be announced at the end of the year in the trial before the (Emergency) Supreme State Security Court of 23 Egyptians and three United Kingdom nationals was postponed until 2004. The 26, all prisoners of conscience, were charged in connection with their alleged affiliation with *Hizb al-Tahrir al-Islami* (Islamic Liberation Party), which is not registered under Egyptian law. Several of the defendants were reportedly tortured or ill-treated following their detention in April and May 2002.

▢ In December, the trial of Ashraf Ibrahim and four other men opened before the (Emergency) Supreme State Security Court. At the opening of the trial, the four other men remained at liberty. Three of the men, including Ashraf Ibrahim, were charged with leadership of an illegal organization and faced up to 15 years' imprisonment. Ashraf Ibrahim faced two additional charges. One of these — harming Egypt's reputation by spreading abroad false information regarding the internal affairs of the country — related to information on alleged human rights violations given to international human rights organizations. The trial was continuing at the end of the year.

Human rights defenders

NGOs continued to operate under the shadow of a restrictive law, passed in June 2002, which regulates their activities. From June, the Ministry for Social Affairs began announcing its decisions on applications put forward by existing and newly established NGOs for registration under the new law. Certain organizations were granted registration while others were reportedly denied it without adequate explanation. In some cases, those denied registration challenged the decision before the courts.

▢ In March, the Court of Cassation acquitted human rights defenders Saad Eddin Ibrahim and Nadia `Abd al-Nur of the Ibn Khaldun Center for Development Studies of all charges. They had been sentenced to seven and two years' imprisonment respectively after previous trials. The main charges against them related to EU-funded projects aimed at promoting participation in elections.

Freedom of religion violated

People continued to be at risk of detention, trial and imprisonment in violation of their right to freedom of religion.

▢ In February, the (Emergency) State Security Court for Misdemeanours sentenced six people to six months' imprisonment for "contempt of religion" in connection with holding private religious gatherings and advocating modifications to basic Islamic rules. The five men and one woman had been tried by the same court in March 2002 and were acquitted. Two other men, Amin Youssef and Ali Mamdouh, who were originally tried with the six and sentenced to three years' imprisonment each, were not included in the retrial ordered by President Mubarak.

Trials in connection with alleged sexual orientation

Dozens of men suffered discrimination, persecution and imprisonment solely in connection with their actual or perceived sexual orientation. Many of those arrested alleged that they were tortured or ill-treated in detention. Although same-sex relations are not explicitly prohibited under Egyptian law, men continued to be sentenced on the charge of "habitual debauchery", which is applied to consensual sexual relations between adult men.

▢ In June and July, 14 men had their sentences reduced on appeal from three to one year's imprisonment. This was the final stage of the retrial, ordered for 50 men by President Mubarak in July 2002, in the case of 52 men tried in 2001 in connection with their alleged sexual orientation.

Several men were detained and tried after they agreed to meet men contacted through the Internet who turned out to be security officers or police informants.

▢ In February, Wissam Tawfiq Abyad was sentenced to 15 months' imprisonment after meeting a man, later believed to be a security officer or police informant, he had contacted through an Internet website for gay men. Private electronic conversations held on the Internet were used as evidence against him.

Unfair trials

Dozens of people faced trial before exceptional courts, such as state security courts, established under emergency legislation. They were charged with a variety of offences, including membership of illegal organizations, contempt for religion, espionage and corruption. The procedures of these courts fell far short of international standards for fair trial.

▢ In February, Nabil Ahmed Soliman was sentenced to five years' imprisonment by the (Emergency) Supreme State Security Court in Cairo, which denies defendants the right to a full review before a higher tribunal, on charges of membership of an illegal organization in connection with his alleged affiliation with the armed Islamist group *al-Gihad* (Holy War). His trial took place after he was deported from the USA to Egypt on 12 June 2002 following a request by the Egyptian authorities on the basis of his alleged affiliation with *al-Gihad*.

Torture and ill-treatment

Torture continued to be used systematically in detention centres throughout the country. Several people died in custody in circumstances suggesting that torture or ill-treatment may have caused or contributed to their deaths.

Torture victims came from all walks of life and included political activists and people arrested during criminal investigations. The most common torture methods reported were electric shocks, beatings, suspension by the wrists or ankles, and various forms of psychological torture, including death threats and threats of rape or sexual abuse of the detainee or a female relative.

▭ Ramiz Gihad was among six men detained in connection with a demonstration against the war on Iraq held on 12 April outside the Egyptian Journalists' Union in Cairo. They were reportedly held incommunicado for between two and 10 days at the State Security Investigations headquarters in Lazoghly Square, Cairo. Ramiz Gihad alleged that he was beaten, slapped, kicked, suspended and subjected to electric shocks.

Inadequate investigations

In the vast majority of cases of alleged torture, no one was brought to justice because the authorities failed to conduct prompt, impartial and thorough investigations. However, some trials of alleged torturers did take place, but only in criminal, not political cases, and generally only after the most serious incidents, usually where the victims had died.

▭ In June, four police officers were sentenced on appeal to a suspended sentence of one year's imprisonment in connection with the case of Farid Shawqy 'Abd al-'Al, who died in al-Muntaza police station in 1999. An autopsy had found injuries on the body consistent with punching and beating with a stick, including on the soles of the feet (falaqa).

▭ In November, the trial of seven police officers opened before Alexandria Criminal Court in connection with the arrest, detention and torture of school bus driver Muhammad Badr al-Din Gum'a Isma'il in Alexandria in 1996.

Extraditions and abuses

The authorities reportedly requested the extradition of Egyptian nationals from several countries, including Bosnia-Herzegovina, Iran and Uruguay. As a result, some people were threatened with extradition or were forcibly returned to Egypt, where they were at risk of human rights violations, including torture or ill-treatment.

▭ On 7 July, the Uruguayan authorities forcibly returned Al-Sayid Hassan Mukhlis to Egypt following an extradition request by the Egyptian authorities. He was reportedly held incommunicado at the headquarters of the State Security Investigations in Cairo where torture has been frequently reported. Al-Sayid Hassan Mukhlis' extradition was sought for his alleged involvement in human rights abuses committed by al-Gama'a al-Islamiya.

AI country reports/visits
Report
· Egypt: Time to implement the UN Committee against Torture's recommendations (AI Index: MDE 12/038/2003)

IRAN

ISLAMIC REPUBLIC OF IRAN
Leader of the Islamic Republic of Iran: Ayatollah Sayed 'Ali Khamenei
President: Hojjatoleslam val Moslemin Sayed Mohammad Khatami
Death penalty: retentionist
UN Women's Convention and its Optional Protocol: not signed

Scores of political prisoners, including prisoners of conscience, continued to serve sentences imposed in previous years following unfair trials. Scores more were arrested in 2003, often arbitrarily and many following student demonstrations. At least a dozen political prisoners arrested during the year were detained without charge, trial or regular access to their families and lawyers. Judicial authorities curtailed freedoms of expression, opinion and association, including of ethnic minorities; scores of publications were closed, Internet sites were filtered and journalists were imprisoned. At least one detainee died in custody, reportedly after being beaten. During the year the pattern of harassment of political prisoners' family members re-emerged. At least 108 executions were carried out, including of long-term political prisoners and frequently in public. At least four prisoners were sentenced to death by stoning while at least 197 people were sentenced to be flogged and 11 were sentenced to amputation of fingers and limbs. The true numbers may have been considerably higher.

Background
The development and fulfilment of human rights in Iran were adversely affected by the political stalemate between supporters and opponents of reform. Socio-political and human rights reforms, favoured by President Khatami and parliament, were often blocked by the Guardian Council (GC), the highest legislative body whose function is to ensure that laws uphold Islamic tenets and the Iranian Constitution. The GC follows a stricter interpretation of political and social conduct and moral codes. Its continued rejection of legislative reforms contributed to a growing sense of despondency and alienation from political affairs among large swathes of society, especially students, and was reflected by a low turnout for municipal elections in March.

In June, the International Labour Organization called on Iran to report on the application of gozinesh (selection) – discriminatory and ideologically-based regulations that stipulate who is eligible to work in the state sector or who can attend university. During the year, discriminatory and arbitrary procedures based on gozinesh were employed in the selection of candidates for parliamentary elections scheduled for February 2004.

Following heightened domestic and international security concerns over Iran's nuclear power program, the country's accession in December to the International Atomic Energy Agency's Additional Protocol contributed to an easing of diplomatic tensions with the European Union (EU) and the USA.

A growing sense in Iran of the importance of international human rights standards was indicated by local initiatives to expose abuses. In June, the leading student body *Daftar-e Tahkim-e Vahdat* (Office for Strengthening Unity – OSU) issued an open letter to the UN Secretary-General describing human rights violations in Iran in terms of the rights set out in the Universal Declaration of Human Rights. Relatives of political prisoners and prisoners of conscience publicized the plight of their loved ones. Non-governmental organizations such as the Iranian Jurists Association for the Defence of Human Rights, and the Association for the Defence of Prisoners' Rights pressed for higher standards in the administration of justice and in prison conditions.

In August, the Secretary General of the parastatal Islamic Human Rights Commission stated that it had received over 12,000 letters from people interested in the human rights situation in Iran.

The judiciary and its security force continued to carry out arbitrary arrests and often held people in secret detention. Detainees were denied access for varying periods to relatives, legal representation and, in a number of cases, medical care.

Legal reforms
Legal reforms addressing human rights concerns that were rejected by the GC included two bills introduced by the Presidency and passed by parliament in 2002. The first was a bill to allow the President to overturn court decisions deemed unconstitutional. The second, which would have removed the GC's powers to select general election candidates, was rejected twice.

In August, citing financial and constitutional reasons, the GC rejected a parliamentary bill providing for Iran's accession to the UN Convention against Torture. In December, parliament clarified concerns raised by the GC but the Convention had not been ratified by the end of the year. Draft legislation aimed at prohibiting torture to obtain confessions or information had been rejected twice in 2002.

A bill put to parliament by the judiciary facilitating the creation of juvenile courts was passed by parliament in December. If upheld by the GC, it would exempt from the death penalty children aged under 18 at the time of the offence.

After many years of debate, the role of prosecutor was reintroduced in early 2003. However, the controversy surrounding the role of Tehran's Chief Prosecutor in connection with the death in custody of Zahra Kazemi in July (see below) indicated that practices in relation to such posts urgently needed to be brought in line with international standards. It remained to be seen whether the introduction of provincial prosecutors would serve the interests of human rights.

In December, legislation providing for equal compensation (*diyeh* – blood money) to non-Muslim victims of crime was concluded by the Expediency Council (an arbitration body that is empowered to finalize legislation) and widely welcomed by Iran's minorities.

Imprisoned students
Following reports that universities would be privatized and tuition costs increased, a protest by a group of students in early June inspired mass demonstrations that continued throughout the month. In the resulting unrest, hundreds of people were arrested, including three members of the OSU who were arbitrarily arrested by plainclothes officials following a press conference. Most detainees were released without charge. However, 132 reportedly remained in detention without charge or trial at the end of the year. An AI request in August for information about their situation received no response.

Students convicted and imprisoned after student demonstrations in July 1999 were reported to have been ill-treated in custody. In several cases, they faced new charges, including some relating to defamation and insult, reportedly based on statements made in prison or given to the media while on temporary leave from prison.

◻ Manuchehr Mohammadi, who had been sentenced to 13 years' imprisonment (reduced to seven years on appeal) following a manifestly unfair trial in October 1999, was reportedly transferred from Evin Prison in June to another prison, raising fears for his safety. He had reportedly been severely beaten by officials in Evin Prison after he gave an interview to a radio station based outside Iran. In July, his sister and father, who had travelled to Tehran from their home in the north of the country, were arbitrarily arrested by plainclothes officials.

◻ Ahmad Batebi, who had been sentenced to death in connection with his participation in student demonstrations in July 1999, was granted temporary leave on medical grounds in October 2003. He went missing on 8 November and his family was subsequently informed that he had been rearrested on 17 November. It was widely believed that he was arbitrarily rearrested for having met the visiting UN Special Rapporteur on the promotion and protection of the right to freedom of opinion and expression. The government stated he had been arrested for violating the terms of his temporary leave.

Administration of justice
Flagrant violations of Iranian and international law continued in the administration of justice. At least one detainee died in custody, reportedly after being beaten. Scores of individuals were held in arbitrary and incommunicado detention, often for prolonged periods.

◻ Zahra Kazemi, of dual Iranian/Canadian nationality, was arrested on 23 June outside Evin prison in Tehran and accused of taking photographs in a prohibited area. She died in a military hospital, still in custody, on 12 July. During her detention, she had been interrogated for three days by judicial officials and later by Ministry of

Intelligence officials. It was widely believed that she had been tortured. An inquiry ordered by President Khatami found that she died of a brain haemorrhage, apparently caused by beating. On 23 September, a Ministry of Intelligence official was charged with "semi-intentional" murder. In October, parliament's Article 90 Commission — constitutionally charged with investigating citizens' complaints — detailed allegations of irregularities and human rights abuses carried out by Tehran's Chief Prosecutor in the case. The Article 90 Commission argued that his actions perverted the course of justice and referred its report to the disciplinary court for judges.

▭ Three members of a religious group, *Melli Mazhabi* (National Religious Alliance), were denied access to their lawyer and family members from the time of their arrest in June to the end of the year. They were reportedly detained incommunicado for supporting student demonstrators. Their lawyer was not informed of any charges against them or allowed to see their file.

Families who raised concerns about the treatment of their imprisoned relatives were threatened, usually with prosecution, and harassed. Some were also evicted from their homes, at times after their homes had been searched and left uninhabitable.

In December, President Khatami announced that he had agreed with the Head of the Judiciary, Ayatollah Shahroudi, to conduct a probe into prison conditions.

Women's rights

In December, lawyer Shirin Ebadi received the Nobel Peace Prize for her promotion of human rights, especially the rights of women and children. She is a member of the Iranian Jurists Association for the Defence of Human Rights, whose founding members included five lawyers who had previously been imprisoned and banned from practising law for periods by the Revolutionary Court.

In August, the GC rejected legislation passed by parliament providing for Iran's accession to the UN Women's Convention. In December, citing irreconcilable differences between parliament and the GC, the bill was sent to the Expediency Council.

Death penalty and other cruel, inhuman and degrading punishments

At least 108 people were executed, often in public. The death penalty was carried out on long-term political prisoners, apparently to intimidate political or ethnic groups such as Kurds and Arabs.

At least 197 people were flogged or sentenced to be flogged, often in large groups. At least 11 people were sentenced to have fingers and limbs amputated as judicial punishments. The total figures may have been considerably higher.

In March, EU officials were reportedly informed that the Head of the Judiciary had called on judges not to pass sentences of stoning and to find alternative punishments. Nevertheless, in November, four men in Mashhad, northeastern Iran, were sentenced to death by stoning in connection with allegations of rape and adultery.

▭ Stays of execution were announced in the cases of two women, Afsaneh Nourouzi and Kobra Rahmanpour, who had been sentenced to death for murder. Both said they had been acting in self-defence. The stays of execution were announced following widespread public opposition to the sentences.

▭ In February, long-term political prisoner Sasan Al-e Ken'an, a supporter of the banned *Komala* party, was executed. At the time of his execution his mother was in Tehran seeking a meeting with members of the UN Working Group on Arbitrary Detention (WGAD) who were visiting Iran. On her return home to the town of Sanandaj, she went to visit her son in prison. She was informed that he had been hanged and told not to make a "fuss" but to bury him quickly.

International and regional organizations

The visits by UN human rights experts contributed to increasing awareness of human rights issues in Iran. However, judicial and other authorities made no public response to their recommendations. In November, the Third Committee of the UN General Assembly adopted a resolution welcoming developments in the human rights situation in Iran, but noted ongoing, grave abuses. The resolution urged the government to, among other things, abide by its international obligations, speed judicial reform and guarantee the dignity of the individual.

The WGAD visited Iran in February. The scope of the visit was limited by restrictions apparently imposed by the authorities. The WGAD recommended, among other things, comprehensive reforms of the criminal justice system, in particular the abolition of Revolutionary Courts and the Special Court for the Clergy, and strengthening the position of lawyers.

In November, following a four-month postponement, the UN Special Rapporteur on the promotion and protection of the right to freedom of opinion and expression visited Iran. He met a limited number of political prisoners and did not appear to have the full cooperation of judicial officials.

After an encouraging start in November 2002, further sessions of the EU-Iran Human Rights Dialogue took place in February and October in Belgium, not Iran as originally planned. The venue was changed after the Iranian authorities objected to the participation of AI and Human Rights Watch. Although the dialogue did not lead to substantive change in judicial practices in Iran, the increased contact between individuals and groups in the countries concerned resulted in greater understanding of the human rights situation in Iran.

AI country reports/ visits
Reports
- International Labour Organization: AI's concerns relevant to the 91st session of the International Labour Conference, 3 to 19 June 2003, Iran (AI Index: IOR 42/003/2003)
- Iran: An independent inquiry must be opened into the death of Zahra Kazemi (AI Index: MDE 13/022/2003)

• Iran: Fear of imminent execution – Afsaneh Nourouzi (AI Index: MDE 13/032/2003)

Visits

Despite increasing communications with the authorities at various levels, AI requests to visit Iran were not granted.

IRAQ

REPUBLIC OF IRAQ
Head of state and government: (until April) Saddam Hussain
Head of the Coalition Provisional Authority: (from May) Paul Bremer
Death penalty: retentionist until April, then suspended
UN Women's Convention: ratified with reservations
Optional Protocol to UN Women's Convention: not signed

Hundreds of civilians were killed and thousands injured as a result of bombing by US-led Coalition forces during a war on Iraq launched in March. Mass graves containing thousands of bodies of victims of human rights violations committed under the government of President Saddam Hussain were unearthed. Thousands of people were arrested and detained without charge or trial during the year. Many civilians were killed as a result of excessive use of force by Coalition forces. Scores of women were abducted, raped and killed as law and order broke down after the war. Torture and ill-treatment by Coalition forces were widespread. Armed groups were responsible for gross human rights abuses: scores of civilians, including foreigners, were killed in attacks. A bomb attack on the UN headquarters in August killed 22 people.

Background

The threat of military intervention in Iraq mounted early in the year. The US and United Kingdom (UK) government accused Iraq of possessing weapons of mass destruction. In January, February and March the heads of the UN weapons inspection teams, Hans Blix and Mohammed al-Baradei, presented their reports on Iraq to the UN Security Council. They reported no evidence of weapons of mass destruction but expressed concern that Iraq had not fully accounted for large quantities of chemical and biological agents. They asked for more time to continue inspections. During this period there were major disagreements at the UN level with many countries urging that all peaceful means be exhausted in the dispute between Iraq and the USA. There were also mass anti-war demonstrations in major cities worldwide.

On 20 March a US-led Coalition invaded Iraq from Kuwait, beginning a sustained war by air and land by Coalition forces. In early April US forces took control of Baghdad, ending the 25-year rule of President Saddam Hussain. UK forces took control of the south. On 1 May US President George W. Bush declared the main combat operations over. A former US diplomat, Paul Bremer, was appointed as US Administrator for Iraq and Head of the Coalition Provisional Authority (CPA).

In May the UN Security Council adopted resolution 1483 which lifted the sanctions that had been imposed on Iraq in 1990. However, the human rights provisions in the resolution were few and weak. The Security Council, through this resolution, ignored the appeal of several non-governmental organizations (NGOs) to establish a UN commission of experts to consult Iraqi society, analyse past human rights crimes and recommend the best options to address them. The same month a UN Special Representative for Iraq was appointed.

In July the CPA appointed a 25-member Iraqi Governing Council (IGC) from the various religious and ethnic groups. The Council had some executive powers, but Paul Bremer retained power to overrule or veto its decisions. In early September the IGC appointed an Iraqi interim government, comprising 25 ministerial portfolios, including a Human Rights Ministry.

After May many former Iraqi officials were arrested by or surrendered to Coalition forces. In July, the two sons of former President Saddam Hussain, 'Uday and Qusay, were killed by US troops in Mosul. On 13 December Saddam Hussain was arrested by US soldiers near the town of al-Dawr, south of Tikrit.

Coalition forces failed to live up fully to their responsibilities under international humanitarian law as occupying powers, including their duty to restore and maintain public order and safety, and to provide food, medical care and relief assistance. Widespread looting of public and private buildings and a sharp rise in criminal activities were seen across the country in the aftermath of the war. Many people faced grave dangers to their health owing to power cuts, shortages of clean water and lack of medical services.

Insecurity quickly became the major concern for the Iraqi population, a problem heightened by the lack of appropriate policing and the wide availability of arms. An increase in serious abuses against women, including rape and murder, was reported, and scores of former Ba'ath Party and security force members were targeted in revenge attacks, particularly in the Shi'a dominated districts of Baghdad and in southern Iraq.

In August fighting erupted between Kurds and Turkmen in the town of Tuz Khurmatu, near Kirkuk, leading to eight deaths.

Mass graves containing thousands of bodies were uncovered in many parts of Iraq. The victims were believed to have been executed by Iraqi security forces in the 1980s, in the aftermath of the 1991 uprisings, and in early 2003. Many bodies were exhumed by people desperate to locate missing relatives.

Many new Iraqi human rights NGOs, including women's groups, were formed and began a wide range of human rights activities, including documenting past and present violations. They worked in difficult circumstances and lacked resources and training.

In October the International Donors' Conference for the reconstruction of Iraq was held in Madrid. Donor nations pledged US$33 billion for the reconstruction of Iraq.

In November the CPA signed an agreement with the IGC paving the way for a transfer of power to an Iraqi interim government by mid-2004.

Coalition forces continued to face regular attacks after May. Most took place in central and northern Iraq, as well as in Baghdad, and led to scores of deaths of US and other nationals. There were increasing attacks on international NGOs and UN agencies, leading to the withdrawal of most or all of their staff.

Little action was taken to address past human rights violations, including mass "disappearances", or to investigate and bring to justice those found responsible for committing crimes against humanity, genocide and war crimes, or to provide compensation and restitution to victims. However, in December the IGC established the statute of the Iraqi Special Tribunal in order to try Saddam Hussein and other former Iraqi officials. The tribunal may impose the death penalty. Also in December the IGC set up a Committee on Truth and Reconciliation.

Iraqi Kurdistan

In February, prior to the invasion of Iraq, opposition groups met in Salahuddin and appointed a six-member leadership council. Widespread anti-Turkish demonstrations were held in April to protest against Turkey's stated intention to send troops to northern Iraq. A leading military commander of the Patriotic Union of Kurdistan (PUK) and member of the Kurdish parliament, Shawkat Haji Mushir, was killed by members of the Islamist group *Ansar al-Islam* near Halabja. Five other people were killed in the ambush.

In the immediate aftermath of the war, PUK forces took control of the city of Kirkuk, reportedly to prevent clashes between the various ethnic groups. However, many Arab villagers who had been brought to northern Iraq by the previous Iraqi government fled their homes. PUK forces withdrew from Kirkuk at the end of April and were replaced by US forces.

After May, US military forces and others were targeted in attacks. In September, one person was killed and scores injured, including US military officials, in a car bomb attack in Arbil.

Human rights concerns during the war

Hundreds of civilians were killed during the war by US and UK forces. Some were victims of cluster bombs, others were killed in disputed circumstances. Unexploded bomblets from cluster bombs posed a threat to civilians, particularly children.

Iraqi forces used unlawful tactics during the war that endangered civilians, including siting weapons near civilian facilities and wearing civilian clothes in order to launch surprise attacks.

▭ On 31 March US soldiers opened fire on an unidentified vehicle as it approached a US checkpoint near al-Najaf. Ten of the 15 passengers, including five children, were killed.

▭ On 1 April at least 33 civilians, including many children, were reportedly killed and around 300 injured in US attacks allegedly involving cluster bombs on the town of al-Hilla, southeast of Baghdad.

Human rights violations after the war
Excessive use of force

Scores of civilians were killed apparently as a result of excessive use of force by US troops or were shot dead in disputed circumstances.

▭ US troops shot dead or injured scores of Iraqi demonstrators in several incidents. For example, seven people were reportedly shot dead and dozens injured in Mosul on 15 April; at least 15 people were shot dead, including children, and more than 70 injured in Fallujah on 29 April; and two demonstrators were shot dead outside the Republican Palace in Baghdad on 18 June.

▭ On 14 May, two US armed vehicles broke through the perimeter wall of the home of Sa'adi Suleiman Ibrahim al-'Ubaydi in Ramadi. Soldiers beat him with rifle butts and then shot him dead as he tried to flee.

▭ US forces shot 12-year-old Mohammad al-Kubaisi as they carried out search operations around his house in the Hay al-Jihad area in Baghdad on 26 June. He was carrying the family bedding to the roof of his house when he was shot. Neighbours tried to rush him by car to the nearby hospital, but US soldiers stopped them and ordered them to go back. By the time they reached his home, Mohammad al-Kubaisi was dead. CPA officials told AI delegates in July that Mohammad al-Kubaisi was carrying a gun when he was killed.

▭ On 17 September a 14-year-old boy was killed and six people were injured when US troops opened fire at a wedding party in Fallujah. The soldiers reportedly believed they were under attack when shots were fired in the air in celebration.

▭ On 23 September, three farmers, 'Ali Khalaf, Sa'adi Faqri and Salem Khalil, were killed and three others injured when US troops opened a barrage of gunfire reportedly lasting for at least an hour in the village of al-Jisr near Fallujah. A US military official stated that the troops came under attack but this was vehemently denied by relatives of the dead. Later that day, US military officials reportedly went to the farmhouse, took photographs and apologized to the family.

Incommunicado detention

People held in prisons and detention centres run by Coalition forces – such as Camp Cropper in Baghdad International Airport (which closed in October), Abu Ghraib Prison and the detention centres in Habbaniya Airport and Um Qasr – were invariably denied access to family or lawyers and any form of judicial review of their detention. Some were held for weeks or months; others appeared to be held indefinitely.

▭ Qays Mohammad Abd al-Karim al-Salman, a businessman with Danish citizenship, returned to Iraq 10 days before his arrest by the US army on 6 May. He alleged he was forced to lie down on the road, then taken to the Holding Centre at Baghdad Airport where he was held for 33 days on suspicion of murder. He was denied contact with the outside world and subjected to cruel, inhuman and degrading treatment.

Torture or ill-treatment

Torture or other ill-treatment by Coalition forces was frequently reported. Detainees suffered extreme heat while housed in tents and were supplied with insufficient water, inadequate washing facilities, open trenches for toilets, no change of clothes, and no books, newspapers, radios or writing materials. Detainees were routinely subjected to cruel, inhuman or degrading treatment during arrest and the first 24 hours of detention. Plastic handcuffs used by US troops caused detainees unnecessary pain. Former detainees stated they were forced to lie face down on the ground, were held handcuffed, hooded or blindfolded, and were not given water or food or allowed to go to the toilet. Allegations of torture and ill-treatment by US and UK troops during interrogation were received. Methods reported included prolonged sleep deprivation; prolonged restraint in painful positions, sometimes combined with exposure to loud music; prolonged hooding; and exposure to bright lights. There were frequent reports of abuses by US forces during house searches, including allegations of looting and wanton destruction of property. Virtually none of the allegations of torture or ill-treatment was adequately investigated.

⌷ Abdallah Khudhran al-Shamran, a Saudi Arabian national, was arrested in al-Rutba in early April by US and allied Iraqi forces while travelling from Syria to Baghdad. On reaching an unknown site, he said he was beaten, given electric shocks, suspended by his legs, had his penis tied and was subjected to sleep deprivation. He was held there for four days before being transferred to a camp hospital in Um Qasr. He was then interrogated and released without money or passport. He approached a British soldier, whereupon he was taken to another place of detention, then transferred to a military field hospital and again interrogated and tortured. This time torture methods included prolonged exposure in the sun, being locked in a container, and being threatened with execution.

⌷ Nine Iraqis arrested on 14 September by the British military in Basra were reportedly tortured. The men all worked for a hotel in Basra where weapons were reported to have been found. Baha' al-Maliki, the hotel's receptionist, died in custody three days later; his body was reportedly severely bruised and covered in blood. Kefah Taha was admitted to hospital in critical condition, suffering renal failure and severe bruising.

Violence against women

In the aftermath of the war, women and girls increasingly faced violent attacks, including abduction, rape and murder, as law and order broke down. Many women became too afraid to leave their homes, and girls were kept away from school. Women who were victims of violence in the street or home had virtually no hope of obtaining justice.

⌷ In May, Asma, a young engineer, was abducted in Baghdad. She was shopping with her mother, sister and a male relative when six armed men started shooting around them. Asma was forced into a car and driven to a farmhouse outside Baghdad, where she was repeatedly raped. A day later she was driven back to her parents' neighbourhood and pushed out of the car.

Human rights abuses by armed groups

From May onwards there was an increasing incidence of attacks by armed groups on US military targets, Iraqi security personnel, Iraqi-controlled police stations, religious leaders and buildings, media workers, NGOs and UN agencies. These resulted in the death of hundreds of civilians, including foreign nationals.

⌷ In August the UN headquarters in Baghdad was bombed, killing 22 people including Sergio Vieira de Mello, the UN Special Representative in Iraq. In September a bomb attack killed the bomber and a security guard, and injured 19 others, near the UN headquarters.

⌷ Ayatollah Muhammed Baqer al-Hakim, Head of the Shi'a Muslim Supreme Council for the Islamic Revolution in Iraq, and 80 other people were killed in a car bomb attack in August in al-Najaf. At least 240 people were injured.

⌷ In September 'Aqila al-Hashimi, a woman member of the Iraqi Governing Council, died in hospital a few days after her car came under fire in Baghdad.

⌷ In September UK national Ian Rimell, an employee of the Mines Advisory Group, was killed in his car near Mosul.

⌷ In October a bomb attack on the headquarters of the International Committee of the Red Cross (ICRC) killed 12 people and injured at least 15.

Review of legislation

There was a continuing lack of clarity about the arrangements to establish a permanent governmental authority in Iraq and about the process for reviewing and amending legislation. The CPA undertook a review of the Iraqi Penal Code of 1969 and the Criminal Procedure Code of 1971 to evaluate their compatibility with international human rights standards. It also introduced legal amendments; these entered into force prior to their publication in Arabic in the *Official Gazette*, in contravention of Article 65 of the Fourth Geneva Convention. The amendments did, nevertheless, include some welcome reforms. Section 9 of CPA Memorandum No. 7 prohibited the use of torture and cruel, inhuman or degrading treatment or punishment. The Revolutionary, Special and National Security Courts, which had conducted grossly unfair trials, were abolished, and Order No. 13 established a new Central Criminal Court with jurisdiction over crimes committed since 19 March 2003 and applying the Iraqi Criminal Code and the Code of Criminal Procedure. However, Order No. 13 contained provisions that violate the principle of judicial independence. Section 2(3) of CPA Memorandum No. 3 removed the jurisdiction of Iraqi courts over any Coalition personnel in both civil and criminal matters, resulting in a lack of accountability for such personnel.

There were no proper mechanisms to ensure competent, impartial investigations into allegations of violations of international human rights and humanitarian law by the CPA or Coalition forces.

AI country reports/visits

Reports
- Iraq: The need to deploy human rights monitors (AI Index: MDE 14/012/2003)
- Iraq: People come first – Amnesty International's 10-point appeal to all parties involved in possible military action in Iraq (AI Index: MDE 14/022/2003)
- Iraq: Civilians under fire (AI Index: MDE 14/071/2003)
- Iraq: Ensuring justice for human rights abuses (AI Index: MDE 14/080/2003)
- Iraq: Looting, lawlessness and humanitarian consequences (AI Index: MDE 14/085/2003)
- Iraq: Responsibilities of the occupying powers (AI Index: MDE 14/089/2003)
- Iraq: People come first – Protect human rights during the current unrest (AI Index: MDE 14/093/2003)
- Iraq: On whose behalf? Human rights and the economic reconstruction process in Iraq (AI Index: MDE 14/128/2003)
- Iraq: The need for security (AI Index: MDE 14/143/2003)
- Iraq: Memorandum on concerns relating to law and order (AI Index: MDE 14/157/2003)
- Iraq: Memorandum on concerns related to legislation introduced by the Coalition Provisional Authority (AI Index: MDE 14/176/2003)

Visits
AI delegates visited Iraq in April for the first time in 20 years. Based in Basra, the delegates researched current and past human rights violations. They met victims of past and recent abuses, Iraqi political groups and British military officials.

Between May and August AI delegates maintained a permanent presence in Baghdad. They met former detainees held by the Coalition forces, researched past human rights violations, particularly "disappearances", raised human rights concerns with civil and military officials at the CPA, and met international and local NGOs. They were denied access to Coalition-run detention centres in Um Qasr in the south and in Baghdad.

In June AI delegates visited the Kurdish-controlled city of Arbil and met police officials, women's organizations and human rights representatives. They travelled to Kirkuk and Mosul to carry out research on internally displaced persons as well as to meet US military officials, former Coalition detainees, and local and international NGOs. They also visited police stations, prisons and hospitals.

ISRAEL AND THE OCCUPIED TERRITORIES

STATE OF ISRAEL
Head of state: Moshe Katzav
Head of government: Ariel Sharon
Death penalty: abolitionist for ordinary crimes
UN Women's Convention: ratified with reservations
Optional Protocol to UN Women's Convention: not signed

The Israeli army killed around 600 Palestinians, including more than 100 children. Most were killed unlawfully – in reckless shooting, shelling and bombing in civilian residential areas, in extrajudicial executions and through excessive use of force. Palestinian armed groups killed around 200 Israelis, at least 130 of them civilians and including 21 children, in suicide bombings and other deliberate attacks. Increasing restrictions on the movement of Palestinians imposed by the Israeli army throughout the Occupied Territories caused unprecedented poverty, unemployment and health problems. The Israeli army demolished several hundred Palestinian homes and destroyed large areas of cultivated land and hundreds of commercial and other properties. Israel stepped up the construction of a fence/wall, most of which cut deep into the West Bank. As a result, hundreds of thousands of Palestinians were confined in enclaves and cut off from their land and essential services in nearby towns and villages. Israel's expansion of illegal settlements in the Occupied Territories continued, further depriving Palestinians of natural resources such as land and water. Thousands of Palestinians were detained by the Israeli army. Most were released without charge, hundreds were charged with security offences against Israel and at least 1,500 were held in administrative detention without charge or trial. Trials before military courts did not meet international standards. Allegations of torture and ill-treatment of Palestinian detainees were widespread and Israeli soldiers used Palestinians as "human shields" during military operations. Certain abuses committed by the Israeli army constituted war crimes, including unlawful killings, obstruction of medical assistance and targeting of medical personnel, extensive and wanton destruction of property, torture and the use of "human shields". The deliberate targeting of civilians by Palestinian armed groups constituted crimes against humanity. Scores of Israeli conscientious objectors who refused to perform military service were imprisoned and some were court-martialled.

Background

In June a peace plan sponsored by the USA, the UN, the European Union and the Russian Federation and known as the "road map" was agreed by Israel and the Palestinian Authority (PA). It called for the establishment of a Palestinian state by 2005 but contained no mechanism to ensure the parties' compliance with their obligations under international law. It called on the Palestinians to stop attacks against Israelis and called on Israel to stop expanding settlements and to dismantle recently established ones, to halt the destruction of Palestinian homes and assassinations of Palestinians, and to ease closures and blockades in the Occupied Territories. In June the main Palestinian armed groups, *al-Aqsa* Martyrs Brigades (an offshoot of *Fatah*), *Hamas* and Islamic *Jihad*, declared a unilateral cease-fire. Israel released some 600 Palestinian detainees, most of whom had almost served their sentences. Negotiations on the "road map" plan collapsed in September and in November attempts were made to resume negotiations when the UN Security Council adopted a resolution approving the "road map". In December the UN General Assembly adopted a resolution seeking an advisory opinion from the International Court of Justice on the legality of Israel's construction of the fence/wall inside the West Bank.

Killings and attacks by the Israeli army

Around 600 Palestinians, most of them unarmed and including more than 100 children, were killed by the Israeli army in random and reckless shooting, shelling and bombings or as a result of excessive use of force. Some 90 Palestinians were killed in extrajudicial executions, including more than 50 uninvolved bystanders, of whom nine were children. Others were killed in armed clashes with Israeli soldiers.

▢ On 25 June, 19-year-old Nivin Abu Rujaila was killed when an Israeli army helicopter gunship fired a missile that struck the taxi she was travelling in. The taxi driver, Akram 'Ali Farhan, was also killed. The target of the strike was travelling in another car.

▢ On 12 June Islam Taha, who was pregnant, and her 18-month-old daughter were killed in Gaza city by rockets launched from an Israeli army helicopter gunship at their car to assassinate her husband, Yasser Taha, who was in the car and who was also killed. Four bystanders were killed and some 20 bystanders, including several children, were wounded. In three similar attacks by the Israeli army in the previous two days, 11 passers-by were killed and scores were injured, including more than 10 children.

Several international activists with the International Solidarity Movement (ISM), journalists and medical workers were killed and injured by Israeli soldiers.

▢ In March ISM activist Rachel Corrie, a US national, was crushed to death by an Israeli army bulldozer in Rafah in the southern Gaza Strip. In April ISM activists Tom Hurndall, a United Kingdom (UK) national, and Brian Avery, a US national, were both shot in the head by Israeli soldiers in Rafah and Jenin respectively. Both were gravely injured. In May UK journalist James Miller was shot in the neck and killed by Israeli soldiers in Rafah.

Israeli soldiers continued to use Palestinians as "human shields" during military operations, forcing them to carry out tasks that endangered their lives.

Most Israeli soldiers and security force members continued to enjoy impunity. Investigations, prosecutions and convictions for human right violations were rare. According to the Israeli army, since the beginning of the *intifada* (uprising) in September 2000, 61 soldiers had been indicted. Of these, 17 were found guilty of violence, two of improper use of weapons, and 22 of looting or damage to property. In the overwhelming majority of the thousands of cases of unlawful killings and other grave human rights violations committed by Israeli soldiers since the *intifada* began, no investigations were known to have been carried out.

Killings and attacks by Palestinian armed groups

At least 130 Israeli civilians, including 21 children, were killed by Palestinian armed groups. Almost half of the victims were killed in suicide bombings and the others were killed in shooting attacks. Some 70 Israeli soldiers were also killed in similar attacks by Palestinian armed groups. Most of the Israeli civilians were killed inside Israel whereas most of the soldiers were killed in the Occupied Territories.

▢ Lilah Kardi, a 22-year-old woman, was killed along with 19 other civilians, including several children, by a Palestinian suicide bomber on a bus in Jerusalem on 19 August. Both *Hamas* and Islamic *Jihad* were reported to have claimed responsibility for the attack.

▢ On 5 October, three female members of the same family — Bruria, Keren and Noya Zer-Aviv, aged 54, 29 and one, respectively — and two other relatives were among those killed in a suicide bomb attack which claimed the lives of 20 Israeli civilians and left scores of others injured. The attack, which was carried out by a Palestinian woman in a restaurant in Haifa, was claimed by Islamic *Jihad*.

Palestinian armed groups repeatedly fired mortars from the Gaza Strip towards nearby Israeli cities and into Israeli settlements in the Gaza Strip. The attacks did not usually result in injuries to Israelis.

Attacks by Israeli settlers on Palestinians in the Occupied Territories

Israeli settlers in the Occupied Territories repeatedly attacked Palestinians and their property. Such attacks increased in October, during the olive harvest, when Israeli settlers destroyed and damaged trees owned by Palestinians in several villages in the West Bank. In most cases attacks by Israeli settlers on Palestinians and their property were not investigated and those responsible were not brought to justice.

▢ On 27 October Israeli settlers attacked a group of Israeli human rights activists who were helping Palestinian farmers to pick their olives near the village of Einabus in the West Bank. Rabbi Arik Asherman, director of Rabbis for Human Rights, and 66-year-old journalist John Ross were among those assaulted by the Israeli settlers.

In October, three Israeli settlers were sentenced to 12 to 15 years' imprisonment for the attempted bombing of a Palestinian girls' school in 2002.

Destruction of Palestinian property in the Occupied Territories

The Israeli army destroyed several hundred Palestinian homes and scores of commercial and public facilities, and destroyed or damaged water, electricity and communication infrastructure throughout the Occupied Territories. Often, the destruction was carried out by the Israeli army as a form of collective punishment on the local population in the wake of attacks carried out by Palestinian groups known or suspected of having operated from or near the targeted areas.

The Israeli army stepped up the destruction of the homes of relatives of Palestinians known or suspected to have carried out attacks against Israeli soldiers or civilians.

Frequently, neighbouring houses were also destroyed or damaged by the large explosive charges usually employed by the soldiers to blow up the houses, and in some cases the inhabitants were killed or injured. The army usually did not allow the inhabitants time to salvage their possessions before destroying their homes.

⌧ On 3 March, Noha Makadmeh, a mother of 10 children who was nine months pregnant, was killed in her bed when her home collapsed as Israeli soldiers blew up a neighbouring house in the middle of the night in Bureij refugee camp in the Gaza Strip. Her husband and most of her children were injured, some of them seriously. Six other nearby houses were destroyed by the blast, leaving some 90 people homeless.

⌧ On the night of 9 September the Israeli army blew up an eight-storey apartment building in Hebron, leaving 68 people homeless, 53 of them women and children. Soldiers evacuated the inhabitants without allowing them to take any of their property and later killed two Palestinian gunmen who had entered the building while fleeing from the soldiers. After the bodies of the two gunmen had been removed from the building the soldiers blew it up. Tartil Abu Hafez Ghaith, an 18-year-old student living in a nearby building, was seriously injured and her neighbour, nine-year-old Tha'ir Muhammad al-Suri, was killed by shrapnel from a shell fired by an Israeli army tank during the attack.

⌧ In October the Israeli army destroyed more than 100 homes and damaged scores of others in a refugee camp in Rafah, leaving hundreds of Palestinians homeless. The Israeli army claimed that it carried out the destruction to uncover three tunnels used by Palestinian armed groups to smuggle weapons from Egypt to the Gaza Strip.

⌧ In a prolonged incursion in the north of the Gaza Strip in June the Israeli army destroyed scores of buildings as well as bridges, roads and other infrastructure. One of the properties destroyed was the Abu Ghaliun tile factory, the largest and most sophisticated such facility in the Occupied Territories. Israeli soldiers destroyed all the machinery and the stock of finished tiles, causing about US$6 million worth of damage.

Collective punishment, closures and violations of economic and social rights

Increasing restrictions imposed by the Israeli authorities on the movement of Palestinians in the Occupied Territories caused unprecedented hardship for Palestinians, hindering or preventing their access to work, education, medical care, family visits and other activities of daily life. Closures, military checkpoints, curfews and a barrage of other restrictions confined Palestinians to their homes or immediate surroundings most of the time.

The restrictions were a major cause of the virtual collapse of the Palestinian economy, resulting in a dramatic increase in unemployment, which stood at close to 50 per cent, and poverty, with two thirds of the Palestinian population living below the poverty line and an increasing number suffering from malnutrition and other health problems.

Hundreds of Israeli army checkpoints and blockades prevented Palestinians from using main roads and many secondary roads that were freely used by Israeli settlers living in illegal settlements in the Occupied Territories. Closures and restrictions on movement were routinely increased in reprisal for attacks by Palestinian armed groups.

Restrictions on the movement of Palestinians were further increased by the construction by Israel of a fence/wall in the western part of the West Bank and around Jerusalem. Israel claims that the fence/wall, composed of fences, concrete walls, deep trenches and tank patrol roads, is intended to stop Palestinians entering Israel to carry out attacks. However, the fence/wall is mostly being built on Palestinian land deep inside the West Bank, cutting off hundreds of thousands of Palestinians from essential services in nearby towns and villages and from their farming land — a main source of subsistence for Palestinians in this region. The Israeli army declared the areas of the West Bank between the fence/wall and Israel closed military areas and required Palestinians living or owning land in these areas to obtain special permits to move in and out of their homes and land. Israeli soldiers frequently denied passage to residents and farmers in these areas, preventing them from going to work or returning home.

To enforce closures and curfews, Israeli soldiers routinely fired live ammunition, tear gas and stun grenades, detained or ill-treated Palestinians and confiscated vehicles and identity cards. Israeli soldiers frequently refused or delayed the passage through checkpoints of Palestinian ambulances and of patients travelling in ordinary vehicles or on foot, forcing some women to give birth at checkpoints.

⌧ On 28 August, 29-year-old Rula Ashtiya from Salem village was denied passage by the Israeli soldiers at Beit Furik checkpoint separating the village from the city of Nablus. She gave birth on the dirt road by the checkpoint. Her baby girl died shortly after and only then did soldiers allow Rula Ashtiya through the checkpoint on foot to go to the hospital in Nablus.

Conscientious objectors
Scores of Jewish Israelis who refused to perform military service or to serve in the Occupied Territories were sentenced to terms of imprisonment of up to six months. Six others who were court-martialled before a military court for refusing to serve in the Israeli army were awaiting sentence. All were prisoners of conscience.

Forcible transfers
In October the Israeli army ordered the forcible transfer from their native West Bank to the Gaza Strip of at least 18 Palestinians detained administratively without charge or trial. All were forcibly transferred by the end of the year.

Concerns of UN bodies
In August the UN Committee on the Elimination of Racial Discrimination and the UN Human Rights Committee called on Israel to revoke a law, passed in July, which banned family reunification for Israelis marrying Palestinians from the Occupied Territories. The Human Rights Committee also called on Israel to halt the construction of the fence/wall inside the Occupied Territories and allow freedom of movement, end house demolitions, stop using Palestinians as "human shields" and investigate allegations of torture, unlawful killings and other violations.

Administration of justice
Petitions were filed by human rights groups to the Israeli Supreme Court on issues including the use by Israeli soldiers of Palestinians as "human shields", the extrajudicial executions of Palestinians, the construction of the fence/wall inside the Occupied Territories, the law banning family reunification for Israelis married to Palestinians, the lack of investigations into killings by the Israeli army of Palestinian civilians, and the existence of an Israeli secret detention centre, known as "facility 1391". All the petitions were pending at the end of the year.

AI country reports/visits
Reports
- Israel/Occupied Territories: Surviving under siege — the impact of movement restrictions on the right to work (AI Index: MDE 15/001/2003)
- Israel/Occupied Territories: Israel must end its policy of assassinations (AI Index: MDE 15/056/2003)
Visits
AI delegations visited Israel and the Occupied Territories in May and August/September. AI delegates met Israeli government officials and raised the organization's concerns.

JORDAN

HASHEMITE KINGDOM OF JORDAN
Head of state: King 'Abdallah II bin al-Hussein
Head of government: Faisal Fayez (replaced 'Ali Abu al-Ragheb in October)
Death penalty: retentionist
UN Women's Convention: ratified with reservations
Optional Protocol to UN Women's Convention: not signed

At least 15 women were reportedly victims of family killings for which leniency in sentencing of the perpetrators continued. At least 15 people were sentenced to death and seven executed. Restrictions continued to be imposed on the right to freedom of expression and on the press. Dozens of possible prisoners of conscience were arrested following demonstrations against the US-led war on Iraq; some were held incommunicado in the General Intelligence Department (GID) and released without charge days later. Dozens of political prisoners were arrested in connection with alleged involvement with Islamist groups and "terrorist" activities. There were reports of torture and ill-treatment of detainees. Political trials continued before the State Security Court (SSC) whose procedures failed to meet international fair trial standards. By the end of 2003 more than 1,500 people fleeing US-led military action on Iraq remained in refugee camps.

Background
In March AI's Secretary General met King 'Abdallah bin al-Hussein and raised concerns about the impending military intervention in Iraq and its potential humanitarian and human rights impact, including on refugee protection. The King gave assurances that Jordan would provide protection for refugees in the event of war on Iraq and give access to international organizations. AI's Secretary General also raised concerns about amendments made to Article 150 of the Penal Code after the dissolution of parliament in 2001. The amendments eroded the right to freedom of expression. The King pledged to look into the matter. In April the amendments to Article 150 were scrapped by a decree issued by the Council of Ministers.

Parliament was re-established after the June general elections and a new cabinet approved. A quota system was invoked which allowed six women with the largest number of votes to take seats in parliament. In October Faisal Fayez replaced 'Ali Abu al-Ragheb as Prime Minister and a new cabinet was formed that included three women. Temporary amendments to the law banning public meetings, introduced in 2001 after the dissolution of parliament, remained in place.

Violence against women and discrimination
At least 15 women were reported to have been victims of family killings. In September, Queen Rania

condemned family killings and continued her support for amendments to Article 340 of the Penal Code, made in the absence of parliament. The amendments stipulate that men who murder their wives or female relatives on grounds of adultery are not exempt from penalty, and that women, like men, who kill their spouse found in an "adulterous situation" can also benefit from a reduced sentence on grounds of mitigating circumstances. However, after the re-establishment of parliament the Lower House twice rejected the amendments. Article 98, which was invoked more often than Article 340 in such cases, allows for a reduced sentence for crimes committed in a "fit of rage" caused by unlawful or dangerous acts on the part of the victim. At least five men benefited from Article 98 in 2003.

◻ In mid-2003 a man reportedly received a one-year prison sentence for killing his sister in 2002. The killing apparently took place after the man learned that his sister had been raped by a neighbour whom she later married on finding that she was pregnant. The Criminal Court found that he strangled his sister in a "fit of fury" as stipulated under Article 98 and that the killing was not premeditated because the woman had tarnished her family's "honour".

Death penalty

At least 15 people were sentenced to death and seven executed during 2003.

◻ Jamal Darwish Fatayer, a Palestinian, was executed in August at Swaqa prison. He was convicted by the SSC on charges related to the killing of Jordanian diplomat Na'ib 'Umran al-Ma'aytah in Beirut in 1994, and membership of the unauthorized Fatah Revolutionary Council. The conviction was upheld in April by the Court of Cassation. Jamal Darwish Fatayer's trial fell seriously short of international standards; claims that he "confessed" under torture were ignored by both the SSC and the Court of Cassation.

Arrests of political prisoners

Dozens of political prisoners were arrested during the year, some of whom may have been prisoners of conscience. Prior to the US-led war on Iraq, people expressing their opposition to the conflict and Jordan's role in it were arrested. Among them were about 19 people detained at the end of March and apparently held incommunicado in the GID. All were released without charge days later. Dozens of others were arrested on suspicion of involvement with Islamist groups or "terrorist" activity.

◻ Fawaz Zurayqat, a leading member of the National Mobilization Committee for the Defence of Iraq, a non-governmental organization which campaigned against the sanctions and war on Iraq, was arrested in March. He was held by the GID and denied access to a lawyer for three days and released without charge after one month. Fawaz Zurayqat was probably a prisoner of conscience and his detention was thought to be linked to his political activities, including those related to opposition to the imposition of sanctions on Iraq.

Trials before the State Security Court

Political trials continued before the SSC whose procedures do not meet international fair trial standards. Cases referred to the SSC concerned allegations of "terrorist" activity and the publication of materials deemed to be "detrimental to the reputation of the state" and participation in unlicensed demonstrations. At least 20 defendants alleged that they had made "confessions" under duress.

◻ Journalist Muhammad Mubaidin served a six-month sentence in Jweidah prison after being convicted by the SSC in February in connection with an article he had written for al-Hilal weekly. Charges included publishing material defaming the Prophet Muhammad, insulting the dignity of the state and individuals leading to incitement, and publishing false information. Two other al-Hilal journalists were released following the trial after being in prison for over a month.

◻ In October the SSC began hearing the case of 15 men charged in relation to belonging to "terrorist" organizations. The organizations in question were al-Qa'ida and Ansar al-Islam (Partisans of Islam). According to reports, all were being tried in absentia except Ahmad al-Riyati who was reportedly arrested at the end of March by US troops in northern Iraq. During his trial, he said he had been tortured by US, Kurdish and Jordanian security forces. His defence lawyers argued that he was mentally unfit to stand trial. One of those being tried in absentia was apparently Mullah Najmuddin Fatih Krekar, said to be the founder of Ansar al-Islam and living in Norway. Jordan's requests for his extradition for drug offences were refused by the Norwegian authorities owing to lack of evidence.

Torture and ill-treatment

Reports of torture and ill-treatment of detainees were received, mainly in relation to those being held by the GID in connection with "terrorism". There were also reports of "confessions" extracted under duress made by people held on murder charges by the Criminal Investigation Department.

◻ Three Jordanian and two Libyan men charged in connection with the killing of US diplomat Laurence Foley in 2002 claimed during their trial before the SSC that they had been tortured under interrogation in the GID. According to reports, five prison inmates gave evidence saying that the men bore signs of torture on their bodies. The National Institute of Forensic Medicine, which examined the case of Muhammad Du'mus, one of the five defendants, apparently concluded that he had suffered injuries, including a missing toenail. The five defendants denied the charges.

◻ In October Maher Arar, a dual Syrian/Canadian national who was forcibly returned to Syria from the USA via Jordan in 2002 on suspicion of involvement with "terrorist" groups, held a press conference in Canada following his release from prison in Syria. He said that Jordanian officials had collected him from Amman airport in October 2002, held him blindfolded in a van, and beat him. He was then detained and questioned in Jordan before being sent to Syria. In Syria he was held incommunicado and tortured (see Syria entry).

Refugees

More than 1,500 people fleeing Iraq during and after the war remained in refugee camps in Jordan and in the "neutral zone" between Jordan and Iraq. Around 500 people, including Somali and Sudanese nationals (some of them recognized refugees) and Palestinians, were in Ruweished refugee camp. There were apparently more than 1,000 people in a refugee camp in the "neutral zone" near Iraq and Jordan's al-Karama border crossing, many of whom were said to be Iranian Kurds who had been refused entry into Jordan. Reportedly, some had travelled there from al-Tash Camp in Iraq, which is administered by the UN High Commissioner for Refugees.

There were no reports of large numbers of Iraqi refugees fleeing the war. It appeared that from the beginning of 2003 the Jordanian authorities operated a policy of refusing entry to many Iraqis.

AI country reports/ visits
Visit

AI visited Jordan in February and March to assess the preparedness of humanitarian non-governmental organizations and UN agencies for the anticipated war on Iraq, and to look at the situation of Iraqi refugees and asylum-seekers in Jordan.

KUWAIT

STATE OF KUWAIT
Head of state: al-Shaikh Jaber al-Ahmad al-Sabah
Head of government: al-Shaikh Sabah al-Ahmad al-Sabah (replaced al-Shaikh Sa'ad al-'Abdallah al-Sabah in October)
Death penalty: retentionist
UN Women's Convention: ratified with reservations
Optional Protocol to UN Women's Convention: not signed

The ongoing impact of the US-led military intervention in Iraq saw a rise in the number of attacks on US forces in Kuwait followed by the arrests of dozens of men. Some of the alleged attackers were linked by the authorities to *al-Qa'ida*. There were unconfirmed reports of torture or ill-treatment of political and criminal detainees. Political prisoners, including prisoners of conscience, continued to be

held. However, four of them were released on expiry of sentence; they had been convicted after manifestly unfair trials in previous years. No executions were reported, but death sentences continued to be handed down.

Background

On 6 July, following parliamentary elections, the government resigned and on 13 July, the Emir of Kuwait, al-Shaikh Jaber al-Ahmad al-Sabah, split the posts of crown prince and prime minister. He announced that al-Shaikh Sabah al-Ahmad al-Sabah, his half brother and long-serving Foreign Minister, would be Prime Minister. In October, a new government was formed. Its priorities were said to include "security issues and the fight against terror" and revitalizing the economy. In December, the new members of the parliamentary human rights committee visited Kuwait's Central Prison to examine conditions there and to follow up on recommendations made by the committee following its 2001 visit.

Arrests and trials

Security measures were strengthened in Kuwait during the year with coordination between the military, police and National Guard. Dozens of men were arrested following the war on Iraq on charges of attacking US military interests or spying for Iraq, or on suspicion of having links with *al-Qa'ida*. Some of the detainees reportedly made confessions under duress.

On 5 March, Khaled Messier al-Shimmari, a police officer, was sentenced to 15 years' imprisonment by a court in Kuwait. He was convicted of wounding two US soldiers in November 2002. However, according to reports, he had previously been admitted to hospital for psychiatric treatment. On 24 June, the Court of Appeal upheld his sentence. His lawyer said he would appeal to Kuwait's highest court, the Court of Cassation.

On 28 October, the Court of Appeal commuted the death sentence of Sami Mohammad Marzook Obaid al-Mutairi to life imprisonment and reduced to two and a half years' imprisonment the sentences of Badi Karuz al-Ajami and Khalifa al-Dihani. Sami al-Mutairi had been sentenced to death on 6 April by the Criminal Court for the premeditated murder of US national Michael Rene Pouliot, a locally recruited civilian contract worker, on 21 January near Camp Doha, the main US military base in Kuwait. He had reportedly "confessed" to the killing and that he had "adopted the *al-Qa'ida* ideology". He was extradited from Saudi Arabia after fleeing there following the attack. His two accomplices had been sentenced to three years in prison for providing him with the murder weapon and ammunition. During his trial, Sami al-Mutairi had denied the validity of his taped "confession" and testified that police officers had prepared the statement and forced him to read it in front of a video camera.

Releases of political prisoners

Following the war on Iraq, at least four of the 30 political prisoners who had been sentenced after manifestly unfair trials in State Security Courts following the Gulf war in 1991 were released and deported after serving their sentences. The four were sisters Rasan and Intisar Khallati; Zannuba 'Abd al-Khadr 'Ashur, who returned to her family in Iraq in April; and Fawwaz Muhammad al-'Awadhi Bseiso, who was resettled in Yemen.

AI received confirmation during the year of the release of two other political prisoners, Rahim Muhammad Najm and Ibtisam al-Dakhil, in 2001 and 2002 respectively. Ibtisam al-Dakhil, a Kuwaiti national by marriage, was stripped of her nationality and resettled by the UN High Commissioner for Refugees in a third country.

Kuwaiti detainees in Guantánamo Bay

On 2 September, lawyers representing the 12 Kuwaiti nationals held in Guantánamo Bay, Cuba, filed a petition asking the US Supreme Court to examine the cases of the detainees. On 10 October, the Supreme Court agreed to hear the appeal filed on behalf of two United Kingdom nationals, two Australians and the 12 Kuwaitis (see also USA entry).

Death penalty

No executions were recorded. However, death sentences continued to be handed down, mainly for murder, rape or drug-related offences.

On 11 March the Court of Cassation reportedly commuted to life imprisonment the death sentence of Khaled al-Azmi, a policeman. He had been convicted of the murder of Hudaya Sultan al-Salem, a prominent woman journalist and member of the royal family, publisher and editor-in-chief of the weekly journal *al-Majalis* in March 2001.

'Disappearances'

On 16 March, Iraqi and Kuwaiti officials held talks in Jordan with Saudi Arabian officials on the fate of at least 600 of their nationals missing since the 1991 Gulf war. Delegates from the International Committee of the Red Cross took part as observers. Following the change of government in Iraq, forensic teams from Kuwait inspected mass graves in Iraq. By the end of the year, the remains of at least 34 Kuwaiti prisoners of war were identified through DNA testing and returned to their families. The process of identifying remains was continuing at the end of the year.

Women's rights

Parliamentary elections in July continued to deny women the right to stand as candidates or vote, and women staged protests against their exclusion from the polls. According to reports, hundreds of women held their own mock election at a makeshift booth at the Kuwait Journalists' Association. On 20 July the new Prime Minister, al-Shaikh Sabah al-Ahmad al-Sabah, promised to renew efforts to grant women more political rights in Kuwait. In September the government announced it had finalized a draft municipality law which would give women for the first time the right to vote and run for office in polls for a new municipal council. The draft law had not been submitted to parliament by the end of the year.

Towards the end of the year, several women were selected to act on a voluntary basis as "environmental mayors" to promote awareness of environmental issues in cities.

LEBANON

LEBANESE REPUBLIC
Head of state: Emile Lahoud
Head of government: Rafiq al-Hariri
Death penalty: retentionist
UN Women's Convention: ratified
Optional Protocol to UN Women's Convention: not signed

Scores of people, including prisoners of conscience, were arrested, many of them arbitrarily. Most were released within hours or days. Many were Islamist activists held in connection with alleged "terrorism"; some were held for alleged "collaboration" with Israel. Scores of civilians were tried before military courts, whose procedures fall short of international standards for fair trial. Curtailments of the activities of human rights defenders increased and there were restrictions on freedom of expression, but generally a high level of human rights debate and activity was allowed. There were reports of torture and ill-treatment of detainees; none was known to have been investigated. At least three people were sentenced to death; the *de facto* moratorium on executions – in force for five years – appeared fragile at the end of the year.

Background

Prime Minister Rafiq al-Hariri submitted the resignation of his government to the President in April. However, he stayed on as Prime Minister and formed a new cabinet with minor ministerial changes.

Major amendments were proposed to the Penal Code by the parliamentary justice committee. Human rights activists led a vigorous campaign against the proposals. If adopted, they could lead to serious restrictions on freedom of association and expression, and further erode the rights of women.

There were wide and lively discussions within the community of non-governmental organizations (NGOs) and human rights groups on issues of human rights and freedoms. Women's rights and violence against women were the subjects of media discussions as well as several national and regional meetings held in Lebanon during the year. In October, the Minister of Justice reiterated the commitment of Lebanon to make its legislation compatible with the UN Women's Convention, which Lebanon ratified in 1996.

Thousands of Syrian troops were redeployed within Lebanon or back to Syria during the year. There were mixed reactions among Lebanese political circles to the Syria Accountability and Lebanese Sovereignty Restoration Act, which was adopted by the US Congress in November (see Syria entry). Exiled opposition leader General Michel Aoun, who testified before the US Congress on the draft Act, was charged by the Lebanese authorities in November with harming relations with a friendly state (Syria), among other offences.

Violence against women

Lebanese women's groups stepped up their campaigns against violence against women, such as "honour killings" and domestic violence including rape. Grave concerns were expressed by human rights activists and women's groups about the proposed revisions of the Penal Code. They feared that the revisions would further enhance the subjugation of women and perpetuate a culture of impunity for family crimes as the proposed Code would still allow for reduced sentences for men and women who commit murder in "honour crimes", and for women who kill their children born out of wedlock.

Unfair trials before military courts

Trials before military courts continued to fall short of international fair trial standards.

On 6 May, Muhammad Ramiz Sultan, Khaled 'Umar Minawi, 'Abdallah Muhammad al-Muhtadi and a Saudi Arabian national, Ihab Husayn Dafa, were sentenced by the Military Court to three years in prison with hard labour for vaguely defined "terrorist" offences. Khaled 'Umar Minawi was reportedly tortured in 2002 while held at the Ministry of Defence detention centre at al-Yarze. There was no known investigation into the allegation.

On 20 December, Khaled 'Ali and Muhammad Ka'aki were reportedly sentenced to 20 years' imprisonment by the Military Court for planning to bomb US and other "Western" targets in the country. The defendants were believed to be leaders of an alleged "terrorist" organization suspected of planning attacks on fast food restaurants in Lebanon between the second half of 2002 and April 2003. Sixteen co-defendants in the case received prison sentences ranging between two months and 12 years. Some of the accused alleged in court that they had broken ribs as a result of torture; no investigation was ordered by the court. There were concerns that all were convicted as a result of "confessions" extracted under torture. Eight others were acquitted; all had spent eight months in pre-trial detention and were reportedly tortured.

Harassment of human rights defenders

Many human rights NGOs continued to operate freely, but there was an increase in harassment of human rights defenders with the aim of curtailing their rights to freedom of expression and association.

Muhammad al-Mugraby, a lawyer and human rights defender, was arrested on 8 August for "impersonating a lawyer" and held for three weeks in Beirut. He was released on bail on 29 August. He had criticized sections of the judiciary and the Beirut Bar Association, and called for reforms of both. In January, the Beirut Bar Association had struck his name off the Association's register *in absentia*. However, the decision should become final only after appeal, which had yet to be concluded by the end of the year.

Samira Trad, director of Frontiers, a human rights organization that defends refugees and marginalized people in Lebanon, was detained overnight on 10 September and questioned by the General Security about Frontiers' work and the legality of the organization. She was charged under Article 386 of the Penal Code with "harming the honour and integrity" of the Lebanese authorities, which carries a sentence of up to one year's imprisonment. The Director of General Security told AI representatives that Samira Trad did not follow proper legal procedures in notifying relevant government authorities about the formation and activities of Frontiers.

Restrictions on freedom of expression

Lively and critical debate continued in the media, but there were some incidents of restriction of the freedom of the press and publication.

Adonis Akra, a philosophy professor, was forced to cancel a book-signing ceremony for the launch of his prison memoirs after being detained for seven hours. Several hundred copies of his book were seized and the authorities ordered the closure of the book's publishing company Dar al-Tali'ah.

Tahsin Khayyat, the owner of a private television channel, NTV, was detained by military police for a day in December for allegedly having links with Israel. He was released without charge. NTV, other media organs and some politicians protested against his arrest, saying it was an attempt to exert pressure on the television channel. NTV had been banned from broadcasting at least once during 2003 apparently after airing a program about US military bases in Saudi Arabia.

Update

In April, the Court of Cassation turned down appeals against a previous ruling to close down the opposition-oriented television station MTV and its sister radio station, *Radio Mont Liban*, for allegedly broadcasting unlicensed election advertisements. This followed an eight-month legal battle over an alleged contravention of Article 68 of the Parliamentary Election Law which revealed major errors in the legal process, suggesting that the closure was politically motivated.

Torture and ill-treatment

Torture and ill-treatment continued to be reported. The authorities refused to allow the International Committee of the Red Cross (ICRC) unfettered access to all prisons, especially those operated by the Ministry of Defence where civilians are held. This was despite a presidential decree in 2002 authorizing the ICRC such access. In October, at least one member of parliament, Saleh Honein, demanded a parliamentary investigation into why the ICRC was not allowed access to military prisons.

On 17 January security forces reportedly used batons and tear gas in closed areas against 17 detainees refusing to attend a court hearing. Ihab al-Banna and Sa'id Minawi needed hospital treatment for serious injuries. The 17 detainees, all held in Rumieh Prison in connection with clashes with security forces in the Dhinniyyah plateau in February 2000, were subsequently held in solitary confinement as punishment. However, in July the Public Prosecutor allowed the detainees to have access to facilities to practise religion, to exercise outside their cells and to grow beards.

Husayn Ahmad al-Qarahani, who was acquitted in December of involvement in the bomb attacks on US restaurants, and earlier of the June attack on *al-Mustaqbal TV* station, stated that he was one of a number of detainees tortured while held incommunicado at the Ministry of Defence detention centre in al-Yarze. He told the Military Court in October that the *ballanco* method of torture (hanging by the wrists which are tied behind the back), and beatings were used against him and other detainees, apparently aimed at coercing them to "confess". No investigations were known to have been carried into his allegations or into other cases of torture reported in 2003.

Government responses

In September, in response to AI's reporting of alleged ill-treatment of detained foreign nationals, the government stated that foreign detainees were being treated well and in accordance with international standards. The same month the government criticized AI's report on the Dhinniyyah detainees (see below) for relying on "untrustworthy sources", and rejected the report's allegations of torture and lack of legal safeguards. AI remained concerned that no independent judicial investigation had yet been ordered into the alleged torture and ill-treatment of the Dhinniyyah detainees.

Death penalty

At least three people were sentenced to death. A *de facto* moratorium on executions since 1998 continued, but appeared under threat in December when it was reported that the President might soon sign the execution papers for 27 or more people convicted of murder in previous years.

Civilian killings

Civilians were victims of what may have been direct or indiscriminate attacks.

Five-year-old 'Ali Nadir Yassin was killed on the night of 6 October when a missile apparently fired at Israeli military forces struck his family's house in the southern village of Hula. The UN Interim Force in Lebanon (UNIFIL) said the missile was a Katyusha, a type typically used by Lebanese resistance groups. *Hizbullah* (Party of God), the Islamist group which occasionally launches attacks on Israeli forces stationed in the Israeli-occupied Sheba'a Farms territory, denied any connection with the killing.

On 9 December, student Mahmoud Hadi and mechanic Khodr 'Arabi were shot dead in their car by Israeli troops near the village of Ghajar, which is split between Lebanon and the Israeli-occupied Syrian Golan Heights.

Refugees
Palestinian refugees

Palestinian refugees continued to face systematic discrimination, including wide prohibitions on the rights to work and own property, and on the freedom of movement. Draft legislation submitted to parliament to lift the ban on Palestinians owning property was withdrawn in October by the Parliamentary Speaker.

Other refugees

There were concerns that convoys organized by the Lebanese authorities to return Iraqis on a voluntary basis to Iraq may have included refugees and asylum-seekers who believed they were at risk of serious human rights violations if returned. A Memorandum of Understanding was signed in September by the Lebanese government and the UN High Commissioner for Refugees (UNHCR). It was seen to represent an important step in formalizing UNHCR's role in the protection of refugees and asylum-seekers in Lebanon. However, there were concerns expressed about the Memorandum, including that it denies asylum-seekers access to refugee status determination procedures after a certain time limit, thereby excluding some people who need protection from being able to access it.

AI country reports/visits
Report
· Lebanon: Torture and unfair trial of the Dhinniyyah detainees (AI Index: MDE 18/005/2003)
Visits

AI delegates visited Lebanon in May/June. They participated in a regional conference on violence against women, investigated the situation of Palestinian refugees and other human rights issues, and met government officials, local human rights organizations and lawyers. Other meetings with government officials took place in October.

LIBYA

SOCIALIST PEOPLE'S LIBYAN ARAB JAMAHIRIYA
Head of state: Mu'ammar al-Gaddafi
Death penalty: retentionist
UN Women's Convention: ratified with reservations
Optional Protocol to UN Women's Convention: not signed

There continued to be widespread human rights violations. Legislation criminalizing peaceful political activities remained in force. The security forces continued to arbitrarily arrest real or alleged political opponents, and to detain them incommunicado for long periods without charge. There were reports of torture and ill-treatment. Unfair trials before People's Courts continued to lead to the imprisonment of political opponents. There was no significant progress in shedding light on the human rights violations of the past, including deaths in custody and "disappearances". Political prisoners detained in previous years remained in prison.

Background

In January, the election of Libya as Chair of the UN Commission on Human Rights became highly politicized. While the Libyan authorities were reported to consider the election as evidence of a good human rights situation in the country, some countries, notably the USA, voiced their opposition.

AI called on all members of the Commission's bureau, including Libya, to take a number of concrete steps to demonstrate their commitment to human rights, including extending a standing invitation to the independent human rights experts of the UN to visit their countries. By the end of the year, this recommendation had not been acted on by Libya.

In Libya, a campaign "No To Torture" was launched by the Gaddafi International Foundation for Charitable Associations (GIFCA) headed by Saif al-Islam al-Gaddafi, one of the sons of Colonel Mu'ammar al-Gaddafi.

In December, in an address to civil servants of the General People's Committee for Justice and Public Security reported by the media, Colonel al-Gaddafi reiterated that Libya had no prisoners of conscience and that prisoners were of two kinds only, either "ordinary criminal" or "heretic".

Further steps were noted towards Libya's reintegration into the international community. On 12 September, the UN Security Council lifted sanctions which had been imposed on Libya after the bombing of a Pan Am flight which exploded over the town of Lockerbie in Scotland, United Kingdom (UK), in 1988, killing 270 people. Libya accepted "civil responsibility" for the bombing and offered compensation under a deal with the USA and the UK. Relatives of victims of the US air raids in Libya in 1986, in which 37 people were killed, called on the Libyan authorities to suspend payment to the victims of the Lockerbie bombing until they received similar compensation from the USA.

In December, Colonel al-Gaddafi declared that Libya was giving up its attempts to develop chemical, biological and nuclear weapons. Libya also announced that it would cooperate with the International Atomic Energy Agency.

The large numbers of Sub-Saharan Africans in Libya hoping to migrate to Europe led some European countries, especially Italy, to take initiatives aimed at building cooperation with Libya to deal with the issue of illegal immigration from Africa to Europe.

Deaths in custody

No independent investigation was known to have been initiated after families of many political prisoners were informed in 2002 that their relatives had died in prison, sometimes years earlier. In September, the Secretariat of the General People's Committee for Justice and Public Security reportedly declared that the cases of "death of some persons who were arrested and detained in police stations" are "limited and well known", and were being "investigated by the General Prosecution". However, this statement did not seem to address the cases of those who died in prisons in previous years.

Arbitrary and incommunicado detention

In January the Secretariat of the General People's Committee for Foreign Liaison and International Cooperation stated in a letter sent to AI that allegations of arbitrary arrest and detention were partial and groundless. However, there were continuing reports that the security forces, notably the Internal Security, continued to arbitrarily detain individuals and hold them incommunicado and without charge, sometimes for several months in breach of the provisions of Libyan law and international standards.

▢ At least three Libyan nationals were reportedly detained without charge after they were forcibly returned from Sudan in October 2002. Abd al-Mun'im Abd al-Rahman, Mohamed Rashid al-Jazawi and Ismail al-Lawati had been deported back to Libya with their wives and children. Upon arrival at Tripoli airport, they were reportedly transferred to Abu Salim prison. It was believed that they were detained incommunicado and without charge for several months. They were believed to remain in detention without charge or trial at the end of the year.

Unfair trials before People's Courts

The authorities continued to deny the existence of political prisoners or prisoners of conscience. However, unfair trials before People's Courts leading to political imprisonment continued to be reported. Basic rights, including the right of a defendant to choose a lawyer and the right to a public hearing, continued to be disregarded.

▢ Hearings continued to be repeatedly postponed in connection with the appeal before a People's Court in Tripoli, opened in mid-2002, of 151 professionals and students arrested in 1998 on suspicion of supporting or sympathizing with the banned Libyan Islamic Group, *al-Jama'a al-Islamiya al-Libiya*, also known as the Muslim Brothers. In February 2002, after a first unfair trial before a People's Court in Tripoli, two possible prisoners of conscience, Abdullah Ahmed Izzedin and Salem Abu Hanak, had been sentenced to death, while scores of others received sentences ranging from 10 years to life imprisonment. In a communiqué issued in September, the Human Rights Society of the GIFCA stated that it had called on the authorities "to work towards the release of the group of the so-called 'Muslim Brothers', and this in order to re-integrate them into society [...], given that they have not used or advocated violence."

Developments in the 'HIV trial'

The trial of six Bulgarians and a Palestinian, arrested in 1999 and charged with deliberately infecting at least 393 children with the HIV virus in al-Fateh hospital in Benghazi, continued before the Criminal Court. In a report submitted to the court, two foreign AIDS experts said that the infections were probably caused by poor hygiene, and not by the seven medical workers. According to media reports, at the end of December, five Libyan medical experts submitted a report to the Benghazi Criminal Court stating that deliberate actions were the likelier cause of the infection.

Unlawful detention of migrants at risk of deportation

Among the thousands of migrants living in Libya or passing through the country were scores of people who were believed to have fled their countries to escape persecution. Possible asylum-seekers were unlawfully detained and remained at risk of forcible deportation. Libya had still not ratified the UN Refugee Convention and its 1967 Protocol.

☐ Seven Eritrean nationals who had reportedly deserted the Eritrean army at different times during 2002 and fled from Eritrea to Sudan and then to Libya were at risk of deportation. They had been arrested by the Libyan authorities on 11 August 2002 as they attempted to cross the Mediterranean Sea. They were subsequently convicted of illegal entry but not released after the expiry of their three-month sentences. They had sought access to the UN High Commissioner for Refugees but it was unclear whether this had been granted by the Libyan authorities. They reportedly remained in detention at the end of the year.

☐ Another Eritrean national, Binyam Abraha, who was in his early twenties and detained in the same detention centre near Janzour, approximately 30km from the capital, Tripoli, died in custody on the night of 16-17 September. He had reportedly been detained in Libya for over a year and a half, apparently without charge or trial. Although he was reported to be seriously ill and to suffer from poor prison conditions, he was allegedly denied access to medical care.

'Disappearances'

2003 marked the 25th anniversary of the "disappearance" of Imam Musa al-Sadr, a prominent Iranian-born Shi'a cleric who had been living in Lebanon and was last seen in Libya during a visit in 1978. It also marked the 10th anniversary of the "disappearance" of

Mansur Kikhiya, former Libyan Foreign Affairs Minister and prominent human rights defender, who was last seen in Cairo, Egypt, in December 1993. The authorities failed to disclose information on these and other cases of "disappearances", including the case of Jaballah Matar and Izzat Youssef al-Maqrif, both prominent Libyan opposition activists, who "disappeared" in Cairo in March 1990.

AI country reports/visits
Visit

In March, AI delegates met the Libyan Ambassador to the UN in Geneva in her capacity as Chair of the UN Commission on Human Rights and discussed the reform of the Commission and issues relating to the human rights situation in Libya, including the issue of AI's access to the country for government talks and research.

MOROCCO/ WESTERN SAHARA

KINGDOM OF MOROCCO
Head of state: King Mohamed VI
Head of government: Driss Jettou
Death penalty: retentionist
UN Women's Convention: ratified with reservations
Optional Protocol to UN Women's Convention: not signed

Forty-five people were killed in several bomb attacks in Casablanca on 16 May. The authorities intensified their clampdown on suspected Islamist activists, begun in 2002, passing a new "anti-terrorist" law on 28 May. Judicial proceedings were brought against over 1,500 people suspected of involvement with the attacks or other "terrorist" activities. At least 16 were sentenced to death and hundreds more to prison terms. Dozens of those sentenced said they had been tortured or ill-treated, in some cases in secret detention, but investigations were generally not carried out into the allegations. Curbs on the rights to freedom of association and expression were felt most acutely by Sahrawi human rights activists and those perceived to be questioning the authority of the monarchy. A draft personal status law proposed significant improvements to women's rights. A commission was established to look into "disappearances" and arbitrary detention in previous decades. The fate of hundreds of people, mainly Sahrawis, who "disappeared" between the 1960s and early 1990s remained unclarified. Dozens of political prisoners sentenced after unfair trials in previous years remained in detention.

Background

Bomb attacks against five separate civilian targets in Casablanca on 16 May killed 45 people, including the 12 assailants. King Mohamed VI announced "the end of the era of leniency", while reaffirming Morocco's commitment to democracy, development and its international obligations.

In July the UN Security Council ratified a new plan on the status of Western Sahara, a disputed territory claimed by both Morocco, which annexed it in 1975, and the Polisario Front, which calls for an independent state there and has set up a self-proclaimed government-in-exile in refugee camps near Tindouf, southwestern Algeria. The plan would make Western Sahara a semi-autonomous part of Morocco for a transition period of up to five years, before a referendum would allow voters to choose between independence, continued semi-autonomy or integration with Morocco. The Moroccan government rejected the plan.

Security legislation

Following the 16 May bomb attacks, a new law on "combating terrorism" was adopted by parliament and entered into force on 28 May. The law contained a broad and unspecific definition of "terrorism". It extended the legal limits for pre-arraignment detention, when a suspect is held without charge or judicial review in the custody of the security forces, to a maximum of 12 days in "terrorism" cases, four days more than the previous maximum. It also restricted the suspect's access to legal counsel during this period, when detainees are most at risk of torture or ill-treatment. In addition, the law widened the scope of the death penalty.

Clampdown on Islamists

According to official statements, judicial proceedings were brought against over 1,500 people suspected of involvement in the May attacks or of planning or inciting other violent acts attributed to Islamists. Several hundred were sentenced to prison terms ranging from a few months to 30 years, and at least 50 were sentenced to life in prison. At least 16 people were sentenced to death and remained in custody. No executions have taken place in Morocco/Western Sahara since 1993.

Dozens of those sentenced were allegedly tortured in custody to extract confessions or to force them to sign or thumbprint statements they rejected. In many cases, suspects were reportedly tortured while held in secret and unacknowledged detention by the Directorate for the Surveillance of the Territory (the internal intelligence service), even though this body had no authority to carry out criminal investigations. The torture allegedly took the form of beatings, forced insertion of objects into the anus, suspension of the body in contorted positions, and the threat of rape of the detainee or the detainee's relatives (usually female). Since 2002 there has been an alarming upsurge in the number of allegations of torture and ill-treatment, after a period in which reported cases had dropped significantly.

▭ Abdelhak Bentassir was arrested in May, accused of being the coordinator of the Casablanca attacks. According to the authorities, he was arrested on 26 May

and died of pre-existing heart and liver complaints as he was being taken to hospital on 28 May before his questioning had been completed. The authorities announced that an autopsy had concluded that he had died of natural causes. The family of Abdelhak Bentassir said that he had been in good health before the arrest and was actually detained on 21 May, five days before the officially announced date of detention. The family was apparently not informed in advance that the autopsy would be performed so they were denied the opportunity to have their own independent doctor present.

Harassment of human rights and civil society activists

Dozens of Sahrawi human rights and civil society activists, particularly those perceived to advocate the independence of Western Sahara, were harassed and intimidated by the authorities. Some were arrested, remanded in custody and brought to trial on apparently politically motivated charges. Others were prevented from leaving the country to raise human rights concerns outside Morocco and had their passports confiscated. Some were members of the Western Sahara branch of the human rights organization Forum for Truth and Justice. The branch was dissolved by the authorities in June on the grounds that the organization had undertaken illegal activities that were likely to disturb public order and undermine the territorial integrity of Morocco. The activities deemed to be illegal appeared to relate solely to members of the organization exercising their right to express peacefully their opinions on self-determination for the Sahrawi people and disseminate views relating to human rights issues.

▭ Salek Bazid, a member of the Western Sahara branch of the Forum for Truth and Justice, was sentenced in March to 10 years' imprisonment. His conviction was based solely on a statement that he was allegedly forced to sign following torture in police custody in September 2002 and which he later withdrew in court. The statement recorded him "confessing" to having instigated outbreaks of violence in Western Sahara between 2000 and 2002. Salek Bazid said he was beaten while his feet and hands were tied together.

Although Moroccan human rights organizations and civil society activists were generally able to carry out their activities without harassment, at least two members of the Moroccan Association of Human Rights were allegedly tortured while being questioned in police custody following arrest.

Restrictions on freedom of expression

The monarchy and the status of Western Sahara remained forbidden subjects for public discussion, including by the press. Several people, including journalists and political activists, were imprisoned after peacefully expressing views on these issues.

▭ Prisoner of conscience Ali Lmrabet, editor of two independent newspapers, *Demain Magazine* and *Doumane*, was sentenced in June to three years' imprisonment and a fine of 20,000 dirhams (approximately US$2,000), and his newspapers were banned. He was convicted of "insulting the King", "undermining the monarchy" and "threatening [Morocco's] territorial integrity". The charges were based on several articles, cartoons and a photo-montage that appeared in his newspapers.

In the wake of the May attacks in Casablanca, several journalists were sentenced to up to three years' imprisonment on charges such as disseminating false information and inciting violence after publishing the views of suspected Islamists.

Women's rights

In October King Mohamed VI announced a series of proposed reforms to the Personal Status Code aimed at improving women's rights. These included raising the legal age for women to marry from 15 to 18, imposing severe restrictions on polygamy, and giving husband and wife equal and joint responsibility over the family. Provisions governing inheritance rights, which discriminate against women, were to remain largely unchanged.

Redress for crimes in previous decades

In November King Mohamed VI approved a recommendation by the official human rights body to establish an Equity and Reconciliation Commission to look into "disappearance" and arbitrary detention cases in previous decades. The Commission would follow up work already undertaken by the Arbitration Commission on Compensation, which, according to an official statement in November, had awarded compensation to some 4,500 victims or family members since being set up in 1999. The new Commission would extend the scope of reparations given to victims and their families, try to locate the remains of those who died in detention, and produce a report summarizing the findings of up to a year's research into "disappearances" and arbitrary detentions. However, the proposal indicated that thorough investigations were not being planned, the identification of individual responsibilities had been categorically excluded and criminal prosecutions had been rejected.

Despite an increased willingness by the authorities to engage with the issue of "disappearances", several hundred people who "disappeared" after arrest between the mid-1960s and early 1990s remained unaccounted for. The vast majority were Sahrawis, arrested in the turbulent period immediately following Morocco's annexation of Western Sahara in 1975. Their families have not received any information from the authorities about their relatives, let alone an acceptance of responsibility. Not one person responsible for ordering or carrying out these "disappearances" has been prosecuted. Some perpetrators allegedly committed gross violations over long periods, including some who were still members or even high-ranking officials of the security forces.

UN human rights mechanisms

In November the UN Committee against Torture expressed concern at the increase in the number of allegations of torture and "the considerable extension of the limit of pre-arraignment detention, the period during which the risk of torture is greatest". The Committee called for prompt and impartial investigations into all torture allegations and an end to impunity.

In July the UN Committee on the Elimination of Discrimination against Women called for Morocco to address the issue of violence against women, including domestic violence, by adopting specific legislation on domestic violence, prosecuting and punishing adequately those responsible, and ensuring victims have immediate means of redress and protection.

In June the UN Committee on the Rights of the Child expressed concern that the "incidence of economic exploitation [of children] remained widespread" and that domestic servants, mostly girls, were "subjected to harsh work conditions and abuses".

Polisario camps

The Polisario Front freed nearly 550 Moroccan prisoners of war who had been detained in its camps, some for over 20 years. However, more than 600 remained in detention, despite an end to armed hostilities between the Polisario Front and the Moroccan authorities in 1991 following a cease-fire brokered by the UN.

Those responsible for human rights abuses in the camps in previous years continued to enjoy impunity. The Polisario authorities failed to hand over perpetrators still resident in the camps to the Algerian authorities to be brought to justice, and the Moroccan government failed to bring to justice the perpetrators of abuses in the Polisario camps present on its territory.

AI country reports/visits

Report

- Morocco/Western Sahara: Briefing to the Committee against Torture (AI Index: MDE 29/011/2003)

Visit

In October AI delegates met victims of torture and their families, human rights activists and members of Morocco's human rights body, and lawyers in Rabat, Casablanca and Laayoune.

PALESTINIAN AUTHORITY

PALESTINIAN AUTHORITY
President: Yasser 'Arafat
Prime Minister: Ahmad Quray (replaced Mahmud 'Abbas in September)
Death penalty: retentionist

Hundreds of Palestinians remained in detention without charge or trial. They included alleged members of armed groups and people suspected of "collaborating" with Israeli intelligence services. Some alleged "collaborators" were killed by armed Palestinians. Palestinian members of armed groups killed some 200 Israelis, most of them civilians. Adequate investigations into such attacks were not carried out and none of those responsible was brought to justice.

Background

The *al-Aqsa intifada* (uprising), which started on 29 September 2000, continued. Some 600 Palestinians were killed by Israeli security forces, the majority of them unlawfully. Palestinian members of armed groups killed some 200 Israelis, including at least 130 civilians, among them 21 children, and around 70 soldiers. Many were killed in suicide bombings claimed by the *al-Aqsa* Martyrs Brigades (an offshoot of *Fatah*), the *Izz al-Din al-Qassam* Brigades (*Hamas*), Islamic *Jihad* and the Popular Front for the Liberation of Palestine. Palestinian armed groups also repeatedly launched mortar attacks from the Gaza Strip towards nearby Israeli cities and into Israeli settlements inside the Gaza Strip. Thousands of Israelis and Palestinians were injured in the conflict.

A peace plan, known as the "road map", sponsored by the European Union, the UN, the Russian Federation and the USA was agreed by the Palestinian Authority (PA) and Israel in June. It envisaged a three-phase process and a set of goals including the establishment of a Palestinian state by 2005, an end to Palestinian violence and Israeli occupation, and a final resolution to the conflict. Human rights organizations expressed concern that the "road map" repeated the failure of previous Israeli-Palestinian agreements to address the protection of fundamental human rights, and did not include provisions to establish specific mechanisms to ensure compliance with obligations under international human rights and humanitarian law.

In the framework of the "road map", some 600 Palestinian detainees and prisoners were released by Israel and on 25 June *Fatah*, *Hamas* and Islamic *Jihad* agreed a three-month cease-fire. In July Israel transferred control of security in Bethlehem and Gaza to the PA. However, the Israeli army maintained its presence around the city of Bethlehem, cutting it off from neighbouring villages and the rest of the West

Bank. Fewer than 10 Israeli army checkpoints and roadblocks were removed while hundreds remained in place throughout the Occupied Territories. The construction by Israel of a fence/wall inside the West Bank continued. Palestinian towns continued to be raided, and closures and curfews were routinely imposed on Palestinian towns and villages, effectively blocking them off from each other (see Israel and the Occupied Territories entry).

The "road map" process collapsed after three consecutive Palestinian suicide bombings in Israel in August and a stepping up by Israeli security forces of extrajudicial executions of Palestinian militants in August and September. The Israeli security cabinet in September approved in principle the forcible expulsion of PA President 'Arafat, but left the timing of such a move open. Throughout 2003, President 'Arafat continued to be confined to his headquarters in the West Bank town of Ramallah.

Attempts to revive the "road map" were made in November, when the UN Security Council adopted a resolution endorsing the plan. In a bid to convince *Hamas* to agree to a new cease-fire, the PA in November unfroze the bank accounts of six charity organizations linked to *Hamas* which had been blocked in August.

On 18 March the Palestinian Legislative Council (PLC) passed a bill creating a new post of prime minister. Mahmud 'Abbas (Abu Mazen) was appointed to the post and formed a cabinet that was approved by the PLC on 29 April. However, a power struggle between President 'Arafat and Prime Minister 'Abbas over control of the PA security services eventually led to the resignation of Mahmud 'Abbas in September. Parliamentary Speaker Ahmad Quray was subsequently appointed as Prime Minister. The new cabinet presented by him was approved by the PLC in November. The Palestinian security forces were unified under a National Security Council, chaired by President 'Arafat.

Administration of justice and impunity

President 'Arafat and other PA officials regularly condemned suicide bombings and other attacks against Israelis and called on Palestinian armed groups to end such attacks. However, those responsible for ordering, planning or carrying out attacks were not brought to justice and no investigations were carried out, and no measures were known to have been taken by the PA to stop Palestinian armed groups from carrying out these attacks.

It remained unclear to what extent the PA could exercise effective control over any of the armed groups involved in attacks against Israelis. The destruction by the Israeli army of most of the PA infrastructure, including prisons and security installations, substantially reduced the PA's capacity and willingness to exercise control over armed groups. The stringent restrictions imposed by the Israeli army on the movement and activities of the Palestinian security forces further undermined their ability to investigate killings and other attacks by Palestinian armed groups and to bring those responsible to justice. Restrictions on movement within the Occupied Territories also prevented or restricted the functioning of PA courts because judges, lawyers and witnesses could not travel freely or at all. There were some reports of Israeli forces breaking into Palestinian prisons and detention centres.

The collapse of internal order and security in several West Bank and Gaza Strip towns created a situation where groups of armed Palestinians had almost free rein to carry out unlawful killings and other abuses.

At least 10 Palestinians suspected of "collaborating" with Israeli intelligence services were unlawfully killed by members of armed groups or by armed individuals. Most of the killings were carried out by members of *al-Aqsa* Martyrs Brigades. The PA consistently failed to investigate these killings and none of the perpetrators was brought to justice.

◻ On 20 July, the acting Governor of Jenin District, Haidar Irshid, was abducted by members of *al-Aqsa* Martyrs Brigades, beaten and then taken to Jenin's refugee camp. He was released after a few hours, reportedly after intervention by President 'Arafat. The group reportedly accused Haidar Irshid of "collaborating" with Israeli security forces.

Several national and international media institutions in the West Bank were raided by groups of armed Palestinians, who reportedly accused them of giving undue prominence in their coverage to internal PA political tensions. During the raids, employees were assaulted and equipment was destroyed. No official investigation was known to have been instigated into these raids.

State Security Courts

On 27 July, the Palestinian Minister of Justice issued a decision, published in the PA's official gazette, abolishing State Security Courts with immediate effect and transferring their responsibilities to regular courts and the Attorney General. Local human rights groups welcomed this decision as a step towards creating an independent Palestinian judiciary, and called on President 'Arafat to cancel Presidential Decree 49 (1995) that had established the courts. They also called on the Minister of Justice to review the cases previously tried before State Security Courts and order their retrial before civil courts. However, there were reports that the State Security Courts in the Gaza Strip continued to operate after the decree abolishing them was issued.

Arbitrary detention

More than 600 Palestinians were held in Palestinian prisons, detention centres or makeshift detention centres at undisclosed locations (so-called "safe houses"). Most were held on criminal charges, and about 100 were detained on charges of "collaborating" with Israeli intelligence services. Some 470 remained held without trial. There were some reports of torture and ill-treatment by various Palestinian security forces.

Death penalty

One person was sentenced to death by a military court after court proceedings that failed to meet international standards for fair trial. Three others were sentenced to death for murder by a civil court. Those sentenced to death can only be executed after the sentence is ratified by the PA's President. During 2003, President 'Arafat did not ratify any death sentences. At least 11 Palestinians remained on death row.

◻ Sergeant Rani Darwish Khalil Shaqqura, a member of the Palestinian security services from the Gaza Strip, was sentenced to death by firing squad by a military court on 17 May for the killing on 15 April of another member of the security services, Captain Hani 'Atiya al-Madhoun.

AI country reports/visits
Visits
AI delegates visited areas under the jurisdiction of the PA in May and August/September.

QATAR

STATE OF QATAR
Head of state: al-Shaikh Hamad Ibn Khalifa Al-Thani
Head of government: al-Shaikh Abdullah Ibn Khalifa Al-Thani
Death penalty: retentionist
UN Women's Convention and its Optional Protocol: not signed

At least one possible prisoner of conscience was released but 39 others, including 19 under sentence of death, remained held. A number of Yemeni nationals were feared to be at risk of *refoulement*.

Background
The government adopted a permanent written Constitution following a referendum held in April. Unlike the previous Constitution, it contained a number of human rights clauses, including guarantees for the rights to freedom of opinion, assembly, association, worship, political asylum, privacy and presumption of innocence, and the independence of the judiciary. The clauses also included prohibition of unlawful detention, torture, *refoulement* (forcible return) and forcible exile of Qatar nationals. However, most of these clauses are formulated in ways that leave their interpretation in practice dependent on existing or future laws. As such, the letter and spirit of the clauses can be seriously undermined by other laws.

The Constitution makes no reference to women's rights although Article 8 expressly excludes female members of the ruling family from accession to the throne. However, two women were appointed to public office in May – Sheikha bint Ahmed al-Mahmud as Minister for Education and Teaching, and Sheikha Ghaila bint Mohammad bin Hamad Al-Thani, a member of the ruling family, as Deputy Chairperson of the National Committee for Human Rights (NCHR).

The NCHR, which was set up in May on the basis of Law 28 of 2002, comprises 13 members including eight officials from government ministries and five prominent Qatar nationals. The tasks as stipulated by the Law include acting as an advisory body to the government on the promotion of human rights and responding to individual complaints concerning human rights.

Possible prisoners of conscience and other political prisoners

At least one possible prisoner of conscience was freed. Firas Nassuh Salim al-Majali, a Jordanian journalist with Qatar's television station, was sentenced to death in October 2002 on charges of spying for Jordan. On 17 March the Emir issued a decree pardoning him and ordering his immediate release.

The status of 39 other political prisoners, including possible prisoners of conscience, sentenced in connection with a coup attempt in 1996, remained unchanged. Twenty were serving life imprisonment and 19 were under sentence of death. They were originally sentenced to life imprisonment but this was changed to capital punishment by the Court of Appeal in May 2001. The final decision rests with the Emir who has the power to commute the death sentences. By the end of the year no decision was known to have been taken by the Emir. All 39 were sentenced after trials that fell far short of international standards of fair trial.

Risk of *refoulement*

A number of Yemeni nationals were reportedly detained on the basis of an "anti-terrorism" policy and were at risk of *refoulement* to Yemen where they could face torture and ill-treatment or other serious human rights violations.

In October Yemen's Interior Minister reportedly said that Yemen was negotiating with Qatar for the transfer of an undisclosed number of Yemeni nationals detained in Qatar in connection with "terrorism". He apparently added that the Qatar government had indicated its willingness to hand over the individuals to Yemen. The detainees were not known to have been given access to lawyers or the judiciary to challenge their *refoulement* in light of the risks of human rights violations they could face in Yemen.

SAUDI ARABIA

KINGDOM OF SAUDI ARABIA
Head of state and government: King Fahd Bin 'Abdul 'Aziz Al-Saud
Death penalty: retentionist
UN Women's Convention: ratified with reservations
Optional Protocol to UN Women's Convention: not signed

Gross human rights violations continued and were exacerbated by government "anti-terrorism" policies and acts of violence, some of which the authorities blamed on *al-Qa'ida* sympathizers. Hundreds of suspected religious activists, critics of the state and protesters were arrested or detained following their forcible return from other countries, and the legal status of those held from previous years remained shrouded in secrecy. Women played an unprecedented role in challenging discrimination against women, which nevertheless continued to be endemic. Torture and ill-treatment remained rife. At least 50 people were executed. Over a dozen foreign nationals were forcibly handed over to their governments. Around 3,500 Iraqi refugees remained as virtual prisoners in Rafha camp. The government continued to deny AI access to the country.

Background

Against a background of protests and violence the government intensified its advocacy of legal and political reforms while simultaneously exacerbating its already dire human rights record in the name of security and "combating terrorism".

In January and September intellectuals submitted two petitions to the government calling for reform. The first, signed by over 100 intellectuals, called for the separation of state powers, the establishment of an elected legislative body with a supervisory role over the government, and the creation of civil society institutions to spread the culture of tolerance and dialogue. In response the government met some signatories of the petition and in June the Crown Prince held a National Dialogue conference attended by some 50 intellectuals and clerics from different sections of society to discuss political and legal reforms. The second petition, signed by over 350 intellectuals, including 51 women, repeated the calls in the first petition and added other demands, notably the recognition of women's rights and fair distribution of wealth.

In October the government announced that it was planning to introduce popular participation in the election of 14 municipal councils, but no details were provided. The announcement coincided with an international conference in Riyadh entitled "Human Rights in War and Peace?" The conference, to which AI was not invited, was said to have avoided touching on the human rights situation in the country.

The reform activities were marred by acts of violence

which resulted in scores of deaths. During the first quarter of the year several officials were murdered in al-Jawf Governorate. They included the Deputy Governor who was shot dead in February in front of his office in Sakakah. The government said it had arrested suspects and that they had confessed to the crime, but did not release any details as to whether this killing or others were politically motivated.

The violence escalated when on 12 May bombers attacked a residential area in Riyadh killing about 35 people, including about nine bombers, and injuring hundreds of residents. The government blamed the attack on suspected al-Qa'ida sympathizers. Security forces embarked on house raids and street chases of alleged suspects in different parts of the country, particularly in the holy cities of Mecca and Medina. Many of the house raids and street chases led to armed clashes and resulted in the killing of dozens of people, including members of the security forces.

Prisoners of conscience and political prisoners

Hundreds of suspected religious activists, critics of the state and protesters, including women, were detained following waves of arrests carried out throughout most of the year. Dozens of them were detained after their forcible return to Saudi Arabia by other governments, including Sudan, Syria, the USA and Yemen. Their conditions of detention and legal status, like those detainees held from previous years, remained unclear due to the secrecy of the criminal justice system which also lacks the most basic standards of fair trial.

Most of the detainees were targeted for arrest in the context of a government policy of "combating terrorism", the implementation of which was intensified in the aftermath of the bombings in Riyadh and other acts of violence. However, hundreds of people were arrested solely as critics of the state or following demonstrations held during and after the human rights conference in October.

📁 Um Sa'ud, a 60-year-old woman, was arrested on 14 October for having taken part in a demonstration that took place that day in Riyadh. She was reportedly beaten and ill-treated on arrest. During the demonstration she carried a picture of her son, Sa'ud al-Mutayri, who reportedly died during a fire in al-Ha'ir Prison on 15 September. She was apparently calling for the return of her son's body to the family. She and two other women were among more than 270 people arrested during the demonstration. The Interior Minister reportedly said that those arrested would be treated as "outlaws" and would receive a "deterrent" punishment. Most of them were released after interrogation, but the three women and 80 men were reportedly sentenced to 55 days in prison. They were believed to have been released on 17 December on completion of sentence.

📁 Abd al-'Aziz al-Tayyar, a 44-year-old former public relations director at Riyadh Chamber of Commerce, was arrested in September for criticizing the government during a television program broadcast by the satellite television station of the UK-based Saudi Arabian opposition group, the Movement of Islamic Reform in Arabia (MIRA). Police reportedly raided his house and arrested him while he was talking by telephone to a live program on the Qatar-based al-Jazeera television station. He remained held in a Riyadh prison, reportedly without charge or trial. Three other people arrested with him also remained in detention at the end of the year.

📁 Muhammad Rajkhan, a 33-year-old father of seven children, was arrested on 8 February near his house in Jeddah. He was reportedly held incommunicado in al-Mabahith al-'Amma (General Intelligence) in Riyadh and allegedly tortured (see below). He was said to have been transferred to al-Ruwais Prison in Jeddah where he remained held at the end of the year.

Women challenge discrimination

Women's rights were a constant theme in the debate on political and legal reform, with women playing an unprecedented role. However, concrete change to the severe forms of discrimination against women remained a distant hope.

Throughout the year government officials, advocates of reform and the media in general touched on almost all forms of discrimination that devalue women, such as the prohibition of women's participation in public life, the subordination of women to men, and domestic violence, particularly with regard to female domestic workers. Women themselves seized the opportunity of the reform debate to advance their cause. Some signed the second reform petition. Some took part in demonstrations. Some had their own or other women's stories published to illustrate the suffering of women caused by the severe forms of discrimination and to challenge the rationale of such discrimination.

Torture and ill-treatment
Torture in detention

Because of the strict secrecy surrounding arrests and incommunicado detention, it was not possible to assess the scale of torture used against those arrested in connection with or following the violent incidents which took place. However, allegations of torture and ill-treatment of those detained in the name of security and "fighting terrorism", as well as of prisoners arrested in previous years, were reported.

📁 Muhammad Rajkhan was said to have suffered damage to his eardrum and loss of weight reportedly as a result of torture and ill-treatment after his arrest in February (see above).

📁 Five UK nationals and one Canadian national who were released from prison in August following a royal pardon provided detailed accounts of their treatment in prisons in Riyadh. They claimed that they repeatedly suffered various forms of torture during interrogation in order to force them to confess to police accusations against them. These included beatings all over the body and on the soles of the feet, sleep deprivation, and shackling and handcuffing for long periods.

Flogging and amputation

Flogging and amputation continued to be imposed by courts as judicial corporal punishment. Among those sentenced to flogging during the year was a woman schoolteacher who received 120 lashes in addition to three and a half months in prison. She was reportedly convicted of planting drugs in the briefcase of her fiancé and reporting him to the police in order to have him imprisoned and facilitate her separation from him. According to one press report she was forcibly engaged to him by her family who refused her request to go back on the marriage.

At least one person, Ghazi Muhammad Mohsen Abdul-Ghani, a Bangladeshi national, had his right hand amputated in March in Mecca. He was convicted of theft.

Refugees

Over a dozen foreign nationals, most of them Yemenis, were handed over to their governments. The Saudi Arabian authorities said that the handover was part of bilateral security cooperation agreements to "fight terrorism", but did not provide details of the names of those handed over or any criminal accusations against them. The detainees were not known to have been given the opportunity to challenge the decision of their forcible return on the grounds that they faced serious risk of human rights violations in their countries.

Up to 1,500 Iraqi refugees from the Gulf war of 1991 were, according to the UN High Commissioner for Refugees, voluntarily repatriated to Iraq after the fall of the Iraqi government in April. They were among more than 5,000 Iraqis who spent over 12 years as virtual prisoners in the Rafha military camp in the northern desert near the border with Iraq and who were denied the opportunity to seek asylum in Saudi Arabia. Around 3,500 remained in the camp at the end of the year.

Death penalty

At least 50 people were executed. Nineteen of them were Saudi Arabian nationals; the rest were foreign nationals, including 19 Pakistani and six Afghan nationals. Twenty-six were convicted of drug-related offences and 24 were found guilty of murder. The number of those who remained under sentence of death was not known but they included two female domestic workers, Sara Jane Dematera, a Philippine national, and Sit Zainab, an Indonesian national. They had both been accused of murdering their employers and were sentenced to death after secret and summary trials in 1993 and 1999 respectively. Alexander Mitchell, a UK national, and William Sampson, a Canadian national, who were both sentenced to death on charges of lethal bombings in Saudi Arabia in 2000, were pardoned and released in August.

AI country reports/visits
Visits
AI made several requests to visit Saudi Arabia, including a request to attend the human rights conference held in October, but received no positive response.

SYRIA

SYRIAN ARAB REPUBLIC
Head of state: Bashar al-Assad
Head of government: Muhammad Naji 'Otri (replaced Muhammad Mustafa Miro in September)
Death penalty: retentionist
UN Women's Convention: ratified with reservations
Optional Protocol to UN Women's Convention: not signed

Scores of people were arrested for political reasons, including for their involvement in peaceful gatherings and after their voluntary or forced return from exile. At least 20 of those arrested were Syrian Kurds. Hundreds of political prisoners, including prisoners of conscience, and scores of people who had "disappeared" remained in prolonged detention without trial or serving sentences imposed after unfair trials. Torture and ill-treatment remained widespread; at least two men died in custody allegedly as a result. Freedom of expression and association remained severely curtailed. Human rights defenders were harassed although in general they could operate more publicly than in previous years.

Background

Syria was increasingly caught up in the turmoil around the US-led war on Iraq and the international "war on terror". The US government frequently criticized Syria's foreign and domestic policies, culminating in the adoption by the US Congress on 11 November of the Syria Accountability and Lebanese Sovereignty Act. The Act authorized tough new sanctions on Syria for its alleged ties to "militant extremists", its purported efforts to develop weapons of mass destruction, and its "occupation" of Lebanon.

On 18/19 June up to 80 civilians were reportedly killed and a number of houses and buildings were destroyed when a US military strike targeted a convoy travelling from Iraq. On 5 October Israeli fighter jets fired missiles at an alleged Palestinian training camp at 'Ayn Saheb, north of Damascus, reportedly injuring six guards and causing extensive damage to a nearby compound housing several hundred Palestinian refugees.

Several Canadian nationals of Syrian descent were reportedly tortured in apparent attempts to extract information on suspected "terrorist" activities. At least one of these cases involved the USA, which reportedly "rendered" suspected "terrorists" to third countries, including Syria, for "more robust" questioning.

A new government was formed on 18 September under Prime Minister Muhammad Naji 'Otri. The Defence, Foreign and Interior Ministers remained unchanged. The President expressed a strong desire to push forward with economic and political reforms.

On 9 December representatives of the European Union and the Syrian government announced the successful conclusion of negotiations for a Euro-Mediterranean Association Agreement. The Agreement was expected to be signed in early 2004 and reportedly contained a legally binding human rights clause.

Prisoners of conscience and political prisoners

Hundreds of political prisoners, including prisoners of conscience, remained in prolonged detention without trial or serving sentences imposed after unfair trials. Others were arrested during the year and tried before the Supreme State Security Court (SSSC) and other courts whose procedures fall far short of international fair trial standards.

▭ 'Abdel Rahman al-Shaghouri was arrested at a checkpoint between Qunaytra and Damascus on 23 February and held incommunicado. He was reportedly beaten in detention before being transferred to Sednaya Prison and charged with offences connected to his use of the Internet and sending news stories to his friends. In December he appeared before a state security court which set the next court session for March 2004.

▭ Eight Syrian Kurds were arrested following a peaceful demonstration outside the UN Children's Fund (UNICEF) headquarters in Damascus on 25 June. The demonstration, which called for civil and political rights for Syrian Kurds, was dispersed violently by police and security forces, and about 20 people were injured. The eight arrested – Mohammed Mustafa, Khaled Ahmed 'Ali , Sherif Ramadhan, 'Amr Mourad, Salar Saleh, Hosam Muhammed Amin, Husayn Ramadhan and Mas'ud Hamid – were reportedly ill-treated while held without charge at al-Mezze police station in Damascus and at the Political Security Branch, where they remained held, largely incommunicado and in solitary confinement, at the end of the year.

▭ Eight prominent human rights activists sentenced to up to 10 years' imprisonment after unfair trials in 2002 remained held in solitary confinement at 'Adra Prison. On 3 October the international Inter-Parliamentary Union (IPU) called for the immediate release of two of them – Ma'mun al-Homsi and Riad Seif – both independent members of parliament. The IPU also welcomed a general amnesty that reportedly reduced by a third the five-year prison sentences of both men. The six other prisoners are 'Arif Dalila, Walid al-Bunni, Kamal al-Labwani, Habib Salih, Habib 'Issa and Fawaz Tello.

▭ Two Syrian Kurds, Hassan Saleh and Marwan 'Uthman, remained held in 'Adra Prison. They had been arrested on 15 December 2002, five days after a peaceful demonstration in Damascus calling for greater protection for the rights of Syrian Kurds. In March a military court changed the charge against both men from "membership of an unauthorized organization" to "inciting sectarian strife", and transferred the case to the SSSC. The SSSC added a further charge of "attempting to sever a part of the Syrian territories". On 8 December the case was postponed until February 2004.

Hundreds of political prisoners, mostly Islamists, remained in detention without trial or imprisoned after unfair trials by the SSSC or field military courts. Among the 800 or so political prisoners in Sednaya Prison were

about 460 members of the banned Muslim Brotherhood, some of whom had been held beyond their 20-year sentences; around 70 members of *Hizb al-Tahrir* (Islamic Liberation Party); and 24 members of *Al-Takfir wal-Hijra* (Excommunication and Migration). It was reported on 4 December that five members of *Hizb al-Tahrir*, detained since 1999, had been sentenced by a state security court to between eight and 10 years in prison. Eight other members arrested in 2002 were still awaiting trial.

Releases of political prisoners

▭ Hassan Sa'dun, a founding member of the Human Rights Association in Syria (HRAS), was released on 9 September having served a two-year prison sentence. He was arrested during the 2001 crack-down on the emerging human rights movement.

▭ During the year it was learned that Kurdish activist Hussain Daoud had been released on 11 December 2002 after two years of mostly incommunicado detention during which he was allegedly tortured. He had been arrested upon arrival at Damascus airport in December 2000 following his deportation from Germany, where his asylum application had been rejected.

Arrests of returnees

Scores of Syrians were arrested and detained on their voluntary or forced return from exile. Most of them were suspected of having links with the Muslim Brotherhood.

▭ Jamal Mahmud al-Wafa'i and six others were arrested on 18 April on their return from exile in Iraq. Two of the four women in the group were later released. Five of those arrested remained held incommunicado without charge at an unknown location at the end of the year.

▭ 'Abdul Razak Shoullar, aged 81, was arrested on his return from Saudi Arabia in July, following 23 years in exile based on his sons' membership of the Muslim Brotherhood. He was detained for several weeks in the Military Intelligence building in Homs.

▭ Maher Arar, who has dual Canadian/Syrian nationality, was arrested in October 2002 after he was deported from the USA via Jordan to Syria reportedly accused of having links with "terrorist" groups. He was held without charge for around a year at a secret location, where he was tortured and ill-treated. After his release on 5 October he gave evidence of the prolonged torture of 'Abdullah al-Malki, also a Canadian/Syrian, believed to be held on similar grounds to Maher Arar.

▭ Muhammad Sa'id al-Sakhri, his wife Maysun Lababidi and their four children were arrested in November 2002 after their forcible return to Syria from Italy, where they had applied unsuccessfully for political asylum. Maysun Lababidi and the four children were held for several weeks. Muhammad Sa'id al-Sakhri was detained until 13 October on charges of belonging to the Muslim Brotherhood. He was reportedly tortured and ill-treated.

Harassment of human rights defenders

Human rights defenders were harassed, although in general they could operate publicly. On 23 August, after 25 years in exile, Haytham Manna' of the France-based

Arab Commission for Human Rights returned to Syria for 12 days after a governmental decision to rehabilitate all of his rights.

▢ Aktham Nu'aysa, a former prisoner of conscience and a director of the Committee for the Defence of Human Rights was repeatedly harassed. His colleagues and family were also targeted, including his 75-year-old mother.

▢ Human rights lawyer Anwar al-Bunni was refused a travel permit to attend a human rights symposium in Germany. The symposium on 10 December presented a human rights award to the imprisoned Syrian parliamentarian Riad Seif. However, human rights lawyer Haytham al-Maleh, Chairman of the HRAS, was granted permission to travel to the symposium. Anwar al-Bunni and Haytham al-Maleh were still awaiting a decision by the Syrian Bar Council regarding charges brought against them by the Damascus Bar Association (DBA). If the DBA's charges are upheld, both men will be barred from practising law for up to three years, although in the meantime they may continue to work as lawyers.

Freedom of expression

Freedom of expression continued to be severely curtailed. The country's only independent satirical weekly *Al-Domari* was reportedly banned in August.

▢ 'Aziza and Shireen al-Sabini, both of whom worked for *al-Muharir al-'Arabi* newspaper, were released between March and June after serving one year in prison. The SSSC had charged the sisters with "obtaining information that should be kept confidential for the integrity of the state". 'Aziza al-Sabini was additionally charged with "promoting news that may weaken the morale of the nation".

▢ Ibrahim Humaydi, chief of the Damascus office of the newspaper *Al-Hayat*, was detained on 23 January for publishing "false information", apparently related to an article written about Syria's contingency plans to receive Iraqi refugees during the impending war, and to an alleged "misuse" of a security source. On 25 May, reportedly after a ruling by the SSSC, he was released on bail and resumed journalistic activities. A further session in December, also reportedly before the SSSC, postponed his trial for a further six months.

▢ Fateh Jamus and Safwan 'Akkash, both former prisoners of conscience, were among 14 human rights activists awaiting trial on charges relating to a lecture – which was cancelled before it started – marking the 40th anniversary of the declaration of the state of emergency in Syria. The men were arrested on 23 August and reportedly charged with "affiliation to a secret organization and carrying out acts which could incite factional conflict within the nation". Sessions of the military court in Aleppo scheduled to hear the case in October, November and December were postponed for procedural reasons.

Torture and ill-treatment

Torture and ill-treatment were widespread and allegations of such treatment were not investigated by the authorities.

Deaths in custody

▢ Lebanese national Joseph Huways, aged 43, died in custody in June. He was arrested by Syrian military forces operating in Lebanon after his car collided with a Syrian army jeep in 1992 to the east of Beirut and subsequently transferred for detention in Syria. He was at least the third Lebanese prisoner to have died in Syrian custody since 1996. Joseph Huways suffered from epilepsy and was reportedly denied access to medical treatment.

▢ Khalil Mustafa, a Syrian Kurd, died in August, apparently as a result of torture, in the Military Intelligence detention centre in Aleppo. He was arrested on 6 August, reportedly in connection with an alleged debt. On 14 August his body was handed over to his family. According to reports, the body had serious injuries, including a broken leg, a missing eye and a fractured skull. On 18 October, following media reports of his death, Political Security officers reportedly questioned his relatives and took his brother, Hasan Mustafa, to an unknown location, where he remained held incommunicado at the end of the year. Neither Hasan nor Khalil Mustafa was known to have any political affiliation.

'Disappearances'

The fate of scores of Lebanese nationals who "disappeared" following their arrest in Lebanon or transfer to Syria by Syrian military or intelligence forces in previous years remained unclear. Some were believed to be still held at unknown locations throughout the country. On 5 July, the Interior Minister reportedly said there were no Lebanese political detainees in Syria. The fate of a number of "disappeared" Palestinians and other Arab nationals also remained unknown.

Refugees

Twelve Iraqis were reportedly sent back to Iraq on 13 April, and 32 Iraqi refugees were forcibly returned home from al-Hol refugee camp near the Syrian-Iraqi border on 21 April. The authorities reportedly cited "security concerns" for the moves.

Violence against women

The Syrian Penal Code continued to allow the suspension of punishment for a rapist if the rapist and victim marry, unless such a marriage is dissolved within three years. There was still no systematic recording or reporting of rape or "family" crimes nor any known shelters for victims of rape and domestic violence. Cases were reported where husbands who had been convicted of killing their wives were given lenient sentences – five to seven years in prison – based on allegedly mitigating circumstances such as the "sexual conduct" of the wife.

TUNISIA

REPUBLIC OF TUNISIA
Head of state: Zine El 'Abidine Ben 'Ali
Head of government: Mohamed Ghannouchi
Death penalty: abolitionist in practice
UN Women's Convention: ratified with reservations
Optional Protocol to UN Women's Convention: not signed

A law on combating "terrorism" was promulgated in December which raised concerns that human rights would be further eroded. Torture continued to be reported, including in the premises of the Ministry of the Interior. Hundreds of political prisoners, including prisoners of conscience, remained in prison. Many had been held for more than a decade. Real and alleged political opponents of the government continued to face unfair trials, often resulting in long prison sentences. Released political prisoners continued to be subjected to administrative control and other arbitrary measures, affecting their freedom of movement and right to work. The government recommended improvements in conditions in prisons and detention centres; however, solitary confinement and denial of medical care continued to be reported.

Background

In July, President Zine El 'Abidine Ben 'Ali announced his candidacy for the presidential elections of 2004, thereby seeking a fourth five-year term in office. The new Constitution, approved by a referendum in May 2002, allows the incumbent president to stand for an unlimited number of elections and raised the age limit from 70 to 75 years. A law was passed in August amending the electoral code. This forbids the use of privately owned or foreign television channels and radio stations to call on electors to vote for, or abstain from voting for, a candidate or list of candidates. Anyone violating the code would face a fine of 25,000 dinars (US$20,800).

In September the European Union (EU)-Tunisia Association Council met under the presidency of the Tunisian Minister of Foreign Affairs. AI issued a briefing paper detailing its concerns about draft "anti-terrorism" legislation (see below). At the meeting, the EU reportedly encouraged the Tunisian authorities to take steps to improve human rights, including freedom of expression and association.

Hundreds of illegal migrants, mostly from sub-Saharan Africa, were arrested by the Tunisian authorities during attempted journeys across the Mediterranean. Italy and Tunisia signed an agreement to combat illegal migration; under the agreement those caught will face prosecution on their return to Tunisia. In June the government announced a series of measures to control the flow of illegal migrants to Europe.

'Anti-terrorism' measures undermining human rights

On Human Rights Day, 10 December, President Ben Ali promulgated a new "anti-terrorism" law. The law contains a very broad definition of "terrorism", leaving it open to wide interpretation which could further undermine human rights. There were concerns that the exercising of the right to freedom of expression could be considered an act of "terrorism" and therefore lead to long sentences after unfair trials before military courts. The law allows for the extension for an undefined period of pre-trial detention, and lacks safeguards in relation to people facing extradition to countries where they could face serious human rights violations. Existing provisions of Tunisian legislation on "terrorism", especially Article 123 of the Military Justice Code and Article 52 of the Penal Code, have been used to criminalize peaceful opposition activities.

Torture

Torture and ill-treatment of detainees continued to be reported in detention centres, including the premises of the Ministry of the Interior in Tunis.

🗀 Some 20 people arrested in February in the region of Zarzis, south of Tunis, in connection with accessing Islamist websites, were detained incommunicado reportedly by the State Security Department in the Interior Ministry. Four of the men alleged that during the first 10 days of detention, they suffered various forms of physical and psychological torture, including being beaten, suspended from the ceiling and threatened with electric shocks. One detainee reported that he was threatened that his mother and sister would be brought in, stripped naked and tortured in his presence. Their trial had not started by the end of the year.

Human rights defenders

Human rights defenders, including lawyers, continued to be intimidated and harassed in the course of their work. Several human rights associations continued to be denied authorization and were obstructed in their work. The judicial authorities reportedly refused to register several complaints lodged by human rights defenders after ill-treatment by the security forces.

🗀 On 13 July, Radhia Nasraoui, a lawyer and human rights defender, was reportedly pushed against a wall and struck after crossing a police cordon outside a reception organized by the unauthorized Tunisian League of Free Writers. In June the authorities had refused to register the *Association de lutte contre la torture en Tunisie* (Association against Torture in Tunisia), a human rights organization established by Radhia Nasraoui.

Cruel and inhuman prison conditions

After increasing pressure from local and international human rights organizations, a Commission of Inquiry into prison conditions, announced by President Ben 'Ali in December 2002, reported back in February. The Commission reportedly identified overcrowding as a serious problem and concluded that extra equipment and qualified personnel were needed to improve prisoners' health. There was no report of improvements in the situation of political prisoners and prisoners of conscience who continued to suffer discrimination. Political prisoners continued to be subjected to arbitrary measures such as prolonged solitary confinement and denial of access to medical care.

▭ Habib Raddadi, who had been serving a 17-year prison sentence on charges of belonging to the unauthorized Islamist movement *al-Nahda* (Renaissance), died on 22 March in al-Haouareb prison after he was reportedly denied the necessary medical care and diet needed for hypertension. On 11 March he suffered a brain haemorrhage and was hospitalized, first in Kairouan and then in Sousse. According to his family, the prison warders in charge of his surveillance in hospital prevented his transfer to Tunis as recommended by doctors. When his family last saw him on 21 March, one of his arms and both his legs were still chained to the bed. He died the following day.

▭ Zouheir Yahiaoui, who was sentenced after an unfair trial to two years and four months' imprisonment in 2002 for spreading false information and misuse of Internet facilities, started a 42-day hunger strike in mid-May to protest against his continued detention and the prison conditions. He was reportedly being held in an overcrowded cell and denied adequate medical care and water. In July the Cassation Court upheld his sentence. He was conditionally released on 18 November after a national and international campaign.

Harassment and intimidation of former political prisoners

Scores of former political prisoners and prisoners of conscience continued to suffer arbitrary measures after their release. Some were denied basic rights such as the right to work and to have a medical card.

▭ Abdel-Majid Ben Tahar, a former prisoner, died on 12 October. He had been conditionally released in April 2002 with a brain tumour after serving eight years of a sentence of 12 years and nine months for belonging to *al-Nahda*. He had apparently been complaining of severe headaches for a year before being allowed a medical examination. "In the weeks that followed my release, the police would come several times a week to my house. They would walk into my bedroom and up to my bed to see if I had died," Abdel-Majid Ben Tahar told AI before he died. He was denied the right to have a passport and therefore the possibility to travel abroad to get medical treatment.

Former political prisoners who resumed their peaceful political activities or criticized the authorities were routinely put under police surveillance and were at risk of arrest and imprisonment after unfair trials.

▭ In October, Abdallah Zouari, a journalist and former political prisoner, was sentenced to 13 months' imprisonment by an appeal court in the southern town of Médenine. The court confirmed earlier sentences – one of nine months' imprisonment for violating restrictions of movement imposed on former prisoners, and another of four months' imprisonment for

defamation. In September 2002 he had been sentenced to eight months' imprisonment for failing to comply with the conditions of his administrative control, but was released on 5 November 2002 following a national and international campaign on his behalf.

AI country reports/ visits
Reports
- Tunisia: The cycle of injustice (AI Index: MDE 30/001/2003)
- Tunisia: Breaking the cycle of injustice – recommendations to the European Union (AI Index: MDE 30/014/2003)
- Tunisia: New draft "anti-terrorism" law will further undermine human rights (AI Index: MDE 30/021/2003)

UNITED ARAB EMIRATES

UNITED ARAB EMIRATES
Head of state: Al-Sheikh Zayed bin Sultan Al-Nahyan
Head of government: Al-Sheikh Maktum bin Rashid Al-Maktum
Death penalty: retentionist
UN Women's Convention and its Optional Protocol: not signed

Scores of political detainees continued to be held without charge or trial for more than two years in the context of measures taken by the authorities to combat "terrorism". Death sentences were imposed or upheld for murder and drug offences, but no executions were known to have been carried out. A man was reportedly sentenced to hand amputation.

Background
In January the authorities declared an amnesty from prosecution for all those staying in the country illegally. Illegal residents were given four months to leave or face imprisonment and a fine. The amnesty was extended by a further two months and by June up to 80,000 people were said to have left the United Arab Emirates (UAE). Thousands who did not comply were reportedly arrested and expelled from the country.

In January, the judiciary announced plans to establish juvenile courts throughout the UAE. It was not known whether these had been established by the end of the year, nor whether their procedures complied with the UAE's obligations as a state party to the UN Children's Convention.

In April the Emirate of Dubai announced the establishment of district councils, with council members to be elected by popular vote.

In June, the ruler of Ras al-Khaimah, one of the seven emirates in the UAE federation, removed his eldest son from his position as Crown Prince. During demonstrations against this move, at least one person was reported to have been shot and wounded by the police.

In August the Ministry of Labour and Social Affairs announced a draft law for the creation in 2004 of a national labour union. Full union membership was reportedly to be restricted to UAE citizens. The Ministry pledged its commitment to implement International Labour Organization (ILO) Conventions on healthy working environments and accommodation for workers.

In November, the UAE's "National Strategy for the Advancement of Women" was launched. The project, formulated with the UN Development Programme and Development Fund for Women (UNIFEM), aims to develop women's productivity and skills as well as their participation in the private and public sectors.

In November the President, Al-Sheikh Zayed bin Sultan Al-Nahyan, ordered the release of 365 prisoners serving sentences in connection with financial and criminal offences. AI received information that at least one of the 365 remained in detention as he was unable to pay a fine.

Political detainees

Scores of people, all UAE nationals said to be former military or police personnel, remained in detention without charge or trial. They had been arrested in the aftermath of the 11 September 2001 attacks in the USA and continued to be held incommunicado, reportedly in the Emirate of Abu Dhabi. Others who had been arrested with them and released were said to have suffered various forms of torture, including beatings and the use of electric shocks to the genitals, during interrogation.

Possible prisoner of conscience

A Philippine national, the Reverend Fernando Alconga, was arrested in Dubai in November 2002 for handing out material on Christianity to a Muslim man in a public place. He was released on bail after being detained for more than a month. In April he received a suspended prison sentence of one year and was deported to the Philippines in July.

Death penalty and other cruel judicial punishments

Several death sentences were passed but no executions were known to have been carried out.

In January, three Indian nationals, Humaid Sufi Muhyeddine, Sulaiman 'Abdul Rahman Ibrahim and Sebastian Corian, had their death sentences upheld for drug trafficking. In October, four Indian nationals were sentenced to death by a court in Dubai in connection with the murder earlier in the year of an Indian national. Four Pakistani nationals were sentenced to death in November by a court in Dubai for the murder in

2002 of a Pakistani national. The Supreme Court in Dubai upheld the death sentences of two Iranian nationals reportedly convicted of attempting to smuggle 800kg of cannabis into the Emirate in November 2002. The UAE introduced the death penalty for drug trafficking in 1995 but no execution for the offence is known to have been carried out.

In April a court in Ras al-Khaimah reportedly sentenced a 20-year-old Pakistani national to hand amputation after he was convicted of stealing US$70. It was not known whether the sentence was carried out.

YEMEN

REPUBLIC OF YEMEN
Head of state: 'Ali 'Abdullah Saleh
Head of government: 'Abdul Qader Bajammal
Death penalty: retentionist
UN Women's Convention: ratified with reservations
Optional Protocol to UN Women's Convention: not signed

Up to 200 people arrested in the months following September 2001 continued to be detained without charge or trial outside any judicial process. They were denied access to lawyers. Foreign nationals continued to be deported for "security reasons" to countries where they were at risk of human rights violations. Four people were reportedly killed in demonstration against the war on Iraq. There were reports of torture, which appeared not to have been independently investigated. At least 30 people were executed and scores, possibly hundreds, were under sentence of death at the end of the year, including a woman who faced death by stoning.

Background

The General People's Congress retained its position as Yemen's ruling party after elections that began on 27 April. The elections were marred by violence, during which five people were killed, and reported electoral irregularities. Women remained under-represented; only 13 stood for election and none was elected.

The Office of the State Ministry for Human Rights was upgraded into a full Ministry of Human Rights.

On 22 May the President declared an amnesty for 16 exiled political leaders who had fled Yemen in 1994 after the north-south civil war. Some of the 16 had been sentenced to death *in absentia*. Many of the 16 had reportedly returned to Yemen by the end of 2003.

Scores of people were reportedly killed in clashes between tribes, and between government forces and tribal groups, in different parts of Yemen.

Indefinite detention without charge or trial

Up to 200 people continued to be detained without charge or trial outside any judicial process since their arrest in the wake of the attacks in the USA on 11 September 2001. There appeared to be no plans to bring them to trial. The government said they were being detained because they held "extremist" religious views and would only be released if they changed their views.

At the end of the year, more than a dozen of those arrested in connection with the October 2000 attack on the destroyer USS Cole had been detained for more than three years without being formally charged and without access to a lawyer.

Political arrests

Hundreds of political arrests were reported during the year. Most of those arrested were held for several months without charge or trial, and without access to the outside world. Arrests were carried out without the judicial supervision required by law. Those targeted included people believed to be members of Islamist organizations or suspected of involvement in "terrorism".

▭ Several suspected members of al-Qa'ida were reportedly arrested in March. Among them were Kamal Saleh Ba Jabia, Sheikh Salah Salem al-Shibani and Sheikh Ammar bin Nasher, all Yemeni nationals, who were suspected of involvement in the bombing of the USS Cole in October 2000. They were believed to be still held at the end of the year.

▭ In April, following the escape of 10 Yemenis held in connection with the attack on the USS Cole, dozens of people were reportedly arrested, including relatives and friends of the escapees. It was not known whether they were still held at the end of the year.

▭ In October, several alleged members of al-Qa'ida were reportedly arrested in Sana'a; those arrested were said to include foreign nationals. They were believed to be still held at the end of the year.

▭ Ghanim al-Malaki, a Saudi Arabian national, and two Yemeni nationals were reportedly arrested on 20 October at the border with Saudi Arabia for suspected membership of al-Qa'ida. The Yemeni authorities were reported to have stated that the suspects would appear before a judge; however by the end of the year AI was not aware of any charges being brought against them.

▭ On 20 October, President 'Ali 'Abdullah Saleh announced that those detained in connection with al-Qa'ida "with no blood in their hands" would be released during the month of Ramadan. At least 34 suspected members of al-Qa'ida were released in November after they "expressed regret for their radical past".

Refugees and forcible deportation of foreign nationals

Dozens of Somali and Ethiopian possible asylum-seekers reportedly drowned in three separate incidents in the Gulf of Aden. The UN High Commissioner for Refugees (UNHCR) said that some of them drowned after they were forced at gunpoint to jump into the sea by crew members. Others were reportedly killed following arguments between the crew and the passengers.

More than 1,000 foreign nationals were reportedly deported for security reasons, many to countries where they were at risk of human rights abuses. Most were targeted because of their nationality and were held for weeks or months incommunicado before being expelled. They included Ethiopian, Indian, Libyan, Somali, Sudanese and Syrian nationals, as well as Saudi Arabian nationals who were exchanged for Yemeni nationals arrested in Saudi Arabia.

▭ In September, Yemen handed over to the Saudi Arabian authorities eight Saudi Arabian nationals, including Bandar al-Ghamdi, who was reportedly detained in connection with bombings in Riyadh in May, and his wife and daughter. The group was reported to have been forcibly returned following a visit by a Saudi Arabian security team to Yemen.

Demonstrations during the Iraq war

On 21 March, thousands of people demonstrated in Sana'a against the war on Iraq. Four Yemenis, including an 11-year-old boy, were reportedly killed and scores injured when security forces fired on the demonstrators using live ammunition and tear gas. Dozens of demonstrators were arrested and subsequently released. Among them were four opposition party leaders. The government announced that an investigation would be carried out into the deaths and injuries. By the end of the year no further information had been made available.

Harassment of journalists

Restrictions on the freedom of the press and harassment of journalists continued.

▭ In March, three journalists – 'Ali al-Saqaf, Ahmad Said Nasser and Abdel 'Aziz Ismail – were each given four-month suspended prison sentences for "harming Yemeni-Saudi relations". The accusation was based on articles in the newspaper al-Wahdawi that allegedly insulted the Saudi Arabian royal family. However, on 27 January, the Appeal Court lifted a life ban on working as a journalist imposed on Jamal Amer, a journalist on al-Wahdawi. Jamal Amer had been found guilty in 2000 of writing an article which was deemed insulting to Saudi Arabia.

Torture and ill-treatment

In September, the Yemeni government submitted a report to the UN Committee against Torture. The Committee welcomed Yemen's reform of its legal system but expressed concerns, including about the lack of definition of torture in the law, the practice of incommunicado detention by the Political Security, the lack of detainees' access to lawyers, and Yemen's failure to investigate promptly allegations of torture. It urged Yemen, among other things, to ensure that all "counter-terrorism" measures would be taken in full conformity with the UN Convention against Torture.

Torture and ill-treatment continued to be reported. Yemen submitted examples of cases to the Committee where investigations into torture allegations were carried out. However, no independent investigations into torture allegations submitted by AI were known to have been carried out.

🗀 Sami Yassin al-Sharjabi was reportedly tortured while held incommunicado in police custody between 26 December 2002 and 14 January 2003 on suspicion of murder. A complaint was submitted and in January the Attorney General requested an investigation into the torture allegations. However, no investigation was known to have been initiated by the end of the year.

🗀 Fourteen-year-old Mohammad Sa'id al-Zaidi was allegedly subjected to psychological torture after he was detained by security officers outside his home in Sana'a on 5 August. He was held with adult prisoners in an underground location until his release on 2 September. Mohammad al-Zaidi was reportedly arrested to try and force his brother, Hassan al-Zaidi, to hand himself in to the authorities. Hassan al-Zaidi, a journalist with the *Yemen Times* newspaper, had written articles criticizing the government.

Death penalty

Death sentences continued to be passed and at least 30 people were executed. Hundreds of people remained under sentence of death at the end of 2003.

🗀 On 26 May the Appeal Court in Ta'iz commuted the death sentence of Hammoud Murshed Hassan Ahmad, a possible prisoner of conscience, to 12 years' imprisonment and the payment of *diya* (blood money) of around US$15,000. An army captain in the former Democratic Republic of Yemen, he had been convicted of a murder that allegedly took place in 1982. He continued to appeal against his conviction.

🗀 Fuad Ali Muhsin al-Ashahari was reported to have been verbally informed at the beginning of December 2002 by the Public Prosecutor that his appeal was missing 24 pages. His case was sent to the Supreme Court of Justice.

🗀 Ali Jarallah was sentenced to death on 14 September. He was convicted of the murder of Jarallah Omar, assistant Secretary General of the Yemeni Socialist Party, in December 2002.

🗀 Nabil al-Mankali, a Spanish national, was at risk of imminent execution after President 'Ali 'Abdullah Saleh reportedly ratified the death sentence against him in September. It was subsequently reported that the President had reprieved him at the last minute, but the status of his death sentence was not clear at the end of the year. Officials from the European Union and a number of Spanish officials called on the Yemeni authorities to show clemency.

🗀 Mohammed Qasim Ragih was executed on 7 May after he was convicted of murdering his pregnant wife and two children.

🗀 At least one woman, 20-year-old Layla Radman 'A'esh, remained under sentence of death by stoning. She had been convicted of adultery in 2000; her appeal was still pending at the end of 2003.

Violence against women

The very active women's movement in Yemen continued its efforts to further women's rights and campaign against violence against women.

In May, the Women's Association in cooperation with Oxfam and the World Bank organized a training workshop in Aden on putting an end to violence in the family. The training workshop dealt with the definition of violence against women, the different forms of domestic violence, and the underlying causes of violence against women. A further workshop in June focused on the role of women in the judiciary.

In September, the Civic Democratic Initiatives Support Foundation held a workshop attended by members of civil society. The workshop called for the enactment of laws amending discriminatory legislation, and the drawing up of projects and programs to limit violence against women.

AI country reports/visits

Report

- Yemen: The rule of law sidelined in the name of security (AI Index: MDE 31/006/2003)

Visit

AI delegates visited Yemen in September and explored cooperation with non-governmental organizations in the campaign to end violence against women.

AI REPORT 2004

WHAT IS AI?

Amnesty International (AI) is a worldwide voluntary activist movement working for human rights. It is independent of any government, political persuasion or religious creed. AI does not support or oppose the views of the victims whose rights it seeks to protect. It is concerned solely with the impartial protection of human rights.

AI mobilizes volunteer activists – people who give freely of their time and energy in solidarity with the victims of human rights abuses. AI has a varied network of members and supporters around the world. At the latest count there were more than 1.8 million members, supporters and subscribers in over 150 countries and territories in every region of the world. AI members come from many different backgrounds, with widely different political and religious beliefs, united by a determination to work for a world where everyone enjoys human rights.

AI members may be organized in one of several thousand groups in local communities, schools and colleges in more than 100 countries and territories. Tens of thousands of members also participate in networks working on particular countries and themes or using particular campaigning techniques. Listed below are the addresses of recognized AI sections in 53 countries and territories and pre-section AI structures in 22 countries and territories; sections and structures coordinate the work of AI members. Also listed are other AI offices around the world; these offices exist for a variety of purposes including research, lobbying, core language translation and coordination at a regional level.

What does AI do?

AI forms a global community of human rights defenders with the principles of international solidarity, effective action for the individual victim, global coverage, the universality and indivisibility of human rights, impartiality and independence, and democracy and mutual respect.

AI's vision is of a world in which every person enjoys all the human rights enshrined in the Universal Declaration of Human Rights and other international human rights standards.

AI's mission is to undertake research and action focused on preventing and ending grave abuses of the rights to physical and mental integrity, freedom of conscience and expression, and freedom from discrimination, within the context of its work to promote all human rights. In this context:

- It campaigns for an end to political killings and "disappearances".
- It opposes without reservation the death penalty, torture and other cruel, inhuman or degrading treatment or punishment.
- It campaigns for perpetrators of human rights abuses to be brought to justice.
- It seeks the release of prisoners of conscience. These are people detained for their political,

religious or other conscientiously held beliefs or because of their ethnic origin, sex, colour, language, national or social origin, economic status, birth or other status – who have not used or advocated violence.
- It works for fair and prompt trials for political prisoners.
- It campaigns for an end to violence against women.
- It opposes certain grave abuses of economic, social and cultural rights.
- It seeks to persuade companies and economic institutions to respect and promote human rights.
- It opposes abuses by non-state actors where the state has failed to fulfil its obligations to provide effective protection.
- It works against grave abuses of the right to freedom from discrimination.
- It seeks to assist asylum-seekers who are at risk of being returned to a country where they might suffer serious abuses of their human rights.
- It calls on governments to refrain from unlawful killings in armed conflict.
- It calls on armed political groups to end abuses such as the detention of prisoners of conscience, hostage-taking, torture and unlawful killings.
- It campaigns for an end to the use of child soldiers.

AI also seeks to:

- cooperate with other non-governmental organizations, the UN and regional intergovernmental organizations;
- ensure control of international military, security and police relations, to prevent human rights abuses;
- organize human rights education and awareness-raising programs.

AI: a democratic movement

AI is a democratic, self-governing movement. Major policy decisions are taken by an International Council made up of representatives from all national sections. The Council meets every two years, and has the power to amend the Statute which governs AI's work and methods. Copies of the Statute are available from the International Secretariat.

The Council elects an International Executive Committee of volunteers which carries out its decisions and appoints the movement's Secretary General, who also heads up the International Secretariat and is the movement's chief spokesperson.

The movement's Secretary General is Irene Khan (Bangladesh), and the members of its International Executive Committee are Margaret Bedggood (New Zealand), Alvaro Briceño (Venezuela), Ian Gibson (Australia), Paul Hoffman (USA), Mariam Lam (Senegal), Claire Paponneau (France), Marian Pink (Austria), Hanna Roberts (Sweden) and Jaap Rosen Jacobson (Netherlands).

Finances

AI's national sections and local volunteer groups and networks are primarily responsible for funding the movement. No funds are sought or accepted from governments for AI's work investigating and campaigning against human rights violations. The donations that sustain this work come from the organization's members and the public. The international budget adopted by AI for the financial year April 2003 to March 2004 was £25,375,000. This sum represents approximately one quarter of the estimated income likely to be raised during the year by the movement's national sections to finance their campaigning and other activities.

AI's ultimate goal is to end human rights violations, but so long as they continue AI tries to provide practical help to the victims. Relief (financial assistance) is an important aspect of this work. Sometimes AI provides financial assistance directly to individuals. At other times, it works through local bodies such as local and national human rights organizations so as to ensure that resources are used as effectively as possible for those in most need.

During the financial year April 2003 to March 2004, the International Secretariat of AI distributed an estimated £53,000 in relief to victims of human rights violations such as prisoners of conscience and recently released prisoners of conscience and their dependants, and for the medical treatment of torture victims. In addition, the organization's sections and groups distributed a further substantial amount, much of it in the form of modest payments by local groups to their adopted prisoners of conscience and dependent families.

Information about AI is available from national section offices and from: International Secretariat, Peter Benenson House, 1 Easton Street, London WC1X 0DW, United Kingdom.

AI online — www.amnesty.org

AI's international website is dedicated to providing AI's human rights resources on the Internet and enabling people to take action to prevent human rights abuses. The site contains more than 38,000 pages. During 2003 there were approximately 15,000 visits to the site per day and there were over 50 million page views over the year.

The website holds most AI reports published since 1996 detailing AI's concerns about human rights issues around the world. Additionally, there is information on the latest campaigns and appeals for action to help protect human rights.

During 2003 increased international resources were devoted to web development, resulting in an improved website with better accessibility, more multilingual content and more action tools to encourage AI supporters to participate in campaigning. The website is also available in: French (http://www.amnesty.org/francais), Spanish (http://www.amnesty.org/espanol), and Arabic (http://www.amnesty.org/arabic)

During 2003 the website featured a number of appeals on behalf of individual prisoners of conscience, victims of torture and prisoners facing the death penalty, as well as campaigns on issues such as torture, the arms trade, and on economic relations and human rights. Special web pages and multimedia content were also created to highlight the continuing human rights crises in specific countries, including Democratic Republic of the Congo (DRC), Iraq and Myanmar. Over 40,000 people used the website to sign a petition to stop the funding of armed groups in the DRC. For the most recent appeals please visit: http://www.amnesty.org/actnow/

In October 2003, AI, Oxfam and the International Action Network on Small Arms (IANSA) launched a worldwide campaign — Control Arms (http://www.controlarms.org) — to press governments worldwide to introduce a binding arms trade treaty. At the heart of the online campaign is the Million Faces Petition (http://www.controlarms.org/million_faces) which aims to collect one million photographs and self portraits by 2006 as a powerful visual message of support for tougher arms controls.

AI's campaign for justice in the Russian Federation (http://www.amnesty.org/russia) continued to be an online success, with almost 650,000 page views over the course of the year. A dedicated Russian language website (http://www.amnesty.org.ru) was also launched to promote respect for human rights in the Russian Federation.

In November a new website for the Asia-Pacific region was launched (http://asiapacific.amnesty.org).

AI's international website also contains contact details for AI's offices worldwide (http://www.amnesty.org/contact/) and links to thousands of human rights-related websites.

AI sections

Algeria Amnesty International, BP 377, Alger, RP 16004
e-mail: amnestyalgeria@hotmail.com
Argentina Amnistía Internacional, Av. Rivadavia 2206 - P4A, C1032ACO Ciudad de Buenos Aires
e-mail: info@amnesty.org.ar
http://www.amnesty.org.ar
Australia Amnesty International, Locked Bag 23, Broadway, New South Wales 2008
e-mail: adminaia@amnesty.org.au
http://www.amnesty.org.au
Austria Amnesty International, Moeringgasse 10, A-1150 Vienna
e-mail: info@amnesty.at
http://www.amnesty.at
Belgium Amnesty International (Flemish-speaking), Kerkstraat 156, 2060 Antwerpen
e-mail: directie@aivl.be
http://www.aivl.be
Belgium Amnesty International (francophone), rue Berckmans 9, 1060 Bruxelles
e-mail: aibf@aibf.be
http://www.aibf.be
Benin Amnesty International, 01 BP 3536, Cotonou
e-mail: aibenin@leland.bj
Bermuda Amnesty International, PO Box HM 2136, Hamilton HM JX
e-mail: aibda@ibl.bm

Canada Amnesty International (English-speaking),
312 Laurier Avenue East, Ottawa, Ontario, K1N 1H9
e-mail: info@amnesty.ca
http://www.amnesty.ca
Canada Amnistie Internationale (francophone),
6250 boulevard Monk, Montréal, Québec, H4E 3H7
e-mail: info@amnistie.qc.ca
http://www.amnistie.qc.ca
Chile Amnistía Internacional, Oficina Nacional,
Huelén 188 A, 750-0617 Providencia, Santiago
e-mail: info@amnistia.cl
http://www.amnistia.cl
Côte d'Ivoire Amnesty International, 04 BP 895,
Abidjan 04
e-mail: amnestycotedivoire@aviso.ci
Denmark Amnesty International, Gammeltorv 8, 5,
1457 Copenhagen K.
e-mail: amnesty@amnesty.dk
http://www.amnesty.dk
Ecuador Amnistía Internacional, Av. 10 de Agosto
N 14-43 y Checa Edificio UCICA, Piso 8, Ofic. #807,
CP 17-15-240-C, Quito
e-mail: admin-ec@amnesty.org
http://www.amnistia.org.ec
Faroe Islands Amnesty International, PO Box 1075,
FR-110 Tórshavn
e-mail: amnesty@amnesty.fo
http://www.amnesty.fo
Finland Amnesty International, Ruoholahdenkatu 24,
D 00180 Helsinki
e-mail: amnesty@amnesty.fi
http://www.amnesty.fi
France Amnesty International, 76 Bd de La Villette,
75940 Paris, Cédex 19
e-mail: info@amnesty.asso.fr
http://www.amnesty.asso.fr
Germany Amnesty International, Heerstrasse 178,
53111 Bonn
e-mail: info@amnesty.de
http://www.amnesty.de
Ghana Amnesty International, Private Mail Bag,
Kokomlemle, Accra - North
e-mail: amnesty@ighmail.com
Greece Amnesty International, Sina 30,
106 72 Athens
e-mail: info@amnesty.gr
http://www.amnesty.gr
Guyana Amnesty International, PO Box 101679,
Georgetown
Hong Kong Amnesty International, Unit B3,
Best-O-Best Commercial Centre, 32-36 Ferry Street,
Kowloon
e-mail: admin-hk@amnesty.org
http://www.amnesty.org.hk
Iceland Amnesty International, PO Box 618,
121 Reykjavík
e-mail: amnesty@rhi.hi.is
http://www.amnesty.is
Ireland Amnesty International, Sean MacBride House,
48 Fleet Street, Dublin 2
e-mail: info@amnesty.iol.ie
http://www.amnesty.ie

Israel Amnesty International, PO Box 14179,
Tel Aviv 61141
e-mail: amnesty@netvision.net.il
http://www.amnesty.org.il
Italy Amnesty International, Via Giovanni Battista De
Rossi 10, 00161 Roma
e-mail: info@amnesty.it
http://www.amnesty.it
Japan Amnesty International,
2-7-7F Kanda-Tsukasa-cho, Chiyoda-ku, Tokyo,
101-0048
e-mail: info@amnesty.or.jp
http://www.amnesty.or.jp
Korea (Republic of) Amnesty International, Daegu
Susong PO Box 36, Daegu 706-600
e-mail: amnesty@amnesty.or.kr
http://www.amnesty.or.kr
Luxembourg Amnesty International, Boîte
Postale 1914, 1019 Luxembourg
e-mail: amnesty@pt.lu
http://www.amnesty.lu
Mauritius Amnesty International, BP 69,
Rose-Hill
e-mail: amnestymtius@intnet.mu
Mexico Amnistía Internacional,
Zacatecas 230, Oficina 605, Colonia Roma Sur,
Delegación Cuahutemoc, CP 06700,
Mexico DF
e-mail: comitedirectivo@amnistia.org.mx
http://www.amnistia.org.mx
Morocco Amnesty International, Place d'Angleterre,
Rue Souissra, Immeuble No. 11, Appt No. 1,
Rabat - L'Océan
e-mail: admin-ma@amnesty.org
Nepal Amnesty International, PO Box 135, Balaju,
Kathmandu
e-mail: amnesty@ccsl.com.np
http://www.amnestynepal.org
Netherlands Amnesty International, PO Box 1968,
1000 BZ Amsterdam
e-mail: amnesty@amnesty.nl
http://www.amnesty.nl
New Zealand Amnesty International, PO Box 5300,
Wellesley Street, Auckland
e-mail: campaign@amnesty.org.nz
http://www.amnesty.org.nz
Norway Amnesty International, PO Box 702, Sentrum,
0106 Oslo
e-mail: info@amnesty.no
http://www.amnesty.no
Peru Amnistía Internacional, Enrique Palacios 735-A,
Miraflores, Lima
e-mail: admin-pe@amnesty.org
http://amnistia.org.pe
Philippines Amnesty International,
17-B Kasing Kasing Street, Corner K-8th, Kamias,
Quezon City
e-mail: amnestypilipinas@meridiantelekoms.net
Poland Amnesty International, ul. Jaśkowa Dolina 4,
80-252 Gdańsk
e-mail: amnesty@amnesty.org.pl
http://www.amnesty.org.pl

Portugal Amnistia Internacional, Rua Fialho de Almeida 13-1, PT-1070-128 Lisboa
e-mail: aiportugal@amnistia-internacional.pt
http://www.amnistia-internacional.pt

Puerto Rico Amnistía Internacional, Calle El Roble 54-Altos, Oficina 11, Río Piedras, 00925
e-mail: amnistiapr@amnestypr.org

Senegal Amnesty International, BP 269 Dakar Colobane
e-mail: aisenegal@sentoo.sn

Sierra Leone Amnesty International, PMB 1021, 16 Pademba Road, Freetown
e-mail: aislf@sierratel.sl

Slovenia Amnesty International, Beethovnova 7, 1000 Ljubljana
e-mail: amnesty.slo@guest.arnes.si
http://www.amnesty.si

Spain Amnistía Internacional, Apdo 50318, 28080 Madrid
e-mail: amnistia.internacional@a-i.es
http://www.es. amnesty.org

Sweden Amnesty International, PO Box 4719, S-11692 Stockholm
e-mail: info@amnesty.se
http://www.amnesty.se

Switzerland Amnesty International, PO Box 3001, Bern
e-mail: info@amnesty.ch
http://www.amnesty.ch

Taiwan Amnesty International, No. 89, 7th floor #1, Chung Cheng Two Road, Kaohsiung
e-mail: aitaiwan@seed.net.tw
http://www.aitaiwan.org.tw

Tanzania Amnesty International, Luther House 3rd Floor, PO Box 4331, Dar es Salaam
e-mail: aitanz@simbanet.net

Togo Amnesty International, BP 20013, Lomé
e-mail: aitogo@cafe.tg

Tunisia Amnesty International, 67 rue Oum Kalthoum, 3ème étage, Escalier B, 1000 Tunis
e-mail: admin-tn@amnesty.org

United Kingdom Amnesty International, 99-119 Rosebery Avenue, London EC1R 4RE
e-mail: info@amnesty.org.uk
http://www.amnesty.org.uk

United States of America Amnesty International, 322 8th Ave, New York, NY 10001
e-mail: admin-us@aiusa.org
http://www.amnestyusa.org

Uruguay Amnistía Internacional, Colonia 871, apto. 5, CP 11100, Montevideo
e-mail: amnistia@chasque.apc.org
http://www.amnistiauruguay.org.uy

Venezuela Amnistía Internacional, Apartado Postal 5110, Carmelitas, Caracas 1010A
e-mail: admin-ve@amnesty.org
http://www.amnistia.int.ve

AI structures

Belarus Amnesty International, PO Box 10P, 246050 Gomel
e-mail: amnesty@tut.by

Bolivia Amnistía Internacional, Casilla 10607, La Paz
e-mail: perescar@ceibo.entelnet.bo

Burkina Faso Amnesty International, 08 BP 11344, Ouagadougou
e-mail: aburkina@sections.amnesty.org

Croatia Amnesty International, Martičeva 24, 10000 Zagreb
e-mail: admin@amnesty.hr
http://www.amnesty.hr

Curaçao Amnesty International, PO Box 3676, Curaçao, Netherlands Antilles
e-mail: eisdencher@interneeds.net

Czech Republic Amnesty International, Palackého 9, 110 00 Praha 1
e-mail: amnesty@amnesty.cz
http://www.amnesty.cz

Gambia Amnesty International, PO Box 1935, Banjul
e-mail: amnesty@gamtel.gm

Hungary Amnesty International, Arany Janos utca 25, Budapest 1051
e-mail: info@amnesty.hu
http://www.amnesty.hu

India Amnesty International, C-161, 4th Floor, Guatam Nagar, New Delhi 110-049
e-mail: admin-in@amnesty.org

Malaysia Amnesty International, E6, 3rd Floor, Bangunan Khas, Jalan 8/1E, 46050 Petaling Jaya, Selangor
e-mail: amnesty@tm.net.my
http://www.crosswinds.net/~aimalaysia/

Mali Amnesty International, BP E 3885, Bamako
e-mail: amnesty-mli@djom.net.ml

Moldova Amnesty International, PO Box 209, MD-2012 Chişinău
e-mail: amnestyrm@araxinfo.com

Mongolia Amnesty International, PO Box 180, Ulaanbaatar 21 0648
e-mail: aimncc@magicnet.mn
http://www.amnesty.mn

Pakistan Amnesty International, B-12, Shelezon Centre, Gulsan-E-Iqbal, Block 15, University Road, Karachi - 75300
e-mail: amnesty@cyber.net.pk
http://www.amnestypakistan.org

Paraguay Amnistía Internacional, Tte. Zotti No. 352 e/Hassler y Boggiani, Asunción
e-mail: ai-info@py.amnesty.org
http://www.amnistia.org.py

Slovakia Amnesty International, Staromestská 6/D, 811 03 Bratislava
e-mail: amnesty@amnesty.sk
http://www.amnesty.sk

South Africa Amnesty International, PO Box 29083, Sunnyside 0132, Pretoria, Gauteng
e-mail: info@amnesty.org.za
http://www.amnesty.org.za

Thailand Amnesty International, 641/8 Ladprao Road, Ladyao Chatujak, Bangkok 10900
e-mail: info@amnesty.or.th
http://www.amnesty.or.th

Turkey Amnesty International, Muradiye
Bayiri Sok, Acarman ap. 50/1, Tesvikiye 80200,
Istanbul
e-mail: amnesty@superonline.com
http://www.amnesty-turkiye.org
Ukraine Amnesty International, PO Box 60,
Kiev 01015
e-mail: office@amnesty.org.ua
Zambia Amnesty International, PO Box 40991, Mufulira
e-mail: azambia@sections.amnesty.org
Zimbabwe Amnesty International, Office 25 E, Bible
House, 99 Mbuya Nehanda Street, Harare
e-mail: amnestyzimbabwe@yahoo.com

AI groups
There are also AI groups in:
Albania, Angola, Aruba, Azerbaijan, Bahamas, Bahrain,
Barbados, Bosnia-Herzegovina, Botswana, Cameroon,
Chad, Cyprus, Dominican Republic, Egypt, Estonia,
Grenada, Jamaica, Jordan, Kuwait, Kyrgyzstan,
Lebanon, Liberia, Lithuania, Malta, Mozambique,
Palestinian Authority, Romania, Russian Federation,
Serbia and Montenegro, Trinidad and Tobago, Uganda,
Yemen

AI offices
International Secretariat (IS) Amnesty
International, Peter Benenson House, 1 Easton Street,
London WC1X 0DW, United Kingdom
e-mail: amnestyis@amnesty.org
http://www.amnesty.org
ARABAI (Arabic translation unit) c/o International
Secretariat, Peter Benenson House, 1 Easton Street,
London WC1X 0DW, United Kingdom
e-mail: arabai@amnesty.org
http://www.amnesty-arabic.org
Editorial de Amnistía Internacional (EDAI)
Calle Valderribas 13, 28007 Madrid, Spain
e-mail: mlleo@amnesty.org
http://www.edai.org
**Éditions Francophones d'Amnesty
International (EFAI)** 17 rue du Pont-aux-Choux,
75003 Paris, France
e-mail: ai-efai@amnesty.org
http://www.efai.org
IS Geneva — UN Representative Office Amnesty
International, 22 rue du Cendrier, 4ème étage,
CH-1201 Geneva, Switzerland
e-mail: gvunpost@amnesty.org
IS New York — UN Representative Office Amnesty
International, 777 UN Plaza, 6 Floor, New York,
NY 10017, USA
e-mail: ai-un-ny@amnesty.org
European Union (EU) Office Amnesty
International, Rue d'Arlon 37-41, B-1000 Brussels,
Belgium
e-mail: amnesty-eu@aieu.be
http://www.amnesty-eu.org
IS Dakar — Development Field Office Amnesty
International, Amadou Shour, Sicap Liberté II,
Villa 1608, Dakar, Senegal
e-mail: ashour@amnesty.org

IS Kampala — Africa Regional Office Amnesty
International, Plot 20A, Kawalya Kaggwa Close, Kololo,
Uganda
e-mail: admin-kp@amnesty.org
IS Pretoria — Development Field Office Amnesty
International, Njeri Kabeberi, PO Box 29083,
Sunnyside 0132, Gauteng, South Africa
e-mail: nkabeber@amnesty.org
Caribbean Regional Office Amnesty International,
PO Box 1912, St. George's, Grenada
e-mail: amnestycro@amnesty.org
IS San José — Americas Regional Office Amnistía
Internacional, 75 metros al norte de la Iglesia de
Fatima, Los Yoses, San Pedro, San José, Costa Rica
e-mail: admin-cr@amnesty.org
IS Hong Kong — Asia Pacific Regional Office
Amnesty International, Unit D, 3F, Best-O-Best
Commercial Centre, 32-36 Ferry Street, Kowloon,
Hong Kong
e-mail: admin-ap@amnesty.org
IS Moscow — Russia Resource Centre Amnesty
International, PO Box 212, Moscow 121019, Russian
Federation
e-mail: russiaresourcecentre@amnesty.org
IS Paris — Research Office Amnesty International,
76 Bd de la Villette, 75940 Paris, Cédex 19, France
e-mail: adminpro@amnesty.org
**IS Beirut — Middle East and North Africa Regional
Office** Amnesty International, PO Box 13-5696,
Chouran Beirut 1102 - 2060, Lebanon
e-mail: mena@amnesty.org

AI'S APPEALS

The country entries in this report include numerous examples of human rights abuses that AI is dedicated to opposing. AI urges those in authority in all countries where abuses occur to take the steps recommended below. More detailed additional recommendations are included where necessary in the specific country entry.

The right to life and physical integrity
Political killings and 'disappearances'

AI calls on governments to end extrajudicial executions and "disappearances". AI calls for prompt, thorough, independent and effective investigations into political killings and "disappearances", and for the families of the victims to know the fate of their loved ones. AI calls on governments to ensure that those responsible for such human rights violations are brought to justice.

AI calls on governments to:

- demonstrate their total opposition to extrajudicial executions and "disappearances" and make clear to security forces that these abuses will not be tolerated in any circumstances;
- end secret or incommunicado detention and introduce measures to locate and protect prisoners;
- provide effective protection to anyone in danger of extrajudicial execution or "disappearance", including those who have received threats;
- ensure that law enforcement officials use force only when strictly required and to the minimum extent necessary – lethal force should be used only when unavoidable to protect life;
- ensure strict chain-of-command control of all security forces;
- ban "death squads", private armies and paramilitary forces acting outside the official chain of command;
- ensure reparations to victims and their families.

Torture and ill-treatment

AI calls on governments to take steps to eradicate torture and ill-treatment. Such steps include initiating impartial, prompt and effective investigations into all allegations of torture and bringing to justice those responsible for torture.

Further safeguards against torture and ill-treatment which AI promotes include:

- policies making clear that torture and ill-treatment will never be tolerated;
- an end to incommunicado detention, including by giving detainees access to independent medical examination and legal counsel;
- abolishing all judicial and administrative corporal punishments;
- outlawing the use of confessions extracted under torture as evidence in any proceedings;
- independent inspection of all places of detention;
- informing detainees of their rights;
- human rights training for law enforcement personnel;
- compensation, medical treatment and rehabilitation for the victims of torture.

Death penalty

AI calls on governments to abolish the death penalty in law and practice.

Pending abolition, AI calls on governments to commute death sentences, to introduce a moratorium on executions, to respect international standards restricting the scope of the death penalty and to ensure the most rigorous standards for fair trial in capital cases.

Criminal justice issues
Impunity

Impunity literally means exemption from punishment. When used by AI it refers to the failure of the state to redress human rights abuses by bringing suspected perpetrators to justice before courts to determine their innocence or guilt, to discover the truth and to provide full reparations. When human rights crimes go unpunished, they can be repeated without fear.

Impunity denies the victims and their relatives the right to have the truth established and acknowledged, the right to see justice done, and the right to an effective remedy. Impunity deprives whole societies of their right to know the truth about their past, and to protect themselves from any recurrence of oppression in the future.

AI calls on governments to ensure that reports of human rights abuses are promptly, thoroughly and impartially investigated and that those suspected of responsibility are brought to justice in a court of law in accordance with international standards.

AI opposes amnesties for perpetrators of human rights abuses. Only by clarifying the truth about what has happened, establishing accountability for human rights abuses, and bringing to justice those responsible can confidence in the justice system be restored and human rights be guaranteed.

Prisoners of conscience

AI calls for the immediate and unconditional release of all prisoners of conscience. Prisoners of conscience are people detained anywhere for their political, religious or other conscientiously held beliefs or because of their ethnic origin, sex, colour, language, national or social origin, economic status, birth or other status – who have not used or advocated violence.

Fair trials

AI calls for prisoners whose cases have a political aspect to be given a prompt and fair trial on recognizably criminal charges, or released.

AI calls for trials to meet minimum international standards of fairness. These include, for example, the right to a fair hearing before a competent, independent and impartial tribunal, the right to have adequate time and facilities to prepare a defence, and the right to appeal to a higher tribunal.

Prison conditions

AI calls on governments to ensure that prison conditions do not amount to cruel, inhuman or degrading treatment or punishment, and that they are in line with international human rights standards for the treatment of prisoners.

Economics and human rights protection
Economic, social and cultural rights
As all human rights are indivisible and interdependent, effective work on civil and political rights cannot be conducted without addressing abuses of economic, social and cultural rights. AI is developing a program of work for the implementation of economic, social and cultural rights.

Economic, social and cultural rights are grounded in international law. National jurisprudence in many countries – and trends to include these rights in constitutional reforms – shows that many of these rights can be realized through legal remedies. Furthermore, numerous international standards permit individuals and groups to present complaints about violations of economic, social and cultural rights to intergovernmental organizations such as the International Labour Organisation, the UN Educational, Scientific and Cultural Organization and the regional African and Inter-American systems.

AI activities in this area have included projects relating to the right to health, food, education and employment.

Companies and economic institutions
Economic interests are increasingly influencing and dominating political agendas, and all too often economic development is pursued without paying attention to human rights. AI believes that economic actors (companies, international financial institutions, international and regional economic forums and relevant non-governmental organizations and intergovernmental organizations) have to be made accountable and that they should ensure that their activities do not impair human rights.

AI seeks to increase the number of economic actors agreeing and taking practical measures to protect and promote human rights.

Non-state actors
AI uses the term "non-state actors" to refer to those acting as private individuals or groups, not as representatives of a government or of an armed political group.

Under international human rights standards, governments have a responsibility to respect, protect and fulfil human rights. If a government does not fulfil its obligation to protect and ensure the rights of its people, it becomes legally responsible for its failure to prevent the violation or to respond to it in an appropriate manner. AI may take action when governments breach their duty to safeguard those in their territory from human rights abuses by non-state actors.

AI takes action against abuses by non-state actors:
- when the harm they cause is similar in severity and nature to violations that AI would oppose if perpetrated by a government (for example "honour killing", slavery and forced prostitution); and
- there is clear evidence that the government has not fulfilled its obligations, under international law, to take the necessary steps to eradicate the abuse. Such evidence may include failure to punish or

prevent the abuses; the absence of legal prohibition or other measures to eradicate the abuses; and failure to provide remedies or compensation to victims.

Discrimination
AI works against grave abuses of the right to freedom from discrimination. Those who are imprisoned solely on grounds such as race, sex, sexual orientation, religion or ethnicity are considered by AI to be prisoners of conscience.

AI calls on all states to take measures to prevent discrimination, not only by their own officials but also by private individuals. States can do this by ratifying international standards against discrimination, such as the International Convention on the Elimination of All Forms of Racial Discrimination and the UN Convention on the Elimination of All Forms of Discrimination against Women, and by ensuring that national legislation outlaws discrimination. Both these international standards and national laws against discrimination must be fully implemented.

Violence against women
AI campaigns to end violence against women.

AI calls for laws to be adopted and enforced to protect women, to ensure that violence in the family is treated as seriously as assaults in other contexts, and that rape and other violence against women is criminalized.

AI demands the abolition of all laws that:
- facilitate impunity for the rape or murder of women;
- criminalize consensual sexual relations in private;
- restrict a woman's right to choose her partner and restrict women's access to reproductive health care and family planning.

AI calls on national and local authorities to fund and support measures to enable all women to live free from violence, such as programs of civic education, training and systems to support and protect victims of violence and women's human rights defenders.

AI urges governments, financial institutions and corporate actors to counter women's impoverishment by ensuring equal access to economic and social rights, including food, water, property, employment and social entitlements and by safeguarding social safety nets, particularly in times of economic stress and dislocation.

AI demands that states end impunity for violence against women in armed conflict.

AI calls on armed political groups to end violence against women by their members.

Asylum-seekers and refugees
AI calls on governments to ensure that asylum-seekers are not returned to countries where they might suffer violations of their fundamental human rights.

AI calls on governments to ensure that all asylum-seekers have access to a fair and impartial individual asylum determination, and to ensure that they are not arbitrarily detained or otherwise put under undue pressure.

Armed conflict
Human rights in wartime
In armed conflict situations, AI continues to oppose human rights violations including the death penalty, torture and ill-treatment, "disappearances", unlawful killings and the imprisonment of prisoners of conscience.

AI takes no position on the reasons behind a particular armed conflict. It is concerned to ensure that the conflict is conducted in accordance with international humanitarian law. AI opposes direct attacks on civilians and indiscriminate or disproportionate attacks, in line with international humanitarian law.

AI does not oppose conscription, except in the case of under 18s, although it insists that conscientious objectors to military service be allowed to perform appropriate alternative civilian service. When such an alternative is not available, and conscientious objectors are imprisoned for their refusal to serve, AI regards them as prisoners of conscience.

Child soldiers
AI campaigns for an end to the recruitment of child soldiers and for the protection of children in armed conflicts. AI opposes both recruitment (voluntary or compulsory) into armed forces and participation in armed conflict by children under 18.

Armed political groups
AI opposes torture, hostage-taking, unlawful killings, and other breaches of international humanitarian law by armed political groups. In opposing these practices, the movement makes its protest known through direct appeals, its own publications and the news media.

Military, security and police (MSP) transfers
AI urges governments to adopt and implement laws and regulations to prohibit the transfer of arms or security equipment or services unless it can be reasonably demonstrated that such transfers will not contribute to serious human rights violations, crimes against humanity or war crimes. In particular, AI calls on all governments to:

- support the establishment of suitable mechanisms at the international level to provide effective control of the trade in arms, including an arms trade treaty based upon international human rights and humanitarian law, and to prohibit indiscriminate weapons (e.g. anti-personnel landmines) and weapons of a nature to cause superfluous injury or unnecessary suffering;
- introduce special legal measures to control the export of foreign licensed arms production, arms brokering and arms trafficking to ensure that such activities do not assist in the violation of human rights;
- implement stringent national controls on the transfer and use of security and crime control equipment, including mechanical restraints (e.g. handcuffs) and riot control equipment (e.g. water-cannon, plastic and rubber bullets, and tear gas) to prevent such equipment being used for human rights violations;
- ban the production, transfer and use of equipment ostensibly for use in law enforcement but whose primary practical use is for the death penalty or for torture or cruel, inhuman or degrading treatment (e.g. electric chairs, leg-irons, serrated cuffs, electro-shock stun belts);
- suspend the transfer and use of security equipment whose effects could pose a substantial risk of human rights abuse (e.g. electro-shock stun guns, pepper sprays, restraint chairs and shackle boards) pending the results of rigorous, independent investigation by experts based on international human rights standards;
- establish stringent regulation and monitoring of MSP training to ensure full respect for international human rights standards.

Promotion of human rights
AI calls on states to ratify international and regional human rights instruments without reservations, and calls on all governments to promote and respect the provisions of these instruments.

AI IN ACTION

AI is about achieving change. All activities by AI's members, supporters and staff seek to support the victims of human rights abuses and others working on their behalf and to influence those who have the power to make a difference. To do this AI confronts governments with its research findings; raises awareness of rights and ways to defend them; shows how widely its concerns are shared through millions of letters, e-mails and petitions; uses the media and the Internet to throw light on hidden abuses; and persuades decision-makers and opinion-formers to add their weight to that of millions of human rights activists worldwide.

AI's action is brought to bear in targeted appeals on behalf of individuals in immediate danger and in global campaigns for the systemic change needed to protect millions.

AI action works. For those who have told AI how an Urgent Action saved their lives and for the many others protected by laws or practice reformed only after sustained pressure, AI's work has had a real impact.

This report cannot hope to capture the full range of AI's activities at the international, national or community level. More information about action being taken around the world, and on how supporters can get involved in making a difference, is available from sections and on AI's websites (for contact details and website addresses see **What is AI?**).

AI visits

During 2003, AI delegates visited 69 countries and territories to conduct research, to meet victims of human rights violations, to observe trials, to contact local human rights activists, and to meet government officials.

Campaign on the Russian Federation

In its year-long worldwide campaign AI highlighted serious violations of human rights in the Russian Federation. During 2003 it published two major reports, *'Dokumenty!' Discrimination on grounds of race in the Russian Federation* (AI Index: EUR 46/001/2003) and *Rough Justice: The law and human rights in the Russian Federation* (AI Index: EUR 46/054/2003).

Throughout the year AI members around the world launched a range of actions aimed at putting pressure on the Russian government to end human rights abuses.

■ In February, the AI health professional network appealed to the Russian authorities concerning the serious problem of prison conditions, tuberculosis and HIV in Russian prisons.

■ A media competition launched by AI in conjunction with the Russian Union of Journalists, with the aim of encouraging better reporting within the Russian Federation of human rights issues, attracted over 300 pieces of work from journalists, newspapers, broadcasters and NGOs from all over the country.

■ On International Women's Day, 8 March, AI members in many countries campaigned on behalf of women subjected to violence within the family in the Russian Federation, by holding vigils, demonstrations and public meetings with representatives of Russian women's organizations, and calling on the Russian government to address and prevent such human rights abuses.

■ After a violent attack on members of ethnic minority communities in Krasnodar territory, local human rights activists and AI supporters around the world sent appeals to the Russian authorities. News of the incident appeared in the Russian media, which noted the attention brought to the case by AI. A criminal investigation was subsequently opened which was still ongoing at the end of the year.

■ AI's campaigning helped to reopen the investigation into allegations of torture and ill-treatment of two boys in Nizhnyi Novgorod. The Regional Procuracy confirmed that "international pressure" had led them to reopen the investigation.

■ AI called on the Russian authorities to conduct a prompt, impartial and thorough investigation into a racially motivated attack on a Zambian student in the town of Vladimir, after the local procuracy attempted to close the case due to lack of evidence. In its response the General Procuracy informed AI that the "unfounded decision" by the Vladimir Procuracy had been revoked and that the investigation was continuing.

■ In October a petition with more than 16,000 signatures collected by AI's worldwide membership was delivered to the administration of President Putin. The petition — designed as a symbolic passport — urged President Putin to address the plight of hundreds of thousands of former Soviet citizens in Russia who are being denied their legal right to obtain Russian citizenship or permanent residency rights.

■ In July, AI Switzerland launched a 100-day educational bus tour to raise awareness about human rights abuses in the Russian Federation. The brightly decorated bus passed through 14 European countries on its way from Switzerland to Moscow.

■ A speakers tour of several Russian cities involved students, academics and future law enforcement officials, among others, in discussions about international mechanisms for human rights protection and actions to end impunity.

■ On International Children's Day, 20 November, AI members around the world sent postcard appeals to President Putin, calling on him to improve the situation for children with mental disabilities in state institutions. This action formed part of a broader campaign, worked on by many AI members, including the youth and student network and the health professional network.

■ At the World Economic Forum in January, AI launched a booklet, *Doing business in the Russian Federation: the human rights approach* (AI Index: EUR 46/059/2002), which identified key human rights issues facing companies operating in the Russian Federation, including security, corruption, and the non-fulfilment of economic, social and cultural rights in a transition economy. The booklet pointed companies to principles and tools they could apply in order to operate in such a way as to protect human rights.

▦ Throughout the year pages on AI's Russia Campaign website were accessed almost 650,000 times.

Iraq Crisis Response

Early in 2003 AI mobilized its members and supporters around the world to bring human rights concerns to the forefront during the unfolding Iraq crisis.

▦ As the war on Iraq loomed, AI called on all its supporters to urge the governments concerned to consider carefully the impact of such a war on the human rights of Iraqis. On 18 March, hours before the start of the conflict, AI Secretary General Irene Khan published an open letter to US President George W. Bush, British Prime Minister Tony Blair, Spanish Prime Minister José María Aznar and Iraqi President Saddam Hussain, urging them to do everything in their power to avoid conflict and warning them that "one of the first casualties of any war in Iraq will be human rights."

▦ During the war, AI members and supporters participated in on-line petitions, met ambassadors from the warring countries, held candlelit vigils, and organized protests. Many of these actions were carried out jointly with other organizations. More than 80 public reports, documents and press statements were released during an eight-month period. AI called on the warring parties to adhere to international humanitarian law, to respect the rights of civilians and prisoners of war in all circumstances, and to protect and assist refugees and internally displaced people. AI highlighted breaches of the rules of war by both sides, for example by urging US and UK forces to refrain from using cluster bombs.

▦ AI activists from around the world handed a petition to Prime Minister Blair asking for assurances that indiscriminate weapons would not be used, that prisoners of war would be treated humanely and that the humanitarian needs of civilians would be met.

▦ As soon as the security situation allowed, AI established a field presence in Iraq. This enabled AI delegates to engage in dialogue with emerging civil society organizations, religious and political leaders, officials from the Coalition Provisional Authority and military officials. The delegates also met victims of recent and past human rights violations committed by former Iraqi government forces and the occupying powers, as well as relatives of victims. The delegates visited hospitals and police stations in order to assess the security situation. AI's delegates were in the field when the first mass graves were discovered. AI urged the occupying powers to take action to protect evidence being uncovered at the sites of mass graves and to investigate suspected places of detention.

▦ AI issued recommendations to the occupying powers, the international community and companies interested in investing in Iraq to ensure that the reconstruction process was transparent, accountable and consistent with human rights obligations. In June AI delegates attended the Extraordinary Annual Meeting of the World Economic Forum in Jordan to urge business leaders to take into account these recommendations. In June a delegation met the UN Special Envoy to Iraq, Sergio Vieira de Mello, who was later tragically killed in a bomb attack on the UN headquarters in Baghdad.

▦ AI made sure that those with power in Iraq heard the concerns of Iraqi people. Having achieved this single aim was worth all the hard work of the movement around the world.

Crisis Alert on the Democratic Republic of the Congo

Eastern Democratic Republic of the Congo (DRC) was the scene of multiple atrocities by armed groups in 2003. The abuses included mass killings and mutilations, rape and the widespread use of child soldiers.

AI responded by launching a period of intensive campaigning, with the primary goals of securing effective international protection of civilians in the region and ending support by regional governments to those committing atrocities. AI members worldwide drew public attention to the crisis and lobbied their governments to strengthen the size and mandate of UN peace-keepers in the areas worst affected by the violence.

▦ An AI report, video and website animation on the widespread use of child soldiers in the DRC were produced, as well as a series of reports on the violence in Ituri district.

▦ In October a high-level AI delegation travelled to the DRC, Rwanda and Uganda to urge these governments to rein in the armed groups responsible for human rights abuses in eastern DRC. A petition of over 40,000 signatures collected from the campaign website was handed to the three governments calling on them to end all support for the armed groups.

▦ As a result of pressure from AI and other organizations, UN peace-keepers in the DRC were given a strengthened protection mandate, their numbers were reinforced in Ituri and more were redeployed to eastern DRC. Regional governments' relations with the armed groups came under increased international scrutiny.

▦ In November, AI launched a keynote memorandum, *DRC: Addressing the present and building a future* (AI Index: AFR 62/050/2003), detailing measures that the DRC government, regional governments, the UN and the international community need to take if the legacy of mass human rights abuse in the DRC is to be finally overcome. Central to this will be effective national and international judicial mechanisms to bring perpetrators of abuses in the region to justice.

Myanmar web action

Following the violent attack on 30 May on members of the National League for Democracy and the arrest over the following weeks of over 100 of the party's members and supporters, AI launched an online petition for their release, which was signed by more than 20,000 people.

AI Japan tried to hand the petition over to the Myanmar embassy in Tokyo on 30 July, the day AI published its report *Myanmar: Justice on trial* (AI Index: ASA 16/019/2003) about political imprisonment and the need for reforms to the administration of justice. Authorities at the embassy refused to take delivery of the petition, which was subsequently posted to them. AI Japan staged a demonstration outside the embassy. At the end of the year most of those detained on 30 May had been released and dozens of those detained after 30 May had been sentenced to prison terms.

Ecuador country action

In October, AI Ecuador launched the campaign "Commit yourself to know your rights and demand the law is upheld" with a public forum in Quito at which an AI delegation presented the report *Ecuador: With no independent and impartial justice there can be no rule of law* (AI Index: AMR 28/010/2003) to representatives of civil society.

- The campaign, which will continue into 2004, will raise awareness in Ecuadorian society of the rights and duties guaranteed under the constitution and in international human rights standards. It is hoped that such awareness-raising will better enable the public to demand that the authorities protect their rights and prosecute members of the security forces in civil courts.
- Throughout the country hundreds of signatures were collected on large pieces of fabric which will be displayed and presented to the authorities in 2004.

Work on behalf of individuals

"I was beaten and verbally abused in detention. After a few days, the guards asked me, 'Do you know your name is all over the Internet?' After that, I was treated better by the guards before being released. The appeals sent by Amnesty members definitely had an impact on my case."
Rehab Abdel Bagi Mohamed Ali, speaking to AI in October about the three weeks she spent in detention in Sudan in September 2002.

One of AI's strengths is the ability of its members and supporters to effect change not just at an institutional level, but also on an individual one. Throughout 2003, mass action by AI members on behalf of individuals across the globe made a positive difference to hundreds of lives.

Over two million letters, faxes and emails were sent by the members of AI's Urgent Action network on behalf of people in 74 countries or territories in imminent danger of serious human rights violations. In over 40 per cent of cases, there were some positive developments after the Urgent Action was issued.

After her release from prison, Turkish human rights defender Sevim Yetkiner told AI she had noted a huge difference in her treatment after an Urgent Action was issued. She also attributed her swift release to the pressure brought about by AI's campaigning.

AI's membership also campaigns effectively on longer-term cases. AI groups around the world meet regularly to work on behalf of particular individuals. Many groups adopt cases of prisoners of conscience and political prisoners and in many cases their action contributes to the release of prisoners or improved conditions, as well as supporting the prisoners and their families through difficult times.

AI groups also adopt cases to fight for justice on behalf of other individuals. For instance, long-term campaigning by membership groups on behalf of scores of people who were beaten and tortured by police in 2000 in Abepura, Indonesia, contributed to pressure on the authorities to investigate the case. In February, two police officers were named as suspects in the case and at the end of the year a trial was pending.

Human rights defenders

The overall aim of AI's work on human rights defenders is to improve the local context so that human rights activists attain the space and freedom to carry out work to protect the rights of others.

Human rights defenders in Africa

Throughout 2003 much was done to strengthen networks and improve information sharing among human rights defenders in Africa.

- In June, training was provided to 20 human rights defenders from throughout central and southern Africa in the use of the UN Special Procedures for supporting defenders and on concrete strategies for personal and institutional security.
- In August, AI Germany organized training on monitoring and documentation for human rights defenders in Cameroon.
- AI supported the participation of the UN Special Representative on Human Rights Defenders, Hina Jilani, in the July 2003 Consultative Forum on human rights defenders in Durban, South Africa, where she raised the particular plight of women defenders in Africa.
- AI collaborated with NGOs in Botswana, South Africa and Uganda to assist and support human rights defenders fleeing from a number of countries, including the DRC, Rwanda, Uganda and Zimbabwe.
- Campaigning by network members and a coalition of international NGOs resulted in a November agreement by the African Commission on Human and Peoples' Rights to establish a "focal point" on human rights defenders within its Secretariat, to better respond to the needs of human rights defenders in Africa.

Human rights defenders in the Americas

In a report '*Essential actors of our time': Human rights defenders in the Americas* (AI Index: AMR 01/009/2003), AI concluded that human rights defenders in Latin America and the Caribbean were enjoying no more – and in some cases less – protection than they had in the past. The report also highlighted cases from North America in which the rights of human rights defenders had been infringed.

Ongoing reports of killings, torture and intimidation were paralleled by a rise in the number of raids on the premises of human rights organizations, theft of important human rights information and increasing restrictions on the right to peaceful assembly.

▓ In March, AI wrote to all European Union (EU) member states asking them to develop foreign policy on the implementation of the principles of the UN Declaration on Human Rights Defenders. While some countries demonstrated interest in the idea, no concrete policies were announced.

▓ The Guatemalan government signed an agreement to establish a *Comisión para la Investigación de Cuerpos Ilegales y Aparatos Clandestinos de Seguridad* (CICIACS), Commission to Investigate Illegal Armed Groups and Clandestine Security Apparatus, aimed at investigating those who perpetrate attacks against members of the judiciary, human rights defenders and others. The Commission, which came about as a result of lobbying by local human rights organizations, was due to be established in 2005.

▓ The Brazilian government announced its intention to set up the *Coordenação Nacional de Proteção aos Defensores de Direitos Humanos*, National Coordination for the Protection of Human Rights Defenders, made up of government officials and representatives from civil society. The National Coordination will facilitate the creation of commissions in states where insecurity for human rights defenders is greatest. Other new proposals included a campaign to raise awareness of work carried out by human rights defenders.

▓ In November, during a high-level mission to Brazil, AI received a pledge of support from President Lula for the protection of human rights defenders across the Americas region.

Human rights defenders in the Middle East/North Africa

Human rights defenders were persecuted in many countries in the region and some were prosecuted on charges ranging from "public order offences" to "undermining the state" and "acts of terrorism". In some countries restrictions imposed by governments have increasingly hampered the activities of human rights defenders. The human rights defenders community in the region is relatively small and at risk and it is important that AI expresses solidarity with them and supports them in all ways that it can.

▓ During 2003, AI took action on behalf of human rights defenders in Algeria, Egypt, Israel and the Occupied Territories, Lebanon, Morocco/Western Sahara, Syria and Tunisia.

▓ Actions taken included issuing press statements, launching appeals on behalf of threatened or detained human rights defenders and sending delegates to observe trials.

▓ In March, Egyptian human rights defender Saad Eddin Ibrahim was acquitted on all charges. AI had adopted him as a prisoner of conscience after he had been sentenced to seven years' imprisonment in a previous trial in May 2001.

▓ In July charges were dropped and travel restrictions lifted against the Syrian human rights defender Haytham al-Maleh.

▓ In October, Algerian human rights defender Salaheddine Sidhoum's earlier conviction (*in absentia*) of 20 years' imprisonment was overturned.

Refugees and asylum-seekers

AI's activities aimed at defending the rights of refugees and asylum-seekers have many aspects worldwide. To assist in this work, and as a campaigning and information-sharing tool, AI launched a new multilingual website in 2003, "Refugees have rights" (http://www.amnesty.org/refugees).

Building protection alliances

▓ On World Refugee Day, 20 June, AI Germany and the UN High Commissioner for Refugees (UNHCR) co-organized a symposium on refugee protection in Europe.

▓ AI Malaysia organized an NGO meeting in September to discuss protection concerns for Indonesian asylum-seekers from the province of Nanggroe Aceh Darussalam. They also organized a public forum on detention of asylum-seekers.

▓ AI Netherlands published a book aimed at informing the Dutch and European debate on protection of refugees in their regions of origin.

Working for individuals

AI continues to support individual refugees and asylum-seekers around the world, providing independent analysis about human rights conditions in countries people flee, and protesting against human rights abuses faced by refugees both in the countries where they seek protection and in their countries of origin. During 2003, AI interventions in individual cases in countries throughout the world ensured that many people were provided protection against return to their persecutors.

▓ AI New Zealand urged the New Zealand government either to release or charge Ahmed Zaoui, an Algerian who sought asylum in New Zealand in December 2002. He was recognized as a refugee in August but at the end of 2003 continued to be held in detention because of a national security assessment – based on secret evidence – made by New Zealand intelligence services.

Rights of children in detention

▓ AI Australia led protests against the continued detention of child asylum-seekers in Australia and on the Pacific island, Republic of Nauru. Those on Nauru had been detained there at the behest of the Australian government. Some of them have now been reunited with immediate family living in Australia. AI Australia also submitted a legal opinion on international law to the High Court in a landmark case about detention of child asylum-seekers in Australia.

▓ AIUSA undertook a joint action against a private hotel chain whose rooms were rented by the government to detain Haitian child asylum-seekers and refugees. Within weeks, all children were moved from the hotel. A letter-writing campaign for a Guatemalan child asylum-seeker resulted in his release after 16 months in detention.

Lobbying activities

▓ AI's EU Office continued to advocate for a more principled approach by EU Member States to agreeing a Common European Asylum System (CEAS). With negotiations due to be finalized by May 2004, there was significant political pressure to adopt common standards that fell short of international legal standards.

A proposal of the UK government to establish extra-territorial processing centres further threatened prospects of agreeing a CEAS which would meet acceptable standards. AI published a report in June critiquing the UK proposals as well as UNHCR and EU counter-proposals that emerged in the early part of the year. Pressure from a number of quarters, including AI, ensured that the most controversial elements of the UK proposals were rejected at an EU Summit in June.

- AI lobbied actively in a number of affected countries, and at EU and UN level, in order to stop forcible returns to Afghanistan, following research findings which showed that in many instances return was neither voluntary nor sustainable.
- AI published a briefing paper prepared for EU decision-makers on continuing protection concerns for Algerian asylum-seekers.

Children's human rights

Every day, children across the world are harmed in war zones, in detention, in care homes, and in the community. In 2003, AI took action on a number of concerns, including those listed below.

- All the warring parties to the conflict in the DRC use children as soldiers. Child soldiers usually receive violent treatment during their training, and in some camps children have died from the deplorable conditions. They are often sent into combat on the frontlines. Many are raped. Children are often given drugs and alcohol to cloud their emotions whilst fighting. Children interviewed by AI after they escaped from the army or were demobilized have given horrifying accounts of how the armed conflict affected them.
- At least four children between the ages of 13 and 16 were among the more than 650 foreign nationals being held at Guantánamo Bay without access to their families or legal counsel.
- In Honduras, hundreds of children have been murdered: some by security forces in extrajudicial executions, some by unidentified persons, some in gang warfare. AI called on the Honduran government to investigate all these deaths and to bring those responsible to trial.
- AI made appeals on behalf of the families of the "disappeared" children of El Salvador. During the armed conflict in El Salvador in the 1980s, many children who became separated from their families were taken by the army to orphanages or put up for adoption. Their families have been searching for them ever since.
- Increasingly severe restrictions imposed by Israel on the movement of Palestinians in the Occupied Territories prevented children from attending school and caused a sharp rise in poverty which led to the emergence of malnutrition in young

children and an increase in the number of child labourers.

- In the Philippines there were persistent reports of children being detained before trial for periods that exceeded explicit domestic standards and frequently in the same cells or facilities as adults.
- Most children with mental disabilities in the Russian Federation are confined to state institutions, many of them in cruel and degrading conditions. AI highlighted the plight of these children as part of its campaign on human rights in the Russian Federation and appealed to the Russian authorities to improve their situation.
- As part of AI's activities to mark International Children's Day, 20 November, a series of web actions were issued, covering many of the concerns detailed above. By the end of the year these pages had been visited nearly 90,000 times.

Lesbian, gay, bisexual and transgender human rights

AI activists have continued to campaign for lesbian, gay, bisexual and transgender (LGBT) rights, tackling cases from Egypt, Honduras, Puerto Rico, the USA and Uzbekistan, amongst others.

- AI considered Wissam Tawfiq Abyad, sentenced by an Egyptian appeal court in February to 15 months' imprisonment for "habitual debauchery", to be a prisoner of conscience. He was one of dozens of alleged gay men detained or imprisoned during 2003 solely for their actual or perceived sexual orientation.
- Eddie Hartman was executed in North Carolina, USA, on 3 October. The prosecution had used Eddie Hartman's homosexuality against him at the trial as part of its successful bid to obtain a death sentence.
- In Uzbekistan, journalist and human rights activist Ruslan Sharipov was found guilty in August of all the charges against him, including homosexuality and sexual relations with minors, following an unfair trial. He had reportedly confessed to the charges against him under duress.
- In Honduras, according to NGO sources, some 200 homosexual and transsexual sex workers were murdered between 1991 and 2003. Few cases have been investigated or seen those responsible brought to justice.
- At the 2003 Commission on Human Rights, reference to "sexual orientation" in the resolution on extrajudicial, summary or arbitrary executions was fiercely contested and forced to a vote. Likewise, a new Brazilian initiative calling on states to promote and protect the human rights of all people regardless of their sexual orientation proved controversial. AI lobbied to support both resolutions and issued a press release welcoming the Brazilian initiative. Fifty-five possible amendments were proposed to the Brazilian draft resolution, aimed at eliminating reference to sexual orientation. On the last day of the Commission the Chair proposed that the issue be postponed to the 2004 session and the vote was passed. AI will continue to campaign in support of the resolution.

There was good news from the USA in June when the ruling in *Lawrence v Texas* effectively overruled all existing sodomy laws in US states and territories, including Puerto Rico, on grounds that such laws were an unconstitutional violation of privacy.

Women's human rights

In all countries of the world, women are treated as second-class citizens, all too often facing violence as a result. In all countries of the world, women are taking action to claim their human rights. In 2003, AI strengthened its capacity to work on gender-based violations through forging alliances with partners in the women's movement and the establishment of a Gender Unit and a dedicated campaign team at the International Secretariat as part of its preparation for the 2004 launch of a major global campaign to *Stop Violence against Women*. Throughout the year the organization campaigned for women in many countries including Afghanistan, Colombia, DRC, India, Mexico, Myanmar, Nigeria, the Russian Federation, Slovakia, Sudan, Turkey and Venezuela.

Among the many concerns that AI took action on were the following:

AI was gravely concerned by the extent of violence faced by women and girls in Afghanistan two years after the ending of the *Taleban* regime. The risk of rape and sexual violence by members of armed factions and former combatants remained high. Forced marriage, particularly of girl children, and violence against women in the family were widespread in many areas of the country.

AI campaigned on behalf of the tens of thousands of women and girls who have been raped during the long-running conflict in the DRC. Almost all girl soldiers have reported being raped or sexually exploited by their commanders and other soldiers in their unit.

On 25 September the Sharia Court of Appeal of Katsina, Nigeria, overturned Amina Lawal's sentence to death by stoning. Both her confession and the conviction were held to be not legally valid. AI maintains that consensual sexual relations between people over the age of consent should not be criminalized and Amina Lawal should never have been brought to court in the first instance.

Every day about 36,000 women in the Russian Federation are beaten by their husbands or partners. The law does not recognize domestic violence as a distinct crime, and does not even allow officials to give perpetrators a warning through an administrative sentence or a fine.

In September, members of AI's health professional network appealed to the Slovak authorities about allegations of forcible sterilization of Roma women.

Ciudad Juárez, Mexico

More than 370 women have been killed over the last 10 years in the cities of Ciudad Juárez and Chihuahua, Mexico, at least 137 of them showing signs of sexual violence prior to death, and at least a further 70 women remain unaccounted for. Local women's organizations believe the figure could be much higher.

In August, AI published the report, *Intolerable Killings: 10 years of abductions and murder of women in Ciudad Juárez and Chihuahua* (AI Index: AMR 41/026/2003) during a high-level visit to Mexico by the Secretary General, Irene Khan. The report examined the context in which the abductions and murders occurred and analysed the state's failure to take effective steps to prevent, investigate and punish the crimes.

Launched simultaneously in Ciudad Juárez and Mexico City, the report gained huge publicity in Mexico and internationally and generated intense pressure on the federal and state authorities. Irene Khan met with President Fox and other ministers who committed themselves to taking action.

Sections around the world secured extensive media coverage of the launch. Successful public events were held by sections including Ireland, Spain and AIUSA on 1 November, Day of the Dead, and 25 November, the International Day for the Elimination of Violence against Women. These initiatives have played an important part in building pressure for real change in Mexico.

AI will continue to develop this work in the forthcoming *Stop Violence against Women* campaign, which will be launched to coincide with International Women's Day in March 2004.

Military, security and police transfers

Amnesty International's Military, Security and Police (MSP) Transfers Network continued to campaign to increase the accountability of governments and businesses involved in the manufacture and trading of arms and security equipment, and those providing military, police or security training. AI's members urged all those involved in military, security and police transfers to consider the human rights implications of their operations.

Control Arms

On 9 October, AI joined forces with Oxfam International and the International Action Network on Small Arms (IANSA) to launch *Control Arms*, a major global campaign calling for control of the international arms trade. The campaign aims to reduce armed violence by:

calling for an International Arms Trade Treaty, which would impose minimum standards, based on existing international human rights and humanitarian law, to strictly control the international supply of arms.

calling on all governments to ensure that their security forces uphold the rule of law and do not abuse their legitimate right to use arms in exceptional circumstances.

Control Arms was launched in 63 countries. Among the many ways sections marked the launch were a press conference in Peru attended by representatives from many Latin American countries and a multi-media concert organized by AI Philippines. In Zambia, AI members marched through Lusaka alongside members of the police and the Zambian army.

The campaign report, *Shattered Lives – the case for tough international arms control* (AI Index: ACT 30/001/2003) was launched at an international press conference in Trafalgar Square in London, transformed for the occasion into a "cemetery" with hundreds of mock gravestones to represent the enormous number of people who die every day from armed violence.

On the same day the Million Faces petition was launched. This action invites people to "sign" the petition by submitting a photo and aims to collect one million "faces" from around the world by 2006, in support of the campaign. The photos are collected and posted on the www.controlarms.org website.

- In November, AI France, the IS MSP team and other international NGOs hosted a *Control Arms* seminar at the European Social Forum in Paris.
- On International Human Rights Day, 10 December, AI members lobbied their parliamentarians, urging them to support the call for an international arms trade treaty. Several governments, including those of Brazil, Cambodia, Costa Rica, Finland, Mali, the Netherlands and Slovenia, made public statements of support for the establishment of legally binding international controls on arms transfers.

Other actions during 2003 included:

- During the war in Iraq, AI was active in campaigning for the US and UK to refrain from using cluster bombs.
- In June, AI attended the G8 Counter-Summit in France and organized a seminar as a prelude to Control Arms. A new edition of the *Terror Trade Times* and a report, *A Catalogue of Failures – G8 arms exports and human rights violations* (AI Index: IOR 30/003/2003) were launched for the occasion.
- In July, at the UN Biennial Meeting of States on Small Arms, held in New York, AI organized a fringe meeting with the participation of the UN Special Rapporteur on Small Arms.
- In December, AI produced a report and action on security equipment, *The Pain Merchants – Security equipment and its use in torture and other ill-treatment* (AI Index: ACT 40/008/2003). European governments were lobbied to implement draft legislation to control and ban the export of security equipment from EU member states.

Human rights and economic relations

In addition to making valuable contributions to AI's campaign on the Russian Federation and expressing its concerns over the reconstruction process in post-conflict Iraq, AI's Business and Economic Relations Network continued to lobby on a number of issues throughout the year.

UN Human Rights Norms for Business

Human rights organizations have addressed concerns to businesses for a number of years, seeking to ensure that companies, like all significant actors, respect and are bound by international human rights standards. AI therefore welcomed as a positive development the approval of the UN Norms on the Responsibilities of Transnational Corporations and Other Business Enterprises with Regard to Human Rights (UN Human Rights Norms for Business) by the UN Sub-Commission on the Promotion and Protection of Human Rights in August. AI had campaigned for the adoption of the UN

Human Rights Norms for Business, with wide support from the NGO community.

Right to water

AI expressed deep disappointment at the failure of the international community to recognize the right to water in the final Ministerial Declaration of the World Water Forum that took place in Kyoto in March. AI believes that a human rights framework has much to offer efforts to tackle critical water issues and has stated that affirming the right to water would help address issues of water scarcity, climate change, water quality, and the spread of water-borne diseases.

Youth and student networks

During 2003, AI's Youth and Student groups from 70 countries campaigned on a wide range of concerns. Their activities included:

- campaigning on behalf of juvenile prisoners in Guantánamo Bay, child soldiers in the DRC, "disappeared" children in El Salvador, administrative detention in Israel/OT, "disappeared" students in Nepal, young human rights defenders around the world and HIV/AIDS-related human rights abuses.
- working on racial discrimination in the Russian Federation during the International Week of Student Action, and on the rights of children with mental disabilities in the Russian Federation.
- organizing several youth camps and workshops to bring together young AI activists from many countries to share activism and leadership skills.

In August the first AI International Youth Assembly gathered 31 AI youth members from around the world in Mexico. The assembly provided a space for youth to discuss AI's role within the wider human rights context; to contribute to AI's strategic plan and youth strategy; and to empower youth leaders to participate in decision-making bodies.

Trade union network

AI's trade union network works for basic labour rights; on behalf of those threatened or imprisoned because of their defence of workers' rights; and with trade unions on all human rights concerns.

- During 2003 network members took up cases of individual trade unionists in danger of human rights abuses in many countries including Brazil, China, Colombia, Peru and Sudan, as well as campaigning on the impact of movement restrictions on the right to work in Israel and the Occupied Territories.
- In May, AI launched a campaign to work with trade unions internationally on the situation of killings and death threats against trade unionists in Colombia.
- AI received good news in April when Dan Byung-ho, President of the Korean Confederation of Trade Unions, was released after 20 months' imprisonment. AI had issued a Worldwide Appeal the previous year calling for his release.
- Two men accused of ordering the murder of trade unionist João Canuto in Brazil in 1985 were convicted and sentenced to 19 years in prison. AI's trade union network had worked on this case for many years.

Health professional network

AI's network of health professionals in more than 30 countries takes action on cases of prisoners in detention, health professionals at risk, those in institutions being denied adequate care, and in cases of the death penalty.

- More than 50 medical actions and updates, as well as relevant Urgent Actions, were sent to network members during 2003.
- Twice during the year the network made direct appeals to the Russian authorities as part of AI's campaign on the Russian Federation.
- In October, representatives of the network met in London to discuss human rights issues – particularly the AI's developing work on the right to health, HIV/AIDS and violence against women.

Human rights education

Human rights education (HRE) is preventative human rights work promoting awareness and understanding of human rights to equip people with the knowledge and skills necessary to respect and defend those rights.

Internationally, HRE programs reach judges, police, women's groups, teachers, schoolchildren, AI members and others using a range of methods and lobby for the inclusion of human rights education in national curricula.

- In the lead-up to AI's *Stop Violence against Women* campaign, HRE packages and training workshops were used to build the capacity of AI members and those of other NGOs.
- AI's Rights Education Action Program (REAP) supported a range of projects, from working with Scout groups in Poland and indigenous communities in Mexico to training prison officials in Morocco. The key aim of this work is to create HRE "multipliers", people who after training are able to take the message forward to wider and more diverse groups.
- AI's most ambitious HRE program to date, "Preventing the Practice of Torture through Education", was launched in June. Funded by the European Commission, this three-year program involves 10 AI sections and structures in West Africa. With the aim of contributing to the eradication of torture in all its forms, including violence against women, the project emphasizes capacity building, the training of trainers and campaigners and the use of theatre for HRE.

INTERNATIONAL AND REGIONAL ORGANIZATIONS

Intergovernmental organizations play an important role in the protection and promotion of human rights worldwide. Throughout 2003, AI continued its efforts to further its human rights work by seeking to influence international and regional organizations both in terms of campaigning against ongoing human rights abuses and in promoting international standards for the protection of human rights. Below are some of the highlights of AI's work with these organizations.

UN Headquarters, New York

AI continued to brief the **Security Council** (SC) about the human rights situation in a number of countries including Afghanistan, Côte d'Ivoire, Democratic Republic of the Congo (DRC), Iraq, Liberia, Sierra Leone and Timor-Leste. AI drew the SC's attention to the human rights abuses in the Ituri region of the DRC, and called for an international force to maintain peace and reinforce the presence of MONUC, the UN peacekeepers already in the region. AI urged the SC to authorize a strong human rights component of the UN Mission in Liberia and made detailed recommendations for mainstreaming human rights to the various UN actors involved. AI briefed an SC delegation visiting Afghanistan and gave informal "Arria style" briefings to SC members on Liberia and Iraq. Calls were made for human rights monitors to be sent to Iraq, for the SC to impress upon the occupying powers their obligations under international humanitarian law, and for a mixed Iraqi/international commission of experts to advise on preservation of evidence, judicial capacity and the best means to bring to justice the perpetrators of crimes under international law. Non-governmental organizations (NGOs), including AI, pressed for an open SC debate on the renewal of Resolution 1422 — which seeks to restrict the powers of the International Criminal Court (ICC) over peacekeepers in UN authorized operations — on the grounds that it was unlawful. Although the resolution was renewed, the open debate reaffirmed support for the ICC. AI persisted in calling for the SC Counter-Terrorism Committee (CTC) to ensure that states observe human rights when taking measures to combat "terrorism". The SC continued to refuse to appoint a human rights expert to advise states on their human rights obligations when implementing SC Resolution 1373, which called for sweeping measures to combat "terrorism". Faced with the SC refusal to act, AI urged UN human rights bodies and mechanisms to increase their communications with the CTC, and called on the CTC to incorporate the human rights observations of these bodies when interacting with countries that report on implementing

Resolution 1373. October saw the third "anniversary" of SC Resolution 1325 on Women, Peace and Security. In advance of the open debate of the SC — which focused on women, peace and security and peacekeeping — AI in collaboration with the NGO Working Group on Women, Peace and Security communicated concerns about implementation of the resolution to all member states. AI and the Women's International League for Peace and Freedom also held a training workshop on Resolution 1325, for NGOs active at the UN.

Before the 58th Session of the UN **General Assembly** (GA), AI called on states to ratify human rights treaties including the Optional Protocol to the Convention on the Elimination of All Forms of Discrimination against Women, the Optional Protocol to the Convention against Torture and Other Cruel, Inhuman or Degrading Treatment or Punishment, and the Optional Protocol to the Convention on the Rights of the Child on the involvement of children in armed conflict. In October AI and Oxfam met UN missions, departments and agencies to discuss their campaign on arms transfers including a call for an international Arms Trade Treaty which would introduce minimum standards to control the supply of arms. AI highlighted its human rights concerns in Iran and Cambodia. The GA adopted new country resolutions on Cambodia, DRC, Iran, Myanmar and Turkmenistan. In the build up to AI's global campaign to *Stop Violence against Women*, AI called on states to support an initiative from the Netherlands for a GA resolution on violence against women. After lengthy negotiations the GA adopted two resolutions: the first requested a study by the Secretary-General on all forms of violence against women which will be presented to the 60th session of the GA in 2005. The second called on states to eliminate domestic violence and to make domestic sexual violence a criminal offence, and stated that custom, tradition or religious consideration could not be invoked to avoid states' obligations. AI called for a strong GA resolution on the protection of human rights when taking measures to counter "terrorism", and in particular called for a report from the Secretary-General on states' implementation of specific recommendations by UN treaty-monitoring bodies. The GA adopted a resolution that called for stronger links between the CTC and UN human rights bodies, and requested a study by the Office of the High Commissioner for Human Rights on strengthening international human rights mechanisms to address the compatibility of counter-terrorism measures with states' human rights obligations.

UN Geneva

Prior to the 59th session in 2003 of the UN **Commission on Human Rights** (the Commission), AI urged the Commission to pay particular attention to the human rights situation in six countries — Colombia, DRC, Iraq, Israel/Occupied Territories, Nepal and Russia (Chechnya) — and five priority themes — the death penalty, refugees and asylum-seekers, human rights and "counter-terrorism", an optional protocol to the International Covenant on Economic, Social and

Cultural Rights, and reform of the Commission. The Commission addressed the human rights situation in Colombia, DRC, Iraq and Israel/Occupied Territories, but failed to take action on Nepal and Russia (Chechnya). AI welcomed the increasing number of states sponsoring the resolution to abolish the death penalty and the Commission's first resolution on human rights and "counter-terrorism". However, AI expressed regret that a new initiative on human rights and sexual orientation was postponed to 2004 because of strong opposition from some states. Under the confidential 1503 procedure, AI submitted information on the human rights situation in Laos, Philippines, USA (Guantánamo detainees) and Zimbabwe.

Responding to the Secretary-General's reform proposal for Special Procedures — independent human rights experts — AI made recommendations for strengthening the special procedures system. AI also welcomed the Commission's first interactive debate with the Special Procedures as a step towards making their reports and recommendations more central to its deliberations. Throughout the year AI submitted information and requests for actions on a range of human rights violations including torture, enforced disappearances, extrajudicial executions, "counter-terrorism" measures, deportations of refugees, gender-based violations and forced evictions. AI briefed some experts prior to country visits, and provided training to Zimbabwean NGOs on using the special procedures system.

AI observed the 55th session of the **Sub-Commission on the Promotion and Protection of Human Rights**. The Sub-Commission adopted Norms on the Responsibilities of Transnational Corporations and Other Business Enterprises with Regard to Human Rights. It also discussed human rights and "terrorism", the trade in small arms and light weapons, the administration of justice through military tribunals, and studies on states' reservations to international human rights treaties and globalization.

AI continued to take action to defend the rights of **displaced persons, refugees, asylum-seekers and migrants**. At the Commission on Human Rights, AI emphasized refugee protection as a human rights issue and lobbied for the inclusion of the rights of refugees and asylum-seekers in resolutions of the Commission. AI, in collaboration with other NGOs, successfully lobbied for a report on the protection of the human rights of refugees and asylum-seekers to be prepared for the 2005 Commission session. AI participated in the first meeting of the UN High Commissioner for Refugees (UNHCR) Forum in June, an intergovernmental meeting to discuss special agreements to resolve refugee situations. In approaches to the European Union (EU) and international bodies during the year, AI opposed initiatives that weakened refugee protection. AI also undertook advocacy and lobbying in UNHCR meetings covering issues including the "strategic use of resettlement". In its second year as observer to the Governing Council of the International Organization for Migration (IOM), AI made an oral statement to its 86th Session in November about human rights and the

work of IOM. As an observer to the International Steering Committee of the Global Campaign for Ratification of the Convention on the Rights of Migrant Workers, on 1 July, AI joined other NGOs and intergovernmental agencies in welcoming the entry into force of the Convention.

During the year considerable attention was given to the UN Secretary-General's proposals for reform of the **treaty-monitoring bodies**. AI participated in discussions on different models for periodic reports by states, at a meeting organized by the government of Liechtenstein and the Office of the High Commissioner for Human Rights (OHCHR), and in a debate at the annual meeting of the chairpersons. The OHCHR was drafting guidelines for an expanded core document and a treaty-specific targeted periodic report, a model favoured by the treaty bodies. In *United Nations: Proposals to strengthen the human rights treaty bodies* (AI Index: IOR 40/018/2003), AI highlighted elements critical to the success of the treaty system, regardless of the model of report. These include the withdrawal of reservations limiting treaty obligations, increased and regular funding, the appointment of independent and expert members, and the systematic integration of gender into the preparation and consideration of reports. AI also recommended measures to improve the reporting process, to facilitate involvement of domestic constituencies in the treaty system. AI continued to update its www.amnesty.org/treatybodies webpage, which includes guidelines and suggestions for NGOs and national human rights institutions on engaging with the treaty system. AI provided treaty bodies with country specific information including: the Committee against Torture (Belgium, Cambodia, Colombia, Morocco, Slovenia and Turkey); the Committee on the Elimination of Discrimination against Women (Canada and Nigeria); and the Human Rights Committee (Belgium, Colombia, Israel, Philippines, Portugal, Russian Federation and Suriname). AI cooperated with the International Coalition to Stop the Use of Child Soldiers in submitting information to the Committee on the Rights of the Child prior to consideration of New Zealand's report under the Optional Protocol on the involvement of children in armed conflict. AI also contributed to the Human Rights Committee's elaboration of a General Comment on Article 2 of the International Covenant on Civil and Political Rights.

In advance of the 2003 **International Labour Conference** (ILC), AI issued *International Labour Organization: 91st session of the International Labour Conference* (AI Index: IOR 42/003/2003). In line with the ILC theme, AI called on member states to ratify the two fundamental International Labour Organization Conventions dealing with discrimination, namely No. 100 (equal remuneration) and No. 111 (employment and occupation), in particular the three permanent members of the Governing Body yet to ratify these treaties — China, Japan and the USA. AI also raised concerns about freedom of association, forced and child labour, and discrimination in Colombia, Iran, Israel/Occupied Territories, Mauritania and Sudan. The ILC failed to establish a commission of inquiry into continuing violations against trade unions and their families in Colombia. However, it requested the Iranian government to report on the practice of *gozinesh*, a form of discrimination affecting employment, and agreed to send a mission to Mauritania.

Regional intergovernmental organizations

AI wrote to the Chairperson of the Commission of the **African Union** (AU) proposing a human rights agenda for the new structure of the AU. As part of the lead-up to AI's *Stop Violence against Women* campaign, AI called on AU states to ratify without delay the Protocol on the Rights of Women in Africa. At sessions of the **African Commission on Human and Peoples' Rights** (African Commission), AI addressed the human rights situation in the DRC and Zimbabwe, human rights defenders in Africa and ratification of the Protocol to the African Charter on Human and Peoples' Rights establishing an African Court on Human and Peoples' Rights. During the year AI provided information to the Special Rapporteur on the rights of women prior to her visit to Sudan and to the African Commission before it considered reports from the DRC and Rwanda, and urged the Commission to intervene in an alleged case of torture in Mauritania.

Through its **European Union** (EU) Office in Brussels and its sections in EU member states, AI continued to press the EU to put human rights into practice more effectively, not only in external relations but also within its own borders. AI maintained a high profile of critical analysis of the EU's restrictive policies on asylum and immigration. Calls were issued for stronger EU action at EU summits with Russia and China, and for support for human rights defenders in Latin America at the EU-Rio meeting. The EU was pressed repeatedly for adequate human rights commitments in connection with the war in Iraq, and cautioned against premature returns of refugees to Afghanistan. Appeals were made to raise human rights concerns in EU dealings with countries such as Algeria, Colombia, DRC, Tunisia, USA, and AI asked the EU to address past "disappearances" through its police mission in Bosnia-Herzegovina. Against the background of the imminent enlargement of the EU to 25 member states in 2004, AI's persistent call for the EU to stop ignoring human rights problems within EU member states began to find resonance in the European Parliament and the European Commission. Comments on legislative initiatives on judicial cooperation between EU member states stressed the need for adequate human rights safeguards. AI continued to participate in NGO efforts to influence the debate on the Future of Europe and to press for stronger incorporation of human rights and sustainable development objectives in the draft new constitutional treaty.

During the year AI participated in meetings of the **Council of Europe** on proposed reforms to the European Court of Human Rights to address the Court's increasing workload and backlog and made joint written submissions with other NGOs on proposals under consideration. AI welcomed some of the proposals aimed at improving the implementation of the European Convention on Human Rights at the national level and at ensuring the long-term effectiveness of the Court. The organization, however, expressed concern about proposals to add new admissibility criteria, which will have the effect of curtailing the possibility of individuals, whose applications to the Court meet current admissibility criteria, to obtain a binding judgment on the merits of whether their rights under the European Convention have been violated. AI stated that such proposals do not address the main challenges facing the Court, are wrong in principle and will make determinations of admissibility more complex and time-consuming. At meetings of the Parliamentary Assembly, AI provided information on country situations and themes including Chechnya, the Guantánamo detainees, political prisoners in Europe and the crisis in Iraq. AI welcomed the entry into force of Protocol No. 13 to the European Convention on Human Rights, which abolishes the death penalty in all circumstances, and campaigned for its ratification by Council of Europe member states.

AI contributed to the discussions at the **Organization for Security and Co-operation in Europe** (OSCE) Supplementary Human Dimension seminars on anti-Semitism and a second seminar on Discrimination, Racism and Xenophobia and made a written statement addressing the seminar on the prevention of torture. AI made oral statements at the OSCE Human Dimension Implementation Meeting on torture, the death penalty and the prevention of discrimination, racism, xenophobia and anti-Semitism. AI also participated in the OSCE meeting on Terrorism, organized by the Dutch Chair-in-Office. During the year, AI also lobbied for the re-establishment of an OSCE presence in Chechnya, provided information to the OSCE Rapporteur on Turkmenistan and to the Chairperson's personal envoy on Central Asia and gave an oral statement to the Supplementary Human Dimension Meeting on the Prevention of Torture.

In preparation for the General Assembly (GA) of the **Organization of American States** (OAS), AI called on OAS member states to strengthen the Inter-American human rights system, protect human rights defenders in the Americas, and respect human rights when taking "counter-terrorism" measures. AI welcomed the GA resolution that governments must fully respect human rights in the fight against "terrorism"; the GA's reiteration of its support for the work of human rights defenders and civil society activists; the development of a treaty against racism, discrimination and intolerance; and the GA's support for ratification and national implementation of the Rome Statute of the International Criminal Court. In October AI attended the Special Conference on Hemispheric Security held in Mexico and, with other NGOs in the region, presented common security concerns in the Americas. The final Declaration of the Conference included a call for the constitutional subordination of all state institutions to the legally constituted civilian authority and respect for the rule of law and human rights. AI and other NGOs from the region participated in a hearing before the

Inter-American Commission on Human Rights concerning *The Situation of the Rights of Women in Ciudad Juárez, Mexico: The Right to be Free from Violence and Discrimination.*

Impunity: the International Criminal Court

In July AI launched a campaign for universal ratification of the Rome Statute, which established the International Criminal Court, and the Agreement on Privileges and Immunities of the Court essential for the Court to operate effectively outside its headquarters in the Netherlands. By the end of 2003, 92 states had ratified the Rome Statute and only four states had ratified the Agreement on Privileges and Immunities. AI urged states to adopt effective implementing legislation, including provisions giving their courts universal jurisdiction over genocide, crimes against humanity, war crimes, torture, extrajudicial executions and "disappearances". AI issued commentaries on draft implementing legislation in Brazil, DRC, Ireland, Malta and Portugal. AI criticized the government of Ghana for not arresting Liberian head of state Charles Taylor following his indictment before the Special Court for Sierra Leone charging him with crimes against humanity and war crimes. When Nigeria granted Charles Taylor asylum, AI called on the authorities to ensure that he answered the charges against him by either surrendering him to the Special Court for Sierra Leone or investigating whether there should be criminal proceedings in the Nigerian courts. Governments were urged not to sign impunity agreements with the USA preventing the surrender of accused persons to the ICC, and parliaments not to ratify them. AI supported the effective operation of the ICC, in particular, by making submissions to the Assembly of States Parties, the Judges, Registrar and the Prosecutor on a range of subjects, including participation of victims and reparations.

Selected AI reports

- 2003 UN Commission on Human Rights: A time for deep reflection (AI Index: IOR 41/025/2002)
- International Criminal Court: The unlawful attempt by the Security Council to give US citizens permanent impunity from international justice (AI Index: IOR 40/006/2003)
- United Nations: Proposals to strengthen the human rights treaty bodies (AI Index: IOR 40/018/2003)
- Statements and press releases issued by Amnesty International during the 59th Session of the UN Commission on Human Rights (AI Index: IOR 41/016/2003)
- Preventing torture worldwide: The Optional Protocol to the Convention against Torture (AI Index: IOR 51/002/2003)
- Universal jurisdiction: Belgian prosecutors can investigate crimes under international law committed abroad (AI Index: IOR 53/001/2003)
- Time to commit to human rights promotion and protection in Africa: Amnesty International recommendations to the 2nd AU Ministerial Conference on Human Rights (AI Index: IOR 63/001/2003)

- Special Court for Sierra Leone: Denial of right to appeal and prohibition of amnesties for crimes under international law (AI Index: AFR 51/012/2003)

AI treaty bodies webpage:
www.amnesty.org/treatybodies
AI International Criminal Court webpage:
www.amnesty.org/icc/

EU Office – www.amnesty-eu.org

- Standing up for human rights in Europe and throughout the world: AI memorandum to the Greek Presidency (EU Office, January 2003)
- EU-Rio Meeting: Human rights defenders in Latin America and Caribbean need urgent support from EU (EU Office, March 2003)
- Strengthening fortress Europe in time of war (EU Office, March 2003)
- Respect for fundamental rights within the EU, presentation to European Parliament Public Hearing (EU Office, April 2003)
- Briefing on EU Return Plan to Afghanistan (EU Office, May 2003)
- Response to the European Commission's Green Paper on procedural safeguards for suspects and defendants in criminal proceedings (EU Office, May 2003)
- Open letter to the EU on the EU-Russia Summit (EU Office, May 2003)
- EU-US extradition agreement still flawed on human rights (EU Office, May 2003)
- Losing direction: The EU's common asylum policy – Open Letter to EU Heads of State and Government at the Thessaloniki Summit (EU Office, June 2003)
- Wanted: A new EU agenda for human rights, benchmarks for the Italian Presidency (EU Office, June 2003)
- Colombia: Briefing to the European Union (EU Office, July 2003)
- Algeria: Steps towards change or empty promises? (EU Office, September 2003)
- Tunisia: New draft "anti-terrorism" law will further undermine human rights (EU Office, September 2003)
- Towards a Constitution for Europe: Justice and Home Affairs (EU Office, October 2003)
- China: Continuing abuses under new leadership (EU Office, October 2003)

Selected international human rights treaties

(AT 31 DECEMBER 2003)

States which have ratified or acceded to a convention are party to the treaty and are bound to observe its provisions. States which have signed but not yet ratified have expressed their intention to become a party at some future date; meanwhile they are obliged to refrain from acts which would defeat the object and purpose of the treaty.

Key

- ● became a state party in 2003
- ○ state is a party
- ◗ signed in 2003
- D signed but not yet ratified
- [10] Countries making a declaration under Article 10 of the Optional Protocol to CEDAW do not recognize the competence of the Committee on the Elimination of Discrimination against Women to undertake confidential inquiries into allegations of grave or systematic violations of the Convention
- [22] Countries making a declaration under Article 22 recognize the competence of the Committee against Torture to consider individual complaints
- [28] Countries making a reservation under Article 28 do not recognize the competence of the Committee against Torture to undertake confidential inquiries into allegations of systematic torture if warranted

Country	International Covenant on Civil and Political Rights (ICCPR)	(first) Optional Protocol to the ICCPR	Second Optional Protocol to the ICCPR, aiming at the abolition of the death penalty	International Covenant on Economic, Social and Cultural Rights	Convention on the Elimination of All Forms of Discrimination against Women (CEDAW)	Optional Protocol to CEDAW	Convention on the Rights of the Child (CRC)	Optional Protocol to the CRC on the involvement of children in armed conflict	International Convention on the Elimination of All Forms of Racial Discrimination	Convention relating to the Status of Refugees (1951)	Protocol relating to the Status of Refugees	Rome Statute of the International Criminal Court	Convention against Torture and Other Cruel, Inhuman or Degrading Treatment or Punishment
Afghanistan	○			○	●		○	●	○			●	○[28]
Albania	○			○	○	●	○		○	○	○	●	
Algeria	○	○			○		○		○	○	○	D	[22]○
Andorra	D	D	D		○	○	○	○	D			○	D
Angola	○	○		○			○			○	○	D	
Antigua and Barbuda					○		○		○	○	○		○
Argentina	○	○	○	○	○	D	○	○	○	○	○	○	[22]○
Armenia	○	○		○	○		○	◗	○			D	○
Australia	○	○	○	○	○		○	D	○	○	○	○	[22]○
Austria	○	○	○	○	○	○	○	○	○	○	○	○	[22]○
Azerbaijan	○	○	○	○	○	○	○	○	○	○	○		[22]○
Bahamas					○		○		○	○	○	D	
Bahrain					○		○		○			D	○
Bangladesh	○			○	○	10○	○	○	○			D	○
Barbados	○	○		○	○		○		○			○	
Belarus	○	○		○	○	D	○		○	○	○		○
Belgium	○	○	○	○	○	D	○	○	○	○	○	○	[22]○
Belize	○			D	○	10○	○	●	○	○	○	○	[22]○
Benin	○	○		○	○	D	○	D	○	○	○	○	
Bhutan					○		○		D				
Bolivia	○	○		○	○		○		○	○	○	○	○
Bosnia and Herzegovina	○	○	○	○	○	○	○	●	○	○	○	○	[22]○
Botswana	○				○		○	◗	○	○	○	○	○
Brazil	○			○	○		○	D	○	○	○	○	○
Brunei Darussalam							○						
Bulgaria	○	○	○	○	○	D	○	○	○	○	○	○	[22]○
Burkina Faso	○	○		○	○	D	○	D	○	○	○	D	[22]○
Burundi	○			○	○	D	○	D	○	○	○	D	[22]○
Cambodia	○			○	○	D	○	D	○	○	○	D	
Cameroon	○	○		○	○		○	D	○	○	○	D	[22]○
Canada	○	○	○	○	○	○	○	○	○	○	○	○	[22]○
Cape Verde	○	○	○	○	○		○		○	○	○	D	○
Central African Republic	○	○		○	○		○		○	○	○	○	
Chad	○	○		○	○		○		○	○	○	D	○
Chile	○	○	D	○	○	D	○	●	○	○	○	D	○
China	D			○	○		○	D	○	○	○		○[28]

SELECTED INTERNATIONAL HUMAN RIGHTS TREATIES

	International Covenant on Civil and Political Rights (ICCPR)	(first) Optional Protocol to the ICCPR	Second Optional Protocol to the ICCPR, aiming at the abolition of the death penalty	International Covenant on Economic, Social and Cultural Rights	Convention on the Elimination of All Forms of Discrimination against Women (CEDAW)	Optional Protocol to CEDAW	Convention on the Rights of the Child (CRC)	Optional Protocol to the CRC on the involvement of children in armed conflict	International Convention on the Elimination of All Forms of Racial Discrimination	Convention relating to the Status of Refugees (1951)	Protocol relating to the Status of Refugees	Rome Statute of the International Criminal Court	Convention against Torture and Other Cruel, Inhuman or Degrading Treatment or Punishment
Colombia	○	○	○	○	○	D	○	D	○	○	○	○	○
Comoros					○		○		D			D	D
Congo (Democratic Republic of the)	○	○		○	○		○	○	○	○	○	○	○
Congo (Republic of the)	○	○		○	○		○		○	○	○	D	●
Cook Islands							○						
Costa Rica	○	○	○	○	○	○	○	●	○	○	○	○	○[22]
Côte d'Ivoire	○	○		○	○		○		○	○	○	D	
Croatia	○	○	○	○	○	○	○	○	○	○	○	○	○[22]
Cuba					○	D	○	D	○				○
Cyprus	○	○		○	○	○	○		○	○	○	○	○[22]
Czech Republic	○	○		○	○	○	○		○	○	○	D	○[22]
Denmark	○	○	○	○	○	○	○	○	○	○	○	○	○[22]
Djibouti	○	○	○	○	○		○		○	○	○		
Dominica	○				○		○		○				
Dominican Republic	○	○		○	○	○	○	D	○	○	○	D	D
Ecuador	○	○	○	○	○	○	○	D	○	○	○	○	○[22]
Egypt	○			○	○		○		○	○	○	D	○
El Salvador	○	○		○	○	D	○	○	○	○	○		○
Equatorial Guinea	○	○		○	○		○		○	○	○		○[28]
Eritrea	○			○	○		○		○			D	
Estonia	○	○		○	○		○	▶	○	○	○	○	○
Ethiopia	○			○	○		○		○	○	○		○
Fiji					○		○		○	○	○	○	
Finland	○	○	○	○	○	○	○	○	○	○	○	○	○[22]
France	○	○		○	○	○	○	●	○	○	○	○	○[22]
Gabon	○			○	○		○	D	○	○	○	○	○
Gambia	○	○		○	○		○	D	○	○	○	○	D
Georgia	○	○	○	○	○	○	○		○	○	○	●	○
Germany	○	○	○	○	○	○	○	D	○	○	○	○	○[22]
Ghana	○	○		○	○	D	○	▶	○	○	○	○	○[22]
Greece	○	○	○	○	○	○	○	●	○	○	○	○	○[22]
Grenada	○				○		○		D				
Guatemala	○	○		○	○	○	○		○	○	○		○[22]
Guinea	○	○		○	○		○		○	○	○	●	○
Guinea-Bissau	D	D	D	○	○	D	○	D	D	D	○	D	D
Guyana	○	○		○	○		○		○			D	○
Haiti	○				○		○	D	○	○	○	D	
Holy See							○	○	○	○	○		
Honduras	○	D	D	○	○		○		○	○	○	○	○
Hungary	○	○	○	○	○	○	○	D	○	○	○	○	○[22]
Iceland	○	○		○	○	○	○		○	○	○	○	○[22]
India	○			○	○		○		○				D
Indonesia					○	D	○	D	○				○
Iran (Islamic Republic of)	○			○			○		○	○	○	D	
Iraq	○			○	○		○		○	○			
Ireland	○	○	○	○	○	○	○	○	○	○	○	○	○[22]
Israel	○			○	○		○	D	○	○	○	D	○[28]
Italy	○	○	○	○	○	○	○	○	○	○	○	○	○[22]

Legend

● became a state party in 2003

○ state is a party

▶ signed in 2003

D signed but not yet ratified

22 Countries making a declaration under Article 22 recognize the competence of the Committee against Torture to consider individual complaints

28 Countries making a reservation under Article 28 do not recognize the competence of the Committee against Torture to undertake confidential inquiries into allegations of systematic torture if warranted

SELECTED INTERNATIONAL HUMAN RIGHTS TREATIES

Country	International Covenant on Civil and Political Rights (ICCPR)	(first) Optional Protocol to the ICCPR	Second Optional Protocol to the ICCPR, aiming at the abolition of the death penalty	International Covenant on Economic, Social and Cultural Rights	Convention on the Elimination of All Forms of Discrimination against Women (CEDAW)	Optional Protocol to CEDAW	Convention on the Rights of the Child (CRC)	Optional Protocol to the CRC on the involvement of children in armed conflict	International Convention on the Elimination of All Forms of Racial Discrimination	Convention relating to the Status of Refugees (1951)	Protocol relating to the Status of Refugees	Rome Statute of the International Criminal Court	Convention against Torture and Other Cruel, Inhuman or degrading Treatment or Punishment
Jamaica	○			○	○		○	○	○	○	○	D	
Japan	○			○	○		○	D	○	○	○		○
Jordan	○			○	○		○	D	○			D	○
Kazakstan	▶			▶	○	○	○	●	○	○	○		○
Kenya	○			○	○		○	○	○	○	○	D	○
Kiribati							○						
Korea (Democratic People's Republic of)	○			○	○		○						
Korea (Republic of)	○	○		○	○		○	D	○	○	○	○	○
Kuwait	○			○	○		○		○			D	○[28]
Kyrgyzstan	○	○		○	○	○	○	●	○	○	○	D	○
Lao People's Democratic Republic	D			D	○		○		○				
Latvia	○	○		○	○		○	D	○	○	○	○	○
Lebanon	○			○	○		○	D	○				○
Lesotho	○	○		○	○	D	○	●	○	○	○	○	○
Liberia	D			D	○		○		○	○	○	D	
Libyan Arab Jamahiriya	○	○		○	○		○		○				○
Liechtenstein	○	○	○	○	○	○	○	D	○	○	○	○	○[22]
Lithuania	○	○	○	○	○	○	D	●	○	○	○	●	○[22]
Luxembourg	○	○	○	○	○	●	○	D	○	○	○	○	○[22]
Macedonia (former Yugoslav Republic of)	○	○	○	○	○	●	○	D	○	○	○	○	○
Madagascar	○	○		○	○	D	○	D	○	○	○	D	D
Malawi	○	○		○	○	D	○	D	○	○	○	○	○
Malaysia					○		○						
Maldives					○		○	D	○				
Mali	○	○		○	○	○	○	○	○	○	○	○	○
Malta	○	○	○	○	○		○		○	○	○	○	○[22]
Marshall Islands							○					○	
Mauritania					○		○		○	○	○		
Mauritius	○	○		○	○	D	○	D	○			○	○
Mexico	○	○		○	○	○	○	○	○	○	○	D	○[22]
Micronesia (Federated States of)							○	D					
Moldova	○			○	○		○	D	○	○	○	D	○
Monaco	○		○	○	○		○	○	○			D	○[22]
Mongolia	○	○		○	○	○	○	D	○			○	○
Morocco	○			○	○		○	D	○	○	○	D	○[28]
Mozambique	○		○		○		○		○	○	○	○	○
Myanmar					○		○						
Namibia	○	○	○	○	○	○	○	○	○	○	○	○	○
Nauru	D	D					○		D			○	D
Nepal	○	○	○	○	○		○	D	○			○	○[22]
Netherlands	○	○	○	○	○	○	○	○	○	○	○	○	○[22]
New Zealand	○	○	○	○	○	○	○	○	○	○	○	○	○[22]
Nicaragua	○	○	D	○	○		○		○	○	○		D
Niger	○	○		○	○		○		○	○	○	○	○
Nigeria	○			○	○	D	○	D	○	○	○	○	○
Niue							○						
Norway	○	○	○	○	○	○	○	●	○	○	○	○	○[22]
Oman							○		●			D	
Pakistan					○		○	D	○				

SELECTED INTERNATIONAL HUMAN RIGHTS TREATIES

	International Covenant on Civil and Political Rights (ICCPR)	(first) Optional Protocol to the ICCPR	Second Optional Protocol to the ICCPR, aiming at the abolition of the death penalty	International Covenant on Economic, Social and Cultural Rights	Convention on the Elimination of All Forms of Discrimination against Women (CEDAW)	Optional Protocol to CEDAW	Convention on the Rights of the Child (CRC)	Optional Protocol to the CRC on the involvement of children in armed conflict	International Convention on the Elimination of All Forms of Racial Discrimination	Convention relating to the Status of Refugees (1951)	Protocol relating to the Status of Refugees	Rome Statute of the International Criminal Court	Convention against Torture and Other Cruel, Inhuman or Degrading Treatment or Punishment
Palau							○						
Panama	○	○	○	○	○	○	○	○	○	○	○	○	○
Papua New Guinea					○		○		○	○	○		
Paraguay	○	○	●	○	○	○	○	○	●	○	○	○	22○
Peru	○	○		○	○	○	○	○	○	○	○	○	22○
Philippines	○	○		○	○	●	○	●	○	○	○	D	○
Poland	○	○	D	○	○	●	○	D	○	○	○	○	22○28
Portugal	○	○	○	○	○	○	○	●	○	○	○	○	22○
Qatar					○		○		○				○
Romania	○	○	○	○	○	●	○	○	○	○	○	○	○
Russian Federation	○	○		○	○	D	○	D	○	○	○	D	22○
Rwanda	○			○	○		○	○	○	○	○		
Saint Kitts and Nevis					○		○			○			
Saint Lucia					○		○		○				D
Saint Vincent and the Grenadines	○	○		○	○		○		○	●	●	○	○
Samoa					○		○			○	○	○	
San Marino	○	○	◗	○	●		○	D	○			○	D
Sao Tome and Principe	D	D	D	D	●	D	○		D	○	○	D	D
Saudi Arabia					○		○		○				○28
Senegal	○	○		○	○	○	○	D	○	○	○	○	22○
Serbia and Montenegro	○	○	○	○	○	●	○	●	○	○	○	○	22○
Seychelles	○	○	○	○	○	D	○	D	○	○	○	D	22○
Sierra Leone	○	○		○	○	D	○	D	○	○	○	○	
Singapore					○		○	D					
Slovakia	○	○	○	○	○	○	○	D	○	○	○	○	22○
Slovenia	○	○	○	○	○	D	○	D	○	○	○	○	22○
Solomon Islands				○	○	○	○		○	○	○	D	
Somalia	○	○		○			D		○	○	○		○
South Africa	○	○	○	D	○		○	D	○	○	○	○	22○
Spain	○	○	○	○	○	○	○	○	○	○	○	○	22○
Sri Lanka	○	○		○	○	○	○		○				○
Sudan	○			○			○	D	○	○	○	D	D
Suriname	○	○		○	○		○	D	○	○	○		
Swaziland					○		○			○	○		
Sweden	○	○	○	○	○	●	○	●	○	○	○	○	22○
Switzerland	○		○	○	○		○		○	○	○	○	22○
Syrian Arab Republic	○			○	●		○	●	○			D	
Tajikistan	○	○		○	○	D	○	○	○	○	○	○	○
Tanzania	○			○	○		○		○	○	○	○	
Thailand	○			○	○	○	○		●			D	
Timor-Leste	●		●	●	●	●	●		●	●	●	○	●
Togo	○	○		○	○		○	D	○	○	○		22○
Tonga							○		○				
Trinidad and Tobago	○			○	○		○		○	○	○	○	
Tunisia	○			○	○		○	●	○	○	○		22○
Turkey	●			●	○	○	○	○	○	○	○		22○
Turkmenistan	○	○		○	○		○		○	○	○		○
Tuvalu					○		○			○	○		
Uganda	○	○		○			○	○	○	○	○	○	○

● became a state party in 2003

○ state is a party

◗ signed in 2003

D signed but not yet ratified

22 Countries making a declaration under Article 22 recognize the competence of the Committee against Torture to consider individual complaints

28 Countries making a reservation under Article 28 do not recognize the competence of the Committee against Torture to undertake confidential inquiries into allegations of systematic torture if warranted

	International Covenant on Civil and Political Rights (ICCPR)	(first) Optional Protocol to the ICCPR	Second Optional Protocol to the ICCPR, aiming at the abolition of the death penalty	International Covenant on Economic, Social and Cultural Rights	Convention on the Elimination of All Forms of Discrimination against Women (CEDAW)	Optional Protocol to CEDAW	Convention on the Rights of the Child (CRC)	Optional Protocol to the CRC on the involvement of children in armed conflict	International Convention on the Elimination of All Forms of Racial Discrimination	Convention relating to the Status of Refugees (1951)	Protocol relating to the Status of Refugees	Rome Statute of the International Criminal Court	Convention against Torture and Other Cruel, Inhuman or Degrading Treatment or Punishment
Ukraine	○	○		○	○	●	○	D	○	○	○	D	22○
United Arab Emirates							○		○			D	
United Kingdom	○		○	○	○		○	●	○	○	○	○	○
United States of America	○			D	D		D	○	○		○	D	○
Uruguay	○	○	○	○	○	○	○	●	○	○	○	○	22○
Uzbekistan	○	○		○	○		○		○			D	○
Vanuatu					○		○						
Venezuela	○	○	○	○	○	○	○	●	○		○	○	22○
Viet Nam	○			○	○		○	D	○				
Yemen	○			○	○		○		○	○	○	D	○
Zambia	○	○		○	○		○		○	○	○	○	○
Zimbabwe	○			○	○		○		○	○	○	D	

● became a state party in 2003

○ state is a party

◗ signed in 2003

D signed but not yet ratified

22 Countries making a declaration under Article 22 recognize the competence of the Committee against Torture to consider individual complaints

28 Countries making a reservation under Article 28 do not recognize the competence of the Committee against Torture to undertake confidential inquiries into allegations of systematic torture if warranted

Selected regional human rights treaties
(AT 31 DECEMBER 2003)

African Union (formerly the Organization of African Unity)

States which have ratified or acceded to a convention are party to the treaty and are bound to observe its provisions. States which have signed but not yet ratified have expressed their intention to become a party at some future date; meanwhile they are obliged to refrain from acts which would defeat the object and purpose of the treaty.

This chart lists countries which were members of the African Union at the end of 2003.

Legend:
- ● became a state party in 2003
- ○ state is a party
- ◗ signed in 2003
- D signed but not yet ratified

	African Charter on Human and Peoples' Rights (1981)	African Charter on the Rights and Welfare of the Child	Convention Governing the Specific Aspects of Refugee Problems in Africa
Algeria	○	●	○
Angola	○	○	○
Benin	○	○	○
Botswana	○	○	○
Burkina Faso	○	○	○
Burundi	○		○
Cameroon	○	○	○
Cape Verde	○	○	○
Central African Republic	○	◗	○
Chad	○	○	○
Comoros	○		
Congo (Democratic Republic of the)	○		○
Congo (Republic of the)	○	D	○
Côte d'Ivoire	○		○
Djibouti	○	D	
Egypt	○	○	○
Equatorial Guinea	○	●	○
Eritrea	○	○	
Ethiopia	○	○	○
Gabon	○	D	○
Gambia	○	○	○
Ghana	○	D	○
Guinea	○	○	○
Guinea-Bissau	○		○
Kenya	○	○	○
Lesotho	○	○	○
Liberia	○	D	○
Libya	○	○	○
Madagascar	○	D	D
Malawi	○	○	○
Mali	○	○	○
Mauritania	○		○
Mauritius	○	○	D
Mozambique	○	○	○
Namibia	○	D	
Niger	○	○	○
Nigeria	○	●	○
Rwanda	○	○	○
Sahrawi Arab Democratic Republic	○	D	
Sao Tome and Principe	○		

African Union (formerly the Organization of African Unity)

	African Charter on Human and Peoples' Rights (1981)	African Charter on the Rights and Welfare of the Child	Convention Governing the Specific Aspects of Refugee Problems in Africa
Senegal	○	○	○
Seychelles	○	○	○
Sierra Leone	○	○	○
Somalia	○	ⅅ	ⅅ
South Africa	○	○	○
Sudan	○		○
Swaziland	○	ⅅ	○
Tanzania	○	●	○
Togo	○	○	○
Tunisia	○	ⅅ	○
Uganda	○	○	○
Zambia	○	ⅅ	○
Zimbabwe	○	○	○

● became a state party in 2003

○ state is a party

◗ signed in 2003

ⅅ signed but not yet ratified

Organization of American States (OAS)

States which have ratified or acceded to a convention are party to the treaty and are bound to observe its provisions. States which have signed but not yet ratified have expressed their intention to become a party at some future date; meanwhile they are obliged to refrain from acts which would defeat the object and purpose of the treaty.

This chart lists countries which were members of the OAS at the end of 2003.

	American Convention on Human Rights (1969)	Protocol to the American Convention on Human Rights to Abolish the Death Penalty	Additional Protocol to the American Convention on Human Rights in the area of Economic, Social and Cultural Rights	Inter-American Convention to Prevent and Punish Torture (1985)	Inter-American Convention on Forced Disappearance of Persons (1994)	Inter-American Convention on the prevention, punishment and eradication of violence against women
Antigua and Barbuda						○
Argentina	○ 62		●	○	○	○
Bahamas						○
Barbados	○ 62					○
Belize						○
Bolivia	○ 62		D	D	○	○
Brazil	○ 62	○	○	○	D	○
Canada						
Chile	○ 62	D	D	○	D	○
Colombia	○ 62		○	○	D	○
Costa Rica	○ 62	○	○	○	○	○
Cuba*						
Dominica	○					○
Dominican Republic	○ 62		D	○		○
Ecuador	○ 62	○	○	○	D	○
El Salvador	○ 62		○	○		○
Grenada	○					○
Guatemala	○ 62		○	○	○	○
Guyana						○
Haiti	○ 62		D	D		○
Honduras	○ 62			D	D	○
Jamaica	○					
Mexico	○ 62		○	○	○	○
Nicaragua	○ 62	○	D	D	D	○
Panama	○ 62	○	○	○	○	○
Paraguay	○ 62	○	○	○	○	○
Peru	○ 62		○	○	○	○
Saint Kitts and Nevis						○
Saint Lucia						○
Saint Vincent and the Grenadines						○
Suriname	○ 62		○	○		○
Trinidad and Tobago						○
United States of America	D					
Uruguay	○ 62	○	○	○	○	○
Venezuela	○ 62	○	D	○	○	○

● became a state party in 2003

○ state is a party

◗ signed in 2003

D signed but not yet ratified

62 Countries making a Declaration under Article 62 recognize as binding the jurisdiction of the Inter-American Court of Human Rights (on all matters relating to the interpretation or application of the American Convention)

* In 1962 the VIII Meeting of Consultation of Ministers of Foreign Affairs decided to exclude Cuba from participating in the Inter-American system.

Council of Europe

States which have ratified or acceded to a convention are party to the treaty and are bound to observe its provisions. States which have signed but not yet ratified have expressed their intention to become a party at some future date; meanwhile they are obliged to refrain from acts which would defeat the object and purpose of the treaty.

This chart lists countries which were members of the Council of Europe at the end of 2003.

● became a state party in 2003

○ state is a party

◗ signed in 2003

D signed but not yet ratified

* Protocol No. 6 to the European Convention for the Protection of Human Rights and Fundamental Freedoms concerning the abolition of the death penalty in times of peace (1983)

** Protocol No. 12 to the European Convention for the Protection of Human Rights and Fundamental Freedoms concerning the general prohibition of discrimination (2000). The Protocol will enter into force after 10 ratifications.

*** Protocol No. 13 to the European Convention for the Protection of Human Rights and Fundamental Freedoms concerning the abolition of the death penalty in all circumstances. The Protocol will enter into force after 10 ratifications.

	European Convention for the Protection of Human Rights and Fundamental Freedoms (1950)	Protocol No. 6*	Protocol No. 12**	Protocol No. 13***	European Convention for the Prevention of Torture and Inhuman or Degrading Treatment or Punishment (1987)
Albania	○	○	◗	◗	○
Andorra	○	○		●	○
Armenia	○	●			○
Austria	○	○	D	D	○
Azerbaijan	○	○	◗		○
Belgium	○	○	D	●	○
Bosnia and Herzegovina	○	○	●	●	○
Bulgaria	○	○		●	○
Croatia	○	○	●	●	○
Cyprus	○	○	○	●	○
Czech Republic	○	○	D	D	○
Denmark	○	○		○	○
Estonia	○	○	D	D	○
Finland	○	○	D	D	○
France	○	○		D	○
Georgia	○	○	○	●	○
Germany	○	○	D	D	○
Greece	○	○	D	D	○
Hungary	○	○	D	●	○
Iceland	○	○	D	D	○
Ireland	○	○	D	○	○
Italy	○	○	D	D	○
Latvia	○	○	D	D	○
Liechtenstein	○	○	D	○	○
Lithuania	○	○		D	○
Luxembourg	○	○	D	D	○
Macedonia	○	○	D	D	○
Malta	○	○		○	○
Moldova	○	○	D	D	○
Netherlands	○	○	D	D	○
Norway	○	○	◗	D	○
Poland	○	○		D	○
Portugal	○	○	D	●	○
Romania	○	○	D	●	○
Russian Federation	○	D	D		○
San Marino	○	○	●	●	○
Serbia and Montenegro	◗	◗	◗	◗	
Slovakia	○	○	D	D	○
Slovenia	○	○	D	●	○
Spain	○	○		D	○
Sweden	○	○		●	○
Switzerland	○	○		○	○
Turkey	○	●	D		○
Ukraine	○	○	D	●	○
United Kingdom	○	○		●	○